THE ESSENTIAL HISTORY OF
CELTIC

FOREWORD BY BOBBY LENNOX

GRAHAM McCOLL AND GEORGE SHERIDAN

First published in 2002
by HEADLINE BOOK PUBLISHING
for WHSmith, Greenbridge Road, Swindon SN3 3LD

1 3 5 7 9 10 8 6 4 2

ISBN 0 7553 1141 8

Design by designsection, Frome, Somerset.
Picture on page 9 courtesy of Tempus Publishing Limited. Pictures on pages 10, 16 and 33 D.C. Thomson & Co Ltd.

Graham McColl would like to thank all who have helped with this book, in particular Cliff Butler, Julian Flanders, Adrian Besley, Bobby Lennox and Betty Murray. Special thanks to Eugene MacBride for providing most of the fact files.

Printed and bound in Great Britain by Clays Ltd, St Ives PLC, Bungay, Suffolk

HEADLINE BOOK PUBLISHING
A division of Hodder Headline
338 Euston Road
London NW1 3BH

www.headline.co.uk
www.hodderheadline.com

Contents

Foreword
By Bobby Lennox

Celtic has been my life ever since I went full-time at the club in the early 1960s. I loved playing for the club and I still love going to see Celtic. The modern Celtic Park is a fantastic place to watch football and it is great to see now so many women and children attending matches. I also have fond memories of the 'Jungle' – when I was a player the support from that section of the ground really inspired us. The Celtic fans are extraordinary – they are always so warm and friendly towards Celtic players, past and present. I hope *The Essential History of Celtic*, as it chronicles the history of this marvellous club, brings back as many cherished moments to them as it has done for me.

I have great memories of my playing career but no matter what profession you are in, you need a wee bit of luck. Shortly after I first signed for the club as a boy and was training with them twice a week, I got a phone call to tell me I had been selected to play for the third team in a match at Barrowfield the following Saturday morning. It was to be the first time I would turn out for a Celtic team, but I have to admit I wasn't looking forward to it because Barrowfield had an ash pitch whereas in Ayrshire we only played on grass parks.

On the Friday, I was hugely relieved when, instead, I was told to go to Parkhead that night to play in a reserve game. I did well enough in that game to stay

August 1964: a 20-year-old Bobby Lennox in Scottish League Cup action against Kilmarnock.

Bobby Lennox scores the opening goal in the 1971 Scottish Cup final against Rangers.

in the second team. If I had played for the third team, on the ash pitch, who knows what might have happened? A few weeks later I received a letter from the club asking me to go full-time and that made life perfect for me.

Attacking football was the only option at Celtic: if you have got players like Jimmy Johnstone, Stevie Chalmers, Willie Wallace, Joe McBride and Dixie Deans for team-mates, the only thing you can do, really, is to play the type of football that will entertain people. We also had full backs and midfielders who were constantly looking to push forward and a centre half who would score a good number of goals every season. Our players were built to attack.

Jock Stein was an inspirational manager – he knew his football inside out and he was very much the boss. On the mornings after European matches we would come in at about 11 o'clock and we would all be having massages and relaxing in soapy baths and he would come in and have a sing-song – he liked to have a good time and a laugh – but as soon as he went out the door you knew he was the gaffer again. His man-to-man motivational skills were unbeatable. I would maybe play in a game where I did a lot of running off the ball and people would say to me that I hadn't played too well, but on the Monday morning big Jock would tell me I had been great for the team by chasing all over the place and making room for other people; things that the football punter maybe would not see.

We had incredible success under Jock, winning nine Scottish League titles in a row and reaching two European Cup finals. It was a major achievement to reach that stage twice and to defeat Inter Milan in the 1967 final was just incredible. There were so many great European nights at Celtic Park and I remember those matches vividly. Jock never allowed us to become complacent and that helped us to reach the latter stages of European competition throughout his time as manager.

I can still remember clearly the thrill of being in a huge, noisy, colourful crowd at my first Celtic match – it was in the 1953 Coronation Cup when Bobby Collins scored direct from a corner against Arsenal. That schoolboy memory remains fresh. I was actually very shy as a youngster, but being at the club brought me out of myself to the point where I now enjoy socialising, chatting and joking with people through hosting the corporate hospitality at home games. It's great fun. I loved every minute of my career with Celtic and I love every minute I spend at the club nowadays. There is no place like Celtic Park and no club like Celtic.

Bobby Lennox

Chapter One: 1888-1903
Romantic Roots

There were no signs of age having wearied Celtic as the club approached its 100th birthday in the spring of 1988. They had just captured a glorious centenary League and Cup 'double' under manager Billy McNeill and as the celebrations began, following a dramatic 2-1 Cup final victory over Dundee United at Hampden Park, McNeill took time to pause and ponder the nature of the Celtic spirit that had driven the club from success to success. 'There's an ingredient about this club,' he said, 'that you can't quite put into words. I think it goes back to the very early days. I think it was founded for the very right reasons and I think those reasons have stayed with us.'

The reasons for the club's foundation, to which McNeill was referring, were borne out of the hardships suffered by Irish immigrants in the East End of Glasgow. Many of the poor were refugees from the Great Famine that had struck Ireland in the mid-19th century, but they received little sympathy for their plight in Scotland and faced discrimination for their racial origins and Catholic religion. Those who sought work in Glasgow, Scotland's industrial heart, had found themselves crammed into slums in its poorest districts.

In an effort to help relieve the Irish immigrants' harsh conditions, Brother Walfrid, the figurehead of the Marist Order in the city, had established a charity – The Poor Children's Dinner Table – to provide meals for East End children. After attending a reception for Hibernian's 1887 Scottish Cup final victory over Dumbarton, he came up with the idea of starting a football club to raise funds for that charity. The Edinburgh club had been founded by Catholic priests in 1875 and the Hibs secretary John McFadden, at that Cup-winning reception, exhorted Glasgow people to found an equivalent of Hibernian in the West of Scotland.

A man of initiative, Walfrid soon enlisted the services of two of the East End's best-known parishioners, John McLaughlin and John Glass, to help establish a Catholic football club in the East End. A site for the club's new ground was found, close to the Eastern Necropolis in the district of Parkhead, and the local East End Irish put in a mammoth effort to build a stadium from scratch. It was a radical move at the time for a football club to construct their stadium prior to kicking a ball; most teams would play in a park until the increasing number of spectators led them to build a suitable ground.

Walfrid's cleverness and expansiveness was further reflected in the name he chose for the club, Celtic. Hibernian, a zealously Irish-Catholic club, had named themselves by adapting the Roman name for Ireland. In a similar spirit, the new Glasgow club took the generic name given to the historical inhabitants of Scotland, Ireland, Wales, Brittany and Iberia: Celtic. This association with the ancient Celts gave the club an identity that was romantic and, importantly, could make it simultaneously attractive to both Scottish and Irish followers.

In just six months the ground was ready for the club's first match. Glasgow Rangers, a club 15 years older than Celtic, had been invited across the city for a friendly match. On 28 May 1888, a crowd of 2,000, paying sixpence entry money, saw Celtic turn out in white shirts with a green collar and a red Celtic cross emblazoned on the breast. Neil McCallum scored the club's first goal when he steered the ball between the Rangers posts after just ten minutes and the new club went on to record a 5-2 victory.

Those early days saw the two clubs maintain excellent relations – John McLaughlin, the Celtic treasurer, would sit in on piano at the Rangers Glee Club and both teams would often share the same train compartment when journeying south to play friendly matches against English clubs.

Celtic Enter the Scottish Cup

Competitive football in their first national tournament was to begin for Celtic in September 1888, with a Scottish Cup tie against Shettleston. In order to strengthen the team, Tom and Willie Maley were entrusted with the recruitment of new players. Tom soon brought in half-a-dozen top performers from Hibernian, where he himself had played for two years, while John Glass stole the outstanding centre half James Kelly away from Renton. Scottish football was nominally amateur, but clubs still found ways of paying players and Celtic soon established themselves as sharp dealers and good payers.

Those players gelled to such an extent that they took Celtic all the way to the Scottish Cup final in the club's debut season. After eight rounds that stretched from September 1888 to February 1889, they faced Third Lanark in the final at Hampden Park. A crowd of 18,000 gathered to see Celtic tumble to a 3-0 defeat. However, a heavy snowfall had made the game a lottery and when the Scottish Football Association convened to review the proceedings it was decided that the match should be replayed. The following Saturday saw the two teams meet again. The scoreline was different, but the eventual outcome remained the same: Third Lanark took the cup, this time after a 2-1 victory.

Willie Maley, many years later, looked back on that opening year with nothing but admiration for Celtic's founders: 'An extraordinary fact in connection with the start of Celtic is that not a man among the founders knew anything about the practical side of football. None had ever played the game. Some, perhaps, had never seen a match. Yet in the first year of the club's life, Celts were within an ace of winning the Scottish Cup.'

Celtic had sprinted to the forefront of Scottish football. The club had only been in existence for nine months and had competed in the final of the country's national competition at the first attempt. Brother Walfrid's purpose of founding a club for charitable purposes was also proving a success as the club presented the grand sum of £421 to Catholic charities at the end of that season.

Brother Walfrid was solely responsible for the birth of Celtic Football Club.

Celtic's success had an immediate impact. When they were drawn to play Queen's Park in the opening round of the 1889-90 Scottish Cup, the match drew a crowd of 26,000, the highest attendance, up to that point, for a football match in Scotland. Queen's Park, the amateur side from the south side of Glasgow, had won the Cup eight times in their 16-year history and as Scotland's oldest club represented the establishment. The game had drawn such numbers to Celtic Park that Queen's Park found their route to the dressing rooms blocked and had to enter the ground through some adjacent gardens. The match ended in a 0-0 draw, although Celtic felt themselves unlucky in having a goal disallowed. The replay brought a 2-1 defeat for the Celts.

That reverse for Celtic in September 1889 threw into sharp relief one of the problems facing ambitious teams in the fledgling years of football. An early knockout in the cup would result in a club just playing friendlies and local cup competitions for the rest of the season. The leading English clubs had found a solution in 1888 when Scotsman William McGregor, the chairman of Aston Villa, had driven through the creation of the world's first football league. It had proved a success, guaranteeing increased, regular income through a series of fixtures that would maintain ongoing competitive interest and stretch over each season.

Two years later, on 20 March 1890, Scotland's leading clubs met at Holton's Hotel in Glassford Street, Glasgow. Celtic committee member John McLaughlin proposed a motion that they form a Scottish League along similar lines to the English model. English football had been openly professional since 1885, but the Scottish game was still nominally amateur. The proposed establishment of a league looked like a serious step in the direction of professionalism and Queen's Park objected strenuously to the idea. McLaughlin's response was succinct: 'You might as well attempt to stop the flow of Niagara with a kitchen chair as to stem the tide of professionalism.' He was correct, although many in the Scottish game regretted the passing of the more relaxed, unstructured approach to the game and the disappearance of such traditions as clubs sharing afternoon tea together after a match.

Willie Maley, one of Celtic's earliest players, became the club's first manager in 1897.

McLaughlin's motion was adopted and on 16 August 1890, Celtic kicked off in Scottish League football with a home fixture against Renton. A sizeable crowd of 10,000 turned up to Celtic Park to see a match that ended in a 4-1 defeat for the home side. Circumstances had forced Jimmy McLaren, a half back, to play in goal, a factor that possibly influenced the scoreline. The following week's fixture, in Edinburgh against Hearts, produced a better result, 5-0 to Celtic, and the Celts ended August by scoring five again when they defeated Cambuslang 5-2. Celtic had, however, fielded a new goalkeeper, Jamie Bell, who had been ineligible under league rules for both of the latter fixtures. Despite being deducted four points, Celtic still strode on undaunted until the end of the season, eventually finishing in third position.

Dumbarton and Rangers shared that first Scottish League title at the end of the 1890-91 season, and it was Dumbarton who eliminated Celtic from the Scottish Cup in the quarter-finals. The following season Celtic improved even further, taking the 1892 Scottish Cup by beating Queen's Park in the final and finishing second in the league to Dumbarton. The Celts had been in contention for the title throughout the season and it was only defeats to Leith Athletic and Dumbarton late in the season that finally quenched their hopes.

The 1892-93 season saw a switch in Celtic's fortunes: they lost 2-1 to Queen's Park in the Scottish Cup final but kept their nerve in the league to

Great Matches

SCOTTISH CUP FINAL		Ibrox Park, 9 April 1892
Celtic 5	**Queen's Park 1**	**Attendance: 23,000**
Campbell 2	Waddell	
McMahon 2		
Sellar o.g.		

Pitch invasions are not a modern phenomenon. The initial staging of the 1892 Scottish Cup final, in which Celtic triumphed 1-0 through a Johnny Campbell goal, was played out as a friendly after incessant pitch intrusions from the 40,000 present caused both captains to inform the referee that they would be requesting that the final be replayed.

The clubs duly agreed, with the blessing of the Scottish Football Association, to meet again four weeks later to try again. The advertised entrance fee was increased from one shilling to two and, although the previous price was restored in the hours prior to the match, it was too late and the crowd was duly reduced to 23,000. This time, the spectators confined themselves to the terraces and Queen's Park held the lead at half-time, inside right Waddell having put them 1-0 up.

The Celts would have the wind behind them for the second half and after the restart a quick double from Johnny Campbell put them ahead. Sandy McMahon added to the tally with an individualistic effort, weaving past several Queen's Park defenders before planting the ball in the net. Half back Willie Maley and centre back James Kelly did much to ensure the lead remained intact, before Kelly's free-kick penetrated the heart of the Spiders' defence and Sellar sent the ball between his own posts. All that remained was for McMahon's late, brave header to underline Celtic's dominance on the day. Celtic had captured their first-ever national trophy – and they had done it in style.

Celtic: Cullen, Reynolds, Doyle, Maley, Kelly, Gallagher, McCallum, Brady, Dowds, McMahon, Campbell.

Queen's Park: Baird, Sillars, Sellar, Gillespie, Robertson, Stewart, Grilland, Waddell, J. Hamilton, W. Lambie, J. Lambie.

become Scottish champions for the first time. Two more titles would follow swiftly, in 1894 and 1896. Celtic also reached the Cup final in 1894, losing 3-1 to Rangers. The 1895-96 championship-winning season saw Celtic chalk up their record victory; an 11-0 home win over Dundee. Their opponents finished the match with nine men, two of them having left the field due to injury, but most of the scoring had been done before those players had left the action. Celtic threw away many chances and could have doubled the scoreline. Outside left Willie Ferguson scored five that day, four of them penalties. Celtic even managed their total without centre forward Allan Martin scoring, although he put away five of the goals the following week as the Celts won 7-0 at Third Lanark.

This succession of triumphs coincided with Celtic settling in to a new stadium in 1892, after their landlord declared his intention to raise the annual rent on the original site from £50 to £450. Local East End Irish volunteers again took part in the work to build a new arena for Celtic: more than 100,000 barrowloads of soil were used to prepare a playing surface. There was little chance of supporters failing to find the new venue; Celtic had moved just yards to a site adjacent to Janefield Street.

Celtic were now wearing green and white stripes and had a team packed with talent. Equally importantly, the club had fully embraced professionalism, which had been introduced officially in Scotland in 1893. The players were

50 Greatest Players

SANDY McMAHON Inside left

Born: Selkirk

Joined Celtic: 1890   **From:** Hibernian

Debut: v Vale of Leven, League, 24 January 1891

Appearances: 217   **Goals:** 177

Left Celtic: 1903   **For:** Partick Thistle

Honours won with Celtic: 4 league championships; 3 Scottish Cups; 6 caps (Scotland)

Sandy McMahon was an inside left of tremendous pace and power. A clever dribbler and a finisher of power and precision, he totted up 171 goals in 217 appearances for the Celts. Nicknamed 'Duke', he stood six feet (1.83m) tall and could at times look ungainly, but in full flow he graced the forward line with his shooting and heading.

Manager Willie Maley always regarded McMahon as the most accomplished header of a ball with whom he had ever worked. One of Celtic's earliest crowd-pullers, his swashbuckling style was vital to the teams that enjoyed a series of successes in the Scottish Cup and the Scottish League during the 1890s.

The great Johnny Campbell was one of Celtic's first master goalscorers.

paid handsomely, but in return demands were made upon them to ensure they would be in peak condition on the park. Training was stringent and exacting and the players were even provided with diet sheets. This disciplined, forward-looking approach required dedication from the Celtic players, but it did nothing to stifle their instincts to provide entertainment on match day.

The club's dedication to professional behaviour helped to build a strong team that contained numerous well-loved characters, including such stars as Dan Doyle, Johnny Campbell and Sandy McMahon. Keeper Dan McArthur was a defiant shot-stopper, whose bravery was outstanding in an era when goalkeepers received little protection. James Kelly, a rock at centre half, held the defence together. Other dependables included industrious inside-right Jimmy Blessington and half-back Willie Maley.

Celtic Enter Paradise

The club's new ground held 70,000 and was distinguished by an ornate stand on the northern part of the ground that could hold 3,500. Adjacent to that was a neat pavilion, similar in style to the one at Fulham's Craven Cottage, containing ultra-modern changing rooms together with leisure facilities for the players and offices for the club's committee men. It was further evidence that Celtic meant business on and off the field. One local quipped that it was 'like leaving the graveyard to enter Paradise' and the latter label soon became a popular nickname for Celtic Park.

The club were now in fine new surroundings, but behind the scenes things were far from idyllic. Throughout the 1890s, as the club was gathering more and more trophies, a split was developing among the members of the club. At the centre of the debate between two opposing groups of members was the club's original status as a charitable institution. Some wished for that to remain the case, whilst others argued that if Celtic were to progress as a club it was necessary for it to become a limited company. Annual general meetings throughout the 1890s had featured heated debates amongst the membership over this matter.

The Celtic committee, the administrators who ran the club, were in no doubt as to the way forward – they wanted the club to become a limited company. They needed an excuse to force the issue their way, however, and in 1895 the perfect situation presented itself. The Scottish Cyclists Union proposed the sum of £500 in return for Celtic staging their 1897 World Cycling Championship event. The new Celtic Park, in common with many Victorian football grounds, had been designed complete with a cycling track, but it was not up to international standards. The committee seized this opportunity to declare that the track required an investment of £900 if it was to be brought up to the required specifications. Once that investment was made, they said, the club would then be able to hold numerous prestigious and lucrative cycling events in the future. They would not, however, authorize the necessary expenditure, which would plunge the club into deep debt, unless members agreed to the club becoming a limited company. At a meeting held at St Mary's Hall on 4 March 1897 the membership agreed to those demands. It was a natural conclusion to a process that had been underway almost from the club's earliest days. The sizeable donations of club profits to charity in its earliest years had been eroded by increasingly greater payments to players and officials.

Glass-fronted Grandstand

The end of 1897 was marked by the Celtic committee taking even greater control of the club's destiny by purchasing the lease on the ground from their landlord for the sum of £10,000. The following year, 1898, an elaborate, glass-fronted grandstand was erected on the south side of the stadium, built by director James Grant. In an unusual arrangement, Grant was given permission by the board of directors to run this stand as his own private enterprise, taking profits from those patrons who wished to watch their football in luxurious surroundings. It provided an early version of corporate hospitality, with the well-heeled watching the match from behind a glass frontage. This adventurous idea proved less than practical as the wealthy spectators created condensation that would mist-up the windows and prevent them following the action.

Discipline remained strong at the club – the committee had shown their mettle after some players had attempted to exercise power a couple of years earlier. Barney Battles, John Divers and Peter Meechan had staged an on-the-spot strike prior to a fixture against Hibernian in November 1896. The trio had objected strenuously to the way some papers had reported Celtic's play against Rangers in the final of the Glasgow Cup the previous week. Reports had painted Celtic's play as being overly aggressive in pursuit of a result.

The reporting had irritated the entire Celtic team but, shortly before kick-off, Battles, Divers and Meechan informed the Celtic committee that they would not take the field unless reporters from two papers, the *Glasgow Evening News* and the *Scottish Referee*, were ejected from the press box.

The Celtic committee was not about to give in to such demonstrations of player power and acted swiftly. Willie Maley, who had by then ceased to figure in the first team, got stripped for action, a reserve player was brought into the team and, rather than accede to the demands of the strikers, Celtic took the field with ten men. They later made up the numbers with another reserve, who arrived at the ground in time to play the second half.

The aftermath of that incident saw the trio suspended indefinitely and their wages heftily reduced. By season's end they had all moved on to other clubs. Maley's fate was quite different: on 3 April 1897 he was appointed Celtic's secretary-manager. The appointment of a man to control team matters was in keeping with the club's new status as a limited company and it was a duty that Maley would undertake with extreme dedication.

50 Greatest Players

DAN DOYLE Left back

Born: Paisley

Joined Celtic: 1891   **From:** Everton

Debut: v Hearts, League, 15 August 1891

Appearances: 123   **Goals:** 5

Left Celtic: 1899 (retired)

Honours won with Celtic: 3 league championships; 3 Scottish Cups; 8 caps (Scotland)

Dan Doyle enjoyed a very good season with Everton in 1890-91. The left back had helped them to become League champions for the first time, he had been made club captain, and he was a fully fledged professional earning good money. Yet when Celtic approached him he was prepared to uproot himself from Liverpool and return to Glasgow, where Celtic were still, nominally, an amateur club. It was clear that financial inducements had been involved and the English League subsequently ruled that its clubs should not deal with Celtic on transfer business.

Once the din had died down, Dan proved himself well worth all the fuss. A superbly accurate tackler, he also possessed excellent powers of distribution and his long-range passes were anticipated and treasured by the early Celtic supporters. 'The inimitable Dan,' was how Willie Maley described him. 'A sure two-footed back. Splendid with his head. A mighty quick thinker... Doyle was seen at his best on the football field when the tide was going against his side.'

Celtic pose for the 1898-99 season teamshot with the championship trophy and the Glasgow Charity Cup.

Maley's first season in management, 1897-98, brought a fourth title to Celtic Park. McArthur, Doyle, McMahon and Blessington were still starring for Celtic and Campbell had returned to the club after a two-year spell with Aston Villa. He chipped in with eight goals on the way to the title, working principally as the inside right to the powerful centre forward George Allan.

Glittering Whirl

Allan had signed from Liverpool in the summer of 1897 and ended his only season at Celtic with 16 goals, including five in a 9-1 victory over Clyde. He returned to Liverpool for a fee of £50 before the end of the 1897-98 season, but another newcomer, 24-year-old Willie Orr, would remain at the club for many years to come. A cultivated left half, his promptings from midfield provided much of the service for the Celtic forwards to begin the glittering whirl of their attacks.

The title would elude Celtic for the succeeding six seasons, but the Scottish Cup was to provide better fare. In the four years after losing to Rangers in the 1894 final, Celtic had exited the Cup in the early rounds. An ignominious 4-2

50 Greatest Players

JOHNNY CAMPBELL Forward

Born: Glasgow

Joined Celtic: 1890   **From:** Benburb

Debut: v Carfin Shamrock, Scottish Cup, 4 October 1890

Left Celtic: 1895   **From:** Aston Villa

Rejoined Celtic: 1897   **From:** Aston Villa

Appearances: 215   **Goals:** 113

Left Celtic: 1903   **For:** Third Lanark

Honours won with Celtic: 2 league championships; 3 Scottish Cups; 12 caps (Scotland)

Johnny Campbell was decades ahead of his time. He was a deft, clever forward who used his intelligence to manoeuvre himself into scoring positions in an era when centre forwards were expected to be battering rams. He was still a very brave player, with exceptional balance, close control and dribbling skills.

His career at Celtic began in 1890 with him playing on the left wing and helping the club to the Scottish Cup triumph of 1892 and the League championships of 1893 and 1894. He was still an outside left when he quit Celtic Park to join Aston Villa in the summer of 1895, helping the Birmingham club to the outstanding feat of the FA Cup and League double in season 1896-97.

Campbell returned to Celtic in 1897 to be used in the centre forward position. His massive £70 signing-on fee was repaid by him in full. A potent scorer from close range and long distance, he was an integral front man in the team that won the League in 1898 and the Cup in 1899 and 1900. He later moved on to Third Lanark and inspired them to win the Scottish Cup in 1905.

defeat at non-League Arthurlie in January 1897 had even led to several players being shown the door at Celtic Park. However, with the team freshened and revived, the 1899 tournament saw them score 17 goals en-route to the final, which would be contested with Rangers at Hampden Park on 22 April 1899.

The rivalry between Celtic and Rangers had been growing steadily. Rangers had begun life as a club for young, middle-class, football-playing gentlemen and they had rapidly grown in popularity. Unlike Celtic, Rangers did not have clearly identifiable religious or racial roots, but their success had attracted Glasgow football followers who sought an alternative to Celtic and who felt somewhat alienated by the boisterously Irish identity that so many Celtic supporters proudly paraded. The other Glasgow clubs were finding it increasingly difficult to compete with Celtic's well-run, mass-supported football business but Rangers offered realistic rivalry – they had won the Scottish Cup in 1897 and 1898 and were the 1898-99 League champions.

A crowd of 25,000 gathered at Hampden Park for the 1899 Scottish Cup final and they saw Celtic take control of the match from the early stages. It was goalless at half-time but midway through the second half Celtic took advantage of indiscipline in the Rangers team to score. As inside right Johnny Hodge lined up to take a Celtic corner, several Rangers men were still disputing a refereeing decision. Rangers paid heavily for their lack of professionalism as McMahon soared into the air and sent a header screeching into the net. Rangers were protesting again when Celtic scored their second. Jack Bell, who had been limping heavily since the 55th minute after a severe whack from a Rangers man, popped the ball through for Hodge, who controlled it to screams of protest for offside from the Rangers backs. The referee would not be swayed, and Hodge flew goalwards to send a shot zipping into the Rangers net and the Cup to Celtic Park.

Rangers were again swept aside by Celtic when the two teams met in a semi-final of the 1900 Scottish Cup. A 4-0 replay victory put the Celts into a final with Queen's Park on a blustery spring day at Ibrox Park. With a crowd of 17,000 looking on – rather fewer than the combined 60,000 who had watched the two Celtic v Rangers semi-finals – the southsiders opened the scoring early in the first half, but McMahon, with a cross-shot, equalized. John Divers, back in the fold two years after the strike that had seen him transferred to Everton, tapped the ball over the line to make it 2-1 to Celtic. Then, as half-time approached, Jack Bell forced the ball over the Queen's Park line after a bundle of bodies had become tangled up in the goalmouth. The second period began with Divers taking the ball round the Queen's Park goalkeeper to deliver the fourth. The amateurs fought back well, scoring twice, but Celtic held out to win 4-3 and ensure that Maley had taken a trophy in each of his first three years as Celtic manager.

Celtic contested the next two Cup finals but lost both of them: 4-3 to Hearts in 1901 and 1-0 to Hibs in 1902. The following year, 1903, Celtic tumbled out of the Cup after a 3-0 home defeat to Rangers. Campbell and McMahon were in the side that day, but it was to be their swan song, Maley immediately dropping them from the side for the remainder of that season.

As the new century got into its stride, Celtic were struggling to maintain their reputation as winners. Manager Maley had a sizeable task on his hands if he was to mould a team capable of emulating the men who had established Celtic's reputation for fine, winning football. It was a task to which he would quickly prove himself equal.

Chapter Two: 1903-19
Bosses of 'The Firm'

The pattern on the Celtic shirts changed from stripes to hoops for the 1903-04 season and a clear new design was also beginning to show itself in Scottish football. During the decade up to 1903, Celtic had won four League championships and Rangers had also won four. The Scottish Cup had gone to Celtic Park twice and to Ibrox four times. The first decade of professionalism had now created an identifiable establishment.

The stakes had increased as the game had grown in popularity and nowhere in the world was the game of football more popular than in early-20th-century industrial Glasgow. For Celtic and Rangers it was good business to have a rival of similar stature – gates had grown healthily as that rivalry had developed in intensity, leading to commensurate profits for both clubs. It was this mutually beneficial relationship that led to a caustic cartoon appearing in a sports paper called *The Scottish Referee* the day before the 1904 Scottish Cup final between Celtic and Rangers. The cartoon depicted a sandwich-board man advertising a popular product. His board carried the slogan 'Patronize the Old Firm – Rangers, Celtic Ltd'. Thus was born the famous nickname for one of football's longest-running rivalries.

That Cup final was the first to be played on the site of the modern Hampden Park and the Celtic team that took the field was unrecognizable from that of just a few years before. Willie Maley had been busy sourcing young talent from the ranks of junior football, Scottish football's semi-professional game, and the team that took the field for the match with Rangers was bursting with youthful zest. Only Willie Orr, now 30 years old, survived from the Celtic side that had seen out the 19th century.

The pull of the Old Firm produced a gate of 65,323 for the final – a new record attendance for the Scottish Cup – and the fare on offer that day ensured that they would return time and again to see future encounters between these sides. Rangers streaked into a 2-0 lead after only 12 minutes due to two defensive errors on Celtic's part, but 25-year-old Jimmy Quinn, who was making a rare appearance at centre forward, got the two goals that ensured the teams reached half-time on level terms. Seven minutes from full-time, Quinn went past one, two, then three Rangers defenders before slipping the ball slickly past the Rangers goalkeeper. He had secured the first

Jimmy McMenemy (right) and Alec Bennett arrived at Celtic Park in the early 1900s from Rutherglen Glencairn.

hat-trick in a Scottish Cup final and the Parkhead side their first major trophy since 1900.

Rangers were, in one way, architects of their own downfall in that match. The Ibrox club had pursued the signature of Celtic centre forward Alec Bennett to the extent that Maley believed the player might not be in entirely the right frame of mind to play against his admirers in the final. Quinn stepped into Bennett's boots and showed himself more than comfortable with the demands of the centre forward role. Celtic's newly-discovered goalscorer would haunt the Ibrox side for many years to come.

As it transpired, Bennett would not move on to Ibrox until 1908, by which time he had been long since supplanted at centre forward by the mighty Quinn. Willie Maley found the new-look Celtic invigorating. Looking back on that groundbreaking Cup-final triumph years later he stated, 'The team was now a splendid blend of youth and experience and the management looked with considerable confidence to the future.'

Crowd Trouble

Quinn was at the centre of events once again in 1905, when he was sent off in a Scottish Cup semi-final. Tom Robertson, the man who had refereed the 1904 final, sent Quinn off eight minutes from time because, he believed, Quinn had kicked Rangers' Alec Craig in the face. That provoked a pitch invasion from the Celtic Park terraces and no sooner had order been restored and the game restarted than the crowd once again surged on to the turf. Robertson abandoned the match and Celtic – 2-0 down – conceded the tie. The burly Quinn was no pushover, but after the match both he, his club and, perhaps more importantly, Craig refuted the idea that Quinn had been guilty of the stated offence. Regardless, the Scottish Football Association upheld his sending off and served a four-week suspension on him.

There would be a happier outcome to the concluding Old Firm match that 1904-05 season. Both sides had finished their League fixtures on 41 points and a play-off between them was ordered for Hampden Park on 6 May 1905. It ended 2-1 in Celtic's favour thanks to goals from Davie Hamilton, a 22-year-old outside left, and Jimmy McMenemy, the 24-year-old inside left.

Celtic had hold of their first title for seven years and Hamilton and McMenemy were typical of the new team that was taking shape. Both were young and enthusiastic and both had been signed at little expense from junior sides, Hamilton arriving in 1902 from Cambuslang Hibernian and McMenemy in the same year from Rutherglen Glencairn. Maley knew what he

Willie Loney. Such was the power of the centre half, he was nicknamed 'The Obliterator'.

was looking for and painstakingly moulded young players such as those once he had them under his wing at Celtic Park.

Celtic's decision to rely on youth was to be amply rewarded. Crowds flocked to a Celtic Park that had taken on a new look since the Cup-winning season of 1903-04. The stand on the Janefield Street side of the ground had succumbed to fire damage that year and instead of erecting another seated structure, the Celtic committee decided to make that part of the ground a standing section. Simultaneously, they purchased the south stand from James Grant. It had proved a liability to him and he was pleased to give it up.

First League and Cup 'Double'

Seamless successes now followed one after another on the field as Maley's youth policy yielded visible results. The League was captured in style in 1904-05 and 1905-06, with Jimmy Quinn leading the charge for goals. Captain Jimmy Hay, an organizer and motivator from his position of left half, underpinned the efforts of those sides. He had been signed for just £50 from Glossop as a 22-year-old in 1903 and would provide Celtic with the best part of a decade's service. Spurring his team-mates on, he led them to the capture of Scottish football's first League and Cup 'double' with the 3-0 Cup final victory over Hearts in 1907, which went in tandem with a third successive League championship title.

Great Matches

SCOTTISH CUP FINAL   **Hampden Park, 20 April 1907**

Celtic 3   **Heart of Midlothian 0**   **Attendance 50,000**
Somers 2
Orr (pen)

Preston North End and Aston Villa, both inspired by Scottish talent, had captured
League and Cup doubles in England during football's early days, but the Scottish game
had yet to see a team perform the monumentous feat. Such were the stakes when
champions-elect Celtic met Hearts in the Scottish Cup final.

A series of replays had seen Celtic play eight games to get past four clubs – Clyde,
Morton, Rangers and Hibernian – and into the final. It proved that this Celtic team
were genuine battlers as well as being the sophisticated stylists who had romped to the
verge of a third successive League title.

Hearts, the Cup holders, offered stern opposition and the teams went in 0-0 at half-
time after contesting a cagey opening 45 minutes. After the break, Celtic gently
increased the pressure. It resulted in a penalty, disputed by Hearts, that Willie Orr
poked into the net. Hearts' resistance broken, Celtic stormed on to score a second goal.
Alec Bennett slipped away from three defenders on the wing then slid a superb cross
into the path of Peter Somers for the inside left to sidefoot it into the net.

With Hearts now beaten, Somers repeated the feat, again from a Bennett cross, to
seal the victory. Scottish football was about to witness the capture of the elusive double
and it was Celtic, the top team of the early 1900s, who were to achieve it.

Celtic: Adams, McLeod, Orr, Young, McNair, Hay, Bennett, McMenemy, Quinn, Somers,
Templeton.

Heart of Midlothian: Allan, Reid, Collins, Phillips, McLaren, Henderson, Bauchop,
Walker, Axford, Yates, Wombwell.

A second successive double made the 1907-08 season another memorable
one. St Mirren contested the Cup final in April, but they were simply brushed
aside. Two goals from Bennett, who had now switched to the right wing after
the competition from Quinn had proved too fierce at centre forward, and one
each from Quinn himself, crafty inside left Peter Somers and Hamilton allowed
the Celts to coast to a 5-1 victory. A week later Bennett scored the only goal of
the game as Celtic defeated Rangers and took a fourth successive League title.

All five Celtic forwards – Bennett, McMenemy, Quinn, Somers and
Hamilton – were regular goalscorers. Their entertaining efforts in attack
were solidly supported by disciplined defending from the three half backs –

'Sunny Jim' Young, Willie Loney and Hay. The two full backs – McNair and Jimmy Weir – kept opposition wingers firmly in check and goalkeeper Davy Adams was hugely reliable.

The sweet, smooth success of that 1907-08 season would be in contrast with Celtic's experiences the following season, in particular the events of April 1909, which rank among the most turbulent in the club's history. Another Old Firm final in the Scottish Cup reflected the increasing popularity of both clubs as 70,000 teetered on Hampden's terraces in anticipation of yet another engaging encounter. They were not to be disappointed. Jimmy Quinn opened the scoring, but Rangers scored twice to lead until close to the end. Then Rangers goalkeeper Henry Rennie, one of the best in British football, inadvertently took the ball over his own line and into the net whilst attempting to avoid a shoulder-charge from Quinn. It meant a replay a week later and although the additional expense for the fans meant the gate was reduced by 10,000, the tie retained full excitement. Quinn's third goal of that final gave Celtic the equalizer in a 1-1 draw.

Celtic pose with the three Cups they won in 1907-08 (the Charity Cup, the Scottish Cup and the Glasgow Cup). Back row, from left: T. White, J. Kelly, T. Colgan, J. McKillop, J. Grant, M. Dunbar. Middle row, from left: manager Willie Maley, Jim Young, P. Somers, J. McMenemy, D. Adams, J. Mitchell, J. Weir, R. Davis. Front row, from left: D. Hamilton, D. McLeod, W. Loney, J. Hay, J. Quinn, A. McNair.

50 Greatest Players

JIMMY QUINN Centre forward

Born: Croy

Joined Celtic: 1900   **From:** Smithston Albion

Debut: v St Mirren, League, 19 January 1901

Appearances: 331   **Goals:** 217

Left Celtic: 1915 (retired)

Honours won with Celtic: 6 league championships;
4 Scottish Cups; 11 caps (Scotland)

Willie Maley had to be patient and persuasive to obtain the signature of a player content to play junior football around his home village of Croy. Jimmy Quinn may have been slow in signing, but he proved himself no slouch on his arrival at the club. Celtic have had few more explosive talents. His first Cup final, against Hearts in 1901, just three months after he had joined Celtic, saw him dance down the left wing, whirring past six opponents before placing the ball in the net.

Bull-like strength, allied to a keen positional sense, speed, nimble feet, superb heading ability and immense bravery, made Jimmy Quinn the ideal centre forward. Strange, then, that he spent most of his first three years at Celtic on the left wing, scoring only sporadically. His hat-trick in the 1904 Scottish Cup final against Rangers and five goals in a 6-1 win over Kilmarnock a week later confirmed him as a natural target man.

Jimmy's scoring feats over the subsequent decade made this modest gentleman the focal point of the Celtic attack in one of the club's greatest eras. Willie Maley, in the late 1930s, described him as 'the greatest centre forward we have ever possessed'.

Hampden Riot

As the referee blew his whistle for the conclusion of the 90 minutes the supporters of both sides lingered on the terraces. Extra-time was expected – some newspaper quotes from Willie Maley in advance of the replay had appeared to hint that such a method would be employed to settle the final in the event of the scores still being level at full-time. Even some players appeared to be confused, staying on the field of play until they realized there would be no more action that day. The crowd grew restless and angry. A suspicion developed that the Old Firm had colluded to gain a third set of takings from a second replay.

As the anger grew, a trickle of supporters found their way on to the pitch and before long a full-scale invasion was under way. Payboxes, where the fans had earlier given up their precious entrance money, were set alight and when firemen arrived to douse the blazes they were set upon by the crowd. Bottles and bricks were thrown at the police, and, as the frenzy grew, fans ripped up parts of the stadium to obtain weapons, using sections of metal fencing and even parts of the goalposts to attack the police. After hours of destruction and violence, the 1909 Hampden Riot eventually spluttered to an end. Subsequently, the SFA decided to withhold the trophy and Celtic and Rangers were ordered to pay a joint fine of £300 to Queen's Park Football Club towards the cost of repairing their stadium.

Nail-biting Conclusion

The conclusion of the 1908-09 League season also proved frenzied, if somewhat more law-abiding. Celtic were instructed to play their final three fixtures, all away matches, on three successive days at the end of April. The first of those matches resulted in a 5-1 win over Queen's Park in a match played at Cathkin due, ironically, to the damage caused to Hampden in the Cup final. A 1-0 defeat at Hibernian the following day meant that the destination of the 1909 title would hinge on Celtic's visit to Hamilton Academicals on 30 April. McMenemy and Hamilton contributed the goals that gave Celtic a 2-1 victory and moved them on to 51 points for the season, one more than runners-up Dundee.

The 1909-10 title race was another close one as the five-times champions found their rivals resolute in pursuit. It ended with the First Division championship back at Celtic Park once more after Celtic had finished two points clear of second-placed Falkirk. It proved to be the end of the most glorious run of championships that British football had yet seen and in 1911 Celtic were presented with a special shield from their fellow First Division clubs to commemorate their winning six titles in a row.

That Celtic team had been a truly special one. It is no exaggeration to suggest that in those formative years of football they were the world's best. They were a compact unit that blended seamless teamwork with free-flowing football and their magnificent consistency of performance yielded wonderful results. The era's great players, such as Jimmy Quinn, Jim Young and Alec McNair, would live on in Celtic supporters' memories long after those players had retired.

The loss of the League title that they had almost come to call their own was a severe blow for Celtic in the 1910-11 season. It was softened somewhat by the capture of the Cup after a 2-0 victory over Hamilton Academicals in a replayed Scottish Cup final. The League escaped their grasp once again in the 1911-12 season, but once more a Cup triumph – beating Clyde 2-0 in the final – rescued their season.

There was to be no joy for Celtic in 1912-13 – for the first time in a decade they would fail to win a trophy – and Maley was quick to act. Names such as Loney and Quinn began to fade from the scene as the manager rebuilt and remodelled his team, once again recruiting the very best talent on a very modest budget. Charlie Shaw, a goalkeeper who would give the club lengthy service, arrived from Queen's Park Rangers for the start of the 1913-14 season. McNair and Young remained in place, joined by Joe Dodds, a young left back who would grace the club for a dozen years.

Other new arrivals included the daring outside right Andy McAtee and the quite brilliant Patsy Gallacher who joined Jimmy McMenemy in the forward line. This winning blend of experience and excellence brought Celtic their third double in 1913-14 – finishing six points clear of Rangers in the First Division and trouncing Hibernian 4-1 in a replayed Scottish Cup final. As their reward, an 18-strong Celtic party took off on a close-season tour of Central Europe, visiting eastern Germany, Austria and Hungary. It would be the last time for many years that such a tour could be undertaken.

50 Greatest Players

JIMMY McCOLL Centre forward

Born: Glasgow

Joined Celtic: 1913   **From:** St Anthony's

Debut: v Dundee, League, 18 October 1913

Appearances: 169   **Goals:** 123

Left Celtic: 1920   **For:** Stoke City

Honours won with Celtic: 4 league championships; 1 Scottish Cup

Jimmy McColl was the man who broke the ice in the Scottish Cup final of 1914. His double strike in the opening ten minutes against Hibernian put Celtic firmly in control of the replayed tie. McColl had missed the first game, but his role in the 4-1 Cup final replay victory established his reputation and he became a fixture in the forward line for Celtic over four title-winning seasons.

Although an equally intelligent player as his predecessor at centre forward, McColl lacked Jimmy Quinn's powerful physique and stood just five feet seven inches (1.7m) tall. He had to squeeze his shooting trigger as soon as he saw a scoring opening to prevent heavyweight defenders trampling all over him. That talent earned him the nickname 'The Sniper'. It was a subtle approach and it worked: McColl's goalscoring ratio was even better than that of Quinn. Many and various were the teams that were blown away by bullets fired by this quiet assassin.

Celtic's Patsy Gallacher (second left), watched by team-mate Jimmy Quinn (right), attempts an audacious overhead backheel in the 1912 Scottish Cup semi-final against Heart of Midlothian. Celtic won the match 3-0.

Maley had built his second great team but their progress would prove to be limited. World War One broke out in late 1914 and the Scottish Cup competition was suspended. League football continued, however, and the Celts would take four titles in succession from 1914 to 1917. Their triumph in 1915-16 produced a new record title-winning margin in Scottish football, Celtic ending their fixtures 11 points clear of second-placed Rangers.

Those triumphs were achieved against a background of wartime restrictions that deeply affected football. Players had their wages slashed by one-third and were drafted in to do their bit to help the war effort. Some helped out in such spheres as munitions work. Others joined the forces.

Peter Johnstone, a mainstay of the Celtic side, put in supplementary shifts as a miner, whilst continuing to be a fixture for Celtic at the heart of their defence. He was 28 years old as he began the 1916-17 season in his regular position for Celtic, but in late 1916 he joined the Seaforth Highlanders. He would die at the battle of Arras in May 1917. Numerous other Scottish footballers would suffer a similar fate on the frontline.

Football was clearly seriously affected by the ongoing conflict, but the Celtic team was so outstanding that it would almost certainly have dominated the game even under normal circumstances. This was the team that achieved a

50 Greatest Players

JIM YOUNG Half back

Born: Kilmarnock

Joined Celtic: 1903   **From:** Bristol Rovers

Debut: v Partick Thistle, League, 15 August 1903

Appearances: 443   **Goals:** 14

Left Celtic: 1917 (retired)

Honours won with Celtic: 9 league championships; 5 Scottish Cups; 1 Scottish League Cup; 50 caps (Scotland)

'Sunny Jim' Young, the man who had a dour disposition even in celebratory team pictures, was an essential element in Celtic's two lengthy League-winning runs in the opening two decades of the 20th century. With Sunny Jim around, the outlook was usually bright for the Celts. He even knew when to quit, retiring as a 35-year-old at the end of the 1916-17 season after sustaining a severe knee injury in the autumn of 1916. Missing his presence at right half, Celtic would bring home just one of the next four available League titles.

One of Willie Maley's master signings, Young arrived on a free transfer from Bristol Rovers in the spring of 1903. As the essential link between the defence and attack, his promptings from the middle of the park set up Celtic attacks and he used his battling qualities to break up the attacks of the opposition. Captain of Celtic from 1911 until the end of his career, Sunny Jim's five Scottish Cup medals and nine Scottish League championship medals did full justice to his talents.

Scottish League record by going 62 matches unbeaten between 20 November 1915, when they defeated Kilmarnock 2-0, and 21 April 1917, when they lost 2-0 at home to that same team.

This great side also clinched the 1918-19 championship, which was played half in peacetime and half in war after World War One had ended in November 1918. A couple of last-day goals at Somerset Park from McAtee and the dashing outside left Adam McLean were enough to beat Ayr United and to help Celtic pip Rangers by one point in the final First Division standings. The previous season had seen Celtic lose out on the title to their Glasgow rivals by the same margin. It was a pity: six-in-a row – the record set by their illustrious predecessors – would have done full justice to that side. Nevertheless, Celtic supporters returning from the war found their team at the top of the tree and well-equipped to stay there.

Chapter Three: 1919-31
A Duel for Dominance

The 1909 Hampden Riot had seen Celtic and Rangers supporters join together in a violent protest but just a decade later the idea of the two sets of fans presenting a similarly unified front had become unimaginable. Celtic manager Willie Maley suggested that the religious bigotry that inflamed the Old Firm's footballing rivalry first became evident in 1912, but it was in the years after World War One that it began to exert its vice-like grip on so many followers of the Old Firm.

Maley's date of 1912 is significant as it was then that Harland & Wolff, the Belfast shipbuilders, put down roots on the Clyde by opening a new shipyard. They imported Irish Protestants to work there, and their rigid antipathy to Catholics found a highly visible focus in Celtic. Although always recruiting players regardless of religion, the football club from the East End was fiercely proud of its Irish and Catholic roots. Protestants, eager to claim a team of their own, saw Rangers, in the heart of the shipbuilding territory of Govan, and already established as Celtic's major rivals, as an obvious choice.

The growing sectarian divide in Glasgow was exacerbated by the establishment of the Irish Republic in 1921. The breach between the newly independent southern Ireland and Britain was felt with bitterness amongst Irish Protestants in Glasgow, and the Old Firm became a vehicle for extreme emotions on both sides. Unemployment and poverty was rife and Irish Catholics, who as immigrants had traditionally accepted jobs at lower wage rates than native Scottish Protestants, were a convenient scapegoat.

Even the Church of Scotland got in on the act. A report to its General Assembly in 1923 spoke of the 'menace of the Irish race' to Scottish nationality. It suggested the control of immigration from the Irish Free State, deportation, and that preference should be given to native-born Scotsmen in public works because Scotland was 'over-gorged' with Irishmen. It was against this increasingly harsh, intolerant background that Celtic and Rangers would fight for dominance of Scottish football throughout the 1920s and 1930s.

Rangers took the first two League titles of the 1920s, but in the 1921-22 season Celtic pushed them all the way for the championship. On the final day of the season the Celts journeyed to Cappielow to face Morton, knowing that a victory would secure the title. It was an occasion marred by rioting on

50 Greatest Players

JIMMY McMENEMY Forward

Born: Rutherglen

Joined Celtic: 1902   **From:** Rutherglen Glencairn

Debut: v Port Glasgow, League, 22 November 1902

Appearances: 515   **Goals:** 168

Left Celtic: 1920   **For:** Partick Thistle

Honours won with Celtic: 10 league championships; 6 Scottish Cups; 12 caps (Scotland)

Jimmy 'Napoleon' McMenemy marshalled the Celtic forward line for two decades in which Celtic reigned like emperors over Scottish football. A dynamic inside left, his excellence made him intrinsically unpredictable, as he had a host of means at his disposal for making and taking goals. His speed allowed him the option of driving a hole in opponents' defences, he could head a ball with great accuracy, shoot with precision and power or pick out a quick, accurate pass for one of his fellow forwards.

That range of skills was vital to Celtic running up their tally of ten League titles between 1905 and 1917. Seemingly satiated with success, Jimmy then retired at the age of 37 but he was back after his 38th birthday to help inspire Celtic to the 1918-19 League title. 'The football pitch to him was a chess board,' said Willie Maley. 'He was continually scheming and plotting and seldom if ever troubled himself with the physical side of the game – he had no need.' Jimmy had won six Scottish Cup medals with Celtic and added another to that tally by helping Partick Thistle beat Rangers in the 1921 final at the age of 40. He later returned to Celtic Park as a member of Maley's coaching staff between 1935 and 1940.

the terraces – bigotry against Celtic and their supporters was not confined to Glasgow – and players from both sides had to appeal for calm from their supporters. On the pitch, Celtic fought back from being 1-0 behind at half-time and Andy McAtee scored an equalizer with a precise header in the dying minutes of the match. It was just enough for Celtic to take the title by one point from Rangers, who had also drawn their final fixture.

That 1922 title win made up for the 1920-21 season, when Celtic had finished ten points adrift of Rangers, but in the 1922-23 season the men from Ibrox again finished out of sight of the Celts. There was a nine-point gap between the Glasgow rivals. Rangers had appointed a new manager, Bill Struth, in 1920 and had become a streamlined outfit, physically strong and fit; a team ready for the demands of professional football in the 1920s. Airdrie, with former Celt Willie Orr in charge, finished in second place.

That 1922-23 season was also the first since 1911 in which Celtic had ended a season outside the top two in the First Division. Patsy Gallacher, the team's inside right and star creator, had been missing through injury for several matches in the early part of 1923 and key defeats at that stage of the season had torpedoed Celtic's championship chances. Gallacher was, however, an ever-present in the 1923 Scottish Cup and Celtic found consolation in that tournament.

Centre forward Joe Cassidy had scored ten of Celtic's 12 Scottish Cup goals on the way to the 1923 final against Hibernian. His goalscoring run was remarkable in itself, but even more so considering the player had suffered a broken jaw in a League match against Rangers in October 1922. That injury had kept the brave striker out of action for a mere three weeks. He brought his talents to bear on the 1923 Scottish Cup final against Hibs, when a crowd of 80,100 at Hampden saw him head home the only goal of a tight match midway through the second half.

The Celtic squad pose in front of their distinctive grandstand in 1922.

That glimpse of glory was obliterated the following season when Celtic tumbled out of the 1924 Scottish Cup in their opening tie. The Parkhead side's 2-0 Cup defeat at Kilmarnock in January 1924 contained an element of ill-luck in that centre half Willie McStay was forced to leave the action through injury. As no substitutions were allowed at that time, Celtic had to complete the game with only ten men and with Gallacher – all five feet seven inches (1.7m) and nine-and-a-half stones (60kg) of him – as an emergency centre half. That Cup exit effectively ended Celtic's season, because by then they were long out of contention for the 1923-24 League title. For the second successive season they finished third, this time 13 points adrift of Rangers and again with Orr's Airdrie above them.

The gap between Celtic and the champions widened even further in the 1924-25 season. They finished an alarming 16 points behind first-placed Rangers, 13 points behind second-placed Airdrie and eight points behind Hibernian. It was the biggest gap, up to that point, that there had been between Celtic and the League winners. Thankfully, this time, the Scottish Cup did come to their rescue. Victories over Third Lanark, Alloa Athletic and Solway Star led to a quarter-final with St Mirren. The first game ended 0-0, its replay 1-1.

In the second replay, a goal from Jimmy McGrory, an exciting new discovery at centre forward that season, gave Celtic the 1-0 victory that sent

Celtic's mid-1920s forward line. From left: Paddy Connolly, Alec Thomson, Jimmy McGrory, Tommy McInally and Adam McLean.

50 Greatest Players

ALEC McNAIR Right back

Born: Bo'ness

Joined Celtic: 1904   **From:** Stenhousemuir

Debut: v Rangers, League, 25 February 1905

Appearances: 604   **Goals:** 9

Left Celtic: 1925 (retired)

Honours won with Celtic: 10 league championships;
6 Scottish Cups; 15 caps (Scotland)

Alec McNair joined Celtic shortly after the 1904 Scottish Cup
final victory, becoming a key figure in Celtic's remarkable run
of successes and remaining central to the team for the next
20 years. The epitome of steadiness and reliability, he was a
Scottish Cup winner at the age of 39 in 1923 and the oldest player to represent Celtic
when, in 1925, he made his final appearance for the club at the age of 41.

McNair was a clever right back, his ability to dispossess opponents through an
unhurried assessment of their strengths and weaknesses earning him the nickname
'The Icicle'. 'The coolest and most intelligent and thoughtful player I have ever seen,'
was Willie Maley's assessment of a man whose steadiness helped to provide the secure
base on which a succession of more flamboyant team-mates could display their talents.

them through to the semi-finals. As the match had entered its final minute,
St Mirren had claimed for a penalty but the referee had awarded a free-kick
on the edge of the penalty area. The furious St Mirren players had refused to
take the kick as they continued to remonstrate with the referee about his
decision. Tiring of their protests, the referee picked up the ball and blew the
final whistle. Afterwards, Celtic players conceded privately that the St Mirren
players had been justified in their protests – the foul on their player had
indeed taken place inside the penalty area. The tie with St Mirren had been
too tight for comfort and the semi-final was expected to be even tighter as
Celtic had been drawn to face champions-elect Rangers.

The Celtic team of the mid-1920s fully upheld the club's traditions in that
it was a team geared to attack. Centre forward Jimmy McGrory, still only 20,
was already established as a scorer of spectacular goals and bunches of them at
a time; in the 1924-25 season, he twice scored four goals in a match and twice
scored hat-tricks. The individualistic Patsy Gallacher remained the torchbearer
of trickery at inside right, while inside left Alec Thomson contributed refined

touches. Wingers Paddy Connolly and Adam McLean were devastatingly effective. The team was equally well-served in midfield by pass masters Peter Wilson and John 'Jean' McFarlane and the reliable centre half Jimmy McStay. Goalkeeper Peter Shevlin and full backs Willie McStay and Hugh Hilley provided unspectacular support for the more lauded front men.

Record Attendance

It was an entertaining side, but their desire to attack made the 1925 Scottish Cup semi-final against an organized Rangers side a tough prospect. Rangers had won 4-1 at Ibrox on New Year's Day and had also won the Celtic Park League encounter that season. The match drew 102,000 fans to Hampden Park. It was the first time a Scottish club match had drawn a crowd of more than 100,000 and the tension of the occasion was evident early on. Celtic eventually settled down well enough to play their flowing football and duly took the lead. Peter Wilson picked out Connolly with a smooth pass and when the winger served McGrory, the centre forward deposited the ball in the back of the Rangers net.

It remained 1-0 at half-time and after an hour Celtic eased further ahead when Connolly's corner was met by McLean with a header. It then became 3-0 when McGrory scored his second after playing a clever one-two with Connolly. Thompson headed Celtic into a 4-0 lead and, close to the end, McLean notched the fifth. It had been an outstanding victory, a triumph that was entirely unexpected and that 5-0 win lifted the Celtic support enormously in the middle of a decade that had seen Rangers dominate the Scottish League. The final, against Dundee, proved to be more troublesome than the semi, but a moment of brilliance from Patsy Gallacher turned the match in Celtic's favour and they went on to win 2-1 and take the 1925 Scottish Cup.

Patsy Gallacher had shown his importance to Celtic with his goal in that Cup final but it was to be one of his final outings in a Celtic jersey. He managed just one appearance in the entire 1925-26 season but his absence was not felt as badly as might have been expected. Alec Thomson switched from inside left to Patsy's position of inside right and Tommy McInally took over Thomson's previous duties. McInally had been a problem player for manager Maley during the forward's previous three-year spell at the club during the early 1920s. An indisciplined individual, albeit one with unusual ability with a ball, he had been transferred to Third Lanark in 1922. Three years on, Maley was willing to give him a second chance and brought him back to Celtic Park for the start of the 1925-26 season. It proved a masterstroke as McInally, now in his mid-20s and to all appearances a reformed figure, prompted goals galore for Celtic and weighed in with 22 himself as Celtic totted up 97 League goals.

Celtic coasted clear of the pack at the top of the First Division and ended the 1925-26 season as champions, eight points ahead of second-placed Airdrie. Rangers were in seventh position, 14 points behind the Celts. Celtic reached the final of the Scottish Cup, but their defence of the trophy proved ultimately unsuccessful as they lost 2-0 to St Mirren. Goalkeeper Peter Shevlin looked at fault for both of St Mirren's strikes.

Celtic had managed well without Patsy Gallacher in that 1925-26 season, and as Willie Maley looked ahead he decided that the inside forward's services were no longer indispensable. Gallacher was now 33 and had suffered injury problems and was, accordingly, offered reduced terms at a meeting in Maley's Bank restaurant. The player decided he would like to move on rather than

50 Greatest Players

PATSY GALLACHER Centre forward

Born: Ramelton, Co. Donegal

Joined Celtic: 1911   **From:** Clydebank Juniors

Debut: v St Mirren, League, 2 December 1911

Appearances: 464   **Goals:** 192

Left Celtic: 1926   **For:** Falkirk

Honours won with Celtic: 6 league championships; 4 Scottish Cups; 10 caps (N. Ireland)

Patsy Gallacher was reputed to be a dour individual off the field, but his actions in a Celtic shirt brightened many lives. His goal in the 1925 Scottish Cup final against Dundee was a moment of individualism typical of this performing artist. It was his last final for Celtic and the one for which he is understandably best remembered, but he had also made an equally effective impact in his first Scottish Cup final, against Clyde in April 1912. The confident 18-year-old, having made his debut only four months earlier, scored the second goal with a rare header in Celtic's 2-0 victory.

His slim build and lack of height meant that opponents often had the impression that Patsy could be kicked into submission. They would be surprised when he took the initiative and, as he put it, 'got his retaliation in first'. 'The Mighty Atom' was the complete Celtic player: audacious, cheeky, willing to take the gamble that he could defy the odds and that his individual brilliance on the ball would be enough to outdo bigger, stronger opponents. In 1926, manager Willie Maley, deciding he was past his best, offered Patsy the minimum wage. Still only 33, Patsy went to Falkirk, giving them six good years of service, leaving the Celtic support with nothing other than loving memories of his swoops, swerves and special style.

Great Matches

SCOTTISH CUP FINAL   Hampden Park, 11 April 1925

Celtic 2   **Dundee 1**   **Attendance 75,317**
Gallacher   McLean
McGrory

Things had been looking up for Celtic. In the six weeks prior to the final thay had beaten Dundee 4-0, inflicted a 5-0 annihilation on Rangers in the Scottish Cup semi-final and followed up with eight goals in their next two League games. So there was a massive sense of anti-climax when, after 30 minutes, Dundee's centre forward 34-year-old Davie McLean, who had left Celtic all of 16 years previously, smacked the ball into the net from close range.

Celtic pressed hard after the break but nothing they did could break Dundee's resistance until, 15 minutes from time, Patsy Gallacher moved on to the ball inside his own half and went weaving past one desperate Dundee challenge after another, a run that took him deep into the heart of his opponents' penalty area. Finally, a defender succeeded in stopping him and grounded the Celt inside the six-yard box. Incredibly, Patsy then jammed the ball between his feet and, as everyone watched in wonder, performed a somersault that took him over the goal-line to give Celtic the equalizer. The Dundee players could not believe what they had seen and Celtic took advantage of their bewilderment to score a swift second through Jimmy McGrory. That victory, their 11th Scottish Cup final win, meant that Celtic had won the trophy more times than any other club, a distinction that had been achieved in a most distinctive way.

Celtic: Shevlin, W. McStay, Hilley, Wilson, J. McStay, McFarlane, Connolly, Gallacher, McGrory, Thomson, McLean.

Dundee: Britton, Brown, Thomson, Ross, W. Rankine, Irving, Duncan, McLean, Halliday, J. Rankine, Gilmour.

accept a reduction in his status at the club. It did not seem too much of a problem since Tommy McInally had shone for the title-winners, but for the 1926-27 season McInally would revert to type – inconsistent and wasteful in one match, then marvellously effective in the next.

The team did start the season well and were among the title contenders until Christmas, but a disastrous run of defeats in the new year saw Celtic tumble down the table, finishing seven points behind Rangers and two points behind Motherwell. One of those defeats was a 4-1 setback to Falkirk, Patsy Gallacher's new club, although Celtic had triumphed over the same opponents in a Scottish Cup semi-final at Ibrox 11 days earlier. Adam

Jimmy McGrory (in white) puts St Mirren's keeper Morrison under pressure as Celtic go on the attack in the 1926 Scottish Cup final.

McLean had scored the only goal of the game in front of a crowd of 73,000 to take Celtic into the 1927 Scottish Cup final.

Gripping Radio

It looked a formality for Celtic to take the trophy as their opponents were East Fife, who despite being Scottish League football's highest scorers with 103 goals, had finished sixth in the Second Division at the end of that 1926-27 season. As with Celtic, who chalked up just two goals fewer, East Fife were a team geared to attacking football with a defence that was commensurately fragile. For the first time the Cup final was transmitted on radio and it proved a gripping event for the 81,000 crowd and for those listening at home.

Celtic were without Jimmy McGrory through injury and that disadvantage was compounded after just seven minutes when the East Fife centre forward, Wood, opened the scoring. Celtic equalized within a minute when the Fifers' Robertson put through his own goal. It made for an intriguing opening to the match and the seemingly mismatched teams remained on level terms until ten minutes before half-time, when Adam McLean finished off a stylish move, netting a sweet shot and putting Celtic 2-1 up. One minute after half-time, Connolly made it 3-1 when he went through on the goalkeeper and patiently waited for the right moment before slipping the ball into the net. East Fife battled manfully but with no further scoring Celtic ended the season with the Cup and a certain degree of satisfaction.

That Cup run had had the interesting benefit of introducing a new goalkeeper to the Celtic team. John Thomson had been brought into the side in February 1927 after Peter Shevlin's disastrous performance in the 6-3 victory over Brechin City. Shevlin had also conceded three goals to Hibs three days before the Brechin match, in a 3-2 defeat that severely dented the Celts' hopes of taking the 1926-27 championship. Manager Maley was never afraid to put young players into his team and decided to give Thomson, who had just turned 18, a chance to prove himself at the top level. The teenage Thomson performed with panache for the remainder of that season and swiftly established himself as Celtic's number one goalkeeper.

Tommy McInally's form was not quite so pleasing – his attitude to training grew ever more lax as his appetite for nightlife increased and he began to pile on the pounds. The autumn of 1927 saw him incur a suspension from the club for 'a breach of training rules' and his unprofessional attitude saw him dropping in and out of the team throughout the season. In October 1927, he received an SFA suspension after being sent off against Rangers, and in early 1928 he was suspended once again by Celtic, again for a training-related misdemeanour.

Such disciplinary problems handicapped the team and Celtic finished five points behind champions Rangers at the end of the 1927-28 season. Celtic made the Scottish Cup final and not only did they receive a 4-0 defeat at the hands of Rangers but also had to witness the Ibrox men capturing their first Scottish League and Cup double.

Two notable names reached for the exit door at Celtic Park in the summer of 1928. Tommy McInally, inevitably, was transferred, to Sunderland in May 1928, and the skilful outside left Adam McLean, still only 29, joined him at Roker Park in August 1928. McLean had spoken out on behalf of the players, by complaining about unsatisfactory payments for playing some friendly matches that summer. His reward was to discover that the financial terms offered to him for the 1928-29 season were considerably lower than those he had received previously. It proved impossible for Celtic to patch up their forward line after the loss of those two creative types. The team hit just 67 goals in the 1928-29 season, 26 fewer than in 1927-28. Celtic sank in the

The Celtic team about to take part in the 1928 Glasgow Cup final against Queen's Park. From left. Back row: Wilson, McGrory, Gray, McCallum, Donoghue, McFarlane. Front row: Alec Thomson, John Thomson, McStay, McGonagle, Connolly.

League, finishing 16 points behind champions Rangers, who finished the 1920s by celebrating their eighth League title of that decade. The only consolation for Celtic was the ongoing goalscoring excellence of Jimmy McGrory.

The team relied on McGrory's goals more than ever, but he was plagued by injury throughout the following 1929-30 season. Celtic finished fourth in the League, 11 points behind Rangers, and lost to St Mirren in the early stages of the Scottish Cup. At Celtic Park, the drama of that 1929-30 season unfolded in front of a brand new South Stand. It seated 4,800 spectators who overlooked a standing enclosure to either side of the players' tunnel. This stand would remain in place for the succeeding four decades.

Celtic, with a rejuvenated forward line, ran Rangers close for the title in 1930-31 and made it to that season's Scottish Cup final, where they would meet Motherwell, who had taken over from Lanarkshire rivals Airdrie as the team most likely to challenge the Old Firm.

With 105,000 looking on at Hampden, Motherwell zipped into a 2-0 half-time lead. They were the complete superiors of Celtic for most of the match. Ten minutes from time, Jimmy McGrory prodded the ball into the Motherwell net, but it looked like being too little too late. As the seconds

Jimmy McGrory challenges the keeper in Celtic's 1931 Scottish Cup semi-final against Kilmarnock. The Celts won 3-0 to face Motherwell in the final.

drifted away and the Motherwell support prepared to celebrate, outside right Bertie Thomson managed to elude his marker to send a cross whirring dangerously into the Motherwell penalty area. It caused confusion at the heart of the Motherwell defence; so much so that centre half Alan Craig made a desperate attempt to clear the ball only to head it into his own net for a most dramatic Celtic equalizer.

The replay proved less complicated: one goal from McGrory and two from Bertie Thomson had Celtic 3-1 ahead at half-time. Motherwell got one back midway through the second half but with only a few minutes remaining Jimmy McGrory found himself unmarked inside the penalty area with the Motherwell goalkeeper, Alan McClory, well out of position. The centre forward gently guided a header into the net to give Celtic a 4-2 victory and the 1931 Scottish Cup. The Celtic support trooped out of Hampden Park that wet April evening convinced that the good times were back after four, long trophyless years. It would not be long before their cheers turned to tears.

Chapter Four: 1931-45
Testing Times

The Celtic directors had long held an ambition for the club to undertake a tour of North America. That ambition was finally realized in the summer of 1931. It was an extensive undertaking, which involved a sea voyage in both directions and a total of 13 fixtures, which were played over a six-week period. The Celtic party landed in New York and visited such cities as Montreal, Toronto, Philadelphia and Chicago. Their opposition included the New York Yankees, the New York Giants, the Michigan All Stars, Pawtucket Rangers and Ulster United. Celtic won nine, lost three and drew one of their matches, scoring 48 goals and conceding 18.

The opportunity to get a rare glimpse of Celtic in live action brought Scottish and Irish emigrants from far and wide. Yet although Willie Maley, the Celtic manager, was moved to comment on their warm reception, 'Our journey was just like a royal procession', the American adventure also had

The Scottish Cup holders on tour prior to the 1931-32 season. The players, back row, from left, are: A. Thomson, McStay, J. Thomson, Napier, McGonagle. Front row: Wilson, B. Thomson, Scarff, Geatons, Cook.

its troublesome moments. A number of Celtic's opponents resorted to a highly physical approach to the game. Jimmy McGrory had his jaw fractured in a match against Hakoah, and at the final whistle in the 3-1 defeat by Pawtucket Rangers, four Celtic players set upon Pawtucket's Sam Kennedy, a former Clyde player.

Tragedy at Ibrox

The entire party was exhausted by the time of their return to Britain from New York but a strong sense of team spirit had been forged. Five weeks after their final North American tour match, Celtic opened their 1931-32 Scottish League fixtures with a 3-0 victory away to Leith Athletic. Five victories and two draws in their opening seven fixtures primed them perfectly for their first encounter with Rangers that season, on 5 September 1931 at Ibrox. A crowd of 80,000 watched the game, which quickly degenerated into a kicking match. Scoring opportunities were rare as the two great rivals knocked lumps out of each other in a goalless first half.

Five minutes after the interval, Rangers created one of the game's few openings when a quick through pass sent their forward Sam English streaking towards John Thomson's goal. The goalkeeper raced out to close him down. English got to the ball a fraction of a second before Thomson and nicked it round the goalkeeper with his right foot. Thomson's bravery had led him to dive at English's feet and when Thomson missed the ball his head suffered the full impact of the onrushing forward's left knee. Thomson lay perfectly still on the spot. English, who had been hurt in the collision, sportingly hobbled over, to check on the Celt. Jimmy McStay had reached his goalkeeper first to find blood jetting from a wound in Thomson's head and the two players immediately signalled to the touchline for medical attention.

John Thomson was carried from the field on a stretcher, with his head bandaged, and in the dressing room he was diagnosed as having suffered a depressed fracture of the skull. He was rushed to the Victoria Infirmary in Langside. Jimmy McGrory dashed to the hospital after the end of the match and stayed by John Thomson's side in the hospital until the goalkeeper passed away at 9.25pm.

An estimated 30,000 people attended John Thomson's funeral in the mining village of Cardenden in Fife the following Wednesday. Three days later a two-minute silence preceded Celtic's home match with Queen's Park as the Celtic support continued to come to terms with the sudden, untimely passing of one of their great favourites. The Thomson tragedy would be compounded later in the month when Peter Scarff, an inside forward who had made 112 appearances and scored 55 goals for Celtic, was unable to take the field for the second half of a match after having spent the first half gasping for breath. Tuberculosis was diagnosed and after two years of treatment Peter died at the age of 25.

Although Thomson and Scarff would live on long in the memories of the Celtic supporters, the difficult task of finding replacements fell to the manager. Willie Maley already had a solution to the goalkeeping vacancy in mind. Joe Kennaway had impressed him hugely when he had produced a series of fine saves for Fall River in their 1-0 victory over Celtic during the North American tour. Kennaway, a 26-year-old Canadian, was sent for in the aftermath of Thomson's death.

Kennaway soon proved himself worthy of Maley's extensive efforts to recruit him and he was to play one of his greatest games for the club in the 1933 Scottish Cup final. Motherwell, watched by a 102,339 Hampden crowd, took control of the game in the early stages, but several fine saves

50 Greatest Players

JOHN THOMSON Goalkeeper

Born: Buckhaven

Joined Celtic: 1926   **From:** Wellesley Juniors

Debut: v Dundee, League, 12 February 1927

Appearances: 188

Left Celtic: Deceased

Honours won with Celtic: 1 league championship; 2 Scottish Cups; 4 caps (Scotland)

The tragedy that snuffed out John Thomson's life on a September day in 1931 cast a pall over Celtic Park. Thomson was known for his openness and courage and it was poignant that the latter quality ended his life at the age of 22. He had shown in his short life all the qualities of an outstanding goalkeeper: agility, quick reactions and safe, sure handling skills.

John Thomson made his first-team debut as a teenager after a spell on loan at Ayr United. When he got the chance to prove himself in the Celtic first team he grabbed it with both hands. The quiet Fifer made his international debut for Scotland in a 2-0 victory over France in Paris in the spring of 1930. Still the automatic choice for his country when he died, Thomson conceded just one goal in four international appearances. The memorial card printed in his honour after his death was perfect in its emotional accuracy, 'They never die who live in the hearts of those they leave behind.'

from Kennaway kept the scoreline at 0-0 and Celtic gradually began to take a grip on proceedings. Three minutes after half-time, the ball bounced around the Motherwell penalty area as Celtic forwards miskicked and Motherwell defenders half-cleared. It eventually landed at the feet of Jimmy McGrory, who clipped the ball into the net for the only goal of a dour game.

A Barren Spell

Celtic's tilts at the title during the early 1930s proved fruitless. They were well adrift of the leading teams and in 1932 the 18-point gap that separated Celtic from champions Motherwell was the furthest the club had ever finished behind the League winners. They finished fourth at the end of the 1933 Cup-winning season, behind Rangers, Hearts and Motherwell, and third in the 1933-34 season, behind Rangers and Motherwell.

The 18-points deficit of 1932 was superseded in 1934, when Celtic finished the season 19 points behind champions Rangers. Willie Maley put the dousing of Celtic's championship spirit down to the pall of gloom that had been cast over the club by the death of John Thomson. 'The shock had a tremendous effect on our players,' was his analysis, 'one which we firmly

Jimmy McStay leads Celtic out for their first match after the death of John Thomson.

believe was responsible for many failures during the next few years. The team was playing first-class football when the blow fell, and continued to do so, but without any great fire or enthusiasm. It seemed as if they had lost heart.'

The Scottish Cup proved equally fruitless in the three seasons after Celtic took the trophy in the 1933 final. They went out of the tournament in unspectacular fashion in 1934, 1935 and 1936. The third of those exits was brought about by a 2-1 home defeat at the hands of St Johnstone, but by then Celtic were on course for their first League title in ten years.

Joe Kennaway filled the Celtic goalkeeper's jersey consistently well after the tragic death of John Thomson.

A new, youthful team had pushed Rangers close for the 1934-35 title, eventually finishing just three points behind their rivals and the team was strengthened for the 1935-36 season when the indomitable English-born centre half Willie Lyon was signed from Queen's Park in the summer of 1935.

Toughening-up

Lyon's introduction was symptomatic of an all-round toughening-up of the Celtic side. His fellow half backs George Paterson and Chic Geatons were hard workers who would compete like demons to win the ball before using it to maximum effect. Energetic full backs Bobby Hogg and Jock Morrison completed the strong defensive shield in front of keeper Kennaway. They provided a platform for a new Celtic forward line, which embodied the attacking traditions of the club, to display their talents. The exceptionally skilled outside right Jimmy Delaney worked in tandem with Willie Buchan, a clever, inventive inside right who was also prepared to do his share of defending or tackling back. On the left wing, Frank Murphy's explosive pace and crossing power was complemented by the tricky inside left Johnny Crum, whose clever positioning made him an elusive target for despairing defenders. The great Jimmy McGrory, still only in his early thirties, remained the sharp spearhead of the attack.

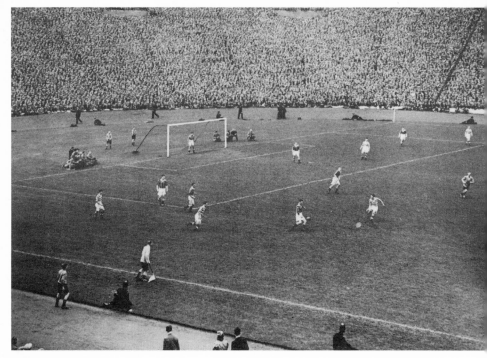

A European record crowd of 146,433 filled Hampden Park for the 1937 Scottish Cup final.

Celtic were now a real handful for their opponents – each of the five fingers of their attack was capable of poking holes in the best-organized defence. Every member of that forward line could win a match on his own and each of them were just as likely to score goals as to make them for their team-mates. After years of fitful performances Celtic were once again Scotland's premier purveyors of top-quality football. That powerful, talented side was irresistible in the 1935-36 season. They scored 115 goals – 48 of them from McGrory – and conceded just 33 as they galloped to the Scottish League title, ending the season five points clear of Rangers and Aberdeen.

Jimmy McGrory played a vital role in Celtic's Scottish Cup triumph in the 1936-37 season, scoring nine of the team's 20 goals on the way to their victory over Aberdeen. He turned 33 just two days after the defeat of Aberdeen at Hampden, but the wear and tear of playing at centre forward was beginning to catch up with him. He had ignored an injury to play in the final, but early in the 1937-38 season decided it was time to retire from the playing side of football. He moved on to become manager of Kilmarnock, but not before scoring a goal in his final appearance as a Celtic player in a 4-3 victory over Queen's Park in October 1937.

Great Matches

SCOTTISH CUP FINAL   Hampden Park, 24 April 1937

Celtic 2   **Aberdeen 1**   Attendance 146,433
Crum   Armstrong
Buchan

The Celtic players were met by a wall of noise that almost shook them off their feet when they took the field for the final of the 1937 Scottish Cup. There were, officially, 146,433 inside the stadium to see Celtic take on Aberdeen, but around 5,000 more had managed to enter for free, packing the terraces at Hampden Park. It is still the record attendance for a European club match and it shows the extent to which football had captured the Scottish public's imagination by the 1930s.

Aberdeen had finished above Celtic in the League, but the Dons looked the more disconcerted by the shuddering sound of the crowd. Celtic's creative maestro Willie Buchan soon began to conduct affairs from his inside forward position. After 11 minutes he shot for goal. The Aberdeen goalkeeper George Johnstone couldn't hold the ball and Johnny Crum stole in to plant it in the net.

In an energetic, engaging game, it took Aberdeen just a minute to equalize. Both sides missed good chances then midway through the second half, Jimmy McGrory, playing despite carrying an injury, trapped the ball on his chest and pushed a pass into the path of Buchan. The forward flew on to the ball and scooped a shot past Johnstone that was slowed when it clipped the inside of the goalkeeper's right-hand post before bouncing over the line and into the net. Celtic and Aberdeen had graced a great occasion and Celtic had captured the Cup for the 15th time.

Celtic: Kennaway, Hogg, Morrison, Geatons, Lyon, Paterson, Delaney, Buchan, McGrory, Crum, Murphy.

Aberdeen: Johnstone, Cooper, Temple, Dunlop, Falloon, Thomson, Bynon, McKenzie, Armstrong, Mills, Lang.

The space vacated by McGrory would soon become filled by a very different type of centre forward. Johnny Crum switched from inside left to become the focal point of the Celtic forward line signalling a turnaround in tactics for Celtic. McGrory had been a bustling physical presence, powerful in the air and prepared to put pressure on goalkeepers with fierce shoulder-charges. In direct contrast, Crum was a lightweight who compensated for his lack of muscle with a keen sense of positioning and a refined touch on the ball. His move had another advantage as it allowed the equally talented John Divers to take his inside forward position.

50 Greatest Players

JIMMY McGRORY Forward

Born: Glasgow

Joined Celtic: 1921   **From:** St Roch's Juniors

Debut: v Third Lanark, League, 20 January, 1923

Appearances: 445   **Goals:** 468

Left Celtic: 1937 (retired)

Honours won with Celtic: 3 league championships; 4 Scottish Cups; 7 caps (Scotland)

'He could hit the ball further with his head than some could with their boot,' states Jackie Watters, a team-mate of Jimmy McGrory in the 1930s. That had been well illustrated in October 1926 when McGrory headed four goals and scored one with his boot in a 6-2 victory over Aberdeen. McGrory had been a regular in the Celtic first team for little over a year, but was already a peerless goalscorer. He ended that 1926-27 season with a new scoring record for the Scottish First Division – 47 goals. He topped that in 1935-36 with a tally of 50.

The broad-shouldered, solid McGrory was built to endure the rigours of the highly physical Scottish game of the 1920s and 1930s. A genial man, he was always prepared to help others, especially younger players, but on the field he was single-minded. That was heavily underlined on 14 January 1928 when he hit a hat-trick in the opening nine minutes of a League match against Dunfermline Athletic at Celtic Park. He scored five more times that afternoon as Celtic won 9-0. Those eight goals remain the record individual scoring tally for a player in Scotland's top division.

Willie Maley tried to sell Jimmy McGrory to Arsenal in the summer of 1928, but McGrory declined a move. The Celtic board, denied a hefty transfer fee, reacted by secretly paying McGrory less than his team-mates for the next decade. It was a mean-spirited way in which to treat a player who never sold anyone short. By the time he left Celtic to become manager of Kilmarnock in 1937 he had scored 468 goals in 445 Scottish League and Cup appearances for the club. He remains the most prolific goalscorer in the history of Celtic.

The other Celtic inside forward, Willie Buchan, meanwhile, was sold to Blackpool for £10,000 in November 1937. Buchan, the hero of the 1937 Cup final, had had no thoughts of a move and was happy at Celtic, but the club decided to cash in on his talents and he was unceremoniously told he was moving south. Malky MacDonald took over from him at inside right.

The changes to the Celtic forward line saw the team begin to play in a new style that was revolutionary for Scottish football. MacDonald, Divers and Crum would switch positions as and when necessary, filling in for each other, and confusing defenders who would be pulled all over the place whenever Celtic went on the attack. With Delaney and Murphy supplying quick service from the wings, Celtic were simply too fast and too tricky for most of their less progressive opponents. 'It all emanated from a wee fellow called John Crum,' recalled MacDonald. 'I think it brought success because it was a different pattern. Previously the pattern had been to have centre forwards like Jimmy McGrory as spearheads. We didn't have a spearhead. John Crum was the fellow who made us because his positional play was phenomenal. There was nothing rehearsed. John was as fly on the field as he was off the field.'

Such intricate, unpredictable play brought the crowds flocking to Celtic Park during the economic boom of the late 1930s. On New Year's Day 1938, a record attendance of 82,500 saw Divers score twice and MacDonald once

Celtic in summer 1937. Back row, from left: Geatons, Hogg, Kennaway, Morrison, Crum, Paterson. Front row: Delaney, MacDonald, Lyon, Divers, Murphy.

July 1937: pre-season training for (from left to right) Divers, Millar, Murphy and Delaney.

in a 3-0 victory over Rangers. Their stunning style helped bring Celtic the League title at the end of the 1937-38 season; the team scoring 114 goals and finishing three points clear of Hearts and 12 ahead of Rangers. It would have been sufficient for the club to celebrate the 50th year of its existence with that triumph, but they were provided with the bonus of also having a special one-off trophy for which to compete in the early summer of 1938.

A celebration of the British Empire was taking place in Bellahouston Park on Glasgow's southside that year and as part of the Empire Exhibition, as it was known, a tournament was held showcasing some of the finest teams in British football. Four clubs represented Scotland – Aberdeen, Hearts, Celtic and Rangers – and four represented England – Brentford, Chelsea, Everton and Sunderland. The tournament was held over a fortnight at Ibrox Park, which was within walking distance of the exhibition, and Celtic faced Sunderland in their opening match. It resulted in a 0-0 draw, which in pre-penalty shootout days meant there would be a replay – the following evening. Sunderland took the lead but after an equalizer from Crum, John Divers scored twice to clinch victory. Crum scored the only goal of Celtic's semi-final with Hearts to set up a final on 10 June 1938 with an Everton side that featured two highly promising young stars in Tommy Lawton and Joe Mercer.

It proved to be a game that had everything and the 82,000 present were enthralled by the football on display. After 90 goalless minutes, extra-time

50 Greatest Players

JIMMY DELANEY Winger

Born: Cleland

Joined Celtic: 1933   **From:** Stoneyburn Juniors

Debut: v Hearts, League, 18 August 1934

Appearances: 160   **Goals:** 74

Left Celtic: 1946   **For:** Manchester United

Honours won with Celtic: 2 league championships; 1 Scottish Cup; 9 caps (Scotland)

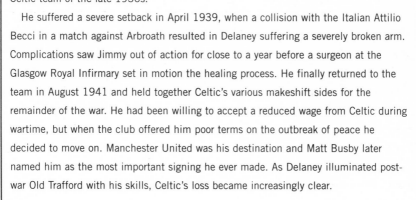

Substance and style made Jimmy Delaney one of the finest and best-loved wingers in Celtic's history. He was fast, he was clever and he carved out superb crosses with marvellous consistency. He was also essentially modest about his own talents and quick to give credit to others for his own success. In truth, Delaney was absolutely vital to the smooth functioning of the winning Celtic team of the late 1930s.

He suffered a severe setback in April 1939, when a collision with the Italian Attilio Becci in a match against Arbroath resulted in Delaney suffering a severely broken arm. Complications saw Jimmy out of action for close to a year before a surgeon at the Glasgow Royal Infirmary set in motion the healing process. He finally returned to the team in August 1941 and held together Celtic's various makeshift sides for the remainder of the war. He had been willing to accept a reduced wage from Celtic during wartime, but when the club offered him poor terms on the outbreak of peace he decided to move on. Manchester United was his destination and Matt Busby later named him as the most important signing he ever made. As Delaney illuminated post-war Old Trafford with his skills, Celtic's loss became increasingly clear.

was played and Celtic sealed victory with a goal of quality. Divers set up Crum who put the ball through the legs of the Everton centre half before placing it in the net. The Empire Exhibition Cup belonged to Celtic.

'We had a great understanding,' was how Jimmy Delaney, Celtic's outside right for that game, remembered those days. 'Johnny Crum was very tricky when he was playing centre forward. Malky MacDonald was one of those boys that could hold the ball. You didn't need to beat men: Malky would beat them for you. He would give you the pass and you would have nothing else to do but cross it. It was the same with Johnny Divers. He would run into great positions and he was a great header of the ball too. Frank Murphy

50 Greatest Players

JOHNNY CRUM Centre forward

Born: Glasgow

Joined Celtic: 1932   **From:** Ashfield Juniors

Debut: v Motherwell, League, 22 October 1932

Appearances: 211   **Goals:** 87

Left Celtic: 1942   **For:** Morton

Honours won with Celtic: 2 league championships; 1 Scottish Cup, 2 caps (Scotland)

An unconventional, individualistic man by nature, Johnny Crum was a groundbreaker in Scottish football. He turned on its head the notion that a centre forward had to be big and tough to get results. Instead, he relied on his football brain to guide him into the most effective position to pounce and score.

He was the fulcrum of the 'Terrible Trio' of Crum, Divers and MacDonald who bamboozled staid defenders in the late 1930s with speedy interchanges of position and quick feet. Johnny was 27 when war broke out and both he and that Celtic team were at their peak but he was surprisingly transferred to Morton in 1942. The war had torn his football career apart, but his feats of the late 1930s ensure that he will be remembered as the focal point of Celtic's revolutionary style of football.

was a great, direct player, a great winger. He could shoot and put over lovely crosses. We had a great forward line; a great team. To me, it was the best Celtic team I ever played in.'

The Empire Exhibition trophy was on display six days after that match, on 16 June 1938, at a Golden Jubilee dinner held by Celtic in the Grosvenor Restaurant, Gordon Street, Glasgow. John Kelly, who had kept goal in Celtic's first League season, was among those present, as were James Bell, another of the club's earliest goalkeepers, Jimmy McGrory, Jimmy Quinn and the prodigal son, Tommy McInally. The toast to the club was proposed by the honorary president of Glasgow Rangers, Sir John Cargill. He paid tribute to Celtic, describing it as an Irish club and stating that the fine characteristics of the Irish race included 'their generosity and large-heartedness' and made them 'the greatest sportsmen in the world'. It was a happy occasion and Willie Maley's long service to the club was marked by the directors presenting him with a gift of 2,500 guineas, which comprised 50 guineas for every year in which he had served the club.

Great Managers – 1897-1939

WILLIE MALEY

'A labour of love' was how Willie Maley described his 50 years of service to Celtic during his speech at the club's Golden Jubilee dinner in 1938. Only 18 months later he found himself exiled from the club he had driven from success to success.

Maley had grown in stature and status in tandem with Celtic. He had been appointed secretary-manager in 1897 and soon proved adept at spotting talented young players in junior football, signing them cheaply and often moving them on for a sizeable profit. As many a player seeking improved terms and conditions found out, Maley was also a strict disciplinarian. One look from Maley could freeze them in their footsteps. Those bold enough still to insist on putting their case forward to the manager often found themselves swiftly ejected from the club.

Painstaking craftsmanship had enabled Maley to put together two excellent Celtic sides in the first two decades of the 20th century, but by the 1920s and 1930s there were signs that his powers were on the wane. A succession of players left the club after petty financial disputes and others were transferred against their will. Rangers dominated Scottish football and Maley found it an ongoing struggle to match the Ibrox club. Success became elusive and when, in the late 1930s, Maley, then 71, fell into dispute with the Celtic directors, he suffered the fate of swift removal that he himself had inflicted on so many players down the years. He is better remembered for his early career as a manager when he built Celtic teams to win with spirit, passion and panache, a tradition that survives to the present day.

That gift to Maley carried within it the seed of his own downfall as Celtic manager. On being presented with the money, he had somewhat pointedly remarked that it had been the first benefit he had received during his long connection with the club. For the next 18 months it would be the source of an ongoing wrangle between him and the Celtic board. Maley wanted Celtic to pay the tax on the gift and made clear his irritation when they refused to do so. Eventually, in December 1939, the Celtic chairman Tom White and his fellow directors took the bold decision to sever ties with their irascible manager. They had grown increasingly tired of his demanding ways and irritable persona; some directors also felt he had acquired too much

Wartime manager Jimmy McStay gets down to work in his office at Celtic Park.

power within the club and they wished to have more of a say in team matters themselves.

Maley's successor, former centre back and captain Jimmy McStay, was a mild-mannered individual, much more likely to yield to the wishes of the directors. By the time of his appointment in February 1940, however, football had been pushed very much to the back of most people's minds. Britain had declared war on Germany and the country was preparing for the ordeal that lay ahead. Football was suspended briefly by the government then allowed to continue as an aide to morale – but only on a regional league basis for financial reasons.

Celtic played in the Western Regional League in the 1939-40 season and in the Southern League from 1940 to 1946, but fielding a consistent team was impossible. Players were called up to the armed services or to work in the mines or factories to help with the war effort. Celtic, like other clubs, also utilized guest footballers who were stationed at bases close to the club.

It was unfortunate for Jimmy McStay to have taken charge at the club during that unstable period, but when the war ended and football looked to resume in a serious way the directorate removed him from his position. He had no idea that he was about to lose his job as manager at Celtic until, on holiday in July 1945, he read about it in the newspaper. It seemed a shoddy way to dispose of the services of a great servant of the club, especially when another great Celtic servant, Jimmy McGrory, was the man the directors had lined up to take his place. It seemed as though the board had seen McStay merely as a caretaker manager in time of war and the difficult task of Celtic's post-war reconstruction would be placed firmly in the hands of Jimmy McGrory. It would prove to be another testing time for everyone at Celtic Park.

Chapter Five: 1945-57
Post-war Reconstruction

There was a fresh look about Celtic as football greeted a new dawn in the years after the Second World War. The team had a new manager: Jimmy McGrory, Celtic's goalscoring hero of the 1920s and 30s. McGrory had been manager of Kilmarnock since 1937, taking them to the 1938 Scottish Cup final against East Fife, which they lost only after a replay. He was a hugely popular figure among the Celtic support who were pleased to welcome home such an illustrious former player and dedicated Celtic servant.

The war years had been undistinguished for Celtic. They had played in the Southern League, a wartime creation, and had hovered around mid-table during its early years, although in the two latter seasons of the war – 1943-44 and 1944-45 – Celtic had finished as runners-up to Rangers. Football remained regionalized for its first post-war season and Celtic finished fourth in the Scottish Southern League.

Despite general excitement at the restart of serious league football, Celtic supporters found the club unable to resume their place at the head of the Scottish game. During the war, the directors had taken the decision to run the club on a most basic level. Wages were reduced and star players from the pre-war years had been jettisoned. Johnny Crum and John Divers had moved to Morton, Malky MacDonald to Kilmarnock and Frank Murphy had been given a free transfer. Only Jimmy Delaney remained from Celtic's exceptional pre-war forward line and during that first post-war season he too would move on, much to the dismay of the Celtic support.

Delaney's wages at Celtic – in common with those of his team-mates – had been stripped to £2 per week during the war and the player had accepted such a cut in good faith. As football regained normality in the first post-war season, he discovered that the directors were unwilling to meet Celtic's star man's modest financial requests and he was transferred to Manchester United in February 1946 for a £4,000 fee.

Jimmy McGrory as Celtic manager.

Delaney had been vital to Celtic during the war, binding the team together as much through his team-mates' confidence in him as through his own inspirational play, sometimes on the wing, sometimes at centre forward. Now that he had gone, only the versatile defensive player Matt Lynch and Bobby Hogg, a sterling servant to the club at right-back, remained from the great Celtic sides of the immediate pre-war period.

The club's wartime policy of limiting team resources has been criticized for short-sightedness. This seems harsh in that no one knew when or how the war was going to end. However, it was not an altogether stagnant time at the club; numerous signings were made during the war years, and almost always these signings were in the Celtic tradition of bringing on board promising local youngsters.

When Scottish League competition resumed in the 1946-47 season, most of the players at McGrory's disposal were eager but untested. Goalkeeper Willie Miller, centre half Jimmy Mallan, inside forward Bobby Evans and John McPhail, who was initially used as a centre half and later as a centre forward, were all in their late teens or early twenties. They were promising players but their inexperience showed through an inconsistency of team

Celtic's young guns of 1948. Back row, from left: Evans, Boden, McAuley, Miller, Milne, Mallan. Front row: Weir, McPhail, Lavery, Tully, Paton.

performance. A mid-table showing in 1946-47 was disheartening, but in the 1947-48 season disaster threatened when the club slipped and slid towards the nether reaches of the League. Hogg made only a handful of appearances that season and Lynch was absent altogether. Delaney, meanwhile, was thriving in Manchester and would end that 1947-48 season with an FA Cup winner's medal. His ability to help that boyish Celtic team knit together was being sorely missed and in the spring of 1948 Celtic became mired in a desperate battle against relegation.

It was the first time in their history Celtic had been threatened with the drop and that prospect so alarmed the Celtic directors that, in February 1948, they sanctioned the £7,000 signing of Jock Weir, a 25-year-old outside right, from Blackburn Rovers. Weir was a colourful character off the field, a ladies' man who enjoyed the high life. He immediately helped Celtic out of a serious run of defeats – two victories and a draw resulting from his first three appearances in League fixtures. Weir then missed three successive League matches, all of which ended in defeats for Celtic, but he was back for the final fixture of that 1947-48 season, an away match against Dundee at Dens Park.

Relegation Trouble
Celtic were still in serious relegation trouble: if they failed to win in Dundee their fate would be in other's hands. With 31,000 looking on, Weir opened the scoring when he forced the ball over the line after a goalmouth melee inside the Dundee penalty area. Dundee, who were placed fourth in the table, fought back to go 2-1 ahead, but Weir came to Celtic's rescue once more, scoring two more goals to give Celtic a 3-2 victory and ensure their standing in the top division for another season.

It transpired that other results did go Celtic's way at the end of that 1947-48 season, but they had still finished only four points above the relegation positions. The only silver lining was a Scottish Cup run that took them to a semi-final against Morton in the spring of that relegation-haunted year of 1948. As the tie went into extra-time, Weir, the hero at Dens Park, missed an easy chance from close-range before Morton went on to scrape a 1-0 victory and progress into the final.

The narrow escape from relegation prompted the board of directors to appoint a new coach. Jimmy Hogan, an Englishman who had been hugely influential in developing football on continental Europe during the 1920s and 1930s, arrived at the club in 1948 with many progressive new ideas on how the players should prepare for matches. The squad would appreciate his input over the following two years, particularly his radical emphasis on ballwork in training. Nevertheless, the real barrier in the way of progress at the club had still to be tackled.

At the time it was quite common for administrators to have a say in team selection and at Celtic, it was the chairman, Robert Kelly, rather than the manager who picked the team. Kelly could look to the precedent of Willie Maley, who, in his time as Celtic secretary-manager, had conferred closely with Celtic board members such as Robert Kelly's father, James, in selecting his Celtic teams. However, James Kelly had been a former Celtic player. Robert Kelly had no such playing experience at the top level. His team selections were based on his own personal whims and not on an in-depth knowledge of football from a playing perspective.

Celtic's Sean Fallon moves on to the ball against Third Lanark in August 1951. Celtic drew the League Cup tie 1-1, with Fallon scoring their goal.

The players were well aware that if the chairman simply took a dislike to a player he would be out of the team. Similarly, a poor player could be favoured because he got on well with the chairman. Jimmy McGrory had taken on the role of a manager, but he was only going through the motions; Kelly held the key to who played and which players moved in and out of the club. This set-up, unsurprisingly, resulted in extreme inconsistency and Celtic

50 Greatest Players

WILLIE MILLER Goalkeeper

Born: Glasgow

Joined Celtic: 1942   **From:** Maryhill Harp

Debut: v Hamilton Ac., Regional League, 22 August 1942

Appearances: 123

Left Celtic: 1950   **For:** Clyde

Honours won with Celtic: 6 caps (Scotland)

The athletic acrobatics of Willie Miller made him one of the best-loved of all Celtic goalkeepers. It was difficult to find a weakness in his goalkeeping: he could deal with all goalscoring efforts, regardless of height, pace or angle, a skill aided enormously by his exceptional powers of anticipation.

His clean handling was complemented by a brave disposition that often saw him plunge at the feet of incoming forwards and he was frequently injured as he did all he possibly could to protect his goal. He lost his place to Johnny Bonnar midway through the 1949-50 season and moved on to Clyde in 1950 while still only 25. He had been unlucky to join Celtic at a time when the team was toiling – better protection from better defenders might have kept him free from injuries and extended his career at a club that has not often had goalkeepers of such a high calibre.

stumbled through the late 1940s, lurching from game to game without any real long-term plan.

Success in League and Cup competition eluded Celtic until the 1950-51 season, when they progressed to the Scottish Cup final. It was Celtic's first appearance in a major Cup final since 1938 and on a bright, sunny April day almost 132,000 supporters descended on Hampden Park to see Celtic face Motherwell. There had been doubts in the approach to the game as to whether centre forward John McPhail would be fit and ready to take the field. McPhail was a powerfully built striker who struggled to maintain his optimum weight and often missed matches because of associated injuries or a lack of overall fitness. He had missed the three League matches since Celtic's semi-final victory over Raith Rovers so the supporters were relieved to see him bustle out on to the field at Hampden for the final.

After just 13 minutes left half Joe Baillie sent an incisive ball slicing through the centre of the Motherwell defence and McPhail, perfectly positioned, controlled it cutely on his heel, took it past two defenders and

Celtic's Jock Weir, Charlie Tully, Johnny Bonnar, Alex Rollo and Bertie Peacock in training during the early 1950s.

then waited for the ball to fall perfectly for him to hook it into the net. It was all Celtic required to win the Cup and for a generation of young Celtic supporters the image of 'Hooky' McPhail chasing that ball through and scoring was the outstanding memory of the immediate post-war period. After 13 barren years Celtic had finally captured some silverware.

The more optimistic Celtic fans felt sure that the Cup victory would spur the team on to better things but it was not to be. The 1951 Cup run had been the result of an inconsistent team hitting patches of form in the right matches. It had been achieved despite the lack of leadership off the field – the many undoubted talents on the Celtic staff had simply struck a rich seam of form. The reality of Celtic's situation was more accurately reflected over the long haul of a League season and in both 1951-52 and 1952-53 the team was stuck firmly in a mid-table position; they actually finished both seasons just four points above the relegation places.

Celtic also made little impact on the domestic cups over those seasons although they could often blame bad luck when they came up against their nemesis, Rangers. A League Cup semi-final in 1952, watched by an 84,000 Hampden crowd, saw both Charlie Tully and Alec Boden strike the Rangers bar, but it was the Ibrox men who put the ball in the net to win 3-0. A similar

Winger Neil Mochan charges the Dundee goalkeeper Bill Brown in Celtic's 5-1 victory at Celtic Park in February 1954.

story could be told of a fourth-round Scottish Cup tie between Celtic and Rangers in March 1953, which was watched by a 95,000 crowd at Ibrox. Rangers took an early lead and in Celtic's desperate search for an equalizer the busy midfielder Bobby Collins struck a post, Tully hit the ball against the Rangers goalkeeper and Collins saw another on-target effort headed off the Rangers line. A classic hard-luck story was completed when Rangers raced away to score a second goal two minutes from time.

There was one last chance of glory at the end of another testing 12 months for Celtic and their support when, in the summer of 1953, the club participated in the Coronation Cup, a tournament in honour of the recent accession to the throne of Queen Elizabeth II. This competition would be played along similar lines to the 1938 Exhibition Cup and it featured four crowd-pulling sides from

England and four from Scotland: Aberdeen, Arsenal, Celtic, Hibernian, Manchester United, Newcastle United, Rangers and Tottenham Hotspur. The matches were to be played at Ibrox and Hampden Park.

Best of British

Celtic were presented with the most difficult opening match possible, against English champions Arsenal, but they took the lead when Bobby Collins drove a corner-kick straight into the Arsenal net. Over the 90 minutes Celtic outplayed the Gunners entirely and the final result of 1-0 was an inaccurate reflection of Celtic's domination of the match in front of a 60,000 crowd. Five days later, 73,000 saw Celtic outmanoeuvre Manchester United in midfield, beating them 2-1 in another impressive victory. It sent Celtic into the Coronation Cup final where they were to face an excellent Hibernian side who had been Scottish champions in 1951 and 1952, and who had lost out on the 1952-53 title to Rangers only on goal average.

Neil Mochan, an outside left signed from Middlesbrough only three days before the tournament began, opened the scoring for Celtic against Hibs with a

powerful, long-range shot 28 minutes into the match. As in their previous two Coronation Cup ties Celtic were overwhelming their opponents and at half-time the majority of the 118,000 crowd believed that the cup was on its way to Celtic Park. The proud Hibs emerged after the break determined to claw their way back into the game and their 'Famous Five' forward line of Gordon Smith, Bobby Johnstone, Lawrie Reilly, Eddie Turnbull and Willie Ormond soon began to test the Celtic defence. Celtic held firm, chiefly through the work of goalkeeper Johnny Bonnar and centre half Jock Stein. Three minutes from time the versatile forward Jimmy Walsh made it 2-0 to Celtic and they had won the Coronation Cup, one of

Jock Stein proved an inspirational captain of Celtic during the 1950s.

the most unexpected but memorable triumphs in the club's history.

Celtic centre half Jock Stein (third right) oversees the situation as goalkeeper Johnny Bonnar clutches the ball during the 1954 Scottish Cup final between Celtic and Aberdeen, which ended 2-1 to Celtic.

Guiding Force

The contribution of Stein to that victory cannot be underestimated. Celtic may have lacked leadership off the park but when they signed Stein in December 1951 they were bringing to Celtic Park not only a useful player, but a man who possessed the ability to guide others. That quality saw him stiffen the Celtic team with his steely presence and his ability to read the game and organize his team-mates was invaluable. Jock Stein himself was always modest about his talents as a player. 'I was fairly good in the air,' he once said, looking back on the early 1950s. 'At that time Celtic needed someone there at the back, but I had good players round about me. I wasn't a bad positional player but I wasn't exceptional as a player; just ordinary – very ordinary.' Stein may have been correct about his technical skills being distinctly average but his ability to inspire the team meant that the Coronation Cup victory sparked off a spectacular 12-month period for the club.

The 1953-54 season began in the fashion to which the Celtic support had become accustomed in those post-war years. A home defeat to Aberdeen, watched by 55,000, was the first of four defeats in their four-team League

50 Greatest Players

CHARLIE TULLY Winger

Born: Belfast

Joined Celtic: 1948   **From:** Belfast Celtic

Debut: v Morton, League, 14 August 1948

Appearances: 319   **Goals:** 43

Left Celtic: 1959   **For:** Cork Hibs

Honours won with Celtic: 1 league championship; 2 Scottish Cups; 2 Scottish League Cups; 10 caps (N. Ireland)

No one embodied the Celtic of the 1950s more than Charlie Tully. He could be repeatedly brilliant in one game and then meander, seemingly uninterested, through the next. As such, he was typical of a team that lacked direction. Inconsistent though he was, at times he could be outrageously consistent: during a Cup tie at Falkirk in 1953 he scored direct from a corner-kick. The referee ordered the kick to be retaken and Tully simply sent the ball directly into the net once again.

The Irishman, who had cost the sizeable fee of £8,000 from Belfast Celtic, was one of the club's first modern cult heroes at a club that has always held individualists in great esteem. Numerous items of memorabilia were peddled on the back of Charlie's name in the Glasgow of the 1950s. His flair for fun was matched off the park and he revelled in partying, sometimes to the detriment of his game. Tully's late nights often resulted in him missing training, which did not always make him popular in the eyes of his team-mates, but his twists, turns and tricks always assured him of the glad eye from the Celtic crowd.

Cup section, which was played over the month of August. Celtic then lost away to newly-promoted Hamilton Academicals on the opening day of the league season, eked out a 1-0 home win over Clyde and then drew 1-1 away to Rangers. Another defeat, away to Queen of the South, meant that Celtic were quickly in danger of losing touch with the teams at the top of the League.

With Jock Stein as their resolute captain, however, the team rallied and defeated Rangers 2-0 in the 1954 New Year's Day match although Rangers were not Celtic's main League rivals that season. Hearts were top of the League from early 1954, and when they met Celtic at Tynecastle in February of that year, a late goal from Jimmy Wardhaugh gave the Edinburgh side a 3-2 win. Their seven-point lead over Celtic in the League now looked close to unassailable, even though Celtic had three games in hand. The title looked

Tynecastle-bound but a remarkable end to the season saw Hearts take just four further points from their final five matches. Celtic won all eight of their League games after the Tynecastle defeat, scoring 23 goals in the process, and finishing, fittingly, with a 1-0 defeat of opening-day opponents Hamilton. It left them five points clear of the unfortunate Hearts at the top of the table as the final curtain fell on that 1953-54 season.

Lethal Injection

Neil Mochan had injected a lethal combination of pace and goalscoring ability to the Celtic attack, scoring 20 goals over the season. It was Stein, though, who had done much to provide the type of steadiness that makes champions. 'There was a wee period when Celtic started to win things and to pick up trophies,' says Billy McNeill, a schoolboy fan in the mid-1950s. 'A lot of it was down to Stein. Not that he was the greatest player in the world, but he was a good captain and a good leader.'

Progress in the Scottish Cup had gone in tandem with the run to the League title and had led to a meeting with Aberdeen in the final. Neil

Bobby Collins hooks home Celtic's third in a 4-4 Scottish Cup thriller with Rangers at Celtic Park in 1957.

Mochan, as so often that season, was the man who engineered the vital breakthrough for Celtic against the Dons. Five minutes after half-time he made an angled run from the right wing and sent a low, hard ball into the centre of the Aberdeen penalty area that caused panic, forcing Aberdeen centre half Young into the error of slicing the ball into his own net. Paddy Buckley equalized for Aberdeen almost from the restart but ten minutes later, Celtic inside right Willie Fernie, another of the stars of the 1953-54 season, glided down the right wing and cut the ball into the Aberdeen goalmouth where Sean Fallon touched the ball into the net. That was enough to give Celtic their first Cup and League double for 40 years.

50 Greatest Players

BOBBY COLLINS Inside right

Born: Glasgow

Joined Celtic: 1949   **From:** Pollok Juniors

Debut: v Rangers, League, 13 August 1949

Appearances: 320   **Goals:** 117

Left Celtic: 1958   **For:** Everton

Honours won with Celtic: 1 league championship; 1 Scottish Cup; 2 Scottish League Cups; 22 caps (Scotland)

The determination of Bobby Collins helped drive Celtic's irregular successes of the 1950s. Nicknamed 'The Wee Barra', he was only five feet and four inches (1.6m) in height and that, allied to his speed and surefootedness on the ball, saw him pigeonholed as a winger in his initial first-team season: 1949-50. The following year he moved to inside right, where better use could be made of his rock-hard shots.

Collins had grown up on the tough streets of Govanhill and was determined not to be pushed around. This fearlessness could lead him into trouble. During the 1955 Scottish Cup final with Clyde he made a heavy challenge on the Clyde goalkeeper. Chairman Robert Kelly was so displeased he dropped Collins for the replay. Without Collins' tenacious services Celtic lost 1-0.

Bobby's winning mentality was badly missed at Celtic Park after his £23,500 departure for Everton, and from Goodison Park he moved on to Leeds United in 1962. Collins was one of Don Revie's first signings as he began to build the great Leeds team of the 1960s and early 1970s. The player's major role for Leeds as Revie's midfield playmaker saw him become the first Scot to be named Footballer of the Year in England when he was given that award in 1965.

Aberdeen had been tigerish opponents for Celtic in that 1954 final and the Dons built on that to take the championship the following year. Encouragingly, Celtic maintained enough good form to challenge them closely for the 1954-55 title, ending the season just three points behind the Pittodrie side. Celtic also reached a second successive Scottish Cup final, to face Clyde. Jimmy Walsh opened the scoring for Celtic late in the first half, but a mistake by goalkeeper Johnny Bonnar three minutes from time, when he misjudged the flight of the ball, gave Clyde's Archie Robertson an equalizer direct from a corner. Tommy Ring scored the only goal of the game for Clyde in the replay.

Stein had, once again, been a prominent provider of morale and organization in another encouraging season. It appeared as though Celtic had finally left behind their days of being mid-table meanderers. They went into the 1955-56 season confident of further progress but in August 1955, during a League Cup match at Celtic Park, Stein suffered a severe ankle injury that meant he would miss much of that season and that would eventually end his career with Celtic. Minus Stein's on-field influence, Celtic could not sustain a good start to the season and finished fifth. They again reached the final of the Scottish Cup, but chairman Kelly intervened prior to the 1956 final with Hearts to make an eccentric team selection that featured right back Mike Haughney at inside right and Billy Craig, a vastly inexperienced 20-year-old, at outside right. The Hearts players drew great confidence simply from hearing Celtic's unusual line-up and rolled on to a 3-1 victory.

Celtic had made little impact on the League Cup, a competition that had become established as Scottish football's third major trophy in the years immediately after the Second World War. The tournament would never quite enjoy the prestige of the Scottish Cup but its unusual format of four-team group sections, which were used as curtain-raisers to the season, followed by swift progress towards an autumnal final, made the League Cup distinctive and won it popularity.

Only twice in the League Cup's first 10 years had Celtic qualified from the League Cup group stages but in 1956 they manoeuvred their way past Aberdeen and Rangers in their group and went weaving towards a final with Partick Thistle. After a 0-0 draw, two goals from Billy McPhail and one from Bobby Collins gave Celtic a 3-1 victory in the replay. The trophy was defended successfully the following year when the club enjoyed its most resounding victory over Rangers. That 7-1 win would long be savoured by the Celtic support, not least because it came in advance of one of the most frustratingly unsuccessful periods in the club's history.

Great Matches

SCOTTISH LEAGUE CUP FINAL   Hampden Park, 19 October 1957

Celtic 7   **Rangers 1**   Attendance 82,293
Wilson   Simpson
Mochan 2
McPhail 3
Fernie (pen)

Bad luck had thwarted several of Celtic's attempts to defeat Rangers during the 1950s and ill-fortune appeared to be plaguing them once again during the early stages of the 1957 League Cup final. Bobby Collins and Charlie Tully each saw scoring efforts smack off the Rangers goal-frame as Celtic poured on the pressure.

As they began to fear that they would pay dearly for missing clear-cut chances, centre forward Billy McPhail, brother of the 1951 Scottish Cup hero John, nodded the ball down to inside left Sammy Wilson, who relaxedly swung his boot at the ball and sent it high into the Rangers net. Celtic continued to exert extraordinary pressure and a Collins free-kick streaked towards goal from a distance of 30 yards before battering off the bar. Just as Rangers felt relieved to be approaching half-time just one down Neil Mochan drove deep into their defence to put an angled shot into the net.

A McPhail header made it 3-0 after the interval and although Billy Simpson netted for Rangers, another McPhail goal put the score at 4-1. Things would only get better. Within another ten minutes, Mochan and McPhail had made it 6-1 and in the final minute McPhail was knocked off his feet inside the penalty area. Willie Fernie, whose perfect passing skills had done much to make the victory possible, stroked a sweet penalty low into the corner of the net to cap a wonderful afternoon on which brain had triumphed supremely over brawn.

Celtic: Beattie, Donnelly, Fallon, Fernie, Evans, Peacock, Tully, Collins, McPhail, Wilson, Mochan.
Rangers: Niven, Shearer, Caldow, McColl, Valentine, Davis, Scott, Simpson, Murray, Baird, Hubbard.

Billy McPhail heads in Celtic's third.

Chapter Six: 1957-66
Reversal of Fortune

The team that had won the 1957 League Cup in such style had drawn on all their considerable experience to achieve that feat. Players such as Charlie Tully and Neil Mochan had started their playing careers in the years towards the end of the Second World War and that trophy win had been an enjoyable overture to their impending retirements from the game. Others, such as Bobby Collins and Bobby Evans would soon be on the move to English football.

A new generation of players were now arriving at Celtic Park, ready to take the club into the 1960s. Youngsters such as Billy McNeill, Stevie Chalmers and John Divers were finding that reserve team football with coach Jock Stein was a lot of fun. Stein, who had been appointed reserve team coach in 1957, would carefully coax the best out of his players, giving them the confidence to maximize their potential and emphasizing ballwork as a major part of their training. As a player, Stein had been known to make himself scarce when he knew there would be some tedious and often pointless hard running at training. Now that he was a coach, Stein was determined to make training enjoyable for his players. The young, receptive individuals at the club responded marvellously to his teachings and soon the reserve team was a more vibrant and exciting one than the first team.

A swinging affair. Frank Haffey relaxes after tipping a shot over the crossbar in a 1-1 draw at Third Lanark in February 1959.

Robert Kelly was still controlling all first-team matters and Celtic plunged back into mediocrity during the late 1950s. The team did manage to finish in the top half of the table but they were never genuine title challengers. A wave of genuine dismay then washed over the club when, in March 1960, Stein quit as reserve-team coach to take up his first position in management, at Dunfermline Athletic.

Stein in the Way

Dunfermline had been facing relegation but Stein swiftly turned round their situation to save them from the drop. By the 1960-61 season he had transformed the attitude of the Dunfermline players so radically that they reached the 1961 Scottish Cup final to face Celtic, who were making their first Cup final appearance since 1957. It was a young Celtic side that lined up in that game, one that featured such undoubted talents as the speedy right back Dunky MacKay, the master passer Pat Crerand at right half, centre half Billy McNeill, inside right Stevie Chalmers and powerful centre forward John Hughes. Only two members of the team were older than 24: inside left Willie Fernie and outside left Alec Byrne. They faced a Dunfermline team that had been knitted together carefully by Stein.

It was clear to the 114,000 present at Hampden that Celtic had the more talented individuals, but that Dunfermline the were better organized and

more purposeful team. The Dunfermline goalkeeper Denis Connachan was in superb form and he did much to thwart the Celtic forwards and win his side a 0-0 draw and a replay. Dunfermline held their nerve and concentration for the second game to win 2-0 and take the Cup, the first trophy in their history. Stein, distinctive in a white coat, could have been mistaken for a rather lively laboratory scientist as he moved among his players on the field at the end of

Celtic's Bertie Auld (right) crosses the ball past Raith Rovers' Willie Pollard in a 1-0 home win in January 1960.

50 Greatest Players

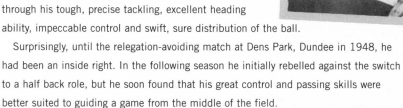

BOBBY EVANS Half back

Born: Glasgow

Joined Celtic: 1944   **From:** St Anthony's Juniors

Debut: v Albion Rovers, Regional League, 19 August 1944

Appearances: 535   **Goals:** 10

Left Celtic: 1960   **For:** Chelsea

Honours won with Celtic: 1 league championship; 2 Scottish Cups; 2 Scottish League Cups, 45 caps (Scotland)

With his red hair and his jersey flapping outside his shorts, Bobby Evans was an instantaneously identifiable figure. He was a tireless half back, linking defence and attack through his tough, precise tackling, excellent heading ability, impeccable control and swift, sure distribution of the ball.

Surprisingly, until the relegation-avoiding match at Dens Park, Dundee in 1948, he had been an inside right. In the following season he initially rebelled against the switch to a half back role, but he soon found that his great control and passing skills were better suited to guiding a game from the middle of the field.

Evans captained Celtic to their first League Cup victory in 1956. He was also captain of Scotland and his 45 appearances for the national team in a 12-year span from 1948 made him the most-capped Celtic player up to that point. He would win three more caps after moving south to wind down his career at Chelsea.

the match. His experiment in teamwork and intense man-management had worked perfectly.

It was an entirely different story at Celtic, where there was a pronounced lack of leadership. The club was bubbling over with talent – in the early 1960s players such as Jimmy Johnstone, Tommy Gemmell, Bobby Lennox and Bobby Murdoch joined Celtic, seeking the type of guidance that would shape their raw abilities into a winning team. That was never forthcoming. The club simply stumbled along in a haphazard fashion. Robert Kelly was still stubbornly selecting the team, Jimmy McGrory was still nominally manager and Sean Fallon, in 1962, was brought on board the coaching staff as assistant to the manager. It was not a winning formula.

John Hughes, who joined the club in 1959, remembers those times vividly. 'It was a nightmare,' he says. 'I was there as a big raw laddie and basically you didn't get any help at all. I just made a lot of mistakes and nobody said anything. Players are playing all the time now at 17 but if you go back to 1960 that wasn't the case and I was in there at 17. I played centre in a bad Celtic team and scored 32 goals one season. I often feel that if I had had some guidance in the early years I'd have been a far better player.'

Celtic remained out of touch in League competition during the early 1960s but they did progress as far as the 1963 Scottish Cup final, where they faced champions Rangers. It was to be another testing occasion for the Celtic support. Ralph Brand opened the scoring for Rangers but Bobby Murdoch equalized from close-range just on half-time. The star for Celtic on the day was goalkeeper Frank Haffey. He had conceded nine goals playing for Scotland against England at Wembley two years previously, but at Hampden he was outstanding, palming off the Rangers forwards time and again.

The most eye-catching of the Celtic forwards on the day was Jimmy Johnstone, the 18-year-old outside right who was playing in only his third match for Celtic after having made his debut in late March 1963. Johnstone did miss one very good chance, sending the ball wide of the Rangers goal as goalkeeper Billy Ritchie lay helpless on the ground.

Celtic's Dunky MacKay runs free as Rangers' Jim Forrest and Celtic's Billy McNeill lie prostrate. Celtic lost this 1963 League Cup tie at Ibrox; one of many disappointments during the early 1960s.

That missed opportunity may have had an influence on Robert Kelly, who was prepared to ignore all the good things Johnstone had done as he dropped the player for the replay 11 days later. His place was taken by Bobby Craig, an inside right who had been signed for £15,000 from Blackburn Rovers the previous October, but who had looked sluggish in his previous performances for Celtic. 'I got dropped for that final,' says Jimmy Johnstone, 'and I feel it wasn't Jimmy McGrory's decision. I think it was really the man above him, Bob Kelly, who was the man who ruled everything. So I think the decision to put Bobby in came from the top and I think I was the youngest so that's how it worked out. It was amazing but these were the kind of decisions that were being made at the time.'

The change backfired as Rangers eased to a comfortable 3-0 victory on the night. It was an uncomfortable evening for the Celtic supporters in the 120,000 crowd and midway through the second half, with their team already three down, thousands of them began pouring towards the exits from Hampden.

Celtic had made interesting progress on another front that season, entering European competition for the first time. Through finishing third in the Scottish First Division at the end of the 1961-62 season they qualified for the Fairs Cup, where they were presented with the toughest possible draw, against the holders, Valencia of Spain.

European Adventures Begin

Celtic's love affair with European football began with, appropriately, a first leg in the Estadio Luis Casanova. A 4-2 defeat was riddled with dubious decisions, including two serious penalty claims from the Celts and a late 'goal' from Stevie Chalmers that was ruled offside. There was much excitement, too, in the return but Valencia played a cunning containing game and a 2-2 draw sent the Spaniards through to the next round; Valencia would end the season by retaining the Fairs Cup.

The defeat by Rangers in the 1963 Scottish Cup final had offered the consolation of another entry into European competition: Rangers were in the European Cup so Celtic, as Scottish Cup runners-up, took their place in the 1963-64 European Cup-Winners' Cup. They defeated FC Basle of Switzerland and Dinamo Zagreb of Yugoslavia. The away leg of that trip provided a worrying moment or two for John Hughes and John Divers when they became stranded on top of a mountain near Zagreb and had to be rescued by the local emergency services. Matters on the field were less alarming – a 2-1 defeat put Celtic through to the quarter-finals on a 4-2 aggregate. They faced Slovan Bratislava of Czechoslovakia in the quarter-final, where 1-0 victories in both the home and away legs brought the reward of a semi-final against MTK Budapest.

So Close, and Yet...

The 1964 Cup-Winners' Cup semi-final with MTK would be entirely typical of the Celtic of the early to mid-1960s in that it would see the team reach opposite extremes of performance. The first leg at Celtic Park saw the home side simply overwhelm the skilful Hungarians. Celtic's relentless attacking, concentration and teamwork saw them power to a 3-0 victory that looked to have guaranteed them a place in the final in Brussels. A fortnight later, in the dressing room before the return in Budapest, chairman Robert Kelly entered and, slapping his glove into his hand, emphasized to the Celtic players how important it was that they went out and did well and won the game. He did not give them any hints as to how they were to achieve that feat.

Tommy Gemmell (right) heads the ball away in the first leg of Celtic's European Cup-Winners' Cup semi-final tie with MTK Budapest.

Lacking realistic tactical guidance from those managing and running the team, Celtic collapsed in the face of incessant pressure from MTK and after an hour the tie was level, the Hungarians having scored three times without reply. A further goal after 70 minutes of the match, from inside left Kuti, put the home side into the final and left serious questions being asked about Celtic's ability to cut the mustard at the top level.

The 1964-65 season did begin encouragingly for Celtic with a 3-0 victory over Rangers that ended a sequence in which Rangers had won six games in a row against their greatest rivals. That early-season optimism soon evaporated as Celtic lost 2-1 in the League Cup final to Rangers, albeit slightly unluckily, went out of the Fairs Cup to Barcelona, and slipped out of contention in the League.

Robert Kelly finally concluded that action had to be taken to redress the situation and, in January 1965, he asked Jock Stein if he would like to return to Celtic as manager. Stein readily agreed to Kelly's request and on Sunday 31 January 1965 the announcement was made to the Scottish public. Jimmy McGrory, after two decades as Celtic manager, was appointed the club's first public relations officer.

The day before that announcement Celtic had met Aberdeen at Celtic Park and had hammered out an 8-0 victory that had been atypical of their season up to that point. The players had become aware that Stein was on his way back to the club and had responded with a show of concerted team work and skill. It was their way of expressing exactly how delighted they had been by the news. Those Celtic players had always been capable of great football, but now they knew that their talents would be moulded and shaped properly through Stein's craftsmanship. He had proved in his two previous managerial posts, at Dunfermline and Hibernian, that he possessed the power to achieve success for his teams and that he would waste no time in doing so.

Jock Stein Arrives

Stein's initial task was to win the Scottish Cup, the only trophy still available to Celtic that 1964-65 season. The team's form fluctuated during their remaining League matches, but he guided them through a tricky Scottish Cup semi-final with Motherwell that went to a replay. Unlike McGrory, Stein had demanded full control of the team and all team selections were now his and his alone. Players found themselves being shifted around from one position to another as Jock Stein meticulously examined all the options that were available to him. He was determined to extract the very best from his playing staff.

It meant that by the time the Scottish Cup final arrived on 24 April 1965 the club had been revitalised with a sparky competitiveness. The opposition that day were Dunfermline, still formidable opponents after Stein's four years of work with them, and it was the Fifers who were 2-1 ahead at half-time. Stein, however, was determined to take the first trophy available to him as Celtic manager and at half time he communicated that determination to his players in no uncertain terms. The second half saw Celtic launch themselves at the Dunfermline defence with wave after wave of attacks. It paid off when a driving run from Bobby Lennox resulted in a cross that saw Bertie Auld brushing aside a pack of defenders to poke home the equalizer.

Nine minutes from time, Billy McNeill climbed high inside the penalty area to smack an unstoppable header into the Dunfermline net. A picture of that moment would take pride of place in Jock Stein's office during the forthcoming years. It was a vitally important moment in the club's history. It had guaranteed victory in the final but more importantly it had ensured that the momentum generated by Stein's arrival would be maintained and showed that Celtic were again capable of triumphing in competitions.

Bertie Auld scores his second goal in the 1965 Scottish Cup final against Dunfermline Athletic.

The players whom Stein had inherited had been highly talented, but that talent had not been properly channelled. Stein now gave them direction. He would tell them exactly what he required from each one of them on the field of play. If they did as he asked he would be effusive in his praise. If they failed to do so, he would be quick to criticize. No player was safe from Stein's severe and accurate assessments of how they were playing and how much effort they were exerting. He drove them on to greater heights than they could have anticipated as he wrung every ounce of effort from them.

Sudden Impact

The sudden impact Stein had made on the players was evident in the way Celtic went close to winning four trophies in the 1965-66 season. The first to fall to them was the 1965 League Cup. Two first half penalties, stroked home in style by John Hughes, were enough to give Celtic a 2-1 victory over Rangers in the final. The tide was beginning to turn in Celtic's favour. Consistency was everything to Stein and his influence propelled Celtic on a run of League victories that saw them drop just three points between August and December 1965. They still found it hard to shake off Rangers – the only team who had beaten them in the League – but when their Glasgow rivals rolled up for their traditional New Year meeting on 3 January 1966 Celtic were well prepared. The playing surface had, in those days before undersoil heating, become hard and rutted but Celtic took to the field in training shoes, an innovation for the time. That gave them a strong grip on proceedings and despite going 1-0 down early on, five superb second-half goals gave them a

Celtic captain Billy McNeill clings on to the Scottish Cup as he is carried shoulder-high by his triumphant team-mates after their 3-2 victory over Dunfermline in 1965.

John Hughes (right) beats Rangers keeper Billy Ritchie to score the winning goal from the penalty spot in the 1965 League Cup final.

splendid 5-1 victory. Celtic went on to take that 1965-66 League title even though Rangers continued to pursue them closely all the way to the end of the season.

The Old Firm's dominance in the 1965-66 season was sealed when they met again in the Scottish Cup final. It went to a replay and although Celtic were the better team, outplaying and outpassing their opponents, Rangers stole the Cup with a fine goal by Kai Johansen. Two out of three domestic trophies was a fine haul for the season and Celtic had also gone close to reaching their first European final. A run to the semi-finals of the European Cup-Winners' Cup produced a classic all-British tie between Celtic and Liverpool. Both sides would win their respective leagues that year and Celtic were more than a match for Liverpool in the first leg at Celtic Park. Shortly after half-time, Bobby Murdoch drove deep into the Liverpool defence and crossed for Lennox to slip the ball into the net.

Liverpool had the better of the return at Anfield and went 2-0 up midway through the second half. Close to the end, Bobby Lennox zipped through and

Great Matches

EUROPEAN CUP-WINNERS' CUP   **Celtic Park, 12 January 1966**
QUARTER-FINAL FIRST LEG
Celtic 3   **Dynamo Kiev 0**   **Attendance 64,000**
Murdoch 2
Gemmell

The imposing figure of Jock Stein materialized on the touchline at Celtic Park as the Dynamo Kiev squad carried out their training session the day before this memorable tie. He signalled to the Kiev coach that his players could have just five minutes more on the pitch – Stein wanted his groundsmen to get on to the pitch before it was too late to tend to the turf and prevent the possibility of it becoming rutted and damaged in the overnight January frost.

It was a meaningful early signal to Kiev that they would be facing assertive, highly professional opponents and although they moved the ball around skilfully during the first half of the tie, full back Tommy Gemmell intervened with a 35-yard shot that raced past goalkeeper Viktor Bannikov to open the scoring. Midway through the second half, Bobby Murdoch burrowed deep into the Russians' penalty area to fire the ball into the narrowest of gaps between Bannikov and his near post. Another Murdoch shot thudded off the crossbar before John Hughes, Stevie Chalmers, Joe McBride and Jimmy Johnstone all made dents in the defence to fire in shots on goal. Six minutes from time, with Kiev weakened and wounded by Celtic's incessant pressure, Murdoch sidefooted the ball into the net after Charlie Gallagher and Johnstone had pierced the defence. It had been the first of Jock Stein's great victories in Europe with Celtic. The involvement of Gemmell as a goalscorer was just one of many hints of the shape of the great European nights to come. The more pessimistic onlookers in a record 64,000 crowd for a European tie recalled the squandering of the 3-0 first leg lead over MTK Budapest in the same competition less than two years previously. Things would be different with Stein at the helm – a fortnight later he calmly steered his team through a 1-1 draw in the second leg and Celtic had taken their first major scalp in European competition.

Celtic: Simpson, Craig, Gemmell, Murdoch, Cushley, Clark, Johnstone, Gallagher, McBride, Chalmers, Hughes.

Dynamo Kiev: Bannikov, Schejolkov, Sosnikhin, Ostrovosky, Medvid, Turyanchik, Brazilevich, Serrebryanikov, Puzach, Biba, Khemenitsky.

Tommy Gemmell arrives back at Prestwick after the second leg.

put the ball in the net only for the referee, Josef Hannet of Belgium, to disallow the goal for offside. Lennox, a superbly speedy player, would often have goals disallowed in his career simply because linesmen could not believe he had the ability to progress several yards in behind a defence so quickly without being offside. On that occasion, as on so many others, Lennox was almost certainly onside. 'It wasn't Liverpool who beat us,' stated Stein after the 2-0 defeat. 'It was the referee. Bobby Lennox was onside. It was a perfectly good goal.'

The Celtic players were, at the time, furious. The final of the Cup-Winners' Cup was scheduled for Hampden Park and they felt aggrieved that their chance of taking a European trophy had been snatched away from them. It felt like a deadly blow to taking of their chances a European trophy. It would actually prove to be a mere overture for many much more dramatic acts involving Celtic in European football.

The Celtic squad in March 1966. From left: Hughes, McCarron, Gemmell, McNeill, Young, Cushley, Fallon, O'Neill, Simpson, Murdoch, Chalmers, Gallagher, Clark, McBride, Brogan, Auld, Lennox, Johnstone.

Chapter Seven: 1966-70
Adventures in Europe

Jock Stein sat poolside in a deck chair, having exchanged his suit for shorts, lightweight shirt and sun hat. He was enjoying the sunshine on Celtic's five-and-a-half week close-season tour of North America in the early summer of 1966. The mood was relaxed and two of his Celtic players, who had been larking around with their team-mates, turned their attentions on Stein, making as if to haul him into the water. Stein's body language quickly told them that this was definitely not an option. The players might be allowed to kid around with one another, but the manager always ensured that he kept his distance and maintained their full respect at all times. Stein had demanded 'full control' of the club on taking over as manager the previous year and he was not going to jeopardize that hard-earned respect under any circumstances. It was vital to his plans for the club in the forthcoming weeks, months and years.

That tour, which took Celtic to Bermuda, Canada and the USA, was a vitally important one for Stein and his players. They were unbeaten in their 11 matches, a series of games that included two wins against Tottenham Hotspur, a draw in another game with the White Hart Lane side and draws with Bayern Munich and Bologna. Stein insisted that his team play those matches in a competitive fashion, so much so that the match with Bayern reached a point where ten players got together to exchange blows.

There were more lighthearted moments for the Celtic party on that trip. Visits to horse-racing meetings, barbecues and nights out further instilled in them the type of team spirit that Stein was always

The Celtic squad leave for their pre-season tour to Bermuda and North America in 1966. From left: Gallagher, Chalmers, Murdoch, Lennox, O'Neill, McNeill, Johnstone, McCarron, Young, Auld, Simpson (squatting), McBride, Cushley and Fallon.

so anxious to engender. 'We have almost been able to see that spirit grow,' said Stein as the tour came to an end. Bobby Lennox recalls those days well. 'It was the trip of a lifetime – in the early sixties it felt as if America was a million miles away. Although we were on tour, we trained hard – and we enjoyed training – and Jock made sure we knew that we had to win the games. The bonding of the team was great on that trip. It was the making of us, really. It brought us all together.'

The benefits of the tour were highly visible at the start of the 1966-67 season as Celtic streaked to 18 successive victories in the League and the League Cup. A moment of speed and style gave Celtic a 1-0 victory in the League Cup final against Rangers on 29 October – centre forward Joe McBride climbed to head Bertie Auld's cross into Bobby Lennox's path and he first-timed his shot into the net.

By then, Celtic had established themselves as the Scottish League leaders and had also eliminated Swiss champions FC Zurich in the opening round of the European Cup. Tommy Gemmell had been the scorer of Celtic's first European Cup goal when he sent a 40-yard shot high into the Swiss net at Celtic Park. The full back had repeated the feat in the return leg as Celtic ran up a 5-0 aggregate victory.

Team Talk

'At that point, we had no thoughts about winning the European Cup,' says Bobby Lennox. 'In fact, it was a big thrill just to go to Zurich. We had never been there. I remember our team talk in Zurich – everyone was crowded into this small room and big Jock said that Zurich would play in the same way as they had done in the first leg. Some of the boys said to him that they thought he was wrong and that Zurich would come out and attack. I think that was the only time I ever heard some of the boys do that: say to Jock that they thought he was wrong. They thought that Zurich would come out and have a go at us, unlike in the first leg in Glasgow. Jock said, "They haven't got the players to have a go at us." As it turned out, Jock was right.'

FC Nantes of France, Celtic's next European Cup opponents, were also swept aside as Celtic won each leg 3-1 in straightforward fashion. It put Celtic into a European Cup quarter-final with Vojvodina Novi Sad, the champions of Yugoslavia. By the time that tie came around in March 1967 Celtic had lost just one match since the start of the season: a 3-2 defeat away to Dundee United in a League game on New Year's Eve. Rangers, however, had remained in close pursuit of the champions and as Celtic travelled to Yugoslavia, the Ibrox side were just two points behind Celtic in the League.

Vojvodina would prove to be the toughest opponents Celtic would face that season. Each of the Vojvodina players was technically accomplished and they were big, strong, fast and fit. 'They had class,' recalls Tommy Gemmell. 'Every one of their players looked comfortable on the ball, they held possession well and they showed a lot of good teamwork. They gave us our two hardest matches in all my years in Europe.' Celtic were more than a match for Vojvodina in the first leg at the Gradski Stadium, Novi Sad, on 1 March 1967, but a slip by sweeper John Clark 20 minutes from the end allowed Stanic to whip the ball into the Celtic net for the only goal of the game.

The second leg at Celtic Park proved equally close and, with the two sides of such a similarly high standard, Celtic struggled to outwit the clever Yugoslavs despite throwing everything into attack. As in the first leg, it required a mistake for the goal to materialize. Pantelic, the Vojvodina goalkeeper, dropped a cross from Tommy Gemmell and Stevie Chalmers nudged the ball into the net. An hour had been played but although Celtic increased the pressure, the aggregate score remained level as the match entered its final minute. A play-off in Rotterdam seemed inevitable until Billy

McNeill soared into the air to meet Charlie Gallagher's corner and send a powerful header high into the Vojvodina net. Celtic had reached the semi-finals of the European Cup in the most dramatic fashion.

'I am not going to say we will win the European Cup,' said Stein as he anticipated the challenge of the semi-finals, 'but there are just three matches and two teams between us and victory. It is not beyond us.' Six British sides had reached the semi-finals of the European Cup previously, but none had advanced further and Celtic found another highly skilful Eastern European side, Dukla Prague, blocking their route to the final.

Keeper Ronnie Simpson swings from the crossbar in celebration of Celtic's second goal in the European Cup quarter-final second leg against Vojvodina Novi Sad.

The first leg was in Glasgow and Dukla approached the match in positive fashion, playing an expansive style of football – goalkeeper Ronnie Simpson had to make an excellent early save from Strunc to prevent the Czech side taking the lead. A brave volley by Jimmy Johnstone, hit into the net as goalkeeper Viktor powered towards him, gave Celtic a 1-0 lead after 27 minutes, but shortly before half-time Strunc got another chance to score and this time Dukla's right winger squeezed the ball past Simpson for the equalizer.

Stein's half-time urgings inspired his team to go up a gear and on the hour, Gemmell's long, high ball dropped nicely for Willie Wallace inside the Dukla penalty area. He balanced himself beautifully before volleying the ball past Viktor. Five minutes on, Bertie Auld played a free-kick sideways to Wallace and he swept the ball across Viktor and into the net.

The 3-1 first-leg lead set Celtic up very nicely for the return in Prague, but Stein refused to take any chances. He sent his team out with five men in

---

50 Greatest Players

JOE McBRIDE Forward

Born: Glasgow

Joined Celtic: 1965   **From:** Motherwell

Debut: v Dundee, League Cup, 21 August 1965

Appearances: 93   **Goals:** 86

Left Celtic: 1968   **For:** Hibernian

Honours won with Celtic: 2 league championships; 2 Scottish League Cups; 2 caps (Scotland)

It is unfortunate that Celtic's European Cup final victory obscures the extraordinary feats of Joe McBride that 1966-67 season. The striker had taken his season's goal tally to 35 when, on Christmas Eve 1966, he suffered a cartilage injury that would sideline him for the next nine months. As his team-mates basked in the glow of European Cup success, McBride, a striker who was equally powerful in the air and on the ground, was pounding round the Parkhead track in a battle to regain his fitness.

McBride had been Jock Stein's first signing for Celtic when he arrived from Motherwell in exchange for a fee of £22,500 in the summer of 1965. He finished the 1965-66 season with 43 goals, making him Scotland's top scorer that season, and he was the Scottish League's leading scorer again in 1966-67, despite missing the entire second half of the First Division fixtures. Sadly, Joe was unable to regain a regular place in the first team after his debilitating injury and those who had enjoyed his stylish scoring could only speculate as to how Jock Stein's late-1960s side might have been even stronger still with McBride as its figurehead.

midfield and with a lone striker, Stevie Chalmers, whose duty was to harass the Dukla defenders when they were in possession. It was contrary to Celtic's traditional style to play in such a fashion, but it yielded the necessary result: a 0-0 draw that took Celtic into the European Cup final.

'They never had any clear-cut chances,' says Tommy Gemmell of that match, 'but they had a lot of half-chances. All it needed was for them to pop one away and they would have hit us like a ton of bricks. We just kept firing balls to the corner flags and Stevie just chased and held it until he got a bit of support. He didn't want to go anywhere or score any goals. We'd hold on to the ball for as long as we could, then go back into defence again.'

Unfinished Business

There was a bit of unfinished business for Celtic to complete prior to the European Cup final. Four days after the match in Prague, Celtic faced Aberdeen in the Scottish Cup final and two goals from Willie Wallace took the trophy to Celtic Park. One week later Celtic travelled to Ibrox needing just one point from the season's second Old firm league match to complete the first domestic treble in the club's history. A crowd of 78,000 saw Jimmy Johnstone tuck the ball into the net after a Bobby Lennox shot had rebounded to him off the foot of the post. That made the score 1-1 at half-time and 15 minutes from time, Johnstone veered infield to strike a stunning 25-yard, left-footed shot high into the Rangers net and give Celtic the lead. Rangers managed to equalize close to the conclusion of the match, but they could not prevent Celtic holding on for the draw that gave them their second successive Scottish championship.

An interested spectator in the stand at Ibrox that day was Helenio Herrera, the manager of Internazionale of Milan, Celtic's opponents in the European Cup final. 'My idea of the ideal final,' he had said earlier in that 1966-67 season, 'would be Inter and Celtic. And we should beat the Scots on neutral ground in Lisbon in May.' As he boarded his private jet back to Milan after watching Celtic clinch the Scottish League title on that rain-rent day in Glasgow, he may have been anticipating that the Celts' energetic, attacking game would be severely curtailed by the sweltering Portuguese heat.

Herrera had been full of Latin braggadocio in the approach to the final, but after Celtic's magnificent 2-1 victory over his Inter side in the 1967 European Cup final, he was moved to admit, 'We can have no complaints. Celtic deserved their victory. We were beaten by Celtic's force. Although we lost, the match was a victory for sport.'

The Celtic team that won the European Cup was beautifully balanced. Stein fielded his players in a 4-2-4 formation, with two expert passers in midfield –

Great Matches

EUROPEAN CUP FINAL   **National Stadium, Lisbon, 25 May 1967**

Celtic 2   **Internazionale 1**   **Attendance 56,000**
Gemmell   Mazzola (pen)
Chalmers

John Fallon, Celtic's sole substitute for the final, carried to the bench a cuddly teddy bear in Celtic's colours. As the teams walked on to the field, Jimmy Johnstone indicated pleadingly to Inter's Giacinto Facchetti that he would like to swap shirts with him after the match. Such actions reinforced the image of Celtic as happy hopefuls against a mighty Inter team that had won the European Cup in 1964 and 1965 and had been World Club champions in both of those years.

The opening minutes of the final offered little to counter such expectations as a flashing header from Sandro Mazzola after three minutes produced a fine save from Ronnie Simpson. Celtic responded well. A left-footed shot and a header, both from Jimmy Johnstone, had Inter's keeper Giuliano Sarti stretching to save. Then, after seven minutes, disaster struck. Jim Craig, under pressure, needlessly fouled Cappellini inside the Celtic penalty area, referee Kurt Tschenscher awarded a penalty, and Mazzola slid the ball smoothly into the left-hand corner of Simpson's net.

Celtic were not dispirited and they attacked hard for the remainder of the half, coming closest to scoring when Bertie Auld shot against the bar. The score remained 1-0 to Inter at half-time but Stein told his men simply to continue playing as they had been doing and they would be rewarded. Instead, his players went out and played even better, with midfielders Bobby Murdoch and Auld steering proceedings magnificently.

The forwards, following Stein's instructions, were constantly on the move to help shift Inter defenders out of position and allow space for the midfielders and full backs to come through for shots. After 63 minutes Tommy Gemmell raced on to a cut-back from Craig to pelt a fearsome shot from the edge of the Inter penalty area high into the Italians' net. Inter began to crumble and five minutes from time, after further sustained Celtic pressure, Bobby Murdoch's low ball into the Inter box was nudged into the net by Stevie Chalmers. As the teams lined up for the restart, the Celtic players could see in the Italians' faces that they were beaten men. Celtic, at the first attempt, had become champions of Europe in masterful fashion.

Celtic: Simpson, Craig, Gemmell, Murdoch, McNeill, Clark, Johnstone, Wallace, Chalmers, Auld, Lennox.

Internazionale: Sarti, Burgnich, Facchetti, Bedin, Guarneri, Picchi, Domenghini, Cappellini, Mazzola, Bicicli, Corso.

Referee: Kurt Tschenscher (West Germany).

...opean Cup final action. Above: Celtic's Bertie Auld fires in a cross that puts the Inter defence ...er pressure. Below: Steve Chalmers (No. 9) turns away to celebrate after scoring the winning goal ...nter keeper Sarti points an accusing finger at his defence.

Captain Billy McNeill receives the European Cup from Americo Thomaz, the President of Portugal.

Bertie Auld and Bobby Murdoch – feeding players of pace in every area of the pitch. Full backs Jim Craig and Tommy Gemmell were expected to overlap, which was a major innovation for a Scottish team. Wingers Jimmy Johnstone and Bobby Lennox were required to drag defenders well wide of their goal, leaving space for quickfire strikers Stevie Chalmers and Willie Wallace to nip in to score. It was a system that had brought Celtic the unique distinction in British football of winning all three domestic trophies plus the European Cup and it would serve them well for the remainder of the 1960s.

'If Inter had not conceded that goal five minutes from time,' says Bobby Lennox, 'I believe we could easily have scored four or five in extra-time. When it went to 2-1, I looked at Facchetti and his face was drained. The score did not matter: I just wanted to win the European Cup. I wouldn't have cared how we won it. If Facchetti had lobbed his own goalie I would have been quite pleased. It is nice, 30-odd years later, to say that we could have won 4-1 or 5-1, but we won the European Cup. That was the only thing that mattered and 2-1 was a great result. It was only weeks later that it really sank in that we were the champions of Europe. It is an incredible thing to look back on and realize that, out of all the thousands of clubs in Europe, you were the best at that time.'

World Club Championship

Celtic's victory over Inter was a triumph for attacking football over catenaccio, the defensive system perfected by Herrera, in which Italian teams would play in an ultra-defensive fashion and hope to nick a goal from a breakaway. As European Cup winners Celtic would now enter the World Club Championship, and Stein intended to play in the same adventurous manner in pursuit of that honour. The World Club Championship was contested between the champions of Europe and South America. It held much prestige in the 1960s and within hours of the European Cup win in Lisbon, Stein was already turning his mind towards that next challenge. 'Whoever we have to play from South America, we shall attack,' he said. 'We want to show South America, as well as Europe, that defensive soccer is finished.'

Billy McNeill (second left) heads the only goal of the match against Racing Club of Buenos Aires in the first leg of the 1967 World Club Championship. Bobby Lennox looks on.

The World Club Championship would be decided over two legs, the first of which would be at Hampden Park on 18 October 1967. Celtic's opponents were to be Argentinian side Racing Club of Buenos Aires. Before that match, Celtic faced Dynamo Kiev in the first round of the European Cup and a wan performance from Celtic in the first leg led to the club's first home defeat in European competition, the Soviet side leaving Glasgow with a 2-1 victory.

Unusual Refereeing

The return match with Dynamo was an unusual one, with Celtic, the away side, playing an attacking game against a defensive Dynamo, desperate to protect their lead despite being at home for the second leg of the tie. The Soviets were assisted by some unusual refereeing decisions from Mr Sbardella of Italy, who appeared to favour the home side. With an hour gone, Bobby Murdoch's frustration with the referee boiled over into real anger and when the Celtic midfielder threw the ball away after a dubious free-kick had been awarded to Dynamo, he was sent off. That only served to stiffen Celtic's resolve and three minutes later Bobby Lennox went zipping on to Bertie Auld's pass to angle the ball into the Kiev net. John Hughes also had the ball in the net minutes later, but Sbardella inexplicably disallowed Hughes' goal. To compound Celtic's misery, a Kiev equalizer in the final minute put the Soviets through.

'The referee was "got at", definitely,' says Jimmy Johnstone. 'He denied us two goals and a penalty.' Celtic had won the great distinction of being the first club from Northern Europe to take the European Cup; now they had the less welcome distinction of being the first holders of that trophy to be eliminated in the first round of the tournament.

Something New, Something Bigger

Jock Stein chose to blot out the memory of that defeat by focusing on the World Club Championship. 'This is something new,' he said, 'something bigger than anything they have been involved in.' The prospect of his side being declared the world's best club side was an enticing one for Stein and his description of the game's status was justified. It was regarded as such a major occasion that the British prime minister Harold Wilson even ventured north to Hampden to join the 103,000 inside the national stadium.

It quickly became clear that the Argentinian side were intent on spoiling the match through incessant fouling. They kicked, spat, gouged and punched their way through the game and were happy to concede just one goal – a superb header by Billy McNeill 20 minutes from time. The Celtic players had never faced anything like the underhand tactics employed by the Argentinians and were now apprehensive about what they might face in the second leg in South America.

The European champions had also found their progress in the League to be less than smooth early in that 1967-68 season. They were in third position – behind Rangers and Hibernian – in late October although they did contest the final of the League Cup on the 28th of that month. An engrossing match with Dundee resulted in a 5-3 Celtic victory – the attack had shone on the afternoon, but some worrying slips in the Celtic defence had helped Dundee to their three goals.

Later that evening, the Celtic squad flew out to Buenos Aires for the return with Racing. A warm welcome awaited them in Argentina. Flowers, sweets and kisses from local girls were doled out to the players on their arrival, but on the day of the match, 1 November 1967, All Saints' Day, the atmosphere inside the Avellaneda Stadium was quite unholy: it was one of naked aggression towards the visiting team.

This time, the Argentinians' underhand tactics kicked in even before kick-off. As the teams warmed up, goalkeeper Ronnie Simpson was struck by a

The Battle of Montevideo. Celtic players look on as Uruguayan police, with batons drawn, keep the two sets of players apart whilst Racing Club captain Martin (No. 4) argues with the referee.

missile that Celtic players were convinced had been launched by one of the Argentinian photographers behind the goal. With a huge gash in his head, Simpson was forced to drop out of the side.

John Fallon replaced Simpson and although Celtic took the lead in the match through a Tommy Gemmell penalty, Racing scored twice to force a play-off in Montevideo, Uruguay, three days later. Once again, Racing had behaved outrageously and by the time the Celtic players took the field in Montevideo on 4 November 1967, their patience with the Argentinians had been stretched to the limit. The players had been determined to take part in this third game because they wanted to prove they were the better team. Stein commented before the play-off, 'The time for politeness is over. We can be hard if necessary and we will not stand the shocking conduct of Racing.'

Jimmy Johnstone had been one of the major targets for abusive treatment from Racing and when Rulli hacked him down during the first half in Montevideo it led to a scuffle involving a number of players who were joined on the field by police armed with batons. When the flare-up was finally calmed, referee Osorio sent off the Argentinian Basile and Bobby Lennox, even though the latter had not been guilty of any misdemeanour.

Celtic's Bobby Murdoch, watched by Billy McNeill, pulls Racing Club's Cardenas along the ground.

'There were a lot of scuffles going on: kicking and all that sort of stuff,' explains Lennox. 'There was an incident and the referee brought the two captains together and he said, "If there is another incident like that, numbers six and eight are going off." I was eight. Next thing, there was a big incident in the middle of the park. The referee came over and said, "Eight – off. Six – off." So I walked to the side and big Jock pushed me back on to the field! "Get back on there!" he said. So I went back on and the referee told me to leave. So I went back off again and Jock said, "I'm telling you to get back on that park!" So I went back on and the referee motioned to this policeman who came on with his sword! That was me decided – I was off straightaway after that.'

Six Dismissed

After the half-time interval, Johnstone, who had been kicked black and blue in all three matches, eventually retaliated mildly and was immediately sent off, leaving Celtic with nine men. Minutes later Cardenas put Racing 1-0 ahead with a long-range shot. As a vicious match reached its climax, John Hughes was dismissed for attempting to kick Cejas, the Racing goalkeeper. Racing's Rulli became the fifth player to be dismissed when he punched John Clark and for a second time Uruguyuan police intervened on the field to try to restore order among the players. Close to the end, Auld became the fourth Celtic player to be sent off after he had punched Maschio. The Celt refused to leave the pitch and he was still on the field when Osorio blew the final whistle.

As the Celtic players returned home, stories flew around Glasgow about the consequences of the game. One of the most disturbing of numerous incorrect rumours was that Stein had been dismissed. Instead, after a Celtic Park board meeting on Monday 9 November, five days after the battle in Montevideo, Celtic chairman Robert Kelly announced: 'We are in this together, from the chairman to the players. We feel that for our reputation and also for the reputation of football, the players must suffer for their conduct. We do not want to individualize and we are taking the unprecedented step of fining the whole team £250 per player.'

50 Greatest Players

RONNIE SIMPSON Goalkeeper

Born: Glasgow

Joined Celtic: 1964   **From:** Hibernian

Debut: v Barcelona, Fairs Cup, 18 November 1964

Appearances: 188

Left Celtic: 1970 (retired)

Honours won with Celtic: 4 league championships; 1 Scottish Cup;
3 Scottish League Cups; 1 European Cup; 5 caps (Scotland)

When Ronnie Simpson heard that Jock Stein was on his way to Celtic in early 1965 the goalkeeper decided that his Celtic career was over before it had barely begun. It had been Stein, after all, who, as Hibernian manager, had transferred Ronnie to Celtic just four months previously. Simpson's fears seemed well-founded. Stein initially did not play him but he was kept on the books over the summer and in the autumn of 1965 he finally got his chance. For the remainder of the 1960s the agile, lithe Simpson would be Celtic's undisputed first-choice number one.

The goalkeeper, who was well into his thirties by the mid-1960s, was nicknamed 'faither' in recognition of his being a decade older than most of his team-mates. Ronnie had joined Queen's Park just as the Second World War ended and had been part of the Great Britain football squad at the 1948 Olympic Games in London. He went on to win FA Cup winner's medals with Newcastle United in 1952 and 1955 before joining Hibs in 1960. Simpson was not the tallest of men but he knew how to fill his goal. Wearing tight, green 'gardening' type gloves, Ronnie tended the turf in front of his goal with such distinction that he was named as Scotland's Player of the Year in the European Cup-winning year of 1967.

This action caused much grievance among the players who felt that the club should have been much more sympathetic to the extreme and unusual pressures they had suffered in the three matches against Racing. The £250 levied on each player was a sizeable sum: it represented a large chunk of their bonus for winning the 1967 European Cup, which had been £1500.

'Racing couldn't have beaten the likes of Vojvodina,' says Bobby Lennox. 'We had played and beaten much better clubs than Racing Club, but they just wouldn't let us play at all. They became world champions, but they were far from the best team we played in that era. They just ran about kicking people. Billy McNeill, when he was manager of Celtic, had a great photo in his office of the equalizing goal in the second game over in Argentina. You can see one of their players going to cross it and Billy and John Clark are standing maybe about 20 yards out and there is a Racing player about eight yards behind them. In the next photograph on the wall you could see their player heading it into the net. It was so far offside it wasn't true.'

A third-round exit from the Scottish Cup after a defeat from Dunfermline in January 1968 allowed Celtic to concentrate on overtaking League leaders Rangers. Their season-long pursuit finally paid off when a 5-2 win over Dundee in mid-April put Celtic one point clear at the top of the League. Celtic had just two games remaining, but Rangers had three so Celtic were in the unusual position during the Stein years of having their fate in others' hands. That situation changed drastically when Rangers could only draw away to Morton, leaving Celtic top of the League on goal average with just two games remaining.

No Easy Conclusion

There would still be no easy conclusion to the 1967-68 season for Celtic: Morton were their next opponents and the Greenock side were at that time an accomplished, top-six side. A 51,000 Celtic Park crowd saw Celtic go a goal ahead through Willie Wallace after 15 minutes but Morton equalized just on half-time. The score was still 1-1 in the 90th minute and a disastrous draw was on the horizon until Bobby Lennox steered a close-range shot into the Morton net to give Celtic a vital victory.

A relieved Jock Stein commented, 'Just before we scored, someone behind the dugout gave us the news that Rangers had won and I said to Neil Mochan, "We've lost it." Then Bobby got the goal. It couldn't have happened in a better way.'

Celtic's final fixture, away to Dunfermline Athletic, was postponed because the Fife club were participating in the 1968 Scottish Cup final. As Stein watched Dunfermline defeat Hearts at Hampden, he was kept up to date with Rangers' progress in their home match with Aberdeen. He beamed with delight when he heard that Aberdeen had won the other match on the south side of Glasgow: it meant Celtic were champions again. Celtic clinched the title with a total of 63 points, a record for the Scottish First Division. It was the first time in more than 50 years that Celtic had won three successive League titles – and the team's record of 106 goals in their favour and just 24 against was their best League record under Jock Stein.

The title win also provided Celtic with entry to the European Cup and after the previous season's lapse in standards against Dynamo Kiev, Stein had his players primed to give of their best in the 1968-69 season's tournament. The first round threw up a difficult tie against French champions St Etienne and Celtic were overwhelmed by the quality of the French side's play in the away leg, which they lost 2-0.

Ice-cool Tommy

The early stages of the home leg with St Etienne proved equally difficult for Celtic and they had to rely on a penalty, awarded against Camerini for a foul on McBride, to put them ahead. The French players were outraged at the penalty award, rubbing their fingers together in the face of the referee to insinuate that he had been 'bought'. As Tommy Gemmell prepared to take the kick, St Etienne players threw clods of earth at the ball in an attempt to distract the Celtic full back. Nothing fazed Tommy and he whacked the ball into the net. That goal upset the French and gave Celtic the momentum to streak on to a 4-0 victory that put them into a second round tie against Red Star Belgrade.

Again Celtic faced highly accomplished opponents and although Bobby Murdoch gave the Celts a third-minute lead in the first leg at Celtic Park, the Yugoslavian side established themselves as the better team during that opening 45 minutes and equalized late in the first half. During the interval, Jock Stein came up with an inspirational idea that would pave Celtic's way into the quarter-finals. Turning to Jimmy Johnstone, he told the player that if Celtic won by a four-goal margin the winger would be exempt from flying to Belgrade for the return.

Two years previously, Johnstone had developed a fear of flying after a turbulent trip from the USA to Britain. With the carrot of being exempt from the flight to the return leg dangling in front of him, Johnstone produced a world-class second-half performance, scoring twice himself and setting up chances for Bobby Lennox and Willie Wallace to score one each and give Celtic an unassailable 5-1 first-leg lead. 'I was everywhere looking for the ball in that second half,' says Johnstone. 'That was great psychology.'

Stein was as good as his word. Johnstone was absent from the squad that travelled to Yugoslavia and which eased to the 1-1 draw that put Celtic into the European Cup quarter-finals. AC Milan awaited them there and in the San Siro a cagey Celtic eked out a useful 0-0 draw. It set them up nicely for the return, but the loss of a 12th minute goal to Pierino Prati allowed Milan to drop back deep into defence. Celtic were unable to score in the face of such concentrated defensive resources and the 0-0 draw meant that they had lost their chance of winning the 1969 European Cup.

'That was a disaster,' says Tommy Gemmell, 'because we had played so well in Milan. We controlled the game at Celtic Park but couldn't put the ball in the pokey hat. Still, you've got to take into account who you are playing and they were a right good side.'

That match against Milan took place in mid-March 1969 and with the excitement of Europe over for another year Celtic settled down to the business of securing the club's second treble. The League Cup final, usually played in the autumn, had been held over until April 1969 because of fire

50 Greatest Players

WILLIE WALLACE Forward

Born: Kirkintilloch

Joined Celtic: 1966   **From:** Hearts

Debut: v Motherwell, League, 10 December 1966

Appearances: 232   **Goals:** 134

Left Celtic: 1971   **For:** Crystal Palace

Honours won with Celtic: 5 league championships; 3 Scottish Cups; 2 Scottish League Cups; 1 European Cup; 4 caps (Scotland)

One of Jock Stein's priorities on taking over as Celtic manager was to fill his forward line with players who combined panache with pace. Willie Wallace, whom Stein signed from Hearts, fitted Stein's requirements to perfection. Willie's nickname of 'Wispy' encapsulated the ghostlike stealth with which he could steal into scoring positions; it mattered little that the nickname was actually a distorted acronym of his initials: William Semple Brown.

Willie was signed by Stein for £30,000 on 6 December 1966, and quickly settled into the inside right position, softening the blow dealt by Joe McBride's absence through injury after that Christmas. Willie played a key role in securing the European Cup, most notably with his two goals against Dukla Prague in the 1967 semi-final.

He remained a consistent scorer for the following four seasons before he lost his place in the team at the start of the 1971-72 season, and left for Crystal Palace. He later emigrated to Australia, where he became a successful businessman.

damage to the stand at Hampden Park. Hibernian stood in Celtic's way in that match, but Hibs were simply outmanoeuvred and outplayed by opponents who were almost flawless in their reading of each other's play as Celtic strolled to a 6-2 victory.

Seamlessly Stylish

Three weeks later Celtic faced Rangers in the Scottish Cup final, having already sewn up the 1968-69 Scottish League title. The treble was secured in style – Celtic were 3-0 up at half-time as they eased to a 4-0 win. Celtic's football was seamlessly stylish as the players moved the ball around at speed – no Scottish side could compete with them that season. It was a reflection of Stein's success in assembling such a superb side that the end of that treble-winning season was tinged with genuine disappointment because of the team's failure to progress further than the quarter-finals of the European Cup.

It was not long before that disappointment eased. Another European Cup tournament began in September 1969 with Celtic easing past FC Basle. Goals from new £40,000 striker Harry Hood, signed from Clyde, and from Gemmell enabled them to eliminate the Swiss club on a 2-0 aggregate and put them into the second round to face Benfica. They warmed up for that encounter by defeating St Johnstone 1-0 at Hampden in the League Cup final, a second-minute Bertie Auld goal giving Celtic their fifth successive League Cup.

Celtic's Jimmy Johnstone fires in a shot in the 1969 League Cup final against Hibernian. Celtic routed the Edinburgh side 6-2.

Another of Tommy Gemmell's long-range free-kicks was the highlight of a stunning 3-0 first-leg victory over Benfica at Celtic Park that seemed sure to have earned Celtic their passage into the quarter-finals. The Portuguese side, however, threw everything at Celtic in the return and a header from Diamentino two minutes into injury-time gave Benfica a 3-0 second-leg victory and levelled the aggregate score in the tie.

Billy McNeill, watched by Willie Wallace, glides on to the ball to head the opening goal in the 4-0 Scottish Cup final victory over Rangers in 1969.

A Toss of the Coin

There was no scoring in extra-time and penalty shoot-outs had yet to be introduced as a means of settling drawn games. So, deep inside Lisbon's Stadium of Light, a coin was tossed by the referee to see which side would progress in the European Cup. Dutch referee Louis van Raavens' two-and-a-half guilder piece was spun in the air by Celtic captain Billy McNeill who called the toss correctly, and Celtic were through to the last-eight of Europe's premier club competition.

'We should never have lost that 3-0 lead,' says Tommy Gemmell. 'We were very careless at the back and gave away silly goals. The luck was with us in winning the toss of the coin, but that ain't the way to win a European Cup tie.'

For the second successive year Celtic were drawn against the champions of Italy in the European Cup quarter-finals. Fiorentina, like Benfica, were overwhelmed by Celtic in another smooth 3-0 Celtic Park European Cup victory, but this time there would be no slackness in the return. 'We have lost games against Benfica and AC Milan because of carelessness and this must be avoided,' said Stein before the match in the Stadio Comunale, Florence. 'We are here to confirm our place in the semi-finals.' His team played cautiously and steadily on the night of the match – Fiorentina did win, but only by 1-0 – and Celtic progressed into the semi-finals.

50 Greatest Players

BERTIE AULD Midfielder

Born: Glasgow

Joined Celtic: 1955   **From:** Maryhill Harp

Debut: v Partick Thistle, League, 16 February 1959

Left Celtic: 1961   **From:** Birmingham City

Rejoined Celtic: 1965   **From:** Birmingham City

Appearances: 275   **Goals:** 79

Left Celtic: 1971   **For:** Hibernian

Honours won with Celtic: 7 league championships; 6 Scottish Cups; 5 Scottish League Cups; 1 European Cup; 3 caps (Scotland)

Few players could displease chairman Robert Kelly during the 1950s and still thrive at Celtic. Bertie Auld had impressive ability, but this native of Maryhill would be pushed around by no one and after a succession of flare-ups on the field Kelly transferred the player to Birmingham in 1961. His spell at St Andrews saw him play against Roma in the final of the 1961 Fairs Cup and gain a League Cup winner's medal in 1963, but in January 1965 he returned to Celtic Park, reportedly after being tipped off that Jock Stein was about to return.

Stein switched him from the left wing to midfield and Auld's neat, intricate passing, in tandem with Bobby Murdoch, undid many a tightly knit defence. Auld could still take care of himself on the field, although maturity meant he now wreaked vengeance through stealth rather than aggression. It is a measure of his quality that he performed even better in his second spell at the club than in his first one, his hard-edged sophistication proving an essential component in all of Celtic's successes during the late 1960s.

As early as March 1970, Celtic had already guaranteed themselves their fifth successive Scottish League title. They would eventually win the title by a massive 12 points from closest challengers Rangers and another treble was in their sights as they had also reached the Scottish Cup final. First, there was the small matter of 'the Battle of Britain'; the first leg of their European Cup semi-final against Leeds United at Elland Road.

A deflected George Connelly shot in the opening minute was enough to give Celtic a 1-0 win. A 45,000 crowd at Elland Road – including 10,000 Celtic supporters – watched the Scottish side control the game from beginning to end. They deserved to win by more and might have done so had a perfectly good goal from star performer Connelly not been disallowed. Nevertheless, they were satisfied with the result – a feeling echoed by the 5,000 ecstatic supporters who welcomed them back to Glasgow's Central Station.

Massive excitement began building in Glasgow in anticipation of Celtic's return match with Leeds, which was to take place at Hampden Park to accommodate the enormous numbers who wished to attend. Four days before that game, however, Celtic had a prior engagement at Hampden. Aberdeen were to be their opponents in the 1970 Scottish Cup final.

George Connelly and John Hughes watch as a drive from Bobby Murdoch (out of picture) beats Leeds keeper David Harvey to seal Celtic's place in the 1970 European Cup final.

Great Matches

EUROPEAN CUP SEMI-FINAL   **Hampden Park, 15 April 1970**
SECOND LEG

Celtic 2   **Leeds United 1**   **Attendance 136,505**
Hughes   Bremner
Murdoch

The Leeds United manager Don Revie had stated in 1965 that Scottish football would be dead by 1970. That year had arrived and Celtic had proved the Scottish game was very much alive and kicking by defeating Revie's champions of England 1-0 in the first leg of the semi-final. The return at Hampden was eagerly anticipated. It had sold out one month previously and the crowd of 136,505 remains the record attendance for any European Cup match anywhere. 'We thought it was going to be the hardest game of our lives,' says Bobby Lennox.

Celtic's advantage from the first leg was quickly erased when, after 14 minutes, Billy Bremner, Leeds' Celtic-supporting Scottish captain, sent a superb, swirling 25-yard shot into the top left-hand corner of goalkeeper Evan Williams' net. It levelled the tie but Celtic soon established themselves as the dominant side, with George Connelly, Bertie Auld and Bobby Murdoch taking hold of the midfield and Jimmy Johnstone and Bobby Lennox bamboozling the Leeds defenders with their trickery.

Two minutes after half-time, Auld curled the ball into the heart of the Leeds penalty area and John Hughes, centre forward on the night, dived to head the equalizer. Stein, remembering that Hughes had always got the better of Jack Charlton in internationals between Scotland and England, had deliberately put him up against the Leeds centre half and once again it had yielded results.

Leeds were a tough, spirited side, but they struggled to cope with the constant invention of Celtic. Five minutes after Hughes' header, Bobby Murdoch collected the ball in midfield and sent a flawless pass into the path of Jimmy Johnstone on the right wing. Leeds defenders Terry Cooper and Norman Hunter went wide to try to smother the threat from Johnstone. That released some space inside the Leeds box and when Johnstone pinged the ball inside, Murdoch, close to the edge of the area, strode on to the ball and shot low and hard past Leeds' substitute goalkeeper David Harvey. The goal sent Celtic into their second European Cup final and, once again, proved beyond reasonable doubt that they were Britain's best.

Celtic: Williams, Hay, Gemmell, Murdoch, McNeill, Brogan, Johnstone, Connelly, Hughes, Auld, Lennox.

Leeds United: Sprake (Harvey), Madeley, Cooper, Bremner, Charlton, Hunter, Lorimer, Clarke, Jones, Giles, Gray.

Three dubious decisions by referee Bobby Davidson gave the Pittodrie side the advantage in the first half of the final. Davidson awarded Aberdeen a penalty for handball against Bobby Murdoch after an Aberdeen cross had struck the midfielder on his upper body. No Aberdeen players had expected a penalty until Davidson pointed to the spot. After four minutes of Celtic protests, Joe Harper put the ball in the net to give the Dons a 1-0 lead. Then, Bobby Lennox appeared to have equalized but the referee ruled out the goal for an infringement on Aberdeen goalkeeper Bobby Clark. Clark had simply dropped the ball nervously in front of the Celt. The Celtic supporters' frustration was complete when Martin Buchan caught Lennox with his boot inside the penalty area only for the referee to rule that the forward had dived.

Eight minutes remained when Aberdeen went 2-0 up, but just as a late Lennox goal for Celtic had given the Glasgow team a chance of saving the match, an Aberdeen strike, in the final minute, finished the game. Following the 3-1 defeat, Stein exploded with fury about the referee's performance and was later fined by the Scottish FA for his comments. 'We played Aberdeen off the park that day and they beat us 3-1,' says Lennox.

Celtic's treble chance had disappeared for the 1969-70 season, but after the epic 2-1 victory over Leeds in the second leg of the European Cup semi-final, the chance of Celtic winning a second European Cup looked exceptionally possible. Feyenoord of Rotterdam were to be their opponents in the final in the San Siro, Milan, on 6 May 1970. The Dutch side had knocked out holders AC Milan in the second round, but they were largely inexperienced in European competition and were widely expected to be unable to face up to the force of the seasoned Celtic players.

Things did not go to plan for Celtic, who started the match shakily. Against Leeds, Celtic had exerted an iron grip on midfield, thanks to the talented central trio of Connelly, Auld and Murdoch. For the final, Stein was convinced that Feyenoord would be overwhelmed if Celtic placed the emphasis on all-out attack. Accordingly, he left Connelly out of the side and fielded an extra forward in a 4-2-4 formation. Feyenoord's midfield three of Franz Hasil, Wim Jansen and Wim van Hanegem soon began to run the game from the middle of the park, although it was Celtic who took the lead on the half-hour.

A free-kick was awarded for a foul on Willie Wallace just outside the Feyenoord penalty area. Murdoch took the kick in unorthodox fashion by putting a clever back-heel into Tommy Gemmell's path. The full back pelted the ball past Feyenoord goalkeeper Eddie Pieters Graafland to open the scoring. It took Feyenoord just two minutes to equalize. Celtic's defence failed to clear a penalty-box ball effectively and Rinus Israel sent a neat

50 Greatest Players

JOHN HUGHES Outside left

Born: Coatbridge

Joined Celtic: 1959   **From:** Shotts Bon Accord

Debut: v Third Lanark, League Cup, 13 August 1960

Appearances: 383   **Goals:** 188

Left Celtic: 1971   **For:** Crystal Palace

Honours won with Celtic: 5 league championships; 1 Scottish Cup; 1 Scottish League Cup; 8 caps (Scotland)

Tears of frustration flooded down John Hughes' cheeks in the aftermath of Celtic's 1961 Scottish Cup final defeat by Dunfermline Athletic. The 18-year-old, Celtic's centre forward in that final, would become even more demoralized over the next few years. The type of coaching and guidance needed to improve his ball skills were not available at Celtic in the early 1960s, so Hughes had to rely on his instinctive talent for the game. That led to his form fluctuating up and down wildly.

Jock Stein turned Hughes' world upside down, transforming him into a powerful outside left. Stein's hunch was that Hughes would blossom if he was allowed to use his exceptional ball control, power and speed on the wing and he was soon proved correct. Hughes developed into a dynamic winger who could still be used as a surprise centre forward and he played a key role in numerous great wins, most notably the European Cup victory over Leeds United in 1970.

Hughes felt Stein's method of motivating players with high bonuses on top of a very modest basic wage was unfair and he confronted the manager to ask for a rise in spring 1971. Stein retorted that Hughes' missed chance against Feyenoord in the 1970 European Cup final had cost Celtic the trophy. 'Yogi' – his nickname derived from the cartoon character who was 'smarter than the average bear' – was soon reluctantly on the move to Crystal Palace.

header over goalkeeper Evan Williams' head to make it 1-1. 'If we had held the lead longer it might have deflated them a bit,' says Bobby Lennox, 'but they got back into the game right away.'

Williams was the outstanding Celt on the night and his interventions on several further occasions saved his team from going behind. At 90 minutes the score was still 1-1 and shortly after the start of extra-time, winger John Hughes was presented with a chance that he admits he should have scored. Instead, he sent his shot against Pieters Graafland and with just three minutes to go Ove Kindvall got in behind the Celtic defence to strike the winner.

Various theories were advanced as reasons for Celtic's defeat. It was suggested that the two-and-a-half-week period between the team's final competitive fixture and the European Cup final had been too long. Centre back Jim Brogan had been weakened by an injury sustained in the opening minute and had struggled throughout the remainder of the match. It was also put forward that the players' attempts to capitalize financially on their appearance in the final through various commercial ventures had distracted them from the task in hand. Another story suggested that there had been a row over bonuses that had continued to rumble up until kick-off.

Some Celtic players, in later years, looking back on the 1970 European Cup final, would suggest that Stein had underestimated the Dutch side, giving the players the impression that they were up against a mediocre team, and failing to galvanize his players with the type of motivation required for such an occasion. Even the 20,000 Celtic fans in the crowd were overwhelmed by their Dutch counterparts, whose rasping klaxons drowned out the songs and chants of the Glasgow contingent. Stein admitted afterwards, 'The better team won. We had too many players off form. I know the reason but I am not going to criticize my players in public. We are disappointed. I was surprised we played so badly but in saying this I don't want to take away any credit from the other side. Every one of their team was a good player.'

Bobby Lennox is quite sure about the major reason for Celtic's defeat. 'I can tell you exactly what happened and I don't care what anybody says: Feyenoord were better than us. Feyenoord played really well that night and we couldn't get ourselves going. Maybe we thought subconsciously that we just had to turn up and we would win, but they played very, very well on the night. We got to within four minutes of a replay, which might have been a big help to us, but they were a good side: make no mistake about it.

'People say that Jock Stein underestimated them but do you know my answer to that? Jock's team talk didn't win us the European Cup in 1967 and his team talk didn't lose us the European Cup against Feyenoord. I can never say that the manager let us down in that situation because we knew that we still had to go out and beat Feyenoord. Team talks help get you going, but they don't win you games – players win you games. That night, when Celtic players got the ball, there didn't seem to be anything on. Feyenoord used the full width of the park and were pinging the ball about brilliantly. They were better than us on the night.' As in the 1967 final, the underdogs had had their day. It was now the task of Stein and his team to bite back.

Chapter Eight: 1970-78
The Challenge of Change

The desire to attack the opposition was a key element of the Celtic teams that achieved so much for the club and its supporters during the 1960s and 1970s. Celtic could also defend when required. They could handle the challenge of any team that wished to take them on in a physical battle and the team was full of tough tacklers who were always keen to notify opponents of their presence. The most important principle for Jock Stein, however, was to entertain the supporters and win matches through attacking football.

The manager was entirely aware of how much the game meant to people and of the need to continually attract them to football grounds. It was that line of logic that led him to announce in late April 1971 that his Lisbon Lions would be taking the field together for the final time on 1 May. Stein made that announcement in the aftermath of his team clinching their sixth consecutive Scottish League title with a victory over Ayr United. It meant they had equalled the feat of the great Celtic team who had won successive titles between 1905 and 1910. Stein, the great showman, immediately promised that the final League fixture of that 1970-71 season would be the fans' last chance to see the greatest Celtic team of all, thus guaranteeing a full house for an otherwise empty fixture.

A crowd of 35,000 materialized to see the Lisbon Lions' final roar. The stand at Celtic Park had been demolished to make way for a brand new structure that would be constructed that summer. Stein and his players stepped gingerly over the rubble of the old edifice as they approached the field of play. Clyde were their unlucky victims as the team turned on the style to win 6-1. Bobby Lennox got a hat-trick, Willie Wallace scored twice and, fittingly, Stevie Chalmers, the scorer of the winner in the 1967 European Cup final, got the other goal. It was a last look back before Stein returned to his ongoing reconstruction of a team fit for the challenges of the 1970s.

Only four of the Lions had remained consistent and regular choices for the first-team in that 1970-71 season: Billy McNeill, Willie Wallace, Jimmy Johnstone and Bobby Lennox. Ronnie Simpson had retired from football in 1970 after sustaining a serious shoulder injury and had made only a token appearance in that final appearance of the Lions against Clyde. Stevie Chalmers, Bertie Auld and John Clark had played only a handful of games in the 1970-71 season and in mid-1971 they would leave Celtic Park to move to new clubs. Others of the Lisbon team, such as Tommy Gemmell and Bobby Murdoch, were finding their places under threat as a stream of new, young players pushed through from the reserves. Among those players were the highly skilled forwards Vic Davidson, Lou Macari and Kenny Dalglish as well as Danny McGrain, a defender with a creative edge to his game. David Hay and George Connelly, who were useful both in defence and in midfield, had both made a name for themselves as ball players with an ability to win the ball and use it imaginatively.

Stein had carefully introduced those young players to the team on a gradual basis. They had come through the reserves together during the late 1960s and

50 Greatest Players

TOMMY GEMMELL Full back

Born: Craigneuk

Joined Celtic: 1961   **From:** Coltness United

Debut: v Aberdeen, League, 5 January 1963

Appearances: 418   **Goals:** 63

Left Celtic: 1971   **For:** Nottingham Forest

Honours won with Celtic: 6 league championships;
3 Scottish Cups; 4 Scottish League Cups; 1 European Cup;
18 caps (Scotland)

Tommy Gemmell was an exciting extrovert whose confidence in his own abilities was reflected in his chosen title for his 1968 autobiography: *The Big Shot*. That title also reflected Gemmell's ability to score spectacular goals, as he had proved three times in the victorious run to the 1967 European Cup. Shortly after taking over as Celtic manager, Jock Stein had spotted Gemmell's scoring potential and had given him extra shooting practice. Gemmell's shot was soon being timed at 70 miles per hour.

Prior to Stein's arrival, Gemmell had been told not to cross the halfway line, but as an overlapping full back, his power, speed and athleticism made him a key man in Stein's game plan of pressing opponents all over the field.

The relationship between Gemmell and his manager sadly soured when Stein dropped the player with little warning before the 1969 League Cup final with St Johnstone. Later that season, Tommy became one of the few players to score in two European Cup finals, with another long-range effort against Feyenoord in the 1970 final, but tension between player and manager continued to simmer and in the autumn of 1971 Gemmell was transferred to Nottingham Forest.

had become known as the Quality Street Gang – a nickname that reflected their collective talent. Stein would bring one of those young players into the team for one or two first-team games, building up the player's experience, before returning him to the reserves. Another youngster would then get his chance to gain experience. Those young players had been introduced on a gradual basis during the late 1960s but by the early 1970s they were worth permanent places in the Celtic team. The fluctuations in personnel did little to hamper the team's ability to gather trophies: Celtic were still able to hold off a strong challenge from Aberdeen, who had led the league for a sizeable chunk of that 1970-71 season, to take the title to Celtic Park again.

Ajax and Cruyff

The European Cup had seen Celtic push on as far as the 1971 quarter-finals, where they encountered Ajax from Amsterdam, a team that featured the marvellously inventive Johan Cruyff among their various talents. Hay was detailed to mark Cruyff closely and did so effectively until midway through the second half when Cruyff managed to slip away to shoot past Evan Williams. The Dutch side increased the pressure and the tie slipped out of Celtic's grasp when they conceded two late goals. The return, played at Hampden, saw

In the European Cup quarter-final second leg against Ajax, John Hughes (left) heads the ball narrowly wide, watched by team-mate Jimmy Johnstone (second right).

Celtic bravely attempt to level Ajax's lead, but they had left themselves too much to do and a single Jimmy Johnstone goal was all they could muster.

Celtic had always won at least two trophies in each of Stein's full seasons with the club prior to that 1970-71 season, but that record looked in jeopardy when, in October 1970, they lost in the final of the League Cup for the first time since the manager's arrival. That 1-0 defeat by Rangers at Hampden meant that if Celtic were to collect a second trophy that season they would have to do so in the Scottish Cup final, where they would face Rangers once again. At Hampden, a Bobby Lennox goal put Celtic 1-0 ahead shortly before half-time, but Derek Johnstone's equalizer late in the match meant the final finished 1-1.

The inexperienced Rangers full back Jim Denny was pitched into the replay and Jimmy Johnstone was detailed by Stein to put extreme pressure on him.

50 Greatest Players

STEVE CHALMERS Forward

Born: Glasgow

Joined Celtic: 1959   **From:** Ashfield Juniors

Debut: v Airdrie, League, 10 March 1959

Appearances: 406   **Goals:** 219

Left Celtic: 1971   **For:** Morton

Honours won with Celtic: 4 league championships; 3 Scottish Cups; 4 Scottish League Cups; 1 European Cup; 5 caps (Scotland)

Jock Stein bought Willie Wallace in December 1966 to play alongside Joe McBride, which would have left Stevie Chalmers sidelined. Stevie had been scoring goals for Celtic since the early 1960s, but was then approaching his 30th birthday. Two days before that date, Joe McBride suffered the injury that put him out for the remainder of the 1966-67 season. Stein had to revise his plans and Stevie Chalmers took the opportunity to go on and score the winner in the 1967 European Cup final.

That goal against Internazionale was a typical Stevie Chalmers strike; he used his swift reflexes and excellent awareness to get just enough on the ball to divert it past Giuliano Sarti in the Inter goal. Subtlety and style were the essential elements in Stevie Chalmers' goalscoring. A true gentleman, highly disciplined on and off the field, Stevie has remained involved with Celtic since his retirement as a player in the mid-1970s. He rejoined Celtic as a coach and latterly was to be found helping the club with commercial activities and acting as a hospitality host on matchdays.

Shortly before kick-off, Lou Macari was told he was in the side as a replacement for Willie Wallace. It would be Macari's first major match for the club.

With 24 minutes played, Billy McNeill let the ball go as it went hurtling into the Rangers penalty area from a corner-kick and Macari nipped in to swipe the ball into the net with his left foot. Within a minute, Jimmy Johnstone was pulled down, rugby-tackle style, by Ron McKinnon inside the Rangers penalty area and Harry Hood poked the resultant penalty home. Jim Craig scored an own goal to put extra pressure on Celtic as Rangers fought back in the second half, but Celtic stayed steady for a 2-1 victory. With the Scottish Cup in their hands, they had maintained Stein's two-trophy record.

It had been a fine achievement for Stein to bring his side through a transitional season in such successful style. The manager had also proved his commitment to Celtic in the spring of 1971 when Manchester United offered him the vacant managerial post at Old Trafford. Stein toyed with the idea

Lou Macari scores his team's seventh goal in a 9-1 win over Clyde at Celtic Park in September 1971.

and even went so far as to meet, in secret, United's general manager Matt Busby. After consideration, however, Stein turned down United's offer. 'I will be staying here as long as I am needed,' he said. 'We have been through a lot together in the last six glorious years and you don't break those links so easily. There is still much to do.'

The urgent need for Stein's reconstruction of Celtic to continue apace was evident in the autumn of 1971. Celtic's seventh successive League Cup final produced disaster when Partick Thistle scored four times without reply inside 25 first-half minutes at Hampden. Billy McNeill had been absent through injury that day and he was badly missed as Celtic tumbled to a shocking 4-1 defeat. Stein described it as 'the biggest blow we ever had as a club' and it prompted the manager to refresh his squad even further.

The weeks following that defeat saw John Hughes and Willie Wallace moved on to Crystal Palace for a combined fee of £50,000 and they were soon followed out of Celtic Park by Tommy Gemmell, signed for £35,000 by Nottingham Forest. Goalkeeper Denis Connaghan, who had played for Stein at Dunfermline, was brought to Celtic from St Mirren while striker Dixie Deans joined from Motherwell for a £17,500 fee.

The impetus of the new signings and the short, sharp shock of the Thistle defeat spurred Celtic on. Aberdeen were again Celtic's closest challengers in the League that 1971-72 season, but by its end they trailed the Celts by a massive ten-point margin. Stein's players' 27-match unbeaten run in the League was a suitably rich means of creating the new Scottish record of seven successive championships.

Stein had altered his side's system of play from 4-2-4 to a more cautious 4-3-3, giving him one fewer forward but an extra midfielder. It had served Celtic well that 1971-72 season, and their steady stroll towards the League title had been matched stride for stride by another successful run in the European Cup. Having beaten BK 1903 Copenhagen and Sliema Wanderers, Celtic were faced with a difficult tie against the powerful Hungarian champions Ujpest Dozsa.

The Celtic players were impressed by the facilities in their dressing room before the first leg in Budapest. It was furnished with sumptuous armchairs and sofas rather than the more traditional wooden benches. They felt comfortable on the field too, playing superbly to win that first leg 2-1. Afterwards, Stein commented of his young, renovated side, 'At this level and when you consider the age of this team of ours, it is probably Celtic's best European Cup display since Lisbon.' A 1-1 second-leg draw put Celtic safely through to the last four.

To the San Siro

There would be a further reminder of that magical 1967 match in Lisbon when Celtic were drawn against Internazionale in the European Cup semi-finals. The away leg in the San Siro proved another step forward for Stein's young side: the manager fielded the team in a 4-5-1 formation, with Macari as their sole attacker, and their disciplined approach earned them a 0-0 draw. The plan had been to hit Inter with the full force of the Celtic attack in the

---

50 Greatest Players

BOBBY MURDOCH Midfielder

Born: Bothwell

Joined Celtic: 1959   **From:** Cambuslang Rangers

Debut: v Hearts, League Cup, 11 August 1962

Appearances: 484   **Goals:** 102

Left Celtic: 1973   **For:** Middlesbrough

Honours won with Celtic: 7 league championships; 4 Scottish Cups, 4 Scottish League Cups; 1 European Cup; 12 caps (Scotland)

Jock Stein described Bobby Murdoch as the best player in Britain in the late 1960s. In the era of George Best, Denis Law and Bobby Charlton many might assume Stein was just talking up of one of his own players. Yet those who watched Murdoch week by week knew that the Celtic manager was not exaggerating. Bobby Murdoch was the complete footballer and his ability to control a match with extreme precision was central to Celtic's vital victories in the 1960s.

The player had been part of the Celtic forward line when Stein arrived at the club in 1965, but the manager immediately moved him back to midfield, where Murdoch became the fulcrum of Celtic's attacks. He passed the ball with perfection, he could read the game like a professor and when he moved upfield in support of the forwards, his shooting from the edge of the area was explosive.

A big, strong man, Bobby Murdoch had a touch on the ball that was surprisingly exquisite and delicate, and that sophistication, along with his strength and stamina, made him a world-class footballer. He was named Scotland's Player of the Year in 1969.

In 1973 Murdoch joined Middlesbrough – 'I only let him move because he had run out of challenges with Celtic,' claimed Stein. He spent nine years at Ayresome Park as player, coach and manager, playing his part in their 1973-74 promotion side and later helping to bring some of the club's emerging talent through to the first team. Tragically, in 2001 Bobby Murdoch became the first Lisbon Lion to pass away, but the memory of one of the greatest Celts of all remains undimmed.

Great Matches

SCOTTISH CUP FINAL   Hampden Park, 6 May 1972

Celtic 6   **Hibernian 1**   Attendance 106,102
McNeill   Gordon
Deans 3
Macari 2

The 1972 Scottish Cup final promised to be a match for the connoisseurs. Hibs – nicknamed 'Turnbull's Tornadoes' in recognition of the galvanizing powers of manager Eddie Turnbull – were playing delightful football and featured outstanding players in John Brownlie, Pat Stanton, John Blackley, Alec Edwards, Jim O'Rourke and Arthur Duncan. There was even some added spice in that they had Bertie Auld on their bench for the final.

It proved to be a classic. Two minutes had passed when Celtic's Tommy Callaghan sent a free-kick to Hibs' back post and Billy McNeill hit the ball on the volley to score from close range. Hibs responded in fiery fashion and ten minutes later Duncan's low cross was turned past Evan Williams by Alan Gordon. Tightly contested, the game was living up to its billing when midway through the first half Dixie Deans headed Bobby Murdoch's free-kick past Jim Herriot in the Hibs goal.

It remained 2-1 to Celtic at half-time and Hibs were still very much in the game, but ten minutes after the break Deans anticipated that John Brownlie's back-header would not reach Herriot. Dixie reached the ball before Herriot, took it past the goalkeeper, evaded a desperate Brownlie tackle, took the ball to the goal-line, edged the ball back inside to beat Herriot a second time and create a scoring angle, then dinked the ball past Eric Schaedler and into the Hibernian net.

A more streamlined goal from Deans 15 minutes from time saw him dart on to a pass from Callaghan to prod the ball past Herriot and put the game beyond Hibs' reach. A couple of poacher's goals from Lou Macari in the closing ten minutes sealed a record scoreline for a 20th-century Scottish Cup final. Dixie Deans had become only the second scorer of a Cup final hat-trick, equalling Jimmy Quinn's treble strike in 1904. It was the highest Scottish Cup final scoreline since Celtic's formation in 1888 and Celtic had emphasized to Hibs and all other pretenders to their crown that they were still the master craftsmen of the Scottish game.

Celtic: Williams, Craig, Brogan, Murdoch, McNeill, Connelly, Johnstone, Deans, Macari, Dalglish, Callaghan.

Hibernian: Herriot, Brownlie, Schaedler, Stanton, Black, Blackley, Edwards, Hazel, Gordon, O'Rourke, Duncan (Auld).

John 'Dixie' Deans on the way to a historic hat-trick.
Opposite: He heads his first and Celtic's second.
This page: Deans' individualistic second goal puts Celtic 3-1 up.

return leg at Celtic Park, but the Italians' own negative approach saw them pack their penalty area and barely venture forward. After extra-time in that second leg, with the aggregate score 0-0, the tie went to a penalty shootout. UEFA had introduced this means of settling matches two years previously, but it was an ordeal Celtic had, until now, avoided.

Sandro Mazzola, one of four Inter players who had also featured in the 1967 final, took the first kick and sent a precise penalty into the net. Dixie Deans stepped up to hit Celtic's first penalty only to lift the ball high over the crossbar. Inter's nominated penalty-takers scored with their next three kicks, as did their Celtic opponents, before Jair slipped Inter's final kick into the net to put Celtic out of the 1972 European Cup. 'No one anticipated our team going as far in the competition this season,' said Stein, 'although we are now disappointed to have been beaten on a technicality at this stage.'

Celtic's 6-1 victory over Hibernian in the 1972 Scottish Cup final had shown that Stein's team remained in robust health despite the defeat by Inter. There seemed no end to the rich seam of success that he had mined since his

Kenny Dalglish (right) scores Celtic's third goal with a diving header in a league match at Heart of Midlothian in October 1973. Celtic won 3-1.

50 Greatest Players

DIXIE DEANS Centre forward

Born: Linwood

Joined Celtic: 1971   **From:** Motherwell

Debut: v Partick Thistle, League, 27 November 1971

Appearances: 184   **Goals:** 124

Left Celtic: 1976   **For:** Luton Town

Honours won with Celtic: 2 league championships; 2 Scottish Cups; 1 Scottish League Cup; 2 caps (Scotland)

The 'Jungle' terracing of Celtic Park, where the hardcore Celtic fans stood before the ground went all-seater, took to John Kelly 'Dixie' Deans from the moment they set eyes on him. They could immediately identify with him – his rotund figure and happy-go-lucky, roguish manner marked him out as less of a lean-limbed Olympian than a punter who had got lucky. Dixie – nicknamed after Everton and England's greatest ever goalscorer – played up to that image, but he was a sharp striker who could be relied on to put the ball in the net with uncanny regularity.

His hat-tricks in two separate Cup finals against Hibernian endeared him further to the support, as did his distinctive celebratory forward rolls. A Celtic folk hero, Dixie is remembered with fond affection by all those who were weaned on the Celtic sides of the early 1970s.

arrival at the club, but the opening months of the 1972-73 season proved stressful for Stein. Celtic were drawn against Ujpest Dozsa in the European Cup once again, this time in the second round, and took a 2-1 first-leg lead to Hungary. There, the Ujpest players sprang at them with stealth from the kick-off and midway through the first half Celtic found themselves 3-0 down. That was the final score and Celtic were out of the tournament disappointingly early. It was the first time Celtic had gone out of the European Cup before Christmas for five years.

An eighth successive League Cup final under Stein matched Celtic against Hibs on 9 December 1972. The Edinburgh side extracted a large measure of compensation for their Scottish Cup thrashing earlier in the year by defeating Celtic 2-1. It was a testing time for Stein, although his side were two points clear of Hibs at the top of the League as Christmas 1972 arrived.

Bill Shankly had told Stein in the dressing room at Lisbon in 1967, after Celtic's greatest triumph, 'John you're immortal.' Sadly, that piece of hyperbole was thrown into sharp relief just after Christmas 1972 when Stein was whisked into hospital suffering from heart trouble. He remained in Glasgow's Victoria Infirmary for 12 days, during which time Celtic had relinquished their leadership of the League to Rangers.

The manager's problems were compounded in the first week of 1973, when Lou Macari, his promising young forward, demanded a transfer. Macari was disillusioned by Celtic's pay structure - a limited basic salary and massive win bonuses – and within days, he had moved to Manchester United for a Scottish record fee of £200,000.

Stein's return to the dugout early in 1973 inspired his players to achieve a 14-match unbeaten run and, once again, their consistency proved too much for their rivals, who melted away, allowing Celtic to clinch the title in some comfort. They lost the 1973 Scottish Cup final 3-2 to Rangers in an even, well-balanced game, but Stein was convinced that his side would be even stronger for the 1973-74 season. The money from the sale of Macari had been invested in three new players. A sum of £40,000 had been spent on obtaining the services of goalkeeper Ally Hunter from Kilmarnock; Andy Lynch cost £35,000 from Hearts; and Steve Murray was bought from Aberdeen for £50,000.

Eight on their Shorts

Celtic's first home League game of the 1973-74 season, against Clyde, saw every player wearing the number eight on their shorts in recognition of the team's eight championships in a row. Their 5-0 victory in that match emphasized the determination of Stein's side to increase that total to nine.

Yet again, they reached the League Cup final and yet again they struggled in that match. Dundee were Celtic's opponents in mid-December 1973 and the miners' strike and resultant energy rationing meant the game kicked off at 1.30 on a dreich day. To complete the misery of the Celtic supporters in the small Cup final crowd, Dundee scored the only goal of the game 15 minutes from time. As if to rub salt into Celtic's wounds, Tommy Gemmell, now captain of the Dens Park side, stepped up to accept the trophy.

The European Cup was proving more enjoyable for Celtic. Victories over TPS Turku of Finland, Vejle of Denmark and Basle of Switzerland took Celtic into the semi-finals of Europe's premier trophy for a fourth time. Their opponents were to be Atletico Madrid and a sell-out Celtic Park crowd anticipated a wonderful night of football. They were to be disappointed. Atletico, managed by Juan Carlos Lorenzo, who had been in charge of the disgraced Argentinian side at the 1966 World Cup, killed the game by whacking and hacking the

Celtic players at every opportunity. The evening ended with three Atletico players having been dismissed and five booked. As the players left the field, Eusebio rapped his knuckles off Jimmy Johnstone's head and the subsequent brawl required police intervention to calm the situation.

That frustrating match had ended in a 0-0 draw, but Celtic expected severe sanctions to be carried out against Atletico by UEFA. It seemed unfair that

50 Greatest Players

BILLY McNEILL Centre half

Born: Bellshill

Joined Celtic: 1957   **From:** Blantyre Victoria

Debut: v Clyde, League Cup, 23 October 1958

Appearances: 790   **Goals:** 35

Left Celtic: 1975 (retired)

Honours won with Celtic: 9 league championships; 7 Scottish Cups; 6 Scottish League Cups; 1 European Cup; 29 caps (Scotland)

Billy McNeill is the ultimate Celtic man. A tough, fearless centre half, he was uncompromising in the tackle and unbeatable in the air, yet he always played the game cleanly – one sending-off in 790 appearances in that most combative of positions testifies to his sportsmanship.

His commitment to the cause was always self-evident and although he did not score many goals, when he did plant the ball in the net it was often at the most vital of times. It was McNeill who scored the winner against Dunfermline in the 1965 Cup final to secure Jock Stein's first trophy as manager. Two years later against Vojvodina in the European Cup quarter-final his last-minute header powered Celtic into the semi-finals. And McNeill's second-minute goal early in the 1969 Scottish Cup final paved the way for a 4-0 win and one of Celtic's most comprehensive and devastating of all victories over Rangers.

When Billy made the solo trip to collect the 1967 European Cup from the president of Portugal, the classical marbled pillars and rostrum of the National Stadium in Lisbon provided a suitable backdrop for the man nicknamed Caesar. He had been tagged with that monicker after a team trip to see the film *Ocean's Eleven*, starring Cesar Romero, but McNeill's regal bearing on the park was more readily identifiable with the Roman emperor.

He was Jock Stein's commander-in-chief on the field, a man of huge presence and an enormously consistent performer during Celtic's most glorious decade. He was 35 when he made his final appearance after almost 800 competitive games for Celtic, a statistic that was fuelled by his great desire to do well for his club. It is a mark of McNeill's appetite for the game that he would later regret having retired too soon.

The familiar sight of Celtic's Kenny Dalglish cutting through a defence. This time it's Rangers' turn to panic in the 1975 Scottish League Cup final.

the farcical first leg might count as a normal result and Celtic hoped and expected that at the very least the return should be played on neutral territory. It was not to be – UEFA contented themselves with a warning-lite to Atletico that consisted of a miniscule fine and a request that they should not behave so badly again.

Celtic were forced to travel to Spain for a tense second leg and both Jock Stein and Jimmy Johnstone received telephone calls at their hotel in Madrid threatening them with assassination if they turned up at the Estadio Vicente Calderon. Both men bravely defied those terrifying threats, but the danger of rioting from the Atletico supporters, who had been stirred up by misleading Spanish press reports of the events in Glasgow, was such that 1,000 riot police were on duty. Atletico, aware their actions were being scrutinized by UEFA, opted to play football on the night and Celtic, unluckily, went down 2-0 and out of the 1974 European Cup after one of the ugliest episodes in its history. It had always been the intention of Lorenzo and his team to kill the first leg and play football in Madrid. Their plan had worked.

Nine-in-a-row

Domestic dealings offered some compensation for that massive disappointment. The Scottish Cup was captured with a straightforward 3-0 victory over Dundee United after a ninth successive League title had been clinched in some comfort. Those nine consecutive title wins meant Celtic shared a world record with MTK Budapest of Hungary and CSKA Sofia of Bulgaria, both of whom had won nine successive titles in their own countries. Neither of those clubs, however, had come anywhere near to matching the type of simultaneous feats that Celtic had achieved in European competition during their nine-in-a-row run.

Billy McNeill could still remember with clarity the difficult days of the pre-Stein era while he was lifting those trophies. The memory of the barren years of the early 1960s helped him to savour the successes of his later years at the club. 'The disappointments are important,' he says, 'because they make the achievements more enjoyable. People used to say to me, "It must have been easy during the nine-in-a-row sequence after you had won the first few titles?" I would say, "No, it gets harder every year." It gets harder because the more successful you are, the harder people try to stop it.'

Other difficulties presented themselves in the second half of 1974. David Hay, who had, like Macari, become disillusioned by his basic wage at Celtic, left the club for Chelsea. George Connelly, Hay's close friend, would suffer

50 Greatest Players

DAVID HAY Full back/Midfielder

Born: Paisley

Joined Celtic: 1966   **From:** St Mirren's Boys Guild

Debut: v Aberdeen, League, 6 March 1968

Appearances: 193   **Goals:** 12

Left Celtic: 1974   **For:** Chelsea

Honours won with Celtic: 3 league championships; 2 Scottish Cups; 1 Scottish League Cup; 27 caps (Scotland)

David Hay got hit in the eye by an arrow when he was a boy and subsequently wore contact lenses. As a young Celtic player he would never tell anybody about that because he felt it was already hard enough getting into the team. By the early 1970s Hay had little need to feel such insecurity. He was indispensable as a hard-tackling ball player who was equally useful at full back or in midfield.

He was a player's player, always available to help out team-mates in trouble, full of stamina and an expert reader of the game. His departure for Chelsea in 1974 followed a world-class display for Scotland in that year's World Cup. Davie's early retirement through an eye injury took him into management at a young age and in 1983 he was appointed Celtic manager aged just 35, a position he held for four years. He returned to the club as chief scout under Tommy Burns for a three-year spell during the mid-1990s.

50 Greatest Players

JIMMY JOHNSTONE Outside right

Born: Viewpark

Joined Celtic: 1961   **From:** Blantyre Celtic

Debut: v Kilmarnock, League, 27 March 1963

Appearances: 515   **Goals:** 130

Left Celtic: 1975   **For:** San José Earthquakes

Honours won with Celtic: 9 league championships; 4 Scottish
Cups; 5 Scottish League Cups; 23 caps (Scotland)

Jimmy Johnstone was once described as a 'flying flea' by an
awestruck continental journalist. It was an appropriate
description of a player who really knew how to get under the
skin of his opponents. The scintillatingly skilful Johnstone
would often torture a distraught defender by beating him once, twice, thrice or
even four times just for the sheer pleasure of it, before streaking off with the ball.

The winger first joined Celtic as a ball boy in the late 1950s and was soon taken on
the playing staff. Only five feet four inches tall, he developed into a ball of muscle by
carrying out practice 100-yard sprints in his miner father's pit boots. Johnstone was an
artist on the ball, but it is easy to overlook just how tough he had to be to resist the
often violent attempts to intimidate him.

Johnstone embodied Celtic – he was an underdog, he defeated big, beefy opponents by
using verve and skill and he could be highly temperamental. Jock Stein knew how to get
the best out of him: the player would be sitting, with his arms folded, in a 'dwam' in the
dressing room until Stein entered. Johnstone would then quickly begin warming up. Stein
also did his best to rein in Johnstone's predilection for partying to excess and the manager
takes much credit for extending Johnstone's career for as long as possible. The player
himself could not believe it when, in 1975, Stein finally told him he was to leave Celtic.
He is one of only a handful of players in Celtic's history to have been entirely irreplaceable.

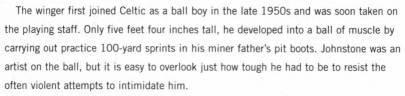

a severe dip in confidence and form following Hay's departure. A first-round
European Cup defeat to a modest Olympiakos side sent Celtic tumbling out
of the tournament in dismal fashion. More positively, the team ended their
long losing sequence in League Cup finals that autumn of 1974 when they
pulled Hibernian apart in a 6-3 win as players on both sides netted hat-
tricks: Dixie Deans for Celtic and Joe Harper for Hibs.

The team performed well during the first half of that 1974-75 season and
entered 1975 two points clear at the top of the League. Then the roof fell in.

A 3-0 New Year defeat at Ibrox, followed by five defeats and two draws in nine-games signalled the end of Celtic's glorious run of title victories. A 3-1 Scottish Cup final victory over Airdrie offered meagre compensation.

If Hay's physical presence and skills had been badly missed in that 1974-75 season, the retirement of inspirational captain Billy McNeill after the Cup final left an even bigger hole in the heart of the side. Then a distraught Jimmy Johnstone was given a free transfer by Stein early in the summer of 1975. Even the manager himself might have moved just a few days after he had handed Johnstone his bad news: he was offered the job of Scotland manager but politely declined.

Stein went off on a well-deserved holiday to Minorca and, on his return, was driving north from Manchester Airport towards Glasgow with his friend Tony Queen and their wives. At Lockerbie, their car was involved in a head-on crash that saw Stein transported to hospital, where surgeons performed emergency surgery to save his life. Stein would recover, gradually, but his

Eyes right. Celtic's Johnny Doyle and Kenny Dalglish watch as Paul Wilson (No. 9) slides the ball past Rangers keeper Peter McCloy during a 2-2 Old Firm draw in September 1976.

50 Greatest Players

GEORGE CONNELLY Midfielder

Born: High Valleyfield

Joined Celtic: 1964   **From:** Tulliallan Thistle

Debut: v Dunfermline, League, 30 April 1968

Appearances: 254   **Goals:** 13

Left Celtic: 1976 (released)

Honours won with Celtic: 4 league championships;

3 Scottish Cups; 2 caps (Scotland)

It is an unfortunate truth that George Connelly's career is remembered as much for his numerous walkouts and extended absences from the game as for his playing ability. Yet his qualities made him the perfect midfielder, whose passes would undermine even the most unified defences.

Connelly was named as Scotland's Footballer of the Year in 1973 and at 24 appeared to have the football world at his feet. He was, however, a particularly shy man who found some of the chicanery involved in professional football overwhelming. Jimmy Johnstone believes Connelly could have been Celtic's equivalent of the great Franz Beckenbauer but suggests, 'I think he thought we were all flymen!' Following the departure of his great friend David Hay in 1974, Connelly announced he was going to quit football. Jock Stein persuaded him to change his mind but it was only stalling the inevitable. Two years later George Connelly finally left Celtic, never to realize fully the limitless potential of his talent.

recuperation meant he would be absent from Celtic Park for the 1975-76 season. Caretaker-manager Sean Fallon took over from him and Celtic failed to win a trophy for the first time since the early 1960s.

A Changed Man

Stein was a changed man when he returned to the club after his year's absence. He was more contemplative, less fiery, than before, but he remained a hugely effective manager and guided a young, fresh-faced side to the finals of both cup competitions and to the League title that 1976-77 season.

The manager's knack of making clever signings was manifested most clearly with the purchase of Pat Stanton from Hibernian. Stanton was in the latter stages of his career, but his steady solidity and expert passing from a deep midfield position underpinned Celtic's enterprising play that season. Dalglish and McGrain excelled and Joe Craig, a £60,000 signing from

Partick Thistle in the autumn of 1976, proved the perfect striker in a good, inventive side. The manager was even able to work a piece of mischief when

50 Greatest Players

KENNY DALGLISH Forward

Born: Glasgow

Joined Celtic: 1968   **From:** Cumbernauld United

Debut: v Hamilton Ac, League Cup, 25 September 1968

Appearances: 320   **Goals:** 167

Left Celtic: 1977   **For:** Liverpool

Honours won with Celtic: 4 league championships;

4 Scottish Cups; 1 Scottish League Cup; 48 caps (Scotland)

Jock Stein was rarely wrong about a footballer so it seems strange that he was not convinced that the teenage Kenny Dalglish had the ability to make it in the professional game. Fortunately, when his coaching staff argued to keep the young Dalglish on Celtic's books, Stein was canny enough to be swayed by their impassioned pleas.

Dedication, single-mindedness and a powerful desire to be the best ensured that Dalglish would return to the ground for extra training sessions in which he honed his skills to perfection. He developed into an outstanding forward who was able to exploit the merest weakness in an opposition defence with his special range of skills. Team-mates appreciated the goals he made for them, both through distracting defenders who paid him special attention and through his highly accurate service.

A prize goalscorer himself, Dalglish specialized in the spectacular, his clever and quick assessment of angles and distances enabling him to squeeze the ball into the net from any position, no matter how difficult. By the mid-1970s, he had developed into one of the greatest players in the British game. Celtic took a long time to recover when he left for Liverpool in a British-record £440,000 transfer during the summer of 1977. It was dispiriting enough for Celtic to lose Dalglish – even more saddening was the realization that he left Celtic Park to fulfil his ambition of winning European trophies.

Dalglish became an Anfield legend, winning three European Cups and five championships. As their player-manager, he was equally successful; leading them to a League and FA Cup double in 1986 and further championships in 1988 and 1990. With Blackburn Rovers, he joined the elite band of men to have taken two clubs to the English championship title. He moved on to Newcastle United and after a shock departure, spent a short spell back at Celtic as director of football operations. He is now enjoying his retirement from the game.

Great Managers – 1965-1978

JOCK STEIN

Earthy wit and wisdom from Jock Stein sent Celtic soaring to unexplored heights during his years as manager. His teams were full of strong-minded individualists sent on to the field to play highly creative, inventive football, yet almost every move they made had been planned to perfection by Stein time and again on the training field.

Stein had transformed Celtic twice even before he took over as manager. As a centre half in the 1950s, he was a prototype player-manager. He compensated for the managerial vacuum at the club by helping to guide his team-mates to the 1954 double. Later that decade, as reserve-team coach, he opened the eyes of a young generation of players by focusing on ball skills in training and taking an interest in their opinions and personalities.

At Dunfermline Athletic, his managerial prowess flourished. After one year at the Fife club, he had pulled the team up from near-relegation to win the Scottish Cup, beating Celtic in the final. Three seasons of European football followed for the Fifers. After a brief stint at Hibernian, Stein, the manager, finally came home.

Stein arrived at Celtic Park as manager in 1965 and almost immediately his grasp of tactics, his meticulous knowledge of all his players' strengths and his marvellous motivational powers inspired his teams. Unrivalled League triumphs were matched by success in European tournaments, a new area of competition in which Stein thrived.

He channelled the talents of his men through simple, sensible maxims – such as 'Play to your strengths and disguise your weaknesses' – but he also managed through fear. He had demanded 'full control' of the club and he got it. Players feared losing out on bonus money by being out of the team and players had to follow his wishes – or they were out.

Even the media were forced to follow Stein's instructions – as he grew in influence and importance, he manipulated reporters mercilessly. Any reporter who displeased Stein would swiftly hear about it from the Celtic manager. Supporters too were in awe of Stein – he always had enormous presence – and on several occasions he plunged into the Celtic crowd to confront those whose behaviour was discrediting the club.

After leaving the club he spent a short time managing Leeds United, before taking the job of Scotland manager. In Cardiff on 10 September 1985, after Scotland had drawn with Wales in a vital World Cup tie, Stein collapsed and died.

'I'm egotistical enough to think that if I'm here we'll have reasonable success,' Stein had said in one masterful understatement. Without the dynamic influence of Jock Stein spurring them on to previously unimaginable peaks, Celtic would not have won the European Cup. Without his relentless demands for consistency from his players, they would never have won nine titles in a row. Jock Stein retains a presence in Celtic's present as the most charismatic, dynamic manager in their history.

Diligent. Jock Stein casually carries the European Cup across the car park at Celtic Park, on the day after his team had won Europe's most prestigious trophy.

Ecstatic. Stein hugs hat-trick hero John 'Dixie' Deans after Celtic's 6-1 win over Hibernian in the 1972 Scottish Cup final.

Disgusted. Jock Stein waits for a word with the referee after seeing his side lose 2-1 after extra time in the League Cup final against Rangers in March 1978. Two months later, he would leave Celtic after 13 years in charge.

he arranged the transfer of Alfie Conn from Tottenham Hotspur; Conn, a former Rangers player, had been expected to return to Scotland that year but to Ibrox rather than Celtic Park.

Celtic took their first Premier Division title with ease, ending the season nine points clear of Rangers. The new Premier Division structure – in which clubs in a ten-team league played each other four times rather than twice – had been introduced in 1975, directly as a result of Celtic's relentless domination of the Scottish League in the previous decade. Through whittling down the number of clubs it was hoped to eliminate the easier games against minnow clubs and make Scottish League football more competitive. Celtic players had initially struggled to adjust to the idea of the reduced league: listening to other results in the bath after a match they would hear just four other scorelines and would be waiting for more before they realised that that was all there was to the new league.

A drab, rainy 1977 Scottish Cup final, matched by a reduced attendance through the game being televised live for the first time since the 1950s, was settled by a penalty kick from left back Andy Lynch after Rangers' Derek Johnstone had handled the ball on the line. A beaming Stein embraced his delighted captain Dalglish on the field at the end of the match. Within weeks, Dalglish had requested a transfer and had departed for Liverpool.

The 1977-78 season began with Stanton suffering an injury that would end his career. McGrain, now the only remaining member of the Quality Street Gang of the early 1970s, sustained a severe ankle knock in early October that meant he would miss the remainder of the season and Scotland's trip to Argentina for the 1978 World Cup finals.

Celtic were forced to rely on young, inexperienced players – whose average age was just 22 – for the remainder of that 1977-78 season and they struggled badly. They did reach a 14th successive League Cup final and lost 2-1 to Rangers, unluckily, after extra-time. A second round European Cup defeat to Innsbruck of Austria and a fourth-round Scottish Cup defeat to First Division Kilmarnock were much less acceptable and, worst of all, the team tottered close to the Premier League relegation zone, although they eventually steadied to finish the season in fifth position.

It was still Celtic's lowest League position since 1965. Jock Stein agreed with the board in the spring of 1978 that it was time to bring to an end his career as Celtic manager. He relinquished his managerial duties in May 1978 having enriched the club with 25 trophies in 13 years that encompassed the greatest era in Celtic's history.

Chapter Nine: 1978-83
A Celtic Revival

Billy McNeill was the only man who had the presence and stature to succeed Jock Stein as the manager of Celtic. He had been indispensable to Stein as team captain during the 1960s and 1970s, and Stein had acknowledged that the club's success during that era would not have been possible without McNeill. It was Stein himself who, in the spring of 1978, approached McNeill with the offer of the job as Celtic manager and McNeill immediately agreed to leave Aberdeen, where he had progressed well during his first year in management.

Across Glasgow, McNeill faced a familiar adversary. John Greig, who had captained Rangers in opposition to McNeill through the 1960s and 1970s, had taken over at Ibrox in the summer of 1978. It made for an intriguing final full season of the 1970s, a decade in which Scottish football had been dominated to a greater extent than ever before by Celtic and Rangers. The 1978-79 season proved no different. It was Rangers who eliminated Celtic from the League Cup in a fraught semi-final that saw Tommy Burns ordered off for Celtic and Rangers' Alex Miller receive the same punishment. The game went to extra-time and an unlucky own goal from Celtic's Jim Casey gave Rangers a 3-2 victory. It resulted in Celtic's absence from the League Cup final for the first time since 1963.

McNeill had filled the team with fire, but their progress was halted when a blanket of atrocious weather settled on Scotland in the midwinter. It meant Celtic did not play a League match between 23 December 1978 and 3 March 1979. The manager kept his team ticking over with two Scottish Cup victories on the east coast and a warm-weather trip to Portugal early in 1979 before they returned to action with a 1-0 League victory over Aberdeen. From that point they hurtled towards the title, sealing their championship win with a dramatic victory over Rangers in their final match of the season. New signings Murdo MacLeod and Davie Provan had done much to inject the liveliness and vigour that McNeill demanded of his teams.

A sign of how far Celtic had fallen prior to McNeill's arrival was that the 1978-79 season had seen them compete for the first time in the Anglo-Scottish Cup, a tournament designed to compensate middle-ranking Scottish clubs who were unable to qualify for European competition. The team had gone out of the Anglo-Scottish Cup competition at the quarter-final stage

Johnny Doyle takes on Rangers' Alex Miller and Alex Forsyth at Parkhead in November 1978.

after a 3-1 aggregate defeat by Burnley, the first leg of which was disfigured by hooliganism at Turf Moor, in which some elements of the travelling Celtic support were not entirely blameless.

The taking of the 1978-79 title ensured that the club would be back in the tournament in which everyone at Celtic Park felt it belonged – the European Cup. The first and second round ties with Partizan Tirana of Albania and Dundalk of Ireland in late 1979 threw up one or two hairy moments, but Celtic progressed past both sides to face Real Madrid in the 1980 quarter-finals.

European Memories Revived

The face of Bobby Lennox featured on the cover of the match programme for the first leg with Real at Celtic Park in March 1980, a reminder of Celtic's greatest nights in Europe. It felt like a long time since that era and despite ticket prices being hiked high for the occasion, Celtic Park was filled to the brim for its first top-drawer European Cup tie since the notorious semi with Real's city rivals Atletico in 1974.

This Madrid encounter was also a memorable one, but for the right reasons – stirring goals from striker George McCluskey and winger Johnny Doyle gave Celtic a 2-0 victory and filled them with confidence for the second leg. McNeill stated before the return in the Bernabeu Stadium that Celtic would be looking to score a vital away goal but after just five minutes

50 Greatest Players

BOBBY LENNOX Forward

Born: Saltcoats

Joined Celtic: 1961   **From:** Ardeer Recreation

Debut: v Dundee, League, 3 March 1962

Left Celtic: March 1978   **For:** Houston Hurricane

Rejoined Celtic: 1961   **From:** Houston Hurricane

Appearances: 589   **Goals:** 273

Left Celtic: 1980 (retired)

Honours won with Celtic: 9 league championships; 6 Scottish Cups; 4 Scottish League Cups; 1 European Cup; 10 caps (Scotland)

Bobby Lennox played through fair times and foul for Celtic and never gave the club anything less than total commitment and dedication. He was part of the team that struggled in the early 1960s, became a Lisbon Lion later that decade and was still scoring and setting up chances in 1980. It was only when a doctor finally instructed him not to play again after a severe pre-season injury that Bobby, then 37, was finally forced to give up the game.

Celtic supporters called him 'buzz-bomb'. Like the Second World War secret weapon, Lennox sped past defences with no warning, but with devastating impact. His exceptional pace, awareness, quick-thinking and reflexes meant that he was always there to pick up loose balls in the penalty area. Alternatively, his swiftness and superb close control could see him pounce on to the ball some distance from goal and carry it at speed before depositing it accurately past the goalkeeper. His enthusiasm for the game, his professional approach and his first-class fitness made him Celtic's greatest post-war goalscorer.

Arsenal manager Bertie Mee wanted to pay a British record fee to bring Bobby Lennox to Highbury in the late 1960s. Bobby Charlton told Jock Stein that he would have loved to have Lennox as a team-mate; Charlton described Lennox as 'one of the best strikers that I have ever seen'. Bobby Lennox knew of the interest from England but he wanted only to remain in his native Saltcoats and play for his beloved Celtic.

of the return, McCluskey prodded the ball past the post and wide from a good position close to goal. Real punished that profligacy severely, rolling on for a 3-0 victory that pushed them into the semi-finals.

'We played well in Glasgow and we didn't play badly over there,' remembers Bobby Lennox. 'Right at the end of the first half in Spain there was a corner, a bit of a scramble and I must have kicked the ball right into the third tier.

Great Matches

SCOTTISH PREMIER LEAGUE		Celtic Park, 21 May 1979

Celtic 4   **Rangers 2**   Attendance 52,000

Celtic 4	Rangers 2
Aitken	MacDonald
McCluskey	Russell
Jackson o.g.	
MacLeod	

Billy McNeill had not expected to be able to turn Celtic round quickly, but after Christmas 1978, a run of 13 victories in 17 League games took the Hoops into their final fixture – a postponed match against Rangers – knowing a victory would secure the title. A draw or a defeat would virtually hand the title to Rangers.

McNeill had exhorted his players not to throw this opportunity away but they made a terrible start. After just nine minutes Alex MacDonald put Rangers 1-0 ahead and with 55 minutes gone Johnny Doyle, Celtic's fiery winger, was dismissed for kicking the grounded MacDonald. Celtic responded by piling on the pressure and were duly rewarded when goals from Aitken and McCluskey gave them a 2-1 lead midway through the second half. But, with just 14 minutes left, Rangers struck back as Bobby Russell's shot scraped in off the post.

Celtic continued to press forward: it was now clear they wanted the win, and the title, more than Rangers. With five minutes remaining, McCluskey's cross was knocked away from Rangers' goal by Peter McCloy, only for centre back Colin Jackson, under pressure, to head it back past him. The game was in its dying seconds when Murdo MacLeod, powered forward and decided to have a long-range shot at goal, knowing that if the ball went off target it would still use up some precious time. Instead his shot zoomed straight into the roof of the net and a delirious Celtic support exuberantly acclaimed the new Scottish champions. 'There are lots of fairytales throughout Celtic's history,' says Billy McNeill, 'and that was one of them.'

Celtic: Latchford, McGrain, Lynch, Aitken, McAdam, Edvaldsson, Provan, Conroy (Lennox), McCluskey, MacLeod, Doyle.

Rangers: McCloy, Jardine, Dawson, Johnstone, Jackson, MacDonald, McLean (Miller) Russell, Parlane, Smith, Cooper.

I thought that by the time it came back from the crowd it would be time up, but Laurie Cunningham whipped in a corner, it hit three or four people and Santillana knocked it into the net. We lost that goal in the 47th minute – they scored right on the half-time whistle – and you could see in the dressing room that the boys had become a bit edgy. That goal had knocked the stuffing out of the team a wee bit. If we had kept it to 0-0 the dressing room would have been really bubbly. We could really have come away with a result that night.'

Celtic celebrate winning the 1978-79 Premier Division title after their 4-2 victory over Rangers. Danny McGrain, arms aloft, is chaired by his team-mates at the end of an exhilarating night.

Prior to the tie with Real, Celtic had opened up an eight-point lead in the Premier League, but a disastrous series of results before the end of the season saw that advantage waste away. Celtic had, to some extent, gone stale in the wake of the disappointment of defeat in Spain and, unusually for a team managed by McNeill, had lowered their standard of performance – perhaps their extensive lead had produced a feeling of complacency.

Most significantly, two home defeats to a hungry Aberdeen side, managed by Alex Ferguson, sandwiched a 3-0 defeat for Celtic from Dundee United at Tannadice. That – together with a dreadful 5-1 defeat at Dundee – cleared the way for a nervy final day of the season on which Celtic could only draw away to St Mirren while Aberdeen stormed to an emphatic victory over Hibs. For the first time since 1955, the League title was bound for Pittodrie. Dundee United's triumph in winning the League Cup that season further emphasized that Aberdeen and United were not prepared to let the Old Firm dominate the 1980s. The teams from the north-east soon went under the joint nickname of the 'New Firm'.

The denouement of that 1979-80 season would, however, have a traditional Glasgow tinge as Celtic and Rangers met at Hampden Park on 10 May in the

Airdrieonians goalkeeper John Martin saves from Danny McGrain during Celtic's 4-1 win at Broomfield in November 1980.

Scottish Cup final. The affair was a lively encounter that contained much good football, but no goals until, shortly into the second half of extra-time, Danny McGrain shot for goal and George McCluskey stuck out a foot to divert the ball past Rangers goalkeeper Peter McCloy. McCluskey launched himself into the air in celebration before a packed Rangers end of the stadium and Celtic held on to the 1-0 lead for the remaining 13 minutes of the match.

Celtic's planned post-match pitch celebrations were curtailed when a riot broke out in which rival supporters confronted each other on the playing surface in the minutes after the Cup had been presented to the players. The root cause of the riot had been the decision by police commanders to redeploy their officers outside the stadium at the final whistle to prevent any possible trouble as the supporters exited Hampden. They overlooked the fact that the police would be absent for a few vital minutes after the match when the supporters would still be on the terraces. The more excitable elements in both camps felt free to clamber off the terraces and confront each other on the pitch.

Mounted police charged in to restore order, as a television commentator indulged in the ridiculously exaggerated comment, 'This is like a scene from *Apocalypse Now!*' in reference to the recently released film about the horrors of the Vietnam War. Deep inside the south stand at Hampden, the Celtic players sat in a state of confusion: they had been told to remain in the dressing room, but had not been made fully aware of the reason why. The riot resulted in the Criminal Justice (Scotland) Act, which came into force in early 1981 and which, among other things, forbade the consumption of alcohol inside Scottish football grounds.

The 1980-81 season saw a new look to Celtic's strike force. Frank McGarvey, a £250,000 signing from Liverpool in the spring of 1980, and 18-year-old Charlie Nicholas teamed up as Celtic's front two and between them scored 57 goals in all competitions. That fresh front-pairing did much to bring the League title back to Celtic Park – Billy McNeill inspired his side to go on an undefeated run that stretched from New Year's Day 1981 through to April of that year, when a 3-2 victory over Dundee United at Tannadice, achieved in considerable style, secured the championship.

Bonner Takes his Chance

A young Irishman, Pat Bonner, had made his debut in the opening game of that 1980-81 season, taking over from Englishman Peter Latchford in goal. Bonner performed so impressively that he missed just one match, the second leg of a second round European Cup-Winners' Cup tie against Politechnica Timisoara of Romania. Latchford returned to action in that game to make his only appearance of the season and found himself the focus of a catastrophic European evening.

Celtic were 1-0 down – after having won the first leg 2-1 – when Latchford was booked for timewasting at a free-kick. Peter could often appear relaxed and laid-back on the field, but it did not make sense for him to be timewasting at a point when Celtic were, because of away goals, behind in the tie. It was, however, consistent with referee Nicolas Langvinus' decisions on a night when he made a whole series of quirky rulings. Free-kicks that should clearly have been awarded Celtic's way went to Politechnica or clear corner-kicks for Celtic were given as goal-kicks to the Romanian side.

The match ended with McGarvey and centre half Roddie MacDonald having been sent off along with the Romanian goalkeeper. Even the Romanians' goal was controversial: Latchford caught a cross ball cleanly then dropped it after receiving a hefty dunt from a Romanian forward who, not being penalized, took advantage by popping the loose ball into the net. The match ended with Politechnica winning by that solitary goal and Celtic making a most unfortunate exit from the tournament.

The Celtic players had been upset by the refereeing in the match against Politechnica Timisoara but they were almost as upset at going out of the European Cup-Winners' Cup to a team they considered their inferiors. There was never any danger of the players feeling that way about their first round opponents in the European Cup at the start of the 1981-82 season. Juventus were defeated 1-0 at a packed Parkhead when Murdo MacLeod's shot was deflected into the air by Juventus sweeper Gaetano Scirea and veered on a crazy curve before finishing its journey high in the Juventus net, leaving goalkeeper Dino Zoff thoroughly perplexed. The second leg fell to Juventus, who won in emphatic fashion by 2-0 to take the tie.

McNeill, having been manager for three years, now had a settled side. Solid left back Mark Reid worked well with Danny McGrain in defence; Tom McAdam stayed steady at centre back while his partner there, Roy Aitken, had licence to roam forward when appropriate. The driving Murdo MacLeod dovetailed neatly with Dom Sullivan and Tommy Burns in midfield. Outside right Davie Provan would work back into midfield when Celtic's opponents had possession and would join the attack when Celtic had the ball. Frank McGarvey and George McCluskey formed an effective forward pairing in that 1981-82 season. Charlie Nicholas had been affected by a mysterious virus in the autumn of 1981 that left him out of the team. Nicholas had been regaining fitness in the reserves when, early in 1982, a leg break put him out of action for the remainder of the season.

To the Wire

Early exits from both the League Cup and the Scottish Cup freed Celtic to concentrate on winning the 1981-82 league title. They remained top of the League from first to last that season, although they reached the final day knowing they had to get a result against St Mirren at Celtic Park. Defeat would open up a possibility of conceding the title on goal difference to Aberdeen, who had won 14 of their 15 fixtures prior to that final day.

There was worrying news from Pittodrie for the Celtic players as they sipped their tea at half-time in the St Mirren match. The Paisley side were holding them to a 0-0 draw while Aberdeen were already 4-0 ahead against Rangers, to whom the match was meaningless. The Celtic players muttered their astonishment at a Rangers side conveniently conceding so many goals. It spurred the Celtic men on to finish the job by swamping St Mirren with attack after attack and three cleanly constructed second half strikes enabled the 39,000 present to celebrate the retention of the title at Celtic Park. A modest presentation ceremony followed – there was none of the fireworks or orchestrated music of later years – and the champagne flowed as captain Danny McGrain took hold of the Premier League trophy.

A rehabilitated Nicholas was fit, sharp and ready for the start of the 1982-83 season and another youngster, the talented midfield playmaker Paul McStay, became a regular starter. Their sophisticated skills enabled them to

Celtic's Dom Sullivan hurdles a tackle from Rangers' Gregor Stevens in Celtic's 2-0 win at Ibrox in September 1981.

slot seamlessly into McNeill's side, which was growing stronger with every passing year. Proof of that was established in the autumn of 1982 when they faced Ajax in the first round of the European Cup. After a 2-2 draw at Celtic Park, McNeill's men travelled to Amsterdam and although they played well, they were drawing 1-1 – and heading out of the tournament on the away goals rule – as the match entered its final minutes. Two minutes from time, George McCluskey raced into the penalty area to slip a shot past goalkeeper Piet Schrijvers to make it 2-1 for the Celts. That gave them overall victory over a superb Ajax side and opened up the prospect of this solid Celtic side making real progress in Europe.

The following round saw Celtic play magnificently against Spanish champions Real Sociedad in the Atocha Stadium, San Sebastian, and they were desperately unlucky to concede two late goals, both of which resulted from wild deflections off Celtic defenders. The 2-0 deficit was too much for the Celts to make up at home and although they won 2-1 at Celtic Park they were out of European competition for another year.

Competition in Scotland was proving equally challenging for Celtic. Aberdeen and Dundee United remained consistently strong opponents, although it was Celtic who were top of the Scottish Premier League as they came face to face with Rangers in the League Cup final of December 1982. Three magnificent goals graced the final – two of them scored for Celtic by

50 Greatest Players

CHARLIE NICHOLAS Forward

Born: Glasgow

Joined Celtic: 1979   **From:** Celtic Boys Club

Debut: v Kilmarnock, League, 16 August 1980

Left Celtic: 1983   **For:** Arsenal

Rejoined Celtic: 1990   **From:** Aberdeen

Appearances: 209   **Goals:** 125

Left Celtic: 1996   **For:** Clyde

Honours won with Celtic: 2 league championships;
1 Scottish Cup; 3 caps (Scotland)

Style and subtlety distinguished Charlie Nicholas as a
special talent from the moment he made his debut as a
teenager in 1980. He was a deft goalscorer, whose strength lay in his ability to drift past
players while keeping the ball at his feet.

The promise that Nicholas showed in his debut season was halted in 1981-82 by
illness and a broken leg. He returned for 1982-83 and hit the net 46 times for the
team. Then the boy with the New Romantic haircut and the leather trousers was
gone – off to Arsenal in a £625,000 transfer that was the talk of British football
that summer.

At Celtic Park, Nicholas had been able to rely on on-field support from team-mates
who made goals and created space for him. But he missed the tight-knit teamwork that
had created so many goals for him and failed to flourish at Arsenal. He returned to
Celtic in 1990 but he could not recapture the youthful zest that had been such an
integral part of his game.

Nicholas and MacLeod, the other by Rangers midfielder Jim Bett – and
McNeill could claim the fifth trophy of his five seasons as manager.

The Old Firm match at New Year 1983 also ended in an impressive 2-1
victory for Celtic, but when Aberdeen arrived in Glasgow in mid-February
1983 their flawless defending, powerful concentration and speedy counter-
attacks saw Celtic come undone. It was a style of football that Celtic
encountered more frequently in Europe than in Scotland and a 3-1 defeat in
front of a 42,000 crowd pushed Celtic down into second place in the League.
Numerous points were squandered by Celtic after that demoralizing setback,
but their chief rivals – Aberdeen and Dundee United – proved equally prone
to pouring away points.

As the final day of the 1982-83 season dawned, the destination of the title remained unknown and three contenders, Celtic, Aberdeen and Dundee United, had the chance to become champions that afternoon. Celtic were scheduled to travel to Ibrox that final day and the outlook became gloomy when Rangers went 2-0 ahead before half-time. A subdued dressing room was revitalized when Billy McNeill reacted to the situation calmly, telling his players that Dundee United were drawing at Dundee. He made it clear to them that since they, the Celtic players themselves, had allowed Rangers to dominate the first half it was up to them to put things right against Rangers in the second half if they were to have a chance of winning the title. That refreshed the players' thinking and sent them out determined to do better. Four second-half goals gave them victory, a heroic effort that, in the end, proved irrelevant: Dundee United defeated their city rivals, leaving them a point above second-placed Celtic, and took the title to Tannadice for the only time in United's history.

So Long, Charlie

Nicholas had scored 46 goals for Celtic that season and, inevitably, the leading English clubs sought the signature of the prodigious youngster. Arsenal, Liverpool and Manchester United all courted Charlie assiduously that summer and he eventually plumped for Highbury, moving to London

Celtic against Rangers in May 1983. Charlie Nicholas sends Rangers goalkeeper Peter McCloy the wrong way from the penalty spot.

for a fee of £625,000. The loss of the striker had been widely anticipated by the Celtic support since the middle of the 1982-83 season. They had not, however, expected Billy McNeill also to leave the club. Behind the scenes, relations between McNeill and the Celtic board – and, in particular, with chairman Desmond White – had always been uneasy.

The latest in a long line of arguments between McNeill and the board arose when McNeill was asked to dismiss his assistant John Clark and replace him with Frank Connor. McNeill was also asked to apologize to the board for newspaper reports that claimed he wanted his salary increased; McNeill was, reportedly, only the fifth-highest-paid manager in the Premier League. McNeill refused to apologize for press-reported statements that, he said, he had not made and he also refused to replace Clark with Connor.

The impasse between McNeill and the directors remained unresolved and a dissatisfied McNeill decided to leave the club in the summer of 1983 to take over as manager of Manchester City. He had maintained the Celtic tradition of fast, attacking football and had done well to lead the team to five trophies – including three championships – in five years during an era in which Scottish football had become highly competitive.

McNeill's departure left the Celtic players and supporters puzzled and disappointed that so little had been done to keep him at the club. With star player Nicholas also having moved on at the first opportunity that season, the reassuring continuity that McNeill had provided in the five years after Jock Stein had now evaporated. The solidity and stability instilled by McNeill had been replaced with uncertainty. The club was now struggling to find a sense of direction.

Pat Bonner in Premier League action against Rangers at Celtic Park in 1983.

Chapter Ten 1983-88
Maintaining Momentum

Celtic swooped swiftly to fill the vacuum that had been created by Billy McNeill's sudden departure from the post of manager. Four days after McNeill had left the club, David Hay, another former Celtic player, was appointed as his replacement. Hay, who was a mere 35 years old, had led Motherwell to promotion to the Premier League in admirable style during the 1981-82 season, but after that had spent a year out of football and had concentrated on running his pub in Paisley.

Hay took over as manager on 4 July 1983 with a precious leaving present from his predecessor. Shortly before leaving for Manchester City, McNeill had signed Brian McClair, who had worked with Hay at Motherwell. McClair slotted swiftly into Hay's team and ended the 1983-84 season as the club's top scorer with 31 goals; a tally that compared favourably with that of the departed Charlie Nicholas, whose 46 goals the previous season had included 14 penalties.

Hay had a public image as a laid-back, relaxed individual that belied the fact that behind the scenes he encouraged his players to compete aggressively. His first season as manager saw Celtic maintain a high standard of performance, but Hay was faced with an Alex Ferguson-inspired Aberdeen side at their peak. Celtic were the Dons' closest challengers in the League but they lacked the consistency of the Pittodrie side and Aberdeen, leaders throughout the season, took the 1983-84 title. Celtic also reached both cup finals but lacked luck on each occasion. An enthralling League Cup final with Rangers ended 2-2 after 90 minutes and was settled in Rangers' favour when the Ibrox side were awarded a debatable penalty in extra-time.

The Scottish Cup final brought Celtic face to face with Aberdeen and the League champions took the lead when Eric Black, looking offside, stretched out a leg to guide the ball past Pat Bonner after 24 minutes. Bob Valentine, the same referee who had awarded Rangers their League Cup final penalty, let the goal stand and then 15 minutes later dismissed Roy Aitken for a heavy challenge on Mark McGhee. It looked like another harsh decision by Valentine – the offence appeared to merit nothing more than a yellow card – but Celtic overcame that obstacle to play the better football in the second half and Paul McStay equalized with a cleanly-struck shot five minutes from time. The extra-time period found Celtic's ten men stretched severely and Mark McGhee took advantage to nick the winning goal for Aberdeen.

In the UEFA Cup Sporting Lisbon, like Aberdeen, had had a taste of Celtic's team spirit earlier that 1983-84 season. The Portuguese side had won the home leg of their UEFA Cup tie 2-0, but Celtic flew at them from the first whistle in the return at Celtic Park and after an awe-inspiring display of attacking football, ended the night with a stunning 5-0 victory. That commitment to attack however, undid Celtic in the following round when a crafty Nottingham Forest side hit the Celts twice on the counter-attack in the second leg of their tie at Celtic Park to knock Celtic out of the 1983-84 UEFA Cup.

50 Greatest Players

DANNY McGRAIN Full back

Born: Glasgow

Joined Celtic: 1967   **From:** Maryhill Juniors

Debut: v Dundee United, League Cup, 26 August 1970

Appearances: 663   **Goals:** 7

Left Celtic: 1987 (released)

Honours won with Celtic: 6 league championships; 5 Scottish Cups; 1 Scottish League Cup; 62 caps (Scotland)

World-class performances on a weekly basis made Danny McGrain a permanent fixture at right back for Celtic for close to two decades. He grew from a precocious youngster in the early 1970s into the father figure of the Celtic team in the 1980s, when his knowledge and guidance helped nurture the talents of numerous young players. McGrain was close to unbeatable as a defender, a powerful tackler with the speed, positional skills and awareness to chase back and block off opposing forwards. He used his speed to equal effect going forward, overlapping in adventurous fashion to push perfect passes into the paths of his team-mates or cross cleverly. Danny combined wonderfully the talents of defender, midfielder and winger and his concentration and application ensured he never allowed any slackness to enter his game.

The added dimension that Danny gave to his position was remarkable in itself – even more extraordinary was the way in which he survived each threat to his career. In 1972 he suffered a fractured skull; in 1974 he was diagnosed diabetic; and in 1977 he suffered an ankle injury that kept him out of action for almost 18 months. A lesser man might have struggled to overcome any one of those setbacks but Danny came back strongly from each one of them. Frequently described as the greatest full back in the world, Danny McGrain was a magnificent player and a man of distinction.

European competition would also be memorable for Hay's team in the 1984-85 season. In the Cup-Winners' Cup they defeated Ghent of Belgium on a 3-1 aggregate then lost 3-1 to Rapid Vienna in the first leg of their second-round tie. That defeat heralded another stirring performance from Celtic in the second leg. As against Sporting in the previous season, the Celts whirled into attack after attack, harnessing skill with aggression, and with just 20 minutes of the match remaining, Celtic zipped into a 3-0 lead when Tommy Burns' committed challenge saw him beat Rapid goalkeeper Ehn to score.

Out of Control

Burns' goal enraged the Rapid players, who protested that Burns had fouled the goalkeeper. Two minutes later, centre back Reinhard Kienast, still raging, punched Burns on the back of the head and Kienast was dismissed. Ehn was next to extract revenge on Burns, kicking the Celtic man inside the penalty area. Matters then threatened to get out of the referee's control when, prior to the resultant penalty being taken, Rapid captain Hans Krankl and his team-mates claimed that one of the Austrian players, Weinhofer, had been struck by a missile thrown from the crowd. At one point the Rapid players appeared ready to walk off the field. Weinhofer eventually left the pitch, alone, and when the Rapid players calmed down, Peter Grant sent a weak spot-kick wide of the post.

Celtic's Davie Provan is held down by Rangers' Dave McPherson in a 1-1 draw at Celtic Park in August 1985.

141

50 Greatest Players

FRANK McGARVEY **Forward**

Born: Glasgow

Joined Celtic: 1980   **From:** Liverpool

Debut: v St Mirren, League, 12 March 1980

Appearances: 245   **Goals:** 109

Left Celtic: 1985   **For:** St Mirren

Honours won with Celtic: 2 league championships; 2 Scottish Cups; 1 Scottish League Cup; 5 caps (Scotland)

Frank McGarvey's predilection for TV wildlife programmes reflected an instinctive, untamed element in much of the forward's play. He was unpredictable in his movement and his wiry frame allowed him to work the ball intricately past defenders. Frank had thrived as a young forward under Alex Ferguson at St Mirren but after a transfer to Liverpool in 1979 he had become frustrated playing reserve-team football. He was a record £250,000 purchase for Celtic when he left Anfield in March 1980 and was soon repaying the fee, scoring the only goal of the game in his first Old Firm match the following month.

Effort etched itself on Frank's face and his hard graft provided a platform for the talents of more glamorous, smooth-moving players, such as Charlie Nicholas. There was no ignoring Frank at the 1985 Scottish Cup final, though, when his superb bending header provided the late matchwinner against Dundee United. It proved to be Frank's final goal for Celtic – he switched to St Mirren that summer after having been disappointed with the new contract offered him by manager David Hay.

The match ended in a 3-0 victory for Celtic but Rapid appealed to UEFA, citing the Weinhofer incident as their main cause of complaint. The Viennese claimed their player had been struck by a bottle from the crowd. UEFA's disciplinary committee threw out their case. Television evidence showed that no bottle had struck Weinhofer. Rapid then changed their story, claiming that their player had been hit by a coin thrown from the crowd. UEFA undermined their own credibility by allowing Rapid to appeal using their changed story and then, to the amazement of all connected with Celtic, upheld their appeal. The match was adjudged by UEFA to have been 'irregular' and the two clubs were ordered to replay the second leg at a stadium that was at least 100 kilometres from Glasgow. With a huge travelling support, Celtic's choice of Old Trafford seemed sure to create an atmosphere similar to Parkhead and, inspired by passion and injustice, Celtic went on the attack from the start.

50 Greatest Players

DAVIE PROVAN Winger

Born: Gourock

Joined Celtic: 1978   **From:** Kilmarnock

Debut: v Partick Thistle, League, 23 September 1978

Appearances: 303   **Goals:** 41

Left Celtic: 1987 (retired)

Honours won with Celtic: 4 league championships, 2 Scottish Cups, 1 Scottish League Cup, 10 caps (Scotland)

Davie Provan was signed from Kilmarnock in the autumn of 1978 for a Scottish record fee of £120,000. He immediately provided a dynamic link between midfield and attack; he would hover wide, augmenting the attack when Celtic were going forward and drop deep to become the extra man in midfield when the opposition had the ball.

Provan combined the intricate ball skills of a traditional winger with a no-nonsense desire to get the ball goalwards as quickly as possible. It had been a long time since Celtic supporters had been treated to the sight of such effective wing play and Davie, who had been Billy McNeill's first signing, was involved in all the great Celtic triumphs of the late 1970s and early 1980s. He is best remembered for his goal direct from a free-kick in the 1985 Scottish Cup final, but the following year he was diagnosed as suffering from ME, which enforced his premature retirement from the game. The exciting sight of the permed Provan, socks round his ankles, accelerating down the wing was badly missed by those fortunate enough to have seen him in his pomp.

If anyone had any doubt that Celtic's luck in the tie was rapidly running out, it was confirmed after 17 minutes when Roy Aitken's scoring effort rebounded from a Rapid post and the Austrians streaked upfield to score. At that moment Hay knew that Celtic were out of the tournament. Paul McStay, in common with all associated with Celtic, was disgusted by Rapid's behaviour. 'It really sickened me,' he says. 'The feigning of the injury sickened me. It was sad.'

Celtic were again second-best to Aberdeen in the League throughout that 1984-85 season and the Pittodrie side comfortably clinched their second title in succession. The end of the season arrived with Celtic seeking success in the 1985 Scottish Cup final and David Hay's position as manager was rumoured to be under threat if he failed to clinch the club's first trophy since mid-December 1982. That 100th Scottish Cup final was to prove another testing

Celtic's Roy Aitken in action in a 1-1 draw against St Mirren in February 1986.

occasion for Hay when, ten minutes after half-time, Stuart Beedie put opponents Dundee United 1-0 ahead.

United were expert at holding on to a lead and they were doing so comfortably until Hay instructed Roy Aitken to move into midfield. Celtic now began surging forward in style and with 14 minutes remaining Murdo MacLeod was fouled on the edge of the United penalty area. Davie Provan stepped up to arc the ball over the defensive wall and into the top corner of the net with an irresistible combination of power and accuracy. Six minutes from time, Aitken forced his way past some heavy challenges on the right wing and whisked the ball into the penalty area where Frank McGarvey flung himself full-length for a diving header that bent into the United net. The Cup belonged to Celtic.

Celtic were now wearing jerseys that carried a sponsor's name for the first time in the club's history. The autumn of 1984 had seen Celtic and Rangers agree to allow double-glazing firm CR Smith to have the company's name on each club's jerseys. In return, Celtic, strangely cash-strapped at the time, were provided with an infusion of cash, some of which Hay had used to purchase Maurice Johnston from Watford for a Scottish record fee of £400,000.

Johnston, in the first tie in European competition for which he was eligible, scored a fine equalizer with a header for Celtic in the 1-1 draw with Atletico Madrid at the Estadio Vicente Calderon in the first round of the 1985-86 European Cup-Winners' Cup. The return at Celtic Park had to be played behind closed doors by order of UEFA. This was a hangover punishment from the Rapid Vienna play-off at Old Trafford the previous season, during which two individuals had left the spectating area to attack Rapid players. The Celtic players were more greatly affected than their Spanish opponents by having to play a European tie without the customary backing of their fanatical supporters and Atletico won 2-1 to progress into the next round.

Celtic had kept their fans hanging on right up until the end of the 1985 Cup final and they repeated the feat in their pursuit of the 1985-86 Premier League title. Celtic trailed the leaders throughout the season and clinched the title only on a nerve-stretching final day of the season with their 5-0 victory over St Mirren at Love Street. Hearts had topped the Premier League for the second half of that 1985-86 season prior to being toppled on the final day by Hay's team and the Edinburgh side's resurgence had been typical of the 1980s up to that point. Clubs outside Glasgow, most notably Aberdeen and Dundee United, had finally risen to challenge the Old Firm's traditional domination of Scottish football.

Celtic's Brian McClair goes past Rangers goalkeeper Chris Woods to score in the 1-1 Premier Division draw at Celtic Park in November 1986.

Great Matches

SCOTTISH PREMIER LEAGUE	St Mirren Park, 3 May 1986
St Mirren 0 Celtic 5	Attendance 17,557

Celtic 5

McClair 2
Johnston 2
McStay

Hope rather than expectation drew a large Celtic support to Paisley on the final day of the 1985-86 season. Celtic started the day second in the Premier League, two points behind Hearts, who had been top since December and who were unbeaten in 1986. Hearts required a single point against Dundee to clinch the championship.

Six minutes into the game, Brian McClair directed a fast-paced header high into the St Mirren net and Celtic went two ahead on the half hour, when a series of short, sharp passes involving MacLeod, McClair and McStay ended with McStay sending Johnston clear on the right. His low shot wriggled under the arm of goalkeeper Jim Stewart.

That goal had a fortunate finish, but Celtic's third, one minute later, was simply superb. Danny McGrain began the approach work with a smart reverse pass to MacLeod, who knocked it back to the advancing McGrain. The right back edged the ball to McStay who bought himself time with a clever heel-flick, looked up and passed to Roy Aitken. He found the moving McGrain who sent McClair motoring down the right wing. His low, searching ball across the face of the goal was met by Johnston, who slid home Celtic's third goal. The speed and control of that move was repeated five minutes later, when McStay lashed the ball into the roof of the net from the edge of the area.

Those goals meant Celtic now had a better goal difference than Hearts, who were drawing 0-0 at Dundee at half-time. Another goal was added by McClair in the 55th minute, but the biggest roars of the afternoon were reserved for the news that Hearts had lost two late goals. Celtic were top of the table for the first time that season, but they were top when it mattered. The title was on its way to Celtic Park.

St Mirren: Stewart, Wilson, D. Hamilton, B. Hamilton, Godfrey, Cooper, Fitzpatrick, Abercrombie, McGarvey, Gallagher (Speirs), Mackie.

Celtic: Bonner, McGrain, Whyte, Aitken, McGugan, MacLeod, McClair, McStay, Johnston, Burns, Archdeacon.

Celtic, under McNeill and then Hay, had battled respectably well against their provincial challengers but Rangers had provided only weak opposition to them. That would all change from mid-1986 when Graeme Souness arrived in Scotland to become player-manager of Rangers. The Ibrox club began spending millions in the transfer market to purchase top-class English internationals and paid them the type of wages that ensured they would be happy to remain at Ibrox. Celtic, in comparison, paid poor salaries in comparison to other major British clubs and had never been consistently serious spenders in the transfer market. The legacy of the Stein years remained: the great manager had extracted maximum value for minimum expenditure and his successors were expected to be able to do the same.

The first decisive clash between Celtic and the revitalized Rangers took place in late October 1986 when the two sides confronted each other in the League Cup final. Ian Durrant sent Rangers 1-0 ahead midway through the second half, but Brian McClair equalized for Celtic 20 minutes from time with a powerful, perfectly-placed drive from 15 yards. The fast, exciting match was well-balanced at 1-1 until, six minutes from time, Aitken and Terry Butcher, one of Rangers' new signings, jostled one another as a Rangers corner was played into the Celtic penalty area. Referee David Syme awarded an extremely soft penalty from which Davie Cooper duly scored to give Rangers the League Cup.

During the closing minutes, Mo Johnston was dismissed and made the sign of the cross as he was leaving the pitch, a gesture less religious than an overt bid to goad the Rangers support into anger. David Hay, normally so laid-back, confronted Syme at the end of the match and was so riled by his refereeing that in the aftermath of the match he stated that if Celtic had a realistic opportunity of joining the English League he would apply immediately.

There was compensation for Celtic in that they were leading the League and at one stage in late 1986 they led Rangers by nine points. At Ibrox on New Year's Day 1987, however, Celtic succumbed to a 2-0 defeat in which Rangers were dominant throughout. It left Celtic just three points

As the 1980s progressed, matches with Rangers grew increasingly fractious. Here Frank McAvennie receives a fist in the face from Rangers goalkeeper Chris Woods in an October 1987 match that saw McAvennie, Woods and Terry Butcher all sent off after the incident.

50 Greatest Players

BRIAN McCLAIR Forward

Born: Airdrie

Joined Celtic: 1983   **From:** Motherwell

Debut: v Brechin City, League Cup, 24 August 1983

Appearances: 142   **Goals:** 121

Left Celtic: 1987   **For:** Manchester United

Honours won with Celtic: 1 league championship; 1 Scottish Cup; 4 caps (Scotland)

Billy McNeill signed Brian McClair for £70,000 from Motherwell, ten days before the manager's sudden departure for Manchester City in the summer of 1983. 'I had felt convinced that this boy would be a scorer,' says McNeill, 'but I can remember people questioning why I had done this.' McClair would go on to fulfil unquestionably the potential that McNeill had spotted. He would be Celtic's top scorer for the next four seasons and a more than adequate replacement for Charlie Nicholas although McClair contrasted severely with his predecessor. His jerky running movement and his brisk, bustling, no-frills approach made him look clumsy at times but he could deliver goals in fine style.

The former Glasgow University student was voted Player of the Year both by his fellow professionals and by football journalists in 1987. That summer he was hunted down by Manchester United manager Alex Ferguson and a fee of £850,000 took him to Old Trafford where, in his debut 1987-88 season, he became the first United player to score more than 20 goals in a season since George Best two decades previously.

ahead of Rangers, who had a game in hand. The Ibrox club were now riding on a wave of confidence and they powered on to take the 1986-87 League title.

Hay paid for that trophyless season with his job, although he felt he had been handicapped by a board of directors who had failed to match the ambitions of their counterparts at Rangers. Billy McNeill, who had been dismissed by Aston Villa early in May 1987 after four years in England, was appointed as the new boss within hours of David Hay being told he was no longer in charge at Celtic.

The purse strings were loosened for McNeill and he purchased several new players for the 1987-88 season, which carried great emotional significance for the Celtic support as it marked the centenary of the club's foundation. Striker Andy Walker was the most expensive acquisition, costing £350,000 from Motherwell. Chris Morris, a full back, joined from Sheffield Wednesday for £125,000 and midfielder Billy Stark proved a bargain at £75,000 from Aberdeen. McNeill also inherited centre back Mick McCarthy, whom Hay, just days before his sacking, had signed for £450,000 from Manchester City.

Maurice Johnston and Brian McClair had left the club that summer of 1987, as had Murdo MacLeod, and with such a high turnover of players it seemed likely that McNeill's new team would require time to settle. Instead, they swept into action with a 4-0 opening day victory away to Morton that set the tone for the remainder of the season. As Paul McStay comments, 'Everything clicked right from the start and after that there was no stopping us.' Celtic lost just twice in their opening 14 games, a run that included a stylish 1-0 victory over champions Rangers to take Celtic to the top of the Premier League. 'During the first half hour,' said McNeill, 'we possibly played the best football I have ever seen in an Old Firm match.'

The second defeat in that run occurred in late October, when Dundee United managed to eke out a 2-1 win at Celtic Park, but after that Celtic did not lose again until April. Mid-season, they received a great boost through signing striker Frank McAvennie, who had joined from West Ham United for a fee of £725,000, and winger Joe Miller, from Aberdeen. Both added finesse

50 Greatest Players

MURDO MacLEOD   Midfielder

Born: Glasgow

Joined Celtic: 1978   **From:** Dumbarton

Debut: v Motherwell, League, 4 November, 1978

Appearances: 395   **Goals:** 82

Left Celtic: 1987   **For:** Borussia Dortmund

Honours won with Celtic: 4 league championships; 2 Scottish Cups, 1 Scottish League Cup; 5 caps (Scotland)

One of Billy McNeill's first tasks on becoming Celtic manager was to address the lack of determination and drive in his midfield. His answer, the human dynamo Murdo MacLeod, signed from Dumbarton for a fee of £100,000 and became the beating heart of the Celtic midfield for nine years.

MacLeod's driving runs forward cut great swathes through the opposition and he could be relied on to choose the correct pass when the time was right.

Work-rate aside, Murdo also scored memorable goals. His strike against Rangers in the 1979 championship decider topped off Celtic's season and a similar goal against the same opponents in the 1982 League Cup final were two of many unforgettable moments. On returning to Celtic Park with his new club Borussia Dortmund shortly after his transfer in 1987, MacLeod was applauded off the field by the whole ground. 'There were tears in my eyes,' he says of that night. 'It was as big a night for me as anything.'

to the forward line and helped Celtic find a consistency that brought them the Scottish League title. McNeill had given the supporters the perfect birthday present for Celtic's centenary celebration.

The followers of the club were given ample opportunity to celebrate the centenary. At the Pavilion Theatre, a musical, *The Celtic Story*, told the tale of the club in a bright, bouncy fashion. At the People's Palace on Glasgow Green, an exhibition showcased Celtic memorabilia down the decades and a new restaurant, The Walfrid, named in honour of the club's founding father, was opened at Celtic Park. The inside of the south stand was modernized at a cost of £2million to incorporate a gym, hospitality suites, a players' lounge and offices.

The directors made efforts to bring Real Madrid to Glasgow to play in a centenary match but the Spanish club's financial demands were too steep. Two centenary matches were played – against Cruzeiro Belo Horizonte and Red Star Belgrade – and while they were entertaining affairs, it had been Celtic's competitive matches that had really got the fans talking.

The money received from the transfers of McClair to Manchester United and Johnston to FC Nantes had been invested in players who ensured McNeill's energetic side was bursting with invention and application. Celtic

Andy Walker scores Celtic's second goal in a 3-0 victory over Dundee at Celtic Park in April 1988.

Great Matches

SCOTTISH CUP FINAL		Hampden Park, 14 May 1988
Celtic 2	**Dundee United 1**	**Attendance 74,000**
McAvennie 2	Gallacher	

Celtic were on the verge of winning the double as the centenary season drew to a close. It was the stuff of dreams, but it soon looked like it was going to prove an anti-climax to an enthralling season. With the game goalless, Dundee United's Kevin Gallacher threatened to score shortly after the half-time break. A desperate Roy Aitken foul sent the United forward tumbling to the turf as he homed in on goal. Minutes later, Gallacher – grandson of Celtic great Patsy Gallacher – was again streaking towards the Celtic goal pursued by Aitken. The Celtic man, perhaps mindful of his earlier booking and of his dismissal in the 1984 final, was careful not to dive into a challenge and Gallacher took advantage to hit a powerful volley past Allen McKnight in Celtic's goal.

Celtic thrust forward energetically despite the strength-sapping heat. With 15 minutes remaining, Billy Stark curled a pass wide to overlapping full back Anton Rogan and he swerved smoothly round Dave Bowman to cross for Frank McAvennie, who outjumped Paul Hegarty to head into the net. It remained 1-1 as the last seconds of the match melted away. Then Joe Miller's corner found Stark, who redirected the ball goalwards. United defender David Narey blocked the shot, but the ball fell to McAvennie who smacked it into the net with the last serious kick of the game. One hundred years of glorious history had been rounded off in magnificent style.

Celtic: Bonner, Morris, Rogan, Aitken, McCarthy, Whyte (Stark), Miller, McStay, McAvennie, Walker (McGhee), Burns.

Dundee United: Thomson, Bowman, Malpas, McInally, Hegarty, Narey, Bannon, Gallacher, Paatelainen (Clark), Ferguson, McKinlay.

Referee: G. B. Smith (Edinburgh).

dominated the four Old Firm matches, especially the contest at New Year where they strolled to a 2-0 victory. The creativity of McStay and the sharpness of McAvennie came to the fore as the striker scored both goals in a victory that eased Celtic into an almost unassailable position at the top of the League. A gritty 2-1 victory at Ibrox in March was equally well deserved and the title was wrapped up with a 3-0 home win over Dundee in April 1988.

Celtic had the best defensive record of any British club that season, having conceded only 23 goals in 44 games. It was the club's best defensive record up to that point since the 1921-22 season. 'We had a great never-say-die attitude,'

We've done it! One hundred years of Celtic football culminates in the double at Hampden. Billy McNeill celebrates on the pitch (left); Tommy Burns gives thanks.

says Andy Walker, top scorer that season with 32 goals. 'It was a magical time for the club and having the chance to play a part in it was extra-special.'

Celtic, coached assiduously by McNeill's assistant Tommy Craig, played a pressing game that season, forcing opponents into errors in every area of the field. It paid off many times over the 1987-88 season, but never more so than in the semi-final of the Scottish Cup against Hearts at Hampden. After an hour of play, the crowd of almost 67,000 saw Hearts' Dave McPherson jump at Celtic goalkeeper Pat Bonner and the ball sail into the Celtic net. Bonner was furious, claiming he had been obstructed, but the goal stood and Celtic were still 1-0 behind with three minutes to go. Celtic continued to press and not only did Mark McGhee – recently signed from SV Hamburg – equalize , but they powered on and Andy Walker struck a winner in the dying minutes.

Such episodes convinced the supporters that their club was predestined to celebrate that centenary year in style and that belief hardened into reality when Celtic won the Scottish Cup by defeating Dundee United in a thrilling final. As the supporters wallowed in their celebrations of the club's first double since 1977 and reflected on the highlights of the club's first 100 years, they felt confident that the good times were back on a permanent basis. None of them could have envisaged that the club was about to descend into one of the darkest passages of its history.

Chapter Eleven: 1988-98
A Difficult Decade

A green Rolls-Royce puttered smoothly round the track at Celtic Park before stopping to allow Billy McNeill to appear to cheers. It was the opening day of the 1988-89 season and the Celtic manager was about to unfurl the championship flag. The ceremonials were followed by a tough match against Hearts, but some nimble work inside the penalty area by Paul McStay set up Frank McAvennie for the goal that produced a 1-0 win. It seemed as though the spirit of the centenary season was going to carry Celtic forward as the club kicked off its second century.

That spirit, however, would soon evaporate as Celtic began a long, steady slide into mediocrity. A 1-0 away defeat to Dundee United in Celtic's next League match was disappointing; a 5-1 defeat at Ibrox one week on from that was devastating.

McNeill had wished to invest in players to maintain the momentum of the team that had won the centenary double, but the cash was not forthcoming and only one new signing had been made in the summer of 1988. Ian Andrews, a goalkeeper, had arrived from Leicester City for a £300,000 fee as cover for Pat Bonner, who had undergone a back operation that summer that would keep him out of action for three months. Andrews' confidence was battered by the Rangers thrashing and after just nine appearances for Celtic he was replaced by Alan Rough, who had joined the club on a short-term basis at the age of 36.

A series of debilitating defeats and another black day at Ibrox, when Rangers won the New Year fixture by 4-1, forced Celtic to wave farewell to the 1988-89 League title. Cracks had begun to appear with frightening regularity in a defence that had been close to flawless the previous season. The restless McAvennie now wanted to leave the club and eventually returned to West Ham United in March 1989 for a £1.25 million fee.

Favourable draws in the Scottish Cup allowed Celtic to make a run to the final where they would face Rangers, but they looked short of scoring power for that encounter – the team was continuing to feel the absence of the departed McAvennie and Andy Walker was forced to miss the match because of a serious eye injury. It forced McNeill to play winger Joe Miller in attack and he showed he had adapted well to that role when, close to

50 Greatest Players

FRANK McAVENNIE Forward

Born: Glasgow

Joined Celtic: 1987   **From:** West Ham United

Debut: v Hibernian, League, 3 October 1987

Left Celtic: 1989   **For:** West Ham United

Rejoined Celtic: 1993 (as free agent)

Left Celtic: 1994 (released)

Appearances: 106   **Goals:** 50

Honours won with Celtic: 1 league championship;

1 Scottish Cup; 2 caps (Scotland)

'The goal I enjoyed most was the first of my double against

Rangers in the Ne'erday game of 1988,' says Frank

McAvennie. It was a classic McAvennie strike – he had

glided into such a perfect position that he only had to extend his foot an inch or two to

tap Chris Morris' pass into the net. Frank's neat header later in that 2-0 victory was a

massive step towards Celtic taking the centenary title and another double in the

Scottish Cup final that ensured the Cup would be added to the League title that year.

Frank also possessed excellent close control and would often drop deep or go wide to

create chances for his fellow forwards. His ability to see openings and make use of

them brought Celtic numerous goals in the late 1980s.

His return to West Ham after just 17 months at Celtic Park was a killer blow to Billy

McNeill's ambitions. By 1992 Frank had become a free agent and was about to be

signed by Partick Thistle when Liam Brady brought him back to Parkhead. It was

strange to see the centenary-year hero now fronting a struggling Celtic team.

half-time, he darted on to a short back-pass from Rangers defender Gary
Stevens and shot low and accurately past goalkeeper Chris Woods for the
only goal of the 1989 Scottish Cup final.

Claiming the Cup provided Celtic with some consolation for relinquishing the
title to Rangers, but an off-field tussle tilted the balance of power in Glasgow
back towards Ibrox in the summer of 1989. McNeill, seeking a striker to
replace McAvennie, looked to have persuaded Maurice Johnston to return to
the club from Nantes, but no sooner had he been announced as a Celtic player
than a 'contractual difficulty' put the signing in doubt. The matter remained
unresolved for weeks until Johnston popped up at another press conference, this
time at Ibrox, to be announced as Rangers' latest signing. Rangers' financial

muscle had persuaded the player to become the first Catholic to play for the club in modern times. It also symbolized their ongoing domination of Scottish football during the late 1980s.

Major Signings

Celtic still made major signings in that summer of 1989. Thwarted in his attempts to purchase Johnston, McNeill brought Polish international striker Dariusz Dziekanowski to Celtic Park for £600,000. Paul Elliott, an English centre back, arrived from Pisa for a fee of £500,000. A battling midfielder, Mike Galloway, cost £500,000 from Hearts and full back Dariusz Wdowcyck, a team-mate of Dziekanowski at Legia Warsaw, arrived early in the season in a £400,000 transfer.

Mick McCarthy threatens Rangers' goal as Butcher and Woods defend a corner in the 1989 Scottish Cup final. A 1-0 victory gave Celtic the trophy.

Dziekanowski made a vivacious start to his Celtic career, scoring four goals in a 5-4 defeat of Partizan Belgrade in the Cup-Winners' Cup on a wild September night. Unfortunately, that second leg saw Celtic concede a fourth Partizan goal two minutes from time that resulted in the club being knocked out on away goals after the tie had ended 6-6 on aggregate.

Soon, however, Dziekanowski's form began to fade and at the end of the 1989-90 season a final against Aberdeen in the Scottish Cup offered Celtic the only chance of salvaging something from a bleak 12 months. It was not to be. After extra-time a dull 0-0 draw went to penalties. It was the first time a Scottish Cup final would be settled in that way and the shootout went

Paul Elliott heads clear from Rangers' Mark Hateley in the 1990 League Cup final. Celtic went down 2-1.

Aberdeen's way, the Dons claiming a 9-8 penalty victory.

The summer of 1990 saw McNeill spend £2million on new players: Charlie Nicholas from Aberdeen, John Collins from Hibs and midfielder Martin Hayes from Arsenal. Collins was a young player of promise – the other two were hoping a fresh start at Celtic Park would perk up their careers. Rangers, meanwhile, had a team packed with experienced, regular English and Scottish internationals. The difference in experience and know-how between the two Old Firm sides meant that the 1990-91 title went to Ibrox and for the first time in a quarter of a century, Celtic ended a second successive season without winning a trophy. Billy McNeill consequently left the post of Celtic manager in the spring of 1991.

Ambition or Drive?

Celtic supporters were now questioning whether the Celtic board of directors had the ambition and drive to match the doings of Rangers, who were being backed by their young, enthusiastic multimillionaire chairman David Murray. David Hay, shortly after his departure as manager in 1987, had revealed that the Celtic board, in his opinion, had been divided by petty squabbles and he claimed that they had been complacent in coming to terms with the new challenge from Rangers that had arisen in the mid-1980s. Now, with the departure of McNeill, and the contrast in the quality of the respective playing staffs at Ibrox and Celtic Park, the Celtic fans questioned how well – or how badly – their club was being run.

Murmurs of discontent began to grow among the supporters. They questioned why the club could not match Rangers in attracting the best players to Glasgow and why Celtic Park remained in a basic condition, with vast, old-fashioned terraces and only 8,000 seats while Rangers supporters enjoyed the comforts of an all-seated, modern stadium. It was against such a background of discontent that McNeill's replacement, Liam Brady, became Celtic manager in the summer of 1991.

50 Greatest Players

ROY AITKEN Centre back

Born: Irvine

Joined Celtic: 1972   **From:** Celtic Boys Club

Debut: v Stenhousmuir, League Cup, 10 September 1975

Appearances: 672   **Goals:** 53

Left Celtic: 1990   **For:** Newcastle United

Honours won with Celtic: 6 league championships; 5 Scottish Cups; 1 Scottish League Cup; 50 caps (Scotland)

'Feed the Bear' was the chant that greeted Roy Aitken's regular forays forward as a young Celtic player and few individuals in the club's history have matched his obvious hunger for Celtic success. Aitken provided a massive presence for Celtic at centre back, from where he would launch his driving runs deep into the opposition defence, or in midfield, where his determination and controlled aggression tended to overshadow the subtle touches that flourished once he had won the ball.

Roy was a mature teenager in the Celtic team that won the double in 1977 and he became the cornerstone of Billy McNeill's vibrant sides of the late 1970s and early 1980s. David Hay found Roy's services equally essential but when McNeill returned as manager in 1987 Roy peaked to perfection. He was by then 28 years old and had enjoyed a successful testimonial against Manchester United, but his appetite for the game was sharpened by the prospect of feasting fabulously on centenary year fare. Time and again in that 1987-88 season, his team-mates would hear the powerful Aitken exhorting them to exert greater and greater effort and no player was more responsible for instilling the hard drive into Celtic that season which resulted in them capturing the double. Aitken, an ace pianist who earned university-standard qualifications at school, moved to Newcastle United in January 1990 with surprising suddenness. It took a long time for Celtic to rediscover the Parkhead passion that went with him.

Great Managers – 1978-83 and 1987-91

BILLY McNEILL

When the call came to become Celtic manager in 1978, it was the fulfilment of a dream for Billy McNeill. He was the ideal man for the vacant position. He commanded the immediate respect of the players through his stature as the captain of Jock Stein's great teams and soon he had galvanized a club that had fallen into torpor in the year prior to McNeill's arrival.

McNeill earned the admiration of the players through his fairness and his practical approach to the game, and his first five years at the club saw Celtic capture a trophy in each year. It was a respectable tally at a time when four clubs were carving up the Scottish domestic game between them. A haul of three championships meant McNeill's Celtic were the most successful team in the Scottish domestic game. McNeill himself, however, had a strained relationship with chairman Desmond White and in June 1983 he walked out on the club after one too many disagreements with the board of directors.

His four-year period in England with Manchester City and Aston Villa tested him to the full and when he returned to Celtic in 1987 he was ready to throw himself back into work in the service of the club he loves so much. 'He was a great enthusiast,' says Tommy Burns, and McNeill used that enthusiasm to fire his players towards the double during the centenary season of 1987-88. The succeeding years saw familiar frustrations emerge for McNeill as he found the ambitions of the directors did not fall in line with his own wishes for the future of the club. He left at the end of the 1990-91 season, disappointed that he had not been given the scope to take the club as far as he wished. Celtic faced consistent, determined challenges on all fronts during Billy McNeill's time as Celtic manager and his record of winning eight trophies in nine seasons bears testimony to his top-class motivational skills and ability to instill in others his desire for Celtic to triumph.

Brady was the first Celtic manager who had not played for the club. The Irish international and former Arsenal and Juventus player was well-known throughout Europe because of his lengthy career as a world-class midfielder and it was the 35-year-old's first post as manager. As with Souness' recruitment by Rangers five years previously, Celtic anticipated that Brady's status would attract top players from outside Scotland to Celtic. Serious money was released to him as the Celtic board threw caution to the wind.

Prior to the 1990s, Celtic had always lived within the club's means and had not gone into debt. Now, the board had decided to do so in an attempt to compete with Rangers. Transfer fees and wages began to increase at a rapid rate. Brady plunged into the transfer market, spending £1.1million on striker Tony Cascarino from Aston Villa; £925,000 on Scottish international centre back Gary Gillespie from Liverpool; and £1million on another centre back, Tony Mowbray from Middlesbrough.

Both defenders suffered badly through injury during that 1991-92 season while Cascarino failed to adjust to the demands of football in Glasgow. The striker, pound for pound, proved to be one of the worst signings in Celtic's history and early in 1992 he was swapped for defender Tom Boyd of Chelsea. In combination with an injury to midfielder Paul McStay, it meant that Brady got off to an unsuccessful start as Celtic manager. The team did not come close to picking up any of the domestic trophies and a second

---

50 Greatest Players

TOMMY BURNS Midfielder

Born: Glasgow

Joined Celtic: 1973   **From:** Maryhill Juniors

Debut: v Dundee, League, 19 April 1975

Appearances: 508   **Goals:** 82

Left Celtic: 1989   **For:** Kilmarnock

Honours won with Celtic: 6 league championships; 4 Scottish Cups; 1 Scottish League Cup; 8 caps (Scotland)

'In the Celtic team, I liked the red-haired man,' said Johan Cruyff after Ajax's 1982 European Cup encounter with Celtic. Many others also liked Burns, not least his team-mates, who benefited from the unselfish midfielder's work. Burns would thread through the right pass at exactly the right moment. He would also make himself available for the ball if a player was in a tight spot. Those skills were appreciated more by fellow players than by fans but Tommy could also contribute eye-catching goals, such as a pelter of a shot against SW Innsbruck in the European Cup in 1977 and his intricately worked left-foot shot at Tannadice in 1981 for the gilt-edged goal that clinched that year's championship title.

Open and approachable off the field, Tommy mixed skill, commitment and aggression on it, inspiring two memorable European victories: the 5-0 victory over Sporting Lisbon in 1983 and the 3-0 defeat of Rapid Vienna in 1984. He threw his boots into the Jungle on his final appearance as a Celtic player in 1989 and, as Kilmarnock manager in the early 1990s, would receive a warm welcome on each return visit to Celtic Park. Between 1994 and 1997 he endured three difficult years as Celtic manager, returning in 2000 as player development officer at Celtic Park, with the duty of overseeing the club's youth system.

50 Greatest Players

BILLY STARK Midfielder

Born: Glasgow

Joined Celtic: 1987   **From:** Aberdeen

Debut: v Morton, League, 8 August 1987

Appearances: 84   **Goals:** 25

Left Celtic: 1990   **For:** Kilmarnock

Honours won with Celtic: 1 league championship; 1 Scottish Cup

The purchase of Billy Stark by Billy McNeill in the summer of 1987 brought to the club a player whose sleek sophistication added control and class to the team during Celtic's classic centenary season.

Stark was 30 years old on his arrival at Celtic Park and had enjoyed a fruitful association with Alex Ferguson at St Mirren and Aberdeen, but Celtic supporters are convinced they saw the best of the player when he returned to his native Glasgow to enjoy an Indian Summer to his career. His top-class positional play and economic but imaginative distribution were vital to the smooth functioning of McNeill's side.

Stark made a noticeable, eye-catching contribution soon after his arrival at Celtic when he curved an expertly judged shot into the Rangers net for the only goal of the season's first Old Firm match. Subtlety from Stark was sprinkled all over that 1987-88 season and in his three years at the club he contributed a respectable number of goals from midfield. Billy joined Tommy Burns at Kilmarnock as assistant manager in 1992 and returned to Celtic with Burns in the same capacity when Burns became manager in 1994.

round 5-1 UEFA Cup defeat to the little-known Neuchatel Xamax of Switzerland was Celtic's worst night ever in European competition.

Another expensive import arrived at Celtic Park in time for the start of the 1992-93 season: England 'B' international forward Stuart Slater cost £1.5million from West Ham United but he, in common with Cascarino, struggled to adjust to life with Celtic. His lack of impact and goals was typical of another dismal season for the team and yet again Celtic were non-contenders for trophies. The pressure began to tell on Brady and when his team picked up just two wins in their first ten League games at the start of the 1993-94 season, he decided to resign.

Brady did, to his credit, always put the emphasis on fine, flowing football but his teams lacked the competitive edge necessary to be winners. Paul McStay, for one, testifies that he enjoyed working with Brady because of the manager's belief in attacking football and the ideas he brought to training.

The Celtic board, by the time of Brady's resignation in October 1993, was under severe pressure on several fronts. The club had dropped deeply into debt after two high-spending years and investment in players that had been visibly unsuccessful. Attendances had plummeted, further reducing the cash flow and making further expensive transfers impossible. The board also had to confront the task of rebuilding Celtic Park. Lord Justice Taylor's report into the Hillsborough disaster meant that, under law, Celtic would have to be playing in an all-seater stadium by the beginning of the 1994-95 season.

Enter the 'Rebels'

There was little sign of the Celtic board of directors having any strategy in place to deal with that stadium dilemma: Celtic Park in late 1993 consisted of two vast terraces and just one purpose-built stand, the South Stand, which held 8,000 seats. The old 'Jungle' terracing had become 'all-seated' in summer 1993 but only with inadequate benches', a crude attempt to deal with the situation that was all to typical of the Celtic board at that time. Furthermore the board had another problem, one that was beginning to snowball. A band of 'rebel' Celtic supporters had organized and were agitating for their removal. Demonstrations against the directors were being held outside the ground on match days and disaffected supporters were holding meetings and rallies to hammer out the best means of toppling the members of the board from their positions.

Two businessmen were prominently at the forefront of those calling for change: Brian Dempsey and Fergus McCann. Dempsey had been on the verge of being accepted on to the Celtic board in late 1990, but directors Christopher White and Michael Kelly had vetoed his appointment at the last minute. From then on Dempsey, a property developer, began to campaign loudly for the board's removal. McCann had emigrated to Canada from central Scotland in the 1960s, where he had made millions. He now wished to reinvest in Celtic, the club he had supported as a boy.

It was against this backdrop that Lou Macari was appointed manager in late October 1993. Macari, a former Celtic player, had left the club for Manchester United in 1973, but as a manager in England's lower divisions during the 1980s and 1990s he had acquired a reputation for building strong teams with scant resources. Macari had been strongly advised not to return to Celtic Park, but his memories of Celtic under Jock Stein two decades earlier overruled the advice he was receiving from friends inside the game about the condition of the club in the early 1990s.

Macari's arrival at a club under siege heralded a stream of cheap signings from the lower reaches of English football. There was a brief improvement in form and hope of a renaissance, but it was a false dawn. The 1994 New Year derby with Rangers resulted in a devastating 4-2 home defeat and missiles were thrown at the directors' box by some angry supporters. After that, the team once again embraced mediocrity.

The plummeting fortunes of Celtic on the field enabled the rebel groups to exert even greater pressure on the Celtic board. A boycott of a League match with Kilmarnock was organized on 1 March 1994. An attendance of just 10,882 was recorded and on the night a fox – symbolic of the hunted directors – raced the length of Celtic Park during the game. With the debt-ridden club's income decreasing drastically, the Bank of Scotland informed the Celtic directors on 3 March 1994 that they were ready to call in the receivers. Within 24 hours the siege of Celtic Park was over as the Celtic directors surrendered their shares. On Friday 4 March 1994, control of the club was finally wrestled from the White and Kelly families who had seized power at Celtic shortly after the club had become a limited company in 1897.

Fergus McCann now took control of Celtic and following the inevitably barren 1993-94 season, new managing director McCann dismissed Lou Macari for failing to observe his instructions. Macari claimed breach of contract and took legal action to claim £400,000 in compensation, but lost his case at the Court of Session in Edinburgh in 1997.

Burns is Back

McCann stated that he would remain at Celtic for a five-year period to oversee the reconstruction of the stadium and to put the club on a stable, business-like footing. He appointed local boy and former Celtic midfielder Tommy Burns as manager. A popular player, Tommy's standing with the support would ensure they would be patient with him if he encountered teething difficulties in resurrecting Celtic's fortunes. At the time of Burns' appointment, in July 1994, it had been five years since Celtic had won a trophy and the 37-year-old Burns looked sure of instant success when he quickly led the club to their first Cup final since 1990.

Celtic's opponents in the 1994 League Cup final were to be Raith Rovers of the First Division and Celtic supporters who turned up at Ibrox Park for the final in November expected nothing less than victory. It was not to be. Raith fought hard for a 2-2 draw and although Celtic had the better of much of the match, by extra-time Raith looked the stronger side. It went to a penalty shootout, which Raith won to take the first major trophy in their history.

Scarves were thrown on to the Ibrox running track by the more emotional Celtic supporters at the end of that match and there was little to console the club's followers in League competition during the remainder of 1994 – a run of 11 matches without a win was a new club record. Furthermore, the team were now playing League fixtures at Hampden Park whilst Celtic Park was being reconstructed, and the national stadium was proving an unpopular alternative venue with the support.

After that dip in the club's fortunes, the redevelopment of Celtic began to gather momentum. A share issue in January 1995 was an overwhelming success and provided the club with a capital base of £20million; 10,000 supporters now owned a little bit of their club. The first phase in the construction of a 60,000 all-seater stadium began and the team pushed on to the final of the Scottish Cup where they would face Airdrie.

That day in May, a match bathed in bright sunshine produced a dour, tense 90 minutes, enlivened only by an early goal from Pierre van Hooijdonk, when he climbed into the air, hovered briefly and headed Tosh McKinlay's cross low

50 Greatest Players

PAT BONNER Goalkeeper

Born: Clochglas, Co. Donegal

Joined Celtic: 1978   **From:** Keadue Rovers

Debut: v Motherwell, League, 17 March 1980

Appearances: 641

Left Celtic: 1994 (retired)

Honours won with Celtic: 4 league championships; 3 Scottish Cups; 1 Scottish League Cup; 80 caps (Rep of Ireland)

The position of goalkeeper had been a transitional one for Celtic throughout the 1970s, with no fewer than eight goalkeepers representing the club during that decade. The 1980s would prove entirely different, with Pat Bonner claiming sole rights to the position from the moment he made his debut at the start of that decade. The supporters enjoyed seeing a Donegal man between the sticks, but although there was a touch of romance about an Irishman achieving success at Celtic it was based entirely on hard work and application from Bonner, who constantly sought ways to improve his game. Celtic's most-capped player – he appeared 80 times for the Republic of Ireland – Bonner was a brilliant shot stopper who would fearlessly throw himself at opponents' feet. 'Scottish goalkeepers are supposed to be bad enough,' he once said, 'but an Irish keeper in Scotland... I just had to go out and try and prove everyone wrong.'

New signings for 1995. Above: Germany's Andreas Thom. Below: Dutchman Pierre van Hooijdonk.

into the Airdrie net. It was enough to win Celtic their first trophy for six long years. 'The game was 90 minutes long,' says Paul McStay, 'but for me the game lasted as long as my five years as captain and our six years without a trophy.'

Dutchman van Hooijdonk had joined Celtic from NAC Breda for a £1.3 million fee in January 1995 and he was followed in August 1995 by German international Andreas Thom, a £2.2 million club-record signing from Bayer Leverkusen. Their arrival heralded a new era in which the club would sign high-grade foreign players to complement domestic talent.

Fantastic Arena

The 1995-96 season would see Celtic perform against the magnificent backdrop of the club's new two-tier north stand, which held 26,000, giving Celtic Park a temporary 34,000 capacity. The sum of £18 million had been spent on reconstruction up to that point and building work now began to fill in the two vacant ends, east and west, with similarly spectacular stands. The result would be one of the greatest arenas in the country, with a capacity of more than 60,000.

The revived, regenerated stadium produced renewed enthusiasm among the support and the team responded by playing fast, attractive football in that 1995-96 season. The resurgent Celtic spirit was symbolized by the players going into a group huddle prior to kick-off in every match. That tradition, introduced by the players themselves in mid-1995, endures to this day.

50 Greatest Players

JOHN COLLINS Midfielder

Born: Galashiels

Joined Celtic: 1990   **From:** Hibernian

Debut: v Ayr United, Scottish League Cup, 22 August 1990

Appearances: 273   **Goals:** 54

Left Celtic: 1996   **For:** Monaco

Honours won with Celtic: 1 Scottish Cup

It takes a special talent to retain enough composure to score a goal of high quality during a pressurized Old Firm encounter. John Collins' stunning left-footed free-kick that bent round the Rangers defensive wall at Ibrox in April 1994 was just that. Even more remarkably, Collins returned to Ibrox four months later to hit home an almost exact replica. It was typical of a player whose football was always measured, controlled and composed.

John Collins possessed a fierce dedication to the game even from his days as a boy in Galashiels. Friends would try to tempt him to celebrate New Year with just one drink but the teetotal Collins would decline, preferring to focus fully on his future as a footballer. He was unfortunate in joining Celtic at a time when the club was about to plunge into trouble, but this smooth-moving, left-sided midfielder proved himself a distinguished Celtic player in an undistinguished era. He became the first major Celtic player to switch clubs on a free 'Bosman' move with his departure to AS Monaco in the summer of 1996, later aiding Everton and then Fulham's venture into the English Premier League.

Thom and van Hooijdonk worked together well in attack and a run of fine form saw the team lose just once in the 1995-96 League season – but 11 draws allowed Rangers to capitalized and take their eighth successive Premier League title. That put pressure on Burns to prevent the Ibrox side equalling or surpassing Celtic's record nine titles in a row under Jock Stein. The manager thus went abroad again in mid-1996, to bring Portuguese striker Jorge Cadete and Italian winger Paolo di Canio to Celtic.

The new players contributed extra flair, but the team was now top-heavy with extrovert attackers and suspect in defence. As the 1996-97 season got underway, van Hooijdonk, Cadete and Di Canio began demanding improved financial terms and news of their squabbles with the club became a continual distraction. Injuries and suspensions also disrupted the club's progress: when Di Canio was sent off after some hysterics in the 2-2 home draw with Hearts on

50 Greatest Players

PAUL McSTAY Midfielder

Born: Hamilton

Joined Celtic: 1981   **From:** Celtic Boys Club

Debut: v Queen of the South, Scottish Cup, 23 January 1981

Appearances: 677   **Goals:** 72

Left Celtic: 1997 (retired)

Honours won with Celtic: 2 league championships; 4 Scottish Cups; 1 Scottish League Cup; 76 caps (Scotland)

Paul McStay was Celtic's premier performer of the 1980s and early 1990s. His composure and creativity made him the ideal central midfield player and his ability was evident from the moment he made his debut. One week later he crowned his League debut against Aberdeen with a left-footed goal, and his first Old Firm game, in October 1982, saw a firm tackle by McStay, inside his own half, start the move that led to him scoring the opening goal. Later in the match, some sublime midfield movement from McStay saw him whip the ball away from three scything challenges and set up Frank McGarvey for Celtic's second goal in their 3-2 Celtic Park victory. Paul had just celebrated his 18th birthday, but the all-round quality of his performances – in particular his acute awareness and flawless passing skills – were such that his place in the team was already secure.

He soon had a nickname – 'The Maestro' – that encapsulated his ability to work magic and orchestrate a match with vision and precision, but one of his most appealing qualities was that Paul always remained a modest, well-rounded individual. His intricate skills were wonderful to watch throughout the 1980s and he peaked in the 1987-88 centenary season. A screeching 20-yard volley at Ibrox in March 1988 was just one of many magnificent moments from McStay that season. 'He drove us on to win that championship that year,' says Pat Bonner.

A deep desire to do well for Celtic underpinned all of Paul McStay's efforts on behalf of the team but when he threw his jersey into the Celtic Park crowd at the end of the final fixture of the 1991-92 season it looked as though he was about to move on. Instead, he decided to remain with Celtic and performances of maturity marked his play until injury forced him to retire in 1997.

Paul's 76 caps make him Celtic's most-capped Scotsman and his finest performances in the dark blue were perhaps those in the 1992 European Championship finals when he hit peak form in top-class company. He left memories of numerous exquisite goals – he seemed to save his best ones for games against Rangers – and of a sublime talent that would have lit up any team.

The dreadlocked Swedish international Henrik Larsson proved the finest of all the continental Europeans to join Celtic in the 1990s.

30 November he became the tenth dismissal of Celtic's season up to that point. Van Hooijdonk was transferred to Nottingham Forest, whilst Di Canio and Cadete were clearly unhappy, and against this unstable background, Rangers held firm to take their ninth successive title. Manager Tommy Burns' three-year contract expired in mid-1997, it was not renewed by McCann, and Burns left the club.

Stand-off

McCann decided, in summer 1997, to try a new way of running football matters at the club. A general manager, Jock Brown, was appointed, to work with a new head coach, Wim Jansen, a Dutchman and the club's first foreign coach. Problems immediately besieged those involved in the new set-up. Di Canio and Cadete refused to return to the club that summer, pleading illness; both players wished to have their contracts improved richly. The stand-off between club and resulted in Di Canio moving to Sheffield Wednesday and Cadete remaining in Portugal. The press then turned against Brown because he had not tipped them off that Di Canio was moving club.

Criticism for Jansen came when Celtic lost their opening league game, away to Hibernian. A stray pass from new £650,000 signing Henrik Larsson led to one of the Hibs goals in the 2-1 defeat. A 2-1 defeat at home to Dunfermline Athletic the following week left Celtic sitting bottom of the Premier League. Jansen, who had been unknown to the press at the time of his recruitment by Celtic, was pilloried for his coaching style and the club was criticized heavily for bringing in a coach whose previous position had been with Sanfrecce Hiroshima in the Japanese J-League.

From that point on, Jansen's thorough coaching methods began to filter through to the players' minds and Celtic stabilized. A run of eight victories took Celtic into second position in the Premier League. They also captured the League Cup, with centre back Marc Rieper, Larsson and midfielder Craig Burley, all new signings, getting the goals in the 3-0 victory over Dundee United at Ibrox in November 1997. It was only the second trophy to have been captured by Celtic in the 1990s. Jansen introduced another new recruit, midfielder Paul Lambert, to the team in late 1997 and a steady stream of results went Celtic's way. A key fixture against Rangers at New Year 1998 ended in a 2-0 Celtic victory – it was the first time since August 1994 that Celtic had beaten Rangers in a League match.

The team maintained steady progress in the second half of the season and moved top of the League at the end of February 1998. Rangers remained in close pursuit, but when Celtic suffered a series of draws in the season's closing fixtures, the Ibrox side simultaneously dropped points. It meant that the destination of the title would be decided on the final day of the season, when Celtic faced St Johnstone at home.

A third-minute goal from Larsson and a 72nd-minute hit from striker Harald Brattbakk, purchased from Rosenborg Trondheim, gave Celtic a 2-0 victory and obliterated the terrifying spectre of Rangers winning a record-breaking ten League titles in a row. It made Jansen a hero with the support, but two days after that triumph he announced his resignation from the position of head coach at Celtic. It emerged that there had been a great deal of friction behind the scenes between Jansen and Brown, and the Dutchman had consequently decided to exercise an option in his contract that allowed him to leave one year after his arrival.

Celtic had secured their first League title for a decade, but the celebrations had been dampened by Jansen's announcement. The club had found some stability under Jansen, only to lose it almost as soon as it had arrived. Now Celtic, a club that had once been a model of continuity, sought a sixth manager in a decade.

Chapter Twelve: 1998-2002
Back on Top

Celtic stars in action for Scotland at the 1998 World Cup in France. Above left: Darren Jackson makes a run against Brazil. Above right: Jackie McNamara (left) battles with Norway's Stale Solbakken.

Record attendances were guaranteed at Celtic Park for the 1998-99 season thanks to the opening of the Jock Stein Stand in the summer of 1998. It completed the stadium redevelopment begun by Fergus McCann four years previously and brought the capacity of Celtic Park up to 60,506. With 53,000 season tickets having been sold, Celtic Park would now have the highest average attendances over a season in the club's history and, for that 1998-99 season, in Britain.

Doctor Jozef Venglos, a 61-year-old Slovakian with coaching experience in a wide variety of countries, had been appointed Celtic's head coach on the eve of the season. As he familiarized himself with the team and adjusted to Scottish football, the August, September and October of 1998 yielded a mediocre set of results that included a defeat by Croatia Zagreb in Celtic's

Great Matches

SCOTTISH PREMIER LEAGUE   **Celtic Park, 21 November 1998**

Celtic 5   **Rangers 1**   **Attendance 59,783**
Moravcik 2   Van Bronckhorst
Larsson 2
Burchill

It was just another Saturday and just another Old Firm game, with a near-60,000 crowd inside the stadium, another 30,000 watching large screens at Ibrox and a worldwide audience of eight million. It was the second encounter between new Old Firm managers Doctor Jozef Venglos of Celtic and Dick Advocaat of Rangers; the first meeting between the two continentals having ended in a 0-0 draw.

Twelve uninspiring minutes had passed when Celtic centre back Alan Stubbs found Phil O'Donnell on the left wing. He pushed a pass into the path of Simon Donnelly, who had made a good run into space and from his swift cross, Lubo Moravcik, hovering 20 yards from goal, sent a low, left-footed shot curling into the corner of the Rangers net. The Slovakian stood stock still as his team-mates acclaimed a goal of rare finesse.

Rangers responded with good efforts from Guivarc'h, Kanchelskis and Wallace and for a spell they were the better side. Then Scott Wilson, Rangers' centre back, made a neanderthal challenge from behind on Moravcik. The consequence was an instant red card and the cue for Moravcik to take control of the game. Shortly before half-time his crafty cross gave Larsson a free header in front of goal but the Swede sent it wide.

As the second half began, crowd pleasing back-heels and tricks showed how much Moravcik was relaxing into the Old Firm experience. Then when Tom Boyd got the ball wide on the right, Lubo got serious, signalling frantically for the ball and meeting Boyd's cross with a stunning, spinning header that streaked into the net. Rangers' misery continued when Donnelly's pass split their defence for Larsson to shrug off a push from Colin Hendry and poke the ball past Niemi to make it 3-0.

Van Bronckhorst's free-kick a minute later revived Rangers briefly before Larsson met O'Donnell's cross with a thumping header to make it 4-1. Only 11 minutes had passed since half-time. Celtic now toyed with their opponents before Mark Burchill nudged the ball past Niemi in the final minute to make it 5-1. It was a win that was particularly sweet for the margin of victory being entirely unexpected.

Celtic: Warner, Boyd, Stubbs, Mjallby, Mahé, Donnelly (Hannah), Lambert, O'Donnell, Riseth, Moravcik (Burchill), Larsson.

Rangers: Niemi, Porrini, Wilson, Hendry, Numan, Kanchelskis (Vidmar), B. Ferguson (I. Ferguson), Van Bronckhorst, Albertz (Durie), Guivarc'h, Wallace.

Referee: Willie Young (Scotland).

Craig Burley scores in Scotland's 1-1 draw with Norway during the 1998 World Cup.

Champions League qualifier and meant that Celtic were already trailing Rangers in the League. There was little in the way of light relief for Celtic fans in those early months, and one of only a few cheering episodes was the introduction of fan club mascot Hoopy the Huddle Hound. Hoopy made his debut before a friendly match with Liverpool on 8 August 1998, at which Lady Stein opened the new stand named after her husband.

Hello Lubo

The thoughtful Venglos introduced fellow Slovakian Lubo Moravcik, an attacking midfielder, to the team in November 1998 and powerful Swedish defender Johan Mjallby also arrived that month. Both contributed to a stunning 5-1 defeat of Rangers that saw Celtic speed off on a five-month spell where they lost just once in the League. The team played some superb football and sustained a serious challenge on Rangers in the second half of that 1998-99 season but, ultimately, the points that had been dropped in the opening months, whilst Venglos was acclimatizing himself to Scottish football, cost Celtic the 1998-99 title.

A 1-0 defeat by Rangers in a dull Scottish Cup final rounded off a season that had seen McCann, his five years as managing director completed, relinquish control of the club. General manager Jock Brown had also left, resigning mid-season after having been placed under severe press pressure. The general manager/head coach set-up was now abandoned. Chief Executive

Allan MacDonald, recruited in spring 1999 as the chief decision-maker in the running of the club, decided instead to appoint a director of football to work with a new head coach. MacDonald chose one of his golfing partner, a friend and ex-Celt Kenny Dalglish, as his director of football. Dalglish, in turn, chose John Barnes as head coach. Barnes had been a player at Liverpool and Newcastle United when Dalglish had been a manager at both of those clubs.

The experienced Venglos – who had been castigated by the press for his advanced years – agreed to move aside to make way for the 35-year-old Barnes. The newspaper men were still not happy. The former England star had gone straight from playing for Charlton Athletic at the end of the 1998-99 season to becoming head coach at Celtic. Now the press's complaint was that the club had chosen a manager with too little experience.

The press were waiting for Barnes to fail and by November 1999 he was under pressure when he lost his first Old Firm game 4-2 to go seven points

50 Greatest Players

JOHAN MJALLBY Centre back

Born: Stockholm

Joined Celtic: 1998   **From:** AIK Solna

Debut: v Rangers, League, 21 November 1998

Appearances: 156*   **Goals:** 12*

Honours won with Celtic: 2 league championships; 1 Scottish Cup; 2 Scottish League Cups; 32 caps (Sweden)*

*Up to end of 2001-02 season

Rock-solid and reliable, Johan Mjallby immediately solidified the Celtic defence with his imposing presence. At just over six feet, the 13 and a half stone Mjallby is the equal of any attacker when it comes to a physical battle. He is also an excellent user of the ball, rarely wasting possession, and his bursts forward from defence are a formidable sight. 'He has got such a big heart and nothing frightens him,' says team-mate Jackie McNamara. When, late in the 1999-2000 season, the club had little to play for, it was impressive to see Mjallby still attacking every ball with gusto and breaking forward with brio.

The arrival of Martin O'Neill as manager in 2000 channelled Mjallby's talents even more productively and he has developed into a world-class centre back. His habit of hovering by jogging lightly on the spot during a game is just one symptom of the keen concentration that ensures opposing strikers are kept on their toes whenever the Swedish international is in close proximity.

50 Greatest Players

STILIAN PETROV Midfielder

Born: Montana, Bulgaria

Joined Celtic: 1999   **From:** CSKA Sofia

Debut: v Dundee United, League, 15 August 1999

Appearances: 111*   **Goals:** 16*

Honours won with Celtic: 2 league championships; 1 Scottish League Cup; 20 caps (Bulgaria)*

*Up to end of 2001-02 season

A fee of £2.2 million brought the young Bulgarian Stilian Petrov to Glasgow from CSKA Sofia in the summer of 1999 but Celtic subsequently did little to ease him into Scottish life. The midfielder, whose English was then limited, felt adrift and lonely. It affected his football and his opening season with the club was less than productive.

The arrival of Martin O'Neill as manager in summer 2000 revived Stilian's fortunes and he began to blossom into a creative dynamo whose quick, precise passing made him the key link man between central midfield and the strikers. His ability to burst into the box to create or score goals was invaluable. Stilian was struck by another setback in March 2001 when he sustained a broken leg at St Johnstone, but he returned to action at the start of season 2001-02 to score spectacular goals, often striking with stunning accuracy from distance.

behind Rangers in the League. A UEFA Cup exit to Olympique Lyon that month gave the press more ammunition to use against him. As he entered 2000, Barnes, now without top scorer Henrik Larsson through a broken leg sustained in Lyon, knew that his only realistic hope of salvaging something from the season lay in the Scottish Cup. Instead, it proved the catalyst for his dismissal. A 3-1 home defeat to underdogs Inverness Caledonian Thistle effectively ended Celtic's season and Barnes' career as head coach at Celtic Park. Dalglish took over as caretaker-manager as Celtic limped through the remainder of the 1999-2000 season.

It meant that Celtic would make a clean start to the first full season of the 21st century. Irishman Martin O'Neill was recruited from Leicester City to become Celtic manager in June 2000 and the title of head coach was now abandoned. 'I'm a bit of a dreamer,' said O'Neill as he contemplated his first season at Celtic, 'but I'm also a realist. I've got a three-year contract and I want to do things relatively quickly. I might get a little bit of time at the start, but that won't last forever. I know the pitfalls.'

Great Matches

SCOTTISH PREMIER LEAGUE		Celtic Park, 27 August 2000
Celtic 6	**Rangers 2**	**Attendance 59,476**
Sutton 2	Reyna	
Petrov	Dodds	
Lambert		
Larsson 2		

The high noon sun beat down on Martin O'Neill as he walked out for his first Old Firm duel. Celtic had not beaten Rangers in their previous seven encounters and Lorenzo Amoruso, fists clenched, could be seen pumping up the Rangers support before kick-off. The Celtic players would reserve their exuberance for the match itself.

The opening seconds saw Lubo Moravcik's probing ball up the left wing spring Bobby Petta free to dink the ball over Rangers right back Fernando Ricksen. Petta then caught the Rangers man's head with his knee as he hurdled him and the referee awarded a dubious corner to Celtic. Moravcik took it and Sutton, near post, flicked the ball down. Alan Stubbs was unable to control it, but Henrik Larsson pounced to whip the ball goalwards. Sutton, offside, diverted the ball into the net and the goal was allowed to stand.

A Billy Dodds header flew across the face of the Celtic goal with goalkeeper Jonathan Gould floundering, before Petta pressed Ricksen into giving away another corner. Moravcik's kick was met by Stilian Petrov who had streaked through a static Rangers defence to pelt a firm, downward header into the net. After ten minutes Petta again teased Ricksen before releasing the ball to Moravcik, whose sudden stop and turn inside the Rangers penalty area unhinged their defence. Lubo's cutback induced a sweet strike from Paul Lambert that saw the Rangers net swaying for a third time.

Minutes before half-time Claudio Reyna was awarded an equalizing goal although there appeared some doubt as to whether the ball had crossed the line. Then Rod Wallace had a goal incorrectly ruled offside. Four minutes into the second half Gould's kick-out was chested down by Sutton for Larsson, 45 yards from goal. He took three touches to tame an unruly, bouncing ball and with his fourth nutmegged Bert Konterman. The Swede was now one-on-one with Stefan Klos and it looked easiest for him to sidefoot the ball past the goalkeeper. Instead, Larsson opted for a spinning, swerving chip that had Klos stumbling around like a sleepwalker. It was one of the finest goals ever seen at Celtic Park. A precise header from Larsson and a close-range strike from Chris Sutton rounded off a six-gun salute from O'Neill's revamped team.

Celtic: Gould, Stubbs, Valgaeren, Mahé, McNamara, Moravcik (Boyd), Lambert, (Mjallby), Petrov, Petta, Larsson (Burchill), Sutton.

Rangers: Klos, Ricksen (Tugay), Amoruso, Konterman, Vidmar, (Kanchelskis), Reyna, Ferguson, Van Bronckhorst, McCann (Lovenkrands), Dodds, Wallace.

O'Neill had favoured a 3-5-2 formation as Leicester manager and he brought that system with him to Celtic. It meant that three central defenders were supplemented by two deep-lying midfield players and it placed the accent heavily on defence. It proved highly effective, however, and four straight victories in their opening League matches sent O'Neill's team confidently into his first Old Firm game, at Celtic Park on 27 August 2000.

A 6-2 victory in that match owed much to the manner in which the powerful Chris Sutton, a record £6million summer purchase from Chelsea, led the line. The striker would combine well with Larsson throughout the 2000-01 season, scoring 67 goals between them, many as a result of Sutton winning the ball in the air and knocking it down into the path of the fully recovered, speedy Larsson. That Old Firm match was typical of O'Neill: the victory was an emphatic one, but Celtic had also been seriously lucky. On the day, Rangers had had a perfectly good goal ruled out for offside and Celtic's first minute opening goal, which helped give the team real impetus, was assisted by two dubious refereeing decisions. Still, Celtic had been the team with the greater desire and had made the most of almost everything that had come their way. That would be an ongoing theme during the O'Neill era. Teamwork and desire would carry the team through the most demanding of matches.

Celtic and Sweden's Johan Mjallby (right) takes on Turkey at Euro 2000. Mjallby is one of a number of top internationals to have been attracted to Celtic in recent years.

175

Top of the League

The League victory over Rangers was followed by a 3-0 home victory over Hibernian, who had been the early-season League leaders. That was enough to send O'Neill's team to the top of the League. They would remain there for the remainder of the 2000-01 season to take the title in some comfort, finishing with a Premier League-record 97 points, 15 ahead of runners-up Rangers. O'Neill had strengthened the team shrewdly when the right signing was available. Goalkeeper Rab Douglas had joined from Dundee in November 2000 and by the end of the season he was behind a seriously

50 Greatest Players

LUBOMIR MORAVCIK Midfielder

Born: Nitra, Slovakia

Joined Celtic: 1998   **From:** Duisburg

Debut: v Dundee, League, 7 November 1998

Appearances: 129   **Goals:** 35

Left Celtic: 2002   **For:** JEF Ichihara (Japan)

Honours won with Celtic: 2 league championships; 1 Scottish Cup; 2 Scottish League Cups; 5 caps (Slovakia)

Lubomir Moravcik is the most technically gifted player to have graced Celtic Park in the past quarter century. 'He is the type of player who makes people come to watch football,' was the effusive tribute paid to him by Rangers' Ronald de Boer, as Lubo prepared to leave Celtic Park at the end of the 2001-02 season.

Doctor Jozef Venglos had heard that Lubo was unhappy with the defensive midfield role he was being forced to play at MSV Duisburg in late 1998 and brought his fellow countryman to Celtic Park. Lubo's departure left some of his Duisburg team-mates in tears and his new Celtic colleagues were soon left open-mouthed at the standard of his technical ability on the ball.

Lubo's touch-perfect passing was sublime and he was equally strong on his left and right foot; his flicks and tricks were delightful cameos that fans could carry around in their minds long after match scorelines had been forgotten. The Lubo-inspired 5-1 demolition of Rangers in November 1998 was one of many magnificent performances and by the time age caught up with him in 2002 – he had been 33 on joining the club for a ridiculously low fee of approximately £200,000 in 1998 – he had endeared himself to the Celtic support. As he made his last appearance in a Celtic jersey in April 2002, even the thunderous standing ovation he received was not enough to do justice as thanks for the marvellous array of skills he had displayed in his four-year stay.

50 Greatest Players

PAUL LAMBERT Midfielder

Born: Glasgow

Joined Celtic: 1997   **From:** Borussia Dortmund

Debut: v Rangers, League, 8 November 1997

Appearances: 197*   **Goals:** 10*

Honours won with Celtic: 3 league championships; 1 Scottish Cup; 2 Scottish League Cups; 21 caps (Scotland)*   *Up to end of 2001-02 season

Paul Lambert became the first Briton to win a European Cup winner's medal with a continental club when he helped Borussia Dortmund defeat Juventus 3-1 in the 1997 final. Six months later, the player was presented at Celtic's door – Lambert and his family had found it difficult to settle in Germany and when they wished to return home, Celtic were only too happy to welcome Paul with open arms.

The midfielder, who had moved to Dortmund from Motherwell, had added a new dimension to his game in Germany. He was now an enormously disciplined player who focused solely on staying steady in his role deep at the back of midfield. Composure and control were the main ingredients in his game, and his determined desire to protect possession made him an inestimably valuable team member.

Paul Lambert's efforts were essential in bringing home three championships in his first five years at the club. He signed a new contract in 2002 that was designed to keep him at the club until 2005. Few around Celtic Park would complain that the man nicknamed 'Victor Meldrew' in the Celtic dressing room could be providing solid service for years to come.

strong defence that consisted of Johan Mjallby, Joos Valgaeren and Ramon Vega. All three of those players were exceptionally useful in the air, whilst Valgaeren and Mjallby were powerful tacklers and good users of the ball.

O'Neill had also purchased midfielder Neil Lennon for £5.75 million from his old club Leicester City. The manager knew what the Irishman could offer and judged that he would form a solid partnership with Paul Lambert in the centre of the park. Two flying wing-backs, in the shape of Bobby Petta and Didier Agathe, provided the team with the pace to turn defence into attack. Agathe had arrived from Hibernian for a token fee of £50,000; Petta had been brought to the club by John Barnes in the 1999-2000 season but had struggled at the start. Another Barnes signing who had also had problems before the arrival of O'Neill was the young Bulgarian Stilian Petrov, who now began to excel in a roving role that linked midfield with the attack.

Lubo Moravcik retained an influential presence in the squad – although now in his mid-thirties the player proved effective either as a substitute or through starting a match and being withdrawn part of the way through the action.

Celtic were simply unstoppable that 2000-01 season. A sublime hat-trick from Larsson in a 3-0 League Cup final victory over Kilmarnock provided O'Neill with his first trophy as Celtic boss. By the time of that final in March 2001, Celtic were as good as assured of the League title and were on course for their first treble since 1969. The season was rounded off in style when, on a warm day in May 2001, Celtic took on Hibs in the Scottish Cup final. A neat goal from ultra-reliable squad member Jackie McNamara, a substitute for the injured Lubo Moravcik, gave Celtic a 1-0 lead at half-time. After the interval, an exceptional strike from Larsson pushed a very one-sided game

Great Managers – 2000-Present

MARTIN O'NEILL

Martin O'Neill looked serious and absorbed in thought as the celebrations got under way at Hampden Park in the wake of the 2001 Scottish Cup final. Celtic had just beaten Hibs 3-0 to win the treble but there was no sign of unrestrained delight from O'Neill at the end of his hugely successful first year as Celtic manager. It was a typical reaction from O'Neill, a university-educated deep thinker who had transformed Celtic, within one season, from being a team that lacked heart and leadership into one that went into every game confident of victory.

The opening two years of O'Neill's management of Celtic had revealed key elements of his style. His instructions to his players are simple and straightforward. He is an astute operator in the transfer market, extracting maximum value for money from his purchases: unheralded buys, such as Didier Agathe and Rab Douglas, showed hitherto hidden qualities under O'Neill. Stability, solidity and encouragement are essential to O'Neill but he has been simultaneously able to work the trick of developing a squad system that has created progressively greater and greater competition for first-team places during his three seasons at the club.

In tandem with assistant manager John Robertson and first-team coach Steve Walford, O'Neill has made Celtic stronger with every passing month that he has been manager. He brought Celtic four trophies in his opening two seasons as the dugout director of affairs. Celtic, under O'Neill, won the title in consecutive years for the first time since 1982 and enjoyed their best run in European football since 1980. It had been a thrilling time for the Celtic supporters and, despite continuous hysterical media speculation about O'Neill's future, they hoped that it had been only the beginning of a long association with this cautious Irishman and his magical management.

almost beyond Hibs' reach and when the Swede scored with a penalty ten minutes from the end it was time for a treble celebration for Celtic.

The momentum was maintained seamlessly into O'Neill's second season. Celtic went top of the League in their third match of the 2001-02 season and victories in the opening two Old Firm matches meant that only a complete disaster would prevent the title arriving at Celtic Park for a second successive year.

Injuries Covered

Injury problems did strike key players in 2001-02. Joos Valgaeren and Chris Sutton were each missing for lengthy periods but their replacements coped admirably. The young Scot Stephen Crainey filled in for Valgaeren on the left side of defence and Welshman John Hartson, a £6 million signing from Coventry City in August 2001, scored 25 goals when Chris Sutton was unavailable.

Parallel to their impressive progress in the League, Celtic enjoyed a fascinating run in

Celtic and Scotland regular Paul Lambert battles for the ball with Belgium's Bart Goor.

Europe. The draw for their third-round qualifying match for the European Champions League could not have been more difficult. Celtic were presented with a tie against Dutch side Ajax and a massive Celtic support travelled to Amsterdam tentatively wondering whether O'Neill's team could translate their effectiveness in Scotland into efficiency in Europe. They witnessed an outstanding performance in the Amsterdam ArenA, with Celtic whizzing into a 2-0 lead after 20 minutes. Smartly-taken goals from wing-backs Didier

Agathe and Bobby Petta were fair reward for a confident, controlled performance. Shota Arveladze pulled a goal back for Ajax before half-time, but in the second half Sutton made it 3-1 with a spectacular header that smacked the underside of the Ajax crossbar on its way into the net.

The competitiveness of European football was emphasized yet again when Ajax travelled to Glasgow for the return and outplayed Celtic with wit and verve. A Wamberto goal after half an hour left the support living on their nerves at the prospect of entry to the Champions League proper drifting away from Celtic, but the team just managed to hold on and qualify for the group stages, chastened by the 1-0 defeat. Rab Douglas, the Celtic goalkeeper, had come in for some harsh, unfair criticism from certain sections of the support since his arrival nine months previously but only some top-class saves from Douglas had enabled Celtic to hurdle that second leg against Ajax.

Juventus, Porto and Rosenborg Trondheim joined Celtic in a challenging Champions League group that always looked as though it would be tight. It set the stage for a fascinating Celtic odyssey across Europe. The Celts were slightly unlucky to lose their opening match, against Juventus in the Stadio

Henrik Larsson celebrates his goal for Sweden against Senegal in the 2002 World Cup finals. After the tournament the Celt announced his retirement from international football.

50 Greatest Players

HENRIK LARSSON   Striker

Born: Helsingborgs, Sweden

Joined Celtic: 1997   **From:** Feyenoord

Debut: v Hibernian, League, 3 August 1997

Appearances: 206*   **Goals:** 157*

Honours won with Celtic: 3 league championships; 1 Scottish Cup; 2 Scottish League
Cups; 48 caps (Sweden)*   *Up to end of 2001-02 season

Great goals, scored in sumptuous style, have made Henrik Larsson a priceless
commodity for Celtic. His chip on the run over Stefan Klos in the 6-2 defeat of Rangers
in 2000 was just one of many world-class strikes to have peppered his Celtic career.
Amidst the glory of his goals, though, it often goes unnoticed just how unselfish a
worker Larsson is for those around him. He is willing to do the type of running that
distracts defenders and rolls them out of the paths of his fellow forwards. Numerous
Celtic goals have resulted from such hard graft.

Henrik's arrival at Celtic in the summer of 1997 did not raise huge expectations.
Larsson had not been a noted goalscorer at Feyenoord but Wim Jansen insisted that the
Swede had to be his first major signing for Celtic. A clause in Larsson's contract with
Feyenoord stipulated that he could leave if any club offered a £650,000 transfer fee for
him and he made a typically low-key bow on the pitch in front of the Celtic support at a
pre-season friendly prior to the 1997-98 season.

It soon became clear that Celtic now possessed a prize talent. Larsson could score all
sorts of goals: long-range free-kicks, thudding, accurate headers, acutely angled drives,
precise chips from distance. He was Celtic's leading scorer that 1997-98 season and his
work did much to prod Celtic in the direction of the championship. He became even
better in the 1998-99 season, with 38 goals in all competitions, so when he suffered a
horrific leg break against Olympique Lyon in autumn 1999 it was an equally severe blow
for player and club. Doubts were thrown up about Henrik's chances of making a complete
recovery from such a dreadful injury but he was back, better than ever, in the 2000-01
season, which he ended with 53 goals in all competitions. His reward was the Golden
Shoe for being Europe's top league goalscorer, the first Celt to win that award. 'Henrik is a
tremendous striker who scores incredible goals from nothing,' says Chris Sutton.

Another outstanding season in 2001-02 saw Henrik again become top scorer at the
club and in the summer of 2002 he became the highest-scoring Celt at a World Cup
finals, with three goals in Sweden's run to the second round. His consistent excellence
had by then made him the highest-paid player ever at the club, and there are few that
begrudge him his well earned rewards.

Delle Alpi. A battling performance from them had seen the score pegged at 2-2 as the game entered its closing stages. Then, as Joos Valgaeren and Nicola Amoruso tussled for a ball that was going across them inside the penalty area, Valgaeren somewhat naïvely allowed his hands to make light contact with the Italian's upper body. Seizing his chance, Amoruso tumbled to the turf, the referee awarded the penalty and Amoruso scored with it to give Juventus a 3-2 victory.

Solid victories over Porto and Rosenborg at home were undone by emphatic defeats from the same sides in Portugal and Norway. It left everything hinging on the final group match, against Juventus, and although a memorable evening ended with an entertaining Celtic victory, the 4-3 triumph at Celtic Park left the team just one point short of qualification for the second phase.

Instead, as the third-placed team in their group, Celtic went into the UEFA Cup. Once again they faced a tough draw, against Valencia, European Champions League finalists the previous season. The away leg ended 1-0 to the Spanish side, thanks, once again, to some exceptional goalkeeping from Douglas, and a cleverly-placed shot from Larsson gave Celtic a 1-0 victory in the return. The score remained 1-1 on aggregate after extra-time so the match went to a penalty shootout. Celtic, rarely successful in shootout situations, came off worst, but as the players trooped off the pitch they were applauded wildly by a Celtic support. After so many seasons in which the anticipation of European competition had resulted only in deflation for the club and its followers, they made it clear that they appreciated the huge strides their team had made in Europe.

'All we needed was one more point away from home and we would have been through,' said Paul Lambert as he looked back on the Champions League campaign. 'It was tough to take because teams from other groups made it to the next stage with fewer points than us and I don't think we really did an awful lot wrong.'

The team suffered a slight dip in form around Christmas 2001 but in the new year, O'Neill told his players it was 'heads down until the end of the season'. They responded with a second successive record Premier League points total – 103 – which was 18 better than that of second-placed Rangers. The defence had conceded just 18 League goals, the lowest total since the 1916-17 season. All those connected with Celtic could now realistically hope they were at the beginning of another of the club's great eras. The 2002-03 season was awaited with relish as the club now had prospects for a future that could match its glorious history.

THE ESSENTIAL HISTORY OF
CELTIC

CLUB STATISTICS

The Celtic Directory

Club Information

- Address: Celtic Park,
  95 Kerrydale Street,
  Glasgow,
  G40 3RE
- Chief Executive: Ian McLeod
- Directors (plc): Eric Riley, Brian Quinn,
  Dermot Desmond, Sir Patrick Sheehy,
  Kevin Sweeney, Tom Allison
- CFAC Directors: Eric Riley, Kevin Sweeney,
  John Keane, Michael McDonald, Jim Hone
- Manager: Martin O'Neill
- Assistant Manager: John Robertson
- Official Supporters Club: Celtic Supporters
  Association, 1524 London Road, Glasgow,
  G40 3RJ
- Celtic Superstore: 0141 554 4231
- Mail Order Hotline: 0141 550 1888
- General Ticket Office: 0141 551 8653
- Facsimile: 0141-551-8106
- Clubcall: 0891 196721
- Credit Card Hotline: 0141 551 8653/8654
- Website: www.celticfc.co.uk
- Ground capacity: 60,832
- Pitch measurements: 110m x 68m
- Year formed: 1888
- Turned professional: 1893
- Club nicknames: The Celts, The Bhoys
- Colours: Emerald green and white hooped
  jerseys, white shorts with emerald green trims,
  and white socks
- Change colours: Gold jerseys with green trims,
  green shorts and gold socks
- Home Shirt Sponsors: NTL
- Away Shirt Sponsors: NTL Home Broadband
- Kit Manufacturers: Umbro

Honours

- Scottish First Division Champions: 1892-93,
  1893-94, 1895-96, 1897-98, 1904-05,
  1905-06, 1906-07, 1907-08, 1908-09,
  1909-10, 1913-14, 1914-15, 1915-16,
  1916-17, 1918-19, 1921-22, 1925-26,
  1935-36, 1937-38, 1953-54, 1965-66,
  1966-67, 1967-68, 1968-69, 1969-70,
  1970-71, 1971-72, 1972-73, 1973-74
- Scottish Premier League Champions: 1976-
  77, 1978-79, 1980-81, 1981-82, 1985-86,
  1987-88, 1997-98, 2000-01, 2001-02
- Scottish Cup winners: 1892, 1899, 1900,
  1904, 1907, 1908, 1911, 1912, 1914,
  1923, 1925, 1927, 1931, 1933, 1937,
  1951, 1954, 1965, 1967, 1969, 1971,
  1972, 1974, 1975, 1977, 1980, 1985,
  1988, 1989, 1995, 2001
- Scottish League Cup winners: 1956-57,
  1957-58, 1965-66, 1966-67, 1967-68,
  1968-69, 1969-70, 1974-75, 1982-83,
  1997-98, 1999-00, 2000-01
- European Cup Winners: 1966-67
- European Cup runners-up: 1969-70
- European Cup semi-finalists: 1971-72, 1973-74
- European Cup quarter-finalists: 1968-69,
  1970-71, 1979-80
- Empire Exhibition Cup winners: 1938
- Coronation Cup winners: 1953
- Glasgow Cup winners: 1890-91, 1891-92,
  1894-95, 1895-96, 1904-05, 1905-06,
  1906-07, 1907-08, 1909-10, 1915-16,
  1919-20, 1920-21, 1926-27, 1927-28,
  1928-29, 1930-31, 1938-39, 1940-41,
  1948-49, 1955-56, 1961-62, 1963-64,
  1964-65, 1966-67, 1967-68, 1969-70,

1974-75 (Celtic were joint winners along with Rangers).

Since 1981-82 the competition has usually involved reserve team players

- Charity Cup winners: 1891-92, 1893-94, 1894-95, 1895-96, 1898-99, 1902-03, 1904-05, 1907-08, 1911-12, 1912-13, 1913-14, 1914-15, 1915-16, 1916-17, 1917-18, 1919-20, 1920-21, 1923-24, 1925-26, 1935-36, 1936-37, 1937-38, 1942-43, 1949-50, 1952-53, 1958-59, 1959-60, 1960-61 (Celtic were joint winners along with Clyde in the final year of the trophy)
- St Mungo Cup winners: 1951
- Glasgow Exhibition Cup winners: 1902
- Scottish League Commemorative Shield winners: 1904-05 1909-10
- Victory in Europe Cup winners: 1945

Celtic's finest achievement. The Lisbon Lions parade the European Cup at Celtic Park in 1967.

Records

- Highest attendance: 82,500 v Rangers, 1 January 1938, Scottish League Division 1
- Record league victory 11-0, v Dundee, 26 October 1895, Scottish League Division 1
- Record league defeat 0-8, v Motherwell, 30 April 1937, Division 1
- In 1967 Celtic won every competition they entered: the European Cup, Scottish League, Scottish Cup and Scottish League Cup
- Most league goals in a season: Jimmy McGrory, 50 goals, Division 1, 1935-36
- Most league appearances: Alec McNair, 548 games
- Most capped player: Paddy Bonner, Republic of Ireland, 80 caps
- Record transfer fee paid: £6,000,000 for Chris Sutton from Chelsea, 2000
- Record transfer fee received: £4,700,000 for Paolo Di Canio to Sheffield Wednesday, August 1997

50 Greatest Players

This list consists of the 50 players who, in the author's opinion, have made the greatest all round contributions to Celtic's history through their skill, consistency and commitment to the teams in which they played and the all-round entertainment they provided for the Celtic support. The majority of the 50 players below would be sure to figure somewhere on everybody's list of all-time Celtic greats.

No. 1 Billy McNeill (Centre half) 790 appearances, 35 goals. Captain of the Lisbon Lions and of the 'nine-in-a-row' side, McNeill was the eyes and ears of Jock Stein on the field. An inspirational figure, and a highly successful Celtic manager (see page 117).

No. 2 Jimmy McGrory (Centre forward) 445 appearances, 468 goals. The greatest goalscorer in Celtic's history with, uniquely, more goals than games played. A dedicated servant of the club as a player in the 1920s and 1930s (see page 48).

No. 3 Henrik Larsson (Centre forward) 206 appearances, 157 goals. Goalscorer of extraordinary consistency whose unselfish play and routine brilliance fired Celtic from the late 1990s onwards and who was indispensable in helping the team to win six trophies (see page 181).

No. 4 Kenny Dalglish (Forward) 320 appearances, 167 goals. Marvellously inventive player who captained the 1977 double-winning team and is Scotland's record cap-holder and goalscorer (see page 123).

No. 5 Bobby Lennox (Forward) 589 appearances, 273 goals. Sizzling speed and lighting-quick reactions made him the club's highest post-war scorer. He clocked up over three decades of quality service at Celtic Park (see page 129).

No. 6 Jimmy Johnstone (Outside right) 515 appearances, 130 goals. Outrageously talented winger whose exceptional flair, magical ball control and ability to produce the unexpected made him a world-class star and an essential element in all Celtic's great triumphs of the 1960s (see page 120).

No. 7 Jimmy Quinn (Forward) 331 appearances, 217 goals. A winger converted into a magnificent, bustling centre forward who became the focal point of the team that won six league titles in a row (see page 24).

No. 8 Bobby Murdoch (Midfielder) 484 appearances, 102 goals. Precision passing, powerful shooting and fearsome tackling made Murdoch the kingpin in the 1960s and early 1970s Celtic midfield (see page 111).

No. 9 Patsy Gallacher (Forward) 464 appearances, 192 goals. A ball-juggling maker and taker of goals. Brimming with self-confidence he brightened the dark days of World War 1 and beyond (see page 35).

No. 10 Tommy Gemmell (Full back) 418 appearances, 63 goals. Master overlapper who performed to perfection the role of attacking full back. His thunderous shots lit up many European nights and saw him score in two European Cup finals (see page 106).

No. 11 Danny McGrain (Full back) 663 appearances, 7 goals. Brought an entirely new dimension to full back play with his adventurous forays up the flank. A great team player who used his outstanding individual skills to the benefit of everyone (see page 140).

No. 12 Paul McStay (Midfielder) 677 appearances, 72 goals. Prize player whose subtle touches and outstanding vision helped him keep the team ticking over smoothly (see page 166).

No. 13 Jimmy Delaney (Forward) 160 appearances, 74 goals. A hugely popular individual, a genuine gentleman and one of the stand-outs in the high-grade team that captured two championships and the Cup in style (see page 51).

No. 14 Bertie Auld (Midfielder) 275 appearances, 79 goals. Crafty passer whose ability to thread the ball through defences to his fast-moving forwards made him vital to Celtic's 1960s successes (see page 99).

No. 15 Steve Chalmers (Forward) 406 appearances, 219 goals. Scored the winner in the European Cup final. A pacey predator with a tendency to put the ball in the net with consummate style (see page 108).

No. 16 Jimmy McMenemy (Forward) 515 appearances, 168 goals. Highly skilled inside forward and an indispensable part of the early 20th-century Celtic, with whom he won 11 championships (see page 30).

No. 17 Bobby Evans (Half back) 535 appearances, 10 goals. Devoted club servant whose composure and class in midfield did much to hold the club together during the difficult 1940s and 1950s (see page 71).

No. 18 Lubomir Moravcik (Midfielder) 129 appearances, 35 goals. Superlative skills and creative vision made Lubo a huge crowd favourite and a vital ingredient in Martin O'Neill's initial successes (see page 176).

No. 19 Ronnie Simpson (Goalkeeper) 188 appearances. European Cup winner with a marvellously reliable pair of hands. He made spectacular and simple saves with equal ease (see page 93).

No. 20 Willie Wallace (Forward) 232 appearances, 134 goals. Pacy inside forward whose sharp scoring and neat touches made him an indispensable part of the great 60s Celtic teams (see page 96).

No. 21 Sandy McMahon (Forward) 217 appearances, 177 goals. Gangly attacker who scored twice in Celtic's first Scottish Cup win and helped Celtic to their first four league titles (see page 12).

No. 22 Jimmy McColl (Centre forward) 169 appearances, 123 goals. Clever goalscorer who netted with exceptional consistency as the centre forward in four championship-winning sides (see page 26).

No. 23 Alec McNair (Full back) 604 appearances, 9 goals. Composed defender whose presence steadied Celtic and who won 12 championship titles with the club in a career lasting over 21 years. (see page 33).

No. 24 David Hay (Full back/Midfielder) 193 appearances, 12 goals. Combative character with the priceless ability to tackle hard and then use the ball with extreme efficiency (see page 119).

No. 25 Murdo MacLeod (Midfielder) 395 appearances, 82 goals. A force in Celtic's midfield for a near-decade. Great fitness and drive were complemented by powerful shooting (see page 149).

No. 26 Jim Young (Midfielder) 443 appearances, 14 goals. Inspirational captain who won ten titles and five Scottish Cups in a 14-year Celtic career (see page 28).

No. 27 Roy Aitken (Central defender/Midfielder) 672 appearances, 53 goals. Tough, determined player who helped drive Celtic to six league titles and the centenary double (see page 157).

No. 28 Johnny Crum (Forward) 211 appearances, 87 goals. A nimble scorer whose elusive style helped win two championships and a Scottish Cup (see page 52).

No. 29 Bobby Collins (Forward) 320 appearances, 117 goals. Multi-talented team player whose driving play was one of the outstanding features of the 1950s Celtic side. A dynamic provider of goals and a frequent scorer with an explosive shot (see page 66).

No. 30 Paul Lambert (Midfielder) 197 appearances, 10 goals. O'Neill's Captain Calm. A steady influence in the Celtic sides that won three league titles. Protects possession and spreads passes with rare assurance (see page 177).

No. 31 Charlie Tully (Forward) 319 appearances, 43 goals. Audacious entertainer who brightened Celtic's 1950s and who played a key role in the 7-1 League Cup final victory over Rangers in 1957 (see page 64).

No. 32 Johan Mjallby (Centre back/Midfielder) 156 appearances, 12 goals. Classic consistency, rugged tackling and power in the air ensure that Johan holds together Martin O'Neill's back three (see page 172).

No. 33 George Connelly (Centre back/Midfielder) 254 appearances, 13 goals. Superb reader of the game who left football far too early (see page 122).

No. 34 Dan Doyle (Full back) 123 appearances, 5 goals. A powerful defender who was strong in the tackle and an accurate long-range passer (see page 15).

No. 35 Tommy Burns (Midfielder) 508 appearances, 82 goals. Hard work and imagination made him a dynamic player and a popular manager (see page 159).

No. 36 John Hughes (Forward) 383 appearances, 188 goals. Powerful, versatile player and scorer of spectacular and often important goals (see page 103).

No. 37 Joe McBride (Centre forward) 93 appearances, 86 goals. Scotland's top striker in his first two seasons at Celtic before injury ended his career (see page 84).

No. 38 Johnny Campbell (Forward) 215 appearances, 113 goals. Preferring brains to brawn, he helped Celtic win three Scottish Cups and three titles (see page 17).

No. 39 Dixie Deans (Centre forward) 184 appearances, 124 goals. Consistent goalscorer who hit hat-tricks in Scottish Cup and League Cup finals (see page 115).

No. 40 John Thomson (Goalkeeper) 188 appearances. Had exceptional handling skills and showed great bravery which led to an untimely death (see page 43).

No. 41 Stilian Petrov (Midfielder) 111 appearances, 16 goals. Determination and drive, allied to neat touches, made Petrov a key attacking midfielder in the teams that won the League in 2001 and 2002 (see page 173).

No. 42 Frank McAvennie (Centre forward) 106 appearances, 50 goals. A fans' favourite who possessed a silky smooth touch in front of goal and who created numerous openings for team-mates (see page 154).

No. 43 Brian McClair (Forward) 142 appearances, 121 goals. Intelligent attacker who was the leading scorer in each of his four seasons with the club (see page 148).

No. 44 Billy Stark (Midfielder) 84 appearances, 25 goals. A quality player whose subtle touches provided a wonderful extra ingredient (see page 160).

No. 45 Charlie Nicholas (Forward) 249 appearances, 125 goals. Skillful, nippy goalscorer who put the ball in the net with aplomb (see page 136).

No. 46 John Collins (Midfielder) 273 appearances, 54 goals. Clever reader of the game and prompter of play who set consistently high standards (see page 165).

No. 47 Willie Miller (Goalkeeper) 123 appearances. Agile athlete whose bravery and fine positioning skills were a valuable asset for Celtic (see page 59).

No. 48 Pat Bonner (Goalkeeper) 641 appearances. Excellent shot-stopper who became the most-capped of all Celts (see page 163).

No. 49 Frank McGarvey (Forward) 245 appearances, 109 goals. Elusive goalscorer and tireless worker who scored and set up numerous goals in the early 1980s (see page 142).

No. 50 Davie Provan (Outside right) 303 appearances, 41 goals. Winger, whose spurts of acceleration injected much-needed pace (see page 143).

Results and Tables 1888-2002

The following pages include details of every official match played by Celtic. Apart from the years 1888-90 when the club only played in the Scottish Cup, each league season has its own page and is dated at the top. League matches appear first, followed by individual cup competitions. The opponents played at home are written in capital letters and appear in upper and lower case for away games. The date of the match, the score, Celtic goalscorers and the match attendance are also included. In the early years of Scottish football, accurate records were not always kept and some details may be missing. Full League and Cup appearances and the goalscorers are featured separately. The final league table is included at the bottom of each page as well as a Fact File which notes particularly interesting facts and figures for the season as well as any notable transfers etc.

The results of matches played during the years 1940-45 are not included. During these wartime years the official league programme was suspended. There was a huge amount of football played during these years, but teams were greatly disrupted. For these reasons, wartime football statistics are not regarded as 'official'.

The skills of Jimmy Johnstone on display against Argentina's Racing Club in Montevideo in the 1967 World Club Championship play-off.

Season 1888-89

Scottish Cup

DATE	OPPONENTS	SCORE	GOALSCORERS	ATTENDANCE
Sep 1	SHETTLESTON	(Rd1) W 5-1	scorers unknown	-
Sep 22	COWLAIRS	(Rd2) W 8-0	Dunbar 3, McCallum 2, Groves, Maley T, Kelly	8,000
Oct 13	ALBION ROVERS	(Rd3) W 4-1	Dunbar, Maley T, Groves, Gallacher	600
Nov 3	St Bernard's	(Rd4) W 4-1	Groves 2, McCallum, Maley T	6,000
Dec 8	CLYDE	(Rd5) W 9-2	Groves 4, Maley T 3, McLarne, McCallum	8,000
Dec 15	East Stirling	(QF) W 2-1	McCallum 2	3,000
Jan 12	Dumbarton	(SF) W 4-1	Groves 2, Dunbar 2	5,000
Feb 9	THIRD LANARK	(F) L 1-2	McCallum	13,000

CAPTAIN: James Kelly

TOP SCORER: Willie Groves

BIGGEST WIN: 8-0 v Cowlairs, 22 September 1888, Scottish Cup

HIGHEST ATTENDANCE: 13,000 v Third Lanark, 9 February 1889, Scottish Cup

MAJOR TRANSFERS IN: James Kelly from Renton, Johnny Madden from Grimsby, Jimmy McLaren from Hibernian, Willie Groves from Hibernian

---

Cup Appearances

PLAYER	CUP COMPETITION	TOTAL
	S CUP	
Coleman Jas	1	1
Coleman Jn	8	8
Collins	2	2
Dunbar M	8	8
Dunbar T	1	1
Dunning	6	6
Gallacher	8	8
Groves	8	8
Kelly Jas	8	8
Kelly John	1	1
McCallum	8	8
McKeown	8	8
McLaren	7	7
McLaughlan	1	1
Maley T	7	7
Maley W	4	4
O'Connor	1	1

Goalscorers

PLAYER	CUP COMPETITION	TOTAL
	S CUP	
Groves	10	10
Dunbar	6	6
McCallum	6	6
Maley T	6	6
McLaren	2	2
Gallacher	1	1
Kelly	1	1

Season 1889-90

Scottish Cup

DATE	OPPONENTS	SCORE	GOALSCORERS	ATTENDANCE
Sep 7	QUEEN'S PARK	(Rd1) D 0-0		26,000
Sep 14	Queen's Park	(R) L 1-2	Groves	-

CAPTAIN: James Kelly

TOP SCORER: Willie Groves

Cup Appearances

PLAYER	CUP COMPETITION	TOTAL
	S CUP	
Coleman	2	2
Dowds	2	2
Dunbar	2	2
Gallagher	2	2
Groves	2	2
Kelly	2	2
McKeown	2	2
McLaren	1	1
McLaughlin	2	2
Madden	2	2
Maley	1	1
Reynolds	2	2

Goalscorers

PLAYER	CUP COMPETITION	TOTAL
	S CUP	
Groves	1	1

Season 1890-91

Scottish Football League

DATE	OPPONENTS	SCORE	GOALSCORERS	ATTENDANCE
Aug 23	Hearts	W 5-0	Madden 2, Groves 2, Dowds	8,000
Aug 30	CAMBUSLANG	W 5-2	Dowds 3, Crossan 2	-
Sep 13	Third Lanark	L 1-2	Dowds	10,000
Oct 25	Abercorn	W 5-1	Dowds 4, Gallagher	5,000
Jan 24	Vale of Leven	L 1-3	Campbell	-
Feb 7	ST MIRREN	W 3-2	Boyle, Dowds, Campbell	3,000
Feb 21	Dumbarton	D 2-2	Dunbar M, unrecorded	-
Feb 28	HEARTS	W 1-0	Campbell	8,000
Mar 7	Cambuslang	L 1-3	Madden	-
Mar 14	COWLAIRS	W 2-0	Dowds 2	6,000
Mar 21	RANGERS	D 2-2	Dowds, Campbell	-
Apr 4	St Mirren	L 0-1		-
Apr 11	DUMBARTON	W 1-0	McMahon	10,000
Apr 25	THIRD LANARK	D 1-1	Unrecorded	-
Apr 29	Cowlairs	W 5-0	Dunbar M 2, rest unrecorded	2,500
May 2	Rangers	W 2-1	Madden, Dowds	10,000
May 5	VALE OF LEVEN	W 9-1	McMahon 3, McGhee 3, Campbell, Dowds	2,000
May 12	ABERCORN	W 2-0	McGhee, McMahon	3,000

Scottish Cup

DATE	OPPONENTS		SCORE	GOALSCORERS	ATTENDANCE
Sep 6	RANGERS	(Rd1)	W 1-0	Groves	16,000
Sep 27	CARFIN SHAMROCK	(Rd2)	D 2-2	Madden 2	-
Oct 4	Carfin Shamrock	(R)	W 3-1	Dowds, Crossan, Groves	5,000
Oct 18	Wishaw Thistle	(Rd3)	W 6-2	Madden 2, Dowds, Campbell, rest unrecorded	-
Nov 8	Our Boys (Dundee)	(Rd4)	W 3-1	Crossan 2, Campbell	4,000
Dec 13	Royal Albert	(S)	W 2-0	Campbell, Crossan	5,000
Dec 20	Dumbarton	(QF)	L 0-3		-

League & Cup Appearances

PLAYER	LEAGUE	CUP COMPETITION S CUP	TOTAL
Bell	15	7	22
Boyle	7		7
Campbell	15	4	19
Coleman	1	1	2
Crossan	3	6	9
Cunningham	1		1
Dolan F		2	2
Dolan M	3		3
Dowds	18	6	24
Dunbar M	12	7	19
Dunbar T	4	1	5
Gallagher H	1		1
Gallagher P	14	5	19
Groves	3	4	7
Kelly	12	5	17
Kyle	1		1
McCallum		2	2
McGhee	9		9
McKeown	14	6	20
McLaren	3	5	8
McMahon	10		10
McPherson		1	1
Madden	16	7	23
Maley T	1		1
Maley W	15	4	19
Reynolds	17	6	23

Goalscorers

PLAYER	LEAGUE	CUP COMPETITION S CUP	TOTAL
Dowds	15	2	17
Madden	4	4	8
Campbell	5	3	8
Crossan	2	5	6
McMahon	6		6
Groves	2	2	4
McGhee	4		4
Dunbar	3		3
Gallagher	1		1

6 league goals unrecorded
2 Scottish Cup goals unrecorded

Fact File

The first Old Firm Scottish Cup match took place in September. The gates were locked with 6,000 supporters still outside.

CAPTAIN: James Kelly

TOP SCORER: Peter Dowds

BIGGEST WIN: 9-1 v Vale of Leven, 5 May 1891, league

HIGHEST ATTENDANCE: 16,000 v Rangers, 6 September 1890, Scottish Cup

MAJOR TRANSFERS IN: Jimmy McGhee from Hibernian, Sandy McMahon from Hibernian

Final Scottish League Table

	P	W	D	L	F	A	Pts
1= DUMBARTON	18	13	3	2	61	21	29
1= RANGERS	18	13	3	2	58	25	29
3 CELTIC	18	11	3	4	48	21	21
4 CAMBUSLANG	18	8	4	6	47	42	20
5 THIRD LANARK	18	8	3	7	38	39	15
6 HEARTS	18	6	2	10	31	37	14
7 ABERCORN	18	5	2	11	36	47	12
8 ST MIRREN	18	5	1	12	39	62	11
8 VALE OF LEVEN	18	5	1	12	27	65	11
10 COWLAIRS	18	3	4	11	24	50	6

DUMBARTON AND RANGERS DECLARED JOINT CHAMPIONS AFTER A 2-2 PLAY-OFF DRAW.
CELTIC, THIRD LANARK AND COWLAIRS FOUR POINTS DEDUCTED FOR RULE INFRINGEMENT.

Season 1891-92

Scottish Football League

DATE	OPPONENTS	SCORE	GOALSCORERS	ATTENDANCE
Aug 15	Hearts	L 1-3	McGhee	-
Aug 22	RANGERS	W 3-0	Madden, Campbell, McMahon	-
Aug 29	Clyde	W 7-2	McMahon 5, McCallum, Brady	-
Sep 5	RENTON	W 3-0	Campbell 3	-
Sep 12	Abercorn	W 5-2	McCallum 2, McMahon 2, Madden	-
Sep 26	DUMBARTON	W 2-0	McMahon, Campbell	-
Oct 3	St Mirren	W 2-1	McCallum 2	-
Oct 17	HEARTS	W 3-1	McMahon 2, Madden	-
Oct 24	VALE OF LEVEN	W 6-1	Madden 4, Brady, McMahon	-
Dec 26	ST MIRREN	W 2-1	Brady, Campbell	-
Jan 30	Cambuslang	W 4-0	Brady, Coleman, McMahon, Campbell	-
Feb 27	THIRD LANARK	W 5-1	Campbell 2, McMahon 2, Coleman	-
Mar 19	CLYDE	D 0-0		-
Apr 2	Vale of Leven	D 2-2	McCallum 2	-
Apr 16	CAMBUSLANG	W 3-1	McCallum, Dowds, Campbell	-
Apr 18	Leith Athletic	L 1-2	McMahon	-
Apr 23	Dumbarton	L 0-1		-
Apr 30	ABERCORN	W 3-1	McCallum, Campbell, McMahon	-
May 5	Renton	W 4-0	McCallum 2, McMahon 2	-
May 7	Rangers	D 1-1	Campbell	-
May 14	LEITH ATHLETIC	W 2-0	McCallum, Foran	-
May 24	Third Lanark	W 3-1	Campbell 2, McMahon	-

Scottish Cup

Nov 28	St Mirren	(Rd1) W 4-2	Maley W, Madden, McMahon o.g.	-
Dec 19	KILMARNOCK ATHLETIC	(Rd2) W 3-0	Brady 2, Dowds	-
Jan 23	COWLAIRS	(Rd3) W 4-1	Brady 2, Madden, McMahon	-
Feb 6	RANGERS	(SF) W 5-3	Brady 2, McCallum, Cunningham, McMahon	-
Apr 9	Queen's Park	(F) W 5-1	Campbell 2, McMahon 2 o.g.	-

League & Cup Appearances

PLAYER	LEAGUE	CUP COMPETITION S CUP	TOTAL
Boyle	2		2
Brady	19	5	24
Campbell	21	5	26
Cassidy	1		1
Clifford	2		2
Coleman	1		1
Cullen	12	3	15
Cunningham	6	1	7
Dolan	1		1
Dowds	15	5	20
Doyle	21	5	26
Duff	8	1	9
Flannigan	2		2
Foran	1		1
Gallagher	11		11
Kelly C	2		2
Kelly Jas	20	5	25
McCallum N	20	5	25
McCallum W	1		1
McGhee	1		1
McLaughlan	1		1
McMahon	19	5	24
Madden	12	4	16
Maley T	1		1
Maley W	15	5	20
O'Connor	1		1
Reynolds	22	5	27

Goalscorers

PLAYER	LEAGUE	CUP COMPETITION S CUP	TOTAL
McMahon	20	5	25
Campbell	14	2	16
McCallum	12	1	13
Brady	4	6	10
Madden	7	2	9
Coleman	2		2
Dowds	1	1	2
Cunningham		1	1
Foran	1		1
Opps' o.gs.		2	2

Fact File

Celtic win their first trophy – the Scottish Cup. The two final teams celebrate together in a Glasgow hotel.

CAPTAIN: James Kelly

TOP SCORER: Sandy McMahon

BIGGEST WIN: 7-2 v Clyde, 29 August 1891, league

MAJOR TRANSFERS IN: Jimmy Blessington from Leith Athletic, Alec Brady from Everton, Dan Doyle from Everton, Neil McCallum from Blackburn

MAJOR TRANSFERS OUT: Mick McKeown to Blackburn

Final Scottish League Table

		P	W	D	L	F	A	Pts
1	DUMBARTON	22	18	1	3	78	27	37
2	CELTIC	22	16	3	3	62	21	35
3	HEARTS	22	15	4	3	65	35	34
4	LEITH ATH.	22	12	1	9	51	40	25
5	RANGERS	22	11	2	9	59	46	24
6	THIRD LANARK	22	8	5	9	44	47	21
6	RENTON	22	8	5	9	37	43	21
8	CLYDE	22	8	4	10	63	61	20
9	ABERCORN	22	6	5	11	44	59	17
10	ST MIRREN	22	5	5	12	43	60	15
11	CAMBUSLANG	22	2	6	14	21	53	10
12	VALE OF LEVEN	22	0	5	17	24	99	5

Season 1892-93

Scottish Football League

DATE	OPPONENTS	SCORE	GOALSCORERS	ATTENDANCE
Aug 20	RENTON	W 4-3	Campbell 2,	15,000
			rest unrecorded	-
Aug 27	Hearts	L 1-2	Gallagher A	
Sep 10	ABERCORN	W 3-2	Madden 2, Flannigan	3,000
Sep 24	Rangers	D 2-2	McMahon, Davidson	12,000
Oct 1	CLYDE	W 3-1	McMahon 2, Campbell	8,000
Oct 15	Dumbarton	W 3-0	Blessington, Dunbar M,	3,000
			Campbell	
Oct 22	St Mirren	W 3-1	Madden, Campbell,	-
			Blessington	
Nov 5	HEARTS	W 5-0	Campbell 2, Davidson,	10,000
			Mulvey, Madden	
Jan 28	Leith Athletic	W 1-0	McMahon	4,000
Feb 11	Abercorn	L 2-4	McMahon, Davidson	-
Mar 18	DUMBARTON	W 5-1	Davidson 2, Mulvey,	-
			Blessington, Kelly	
Mar 25	Renton	W 2-0	Mulvey 2	-
Apr 22	Third Lanark	W 6-0	McMahon 3, Blessington,	-
			Gibb, Campbell	
Apr 29	RANGERS	W 3-0	Kelly, Campbell, McMahon	14,000
May 2	ST MIRREN	W 4-1	Campbell 2, McMahon 2	-
May 6	Clyde	W 2-1	McMahon, Blessington	6,000
May 9	LEITH ATHLETIC	W 3-1	Davidson 2, Madden	5,000
May 18	THIRD LANARK	L 2-5	Kelly, unrecorded	-

Scottish Cup

Nov 26	LINTHOUSE	(Rd1) W 3-1	McMahon 2, Madden	-
Dec 17	5th K.R.V.	(Rd2) W 7-0	Madden 5, Blessington,	-
			Campbell	
Jan 2	THIRD LANARK	(Rd3) W 5-1	McMahon 3, Towie 2	8,000
Feb 4	ST BERNARD'S	(SF) W 5-0	Blessington 2, McMahon 2,	12,000
			Madden	
Mar 11	Queen's Park	(F) L 1-2	Blessington	13,239

League & Cup Appearances

PLAYER	LEAGUE	CUP COMPETITION S CUP	TOTAL
Blessington	15	5	20
Byrne	1		1
Campbell	17	5	22
Clifford	6		6
Coleman	1		1
Cullen	17	5	22
Curran	7		7
Davidson	13		13
Doyle	15	5	20
Dunbar M	3		3
Dunbar T	16	5	21
Fitzsimmons	1		1
Flannigan	2		2
Foran	1		1
Gallagher A	2		2
Gallagher P	5		5
Kelly	17	5	22
Lees	1		1
McArthur	1		1
McCann E	1		1
McCann J	2		2
McMahon	12	5	17
McLaughlan	1		1
Madden	14	5	19
Maley	9	5	14
Mulvey	4		4
Murray	2		2
Reynolds	11	5	16
Scott	1		1
Towie		5	5

Goalscorers

PLAYER	LEAGUE	CUP COMPETITION S CUP	TOTAL
McMahon	12	7	19
Campbell	11	1	12
Madden	5	7	12
Blessington	5	4	9
Davidson	7		7
Mulvey	4		4
Kelly	3		3
Towie		2	2
Dunbar M	1		1
Flannigan	1		1
Gallagher A	1		1
Gibb	1		1

3 league goals unrecorded

Fact File

Celtic clinched their first league title on 9 May 1893 by beating Leith Athletic.

CAPTAIN: James Kelly

TOP SCORER: Sandy McMahon

BIGGEST WIN: 7-0 v 5th Kirkcudbright Rifle Volunteers, 17 December 1892, Scottish Cup

HIGHEST ATTENDANCE: 15,000 v Renton, 20 August 1892, league

MAJOR TRANSFERS OUT: Alec Brady to Sheffield Wednesday, Neil McCallum to Nottingham Forest

Final Scottish League Table

		P	W	D	L	F	A	Pts
1	CELTIC	18	14	1	3	54	25	29
2	RANGERS	18	12	4	2	41	27	28
3	ST MIRREN	18	9	2	7	40	39	20
4	THIRD LANARK	18	9	1	8	53	39	19
5	HEARTS	18	8	2	8	39	41	18
6	LEITH ATH.	18	8	1	9	35	31	17
6	DUMBARTON	18	8	1	9	35	35	17
8	RENTON	18	5	5	8	31	44	15
9	ABERCORN	18	5	1	12	35	52	11
10	CLYDE	18	2	2	14	25	55	6

Season 1893-94

Scottish League Divison 1

DATE	OPPONENTS	SCORE	GOALSCORERS	ATTENDANCE
Aug 12	THIRD LANARK	W 5-0	McMahon 3, Campbell, Madden	8,000
Aug 19	Dundee	W 4-1	McMahon 2, Cassidy, o.g.	8,000
Aug 26	DUMBARTON	D 0-0		10,000
Sep 2	Rangers	L 0-5		13,000
Sep 9	Hearts	W 4-2	Campbell 2, Madden, o.g.	15,000
Sep 23	LEITH ATHLETIC	w 4-1	Cassidy 3, Madden	6,000
Sep 30	St Mirren	W 2-1	Blessington, Cassidy	7,000
Oct 14	ST BERNARD'S	W 5-2	McMahon 3, Cassidy, Madden	8,000
Nov 4	DUNDEE	W 3-1	Campbell 2, Madden	3,000
Nov 11	Renton	W 3-0	Blessington, McMahon, Davidson	-
Dec 2	RENTON	W 3-2	McMahon 3	3,000
Dec 23	Dumbarton	W 5-4	McMahon 2, Cassidy, Blessington, o.g.	-
Dec 30	Third Lanark	W 3-1	Divers, McMahon, Blessington	12,000
Jan 20	St Bernard's	W 2-1	Madden, Blessington	4,000
Feb 10	ST MIRREN	W 5-1	Divers 2, McMahon 2, Campbell	-
Feb 24	RANGERS	W 3-2	McMahon, Blessington, Madden	8,000
Mar 10	HEARTS	L 2-3	Divers, Doyle	7,000
Mar 17	Leith Athletic	L 0-5		-

Scottish Cup

DATE	OPPONENTS		SCORE	GOALSCORERS	ATTENDANCE
Nov 25	HURLFORD	(Rd1)	W 6-0	Campbell 2, Blessington 2 Cassidy, McMahon	2,000
Dec 16	ALBION ROVERS	(Rd2)	W 7-0	McMahon 4, Blessington Madden, Cassidy	1,500
Jan 13	ST BERNARD'S	(Rd3)	W 8-1	McMahon 4, Madden 2, rest unrecorded	-
Feb 3	Third Lanark	(SF)	W 5-3	McMahon 3, Blessington Cassidy	12,000
Feb 17	Rangers	(F)	L 1-3	Maley	17,000

League & Cup Appearances

PLAYER	LEAGUE	CUP COMPETITION S CUP	TOTAL
Blessington	18	5	23
Campbell	13	2	15
Cassidy	18	5	23
Cullen	18	5	23
Curran	13	5	18
Davidson	3		3
Divers	6	4	10
Doyle	12	5	17
Dunbar	8		8
Kelly	17	5	22
Mcdonald	1		1
McEleny	2	1	2
McGinn	2		2
McMahon	15	5	20
Madden	15	4	19
Maley	13	4	17
O'Byrne	13	4	17
Reynolds	18	5	23

Goalscorers

PLAYER	LEAGUE	CUP COMPETITION S CUP	TOTAL
McMahon	18	12	30
Blessington	6	4	10
Cassidy	7	3	10
Madden	7	3	10
Campbell	6	2	8
Divers	4		4
Davidson	1		1
Doyle	1		1
Maley		1	1
Opps' o.gs.	3		3

2 Scottish Cup goals unrecorded

Fact File

Willie Maley played under the pseudonym of 'Montgomery' in a number of games this season.

CAPTAIN: James Kelly
TOP SCORER: Sandy McMahon
BIGGEST WIN: 8-1 v St Bernard's, 13 January 1894, league
HIGHEST ATTENDANCE: 17,000 v Rangers, 17 February 1894, Scottish Cup
MAJOR TRANSFERS IN: John Divers from Hibernian

Final Scottish League Div 1 Table

		P	W	D	L	F	A	Pts
1	CELTIC	18	14	1	3	53	32	29
2	HEARTS	18	11	4	3	46	32	26
3	ST BERNARD'S	18	11	1	6	53	39	23
4	RANGERS	18	8	4	6	44	30	20
5	DUMBARTON	18	7	5	6	32	35	19
6	ST MIRREN	18	7	3	8	49	47	17
6	THIRD LANARK	18	7	3	8	38	44	17
8	DUNDEE	18	6	3	9	47	59	15
9	LEITH ATH.	18	4	2	12	36	46	10
10	RENTON	18	1	2	15	23	57	4

Season 1894-95

Scottish League Divison 1

DATE	OPPONENTS	SCORE	GOALSCORERS	ATTENDANCE
Aug 11	Dundee	L 1-1	Lees	8,000
Aug 18	ST BERNARD'S	W 5-2	Lees 2, Blessington 2, Cassidy	-
Aug 25	Third Lanark	L 1-2	Blessington	-
Sep 8	St Mirren	W 3-0	McMahon 2, Cassidy	8,000
Sep 22	RANGERS	W 5-3	Divers 2, Madden 2, Cassidy	16,000
Oct 18	Clyde	W 4-2	McMahon 2, Maley, Divers	4,000
Oct 20	DUMBARTON	W 6-0	Cassidy 2, Madden 2, Blessington, unrecorded	2,000
Nov 3	HEARTS	L 0-2		20,000
Nov 10	St Bernard's	W 2-0	McMahon, Cassidy	8,000
Dec 22	ST MIRREN	D 2-2	Blessington, Campbell	600
Feb 16	Hearts	L 0-4		8,000
Feb 23	THIRD LANARK	D 4-4	Campbell 2, McMahon, Madden	5,000
Mar 9	Dumbarton	W 2-0	McMahon, Madden	-
Mar 16	LEITH ATHLETIC	W 4-0	Ferguson W 2, Devlin, Madden	-
Mar 23	Rangers	D 1-1	McMahon	5,000
Mar 30	Leith Athletic	W 6-5	Davidson 2, Ferguson W, Madden, Divers, Ferguson J	-
Apr 27	CLYDE	W 2-0	Divers, Dunbar T	-
May 4	DUNDEE	W 2-1	McMahon, Divers	6,000

Scottish Cup

Nov 24	QUEEN'S PARK	(Rd1)	W 4-1	Campbell 2, Cassidy, Dunbar T	15,000
Dec 29	Hibernian	(Rd2)	W 2-0	Divers, Doyle	-
Jan 19	Dundee	(Rd3)	L 0-1		-

League & Cup Appearances

PLAYER	LEAGUE	CUP COMPETITION S CUP	TOTAL
Arnott	1		1
Blessington	12	3	15
Campbell	9	3	12
Cassidy	10	3	13
Cullen	3	1	4
Curran	1		1
Davidson	5		5
Devlin Jas	2		2
Devlin Jn	2		2
Divers	10		10
Dowds	3		3
Doyle	15	3	18
Dunbar	13	2	15
Ferguson J	1		1
Ferguson W	4		4
Jack	1		1
Kelly	12	3	15
Lees	3		3
McArthur	14	2	16
McCann	3		3
McDonald	2		2
McEleny	15	3	18
McElhaney	2		2
McMahon	11		11
Madden	14	3	17
Maley	14	2	16
Morrison	2		2
O'Brien	1		1
O'Rourke	3		3
Powers	1		1
Reynolds	6	2	8
Thom	1		1
Thomas	1		1
Thomson	1		1
Trodden	1		1

Goalscorers

PLAYER	LEAGUE	CUP COMPETITION S CUP	TOTAL
McMahon	9		9
Madden	8		8
Cassidy	6	1	7
Divers	6	1	7
Blessington	5		5
Campbell	3	2	5
Ferguson W	3		3
Lees	3		3
Davidson	2		2
Dunbar T	1	1	2
Devlin John	1		1
Doyle		1	1
Ferguson J	1		1
Maley	1		1

1 league goal unrecorded

Fact File

The stormy weather of 22 December 1894 cut the gate to 600 and full back Jerry Reynolds counted them in as they arrived.

CAPTAIN: James Kelly
TOP SCORER: Sandy McMahon
BIGGEST WIN: 6-0 v Dumbarton, 20 October 1894, league
HIGHEST ATTENDANCE: 20,000 v Hearts, 3 November 1894, league
MAJOR TRANSFERS IN: Peter Dowds from Stoke
MAJOR TRANSFERS OUT: Barney Battles to Hearts

Final Scottish League Div 1 Table

		P	W	D	L	F	A	Pts
1	HEARTS	18	15	1	2	50	18	31
2	CELTIC	18	11	4	3	50	29	26
3	RANGERS	18	10	2	6	41	26	22
4	THIRD LANARK	18	10	1	7	51	39	21
5	ST MIRREN	18	9	1	8	34	34	19
6	ST BERNARD'S	18	8	1	9	37	40	17
7	CLYDE	18	8	0	10	38	47	16
8	DUNDEE	18	6	2	10	28	33	14
9	LEITH ATH.	18	3	1	14	32	64	7
9	DUMBARTON	18	3	1	14	27	58	7

Scottish League Divison 1

DATE	OPPONENTS	SCORE	GOALSCORERS	ATTENDANCE
Aug 10	Dundee	W 2-1	Martin, McMahon	10,000
Aug 17	CLYDE	W 3-0	McMahon, Martin, Blessington	8,000
Aug 24	Hibernian	L 2-4	Battles, McMahon	10,000
Aug 31	ST MIRREN	W 4-0	Martin 3, Madden	5,000
Sep 7	Rangers	W 4-2	Dunbar 2, Ferguson, Crossan	16,000
Sep 14	HEARTS	L 0-5		15,000
Sep 16	St Bernard's	L 0-3		5,000
Sep 28	Dumbarton	W 3-1	Divers, Blessinton, McMahon	-
Oct 5	HIBERNIAN	W 3-1	McMahon, Doyle, Martin	20,000
Oct 12	Clyde	W 5-1	Martin 2, Blessington, McMahon, Madden	7,000
Oct 26	DUNDEE	W11-0	Blessinton 2, Ferguson, Doyle, Battles, Meechan, McMahon, rest unrecorded	10,000
Nov 9	THIRD LANARK	W 7-0	Martin 5, McMahon, Ferguson	3,000
Nov 23	Hearts	W 4-1	Martin 2, McMahon, Blessington	15,000
Nov 30	St Mirren	W 3-1	Blessington 2, Ferguson	5,000
Dec 7	ST BERNARD'S	W 2-1	McMahon, Martin	1,000
Dec 14	RANGERS	W 6-2	McMahon 2, Martin, Blessington, Battles, Morrison	20,000
Dec 21	DUMBARTON	W 3-0	Martin, McMahon, Doyle	1,000
Feb 29	Third Lanark	W 2-1	McMahon, Blessington	8,000

Scottish Cup

Jan 18	QUEEN'S PARK	(Rd1) L 2-4	Doyle, McMahon	28,000

League & Cup Appearances

PLAYER	LEAGUE	CUP COMPETITION S CUP	TOTAL
Battles	16		16
Blessington	16	1	17
Crossan	4		4
Cullen	1		1
Divers	6		6
Doyle	12	1	13
Dunbar	6		6
Ferguson	13	1	14
Kelly	16	1	17
King	8	1	9
McArthur	17	1	18
McEleny	3		3
McIlvenny	1		1
McMahon	15	1	16
McManus	1		1
Madden	13	1	14
Maley	7	1	8
Martin	17	1	18
Meechan	15		15
Morrison	5		5
O'Rourke	6		6

Goalscorers

PLAYER	LEAGUE	CUP COMPETITION S CUP	TOTAL
Martin	18		18
McMahon	14	1	15
Blessington	10		10
Ferguson	4		4
Doyle	3	1	4
Battles	3		3
Madden	2		2
Dunbar	2		2
Crossan	1		1
Divers	1		1
Meechan	1		1
Morrison	1		1

4 league goals unrecorded

Fact File

On 31 August 1895 in a match against St Mirren Johnny Madden was ordered off, then recalled and scored almost immediately.

CAPTAIN: James Kelly

TOP SCORER: Allan Martin

BIGGEST WIN: 11-0 v Dundee, 26 October 1895, league

HIGHEST ATTENDANCE: 28,000 v Queen's Park, 18 January 1896, Scottish Cup

MAJOR TRANSFERS IN: Allan Martin from Hibernian, Peter Meechan from Sunderland

MAJOR TRANSFERS OUT: Johnny Campbell to Aston Villa, Jerry Reynolds to Burnley

Final Scottish League Div 1 Table

		P	W	D	L	F	A	Pts
1	CELTIC	18	15	0	3	64	25	30
2	RANGERS	18	11	4	3	57	39	26
3	HIBERNIAN	18	11	2	5	58	39	24
4	HEARTS	18	11	0	7	68	36	22
5	DUNDEE	18	7	2	9	33	42	16
6	THIRD LANARK	18	7	1	10	47	51	15
6	ST BERNARD'S	18	7	1	10	36	53	15
8	ST MIRREN	18	5	3	10	31	51	13
9	CLYDE	18	4	3	11	39	59	11
10	DUMBARTON	18	4	0	14	36	74	8

Season 1896-97

Scottish League Divison 1

DATE	OPPONENTS	SCORE	GOALSCORERS	ATTENDANCE
Aug 5	Hibernian	L 1-3	Ferguson	12,000
Aug 17	Clyde	W 7-2	King, Doyle, rest unrecorded	3,000
Aug 22	ST BERNARD'S	W 2-0	McMahon, King	8,000
Aug 29	Abercorn	W 6-0	Morrison 2, King 2, McMahon 2	-
Sep 5	HEARTS	W 3-0	Divers 2, McMahon	25,000
Sep 12	St Bernard's	W 2-1	Divers, Blessington	8,000
Sep 26	ST MIRREN	W 2-1	McMahon 2	6,000
Oct 3	Dundee	D 2-2	Russell, McMahon	17,000
Oct 10	RANGERS	D 1-1	McMahon	24,000
Oct 17	THIRD LANARK	W 2-0	McEleny, Russell	10,000
Oct 24	Hearts	D 1-1	Blessington	15,000
Nov 7	ABERCORN	W 5-0	McMahon 2, King 2, Divers	1,000
Nov 28	HIBERNIAN	D 1-1	Gilhooly	15,000
Dec 5	Third Lanark	W 3-0	Ferguson, Gilhooly, Blessington	4,000
Dec 12	CLYDE	W 4-1	Ferguson 2, Groves, Blessington	-
Dec 19	Rangers	L 0-2		15,000
Feb 20	DUNDEE	L 0-1		10,000
Mar 13	St Mirren	L 0-2		-

Scottish Cup

Jan 9	Arthurlie	(Rd1) L 2-4	McIlvenny, Ferguson	-

League & Cup Appearances

PLAYER	LEAGUE	CUP COMPETITION S CUP	TOTAL
Battles	12		12
Blessington	16	1	17
Carlin	1		1
Connachan	1		1
Crossan	1	1	2
Cullen	7	1	8
Divers	7		7
Doyle	16		16
Dunbar	4		4
Farrell		1	1
Ferguson	8	1	9
Gilhooly	4		4
Groves	2		2
Henderson	3	1	4
Hutchison	2		2
Kelly	10	1	11
King A	17	1	18
King J		1	1
McArthur	11		11
McEleny	10		10
McIlvenny	1	1	2
McMahon	12		12
Madden	8		8
Maley	2		2
Meechan	10		10
Morrison	8	1	9
Neilsen	1		1
Orr	6		6
Russell	17		17
Slaven	1		1

Goalscorers

PLAYER	LEAGUE	CUP COMPETITION S CUP	TOTAL
McMahon	10		10
King A	6		6
Ferguson	4	1	5
Blessington	4		4
Divers	4		4
Gilhooly	2		2
Morrison	2		2
Russell	2		2
Doyle	1		1
Groves	1		1
McEleny	1		1
McIlvenny		1	1

5 league goals unrecorded

Fact File

Celtic's Scottish Cup giant-killing defeat by Arthurlie led to two players being released, one fined and the rest having their salaries reduced.

CAPTAIN: James Kelly

TOP SCORER: Sandy McMahon

BIGGEST WIN: 6-0 v Abercorn, 29 August 1896, league

HIGHEST ATTENDANCE: 25,000 v Hearts, 5 September 1896, league

MAJOR TRANSFERS IN: Willie Groves from Hibernian, Alec King from Hearts, Davie Russell from Hearts

MAJOR TRANSFERS OUT: Allan Martin to Hibernian, Peter Meechan to Everton

Final Scottish League Div 1 Table

		P	W	D	L	F	A	Pts
1	HEARTS	18	13	2	3	47	22	28
2	HIBERNIAN	18	12	2	4	50	20	26
3	RANGERS	18	11	3	4	64	30	25
4	CELTIC	18	10	4	4	42	18	24
5	DUNDEE	18	10	2	6	38	30	22
6	ST MIRREN	18	9	1	8	38	29	19
7	ST BERNARD'S	18	7	0	11	32	40	14
8	THIRD LANARK	18	5	1	12	29	46	11
9	CLYDE	18	4	0	14	27	65	8
10	ABERCORN	18	1	1	16	21	88	3

Season 1897-98

Scottish League Divison 1

DATE	OPPONENTS	SCORE	GOALSCORERS	ATTENDANCE
Sep 4	HIBERNIAN	W 4-1	Henderson 2, King, Russell	17,000
Sep 11	Hearts	D 0-0		
Sep 20	St Bernard's	W 2-0	Gilhooly, Campbell	3,000
Sep 25	CLYDE	W 6-1	McMahon 2, Allan 2, King, Russell	5,000
Sep 27	Rangers	W 4-0	McMahon, King, Campbell, Allan	31,000
Oct 2	St Mirren	D 0-0		12,000
Oct 9	Third Lanark	W 1-0	Allan	12,000
Oct 23	HEARTS	W 3-2	Campbell 2, Allan	17,000
Nov 6	Dundee	W 2-1	Henderson 2	11,000
Nov 27	Hibernian	W 2-1	Reynolds, McMahon	12,000
Dec 4	THIRD LANARK	W 4-0	Russell 2, Campbell, Somers	6,000
Dec 11	Partick Thistle	W 6-3	Somers 2, Allan 2, Russell, Campbell	-
Dec 18	ST BERNARD'S	W 5-1	Gilhooly 2, McMahon, Allan	8,000
Dec 25	Clyde	W 9-1	Allan 5, Russell 2, McMahon, Campbell	3,000
Jan 15	DUNDEE	W 2-1	Blessington, Russell (pen)	7,000
Jan 29	PARTICK THISTLE	W 3-1	Allan 2, Campbell	5,000
Feb 12	ST MIRREN	W 3-0	Gilhooly 2, Russell	4,000
Apr 11	RANGERS	D 0-0		16,000

Scottish Cup

Jan 8	Arthurlie	(Rd1) W 7-0	McMahon 2, Henderson 2, Allan, Goldie, Campbell	3,000
Jan 22	Third Lanark	(Rd2) L 2-3	King, Campbell	12,000

League & Cup Appearances

PLAYER	LEAGUE	CUP COMPETITION S CUP	TOTAL
Allan	17	2	19
Blessington	5	2	7
Campbell	18	2	20
Docherty	1		1
Gilhooly	15	1	16
Goldie	13	2	15
Henderson	9	1	10
King	16	2	18
Lynch	1		1
McArthur	17	2	19
McMahon	14	1	15
Orr J	1		1
Orr W	14	1	15
Reynolds	4		4
Russell	18	2	20
Somers	3		3
Welford	16	2	18

Goalscorers

PLAYER	LEAGUE	CUP COMPETITION S CUP	TOTAL
Allan	15	1	16
Campbell	8	2	10
McMahon	7	2	9
Russell	9		9
Henderson	4	2	6
Gilhooly	5		5
King	3	1	4
Somers	3		3
Blessington	1		1
Goldie		1	1
Reynolds	1		1

Fact File

Celtic scored 15 goals in their two league games against Clyde – George Allen scored 7 of them.

SECRETARY-MANAGER: Willie Maley

CAPTAIN: Dan Doyle

TOP SCORER: George Allan

BIGGEST WIN: 9-1 v Clyde, 25 December 1897, league

HIGHEST ATTENDANCE: 31,000 v Rangers, 27 September 1897, league

MAJOR TRANSFERS IN: George Allan from Liverpool, Johnny Campbell from Aston Villa, John Divers from Everton

MAJOR TRANSFERS OUT: George Allan to Liverpool

Final Scottish League Div 1 Table

		P	W	D	L	F	A	Pts
1	CELTIC	18	15	3	0	56	13	33
2	RANGERS	18	13	3	2	71	15	29
3	HIBERNIAN	18	10	2	6	47	29	22
4	HEARTS	18	8	4	6	54	33	20
5	THIRD LANARK	18	8	2	8	37	38	18
5	ST MIRREN	18	8	2	8	30	36	18
7	DUNDEE	18	5	3	10	29	36	13
7	PARTICK T	18	6	1	11	34	64	13
9	ST BERNARD'S	18	4	1	13	35	67	9
10	CLYDE	18	1	3	14	21	83	5

Season 1898-99

Scottish League Divison 1

DATE	OPPONENTS	SCORE	GOALSCORERS	ATTENDANCE
Aug 20	THIRD LANARK	W 2-1	McAuley, King (pen)	17,000
Aug 27	Clyde	D 0-0		13,000
Sep 3	ST MIRREN	W 4-1	Bell, McMahon, Hynds, Gilhooly	10,000
Sep 10	Hibernian	L 1-2	McMahon	12,000
Sep 19	Hearts	D 2-2	Bell, fisher	-
Sep 24	RANGERS	L 0-4		44,868
Sep 26	HIBERNIAN	L 1-2	McMahon	12,000
Oct 1	St Mirren	L 0-4		8,000
Oct 8	ST BERNARD'S	W 1-0	Campbell	12,000
Oct 29	St Bernard's	W 3-2	McMahon, Campbell, Hynds	-
Nov 5	CLYDE	W 9-2	McMahon 3, Battles 2, Bell, Fisher, Divers, o.g.	-
Nov 19	Dundee	W 4-1	Divers, Bell, Somers, fisher	3,000
Nov 26	PARTICK THISTLE	W 4-0	Divers 3, Bell	
Dec 3	Partick Thistle	W 8-3	McMahon 3, Somers 2, Divers, Orr, o.g.	2,000
Dec 17	HEARTS	W 3-2	Somers, Gilhooly, McMahon	6,000
Dec 31	Third Lanark	W 4-2	Divers 2, Bell, McMahon	4,000
Jan 2	Rangers	L 1-4	McMahon	30,000
Jan 7	DUNDEE	W 4-1	Bell 3, Divers	-

Scottish Cup

Jan 14	6th G.R.V.	(Rd1) W 8-1	McMahon 3, Hodge 2, Divers, Campbell, King	700
Feb 4	ST BERNARD'S	(Rd2) W 3-0	Hodge, Campbell, McMahon	4,000
Feb 25	QUEEN'S PARK	(Rd3) W 2-1	McMahon 2	35,000
Mar 11	PORT GLASGOW ATH.	(SF) W 4-2	Bell 2, McMahon, Divers	9,000
Apr 22	Rangers	(F) W 2-0	McMahon, Hodge	25,000

League & Cup Appearances

PLAYER	LEAGUE	CUP COMPETITION S CUP	TOTAL
Battles	8	4	12
Bell	17	5	22
Breslin	1		1
Campbell	11	5	16
Davidson	6	1	7
Divers	9	5	14
Docherty	3		3
Donlevy	1		1
Doyle	5		5
Fisher	10		10
Gilhooly	11		11
Goldie	12		12
Hodge		5	5
Hynds	11	1	12
King	12	3	15
Lynch	1		1
McArthur	15	5	20
McAuley	1		1
McMahon	17	5	22
Marshall		4	4
Moir	1		1
Moran	1		1
Orr	11	3	14
Ross	1		1
Somers	8		8
Stories	14	5	19
Welford	11	4	15

Goalscorers

PLAYER	LEAGUE	CUP COMPETITION S CUP	TOTAL
McMahon	13	8	21
Bell	9	2	11
Divers	9	2	11
Campbell	2	2	4
Hodge		4	4
Somers	4		4
Fisher	3		3
Battles	2		2
Gilhooly	2		2
Hynds	2		2
King	1	1	2
McAuley	1		1
Orr	1		1
Opps' o.gs.	2		2

Fact File

For the second season in a row Celtic put nine goals past Clyde in one match.

SECRETARY-MANAGER: Willie Maley

CAPTAIN: Dan Doyle

TOP SCORER: Sandy McMahon

BIGGEST WIN: 9-2 v Clyde, 5 November 1898, league

HIGHEST ATTENDANCE: 44,868 v Rangers, 24 September 1898, league

MAJOR TRANSFERS OUT: Jimmy Blessington to Preston, Davie Russell to Preston

Final Scottish League Div 1 Table

		P	W	D	L	F	A	PTS
1	RANGERS	18	18	0	0	79	18	36
2	HEARTS	18	12	2	4	56	30	26
3	CELTIC	18	11	2	5	51	33	24
4	HIBERNIAN	18	10	3	5	42	43	23
5	ST MIRREN	18	8	4	6	46	32	20
6	THIRD LANARK	18	7	3	8	33	38	17
7	ST BERNARD'S	18	4	4	10	30	37	12
7	CLYDE	18	4	4	10	23	48	12
9	PARTICK T	18	2	2	14	19	58	6
10	DUNDEE	18	1	2	15	23	65	4

Season 1899-1900

Scottish League Divison 1

DATE	OPPONENTS	SCORE	GOALSCORERS	ATTENDANCE
Aug 19	CLYDE	W 3-2	Marshall, McMahon, unrecorded	10,000
Aug 26	Kilmarnock	D 2-2	Divers, Marshall	12,000
Sep 2	THIRD LANARK	W 5-2	Gilhooly 2, Bell, Hodge, Campbell	10,000
Sep 9	HIBERNIAN	W 2-1	Hodge 2	15,000
Sep 18	Hibernian	D 1-1	Bell	12,000
Sep 23	Clyde	W 5-0	Campbell 2, King, Bell, Hodge	5,000
Sep 25	Third Lanark	W 3-0	Gilhooly 2, Campbell	10,000
Sep 30	HEARTS	L 0-2		10,000
Oct 7	Rangers	D 3-3	Campbell, McMahon, o.g.	40,000
Oct 21	St Mirren	D 2-2	Bell, Gilhooly	7,000
Oct 28	ST BERNARD'S	W 5-0	Hodge 2, Gilhooly 2, McMahon	3,000
Nov 4	Hearts	L 2-3	Gilhooly, McMahon	8,000
Nov 25	Dundee	W 2-1	Divers, o.g.	10,000
Dec 2	St Bernard's	D 1-1	McMahon	4,000
Dec 9	ST MIRREN	W 3-1	Bell 2, Campbell	-
Dec 16	KILMARNOCK	D 3-3	Campbell, Divers, Somers	-
Dec 23	DUNDEE	D 1-1	Divers	-
Jan 1	RANGERS	W 3-2	Bell, Divers 2	30,000

Scottish Cup

Jan 13	BO'NESS	(Rd1) W 7-1	McMahon 2, Somers 2, Orr, Bell, Divers	1,000
Jan 27	Port Glasgow	(Rd2) W 5-1	Campbell 2, Gilhooly 2, McMahon	5,000
Feb 17	Kilmarnock	(Rd3) W 4-0	McMahon, Bell, Gilhooly, Divers	6,000
Feb 24	Rangers	(SF) D 2-2	Campbell, Bell	33,000
Mar 10	RANGERS	(R) W 4-0	McMahon 2, Hodge, Bell	32,000
Apr 14	Queen's Park	(F) W 4-3	Divers 2, McMahon, Bell	18,000

League & Cup Appearances

PLAYER	LEAGUE	CUP COMPETITION S CUP	TOTAL
Battles	14	5	19
Bell	18	6	24
Blackwood	1		1
Campbell	16	6	22
Davidson	8	5	13
Divers	8	5	13
Docherty	7		7
Gilhooly	15	3	18
Hodge	13	2	15
Hynds	2	2	4
King	11		11
McArthur	11	6	17
McMahon	10	6	16
Marshall	8	6	14
Orr	8	4	14
Russell	16	4	20
Somers	3	1	4
Storrier	7	1	8
Turnbull	11	1	12
Welford	11		11

Goalscorers

PLAYER	LEAGUE	CUP COMPETITION S CUP	TOTAL
Bell	7	5	12
McMahon	5	7	12
Gilhooly	8	3	11
Campbell	7	3	10
Divers	6	4	10
Hodge	6	1	7
Somers	1	2	3
Marshall	2		2
King	1		1
Orr		1	1
Opps' o.gs.	2		2

1 league goal unrecorded

Fact File

Jack Bell scored Celtic's first goal in the 20th century in the home match against Rangers on 1 January.

SECRETARY-MANAGER: Willie Maley

CAPTAIN: Harry Marshall

TOP SCORERS: Jack Bell and Sandy McMahon

BIGGEST WIN: 7-1 v Bo'ness, 13 January 1900, Scottish Cup

HIGHEST ATTENDANCE: 40,000 v Rangers, 7 October 1899, league

MAJOR TRANSFERS IN: Davie Russell from Preston

Final Scottish League Div 1 Table

		P	W	D	L	F	A	Pts
1	RANGERS	18	15	2	1	69	27	32
2	CELTIC	18	9	7	2	46	27	25
3	HIBERNIAN	18	9	6	3	43	24	24
4	HEARTS	18	10	3	5	41	24	23
5	KILMARNOCK	18	6	6	6	30	37	18
6	DUNDEE	18	4	7	7	36	39	15
6	THIRD LANARK	18	5	5	8	31	38	15
8	ST MIRREN	18	3	6	9	30	46	12
8	ST BERNARD'S	18	4	4	10	29	47	12
10	CLYDE	18	2	0	16	24	70	4

Season 1900-01

Scottish League Divison 1

DATE	OPPONENTS	SCORE	GOALSCORERS	ATTENDANCE
Aug 15	PARTICK THISTLE	D 3-3	Battles, McMahon, Campbell	4,000
Aug 18	Morton	W 3-2	Campbell, Findlay, Divers	7,000
Aug 25	HIBERNIAN	W 3-1	McMahon 2, Hodge	12,000
Sep 1	Third Lanark	W 2-1	Hodge, Gray	10,000
Sep 8	Queen's Park	W 2-0	McMahon 2	18,000
Sep 17	Hearts	W 2-0	Hodge, Loney	7,000
Sep 24	THIRD LANARK	W 5-1	Findlay 2, McOustra, Divers, Orr	8,000
Sep 29	Hibernian	D 2-2	Findlay, McOustra	12,000
Oct 6	RANGERS	W 2-1	Divers, Campbell	11,000
Oct 13	QUEEN'S PARK	W 2-0	McMahon, Divers	12,000
Oct 27	KILMARNOCK	W 1-0	Campbell	5,000
Nov 3	Kilmarnock	L 1-2	Hodge	4,000
Nov 10	Dundee	D 1-1	Hodge	10,000
Nov 17	HEARTS	L 1-3	Hodge	6,000
Nov 24	MORTON	W 4-2	Campbell 2, McOustra, McMahon	1,000
Dec 1	Partick Thistle	W 6-2	McMahon 2, Campbell 2, Findlay, Divers	7,000
Dec 15	ST MIRREN	W 3-0	Divers, McOustra, McMahon	3,000
Dec 22	DUNDEE	L 1-2	Russell	-
Jan 1	Rangers	L 1-2	McMahon	-
Jan 19	St Mirren	W 4-3	Campbell 2, Quinn, Hodge	-

Scottish Cup

Jan 12	RANGERS	(Rd1)	W 1-0	McOustra	30,000
Feb 9	KILMARNOCK	(Rd2)	W 6-0	Campbell 2, Findlay, McMahon, Divers, McOustra	12,000
Feb 16	Dundee	(Rd3)	W 1-0	Findlay	15,000
Mar 23	ST MIRREN	(SF)	W 1-0	Campbell	18,000
Apr 6	Hearts	(F)	L 3-4	McOustra, Quinn, McMahon	17,000

League & Cup Appearances

PLAYER	LEAGUE	CUP COMPETITION S CUP	TOTAL
Battles	15	5	20
Campbell	20	5	25
Davidson	18	5	23
Divers	16	5	21
Donnelly	3	2	5
Findlay	12	3	15
Gilhooly	1		1
Gray	2		2
Hodge	13		13
Hynds	13		13
Loney	5	5	10
McArthur	17	3	20
McMahon	20	5	25
McNeill	2		2
McOustra	14	5	19
Orr	18	5	23
Quinn	1	2	3
Russell	17	5	22
Storrier	13		13

Goalscorers

PLAYER	LEAGUE	CUP COMPETITION S CUP	TOTAL
Campbell	10	3	13
McMahon	11	2	13
Findlay	5	2	7
Hodge	7		7
Divers	6	1	7
McOustra	4	3	7
Quinn	1	1	2
Battles	1		1
Gray	1		1
Loney	1		1
Orr	1		1
Russell	1		1

Fact File

The scheduled Scottish Cup tie against Kilmarnock on 26 January was played as a friendly because in the telegram to the referee 'Park Playable' was garbled into 'Unplayable' and so he did not turn up. The match was played on 9 February.

SECRETARY-MANAGER: Willie Maley
CAPTAIN: Davie Russell
TOP SCORERS: Johnny Campbell and Sandy McMahon
BIGGEST WIN: 6-0 v Kilmarnock, 9 February 1901, Scottish Cup
HIGHEST ATTENDANCE: 30,000 v Rangers, 12 January 1901, Scottish Cup
MAJOR TRANSFERS IN: Harry Marshall from Hearts

Final Scottish League Div 1 Table

		P	W	D	L	F	A	Pts
1	RANGERS	20	17	1	2	60	25	35
2	CELTIC	20	13	3	4	49	28	29
3	HIBERNIAN	20	9	7	4	29	22	25
4	MORTON	20	9	3	8	40	40	21
5	KILMARNOCK	20	7	4	9	35	47	18
5	THIRD LANARK	20	6	6	8	20	29	18
7	DUNDEE	20	6	5	9	36	35	17
7	QUEEN'S PARK	20	7	3	10	33	37	17
9	ST MIRREN	20	5	6	9	33	43	16
10	HEARTS	20	5	4	11	22	30	14
11	PARTICK T	20	4	2	14	28	49	10

Season 1901-02

Scottish League Divison 1

DATE	OPPONENTS	SCORE	GOALSCORERS	ATTENDANCE
Aug 17	DUNDEE	D 1-1	Divers	5,000
Aug 24	Morton	W 2-1	McOustra, Campbell	6,000
Aug 31	THIRD LANARK	W 3-2	Hodge, Campbell (pen), Quinn	15,000
Sep 7	St Mirren	W 3-2	Hodge 2, Campbell	-
Sep 16	Hibernian	W 2-1	McMahon, Crawford	-
Sep 21	Morton	W 2-1	Campbell, McMahon	-
Sep 23	Third Lanark	W 2-0	Crawford, Hodge	15,000
Sep 28	Kilmarnock	W 1-0	Livingstone	7,000
Oct 5	Rangers	D 2-2	Quinn, o.g.	27,000
Oct 19	QUEEN'S PARK	W 1-0	Findlay	-
Nov 2	Hearts	D 2-2	Drummond, Campbell	10,000
Nov 9	ST MIRREN	W 3-1	Livingstone 3	-
Nov 16	Dundee	W 3-2	Campbell 2, McMahon	10,000
Nov 30	HEARTS	L 1-2	McMahon	-
Dec 7	Queen's Park	L 2-3	McMahon, Campbell	14,000
Dec 14	HIBERNIAN	D 2-2	Campbell (pen), Hodge	7,000
Dec 28	KILMARNOCK	W 4-2	McOustra 3, Hodge	3,000
Jan 1	RANGERS	L 2-4	McMahon, Marshall	40,000

Scottish Cup

Jan 11	THORNLIEBANK	(Rd1) W 3-0	Livingstone 2, Campbell	-
Jan 25	Arbroath	(Rd2) W 3-2	Campbell, Orr, McMahon	6,000
Feb 15	Hearts	(Rd3) D 1-1	Quinn	23,000
Feb 22	HEARTS	(R) W 2-1	McMahon 2	25,000
Mar 22	St Mirren	(SF) W 3-2	Livingstone, Campbell, McDermott	-
Apr 26	HIBERNIAN	(F) L 0-1		16,000

League & Cup Appearances

PLAYER	LEAGUE	CUP COMPETITION S CUP	TOTAL
Battles	13	6	19
Campbell	14	4	18
Crawford	6		6
Davidson	11	2	13
Divers	2		2
Drummond	4		4
Findlay	2		2
Hodge	8	1	9
Hynds	2		2
Livingstone	17	6	23
Loney	11	6	17
McArthur	1		1
McCafferty	2		2
McDermott	2	5	7
McFarlane	17	6	23
McMahon	13	5	18
McOustra	9	2	11
Mair	1		1
Marshall	16	4	20
Moir	8		8
Orr	14	5	19
Quinn	12	6	18
Russell	3	2	5
Walls		1	1
Watson	12	4	16

Goalscorers

PLAYER	LEAGUE	CUP COMPETITION S CUP	TOTAL
Campbell	9	3	12
McMahon	6	3	9
Livingstone	4	3	7
Hodge	6		6
McOustra	4		4
Quinn	2	1	3
Crawford	2		2
Divers	1		1
Drummond	1		1
Findlay	1		1
McDermott		1	1
Marshall	1		1
Orr		1	1
Opps' o.gs.	1		1

Fact File

Johnny Divers, the first Celt to join Hibernian, won a winner's medal in the Scottish Cup final against his former team.

SECRETARY-MANAGER: Willie Maley

CAPTAIN: Davie Russell

TOP SCORER: Johnny Campbell

BIGGEST WIN: 3-0 v Thornliebank, 11 January 1902, Scottish Cup

HIGHEST ATTENDANCE: 40,000 v Rangers, 1 January 1902, league

MAJOR TRANSFERS IN: George Livingstone from Sunderland

Final Scottish League Div 1 Table

		P	W	D	L	F	A	Pts
1	RANGERS	18	13	2	3	43	29	28
2	CELTIC	18	11	4	3	38	28	26
3	HEARTS	18	10	2	6	32	21	22
4	THIRD LANARK	18	7	5	6	30	26	19
4	ST MIRREN	18	8	3	7	29	28	19
6	HIBERNIAN	18	6	4	8	36	23	16
6	KILMARNOCK	18	5	6	7	22	27	16
8	QUEEN'S PARK	18	5	4	9	21	32	14
9	DUNDEE	18	4	5	9	15	31	13
10	MORTON	18	1	5	12	20	41	7

Season 1902-03

Scottish League Divison 1

DATE	OPPONENTS	SCORE	GOALSCORERS	ATTENDANCE
Aug 16	Hibernian	D 1-1	Campbell	7,000
Aug 23	ST MIRREN	D 2-2	Campbell, Crawford	8,000
Aug 30	Third Lanark	W 2-1	McDermott, Marshall	13,000
Sep 6	QUEEN'S PARK	D 1-1	Campbell (pen)	14,000
Sep 15	Hearts	W 2-1	Quinn, Campbell	8,000
Sep 20	Kilmarnock	W 3-1	Campbell 3	-
Sep 27	THIRD LANARK	W 1-0	Campbell	15,000
Sep 29	HEARTS	D 2-2	Campbell, Somers	-
Oct 4	Queen's Park	L 1-2	Campbell	12,000
Oct 18	RANGERS	D 1-1	Campbell (pen)	25,000
Nov 1	KILMARNOCK	W 3-1	Campbell, Somers, unrecorded	-
Nov 15	PARTICK THISTLE	W 4-2	Somers, Murray, Quinn, unrecorded	-
Nov 22	PORT GLASGOW	W 3-0	Loney, Hamilton, McMenemy	-
Nov 29	DUNDEE	D 2-2	Loney, Hamilton	8,000
Dec 6	Partick Thistle	D 0-0		-
Dec 13	St Mirren	L 1-3	Murray	6,000
Dec 20	MORTON	D 1-1	McDermott	-
Jan 1	Rangers	D 3-3	McMahon 2, Campbell	-
Jan 2	HIBERNIAN	L 0-4		14,000
Mar 7	Port Glasgow	D 1-1	McMenemy	-
Mar 14	Morton	W 2-0	Hamilton, Clark	4,000
Mar 21	Dundee	L 0-2		-

Scottish Cup

Jan 24	ST MIRREN	(Rd1) D 0-0		-
Jan 31	St Mirren	(R) D 1-1	McDermott	16,000
Feb 14	ST MIRREN	(R2) W 4-0	Murray, McMahon, Watson, Campbell	35,000
Feb 21	PORT GLASGOW ATH.	(Rd2) W 2-0	Campbell, McDermott	-
Feb 28	RANGERS	(QF) L 0-3		40,000

League & Cup Appearances

PLAYER	LEAGUE	CUP COMPETITION S CUP	TOTAL
Battles	10	4	14
Campbell	15	5	20
Caírk	2		2
Crawford	4		4
Hamilton	17		17
Loney	19	3	22
McCafferty	1		1
McDermott	10	4	14
McLeod	20	1	21
McMahon	6	5	11
McMenemy	4		4
McPherson	22	5	27
Marshall	5	3	8
Moir	19	4	23
Murray	11	5	16
Orr	19	5	24
Quinn	18	5	23
Somers	16	1	17
Walls	4		4
Watson	17	5	22
Watson	3		3

Goalscorers

PLAYER	LEAGUE	CUP COMPETITION S CUP	TOTAL
Campbell	13	2	15
McDermott	2	2	4
Hamilton	3		3
Murray	2	1	3
Somers	3		3
Loney	2		2
McMahon	2		2
McMenemy	2		2
Quinn	2		2
Clark	1		1
Crawford	1		1
Marshall	1		1
Watson		1	1

2 league goals unrecorded

Fact File

Celtic took three matches to dispose of St Mirren in the first round of the Scottish Cup. They eventually won the second replay 4-0.

SECRETARY-MANAGER: Willie Maley

CAPTAIN: Willie Orr

TOP SCORER: Johnny Campbell

BIGGEST WIN: 4-0 v St Mirren, 14 February 1903, Scottish Cup

HIGHEST ATTENDANCE: 40,000 v Rangers, 28 February 1903, Scottish Cup

MAJOR TRANSFERS OUT: George Livingstone to Liverpool

Final Scottish League Div 1 Table

		P	W	D	L	F	A	Pts
1	HIBERNIAN	22	16	5	1	48	18	37
2	DUNDEE	22	13	5	4	31	12	31
3	RANGERS	22	12	5	5	56	30	29
4	HEARTS	22	11	6	5	46	27	28
5	CELTIC	22	8	10	4	36	30	26
6	ST MIRREN	22	7	8	7	39	40	22
7	THIRD LANARK	22	8	5	9	34	27	21
8	PARTICK T	22	6	7	9	34	50	19
9	KILMARNOCK	22	6	4	12	24	43	16
10	QUEEN'S PARK	22	5	5	12	33	48	15
11	PORT GLASGOW A	22	3	5	14	26	49	11
12	MORTON	22	2	5	15	22	55	9

Season 1903-04

Scottish League Divison 1

DATE	OPPONENTS	SCORE	GOALSCORERS	ATTENDANCE
Aug 15	PARTICK THISTLE	W 2-1	Bennett, McMenemy	-
Aug 22	St Mirren	W 1-0	Somers	-
Aug 29	THIRD LANARK	L 1-3	Bennett	15,000
Sep 5	Hibernian	W 2-0	Somers, Bennett	-
Sep 26	HIBERNIAN	W 1-0	Gilligan	-
Sep 28	Third Lanark	L 1-3	Quinn	17,000
Oct 3	QUEEN'S PARK	W 3-0	Orr 2 (1 pen), McMenemy	-
Oct 10	DUNDEE	W 4-2	Gilligan 2, Orr 2 (1 pen)	7,000
Oct 17	Rangers	D 0-0		24,000
Oct 24	HEARTS	W 4-0	Gilligan 2, McMenemy, Bennett	5,000
Oct 31	Queen's Park	L 0-1		-
Nov 14	Kilmarnock	W 6-1	Somers 2, Gilligan 2, o.g., unrecorded	-
Dec 5	Morton	W 1-0	Gilligan	4,500
Dec 12	AIRDRIE	W 3-0	Muir, Orr, Hamilton	-
Dec 19	Partick Thistle	W 4-0	Hamilton 2, Bennett 2	-
Dec 26	PORT GLASGOW	W 4-1	Gilligan 3, Hay	-
Jan 1	RANGERS	D 2-2	Bennett, McMenemy	33,000
Jan 9	Airdrie	L 3-4	Hamilton, McMenemy, Hay (pen)	-
Jan 16	MOTHERWELL	W 6-0	McMenemy 3, Hamilton, Somers, Gilligan	-
Jan 23	MORTON	W 5-1	Muir 3, Bennett 2	-
Jan 30	Dundee	L 1-2	Bennett	15,000
Feb 6	Port Glasgow	W 3-2	Quinn 3	-
Mar 12	ST MIRREN	W 3-1	Quinn, Hamilton, Gilligan	-
Mar 26	Motherwell	W 2-1	Bennett	-
Apr 2	Hearts	L 1-2	McMenemy	-
Apr 23	KILMARNOCK	W 6-1	Quinn 5, McMenemy	3,000

Scottish Cup

Feb 13	ST BERNARD'S	(Rd1) W 4-0	McMenemy 2, Orr 2	-
Feb 20	DUNDEE	(Rd2) D 1-1	Hamilton	-
Feb 27	Dundee	(R) D 0-0		-
Mar 5	DUNDEE	(R2) W 5-0	Muir 2, Bennett, Quinn, McMenemy	-
Mar 19	THIRD LANARK	(SF) W 2-1	Muir, Quinn	36,000
Apr 16	Rangers	(F) W 3-2	Quinn 3	64,323

League & Cup Appearances

PLAYER	LEAGUE	CUP COMPETITION S CUP	TOTAL
Adams	21	6	27
Battles	22	2	24
Bennett	18	5	23
Gilligan	13	1	14
Graham	4		4
Grassam	2		2
Hamilton	13	5	18
Hay	24	6	30
Loney	14	6	20
MacLeod	10	6	16
McMenemy	22	6	28
McPherson	5		5
Moir	6		6
Muir	20	5	25
Orr	18	6	24
Quinn	18	4	22
Somers	20	4	24
Strang	2		2
Watson	17		17
Young	17	4	21

Goalscorers

PLAYER	LEAGUE	CUP COMPETITION S CUP	TOTAL
Quinn	10	5	15
McMenemy	10	3	13
Gilligan	13		13
Bennett	11	1	12
Hamilton	6	1	7
Muir	4	3	7
Orr	6	2	8
Somers	5		5
Hay	2		2
Opps' o.gs.	1		1

1 league goal unrecorded

Fact File

On 15 August 1903 Celtic appeared for the season's opening match against Partick Thistle in their new strip – green and white hoops.

SECRETARY-MANAGER: Willie Maley

CAPTAIN: Willie Orr

TOP SCORER: Jimmy Quinn

BIGGEST WIN: 6-0 v Motherwell, 16 January 1904, league

HIGHEST ATTENDANCE: 64,323 v Rangers, 16 April 1904, Scottish Cup

MAJOR TRANSFERS IN: Jim Young from Bristol Rovers

MAJOR TRANSFERS OUT: Harry Marshall to Clyde, Dan McArthur to Clyde, Sandy McMahon to Partick Thistle

Final Scottish League Div 1 Table

		P	W	D	L	F	A	Pts
1	THIRD LANARK	26	20	3	3	61	26	43
2	HEARTS	26	18	3	5	63	35	39
3	CELTIC	26	18	2	6	69	28	38
3	RANGERS	26	16	6	4	80	33	38
5	DUNDEE	26	13	2	11	55	46	28
6	ST MIRREN	26	11	5	10	45	38	27
6	PARTICK T	26	10	7	9	43	40	27
8	QUEEN'S PARK	26	6	9	11	28	47	21
9	PORT GLASGOW A	26	8	4	14	33	49	20
10	HIBERNIAN	26	7	5	14	31	42	19
11	MORTON	26	7	4	15	31	51	18
11	AIRDRIEONIANS	26	7	4	15	32	62	18
13	MOTHERWELL	26	6	3	17	26	61	15
14	KILMARNOCK	26	4	5	17	27	66	13

Season 1904-05

Scottish League Divison 1

DATE	OPPONENTS	SCORE	GOALSCORERS	ATTENDANCE
Aug 20	Partick Thistle	W 5-0	Young, Hay, McLean, McMenemy, Bennett	9,000
Aug 27	Port Glasgow	W 4-1	Quinn 3, McLean	6,000
Sep 3	HEARTS	D 1-1	Somers	19,000
Sep 17	St Mirren	W 3-2	Quinn 2, Hay	-
Sep 19	Hearts	L 0-2		-
Sep 26	THIRD LANARK	W 2-1	McMenemy 2	10,000
Oct 1	Queen's Park	W 3-2	Quinn, Bennet, o.g.	15,000
Oct 15	RANGERS	D 2-2	McMenemy, Bennett	30,000
Oct 22	Third Lanark	W 2-1	Quinn 2	-
Oct 29	QUEEN'S PARK	D 1-1	Quinn	-
Nov 5	Kilmarnock	W 3-0	Hamilton, Quinn, unrecorded	-
Nov 12	Hibernian	D 2-2	Quinn, o.g.	-
Nov 19	DUNDEE	W 3-0	Bennett 2, Loney	-
Nov 26	Airdrie	W 3-1	McMenemy 2, Bennett	-
Dec 3	MOTHERWELL	W 4-2	Bennett, McLean, Quinn, Somers	5,000
Dec 10	Morton	W 1-0	Quinn	5,000
Dec 17	PARTICK THISTLE	D 2-2	Somers, Hay (pen)	8,000
Dec 24	ST MIRREN	W 1-0	Somers	-
Dec 31	KILMARNOCK	W 3-1	Orr (pen), Loney, McIlvenny	5,000
Jan 3	AIRDRIE	L 2-3	Somers, Loney	8,000
Jan 7	PORT GLASGOW	W 3-0	Hamilton 2, unrecorded	-
Jan 14	Dundee	L 1-2	McLean	-
Jan 21	HIBERNIAN	W 2-0	Somers 2	-
Feb 4	MORTON	W 5-2	Loney 2, Bennett, Quinn, McMenemy	-
Feb 18	Rangers	W 4-1	Quinn 2, Hamilton 2	28,000
Mar 4	Motherwell	W 6-2	Quinn 3, McNair, Loney, Somers	8,000

Scottish Cup

DATE	OPPONENTS		SCORE	GOALSCORERS	ATTENDANCE
Jan 28	Dumfries	(Rd1)	W 2-1	Quinn, Bennett	3,000
Feb 11	LOCHGELLY UNITED	(Rd2)	W 3-0	Somers, Orr (pen), Quinn	2,000
Feb 25	PARTICK THISTLE	(Rd3)	W 3-0	Bennett, Orr (pen), McMenemy	30,000
Mar 25	RANGERS	(SF)	L 0-2		36,000

League & Cup Appearances

PLAYER	LEAGUE	CUP COMPETITION S CUP	TOTAL
Adams	27	4	31
Bennett	22	4	26
Black	10	1	11
Hamilton	25	4	29
Hay	27	4	31
Loney	27	4	31
McIlvenny	7	1	8
McLean	15		15
MacLeod	25	4	29
McNair	6	1	7
Orr	21	4	25
Quinn	22	4	26
Somers	26	4	30
Watson	2		2
Young	19	2	21

Goalscorers

PLAYER	LEAGUE	CUP COMPETITION S CUP	TOTAL
Quinn	19	2	21
Bennett	8	2	10
Somers	8	1	9
McMenemy	7	1	8
Loney	6		6
Hamilton	5		5
McLean	4		4
Hay	3		3
Orr	1	2	3
McIlvenny	1		1
McNair	1		1
Young	1		1
Opps' o.gs.	2		2

2 league goals unrecorded

Fact File

A Jim Young clearance in the match at Third Lanark on 22 October 1904 hit referee Hamilton in the face. The clash of ball and whistle lost him five teeth.

SECRETARY-MANAGER: Willie Maley

CAPTAIN: Willie Orr

TOP SCORER: Jimmy Quinn

BIGGEST WIN: 5-0 v Partick Thistle, 20 August 1904, league

HIGHEST ATTENDANCE: 36,000 v Rangers, 25 March 1905, Scottish Cup

MAJOR TRANSFERS OUT: Barney Battles to Kilmarnock

Final Scottish League Div 1 Table

		P	W	D	L	F	A	PTS
1	CELTIC	26	18	5	3	68	31	41
1	RANGERS	26	19	3	4	83	28	41
3	THIRD LANARK	26	14	7	5	60	28	35
4	AIRDRIEONIANS	26	11	5	10	38	45	27
5	HIBERNIAN	26	9	8	9	39	39	26
5	PARTICK T	26	12	2	12	36	56	26
7	DUNDEE	26	10	5	11	38	32	25
7	HEARTS	26	11	3	12	43	44	25
9	KILMARNOCK	26	9	5	12	29	45	23
10	ST MIRREN	26	9	4	13	33	36	22
11	PORT GLASGOW A	26	8	5	13	30	48	21
12	QUEEN'S PARK	26	6	8	12	28	45	20
13	MORTON	26	7	4	15	27	50	18
14	MOTHERWELL	26	6	2	18	28	53	14

CELTIC BEAT RANGERS 2-1 IN A PLAY-OFF FOR THE CHAMPIONSHIP.

Season 1905-06

Scottish League Divison 1

DATE	OPPONENTS	SCORE	GOALSCORERS	ATTENDANCE
Aug 19	MOTHERWELL	W 3-1	Quinn 2, Bennett	9,000
Aug 26	Kilmarnock	W 4-2	Somers, Hay, McMenemy, Hamilton	-
Sep 2	HIBERNIAN	W 1-0	Bennett	12,000
Sep 11	Hearts	D 1-1	McMenemy	-
Sep 16	Falkirk	W 5-0	Quinn 2, Bennett 2, Loney	6,000
Sep 25	Third Lanark	W 1-0	McNair	16,000
Sep 30	AIRDRIE	W 2-1	Orr (pen), McMenemy	35,000
Oct 14	QUEEN'S PARK	W 5-1	Quinn 3, Hamilton, Young	-
Oct 21	Rangers	L 2-3	Somers, Orr (pen)	35,000
Oct 28	DUNDEE	W 3-1	Orr (pen), McNair, Young	8,000
Nov 4	Partick Thistle	W 3-0	Somers, McNair, o.g.	-
Nov 11	PORT GLASGOW	L 0-1		-
Nov 18	Morton	W 4-0	Bennett 2, Quinn, Hamilton	8,000
Nov 25	ST MIRREN	W 2-1	Somers, o.g.	5,000
Dec 2	Port Glasgow	W 1-0	Loney	8,000
Dec 9	ABERDEEN	W 1-0	McMenemy	12,000
Dec 16	Motherwell	W 4-0	Quinn 2, Hamilton, McMenemy	-
Dec 23	MORTON	W 4-0	McMenemy, Bennett, Quinn, Orr (pen)	5,000
Dec 30	Hibernian	W 1-0	Quinn	11,000
Jan 1	RANGERS	W 1-0	Hamilton	36,000
Jan 2	KILMARNOCK	W 2-0	Hamilton, Bennett	-
Jan 6	FALKIRK	W 7-0	Bennett 3, McMenemy 2, Hay (pen), Bauchop	5,000
Jan 13	Airdrie	W 5-2	Quinn 3, Hamilton, Orr (pen)	10,000
Jan 20	PARTICK THISTLE	W 4-1	Bennett 2, McNair, McMenemy	-
Feb 3	Dundee	L 0-1		9,000
Feb 17	St Mirren	W 3-2	Bauchop, McMenemy, Hay (pen)	12,000
Mar 3	Aberdeen	L 0-1		-
Mar 10	Queen's Park	W 6-0	Quinn 4, Hamilton, Bennett	15,000
Apr 21	HEARTS	W 1-0	Quinn	7,000
May 7	THIRD LANARK	L 0-1		1,500

Scottish Cup

Jan 27	Dundee	(Rd1) W 2-1	Somers o.g.	25,000
Feb 10	BO'NESS	(Rd2) W 3-0	Loney, McMenemy, Quinn	-
Feb 24	HEARTS	(Rd3) L 1-2	McMenemy	50,000

League & Cup Appearances

PLAYER	LEAGUE	CUP COMPETITION S CUP	TOTAL
Adams	30	3	33
Bauchop	4		4
Bennett	28	3	31
Campbell	11		11
Garry	2		2
Hamilton	26	3	29
Hay	30	3	33
Loney	28	3	31
MacLeod	21	3	24
McMenemy	28	3	31
McNair A	22	2	24
McNair W	1		1
Orr	24	3	27
Quinn	27	3	30
Shaw	1		1
Somers	22	3	25
Watson	1		1
Wilson	5		5
Young	19	1	20

Goalscorers

PLAYER	LEAGUE	CUP COMPETITION S CUP	TOTAL
Quinn	20	1	21
Bennett	14		14
McMenemy	10	2	12
Hamilton	8		8
Somers	4	1	5
Orr	5		5
McNair	4		4
Hay	3		3
Loney	2	1	3
Bauchop	2		2
Young	2		2
Opps' o.gs.	2	1	3

Fact File

R.G. Campbell made his debut in the match against Motherwell on the opening day of the season. He was nicknamed 'baby' – short for 'baby elephant'.

SECRETARY-MANAGER: Willie Maley

CAPTAIN: Willie Orr

TOP SCORER: Jimmy Quinn

BIGGEST WIN: 7-0 v Falkirk, 6 January 1906, league

HIGHEST ATTENDANCE: 50,000 v Hearts, 24 February 1906, Scottish Cup

Final Scottish League Div 1 Table

		P	W	D	L	F	A	Pts
1	CELTIC	30	24	1	5	76	19	49
2	HEARTS	30	18	7	5	64	27	43
3	AIRDRIEONIANS	30	15	8	7	53	31	38
4	RANGERS	30	15	7	8	58	48	37
5	PARTICK T	30	15	6	9	44	40	36
6	THIRD LANARK	30	16	2	12	62	38	34
6	DUNDEE	30	11	12	7	40	33	34
8	ST MIRREN	30	13	5	12	41	37	31
9	MOTHERWELL	30	9	8	13	50	64	26
9	MORTON	30	10	6	14	35	54	26
11	HIBERNIAN	30	10	5	15	35	40	25
12	ABERDEEN	30	8	8	14	36	48	24
13	FALKIRK	30	9	5	16	52	68	23
14	KILMARNOCK	30	8	4	18	46	68	20
14	PORT GLASGOW A	30	6	8	16	38	68	20
16	QUEEN'S PARK	30	5	4	21	41	88	14

Season 1906-07

Scottish League Divison 1

DATE	OPPONENTS	SCORE	GOALSCORERS	ATTENDANCE
Aug 18	Motherwell	W 6-0	Quinn 3, Loney, Hay, Somers	12,000
Aug 25	KILMARNOCK	W 5-0	Quinn 2, Hamilton, Orr, Templeton	28,000
Sep 1	Morton	W 2-0	Quinn, somers	8,000
Sep 15	HEARTS	W 3-0	Hamilton 2, Quinn	20,000
Sep 24	THIRD LANARK	W 2-0	Quinn, McMenemy	13,000
Sep 29	Airdrie	W 2-0	Quinn 2	27,000
Oct 13	ABERDEEN	W 2-1	Bennett, Somers	12,000
Oct 20	Dundee	D 0-0		26,000
Oct 27	RANGERS	W 2-1	Somers, Templeton	34,000
Nov 3	Hamilton Ac.	W 5-2	Quinn 3, Somers, Young (pen)	12,000
Nov 10	HIBERNIAN	W 2-1	McMenemy, Templeton	8,000
Nov 17	Falkirk	W 3-2	Bennett 3	9,000
Nov 24	CLYDE	D 3-3	Young 2 (1 pen), Quinn	12,000
Dec 1	PARTICK THISTLE	W 4-1	McMenemy 2, Somers, Quinn	8,000
Dec 8	St Mirren	W 3-0	Quinn 3	10,000
Dec 15	Queen's Park	W 4-0	Templeton 2, McMenemy, Quinn	15,000
Dec 22	PORT GLASGOW	W 4-0	Quinn 2, Bennett, McMenemy	16,000
Dec 29	Kilmarnock	D 2-2	Quinn, Hamilton	-
Dec 31	AIRDRIE	W 2-1	Orr (pen), Quinn	-
Jan 1	Rangers	L 1-2	Somers	50,000
Jan 2	Hamilton Ac.	W 2-0	Young (pen), Hamilton	-
Jan 5	FALKIRK	W 3-2	Quinn 2, McNair	16,000
Jan 12	Clyde	W 2-0	Somers, Bauchop	20,000
Jan 19	MORTON	W 2-1	McMenemy, McNair	10,000
Mar 2	Aberdeen	D 2-2	Somers, Orr (pen)	-
Mar 16	Third Lanark	L 1-2	Quinn	9,000
Mar 23	DUNDEE	D 0-0		32,000
Apr 1	QUEEN'S PARK	W 2-1	Quinn, Hamilton	-
Apr 24	Partick Thistle	W 2-0	Quinn, Bennett	4,000
Apr 27	ST MIRREN	D 1-1	Quinn	7,000
May 4	Port Glasgow	D 1-1	Orr (pen)	2,500
May 8	Hibernian	W 1-0	o.g.	-
May 11	Hearts	D 3-3	Bauchop, Young, Garry	11,000
May 15	MOTHERWELL	D 1-1	Bauchop	-

Scottish Cup

DATE	OPPONENTS		SCORE	GOALSCORERS	ATTENDANCE
Feb 2	CLYDE	(Rd1)	W 2-1	Hamilton, Bennett	25,000
Feb 9	Morton	(Rd2)	D 0-0		12,000
Feb 16	MORTON	(R)	D 1-1	McMenemy	25,000
Feb 23	MORTON	(R2)	W 2-1	McMenemy, Hay	35,000
Mar 9	Rangers	(Rd3)	W 3-0	Somers, Hay, Hamilton	60,000
Mar 30	HIBERNIAN	(SF)	D 0-0		25,000
Apr 6	Hibernian	(R)	D 0-0		-
Apr 13	HIBERNIAN	(R2)	W 3-0	Quinn, Somers, McMenemy	30,000
Apr 20	HEARTS	(F)	W 3-0	Somers 2, Orr (pen)	50,000

League & Cup Appearances

PLAYER	LEAGUE	CUP COMPETITION S CUP	TOTAL
Adams	28	9	37
Bauchop	9		9
Bennett	26	9	35
Craig	9		9
Garry	4		4
Hamilton	22	7	29
Hay	24	9	33
Loney	11		11
MacLeod	25	9	34
McMenemy	31	9	40
McNair	28	9	37
Mitchell	12		12
Morrison	1		1
Orr	17	9	26
Quinn	26	5	31
Sinclair	6		6
Somers	27	8	35
Templeton	25	7	32
Weir	2		2
Wilson	9		9
Young	32		32

Goalscorers

PLAYER	LEAGUE	CUP COMPETITION S CUP	TOTAL
Quinn	29	1	30
Somers	9	4	13
McMenemy	7	3	10
Hamilton	6	2	8
Bennett	6	1	7
Templeton	5		5
Young	5		5
Orr	4		4
Bauchop	3		3
Hay	1	2	3
McNair	2		2
Garry	1		1
Loney	1		1
Opps' o.gs.	1		1

Fact File

Keeper Tom Sinclair joined on loan from Rangers. He played 6 league games during the season and did not concede a single goal.

SECRETARY-MANAGER: Willie Maley

CAPTAIN: Willie Orr

TOP SCORER: Jimmy Quinn

BIGGEST WIN: 6-0 v Motherwell, 18 August 1906, league

HIGHEST ATTENDANCE: 60,000 v Rangers, 9 March 1907, Scottish Cup

MAJOR TRANSFERS IN: Bobby Templeton from Arsenal

Final Scottish League Div 1 Table

		P	W	D	L	F	A	Pts
1	CELTIC	34	23	9	2	80	30	55
2	DUNDEE	34	18	12	4	53	26	48
3	RANGERS	34	19	7	8	69	33	45
4	AIRDRIEONIANS	34	18	6	10	59	44	42
5	FALKIRK	34	17	7	10	73	58	41
6	THIRD LANARK	34	15	9	10	57	48	39
7	ST MIRREN	34	12	13	9	50	44	37
8	CLYDE	34	15	6	13	47	52	36
9	HEARTS	34	11	13	10	46	43	35
10	MOTHERWELL	34	12	9	13	45	48	33
11	ABERDEEN	34	10	10	14	48	55	30
11	HIBERNIAN	34	10	10	14	40	49	30
13	MORTON	34	11	6	17	41	50	28
14	PARTICK T	34	9	8	17	40	60	26
15	QUEEN'S PARK	34	9	6	19	51	66	24
16	HAMILTON A	34	8	5	21	40	64	21
16	KILMARNOCK	34	8	5	21	40	72	21
16	PORT GLASGOW A	34	7	7	20	30	67	21

Season 1907-08

Scottish League Divison 1

DATE	OPPONENTS	SCORE	GOALSCORERS	ATTENDANCE
Aug 15	HAMILTON AC.	W 3-0	Hamilton 2, Somers	-
Aug 17	MOTHERWELL	W 3-0	Quinn 2, Bennett	12,000
Aug 24	Morton	W 3-2	Kivlichan 2, Hamilton	9,000
Aug 31	DUNDEE	W 3-2	Somers 2, Quinn	27,000
Sep 7	FALKIRK	W 3-2	McMenemy, Quinn, Bennett	27,000
Sep 14	Kilmarnock	D 0-0		-
Sep 21	AIRDRIE	D 1-1	Quinn	20,000
Sep 23	Aberdeen	L 1-2	Quinn	10,000
Sep 30	Third Lanark	W 3-1	Hay 2 (2 pens), McMenemy	12,000
Oct 5	Hibernian	W 2-1	Quinn, Hamilton	10,000
Nov 2	PORT GLASGOW	W 5-0	McLean 3, Young, Quinn	6,000
Nov 9	Clyde	W 2-0	Quinn, Loney	-
Nov 16	QUEEN'S PARK	W 4-1	Somers 2, Quinn, Kivlichan	13,000
Nov 23	Hearts	L 0-1		24,000
Dec 7	ST MIRREN	W 4-0	McLean 2, McNair, Quinn	8,000
Dec 14	Hamilton Ac.	W 4-2	Quinn 2, McLean, Hay	6,000
Dec 21	KILMARNOCK	W 4-1	Quinn, Bennett, Somers, Hamilton	10,000
Dec 28	Airdrie	D 0-0		-
Jan 1	RANGERS	W 2-1	Hamilton, McMenemy	50,000
Jan 2	ABERDEEN	W 3-0	Semple, Quinn, o.g.	
Jan 11	CLYDE	W 5-1	McLean 2, Hamilton 2, Somers	8,000
Jan 18	Motherwell	D 2-2	McNair, Somers	10,000
Feb 1	PARTICK THISTLE	W 4-1	McLean 2, McMenemy, Somers	4,000
Feb 15	Port Glasgow	W 3-0	McMenemy 2, Kivlichan	3,000
Feb 29	THIRD LANARK	D 1-1	Quinn	11,000
Mar 7	HIBERNIAN	W 4-0	Loney, McMenemy, Somers, Hamilton	16,000
Mar 14	Partick Thistle	W 3-0	Kivlichan, Somers, Bennett (pen)	-
Mar 28	Dundee	L 0-2		14,000
Apr 4	MORTON	W 2-0	McLean, Loney	3,000
Apr 11	Queen's Park	W 2-0	McMenemy, Quinn	11,000
Apr 20	HEARTS	W 6-0	Quinn 3, McMenemy, Loney, Hamilton	10,000
Apr 25	Rangers	W 1-0	Bennett	40,000
Apr 27	Falkirk	D 1-1	Semple	10,000
Apr 30	St Mirren	D 2-2	Bennett 2	6,000

Scottish Cup

Jan 25	PEEBLES ROVERS	(Rd1) W 4-0	Kivlichan 2, Somers, Hamilton	4,000
Feb 8	Rangers	(Rd2) W 2-1	Kivlichan 2	23,000
Feb 22	Raith Rovers	(Rd3) W 3-0	McMenemy 2, Kivlichan	14,000
Mar 21	Aberdeen	(SF) W 1-0	McMenemy	20,000
Apr 18	St Mirren	(F) W 5-1	Bennett 2, Quinn, Somers, Hamilton	60,000

League & Cup Appearances

PLAYER	LEAGUE	CUP COMPETITION S CUP	TOTAL
Adams	34	5	39
Bennett	32	5	37
Craig	1		1
Hamilton	21	5	26
Hay	22	2	24
Kivlichan	11	3	14
Loney	26	5	31
McLean	10		10
MacLeod	26	1	27
McMenemy	30	5	35
McNair	19	5	24
Mitchell	17	3	20
Orr	1		1
Quinn	24	2	26
Sanderson	1		1
Semple	7		7
Somers	30	5	35
Templeton	4		4
Weir	29	5	34
Young	29	4	33

Goalscorers

PLAYER	LEAGUE	CUP COMPETITION S CUP	TOTAL
Quinn	19	1	20
Somers	11	2	13
Hamilton	10	2	12
Kivlichan	6	6	12
McMenemy	9	3	12
McLean	11		11
Bennett	7	2	9
loney	4		4
Hay	3		3
McNair	2		2
Semple	2		2
Young	1		1
Opps' o.gs.	1		1

Fact File

The Old Firm Scottish Cup tie saw admission prices double to a shilling and the attendance fall by an estimated 35,000.

SECRETARY-MANAGER: Willie Maley

CAPTAIN: Jimmy Hay

TOP SCORER: Jimmy Quinn

BIGGEST WIN: 6-0 v Hearts, 20 April 1908, league

HIGHEST ATTENDANCE: 60,000 v St Mirren, 18 April 1908, Scottish Cup

MAJOR TRANSFERS OUT: Bobby Templeton to Kilmarnock

Final Scottish League Div 1 Table

		P	W	D	L	F	A	Pts
1	CELTIC	34	24	7	3	86	27	55
2	FALKIRK	34	22	7	5	103	42	51
3	RANGERS	34	21	8	5	74	40	50
4	DUNDEE	34	20	8	6	71	28	48
5	HIBERNIAN	34	17	8	9	55	42	42
6	AIRDRIEONIANS	34	18	5	11	58	41	41
7	ST MIRREN	34	13	10	11	50	59	36
8	ABERDEEN	34	13	9	12	45	44	35
9	THIRD LANARK	34	13	7	14	45	50	33
10	MOTHERWELL	34	12	7	15	61	53	31
11	HAMILTON A	34	10	8	16	55	65	28
11	HEARTS	34	11	6	17	50	62	28
13	MORTON	34	9	9	16	43	66	27
14	PARTICK T	34	8	9	17	43	69	25
14	KILMARNOCK	34	6	13	15	38	61	25
16	QUEEN'S PARK	34	7	8	19	54	84	22
17	CLYDE	34	5	8	21	36	75	18
18	PORT GLASGOW A	34	5	7	22	39	98	17

Season 1908-09

Scottish League Divison 1

DATE	OPPONENTS	SCORE	GOALSCORERS	ATTENDANCE
Aug 15	Morton	W 5-0	Quinn 4, McMenemy	7,000
Aug 22	KILMARNOCK	W 5-1	Quinn 2 (1 pen), Munro 2, McMenemy	-
Aug 29	Dundee	L 1-2	Somers	21,000
Sep 5	ST MIRREN	L 0-1		-
Sep 28	THIRD LANARK	W 1-0	Hamilton	-
Oct 10	DUNDEE	W 2-0	Hamilton 2	20,000
Oct 31	Clyde	W 2-0	McMenemy, McLean	18,000
Nov 7	PARTICK THISTLE	W 3-0	McMenemy 3	5,000
Nov 14	PORT GLASGOW	W 2-1	Quinn, Hamilton	3,000
Nov 21	Airdrie	W 2-1	Quinn 2	11,000
Nov 28	QUEEN'S PARK	W 4-0	McMenemy 3, Somers	16,000
Dec 5	Motherwell	W 2-1	Loney, McMenemy	12,000
Dec 12	HIBERNIAN	W 2-0	Quinn, Loney	8,000
Dec 19	Aberdeen	W 2-0	Hamilton, Loney	10,000
Dec 26	CLYDE	L 0-1		10,000
Jan 1	Rangers	W 3-1	Hamilton, McMenemy, Munro	60,000
Jan 2	Kilmarnock	L 1-3	Loney	12,000
Jan 9	HEARTS	D 1-1	Quinn	10,000
Jan 30	FALKIRK	W 2-0	Quinn, Hamilton	10,000
Feb 13	Port Glasgow	W 4-1	Kivlichan 2, Quinn, Hamilton	-
Feb 24	ABERDEEN	W 2-0	Somers, Quinn	-
Mar 6	Falkirk	D 1-1	Dodds (pen)	10,000
Mar 13	RANGERS	L 2-3	Munro, Quinn	30,000
Mar 29	Partick Thistle	W 1-0	Kivlichan	-
Apr 3	St Mirren	W 1-0	McLean	-
Apr 12	Third Lanark	D 1-1	Somers	14,000
Apr 19	Hearts	W 2-1	McMenemy 2	12,000
Apr 21	HAMILTON AC.	D 1-1	Quinn	2,000
Apr 22	MORTON	W 5-1	Atkinson 2, Munro 2, McLean	-
Apr 24	AIRDRIE	D 0-0		-
Apr 26	MOTHERWELL	W 4-0	Quinn 3, McLean	-
Apr 28	Queen's Park	W 5-0	Quinn 3, McLean 2	-
Apr 29	Hibernian	L 0-1		7,000
Apr 30	Hamilton Ac.	W 2-1	Hamilton, McMenemy	8,000

Scottish Cup

Jan 23	Leith Athletic	(Rd1) W 4-2	Quinn 3, Hay	
Feb 6	PORT GLASGOW	(Rd2) W 4-0	Hay 2, Quinn, Hamilton	
Feb 20	AIRDRIE	(Rd3) W 3-1	McMenemy 2, Hamilton	20,000
Mar 20	CLYDE	(SF) D 0-0		40,000
Mar 27	CLYDE	(R) W 2-0	Quinn, o.g.	35,000
Apr 10	Rangers	(F) D 2-2	Quinn, o.g.	70,000
Apr 17	Rangers	(R) D 1-1	Quinn	60,000

League & Cup Appearances

PLAYER	LEAGUE	CUP COMPETITION S CUP	TOTAL
Adams	31	7	38
Atkinson	1		1
Craig	3		3
Dodds	16	4	20
Hamilton	30	7	37
Hay	33	7	40
Johnstone	1		1
Kivlichan	16	4	20
Loney	22	4	26
McLean	14		14
MacLeod	4		4
McMenemy	31	6	37
McNair	26	7	33
Mitchell	5		5
Moran	2		2
Munro	18	4	22
Oliver	2		2
Quinn	30	7	37
Sanderson	1		1
Semple	1		1
Somers	25	7	32
Weir	31	6	37
Young	31	7	38

Goalscorers

PLAYER	LEAGUE	CUP COMPETITION S CUP	TOTAL
Quinn	22	7	29
McMenemy	14	2	16
Hamilton	9	2	11
Munro	6		6
McLean	6		6
Somers	4		4
Loney	4		4
Kivlichan	3		3
Hay		3	3
Atkinson	2		2
Dodds	1		1
Opps' o.gs.		2	2

Fact File

Celtic won the league championship playing their last 8 games in 11 days and winning five of them.

SECRETARY-MANAGER: Willie Maley

CAPTAIN: Jimmy Hay

TOP SCORER: Jimmy Quinn

BIGGEST WIN: 5-0 v Morton, 15 August 1908, league

HIGHEST ATTENDANCE: 70,000 v Rangers, 10 April 1909, Scottish Cup

MAJOR TRANSFERS OUT: Alec Bennett to Rangers, Donald McLeod to Middlesbrough

Final Scottish League Div 1 Table

		P	W	D	L	F	A	Pts
1	CELTIC	34	23	5	6	71	24	51
2	DUNDEE	34	22	6	6	70	32	50
3	CLYDE	34	21	6	7	61	37	48
4	RANGERS	34	19	7	8	91	38	45
5	AIRDRIEONIANS	34	16	9	9	67	46	41
6	HIBERNIAN	34	16	7	11	40	32	39
7	ST MIRREN	34	15	6	13	53	45	36
7	ABERDEEN	34	15	6	13	61	53	36
9	FALKIRK	34	13	7	14	58	56	33
9	KILMARNOCK	34	13	7	14	47	61	33
11	THIRD LANARK	34	11	10	13	56	49	32
11	HEARTS	34	12	8	14	54	49	32
13	PORT GLASGOW A	34	10	8	16	39	52	28
13	MOTHERWELL	34	11	6	17	47	73	28
15	QUEEN'S PARK	34	6	13	15	42	65	25
16	HAMILTON A	34	6	12	16	42	72	24
17	MORTON	34	8	7	19	39	90	23
18	PARTICK T	34	2	4	28	38	102	8

Season 1909-1910

Scottish League Divison 1

DATE	OPPONENTS	SCORE	GOALSCORERS	ATTENDANCE
Aug 17	HAMILTON AC.	W 3-1	Hay, Quinn, McMenemy	-
Aug 21	FALKIRK	W 2-0	McMenemy, Kivlichan	22,000
Aug 28	Hibernian	L 0-1		18,000
Sep 4	MOTHERWELL	D 2-2	Johnstone, McMenemy	-
Sep 11	Morton	L 1-2	Quinn	-
Sep 18	Hamilton Ac.	W 5-1	McMenemy 3, Johnstone, McLean D	9,000
Sep 20	Hearts	W 2-1	McLean D, Kivlichan	-
Sep 27	Third Lanark	W 1-0	McMenemy	-
Oct 2	DUNDEE	W 1-0	Quinn	32,000
Oct 16	Port Glasgow	W 3-2	Johnstone, Weir (pen), Quinn	-
Oct 23	QUEEN'S PARK	W 6-0	Johnstone 2, Quinn 2, Kivlichan, Hamilton	-
Oct 30	Rangers	D 0-0		-
Nov 6	HEARTS	W 1-0	Hamilton	-
Nov 13	Partick Thistle	W 3-1	Quinn 2, Loney	30,000
Nov 20	AIRDRIE	W 3-1	Johnstone 2, Quinn	-
Nov 27	Aberdeen	W 1-0	Johnstone	-
Dec 4	KILMARNOCK	W 2-1	Loney, Quinn	-
Dec 11	ST MIRREN	D 1-1	McMenemy	-
Dec 18	Motherwell	W 3-1	Hay, Quinn, McMenemy	25,000
Dec 25	Kilmarnock	W 1-0	Quinn	-
Jan 1	RANGERS	D 1-1	Hamilton	60,000
Jan 3	Clyde	W 1-0	Quinn	20,000
Jan 8	Airdrie	W 2-0	Kivlichan 2	-
Jan 15	PORT GLASGOW	W 4-0	Quinn 2, Loney, Hamilton	-
Jan 29	St Mirren	L 1-2	Quinn	12,000
Mar 16	THIRD LANARK	W 2-0	Quinn, Johnstone	5,000
Mar 19	Queen's Park	W 1-0	Kivlichan	-
Mar 26	PARTICK THISTLE	W 3-1	Quinn 3	-
Mar 28	CLYDE	W 2-1	Quinn 2 (2 pens)	10,000
Apr 6	MORTON	W 3-0	Johnstone, Quinn, McMenemy	-
Apr 9	ABERDEEN	W 2-0	Quinn, Johnstone	-
Apr 23	Falkirk	L 0-2		-
Apr 25	HIBERNIAN	D 0-0		2,000
Apr 30	Dundee	D 0-0		-

Scottish Cup

Jan 22	Dumbarton	(Rd1) W 2-1	Loney, McMenemy	10,000
Feb 12	THIRD LANARK	(Rd2) W 3-1	Quinn 3	-
Feb 19	ABERDEEN	(Rd3) W 2-1	McMenemy, Quinn	25,000
Mar 12	Clyde	(SF) L 1-3	Kivlichan	38,000

League & Cup Appearances

PLAYER	LEAGUE	CUP COMPETITION S CUP	TOTAL
Adams	25	3	28
Allan	2		2
Dodds	12	1	13
Duncan	9		9
Hamilton	33	2	35
Hay	28	3	31
Johnstone	29	4	33
Kivlichan	24	4	28
Loney	25	4	29
McIntosh	8	3	11
McLean D	4		4
McLean L	3		3
McMenemy	29	3	32
McNair	28	3	31
Mitchell	15	1	16
Munro	7	2	9
Quinn	28	4	32
Robertson	3	1	4
Roose		1	1
Somers	6		6
Weir	20	3	23
Young Jim	34	2	36
Young John	2		2

Goalscorers

PLAYER	LEAGUE	CUP COMPETITION S CUP	TOTAL
Quinn	24	4	28
McMenemy	10	2	12
Johnstone	11		11
Kivlichan	6	1	7
Hamilton	4		4
Loney	3	1	4
Hay	2		2
McLean D	2		2
Weir	1		1

Fact File

On 29 January 1910 over 600 cartloads of snow had to be removed from the pitch before the match against St Mirren could start.

SECRETARY-MANAGER: Willie Maley

CAPTAIN: Jimmy Hay

TOP SCORER: Jimmy Quinn

BIGGEST WIN: 6-0 v Queen's Park, 23 October 1909, league

HIGHEST ATTENDANCE: 60,000 v Rangers, 1 January 1910, league

Final Scottish League Div 1 Table

		P	W	D	L	F	A	Pts
1	CELTIC	34	24	6	4	63	22	54
2	FALKIRK	34	22	8	4	71	28	52
3	RANGERS	34	20	6	8	70	35	46
4	ABERDEEN	34	16	8	10	44	29	40
5	CLYDE	34	14	9	11	47	40	37
6	DUNDEE	34	14	8	12	52	44	36
7	THIRD LANARK	34	13	8	13	62	44	34
7	HIBERNIAN	34	14	6	14	33	40	34
9	AIRDRIEONIANS	34	12	9	13	46	57	33
10	MOTHERWELL	34	12	8	14	59	60	32
10	KILMARNOCK	34	12	8	14	53	59	32
12	HEARTS	34	12	7	15	59	50	31
12	ST MIRREN	34	13	5	16	48	58	31
14	QUEEN'S PARK	34	12	6	16	54	74	30
15	HAMILTON A	34	11	6	17	50	67	28
16	PARTICK T	34	8	10	16	45	59	26
17	MORTON	34	11	3	20	38	60	25
18	PORT GLASGOW A	34	3	5	26	25	93	11

Season 1910-11

Scottish League Division 1

DATE	OPPONENTS	SCORE	GOALSCORERS	ATTENDANCE
Aug 17	AIRDRIE	W 3-0	Quinn 2, Loney	7,000
Aug 20	Falkirk	L 1-2	Quinn (pen)	12,000
Aug 27	MORTON	L 0-1		5,000
Sep 3	Kilmarnock	L 0-1		9,000
Sep 17	DUNDEE	W 2-1	Quinn, McMenemy	25,000
Sep 19	Hibernian	W 4-0	Quinn 2, Johnstone, McMenemy	12,000
Sep 26	Partick Thistle	D 1-1	McMenemy	18,000
Oct 1	Queen's Park	W 1-0	Kivlichan	15,000
Oct 3	Raith Rovers	L 1-2	McAteer	7,000
Oct 15	HEARTS	D 0-0		9,000
Oct 22	Hamilton	W 1-0	Quinn	10,000
Oct 29	RANGERS	L 0-1		32,000
Nov 5	ST MIRREN	W 5-0	Kivlichan 2, Loney, Johnstone, McMenemy	7,000
Nov 12	Airdrie	D 0-0		10,000
Nov 1	THIRD LANARK	D 0-0		8,000
Nov 26	Dundee	L 0-1		20,000
Dec 3	MOTHERWELL	W 3-0	Kivlichan, Quinn, McMenemy	3,000
Dec 10	Clyde	W 2-0	Loney, McMenemy	15,000
Dec 17	KILMARNOCK	W 2-0	Quinn, McMenemy	8,000
Dec 24	Morton	D 1-1	Quinn	7,000
Dec 31	RAITH ROVERS	W 5-0	McMenemy 2, Hastie, Quinn, McAtee	8,000
Jan 2	Rangers	D 1-1	McAtee	60,000
Jan 3	CLYDE	W 2-0	Quinn, McAtee	15,000
Jan 7	PARTICK THISTLE	W 2-0	Quinn, McAtee	12,000
Jan 14	Aberdeen	L 0-1		10,000
Jan 21	FALKIRK	D 0-0		7,000
Feb 4	Motherwell	L 1-2	Hastie	10,500
Feb 18	QUEEN'S PARK	W 2-0	Hastie, McAtee	2,500
Mar 18	St Mirren	D 1-1	McAtee	5,000
Mar 25	HIBERNIAN	W 2-0	McAtee, Kivlichan	4,000
Apr 1	Hearts	D 1-1	McCann	10,000
Apr 17	Third Lanark	D 1-1	McCann	8,000
Apr 26	HAMILTON AC.	W 3-0	McAtee, Johnstone, Quinn	1,000
Apr 29	ABERDEEN	D 0-0		3,000

Scottish Cup

Jan 28	ST MIRREN	(Rd1)	W 2-0	McMenemy, Hastie	15,000
Feb 11	GALSTON	(Rd2)	W 1-0	Quinn	5,000
Feb 25	CLYDE	(Rd3)	W 1-0	McMenemy	40,000
Mar 11	ABERDEEN	(SF)	W 1-0	McMenemy	48,000
Apr 8	Hamilton Ac.	(F)	D 0-0		45,000
Apr 15	Hamilton Ac.	(R)	W 2-0	Quinn, McAteer	25,000

League & Cup Appearances

PLAYER	LEAGUE	CUP COMPETITION S CUP	TOTAL
Adams	34	6	40
Blair	1		1
Dodds	25	6	31
Geechrin	1		1
Hamilton	22	6	28
Hastie	16	3	19
Hay	31	6	37
Johnstone	19	2	21
Kivlichan	25	5	30
Loney	21	2	23
McAtee	17	2	19
McAteer	13	4	17
McCann	7		7
McGregor	2		2
McMenemy	30	6	36
McNair	34	6	40
Mitchell	11		11
Munro	5		5
O'Neill	1		1
Quinn	27	6	33
Young Jim	31	6	37
Young John	1		1

Goalscorers

PLAYER	LEAGUE	CUP COMPETITION S CUP	TOTAL
Quinn	14	3	17
McMenemy	10	2	12
McAtee	6		6
Kivlichan	5		5
Hastie	3	1	4
McAteer	3	1	4
Johnstone	3		3
Loney	3		3
McCann	1		1

Fact File

Celtic won the Scottish Cup without conceding a goal.

SECRETARY-MANAGER: Willie Maley

CAPTAIN: Jimmy Hay

TOP SCORER: Jimmy Quinn

BIGGEST WIN: 5-0 v St Mirren, 5 November 1910, league; 5-0 v Raith Rovers, 31 December 1910, league

HIGHEST ATTENDANCE: 60,000 v Rangers, 2 January 1911, league

MAJOR TRANSFERS OUT: James Weir to Middlesbrough

Final Scottish League Div 1 Table

		P	W	D	L	F	A	Pts
1	RANGERS	34	23	6	5	90	34	52
2	ABERDEEN	34	19	10	5	53	28	48
3	FALKIRK	34	17	10	7	65	42	44
4	PARTICK T	34	17	8	9	50	41	42
5	CELTIC	34	15	11	8	48	18	41
5	DUNDEE	34	18	5	11	54	42	41
7	CLYDE	34	14	11	9	45	36	39
7	THIRD LANARK	34	16	7	11	59	53	39
9	HIBERNIAN	34	15	6	13	44	48	36
10	KILMARNOCK	34	12	10	12	42	45	34
11	AIRDRIEONIANS	34	12	9	13	49	53	33
12	ST MIRREN	34	12	7	15	46	57	31
13	MORTON	34	9	11	14	49	51	29
14	HEARTS	34	8	8	18	42	59	24
14	RAITH R	34	7	10	17	36	55	24
16	HAMILTON A	34	8	5	21	31	60	21
17	MOTHERWELL	34	8	4	22	37	66	20
18	QUEEN'S PARK	34	5	4	25	28	80	14

Season 1911-12

Scottish League Divison 1

DATE	OPPONENTS	SCORE	GOALSCORERS	ATTENDANCE
Aug 15	AIRDRIE	W 3-0	Hamilton, Brown, Dodds (pen)	7,000
Aug 19	FALKIRK	W 3-1	Brown, Hamilton, McMenemy	16,000
Aug 26	Morton	D 1-1	McMenemy	8,000
Sep 2	CLYDE	W 3-2	Quinn 2, McMenemy	16,000
Sep 16	Dundee	L 1-3	McMenemy	22,000
Sep 23	Kilmarnock	W 2-0	McMenemy, Nichol	6,000
Sep 25	PARTICK THISTLE	W 3-0	Nichol 2, McMenemy	8,000
Sep 30	Hearts	L 1-2	McAteer	25,000
Oct 2	Raith Rovers	W 2-1	Nichol, Travers	-
Oct 7	Hamilton Ac.	L 0-1		10,000
Oct 14	ABERDEEN	W 1-0	Donaldson	10,000
Oct 21	Rangers	L 1-3	McAtee	45,000
Oct 28	HIBERNIAN	W 3-1	Brown, McAtee, Donaldson	7,000
Nov 4	Falkirk	D 1-1	Brown	7,000
Nov 11	HAMILTON AC.	W 2-1	Donaldson, Nichol	8,000
Nov 18	Hibernian	D 1-1	Donaldson	11,000
Nov 25	Motherwell	L 2-3	Travers, Black	10,000
Dec 2	ST MIRREN	W 3-1	Donaldson, Johnstone, Loney	12,000
Dec 9	Queen's Park	W 4-1	Quinn 2, Donaldson, Gallacher	15,000
Dec 16	Third Lanark	L 0-1		12,000
Dec 23	MORTON	D 1-1	Johnstone	12,000
Dec 30	Airdrie	D 0-0		8,000
Jan 1	RANGERS	W 3-0	Quinn 3	70,000
Jan 2	Clyde	D 1-1	Dodds	17,000
Jan 6	HEARTS	D 1-1	Travers	20,000
Jan 13	MOTHERWELL	W 2-0	Quinn, McAtee	17,000
Jan 20	St Mirren	D 1-1	Nichol	16,000
Feb 3	THIRD LANARK	W 3-1	Clark, Gallacher, McAtee (pen)	11,000
Feb 17	QUEEN'S PARK	W 2-1	Travers, McAtee (pen)	12,000
Mar 2	DUNDEE	W 2-0	Nichol, Brown	6,000
Mar 16	Partick Thistle	D 1-1	Travers	25,000
Mar 23	Aberdeen	D 1-1	McMenemy	5,000
Apr 13	KILMARNOCK	W 2-0	Gibson, Nichol	6,000
Apr 20	Raith Rovers	D 1-1	McAtee	4,000

Scottish Cup

Jan 27	DUNFERMLINE ATH.	(Rd1) W 1-0	Brown	9,000
Feb 10	EAST STIRLING	(Rd2) W 3-0	Quinn 2, Travers	6,000
Feb 24	Aberdeen	(Rd3) D 2-2	Quinn, McAtee	25,000
Mar 9	ABERDEEN	(R) W 2-0	Travers 2	31,000
Mar 30	Hearts	(SF) W 3-0	McMenemy 2, Brown	43,000
Apr 6	Clyde	(F) W 2-0	McMenemy, Gallacher	46,000

League & Cup Appearances

PLAYER	LEAGUE	CUP COMPETITION S CUP	TOTAL
Adams	18		18
Black	4		4
Brown	27	6	33
Clark	2		2
Dodds	33	6	39
Donaldson	17		17
Gallacher	9	2	11
Gibson	2		2
Hamilton	12		12
Johnstone	27	6	33
Loney	22	6	28
McAtee	32	6	38
McAteer	11		11
McGormack	1		1
McGregor	8		8
McMenemy	21	6	27
McNair	29	6	35
Mitchell	5		5
Mulrooney	16	6	22
Nichol	16		16
Quinn	10	6	16
Travers	18	4	22
Young	34	6	40

Goalscorers

PLAYER	LEAGUE	CUP COMPETITION S CUP	TOTAL
Quinn	8	3	11
McMenemy	7	3	10
Nichol	8		8
Travers	5	3	8
Brown	5	2	7
McAtee	5	1	6
Donaldson	6		6
Gallacher	2	1	3
Dodds	2		2
Hamilton	2		2
Johnstone	2		2
Black	1		1
Clark	1		1
Gibson	1		1
Loney	1		1
McAteer	1		1

Fact File

On 1 January 1912 Jimmy Quinn scored a hat-trick against Rangers, repeating his hat-trick of the 1904 Scottish Cup final, also against Rangers.

SECRETARY-MANAGER: Willie Maley

CAPTAIN: Jim Young

TOP SCORER: Jimmy Quinn

BIGGEST WIN: 4-1 v Queen's Park, 9 December 1911, league

HIGHEST ATTENDANCE: 70,000 v Rangers, 1 January 1912, league

MAJOR TRANSFERS OUT: Jimmy Hay to Newcastle

Final Scottish League Div 1 Table

		P	W	D	L	F	A	Pts
1	RANGERS	34	24	3	7	86	34	51
2	CELTIC	34	17	11	6	58	33	45
3	CLYDE	34	19	4	11	56	32	42
4	HEARTS	34	16	8	10	54	40	40
4	PARTICK T	34	16	8	10	47	40	40
6	MORTON	34	14	9	11	44	44	37
7	FALKIRK	34	15	6	13	46	43	36
8	DUNDEE	34	13	9	12	52	41	35
8	ABERDEEN	34	14	7	13	44	44	35
10	AIRDRIEONIANS	34	12	8	14	40	41	32
11	THIRD LANARK	34	12	7	15	40	57	31
12	HAMILTON A	34	11	8	15	32	44	30
13	HIBERNIAN	34	12	5	17	44	47	29
14	MOTHERWELL	34	11	5	18	34	44	27
14	RAITH R	34	9	9	16	39	59	27
16	KILMARNOCK	34	11	4	19	38	60	26
17	QUEEN'S PARK	34	8	9	17	29	53	25
18	ST MIRREN	34	7	10	17	32	59	24

Season 1912-13

Scottish League Divison 1

DATE	OPPONENTS	SCORE	GOALSCORERS	ATTENDANCE
Aug 17	Falkirk	D 0-0		10,000
Aug 24	HIBERNIAN	D 1-1	McMenemy	12,000
Aug 31	Kilmarnock	W 2-0	Unrecorded	9,000
Sep 7	ABERDEEN	W 2-0	McMenemy, Johnstone, Gray	10,000
Sep 14	Airdrie	W 4-1	McMenemy, Gray, Johnstone, Gallacher	15,000
Sep 21	Dundee	L 1-3	McMenemy	20,000
Sep 30	Partick Thistle	W 3-2	McAtee, Brown, Gray	12,000
Oct 5	MORTON	W 1-0	Quinn	20,000
Oct 19	Raith Rovers	L 1-2	Dodds (pen)	10,000
Oct 26	RANGERS	W 3-2	Brown, Gallacher, Quinn	40,000
Nov 2	Third Lanark	W 1-0	Gallacher	18,000
Nov 9	HEARTS	W 1-0	McMenemy	13,000
Nov 16	Queen's Park	W 1-0	McAtee	13,000
Nov 23	MOTHERWELL	L 1-2	Quinn	5,000
Nov 30	Clyde	D 1-1	Browning	10,000
Dec 7	HAMILTON AC.	W 2-1	McAtee, McMenemy	8,000
Dec 14	Morton	W 2-1	Browning, Loney (pen)	11,000
Dec 21	DUNDEE	W 2-0	Gallacher, Quinn	8,000
Dec 28	St Mirren	W 3-1	Quinn, McAtee, Browning	12,000
Jan 1	Ranger	W 1-0	Quinn	67,000
Jan 2	CLYDE	W 3-0	Quinn, McMenemy, Young (pen)	18,000
Jan 4	PARTICK THISTLE	W 1-0	Gallacher	15,000
Jan 11	QUEEN'S PARK	W 1-0	Gallacher	9,000
Jan 18	Hibernian	L 0-1		14,000
Jan 25	AIRDRIE	D 1-1	Gray	12,000
Feb 1	THIRD LANARK	W 2-0	Gallacher 2	7,000
Feb 15	Aberdeen	L 0-3		12,000
Mar 15	Motherwell	L 0-1		10,000
Mar 22	FALKIRK	L 1-2	Browning	18,000
Mar 24	RAITH ROVERS	W 4-1	Quinn 3, Gallacher	15,000
Mar 29	KILMARNOCK	W 4-1	Browning 2, Quinn, Gallacher	8,000
Apr 5	ST MIRREN	W 2-1	Browning, Gray	10,000
Apr 21	Hearts	D 0-0		-
Apr 26	Hamilton Ac.	W 1-0	Browning	4,000

Scottish Cup

Feb 8	ARBROATH	(Rd1) W 4-0	Johnstone 2, Gallacher, Brown	9,000
Feb 22	PEEBLES ROVERS	(Rd2) W 3-0	McMenemy 2, Quinn	6,000
Mar 8	HEARTS	(Rd3) L 0-1		65,000

League & Cup Appearances

PLAYER	LEAGUE	CUP COMPETITION S CUP	TOTAL
Boyle	8		8
Brown	13	1	14
Browning	21		21
Cassidy	3		3
Dodds	34	3	37
Gallacher	33	3	36
Gray	12	1	13
Jarvis	6		6
Johnstone	28	3	31
Loney	21	3	24
McAtee	32	2	34
McGregor	6		6
McMenemy	21	3	24
McNair	30	3	33
Mitchell	24	2	26
Mulrooney	26	3	29
Quinn	23	6	26
Young	33	3	36

Goalscorers

PLAYER	LEAGUE	CUP COMPETITION S CUP	TOTAL
Quinn	10	1	11
Gallacher	10	1	11
McMenemy	7	2	9
Browning	8		8
Gray	5		5
McAtee	4		4
Johnstone	2	2	4
Brown	2	1	3
Dodds	1		1
Loney	1		1
Young	1		1

2 league goals unrecorded

Fact File

On 2 January 1913 Jim Young took over from regular penalty-taker Joe Dodds and scored his first goal in 6 years.

SECRETARY-MANAGER: Willie Maley

CAPTAIN: Jim Young

TOP SCORER: Jimmy Quinn

BIGGEST WIN: 4-0 v Arbroath, 8 February 1912, Scottish Cup

HIGHEST ATTENDANCE: 67,000 v Rangers, 1 January 1913, league

MAJOR TRANSFERS OUT: Davie Hamilton to Dundee

Final Scottish League Div 1 Table

		P	W	D	L	F	A	Pts
1	RANGERS	34	24	5	5	76	41	53
2	CELTIC	34	22	5	7	53	28	49
3	HEARTS	34	17	7	10	71	43	41
3	AIRDRIEONIANS	34	15	11	8	64	46	41
5	FALKIRK	34	14	12	8	56	38	40
6	MOTHERWELL	34	12	13	9	47	39	37
6	ABERDEEN	34	14	9	11	47	40	37
6	HIBERNIAN	34	16	5	13	63	54	37
9	CLYDE	34	13	9	12	41	44	35
10	HAMILTON A	34	12	8	14	44	47	32
11	KILMARNOCK	34	10	11	13	37	54	31
12	ST MIRREN	34	10	10	14	50	60	30
13	MORTON	34	11	7	16	50	59	29
13	DUNDEE	34	8	13	13	33	46	29
15	THIRD LANARK	34	8	12	14	31	41	28
16	RAITH R	34	8	10	16	46	60	26
17	PARTICK T	34	10	4	20	40	55	24
18	QUEEN'S PARK	34	5	3	26	34	88	13

Season 1913-14

Scottish League Divison 1

DATE	OPPONENTS	SCORE	GOALSCORERS	ATTENDANCE
Aug 16	AYR UNITED	W 5-1	Connolly 2, McAtee 2 Gallacher	20,000
Aug 23	Motherwell	D 1-1	Connolly	20,000
Aug 30	FALKIRK	W 4-0	McAtee, Connolly, McMenemy, Browning	30,000
Sep 6	Hibernian	W 2-1	McMenemy 2	20,000
Sep 13	ST MIRREN	L 0-2		6,000
Sep 15	HEARTS	L 0-2		16,000
Sep 20	Morton	W 4-0	Gallacher 2, Quinn 2	20,000
Sep 29	CLYDE	W 2-0	Gallacher, McMenemy	20,000
Oct 4	ABERDEEN	W 2-1	Browning, McAtee	15,000
Oct 11	Aberdeen	W 1-0	Young	14,000
Oct 18	DUNDEE	W 1-0	McAtee	25,000
Oct 25	Rangers	W 2-0	McAtee, Whitehead	64,000
Nov 1	KILMARNOCK	W 4-0	Gallacher 2, McColl 2	13,000
Nov 8	Queen's Park	W 2-0	McAtee, Dodds (pen)	18,000
Nov 15	Dumbarton	W 4-0	Gallacher 2, Whitehead, Browning	10,000
Nov 22	HAMILTON AC.	W 1-0	Gallacher	15,000
Nov 29	Airdrie	W 1-0	Gallacher	18,000
Dec 6	THIRD LANARK	W 3-0	Gallagher, Owers, Crone	10,000
Dec 13	Raith Rovers	W 2-1	Browning, Owers	12,000
Dec 20	MOTHERWELL	D 0-0		16,000
Dec 27	Ayr United	W 6-0	Owers 4, Browning 2	7,000
Jan 1	RANGERS	W 4-0	Browning 2, Young, McMenemy	75,000
Jan 3	Partick Thistle	D 0-0		30,000
Jan 5	Clyde	W 1-0	Owers	9,000
Jan 10	DUMBARTON	W 4-0	Gallacher 3, Johnstone	11,000
Jan 17	Dundee	W 1-0	Browning	20,000
Jan 24	Airdrie	W 1-0	McMaster	16,000
Jan 31	St Mirren	W 3-0	Owers, Johnstone, Dodds (pen)	16,000
Feb 14	MORTON	W 3-0	McColl, Gallacher, Browning	21,000
Feb 28	Falkirk	L 0-1		10,000
Mar 24	HEARTS	D 0-0		10,000
Apr 1	Third Lanark	W 3-1	Gallacher 2, McMenemy	8,000
Apr 8	Kilmarnock	W 1-0	Gallacher	6,000
Apr 13	QUEEN'S PARK	W 5-0	McColl 2, Gallacher, McMenemy, McAtee	14,000
Apr 18	HIBERNIAN	W 3-0	McMenemy 2, McColl	12,000
Apr 24	Hamilton Ac.	W 2-1	McColl, Crone	7,000
apr 25	PARTICK THISTLE	D 1-1	McMenemy	8,000
Apr 29	RAITH ROVERS	W 2-1	Gallacher 2	-

Scottish Cup

Feb 7	Clyde	(Rd1) D 0-0		46,000
Feb 10	CLYDE	(R) W 2-0	Gallacher 2	40,000
Feb 21	Forfar Athletic	(Rd2) W 5-0	McColl 3, Dodds,	6,000
Mar 7	Motherwell	(Rd3) W 3-1	Gallacher, McColl, McAtee	18,000
Mar 28	Third Larnark	(SF) W 2-0	McAtee, Owers	56,000
Apr 1	Hibernian	(F) D 0-0		40,000
Apr 16	Hibernian	(R) W 4-1	McColl 2, Browning 2	-

League & Cup Appearances

PLAYER	LEAGUE	CUP COMPETITION S CUP	TOTAL
Brown	37	7	44
Cassidy	1		1
Connolly	9		9
Crone	8		8
Davidson	5	1	6
Dodds	36	7	43
Gallacher	37	7	44
Hill	2		2
Johnstone	36	7	43
Loney	2		2
McAtee	36	7	43
McColl	17	4	21
McGregor A	1		1
McGregor T	13	3	16
McMaster	33	6	39
McMenemy	20	6	26
McNair	32	4	36
Owers	13	3	16
Quinn	1	1	2
Shaw	38	7	45
Whitehead	7		7
Young	34	7	41

Goalscorers

PLAYER	LEAGUE	CUP COMPETITION S CUP	TOTAL
Gallacher	21	3	24
McColl	7	6	13
Browning	10	2	12
McMenemy	10	1	11
McAtee	8	2	10
Owers	8	1	9
Connolly	4		4
Dodds	2	1	3
Crone	2		2
Quinn	2		2
Young	2		2
Johnstone	2		2
Whitehead	2		2
McMaster	1		1

Fact File

Celtic won their third league and Scottish Cup 'double' but would have to wait 40 years for another.

SECRETARY-MANAGER: Willie Maley

CAPTAIN: Jim Young

TOP SCORER: Patsy Gallacher

BIGGEST WIN: 6-0 v Ayr Utd, 27 December 1913, league

HIGHEST ATTENDANCE: 75,000 v Rangers, 1 January 1914, league

MAJOR TRANSFERS IN: Charlie Shaw from Queen's Park Rangers

MAJOR TRANSFERS OUT: Willie Loney to Motherwell

Final Scottish League Div 1 Table

		P	W	D	L	F	A	Pts
1	CELTIC	38	30	5	3	81	14	65
2	RANGERS	38	27	5	6	79	31	59
3	HEARTS	38	23	8	7	70	29	54
3	MORTON	38	26	2	10	76	51	54
5	FALKIRK	38	20	9	9	69	51	49
6	AIRDRIEONIANS	38	18	12	8	72	43	48
7	DUNDEE	38	19	5	14	64	53	43
8	THIRD LANARK	38	10	15	13	42	51	36
9	CLYDE	38	11	11	16	44	44	33
9	AYR U	38	13	7	18	56	72	33
11	RAITH R	38	13	6	19	56	57	32
12	KILMARNOCK	38	11	9	18	48	68	31
13	HIBERNIAN	38	12	6	20	58	75	30
13	ABERDEEN	38	10	10	18	38	55	30
15	PARTICK T	38	10	9	19	37	51	29
15	QUEEN'S PARK	38	10	9	19	52	84	29
17	HAMILTON A	38	11	6	21	49	66	28
17	MOTHERWELL	38	11	6	21	46	65	28
19	DUMBARTON	38	10	7	21	45	87	27
20	ST MIRREN	38	8	6	24	38	73	22

Season 1914-15

Scottish League Divison 1

DATE	OPPONENTS	SCORE	GOALSCORERS	ATTENDANCE
Aug 15	Hearts	L 0-2		-
Aug 22	MOTHERWELL	W 1-0	McColl	20,000
Aug 29	St Mirren	D 3-3	Gallacher 2, McColl	18,000
Sep 5	MORTON	W 6-2	McAtee 4, Crone 2	15,000
Sep 19	Hibernian	D 1-1	McColl	14,000
Sep 26	Dundee	W 3-1	McColl 2, Gallacher	12,000
Sep 28	CLYDE	W 3-0	McColl, Browning, McMenemy	14,000
Oct 3	DUNDEE	W 6-0	Browning 3, McMenemy 2, McColl	15,000
Oct 5	Raith Rovers	D 2-2	McColl, McMenemy	10,000
Oct 10	Ayr United	L 0-1		5,000
Oct 17	FALKIRK	W 1-0	Gallacher	10,000
Oct 24	Hamilton Ac.	W 1-0	Quinn	20,000
Oct 31	RANGERS	W 2-1	McMenemy, Gallacher	35,000
Nov 7	Kilmarnock	W 3-1	McMenemy 2, McAtee	12,000
Nov 14	THIRD LANARK	W 1-0	McColl	6,000
Nov 21	AYR UNITED	W 4-0	Gallacher 3, Browning	7,000
Nov 28	Dumbarton	W 4-1	McColl 2, McAtee, McMenemy	4,000
Dec 5	Aberdeen	W 1-0	Browning	7,000
Dec 12	QUEEN'S PARK	W 5-1	Crone 3, Quinn 2	6,000
Dec 19	Airdrie	W 1-0	McColl	7,000
Dec 26	HAMILTON AC.	W 3-1	Gallacher 2, Quinn	8,000
Jan 1	Rangers	L 1-2	Browning	50,000
Jan 2	Clyde	W 2-0	Browning 2	6,000
Jan 4	KILMARNOCK	W 2-0	Mccoll, Johnstone	8,000
Jan 9	PARTICK THISTLE	W 6-1	Gallacher 3, Mccoll, Browning, Dodds	11,000
Jan 16	Falkirk	W 1-0	McAtee	10,000
Jan 30	HEARTS	D 1-1	McAtee	45,000
Feb 6	ST MIRREN	W 2-1	McColl 2	10,000
Feb 13	Morton	W 2-0	McColl, Gallacher	10,000
Feb 20	DUMBARTON	W 1-0	McColl	5,000
Feb 27	Partick Thistle	W 2-0	McColl, Dodds (pen)	30,000
Mar 6	HIBERNIAN	W 5-1	McMenemy 2, Browning, Dodds, McAtee	13,000
Mar 27	RAITH ROVERS	W 3-1	McColl 3	6,000
Apr 3	AIRDRIE	W 3-0	McColl, McMenemy, Browning	10,000
Apr 5	Queen's Park	W 3-0	McColl, McMenemy, Gallacher	15,000
Apr 10	ABERDEEN	W 1-0	McMenemy	20,000
Apr 17	Third Lanark	W 4-0	Browning 2, McColl, McMenemy	12,000
Apr 24	Motherwell	D 1-1		-

The Scottish Cup was suspended for the duration of the First World War.

League Appearances

PLAYER	LEAGUE	TOTAL
Browning	38	38
Crone	5	5
Dodds	36	36
Gallacher	32	32
Gray	1	1
Jarvis	1	1
Johnstone	33	33
McAtee	38	38
McColl	33	33
McGregor	16	16
McMaster	32	32
McMenemy	36	36
McNair	35	35
Quinn	6	6
Shaw	38	38
Young	38	38

Goalscorers

PLAYER	LEAGUE	TOTAL
McColl	25	25
Gallacher	15	15
Browning	14	14
McMenemy	14	14
McAtee	9	9
Crone	5	5
Quinn	4	4
Dodds	3	3
Johnstone	1	1

1 league goal unrecorded

Final Scottish League Div 1 Table

		P	W	D	L	F	A	Pts
1	CELTIC	38	30	5	3	91	25	65
2	HEARTS	38	27	7	4	83	32	61
3	RANGERS	38	23	4	11	74	47	50
4	MORTON	38	18	12	8	74	48	48
4	AYR U	38	20	8	10	55	40	48
6	FALKIRK	38	16	7	15	48	48	39
7	HAMILTON A	38	16	6	16	60	55	38
7	PARTICK T	38	15	8	15	56	58	38
9	ST MIRREN	38	14	8	16	56	65	36
10	AIRDRIEONIANS	38	14	7	17	54	60	35
10	HIBERNIAN	38	12	11	15	59	66	35
12	KILMARNOCK	38	15	4	19	55	59	34
12	DUMBARTON	38	13	8	17	51	66	34
14	ABERDEEN	38	11	11	16	39	52	33
14	DUNDEE	38	12	9	17	43	61	33
16	THIRD LANARK	38	10	12	16	51	57	32
17	CLYDE	38	12	6	20	44	59	30
17	MOTHERWELL	38	10	10	18	49	66	30
19	RAITH R	38	9	10	19	53	68	28
20	QUEEN'S PARK	38	4	5	29	27	90	13

Fact File

Andrew Kerins (aka Brother Walfrid), the founder of the club, died in 1915 aged 76.

SECRETARY-MANAGER: Willie Maley

CAPTAIN: Jim Young

TOP SCORER: Jimmy McColl

BIGGEST WIN: 6-0 v Dundee, 3 October 1914, league

HIGHEST ATTENDANCE: 50,000 v Rangers, 1 January 1915, league

Season 1915-16

Scottish League Divison 1

DATE	OPPONENTS	SCORE	GOALSCORERS	ATTENDANCE
Aug 21	MOTHERWELL	W 3-1	Gallacher, McColl, Dodds	16,000
Aug 28	Airdrie	W 5-0	McColl 4, Browning	8,000
Sep 4	FALKIRK	W 2-1	Gallacher 2	16,000
Sep 11	Morton	W 1-0	Young	10,000
Sep 18	Dundee	W 2-0	Gallacher, Browning	12,000
Sep 27	CLYDE	W 5-0	McColl 2, Browning, McMenemy, McAtee	10,000
Oct 2	Hibernian	W 4-0	McColl, Gallacher, McMaster, McAtee	12,000
Oct 16	Hamilton Ac.	W 3-2	McColl, Young, Gallacher	14,000
Oct 23	ST MIRREN	L 0-2		6,000
Oct 30	Rangers	L 0-3		45,000
Nov 6	ABERDEEN	W 3-1	McColl 2, Gallacher	7,000
Nov 13	Hearts	L 0-2		16,000
Nov 20	KILMARNOCK	W 2-0	McColl, o.g.	4,000
Nov 27	Raith Roves	W 2-0	McColl, Gallacher	5,000
Dec 4	QUEEN'S PARK	W 6-2	McColl 3, Dodds, Johnstone, Browning	6,000
Dec 11	Ayr United	W 4-0	Gallacher 2, McMenemy, Browning	4,000
Dec 18	Partick Thistle	W 4-0	McMenemy 2, McAtee, Browning	22,000
Dec 25	AIRDRIE	W 6-0	Gallacher 3, McColl, Browning, McMenemy	10,000
Jan 1	RANGERS	D 2-2	McColl, McAtee	40,000
Jan 3	Clyde	W 3-1	McColl 2, Crone	12,000
Jan 8	Dumbarton	W 2-1	Browning, Johnstone	7,000
Jan 15	HIBERNIAN	W 3-1	McColl 2, Gallacher	10,000
Jan 22	Third Lanark	W 4-0	McAtee 2, McColl, Dodds (pen)	10,000
Jan 29	AYR UNITED	W 3-1	McColl, McAtee, Gallacher	12,000
Feb 5	Aberdeen	W 4-0	Gallacher 2, McColl, McMenemy	12,000
Feb 12	DUMBARTON	W 6-0	McAtee 3 (1 pen), McMaster 2, Gallacher	6,000
Feb 19	Queen's Park	W 1-0	Gallacher	15,000
Feb 26	DUNDEE	W 3-0	McColl 2, Dodds	10,000
Mar 4	Kilmarnock	W 3-0	McColl, Gallacher, McMenemy	10,000
Mar 11	HAMILTON AC.	W 5-1	McColl 4, McMenemy	7,000
Mar 18	St Mirren	W 5-0	McColl 2, Browning, Gallacher, McAtee	10,000
Apr 1	MORTON	D 0-0		20,000
Apr 8	Falkirk	W 2-0	Crone, O'Kane	8,000
Apr 15	RAITH ROVERS	W 6-0	Gallacher 3, O'Kane 2, Dodds	10,000
Apr 15	Motherwell	W 3-1	McMenemy, Dodds (pen), Browning	10,000
Apr 22	HEARTS	D 0-0		18,000
Apr 24	THIRD LANARK	W 4-1	O'Kane 3, Gallacher	4,000
Apr 29	PARTICK THISTLE	W 5-0	Gallacher 3, O'Kane 2	18,000

League Appearances

PLAYER	LEAGUE	TOTAL
Browning	38	38
Cassidy	4	4
Crone	4	4
Dodds	38	38
Gallacher	37	37
Johnstone	36	36
McAtee	34	34
McCabe	2	2
McColl	32	32
McGregor	15	15
McMaster	37	37
McMenemy	32	32
McNair	31	31
O'Kane	5	5
Shaw	38	38
Young	35	35

Goalscorers

PLAYER	LEAGUE	TOTAL
McColl	34	34
Gallacher	28	28
McAtee	11	11
Browning	10	10
McMenemy	9	9
O'Kane	8	8
Dodds	6	6
McMaster	3	3
Crone	2	2
Johnstone	2	2
Young	2	2
Opps' o.gs.	1	1

Fact File

Celtic played and won two league matches on the same day. On 15 April they beat Raith Rovers 6-0 in the afternoon before going to Motherwell and winning 3-1.

SECRETARY-MANAGER: Willie Maley

CAPTAIN: Jim Young

TOP SCORER: Jimmy McColl

BIGGEST WIN: 6-0 v Airdrie, 25 December 1915, league; 6-0 v Dumbarton, 12 February 1916, league; 6-0 v Raith Rovers, 15 April 1916, league

HIGHEST ATTENDANCE: 45,000 v Rangers, 30 October 1915, league

Final Scottish League Div 1 Table

		P	W	D	L	F	A	Pts
1	CELTIC	38	32	3	3	116	23	67
2	RANGERS	38	25	6	7	87	39	56
3	MORTON	37	22	7	8	86	35	51
4	AYR U	38	20	8	10	72	45	48
5	PARTICK T	38	19	8	11	65	41	46
5	HEARTS	37	20	6	11	66	45	46
7	HAMILTON A	38	19	3	16	68	76	41
8	DUNDEE	38	18	4	16	56	49	40
9	DUMBARTON	38	13	11	14	54	64	37
10	KILMARNOCK	38	12	11	15	46	49	35
11	ABERDEEN	38	11	12	15	51	64	34
12	FALKIRK	38	12	9	17	45	61	33
13	ST MIRREN	38	13	4	21	50	67	30
13	MOTHERWELL	38	11	8	19	55	82	30
13	AIRDRIEONIANS	38	11	8	19	44	74	30
16	THIRD LANARK	38	9	11	18	40	56	29
16	CLYDE	38	11	7	20	49	71	29
18	QUEEN'S PARK	38	11	6	21	53	100	28
19	HIBERNIAN	38	9	7	22	44	71	25
20	RAITH R	38	9	5	24	30	65	23

MORTON AND HEARTS PLAYED ONLY ONCE.

Season 1916-17

Scottish League Divison 1

DATE	OPPONENTS	SCORE	GOALSCORERS	ATTENDANCE
Aug 19	St Mirren	W 5-1	Gallacher 4, O'Kane	13,000
Aug 26	HIBERNIAN	W 3-1	Browning 2, O'Kane	8,000
Sep 2	Ayr United	W 1-0	O'Kane	7,000
Sep 9	AIRDRIE	W 3-1	O'Kane 2, Gallacher	12,000
Sep 16	Motherwell	W 4-0	McAtee 2, Gallacher 2	14,000
Sep 30	HEARTS	W 1-0	Browning	15,000
Oct 14	Falkirk	D 1-1	Gallacher	4,000
Oct 21	MORTON	D 0-0		25,000
Oct 28	RANGERS	D 0-0		40,000
Nov 4	Dundee	W 2-1	Gallacher, Browning	10,000
Nov 11	Queen's Park	W 3-1	Gallacher, McColl, Dodds (pen)	18,000
Nov 18	PARTICK THISTLE	D 0-0		10,000
Nov 25	ABERDEEN	W 1-0	McMenemy	8,000
Dec 2	Raith Rovers	W 4-1	McColl 3, Browning	3,000
Dec 9	AYR UNITED	W 5-0	Gallacher 3, Browning, McMenemy	8,000
Dec 16	Hamilton Ac.	W 4-0	Browning 2, McColl, Dodds (pen)	8,000
Dec 23	Partick Thistle	W 2-0	Browning, McColl	16,000
Dec 30	FALKIRK	W 2-0	Browning, Mccoll	7,000
Jan 1	Rangers	D 0-0		45,000
Jan 2	CLYDE	D 0-0		7,000
Jan 6	MOTHERWELL	W 1-0	Dodds	9,000
Jan 13	Hearts	W 1-0	McColl	15,000
Jan 20	DUMBARTON	D 1-1	McColl	-
Jan 27	Third Lanark	D 0-0		15,000
Feb 3	RAITH ROVERS	W 5-0	McColl 2, Gallacher 2, McAtee	16,000
Feb 10	Morton	W 1-0	McColl	16,000
Feb 17	DUNDEE	W 2-0	McColl 2	10,000
Feb 24	Kilmarnock	D 2-2	McMenemy, Gallacher	7,000
Mar 3	QUEEN'S PARK	W 3-2	McColl, Browning, McMenemy	16,000
Mar 10	HAMILTON AC.	W 6-1	McColl 4, Gallacher, McMenemy	10,000
Mar 17	Airdrie	W 2-1	McAtee, Gallacher	8,000
Mar 24	Aberdeen	D 0-0		25,000
Mar 31	ST MIRREN	W 3-0	McColl, Gallacher, Dodds	8,000
Apr 7	Dumbarton	W 3-1	McColl, Browning, Dodds (pen)	18,000
Apr 9	THIRD LANARK	W 2-0	McColl, Gallacher	10,000
Apr 14	Hibernian	W 1-0	Gallacher	18,000
Apr 21	KILMARNOCK	L 0-2		18,000
Apr 28	Clyde	W 5-0	McColl 2, Gallacher, McLean, Dodds	16,000

League Appearances

PLAYER	LEAGUE	TOTAL
Brown	22	22
Browning	35	35
Cassidy	3	3
Connolly	4	4
Dodds	38	38
Fullerton	1	1
Gallacher	28	28
Hamill	7	7
Johnstone	2	2
McAtee	32	32
McColl	31	31
McGregor	1	1
McLean	6	6
McMaster	4	4
McMenemy	34	34
McNair	37	37
McStay	37	37
O'Kane	15	15
Ribchester	2	2
Shaw	38	38
Wilson	36	36
Young	5	5

Goalscorers

PLAYER	LEAGUE	TOTAL
McColl	24	24
Gallacher	22	22
Browning	12	12
Dodds	6	6
McMenemy	5	5
O'Kane	5	5
McAtee	4	4
McLean	1	1

Final Scottish League Div 1 Table

		P	W	D	L	F	A	Pts
1	CELTIC	38	27	10	1	79	17	64
2	MORTON	38	24	6	8	72	39	54
3	RANGERS	38	24	5	9	68	32	53
4	AIRDRIEONIANS	38	21	8	9	71	38	50
5	THIRD LANARK	38	19	11	8	53	37	49
6	KILMARNOCK	38	18	7	13	69	46	43
7	ST MIRREN	38	15	10	13	49	43	40
8	MOTHERWELL	38	16	6	16	57	59	38
9	PARTICK T	38	14	7	17	44	43	35
9	DUMBARTON	38	12	11	15	56	73	35
9	HAMILTON A	38	13	9	16	54	73	35
12	FALKIRK	38	12	10	16	58	57	34
12	CLYDE	38	10	14	14	41	53	34
14	HEARTS	38	14	4	20	44	59	32
15	AYR U	38	12	7	19	47	59	31
16	DUNDEE	38	13	4	21	58	71	30
16	HIBERNIAN	38	10	10	18	57	72	30
18	QUEEN'S PARK	38	11	7	20	56	81	29
19	RAITH R	38	8	7	23	42	91	23
20	ABERDEEN	38	7	7	24	36	68	21

Fact File

Celtic's 0-2 defeat by Kilmarnock on 21 April 1917 ended a run of 62 undefeated league games.

SECRETARY-MANAGER: Willie Maley

CAPTAIN: Charlie Shaw

TOP SCORER: Jimmy McColl

BIGGEST WIN: 6-1 v Hamilton, 10 March 1916, league

HIGHEST ATTENDANCE: 45,000 v Rangers, 1 January 1917, league

Season 1917-18

Scottish League Divison 1

DATE	OPPONENTS	SCORE	GOALSCORERS	ATTENDANCE
Aug 18	AYR UNITED	W 4-0	McColl 2, Browning 2	15,000
Aug 25	Falkirk	W 3-1	Gallacher, McMenemy, McAtee	6,000
Sep 1	CLYDE	W 3-2	McColl 3	12,000
Sep 15	PARTICK THISTLE	W 2-1	McColl 2	15,000
Sep 24	Third Lanark	W 2-0	McColl, Browning	12,000
Sep 29	Hearts	W 1-0	McLean	10,000
Oct 13	KILMARNOCK	L 2-3	McLean, Gallacher	18,000
Oct 20	Rangers	W 2-1	McColl, McAtee	45,000
Oct 27	QUEEN'S PARK	W 3-0	McAtee, Jackson, Browning	8,000
Nov 3	Airdire	L 0-2		-
Nov 10	HAMILTON AC.	W 1-0	McLean	6,000
Nov 17	Dumbarton	W 2-0	Gallacher, Browning	7,000
Nov 24	HIBERNIAN	W 2-0	McLean, Dodds	7,000
Dec 1	Morton	D 1-1	McLean	12,000
Dec 8	CLYDEBANK	W 3-0	McLean, Jackson, McCormack	12,000
Dec 15	Motherwell	W 4-3	Gallacher, Jackson, McAtee, Browning	7,000
Dec 22	DUMBARTON	W 3-0	Gallacher 2, McMenemy	8,000
Dec 29	Ayr United	W 2-1	McLean 2	4,000
Jan 1	RANGERS	D 0-0		50,000
Jan 2	Clyde	W 4-1	McMenemy, Browning, Gallacher, Cringan	12,000
Jan 5	St Mirren	D 0-0		13,000
Jan 12	FALKIRK	D 0-0		6,000
Jan 26	AIRDIRE	D 3-3	Gallacher, Brown, McLean	15,000
Feb 2	Queen's Park	W 2-0	Gallacher, McMenemy	15,000
Feb 9	HEARTS	W 3-0	Gallacher, McMenemy, McLean	6,000
Feb 16	Hamilton Ac.	W 2-1	McLean 2	10,000
Feb 23	MORTON	W 2-0	Gallacher 2	20,000
Mar 2	Clydebank	W 2-1	Gallacher (pen), Browning	16,000
Mar 9	Partick Thistle	D 0-0		30,000
Mar 16	ST MIRREN	W 1-0	McColl	15,000
Mar 23	THIRD LANARK	L 1-3	Gallacher	12,000
Mar 30	Kilmarnock	W 3-1	Gallacher, McLean, Browning	8,000
Apr 6	Hibernian	W 2-0	Gallacher, McAtee	11,000
Apr 13	MOTHERWELL	D 1-1	Gallacher	30,000

League Appearances

PLAYER	LEAGUE	TOTAL
Bauchop	1	1
Brodei	1	1
Brown	32	32
Browning	31	31
Cassidy	1	1
Cringan	30	30
Dodds	27	27
Gallacher	33	33
Jackson	21	21
Kelly	1	1
Livingstone	6	6
McAtee	28	28
McColl	14	14
McCormack	2	2
McGregro	10	10
McInally	1	1
McLean	23	23
McMaster	8	8
McMenemy	25	25
McNair	31	31
Shaw	34	34
Stewart	1	1
Wilson	11	11
trialist	2	2

Goalscorer

PLAYER	LEAGUE	TOTAL
Gallacher	17	17
McLean	13	13
McColl	10	10
Browning	9	9
McAtee	5	5
McMenemy	5	5
Jackson	3	3
Brown	1	1
Cringan	1	1
Dodds	1	1
McCormack	1	1

Fact File

On 10 November 1917 the Hamilton goalkeeper not only saved a Dodds penalty but also two subsequent rebounds.

SECRETARY-MANAGER: Willie Maley

CAPTAIN: Willie Cringan

TOP SCORER: Patsy Gallacher

BIGGEST WIN: 4-0 v Ayr United, 18 August 1917, league

HIGHEST ATTENDANCE: 50,000 v Rangers, 1 January 1918, league

MAJOR TRANSFERS IN: Willie Cringan from Sunderland

Final Scottish League Div 1 Table

		P	W	D	L	F	A	Pts
1	RANGERS	34	25	6	3	66	24	56
2	CELTIC	34	24	7	3	66	26	55
3	KILMARNOCK	34	19	5	10	69	41	43
3	MORTON	34	17	9	8	53	42	43
5	MOTHERWELL	34	16	9	9	70	51	41
6	PARTICK T	34	14	12	8	51	37	40
7	QUEEN'S PARK	34	14	6	14	64	63	34
7	DUMBARTON	34	13	8	13	48	49	34
9	CLYDEBANK	34	14	5	15	55	56	33
10	HEARTS	34	14	4	16	41	58	32
11	ST MIRREN	34	11	7	16	42	50	29
12	HAMILTON A	34	11	6	17	52	63	28
13	THIRD LANARK	34	10	7	17	56	62	27
13	FALKIRK	34	9	9	16	38	58	27
15	AIRDRIEONIANS	34	10	6	18	46	58	26
16	HIBERNIAN	34	8	9	17	42	57	25
17	CLYDE	34	9	2	23	37	72	20
18	AYR U	34	5	9	20	32	61	19

Season 1918-19

Scottish League Divison 1

DATE	OPPONENTS	SCORE	GOALSCORERS	ATTENDANCE
Aug 17	Hibernian	W 3-0	McLean, Jackson, McColl	15,000
Aug 24	MORTON	D 1-1	McLean	30,000
Aug 31	Clyde	W 3-0	Gallacher 2 (2 pens), McLean	20,000
Sep 7	AYR UNITED	W 1-0	Cringan	15,000
Sep 14	Queen's Park	W 3-0	Gallacher 2, McColl	25,000
Sep 28	Falkirk	W 2-1	McColl, Brodie	7,000
Sep 30	THIRD LANARK	W 3-1	McColl, McLean, Cringan (pen)	15,000
Oct 12	Kilmarnock	D 1-1	Brown W	10,000
Oct 19	Rangers	L 0-3		35,000
Oct 26	Dumbarton	W 5-0	McLen 2, Burns 2, Cringan	7,000
Nov 2	ST MIRREN	W 1-0	McLean	8,000
Nov 9	HEARTS	D 1-1	Gallacher	11,000
Nov 23	Partick Thistle	W 1-0	Gallacher	25,000
Dec 7	Motherwell	L 1-3	McColl	14,000
Dec 14	DUMBARTON	W 2-0	McColl, McMenemy	6,000
Dec 21	Hamilton Ac.	W 2-1	McLean 2	8,000
Dec 28	HIBERNIAN	W 2-0	McColl, Browning	10,000
Jan 1	Rangers	D 1-1	McMenemy	65,000
Jan 2	CLYDE	W 2-0	Gallacher, Burns	15,000
Jan 4	Third Lanark	W 3-2	McColl, McLean, McMenemy	20,000
Jan 11	CLYDEBANK	W 3-1	McColl, Dodds (pen), Cassidy	16,000
Jan 18	St Mirren	W 4-0	McLean, McAtee, Brown H, Gallacher	16,000
Jan 25	MOTHERWELL	D 0-0		25,000
Feb 1	KILMARNOCK	W 2-1	McLean, McAtee	25,000
Feb 8	Airdrie	W 2-1	Brown H, Dodds (pen)	15,000
Feb 15	HAMILTON AC.	W 4-1	McColl 3, McStay	10,000
Feb 22	PARTICK THISTLE	W 2-1	Gallacher, McLean	20,000
Mar 8	Morton	D 0-0		15,000
Mar 22	QUEEN'S PARK	W 2-0	Cassidy 2	16,000
Apr 12	Clydebank	W 2-0	McColl 2	17,000
Apr 19	FALKIRK	W 4-0	Gallacher 3, McColl	20,000
Apr 21	AIRDRIE	W 3-0	Gallacher 2, McMenemy	20,000
Apr 28	Hearts	W 3-2	McColl 2, McAtee	15,000
May 10	Ayr United	W 2-0	McLean, McAtee	1,000

League Appearances

PLAYER	LEAGUE	TOTAL
Barber	4	4
Brodie	1	1
Brown H	25	25
Brown W	9	9
Browning	9	9
Burns	13	13
Cassidy	6	6
Corcoran	3	3
Cringan	29	29
Dodds	13	13
Duncan	2	2
Elliot	1	1
Gallacher	29	29
Jackson	6	6
Kelly	1	1
Livingstone	11	11
McAtee	12	12
McColl	30	30
McEvoy	10	10
McGinnigle	1	1
McGregor	6	6
McLean	32	32
McMenemy	19	19
McNair	31	31
McStay	20	20
Mitchell	5	5
Price	6	6
Shaw	32	32
Shea	1	1
Syme	2	2
Taylor	5	5

Goalscorers

PLAYER	LEAGUE	TOTAL
McColl	17	17
Gallacher	14	14
McLean	14	14
McAtee	4	4
McMenemy	4	4
Burns	3	3
Cassidy	3	3
Cringan	3	3
Brown H	2	2
Dodds	2	2
Brodie	1	1
Brown W	1	1
Browning	1	1
Jackson	1	1
McStay	1	1

Final Scottish League Div 1 Table

		P	W	D	L	F	A	PTS
1	CELTIC	34	26	6	2	71	22	58
2	RANGERS	34	26	5	3	86	16	57
3	MORTON	34	18	11	5	76	40	47
4	PARTICK T	34	17	7	10	62	43	41
5	MOTHERWELL	34	14	10	10	51	40	38
5	AYR U	34	15	8	11	62	53	38
7	HEARTS	34	14	9	11	59	52	37
8	QUEEN'S PARK	34	15	5	14	59	57	35
8	KILMARNOCK	34	14	7	13	61	59	35
10	CLYDEBANK	34	12	8	14	54	65	32
10	ST MIRREN	34	10	12	12	43	55	32
12	THIRD LANARK	34	11	9	14	60	62	31
13	AIRDRIEONIANS	34	9	11	14	45	54	29
14	HAMILTON A	34	9	9	16	49	75	27
15	DUMBARTON	34	7	8	19	31	58	22
16	FALKIRK	34	6	8	20	46	73	20
16	CLYDE	34	7	6	21	45	75	20
18	HIBERNIAN	34	5	3	26	30	91	13

Fact File

Ex-Rangers players David Taylor and Scott Duncan played for Celtic as guests during the season.

MANAGER: Willie Maley

CAPTAIN: Willie Cringan

TOP SCORER: Jimmy McColl

BIGGEST WIN: 5-0 v Dumbarton, 26 October 1918, league

HIGHEST ATTENDANCE: 65,000 v Rangers, 1 January 1919, league

Season 1919-1920

Scottish League Divison 1

DATE	OPPONENTS	SCORE	GOALSCORERS	ATTENDANCE
Aug 16	CLYDEBANK	W 3-1	McInally 3	12,000
Aug 18	DUMBARTON	W 3-1	McInally 2, McMenemy	6,000
Aug 23	Hamilton Ac.	W 2-1	McInally, McMenemy	12,000
Aug 27	KILMARNOCK	W 1-0	McLean	10,000
Aug 30	RAITH ROVERS	W 3-0	McInally 2, Gallacher	10,000
Sep 13	Hearts	W 1-0	Gallacher	40,000
Sep 27	CLYDE	W 3-1	McInally 3	20,000
Sep 29	Third Lanark	W 4-1	McInally 2, McLean 2	-
Oct 11	HIBERNIAN	W 7-3	Gallacher 3, McInally 2, Gilchrist, Watson	15,000
Oct 18	Rangers	L 0-3		75,000
Oct 25	QUEEN'S PARK	W 3-1	Cringan, Watson, McStay	20,000
Nov 1	Morton	W 2-1	McLean, McStay	21,000
Nov 8	FALKIRK	D 1-1	McInally	14,000
Nov 15	Ayr United	D 1-1	McStay (pen)	12,000
Nov 22	PARTICK THISTLE	D 0-0		20,000
Nov 29	Aberdeen	W 1-0	Gilchrist	25,000
Dec 6	MOTHERWELL	W 5-0	McMenemy 2, Gallacher 2, Watson	20,000
Dec 13	Airdrie	D 0-0		12,000
Dec 20	Dumbarton	D 0-0		12,000
Dec 27	THIRD LARNK	W 2-1	McLean 2	12,000
Jan 1	RANGERS	D 1-1	Cringan	80,000
Jan 3	Raith Rovers	W 3-0	McInally, McAtee, Cassidy	15,000
Jan 5	Clyde	W 2-0	McInally, McAtee	20,000
Jan 10	MORTON	D 1-1	McLean	25,000
Jan 17	Kilmarnock	W 3-2	Craig 2, McAtee	10,000
Jan 24	Clydebank	L 0-2		10,000
Jan 31	Dundee	L 1-2	Cassidy	18,000
Feb 14	ALBION ROVERS	W 3-0	McLean 2, McInally	20,000
Feb 28	HAMILTON AC.	W 2-0	Cassidy, McStay (pen)	20,000
Mar 13	Queen's Park	W 2-1	Cassidy, McKay	25,000
Mar 27	Falkirk	W 2-1	Cassidy, McLean	12,000
Apr 3	St Mirren	W 2-0	McInally, Gallacher	16,000
Apr 5	Partick Thistle	W 2-1	McInally, McAtee	30,000
Apr 10	ABERDEEN	W 5-0	Gallacher 2, McInally, Cassidy, McLean	11,000
Apr 14	Albion Rovers	W 5-0	McInally 2, Gallacher, McStay, McLean	11,000
Apr 17	Motherwell	D 0-0		22,000
Apr 19	Hibernian	W 2-1	McInally 2	15,000
Apr 22	ST MIRREN	D 2-2	McInally, McStay (pen)	10,000
Apr 24	AYR UNITED	W 4-0	McKay 2, Craig, Watson	12,000
Apr 25	DUNDEE	D 1-1	McStay (pen)	7,000
Apr 28	AIRDRIE	W 1-0	McKay	7,000
May 1	HEARTS	W 3-0	McKay, McInally, Cringan	10,000

Scottish Cup

Feb 7	Dundee	(Rd1) W 3-1	McLean, McInally, Cringan	34,000
Feb 21	PARTICK THISTLE	(Rd2) W 2-0	McInally, McStay	25,000
Mar 6	Rangers	(Rd3) L 0-1		64,000

League & Cup Appearances

PLAYER	LEAGUE	CUP COMPETITION S CUP	TOTAL
Brown	10		10
Cassidy	28	3	31
Craig	5		5
Cringan	40	3	43
Dodds	13	3	16
Gallacher	22	1	23
Gilchrist	31		31
Lawrie	3		3
Livingstone	14		14
McAtee	22	3	25
McColl	8		8
McFarlane	3		3
McInally	32	2	34
McKay	6		6
McLean	41	3	44
McMaster	27	3	30
McMenemy	27	3	30
McNair	35	3	38
McStay	40	3	43
Pratt	1		1
Shaw	39	3	42
Watson	15		15

Goalscorers

PLAYER	LEAGUE	CUP COMPETITION S CUP	TOTAL
McInally	28	2	30
McLean	12	1	13
Gallacher	11		11
McStay	7	1	8
Cassidy	6		6
McKay	5		5
Cringan	3	1	4
McAtee	4		4
McMenemy	4		4
Watson	4		4
Craig	3		3
Gilchrist	2		2

Fact File

At the Old Firm game on 18 October 1919 many supporters wore German army helmets painted green and white or blue, to celebrate the end of hostilities.

MANAGER: Willie Maley

CAPTAIN: Willie Cringan

TOP SCORER: Tommy McInally

BIGGEST WIN: 5-0 v Motherwell, 6 December 1919, league; 5-0 v Aberdeen, 10 April 1920, league; 5-0 v Albion Rovers, 14 April 1920, league

HIGHEST ATTENDANCE: 80,000 v Rangers, 1 January 1920, league

MAJOR TRANSFERS OUT: John Browning to Chelsea

Final Scottish League Div 1 Table

		P	W	D	L	F	A	Pts
1	RANGERS	42	31	9	2	106	25	71
2	CELTIC	42	29	10	3	89	31	68
3	MOTHERWELL	42	23	11	8	74	53	57
4	DUNDEE	42	22	6	14	79	65	50
5	CLYDEBANK	42	20	8	14	78	54	48
6	MORTON	42	16	13	13	71	48	45
7	AIRDRIEONIANS	42	17	10	15	57	43	44
8	THIRD LANARK	42	16	11	15	56	62	43
8	KILMARNOCK	42	20	3	19	59	74	43
10	AYR U	42	15	10	17	72	69	40
11	DUMBARTON	42	13	13	16	57	65	39
12	QUEEN'S PARK	42	14	10	18	67	73	38
12	PARTICK T	42	13	12	17	51	62	38
12	ST MIRREN	42	15	8	19	63	81	38
15	CLYDE	42	14	9	19	64	71	37
15	HEARTS	42	14	9	19	57	72	37
17	ABERDEEN	42	11	13	18	46	64	35
18	HIBERNIAN	42	13	7	22	60	79	33
19	RAITH R	42	11	10	21	61	83	32
20	FALKIRK	42	10	11	21	45	74	31
21	HAMILTON A	42	11	7	24	56	86	29
22	ALBION R	42	10	8	24	43	77	28

Season 1920-21

Scottish League Divison 1

DATE	OPPONENTS	SCORE	GOALSCORERS	ATTENDANCE
Aug 18	Hamilton Ac.	D 1-1	McInally	10,000
Aug 21	Albion Rovers	W 1-0	McMaster	17,000
Aug 28	Aberdeen	W 2-1	McStay (pen), o.g.	22,000
Sep 1	MORTON	D 1-1	McInally	15,000
Sep 7	MOTHERWELL	W 1-0	McInally	20,000
Sep 11	HAMILTON AC.	W 2-1	McInally, Cassidy	-
Sep 20	Hibernian	W 3-0	McLean, McInally, Cassidy	-
Sep 25	AYR UNITED	W 3-1	McAtee, Cassidy, McInally	8,000
Sep 27	THIRD LANARK	W 3-0	McLean, Gilchrist, McInally	12,000
Oct 9	QUEEN'S PARK	W 5-1	Cassidy 3, Gallacher, o.g.	-
Oct 12	FALKIRK	W 4-1	McInally 2, McLean, Cassidy	-
Oct 16	Dundee	W 2-1	McInally, McAtee	32,000
Oct 23	RANGERS	L 1-2	Cassidy	62,269
Oct 26	ALBION ROVERS	L 0-2		-
Oct 30	Hearts	W 1-0	Cassidy	-
Nov 6	Dumbarton	W 3-1	Cringan, Cassidy, McLean	10,000
Nov 13	KILMARNOCK	W 2-0	Gallacher, Cassidy	12,000
Nov 20	Clyde	L 1-2	McInally	-
Nov 27	RAITH ROVERS	W 5-0	Longmuir 2, Cringan, Gallacher, McAtee	8,000
Dec 4	Falkirk	W 3-1	McInally 2, McLean	-
Dec 11	PARTICK THISTLE	W 1-0	Gallacher (pen)	-
Dec 18	AIRDRIE	W 2-1	Gallacher, McInally	-
Dec 25	St Mirren	W 2-0	McInally, Cassidy	15,000
Jan 1	Rangers	W 2-0	Cassidy 2	69,260
Jan 3	CLYDE	W 1-0	Cassidy	-
Jan 8	Clydebank	W 2-0	McInally, McAtee	-
Jan 15	Morton	D 1-1	McInally	-
Jan 22	Motherwell	D 1-1	o.g.	-
Jan 29	ABERDEEN	W 3-1	McInally, McStay, McLean	12,000
Feb 12	ST MIRREN	W 6-0	McInally 3, Gallacher 2, McLean	-
Feb 23	Third Lanark	W 2-1	McLean, McInally	-
Feb 26	Queen's Park	W 2-0	McMaster, Gallacher	-
Mar 9	DUNDEE	W 2-0	McInally 2	-
Mar 12	Ayr United	L 1-2	McLean	9,000
Mar 19	HEARTS	W 3-2	McStay 2 (2 pens), Cassidy	15,000
Mar 26	Kilmarnock	L 2-3	McInally, Cassidy	8,000
Mar 28	Partick Thistle	W 1-0	Gallacher	-
Apr 2	DUMBARTON	D 1-1	McStay (pen)	10,000
Apr 9	Raith Rovers	L 0-2		-
Apr 20	CLYDEBANK	D 1-1	McKay	-
Apr 23	HIBERNIAN	W 3-0	McInally 2, Miller	-
Apr 30	Airdrie	W 3-2	Gallacher, McInally, McLean	10,000

Scottish Cup

DATE	OPPONENTS		SCORE	GOALSCORERS	ATTENDANCE
Feb 5	Vale of Leven	(Rd1)	W 3-0	Cassidy 2, McLean	3,000
Feb 19	East Fife	(Rd2)	W 3-1	McInally 2, Gallacher	11,000
Mar 5	HEARTS	(Rd3)	L 1-2	Gallacher	37,000

League & Cup Appearances

PLAYER	LEAGUE	CUP COMPETITION S CUP	TOTAL
Cassidy	39	3	42
Craig	1		1
Cringan	25		25
Gallacher	39	3	42
Gilchrist	32	3	35
Glasgow	2		2
Livingstone	13	3	16
Longmuir	2		2
McAtee	29	2	31
McFarlane	13	1	14
McInally	37	3	40
McKay	4		4
McLean	40	3	43
McMaster	33	3	36
McNair	29		29
McStay	37	3	40
Miller	3		3
Murphy	17	3	20
Prattt	20		20
Price	2		2
Shaw	42	3	45
Watson	3		3

Goalscorers

PLAYER	LEAGUE	CUP COMPETITION S CUP	TOTAL
McInally	28	2	30
Cassidy	17	2	19
Gallacher	10	2	12
McLean	10	1	11
McStay	5		5
McAtee	4		4
Cringan	2		2
Longmuir	2		2
McMaster	2		2
Gilchrist	1		1
McKay	1		1
Miller	1		1
Opps' o.gs.	3		3

Fact File

Celtic missed five penalties in the course of the season. Willie McStay was responsible for three of them.

MANAGER: Willie Maley

CAPTAIN: Willie Cringan

TOP SCORER: Tommy McInally

BIGGEST WIN: 6-0 v St Mirren, 12 February 1921, league

HIGHEST ATTENDANCE: 62,269 v Rangers, 23 October 1920, league

MAJOR TRANSFERS OUT: Joe Dodds to Cowdenbeath, Jimmy McColl to Stoke, Jimmy McMenemy to Partick Thistle

Final Scottish League Div 1 Table

		P	W	D	L	F	A	Pts
1	RANGERS	42	35	6	1	91	24	76
2	CELTIC	42	30	6	6	86	35	66
3	HEARTS	42	20	10	12	74	49	50
4	DUNDEE	42	19	11	12	54	48	49
5	MOTHERWELL	42	19	10	13	75	51	48
6	PARTICK T	42	17	12	13	53	39	46
7	CLYDE	42	21	3	18	63	62	45
8	THIRD LANARK	42	19	6	17	74	61	44
8	MORTON	42	15	14	13	66	58	44
10	AIRDRIEONIANS	42	17	9	16	71	64	43
11	ABERDEEN	42	14	14	14	53	54	42
11	KILMARNOCK	42	17	8	17	62	68	42
13	HIBERNIAN	42	16	9	17	58	57	41
14	AYR U	42	14	12	16	62	69	40
14	HAMILTON A	42	14	12	16	44	57	40
16	RAITH R	42	16	5	21	54	58	37
17	ALBION R	42	11	12	19	57	68	34
17	FALKIRK	42	11	12	19	54	72	34
19	QUEEN'S PARK	42	11	11	20	45	80	33
20	CLYDEBANK	42	7	14	21	47	72	28
21	DUMBARTON	42	10	4	28	41	89	24
22	ST MIRREN	42	7	4	31	43	92	18

Season 1921-22

Scottish League Divison 1

DATE	OPPONENTS	SCORE	GOALSCORERS	ATTENDANCE
Aug 15	RAITH ROVERS	W 4-0	Longmuir 2, Cassidy, McAtee	-
Aug 20	HIBERNIAN	W 3-1	Longmuir 2, Cassidy	-
Aug 24	Airdrie	W 2-0	Gallacher, McLean	15,000
Aug 27	Raith Rovers	D 1-1	McLean	15,000
Sep 6	DUMBARTON	W 4-0	McInally 2, Gallacher, Cassidy	-
Sep 10	Aberdeen	D 1-1	McInally	-
Sep 19	Hibernian	L 1-2	Gallacher	16,000
Sep 24	Dumbarton	W 5-0	McInally 2, McLean 2, Gallacher	10,000
Sep 26	MORTON	W 1-0	McLean	10,000
Oct 4	ST MIRREN	W 2-0	Cassidy, Gallacher	12,000
Oct 8	Dundee	D 0-0		35,000
Oct 15	ALBION ROVERS	W 3-1	McInally, Gilchrist, Gallacher	16,000
Oct 22	Rangers	D 1-1	McInally	40,000
Oct 29	AYR UNITED	W 2-1	McInally, McStay (pen)	9,000
Nov 5	HEARTS	W 3-0	Dodds 2, Cassidy	10,000
Nov 12	Kilmarnock	L 3-4	McInally 3	-
Nov 19	QUEEN'S PARK	W 3-2	McStay, Cassidy, McInally	7,000
Nov 26	Motherwell	D 1-1	Cassidy	-
Dec 3	AIRDRIE	W 1-0	Cassidy	10,000
Dec 10	Ayr United	D 0-0		10,000
Dec 17	CLYDEBANK	W 6-0	Cassidy 2, McLean, McFarlane, Dodds (pen), Gallacher	5,000
Dec 24	FALKIRK	D 0-0		14,000
Dec 31	Hamilton Ac.	W 3-1	McStay (pen), Gallacher, McAtee	10,000
Jan 2	RANGERS	D 0-0		-
Jan 3	Clyde	D 1-1	Gallacher	-
Jan 7	THIRD LANARK	W 2-0	Gallacher, McInally	10,000
Jan 14	Clydebank	W 2-0	McFarlane, Gallacher	9,000
Jan 21	ABERDEEN	W 2-0	McInally, McFarlane	12,000
Feb 4	Partick Thistle	D 0-0		-
Feb 14	St Mirren	W 2-0	McInally 2	15,000
Feb 18	CLYDE	W 1-0	Cassidy	-
Mar 1	HAMILTON AC.	W 4-0	McLean 2, Dodds (pen), McInally	-
Mar 4	Third Lanark	D 0-0		12,000
Mar 11	KILMARNOCK	W 1-0	Cassidy	6,000
Mar 15	MOTHERWELL	W 2-0	Gallacher 2	8,000
Mar 18	Falkirk	D 1-1	Cassidy	20,000
Mar 25	Hearts	W 2-1	McAtee, Cassidy	22,000
Apr 1	Queen's Park	W 3-1	Cassidy 2, Gilchrist	-
Apr 8	DUNDEE	W 4-0	Cassidy 2, Gallacher, McAtee	9,000
Apr 15	Albion Rovers	W 2-0	Gallacher, McFarlane	11,000
Apr 17	PARTICK THISTLE	W 3-0	Gallacher 2, McStay	12,000
Apr 29	Morton	D 1-1	McAtee	20,000

Scottish Cup

Jan 28	MONTROSE	(Rd1) W 4-0	McFarlane 2, McInally, McLean	6,000
Feb 11	Third Lanark	(Rd2) W 1-0	McLean	45,000
Feb 25	HAMILTON AC.	(Rd3) L 1-3	Dodds	20,000

Fact File

Willie McStay marketed a matchbox holder with his portrait edged in green and white as part of his benefit.

MANAGER: Willie Maley
CAPTAIN: Willie Cringan
TOP SCORERS: Joe Cassidy and Tommy McInally
BIGGEST WIN: 6-0 v Clydebank, 17 December 1921, league
HIGHEST ATTENDANCE: 45,000 v Third Lanark, 11 February 1922, Scottish Cup
MAJOR TRANSFERS IN: Joe Dodds from Cowdenbeath

League & Cup Appearances

PLAYER	LEAGUE	CUP COMPETITION S CUP	TOTAL
Cassidy	38	2	40
Collins	2		2
Connolly	2		2
Craig	2		2
Cringan	37	3	40
Dodds	30	3	33
Gallacher	39	3	42
Gilchrist	41	3	44
Glancy	1		1
Hilley	1		1
Longmuir	8		8
McAtee	38	3	41
McFarlane	17	1	18
McInally	24	3	27
McLean	34	3	37
McMaster	26	2	28
McNair	39	3	42
McStay	29	1	30
Miller	2		2
Murphy	11		11
Pratt	1		1
Shaw	40	3	43

Goalscorers

PLAYER	LEAGUE	CUP COMPETITION S CUP	TOTAL
Cassidy	18		18
McInally	17	1	18
Gallacher	17		17
McLean	8	2	10
McFarlane	4	2	6
Dodds	4	1	5
McAtee	5		5
Longmuir	4		4
McStay	4		4
Gilchrist	2		2

Final Scottish League Div 1 Table

		P	W	D	L	F	A	Pts
1	CELTIC	42	27	13	2	83	20	67
2	RANGERS	42	28	10	4	83	26	66
3	RAITH R	42	19	13	10	66	43	51
4	DUNDEE	42	19	11	12	57	40	49
5	FALKIRK	42	16	17	9	48	38	49
6	PARTICK T	42	20	8	14	57	53	48
7	HIBERNIAN	42	16	14	12	55	44	46
8	ST MIRREN	42	17	12	13	71	61	46
9	THIRD LANARK	42	17	12	13	58	52	46
10	CLYDE	42	16	12	14	60	51	44
11	ALBION R	42	17	10	15	55	51	44
12	MORTON	42	16	10	16	58	57	42
13	MOTHERWELL	42	16	7	19	63	58	39
14	AYR U	42	13	12	17	55	63	38
15	ABERDEEN	42	13	9	20	48	54	35
16	AIRDRIEONIANS	42	12	11	19	46	56	35
17	KILMARNOCK	42	13	9	20	56	83	35
18	HAMILTON A	42	9	16	17	51	62	34
19	HEARTS	42	11	10	21	50	60	32
20	DUMBARTON	42	10	10	22	46	81	30
21	QUEEN'S PARK	42	9	10	23	38	82	28
22	CLYDEBANK	42	6	8	28	34	103	20

DUNDEE v AYR; BOTH GAMES AT DUNDEE.

Season 1922-23

Scottish League Divison 1

DATE	OPPONENTS	SCORE	GOALSCORERS	ATTENDANCE
Aug 19	Alloa Ath.	W 3-2	McStay W (pen), Cassidy Gallacher	15,000
Aug 26	HAMILTON AC.	W 2-1	McLean, Cassidy	10,000
Sep 9	RAITH ROVERS	W 3-0	Gilchrist, Cassidy, McLean	14,000
Sep 18	Hibernian	L 0-1		-
Sep 23	Dundee	W 1-0	Murphy JF	25,000
Sep 25	Aberdeen	L 1-3	Cassidy	25,000
Oct 7	PARTICK THISTLE	W 4-3	Gallacher 2 (1 pen), McFarlane, Cassidy	10,000
Oct 14	MOTHERWELL	W 1-0	Cassidy	12,000
Oct 21	Morton	W 1-0	Cassidy	
Oct 28	RANGERS	L 1-3	Gallacher	44,000
Nov 4	Clyde	W 1-0	McFarlane	13,000
Nov 11	AYR UNITED	L 1-4	McStay W (pen)	7,000
Nov 18	Airdrie	L 0-1		-
Nov 25	THIRD LANARK	W 3-0	Cassidy 3	10,000
Dec 2	Albion Rovers	W 3-2	Cassidy, Gallacher, o.g.	8,000
Dec 9	FALKIRK	D 1-1	McStay W (pen)	12,000
Dec 16	Hearts	W 3-0	McFarlane, McLean, Gallacher	28,000
Dec 23	KILMARNOCK	L 1-2	McLean	-
Dec 30	Raith Rovers	W 3-0	Cassidy 2, Gilchrist	-
Jan 1	Rangers	L 0-2		30,000
Jan 2	CLYDE	D 0-0		8,000
Jan 6	ABERDEEN	L 1-2	Cassidy	8,000
Jan 20	Third Lanark	L 0-1		-
Jan 31	HIBERNIAN	D 0-0		-
Feb 3	Kilmarnock	L 3-4	McGrory, Cassidy, McAtee	-
Feb 14	ALBION ROVERS	D 1-1	Cassidy (pen)	5,000
Feb 17	Falkirk	D 0-0		10,000
Feb 27	ST MIRREN	W 1-0	Cassidy	-
Mar 3	ALLOA ATH.	W 1-0	Murphy JF	-
Mar 14	Hamilton Ac.	D 1-1	Cassidy	7,000
Mar 17	DUNDEE	W 2-1	McStay W 2 (1 pen)	-
Mar 24	MORTON	W 3-1	Cassidy 3	10,000
Apr 2	Partick Thistle	W 2-0	Gallacher 2	25,000
Apr 7	HEARTS	W 2-1	Thomson, Cassidy	11,000
Apr 10	St Mirren	L 0-1		-
Apr 21	Motherwell	D 0-0		-
Apr 25	Ayr United	W 1-0	Cassidy	6,000
Apr 28	AIRDRIE	D 1-1	McStay W (pen)	10,000

Scottish Cup

DATE	OPPONENTS		SCORE	GOALSCORERS	ATTENDANCE
Jan 13	Lochgelly United	(Rd1)	W 3-2	Cassidy 3	10,000
Jan 27	HURLFORD	(Rd2)	W 4-0	Cassidy 4	5,000
Feb 10	EAST FIFE	(Rd3)	W 2-1	Cassidy 2	12,000
Feb 24	RAITH ROVERS	(QF)	W 1-0	McLean	31,000
Mar 10	Motherwell	(SF)	W 2-0	Cassidy, McAtee	71,506
Mar 31	Hibernian	(F)	W 1-0	Cassidy	82,000

League & Cup Appearances

PLAYER	LEAGUE	CUP COMPETITION S CUP	TOTAL
Cairney	3	1	4
Cassidy	33	6	39
Connolly	25	4	29
Crilly	3		3
Cringan	35	6	41
Gallacher	40	4	34
Gilchrist	23	1	24
Grainger	4		4
Hilley	23	2	25
Hughes	5		5
McAtee	27	6	33
McFarlane	36	6	42
McGrory	3	1	4
McLean	31	6	37
McMaster	4		4
McNair	21	4	25
McStay J	24	6	30
McStay W	33	6	39
Murphy JB	7		7
Murphy JF	6	1	7
Shaw	33	6	39
Thomson	9		9

Goalscorers

PLAYER	LEAGUE	CUP COMPETITION S CUP	TOTAL
Cassidy	23	11	32
Gallacher	8		7
McStay W	6		6
McLean	4	1	5
McFarlane	3		3
Gilchrist	2		2
McAtee	1	1	2
Murphy JF	2		2
McGrory	1		1
Thomson	1		1
Opps' o.gs.	1		1

Fact File

On 22 October 1922, the day after the victory over Morton, Jock Stein was born.

MANAGER: Willie Maley

CAPTAIN: Willie Cringan

TOP SCORER: Joe Cassidy

BIGGEST WIN: 4-0 v Hurlford, 27 January 1923, Scottish Cup

HIGHEST ATTENDANCE: 82,000 v Hibernian, 31 March 1923, Scottish Cup

MAJORS TRANSFERS OUT: Johnny Gilchrist to Preston, Tommy McInally to Third Lanark

Final Scottish League Div 1 Table

		P	W	D	L	F	A	Pts
1	RANGERS	38	23	9	6	67	29	55
2	AIRDRIEONIANS	38	20	10	8	58	38	50
3	CELTIC	38	19	8	11	52	39	46
4	FALKIRK	38	14	17	7	44	32	45
5	ABERDEEN	38	15	12	11	46	34	42
6	ST MIRREN	38	15	12	11	54	44	42
7	DUNDEE	38	17	7	14	51	45	41
8	HIBERNIAN	38	17	7	14	45	40	41
9	RAITH R	38	13	13	12	31	43	39
10	AYR U	38	13	12	13	43	44	38
11	PARTICK T	38	14	9	15	51	48	37
12	HEARTS	38	11	15	12	51	50	37
13	MOTHERWELL	38	13	10	15	59	60	36
14	MORTON	38	12	11	15	44	47	35
15	KILMARNOCK	38	14	7	17	57	66	35
16	CLYDE	38	12	9	17	36	44	33
17	THIRD LANARK	38	11	8	19	40	59	30
18	HAMILTON A	38	11	7	20	43	59	29
19	ALBION R	38	8	10	20	38	64	26
20	ALLOA ATH	38	6	11	21	27	52	23

Season 1923-24

Scottish League Divison 1

DATE	OPPONENTS	SCORE	GOALSCORERS	ATTENDANCE
Aug 18	FALKIRK	W 2-1	Cassidy 2	-
Aug 25	Clydebank	D 0-0		10,000
Sep 1	PARTICK THISTLE	L 1-2	Cassidy	-
Sep 8	Queen's Park	W 2-0	McLean, Cassidy	-
Sep 17	Hibernian	D 0-0		-
Sep 22	Ayr United	L 2-4	McAtee, Gallacher	8,000
Sep 24	MORTON	W 3-0	Cassidy, McAtee, McStay W (pen)	-
Sep 29	Aberdeen	W 2-0	McLean 2	19,000
Oct 6	CLYDE	W 4-0	Cassidy 3, McLean	-
Oct 13	Hearts	D 0-0		26,000
Oct 20	RAITH ROVERS	D 0-0		-
Oct 27	Rangers	D 0-0		38,000
Nov 3	Airdrie	D 2-2	Cassidy, McStay W (pen)	10,000
Nov 10	Hamilton Ac	W 5-2	McLean 2, Gallacher, Cassidy, Thomson	-
Nov 17	DUNDEE	D 0-0		10,000
Nov 24	St Mirren	W 1-0	Cassidy	14,000
Dec 1	THIRD LANARK	W 3-1	Cassidy, McLean, Gallacher	-
Dec 8	Kilmarnock	D 1-1	Thomson	-
Dec 15	MOTHERWELL	W 2-1	McFarlane, Cassidy	-
Dec 22	Dundee	L 1-2	Cassidy	15,000
Jan 1	RANGERS	D 2-2	Thomson, McStay W (pen)	60,000
Jan 2	Clyde	D 0-0		-
Jan 5	HAMILTON AC.	W 1-0	Cassidy	-
Jan 12	Third Lanark	W 3-1	Cassidy 2, McLean	12,000
Jan 19	ABERDEEN	W 4-0	Cassidy 2, Gallacher, McLean	-
Feb 2	Morton	L 0-1		-
Feb 13	Motherwell	W 1-0	o.g.	-
Feb 16	Queen's Park	W 1-0	McLean	-
Feb 26	HEARTS	W 4-1	Cassidy 3, McFarlane	-
Mar 1	Partick Thistle	D 1-1	Cassidy	-
Mar 4	CLYDEBANK	L 1-2	McStay W	-
Mar 8	KILMARNOCK	W 2-1	Connolly, Cassidy	-
Mar 15	Falkirk	L 1-3	Connolly	7,000
Mar 22	Raith Rovers	L 0-1		-
Mar 29	Airdrie	L 0-2		-
Apr 5	AYR UNITED	W 3-0	Gallacher, Cassidy, Connolly	-
Apr 12	ST MIRREN	L 0-1		3,000
Apr 26	HIBERNIAN	D 1-1	Gilgun	-

Scottish Cup

Jan 26	Kilmarnock	(Rd1) L 0-2		17,500

League & Cup Appearances

PLAYER	LEAGUE	CUP COMPETITION S CUP	TOTAL
Cassidy	33	1	34
Connolly	20		20
Cringan	6		6
Gallacher	35	1	36
Gilgun	3		3
Grainger	8		8
Hilley	33	1	34
McAtee	30	1	31
McFarlane	36	1	37
McGhee	1		1
McLaughlin	1		1
McLean	33	1	34
McNair	29	1	30
McStay J	36	1	37
McStay W	32	1	33
Shaw	38	1	39
Thomson	33	1	34
Wilson	11		

Goalscorers

PLAYER	LEAGUE	CUP COMPETITION S CUP	TOTAL
Cassidy	25		25
McLean	10		10
Gallacher	5		5
McStay W	4		4
Connolly	3		3
Thomson	3		3
McAtee	2		2
McFarlane	2		2
Gilgun	1		1
Opps' o.gs.	1		1

Fact File

Between 22 September and 3 November 1923 keeper Charlie Shaw went 644 minutes without conceding a goal.

MANAGER: Willie Maley

CAPTAIN: Willie McStay

TOP SCORER: Joe Cassidy

BIGGEST WIN: 4-0 v Clyde, 6 October 1923, league; 4-0 v Aberdeen, 19 January 1924, league

HIGHEST ATTENDANCE: 60,000 v Rangers, 1 January 1924, league

MAJOR TRANSFERS OUT: Willie Cringan to Third Lanark, Joe Dodds to Queen of the South

Final Scottish League Div 1 Table

		P	W	D	L	F	A	Pts
1	RANGERS	38	25	9	4	72	22	59
2	AIRDRIEONIANS	38	20	10	8	72	46	50
3	CELTIC	38	17	12	9	56	33	46
4	RAITH R	38	18	7	13	56	38	43
5	DUNDEE	38	15	13	10	70	57	43
6	ST MIRREN	38	15	12	11	53	45	42
7	HIBERNIAN	38	15	11	12	66	52	41
8	PARTICK T	38	15	9	14	58	55	39
9	HEARTS	38	14	10	14	61	50	38
10	MOTHERWELL	38	15	7	16	58	63	37
11	MORTON	38	16	5	17	48	54	37
12	HAMILTON A	38	15	6	17	52	57	36
13	ABERDEEN	38	13	10	15	37	41	36
14	AYR U	38	12	10	16	38	60	34
15	FALKIRK	38	13	6	19	46	53	32
16	KILMARNOCK	38	12	8	18	48	65	32
17	QUEEN'S PARK	38	11	9	18	43	60	31
18	THIRD LANARK	38	11	8	19	54	78	30
19	CLYDE	38	10	9	19	40	70	29
20	CLYDEBANK	38	10	5	23	42	71	25

Season 1924-25

Scottish League Divison 1

DATE	OPPONENTS	SCORE	GOALSCORERS	ATTENDANCE
Aug 16	Dundee	D 0-0		18,000
Aug 19	Partick Thistle	D 2-2	McStay W (pen), Thomson	-
Aug 23	AIRDRIE	D 1-1	Gallacher	-
Aug 30	Falkirk	W 2-1	McGrory, Gallacher	16,000
Sep 6	Aberdeen	W 4-0	McLean 3, Thomson	-
Sep 13	ST MIRREN	W 5-0	Thomson, Gallacher, McGrory, McStay W (pen), McLean	15,000
Sep 15	Hibernian	W 3-2	McGrory 2, McLean	-
Sep 27	MOTHERWELL	W 4-0	McGrory 3, Gallacher	18,000
Sep 29	COWDENBEATH	W 3-1	McLean 2, McStay W (pen)	-
Oct 11	HEARTS	W 1-0	Wilson (pen)	-
Oct 18	St Johnstone	D 0-0		12,000
Oct 25	RANGERS	L 0-1		40,000
Nov 1	Morton	L 0-1		-
Nov 8	KILMARNOCK	W 6-0	Fleming 4, Connolly, Wilson	-
Nov 15	Queen's Park	L 1-3	McStay W	-
Nov 22	Third Lanark	D 1-1	Fleming	15,000
Nov 29	PARTICK THISTLE	L 1-2	Thomson	-
Dec 6	AYR UNITED	W 2-0	Thomson, Gallacher	-
Dec 13	Hearts	L 1-3	Gallacher	18,000
Dec 20	HAMILTON AC.	L 0-2		-
Dec 27	Raith Rovers	D 2-2	Fleming, Connolly	-
Jan 1	Rangers	L 1-4	Fleming	34,000
Jan 3	Airdrie	L 1-3	Thomson	-
Jan 5	THIRD LANARK	W 7-0	Connolly 2, McLean 2, Thomson McStay W (pen), McStay J	-
Jan 10	ABERDEEN	W 3-1	Fleming 2, Gallacher	-
Jan 17	Motherwell	L 0-1		-
Jan 31	HIBERNIAN	D 1-1	McLean	-
Feb 11	Ayr United	W 2-0	Thomson, McFarlane	-
Feb 14	ST JOHNSTONE	W 2-1	Connolly, Thomson	-
Feb 24	Hamilton Ac.	W 4-0	McGrory 3, Thomson	-
Feb 28	DUNDEE	W 4-0	McGrory 2, McLean 2	-
Mar 14	Cowdenbeath	L 0-3		-
Mar 24	MORTON	W 2-1	Wilson, Thomson	-
Mar 28	RAITH ROVERS	W 2-0	McGrory, Thomson	-
Apr 1	FALKIRK	W 6-1	McGrory 4, McLean, Thomson	-
Apr 15	Kilmarnock	L 1-2	Fleming	-
Apr 18	QUEEN'S PARK	D 1-1	Connolly	-
Apr 25	St Mirren	L 1-2	Wilson (pen)	-

Scottish Cup

Jan 24	Third Lanark	(Rd1) W 5-1	McGrory 4, Gallacher	42,000
Feb 7	ALLOA ATH.	(Rd2) W 2-1	McGrory 2	12,000
Feb 21	SOLWAY STAR	(Rd3) W 2-0	Thomson, McGrory	-
Mar 7	St Mirren	(Rd4) D 0-0		47,428
Mar 10	ST MIRREN	(R) D 1-1	o.g.	36,000
Mar 16	St Mirren	(R2) W 1-0	McGrory	47,492
Mar 21	Rangers	(SF) W 5-0	McGrory 2, McLean 2 Thomson	101,714
Apr 11	Dundee	(F) W 2-1	Gallacher, McGrory	75,317

League & Cup Appearances

PLAYER	LEAGUE	CUP COMPETITION S CUP	TOTAL
Blair	2		2
Connolly	38	8	46
Corrigan	4		4
Fleming	19		19
Gallacher	28	8	36
Garden	1		1
Grainger	1		1
Healey	2		2
Hilley	37	8	45
Leitch	2		2
McFarlane	37	8	45
McGrogan	5	1	6
McGrory	25	8	33
McLean	27	8	35
McNair	12		12
McStay J	36	8	44
McStay W	33	8	41
Shaw	11		11
Sherlin	27	8	35
Thomson	38	8	46
Wilson	33	7	40

Goalscorers

PLAYER	LEAGUE	CUP COMPETITION S CUP	TOTAL
McGrory	17	11	28
McLean	13	2	15
Thomson	13	2	15
Fleming	10		10
Gallacher	7		7
Connolly	6		6
McStay W	5		5
Wilson	4		4
McFarlane	1		1
McStay J	1		1
Opps' o.gs.		1	1

Final Scottish League Div 1 Table

		P	W	D	L	F	A	Pts
1	RANGERS	38	25	10	3	76	26	60
2	AIRDRIEONIANS	38	25	7	6	85	31	57
3	HIBERNIAN	38	22	8	8	78	43	52
4	CELTIC	38	18	8	12	77	44	44
5	COWDENBEATH	38	16	10	12	76	65	42
6	ST MIRREN	38	18	4	16	65	63	40
7	PARTICK T	38	14	10	14	60	61	38
8	DUNDEE	38	14	8	16	47	54	36
9	RAITH R	38	14	8	16	53	61	36
10	HEARTS	38	12	11	15	64	68	35
11	ST JOHNSTONE	38	12	11	15	57	72	35
12	KILMARNOCK	38	12	9	17	53	64	33
13	HAMILTON A	38	15	3	20	50	63	33
14	MORTON	38	12	9	17	46	69	33
15	ABERDEEN	38	11	10	17	46	56	32
16	FALKIRK	38	12	8	18	44	54	32
17	QUEEN'S PARK	38	12	8	18	50	71	32
18	MOTHERWELL	38	10	10	18	54	63	30
19	AYR U	38	11	8	19	43	65	30
20	THIRD LANARK	38	11	8	19	53	84	30

Fact File

On 18 April 1925 Alec McNair made his final appearance in the match against Queen's Park. At the age of 41 years and 4 months he became the oldest ever Celtic player.

MANAGER: Willie Maley

CAPTAIN: Willie McStay

TOP SCORER: Jimmy McGrory

BIGGEST WIN: 7-0 v Third Lanark, 5 January 1925, league

HIGHEST ATTENDANCE: 101,714 v Rangers, 21 March 1925, Scottish Cup

MAJOR TRANSFERS OUT: Joe Cassidy to Bolton

Season 1925-26

Scottish League Divison 1

DATE	OPPONENTS	SCORE	GOALSCORERS	ATTENDANCE
Aug 15	HIBERNIAN	W 5-0	McGrory 3, Connolly, McLean	22,000
Aug 22	Clydebank	W 2-1	Thomson, McGrory	23,193
Aug 19	HAMILTON AC.	W 2-0	McInally, McStay J	16,000
Sep 12	COWDENBEATH	W 6-1	McLean 2, McGrory 2, Thomson, McInally	-
Sep 19	Dundee United	L 0-1		20,000
Sep 26	FALKIRK	W 3-1	McGrory, McInally, McLean	
Oct 3	Airdrie	L 1-5	McGrory	23,000
Oct 13	QUEEN'S PARK	W 4-1	Connolly, McGrory, Thomson, McInally	5,000
Oct 17	Rangers	L 0-1		35,000
Oct 24	Morton	W 5-0	McGrory 2, McInally, Thomson, McLean	-
Oct 31	DUNDEE	D 0-0		
Nov 7	Aberdeen	W 4-2	Thomson 2, McInally, McGrory	20,000
Nov 14	Raith Rovers	W 2-1	McGrory 2	8,000
Nov 25	HEARTS	W 3-0	McInally, McGrory, Thomson	7,000
Nov 29	St Johnstone	W 3-0	Thomson, McGrory, McLean	-
Dec 5	CLYDEBANK	D 1-1	McGrory	-
Dec 12	St Mirren	W 2-0	Thomson, McGrory	27,000
Dec 19	AIRDRIE	W 3-2	Thomson 2, McGrory	22,000
Dec 26	Cowdenbeath	D 1-1	McLean	8,000
Jan 1	RANGERS	D 2-2	McGrory, McInally	57,000
Jan 2	Queen's Park	W 4-1	McGrory 2, Thomson, McLean	20,000
Jan 4	PARTICK THISTLE	W 3-0	McGrory 3	17,000
Jan 9	RAITH ROVERS	W 1-0	McStay W (pen)	5,000
Jan 16	Hibernian	D 4-4	McGrory 2, McLean, McFarlane	25,000
Jan 30	MOTHERWELL	W 3-1	McLean, McGrory, Thomson	
Feb 10	Kilmarnock	L 1-3	McStay W (pen)	8,000
Feb 13	Falkirk	D 1-1	McLean	-
Mar 3	Hearts	W 2-1	McInally, Connolly	-
Mar 9	ST MIRREN	W 6-1	McGrory 3, McLean 2, McInally	-
Mar 17	Dundee	W 2-1	McGrory, Malloy	10,000
Mar 24	ST JOHNSTONE	W 4-1	McInally, Thomson, McGrory, o.g.	-
Mar 27	Motherwell	L 1-2	McInally	16,000
Mar 30	ABERDEEN	W 4-1	McInally 2, Thomson, McGrory	-
Apr 3	KILMARNOCK	D 0-0		
Apr 5	Partick Thistle	D 0-0		25,000
Apr 14	MORTON	W 3-0	McGrory, Connolly, McInally	-
Apr 17	Hamilton Ac.	W 3-1	Leitch, McGrory, Connolly	6,000
Apr 24	DUNDEE UNITED	W 6-2	McLean 3, McGrory 2, McFarlane	-

Scottish Cup

Jan 23	Kilmarnock	(Rd1) W 5-0	Thomson 2, McLean, McInally, McGrory	24,174
Feb 6	HAMILTON AC.	(Rd2) W 4-0	McInally, Thomson, McGrory, McLean	33,000
Feb 20	Hearts	(Rd3) W 4-0	McInally 2, McGrory, Connolly	50,500
Mar 6	DUMBARTON	(Rd4) W 6-1	McLean 2, McGrory 2, McStay W (pen), Thomson	19,000
Mar 20	Aberdeen	(SF) W 2-1	McInally, McGrory	24,000
Apr 10	St Mirren	(F) L 0-2		98,620

MANAGER: Willie Maley

CAPTAIN: Willie McStay

TOP SCORER: Jimmy McGrory

BIGGEST WIN: 6-1 v St Mirren, 9 March 1926, league; 6-1 v Cowdenbeath,12 September 1925, league; 6-1 v Dumbarton, 6 March 1926, Scottish Cup

MAJOR TRANSFERS IN: Tommy McInally from Third Lanark

MAJOR TRANSFERS OUT: Charlie Shaw to New Bedford (USA)

League & Cup Appearances

PLAYER	LEAGUE	CUP COMPETITION S CUP	TOTAL
Callaghan	6		6
Connolly	36	6	42
Gallacher	1		1
Gilfeather	2		2
Hilley	37	6	43
Leitch	3	1	4
McColgan	2		2
McFarlane	34	6	40
McGrory	37	6	43
McInally	37	6	43
McLean	32	4	36
McStay J	38	6	44
McStay W	35	6	41
Malloy	5	1	6
Shaw	2		2
Shevlin	36	6	42
Thomson	37	6	43
Wilson	38	6	44

Goalscorers

PLAYER	LEAGUE	CUP COMPETITION S CUP	TOTAL
McGrory	36	6	42
McInally	17	5	22
McLean	16	4	20
Thomson	15	4	19
Connolly	5	1	6
McStay W	2	1	3
McFarlane	2		2
Leitch	1		1
McStay J	1		1
Malloy	1		1
Opps' o.gs.	1		1

Fact File

On 12 September 1925 Celtic let in the unemployed for 6d at the Boys' Gate. Cowdenbeath claimed £70 in lost gate money. They were awarded £16 and Celtic were censured.

Final Scottish League Div 1 Table

		P	W	D	L	F	A	Pts
1	CELTIC	38	25	8	5	97	40	58
2	AIRDRIEONIANS	38	23	4	11	95	54	50
3	HEARTS	38	21	8	9	87	56	50
4	ST MIRREN	38	20	7	11	62	52	47
5	MOTHERWELL	38	19	8	11	67	46	46
6	RANGERS	38	19	6	13	79	55	44
7	COWDENBEATH	38	18	6	14	87	68	42
8	FALKIRK	38	14	14	10	61	57	42
9	KILMARNOCK	38	17	7	14	79	77	41
10	DUNDEE	38	14	9	15	47	59	37
11	ABERDEEN	38	13	10	15	49	54	36
12	HAMILTON A	38	13	9	16	68	79	35
13	QUEEN'S PARK	38	15	4	19	70	81	34
14	PARTICK T	38	10	13	15	64	73	33
15	MORTON	38	12	7	19	57	84	31
16	HIBERNIAN	38	12	6	20	72	77	30
17	DUNDEE U	38	11	6	21	52	74	28
18	ST JOHNSTONE	38	9	10	19	43	78	28
19	RAITH R	38	11	4	23	46	81	26
20	CLYDEBANK	38	7	8	23	55	92	22

Season 1926-27

Scottish League Divison 1

DATE	OPPONENTS	SCORE	GOALSCORERS	ATTENDANCE
Aug 14	Kilmarnock	W 3-2	McInally, McGrory, McLean	-
Aug 21	COWDENBEATH	W 2-0	McGrory, Thomson	10,000
Aug 28	Queen's Park	W 6-1	McGrory 4, McStay W (pen), Connolly	-
Sep 4	MORTON	W 3-0	Wilson, Doyle, Thomson	-
Sep 11	Clyde	D 2-2	McGrory, Doyle	-
Sep 18	HAMILTON AC.	D 2-2	Connolly 2	10,000
Sep 25	Hibernian	L 2-3	McGrory, McLean	-
Oct 2	DUNDEE	D 0-0		30,000
Oct 16	St Mirren	L 1-3	McGrory	-
Oct 23	ABERDEEN	W 6-2	McGrory 5, McLean	-
Nov 6	Airdrie	D 2-2	McGrory, Connolly	12,000
Nov 13	HEARTS	W 1-0	McLean	-
Nov 20	Dunfermline Ath.	W 6-0	McGrory 4, McLean 2	-
Nov 27	DUNDEE UTD	W 7-2	McGrory 5, Thomson, McLean	-
Dec 4	Motherwell	W 1-0	McGrory	-
Dec 11	ST JOHNSTONE	W 4-0	McGrory 2, Thomson, Connolly	-
Dec 18	Partick Thistle	W 3-0	McLean 2, McGrory	-
Dec 25	KILMARNOCK	W 4-0	McInally 2, McStay W, McGrory	-
Jan 1	Rangers	L 1-2	Thomson	63,000
Jan 3	QUEEN'S PARK	L 2-3	McLean, Thomson	-
Jan 8	Morton	W 6-2	McInally 3, Thomson, McLean, McGrory	6,000
Jan 15	CLYDE	W 7-0	McGrory 5, McLean 2	10,000
Jan 29	Hamilton Ac.	W 2-1	McLean, McGrory	6,000
Feb 2	HIBERNIAN	L 2-3	McLean, Thomson	-
Feb 12	Dundee	W 2-1	Thomson, McGrory	17,000
Feb 16	Hamilton Ac.	D 3-3	McGrory 3	4,000
Feb 23	FALKIRK	W 3-1	McGrory 2, Thomson	-
Feb 26	ST MIRREN	W 6-2	McGrory 4, McLean, McInally	-
Mar 9	Aberdeen	D 0-0		-
Mar 12	Cowdenbeath	L 1-2	McInally	-
Mar 16	AIRDRIE	W 2-1	McGrory, o.g.	-
Mar 30	Hearts	L 0-3		-
Apr 2	DUNFERMLINE ATH.	W 2-1	Thomson, McGrory	-
Apr 6	Falkirk	L 1-4	Thomson	-
Apr 9	Dundee Utd	D 3-3	Connolly, McMenemy, McInally	-
Apr 18	RANGERS	L 0-1		-
Apr 20	MOTHERWELL	W 3-2	Connolly, McLean, Donoghue	-
Apr 23	St Johnstone	L 0-1		-
Apr 30	PARTICK THISTLE	W 2-1	McLean 2	-

Scottish Cup

DATE	OPPONENTS	SCORE	GOALSCORERS	ATTENDANCE
Jan 22	Queen of the South	(Rd1) D 0-0		8,000
Jan 26	QUEEN OF THE SOUTH	(R) W 4-1	McGrory 2, McLean, Thomson	-
Feb 5	Brechin City	(Rd2) W 6-3	McGrory 4, McLean, McInally	4,000
Feb 19	Dundee	(Rd3) W 4-2	Connolly, McLean, McStay W (pen), McGrory	37,477
Mar 5	Bo'ness	(Rd4) W 5-2	McGrory 2, McLean, Thomson, McInally	9,000
Mar 26	Falkirk	(SF) W 1-0	McLean	73,000
Apr 16	East Fife	(F) W 3-1	McLean, Connolly, o.g.	80,070

League & Cup Appearances

PLAYER	LEAGUE	CUP COMPETITION S CUP	TOTAL
Blair	1		1
Callaghan	5		5
Connolly	38	7	45
Donoghue	17	3	20
Doyle	8	1	9
Hilley	37	7	44
McArdle	1		1
McCallum	3		3
McFarlane	34	6	40
McGrory	33	6	39
McInally	32	7	39
McLean	32	7	39
McMenemy	4	1	5
McNally	1		1
McStay J	26	5	31
McStay W	33	7	40
Malloy	2		2
Shevlin	23	3	26
Thomson A	37	7	44
Thomson J	15	4	19
Turnbull	2		2
Wilson	34	6	40

Goalscorers

PLAYER	LEAGUE	CUP COMPETITION S CUP	TOTAL
McGrory	48	9	57
McLean	19	6	25
Thomson A	12	2	14
McInally	9	2	11
Connolly	7	2	9
McStay W	2	1	3
Doyle	2		2
Donoghue	1		1
McMenemy	1		1
Wilson	1		1
Opps' o.gs.	1	1	2

Fact File

On 14 August 1926 Celtic wore a changed strip of green and white quarters in the match at Kilmarnock.

MANAGER: Willie Maley

CAPTAIN: Willie McStay

TOP SCORER: Jimmy McGrory

BIGGEST WIN: 7-0 v Clyde, 15 January 1927, league

HIGHEST ATTENDANCE: 80,070 v East Fife, 16 April 1927, Scottish Cup

MAJOR TRANSFERS OUT: Patsy Gallacher to Falkirk

Final Scottish League Div 1 Table

		P	W	D	L	F	A	Pts
1	RANGERS	38	23	10	5	85	41	56
2	MOTHERWELL	38	23	5	10	81	52	51
3	CELTIC	38	21	7	10	101	55	49
4	AIRDRIEONIANS	38	18	9	11	97	64	45
5	DUNDEE	38	17	9	12	77	51	43
6	FALKIRK	38	16	10	12	77	60	42
7	COWDENBEATH	38	18	6	14	74	60	42
8	ABERDEEN	38	13	14	11	73	72	40
9	HIBERNIAN	38	16	7	15	62	71	39
10	ST MIRREN	38	16	5	17	78	76	37
11	PARTICK T	38	15	6	17	89	74	36
12	QUEEN'S PARK	38	15	6	17	74	84	36
13	HEARTS	38	12	11	15	65	64	35
14	ST JOHNSTONE	38	13	9	16	55	69	35
15	HAMILTON A	38	13	9	16	60	85	35
16	KILMARNOCK	38	12	8	18	54	71	32
17	CLYDE	38	10	9	19	54	85	29
18	DUNFERMLINE ATH	38	10	8	20	53	85	28
19	MORTON	38	12	4	22	56	101	28
20	DUNDEE U	38	7	8	23	56	101	22

Season 1927-28

Scottish League Divison 1

DATE	OPPONENTS	SCORE	GOALSCORERS	ATTENDANCE
Aug 13	HIBERNIAN	W 3-0	McGrory, Thomson, McLean	18,000
Aug 16	KILMARNOCK	W 6-1	McInally 2, McGrory, McLean, Connolly, o.g.	-
Aug 20	Hamilton Ac.	D 0-0		-
Aug 27	FALKIRK	W 3-0	Thomson, McGrory, McInally	-
Sep 3	Raith Rovers	W 3-0	McGrory 2, McInally	14,000
Sep 10	QUEEN'S PARK	W 3-0	McMenemy, Thomson, McGrory	-
Sep 17	Dunfermline Ath.	D 1-1	McLean	7,000
Sep 24	CLYDE	W 3-0	McGrory 2, Thomson	-
Oct 1	Dundee	W 4-1	McGrory 2, Thomson, Wilson (pen)	15,000
Oct 15	Rangers	L 0-1		50,000
Oct 22	Aberdeen	L 1-3	Wilson	11,000
Oct 29	ST MIRREN	W 6-0	McGrory 4, Connolly 2	-
Nov 5	AIRDRIE	W 3-2	McInally 3	-
Nov 12	Hearts	D 2-2	McGrory 2	32,000
Nov 19	COWDENBEATH	D 1-1	McGrory	-
Nov 26	Bo'ness	W 1-0	Thomson	-
Dec 3	MOTHERWELL	L 1-2	McInally	20,000
Dec 10	St Johnstone	W 5-3	McGrory 3, Wilson, Thomson	6,000
Dec 17	PARTICK THISTLE	D 0-0		-
Dec 24	Hibernian	D 2-2	Thomson, McGrory	-
Jan 2	RANGERS	W 1-0	McGrory	70,000
Jan 3	Queen's Park	W 3-1	McGrory 3	-
Jan 7	Falkirk	W 3-1	McGrory 3	12,000
Jan 14	DUNFERMLINE ATH.	W 9-0	McGrory 8, Thomson	-
Jan 28	Kilmarnock	D 2-2	McGrory, McInally	-
Feb 11	Clyde	W 1-0	McInally	-
Feb 14	DUNDEE	W 3-1	Thomson, McInally, McLean	-
Feb 21	St Mirren	W 2-0	McInally, McLean	20,000
Feb 25	ABERDEEN	D 1-1	McInally	-
Mar 6	HAMILTON AC.	W 4-0	McGrory 3, Connolly	-
Mar 17	HEARTS	W 2-1	McGrory 2	-
Mar 28	COWDENBEATH	W 2-0	McLean, McGrory	-
Mar 31	BO'NESS	W 4-1	McGrory 2, Wilson, McLean	-
Apr 7	Motherwell	L 1-3	McLean	-
Apr 9	Airdrie	L 1-3	Thomson	-
Apr 18	ST JOHNSTONE	W 3-0	McInally 2, McLean	-
Apr 21	Partick Thistle	D 3-3	McGrory 2, McStay W (pen)	-
Apr 23	RAITH ROVERS	L 0-3		-

Scottish Cup

Jan 21	BATHGATE	(Rd1) W 3-1	McLean 2, McInally	3,000
Feb 4	Keith	(Rd2) W 6-1	McGrory 3, McInally 3	5,800
Feb 18	ALLOA ATHLETIC	(Rd3) W 2-0	Connolly, McGrory	7,000
Mar 3	Motherwell	(Rd4) W 2-0	Doyle, McGrory	23,000
Mar 24	Queen's Park	(SF) W 2-1	McLean, McGrory	54,000
Apr 14	Rangers	(F) L 0-4		118,115

League & Cup Appearances

PLAYER	LEAGUE	CUP COMPETITION	TOTAL
		S CUP	
Connolly	38	6	44
Donoghue	7	1	8
Doyle	9	3	12
Geddes	2		2
Hilley	3		3
McCallum	1		1
McFarlane	35	5	40
McGonagle	29	5	34
McGrory	37	6	43
McInally	26	4	30
McLean	36	6	42
McMenemy	9		9
McStay J	38	6	44
McStay W	34	6	40
Sinclair	2		2
Thomson A	36	6	42
Thomson J	38	6	44
Wilson	38	6	44

Goalscorers

PLAYER	LEAGUE	CUP COMPETITION	TOTAL
		S CUP	
McGrory	47	6	53
McInally	15	4	19
McLean	9	3	12
Thomson	11		11
Connolly	4	1	5
Wilson	4		4
Doyle		1	1
McMenemy	1		1
McStay W	1		1
Opps' o.gs.	1		1

Final Scottish League Div 1 Table

		P	W	D	L	F	A	Pts
1	RANGERS	38	26	8	4	109	36	60
2	CELTIC	38	23	9	6	93	39	55
3	MOTHERWELL	38	23	9	6	92	46	55
4	HEARTS	38	20	7	11	89	50	47
5	ST MIRREN	38	18	8	12	77	76	44
6	PARTICK T	38	18	7	13	85	67	43
7	ABERDEEN	38	19	5	14	71	61	43
8	KILMARNOCK	38	15	10	13	68	78	40
9	COWDENBEATH	38	16	7	15	66	68	39
10	FALKIRK	38	16	5	17	76	69	37
11	ST JOHNSTONE	38	14	8	16	66	67	36
12	HIBERNIAN	38	13	9	16	73	75	35
13	AIRDRIEONIANS	38	12	11	15	59	69	35
14	DUNDEE	38	14	7	17	65	80	35
15	CLYDE	38	10	11	17	46	72	31
16	QUEEN'S PARK	38	12	6	20	69	80	30
17	RAITH R	38	11	7	20	60	89	29
18	HAMILTON A	38	11	6	21	67	86	28
19	BO'NESS	38	9	8	21	48	86	26
20	DUNFERMLINE ATH	38	4	4	30	41	126	12

Fact File

The first organized speedway meeting in Britain took place at Celtic Park on 28 April 1928.

MANAGER: Willie Maley
CAPTAIN: Willie McStay
TOP SCORER: Jimmy McGrory
BIGGEST WIN: 9-0 v Dunfermline, 9 January 1928, league
HIGHEST ATTENDANCE: 118,115 v Rangers, 14 April 1928, Scottish Cup

Season 1928-29

Scottish League Divison 1

DATE	OPPONENTS	SCORE	GOALSCORERS	ATTENDANCE
Aug 11	Dundee	W 1-0	McGrory	19,000
Aug 18	AIRDRIE	W 4-1	McGrory 3, McCallum	-
Aug 25	Ayr United	W 2-0	Gray 2 (1 pen)	16,000
Sep 8	KILMARNOCK	W 3-0	McGrory, Gray, Connolly	-
Sep 15	Cowdenbeath	W 1-0	McGrory	-
Sep 22	ST MIRREN	L 0-3		-
Sep 29	Hamilton Ac.	D 1-1	McNally	14,000
Oct 13	Motherwell	D 3-3	Gray 2 (1 pen), Connolly	-
Oct 20	RANGERS	L 1-2	McGrory	-
Oct 27	Queen's Park	D 4-4	McGrory 2, Riley 2	20,000
Nov 3	RAITH ROVERS	W 3-1	McGrory 2, Thomson	7,000
Nov 10	Aberdeen	D 2-2	Connolly, o.g.	18,000
Nov 17	CLYDE	W 4-0	Gray 2, McNally, o.g.	-
Nov 24	Third Lanark	W 2-0	Connolly, Thomson	-
Dec 1	ST JOHNSTONE	D 0-0		-
Dec 8	Falkirk	L 0-3		-
Dec 15	HEARTS	W 1-0	Connolly	20,000
Dec 22	Airdrie	W 1-0	Connolly	-
Dec 29	DUNDEE	W 2-1	Gray, Thomson	-
Jan 1	Rangers	L 0-3		60,000
Jan 5	AYR UNITED	W 3-0	Gray 2, Connolly	8,500
Jan 12	Partick Thistle	L 0-3		-
Jan 26	Hearts	L 1-2	Scarff	-
Feb 9	St Mirren	W 1-0	Scarff	-
Feb 12	COWDENBEATH	W 1-0	McGrory	-
Feb 19	HAMILTON AC.	W 3-0	McGrory 3	-
Feb 23	Hibernian	L 1-2	McGrory	-
Mar 9	Raith Rovers	W 4-1	Scarff 3, Prentice	-
Mar 16	ABERDEEN	D 2-2	McGrory, Connolly	-
Mar 19	MOTHERWELL	W 2-0	Scarff, Connolly	-
Mar 26	Clyde	W 1-0	Thomson	-
Mar 30	Third Lanark	W 3-1	McGrory, McGonagle (pen), o.g.	-
Apr 1	Partick Thistle*	W 1-0	Gray	11,000
Apr 6	St Johnstone	D 1-1	Gray	-
Apr 13	Hibernian*	L 1-4	McGrory	-
Apr 17	Queen's Park*	L 1-2	McGrory	-
Apr 20	Falkirk*	W 3-0	Scarff 2, Hughes	-
Apr 27	Kilmarnock	W 3-2	Connolly, McGrory, Hughes	-

*Played away because of fire damage at Celtic Park.

Scottish Cup

Jan 19	ARTHURLIE	(Rd1) W 5-1	McGrory 3, Connolly, McStay J	8,000
Feb 2	EAST STIRLING	(Rd2) W 3-0	McGrory 2, McStay J	8,000
Feb 16	ARBROATH	(Rd3) W 4-1	McGrory 4	7,000
Mar 6	MOTHERWELL	(Rd4) D 0-0		47,000
Mar 13	Motherwell	(R) W 2-1	Connolly, McGrory	32,000
Mar 23	Kilmarnock	(SF) L 0-1		40,000

League & Cup Appearances

PLAYER	LEAGUE	CUP COMPETITION S CUP	TOTAL
Connolly	35	6	41
Crozier	2		2
Donoghue	14	4	18
Getons	2		2
Gray	26	5	31
hughes	8		8
McCallum	21	1	22
McFarlane	23	2	25
McGonagle	38	6	44
McGrory	21	6	27
McMenemy	2		2
McNally	5		5
McStay J	38	6	44
McStay W	36	6	42
McWilliams	6		6
Nicol	1		1
Prentice	4		4
Riley	10		10
Scarff	16	6	22
Thomson A	37	6	43
Thomson J	37	6	43
Wilson	36	6	42

Goalscorers

PLAYER	LEAGUE	CUP COMPETITION S CUP	TOTAL
McGrory	21	10	31
Gray	12		12
Connolly	10	2	12
Scarff	8		8
Thomson A	4		4
Hughes	2		2
McNally	2		2
McStay J		2	2
Riley	2		2
McCallum	1		1
McGonagle	1		1
Prentice	1		1
Opps' o.gs.	3		3

Fact File

On the morning of 28 March 1929, the pavilion at Celtic Park burnt down. Among the charred remains were strips, 50 pairs of boots and club records.

MANAGER: Willie Maley
CAPTAIN: Willie McStay
TOP SCORER: Jimmy McGrory
BIGGEST WIN: 5-1 v Arthurlie, 19 January 1929, league
HIGHEST ATTENDANCE: 60,000 v Rangers, 1 January 1929, league
MAJOR TRANSFERS OUT: Tommy McInally to Sunderland, Adam McLean to Sunderland

Final Scottish League Div 1 Table

		P	W	D	L	F	A	Pts
1	RANGERS	38	30	7	1	107	32	67
2	CELTIC	38	22	7	9	67	44	51
3	MOTHERWELL	38	20	10	8	85	66	50
4	HEARTS	38	19	9	10	91	57	47
5	QUEEN'S PARK	38	18	7	13	100	69	43
6	PARTICK T	38	17	7	14	91	70	41
7	ABERDEEN	38	16	8	14	81	68	40
8	ST MIRREN	38	16	8	14	78	75	40
9	ST JOHNSTONE	38	14	10	14	57	70	38
10	KILMARNOCK	38	14	8	16	79	74	36
11	FALKIRK	38	14	8	16	68	86	36
12	HAMILTON A	38	13	9	16	58	83	35
13	COWDENBEATH	38	14	5	19	55	69	33
14	HIBERNIAN	38	13	6	19	54	62	32
15	AIRDRIEONIANS	38	12	7	19	56	65	31
16	AYR U	38	12	7	19	65	84	31
17	CLYDE	38	12	6	20	47	71	30
18	DUNDEE	38	9	11	18	59	69	29
19	THIRD LANARK	38	10	6	22	71	102	26
20	RAITH R	38	9	6	23	52	105	24

Season 1929-30

Scottish League Divison 1

DATE	OPPONENTS	SCORE	GOALSCORERS	ATTENDANCE
Aug 10	HEARTS	W 2-1	McGrory 2	40,000
Aug 17	Morton	W 2-1	Scarff 2	-
Aug 24	ABERDEEN	L 3-4	Kavanagh, McGrory, Scarff	-
Aug 31	Hamilton Ac.	W 3-2	McGrory 3	12,000
Sep 14	Airdrie	W 1-0	McGonagle	24,000
Sep 21	DUNDEE	D 1-1	McNally	-
Sep 28	Ayr United	W 3-1	McGrory 3 (1 pen)	-
Oct 5	FALKIRK	W 7-0	McGrory 3, Connolly 2, Scarff, Thomson A	-
Oct 19	QUEEN'S PARK	W 2-1	Scarff, Thomson A	-
Oct 23	Dundee United	D 2-2	Napier, Scarff	6,000
Oct 26	Rangers	L 0-1		-
Nov 2	HIBERNIAN	W 4-0	Connolly, Napier, Kavanagh, NcNally	-
Nov 9	Motherwell	L 1-2	Napier	-
Nov 16	COWDENBEATH	W 2-1	Napier, Wilson (pen)	-
Nov 23	St Johnstone	W 6-1	McGrory 3, Thomson R, Napier, Robertson	-
Nov 30	Partick Thistle	L 2-3	McGrory, Connolly	-
Dec 7	ST MIRREN	W 3-0	McGrory, Napier, McStay J	-
Dec 14	Kilmarnock	D 1-1	McGrory	-
Dec 21	Hearts	W 3-1	McGrory, Connolly, Thomson R	22,000
Dec 28	MORTON	L 0-1		-
Jan 1	RANGERS	L 1-2	Napier	40,000
Jan 2	Queen's Park	L 1-2	Napier	25,000
Jan 4	Aberdeen	L 1-3	Napier	-
Jan 25	Clyde	W 3-2	Wilson (pen), Thomson R, McGrory	-
Feb 5	AIRDRIE	L 1-2	Napier	-
Feb 8	Dundee	D 2-2	Napier, McGrory	-
Feb 18	AYR UNITED	W 4-0	Scarff 4	-
Feb 22	Falkirk	W 1-0	Scarff	-
Mar 1	DUNDEE UNITED	W 7-0	Scarff 4, Hughes, Napier, Thomson A	-
Mar 8	Hibernian	W 2-0	McGrory, Scarff	11,000
Mar 15	MOTHERWELL	L 0-4		-
Mar 22	Cowdenbeath	W 2-1	Scarff, Napier	-
Mar 29	ST JOHNSTONE	W 6-2	McGrory 3, Scarff, Napier, Thomson A	5,000
Apr 5	PARTICK THISTLE	W 2-0	McGrory 2	-
Apr 12	St Mirren	D 0-0		-
Apr 15	HAMILTON AC.	W 3-0	McGrory 2, Napier	-
Apr 19	KILMARNOCK	W 4-0	McGrory 2, Napier, Wilson (pen)	-
Apr 21	CLYDE	L 0-2		-

Scottish Cup

DATE	OPPONENTS		SCORE	GOALSCORERS	ATTENDANCE
Jan 18	Inverness Caledonian	(Rd1)	W 6-0	McGrory 2, Napier, Wilson Connolly, o.g.	6,500
Feb 1	ARBROATH	(Rd2)	W 5-0	McGrory 2, Thomson R, Thomson A, Scarff	6,500
Feb 15	ST MIRREN	(Rd3)	L 1-3	Thomson A	32,000

League & Cup Appearances

PLAYER	LEAGUE	CUP COMPETITION S CUP	TOTAL
Barrie	1		1
Connolly	27	2	29
Cook	11		11
Donoghue	4		4
Gallagher	2		2
Geatons	23	3	26
Hughes	11		11
Kavanagh	17		17
Kelly	9	1	10
McCallum	11		11
McGonagle	35	3	38
McGrory	26	3	29
McNally	5		5
McStay	32	3	35
Napier	29	2	31
Prentice	2		2
Robertson	28	3	31
Scarff	25	2	27
Thomson A	35	3	38
Thomson J	29	2	31
Thomson R	20	2	22
Wilson	36	3	39

Goalscorers

PLAYER	LEAGUE	CUP COMPETITION S CUP	TOTAL
McGrory	31	4	35
Scarff	18	1	19
Napier	16	1	17
Connolly	5	1	6
Thomson A	4	2	6
Thomson R	3	1	4
Wilson	3	1	4
Kavanagh	2		2
McNally	2		2
Hughes	1		1
McGonagle	1		1
McStay J	1		1
Robertson	1		1
Opps' o.gs.		1	1

Fact File

In successive games on 14 and 21 December 1929 goalkeeper John Thomson was concussed after diving at forwards' feet.

MANAGER: Willie Maley

CAPTAIN: Jimmy McStay

TOP SCORER: Jimmy McGrory

BIGGEST WIN: 7-0 v Falkirk, 5 October 1929, league; 7-0 v Dundee United, 1 March 1930, league

HIGHEST ATTENDANCE: 40,000 v Rangers, 1 January 1930, league

MAJOR TRANSFERS OUT: John McFarlane to Middlesbrough, Willie McStay to Hamilton

Final Scottish League Div 1 Table

		P	W	D	L	F	A	PTS
1	RANGERS	38	28	4	6	94	32	60
2	MOTHERWELL	38	25	5	8	104	48	55
3	ABERDEEN	38	23	7	8	85	61	53
4	CELTIC	38	22	5	11	88	46	49
5	ST MIRREN	38	18	5	15	73	56	41
6	PARTICK T	38	16	9	13	72	61	41
7	FALKIRK	38	16	9	13	62	64	41
8	KILMARNOCK	38	15	9	14	77	73	39
9	AYR U	38	16	6	16	70	92	38
10	HEARTS	38	14	9	15	69	69	37
11	CLYDE	38	13	11	14	64	69	37
12	AIRDRIEONIANS	38	16	4	18	60	66	36
13	HAMILTON A	38	14	7	17	76	81	35
14	DUNDEE	38	14	6	18	51	58	34
15	QUEEN'S PARK	38	15	4	19	67	80	34
16	COWDENBEATH	38	13	7	18	64	74	33
17	HIBERNIAN	38	9	11	18	45	62	29
18	MORTON	38	10	7	21	67	95	27
19	DUNDEE U	38	7	8	23	56	109	22
20	ST JOHNSTONE	38	6	7	25	48	96	19

Season 1930-31

Scottish League Divison 1

DATE	OPPONENTS	SCORE	GOALSCORERS	ATTENDANCE
Aug 9	KILMARNOCK	W 3-1	McCallum 2, Napier	8,000
Aug 16	Falkirk	L 2-3	Scarff 2	13,000
Aug 23	HIBERNIAN	W 6-0	Scarff 3, Smith, McStay, Thomson R	8,000
Aug 30	East Fife	W 6-2	Napier 3 (2 pens), Scarff 2, Thomson A	-
Sep 6	ABERDEEN	W 1-0	Napier (pen)	18,000
Sep 13	Hamilton Ac.	D 0-0		
Sep 20	RANGERS	W 2-0	Thomson A, Thomson R	-
Sep 27	Queen's Park	D 3-3	Napier 2 (2 pens), Thomson R	20,000
Oct 4	MORTON	W 4-1	McGrory 3, Thomson R	15,000
Oct 18	ST MIRREN	W 3-1	McGrory 2, Scarff	18,000
Oct 25	Motherwell	D 3-3	Scarff, McGrory, Thomson A	-
Nov 1	PARTICK THISTLE	W 5-1	Scarff 2, McGrory 2, Napier	-
Nov 8	HEARTS	W 2-1	Scarff, Napier	-
Nov 15	Cowdenbeath	D 1-1	Wilson	-
Nov 22	Ayr United	W 6-2	Scarff 2, Napier 2, McGrory 2	-
Dec 6	Airdrie	W 2-1	McGrory, Thomson A	-
Dec 13	LEITH ATHLETIC	W 4-0	Napier 2 (2 pens), Geatons, McGrory	-
Dec 20	Kilmarnock	W 3-0	McGrory 3	-
Dec 27	FALKIRK	W 3-0	McGrory, Thomson A, Napier (pen)	-
Jan 1	Rangers	L 0-1		84,000
Jan 3	Hibernian	D 0-0		22,000
Jan 10	EAST FIFE	W 9-1	McGrory 5, Scarff 3, Thomson A	-
Jan 24	Aberdeen	D 1-1	Cowan	-
Feb 7	Morton	W 1-0	Thomson A	-
Feb 18	CLYDE	L 0-1		-
Feb 21	St Mirren	W 3-1	Thomson R 2, Napier	-
Feb 24	HAMILTON AC.	W 2-1	McGrory, Thomson R	-
Mar 4	MOTHERWELL	W 4-1	McGrory 4	32,000
Mar 7	Partick Thistle	L 0-1		-
Mar 18	Hearts	D 1-1	Hughes	25,000
Mar 21	COWDENBEATH	W 6-0	McGrory 4, McStay, Napier	-
Mar 25	DUNDEE	D 2-2	Hughes, Thomson R	-
Apr 4	AYR UNITED	W 4-1	Scarff, McGrory, 2 o.g.	-
Apr 6	Clyde	W 2-0	Napier (pen), Thomson R	20,000
Apr 18	AIRDRIE	W 3-1	McGrory, Scarff, Napier (pen)	-
Apr 22	Dundee	D 0-0		-
Apr 25	Leith Athletic	W 3-0	McGrory 3	-
Apr 28	QUEEN'S PARK	D 1-1	McGrory	-

Scottish Cup

Jan 17	East Fife	(Rd1) W 2-1	Napier, Scarff	9,000
Feb 4	Dundee United	(Rd2) W 3-2	Scarff 2, Napier	-
Feb 14	Morton	(Rd3) W 4-1	McGrory 3, Napier	20,577
Feb 28	ABERDEEN	(Rd4) W 4-0	Thomson R 3, McGrory	64,699
Mar 14	Kilmarnock	(SF) W 3-0	Napier, Hughes, McGrory	53,973
Apr 11	Motherwell	(F) D 2-2	McGrory, o.g.	104,803
Apr 15	Motherwell	(R) W 4-2	Thomson R 2, McGrory 2	98,579

Fact File

On 27 September 1930 in the match against Queen's Park the referee played a 40-minute first half and blew for full-time two minutes early. The game was restarted and Queen's Park equalized with a 91st-minute penalty.

MANAGER: Willie Maley

CAPTAIN: Jimmy McStay

TOP SCORER: Jimmy McGrory

BIGGEST WIN: 9-1 v East Fife, 10 January 1931, league

HIGHEST ATTENDANCE: 104,803 v Motherwell, 11 April 1931, Scottish Cup

League & Cup Appearances

PLAYER	LEAGUE	CUP COMPETITION S CUP	TOTAL
Cook	33	7	40
Cowan	1		1
Geatons	29	7	36
Hughes	8	2	10
Kavanagh	4	1	5
McCallum	2		2
McGonagle	37	7	44
McGrory	29	6	35
McStay	37	7	44
Morrison	5		5
Napier	37	7	44
Robertson D	2		2
Robertson G	6		6
Scarff	37	7	44
Smith	3		3
Thomson A	36	7	43
Thomson J	36	7	43
Thomson R	34	7	41
Tierney	7		7
Whitelaw	10		10
Wilson	25	5	30

Goalscorers

PLAYER	LEAGUE	CUP COMPETITION S CUP	TOTAL
McGrory	36	8	44
Napier	18	4	22
Scarff	19	3	22
Thomson R	9	5	14
Thomson A	7		7
Hughes	2	1	3
McCallum	2		2
McStay	2		2
Cowan	1		1
Geatons	1		1
Smith	1		1
Wilson	1		1
Opps' o.gs.	2	1	3

Final Scottish League Div 1 Table

		P	W	D	L	F	A	PTS
1	RANGERS	38	27	6	5	96	29	60
2	CELTIC	38	24	10	4	101	34	58
3	MOTHERWELL	38	24	8	6	102	42	56
4	PARTICK T	38	24	5	9	76	43	53
5	HEARTS	38	19	6	13	90	63	44
6	ABERDEEN	38	17	7	14	79	63	41
7	COWDENBEATH	38	17	7	14	58	65	41
8	DUNDEE	38	17	5	16	65	63	39
9	AIRDRIEONIANS	38	17	5	16	59	66	39
10	HAMILTON A	38	16	5	17	59	57	37
11	KILMARNOCK	38	15	5	18	59	60	35
12	CLYDE	38	15	4	19	60	87	34
13	QUEEN'S PARK	38	13	7	18	71	72	33
14	FALKIRK	38	14	4	20	77	87	32
15	ST MIRREN	38	11	8	19	49	72	30
16	MORTON	38	11	7	20	58	83	29
17	LEITH ATH.	38	8	11	19	51	85	27
18	AYR U	38	8	11	19	53	92	27
19	HIBERNIAN	38	9	7	22	49	81	25
20	EAST FIFE	38	8	4	26	45	113	20

Season 1931-32

Scottish League Divison 1

DATE	OPPONENTS	SCORE	GOALSCORERS	ATTENDANCE
Aug 8	Leith Athletic	W 3-0	McGrory 2, Thomson R	-
Aug 15	DUNDEE UNITED	W 3-2	McGrory 2, Thomson A	10,000
Aug 19	HEARTS	W 3-0	Scarff 2, Napier	20,000
Aug 22	Aberdeen	D 1-1	Whitney	28,000
Aug 26	COWDENBEATH	W 7-0	McGrory 4, Napier, Thomson A, Solis	-
Aug 29	HAMILTON AC.	W 6-1	McGrory 3, Scarff 3	-
Sep 2	Third Lanark	D 3-3	McGrory 2, Scarff	-
Sep 5	Rangers	D 0-0		80,000
Sep 12	QUEEN'S PARK	D 2-2	Napier (pen), Solis	-
Sep 19	Morton	D 3-3	Napier 2, Hughes	-
Sep 26	FALKIRK	W 4-1	Napier 2 (1 pen), McGrory, o.g.	-
Oct 3	Kilmarnock	W 3-2	McGrory 2, Napier	-
Oct 10	CLYDE	D 1-1	Hughes	-
Oct 17	Dundee	L 0-2		17,000
Oct 24	AYR UNITED	W 4-2	McGhee 2, McGrory, Napier	-
Oct 31	Motherwell	D 2-2	Napier 2	-
Nov 14	PARTICK THISTLE	L 1-2	Thomson A	-
Nov 21	Hearts	L 1-2	McGrory	-
Nov 28	Cowdenbeath	W 2-1	Thomson R 2	5,000
Dec 5	THIRD LANARK	W 5-0	McGrory 3, Napier 2	-
Dec 12	AIRDRIE	W 6-1	Napier 3, McGrory 2, Solis	-
Dec 19	LEITH ATHLETIC	W 6-0	McGrory 4, Thomson R, Napier	-
Dec 26	Dundee United	L 0-1		15,000
Jan 1	RANGERS	L 1-2	McGrory	55,000
Jan 2	Queen's Park	W 3-0	Napier 2 (1 pen), o.g.	-
Jan 9	ABERDEEN	W 2-0	Hughes, Wilson	-
Jan 23	Hamilton Ac.	L 0-1		-
Feb 6	Falkirk	L 0-2		-
Feb 20	Clyde	L 1-2	Napier (pen)	-
Feb 27	DUNDEE	L 0-2		-
Mar 5	Ayr United	W 3-2	O'Donnell 2, Thomson A	7,000
Mar 12	MOTHERWELL	L 2-4	Thomson A, O'Donnell	25,000
Mar 19	St Mirren	W 2-1	O'Donnell, Kavanagh	-
Mar 28	ST MIRREN	W 1-0	Thomson A	-
Apr 2	MORTON	W 6-3	O'Donnell 4, Thomson A 2	-
Apr 9	Airdrie	D 1-1	O'Donnell	-
Apr 23	KILMARNOCK	W 4-1	Kavanagh 2, Thomson A, Napier (pen)	-
Apr 30	Partick Thistle	W 2-0	McDonald 2	-

Scottish Cup

DATE	OPPONENTS		SCORE	GOALSCORERS	ATTENDANCE
Jan 16	FALKIRK	(Rd1)	W 3-2	Napier 2 (1 pen), o.g.	14,000
Jan 30	St Johnstone	(Rd2)	W 4-2	Napier 3, Thomson A	19,185
Feb 13	Motherwell	(Rd3)	L 0-2		38,000

League & Cup Appearances

PLAYER	LEAGUE	CUP COMPETITION S CUP	TOTAL
Coen	3		3
Cook	33	3	36
Falconer	7	1	8
Geatons	26	3	29
Hughes	11	1	12
Kavanagh	11	2	13
Kennaway	20	2	22
McCallum	1		1
McDonald	1		1
McGhee	5	1	6
McGonagle P	36	3	39
McGonagle T	1		1
McGrory	22	1	23
McStay	37	3	40
McWilliams	1		1
Morrison	10		10
Napier	33	3	36
O'Donnell	9		9
Scarff	19		19
Smith	9	2	11
Solis	9		9
Thomson A	35	3	38
Thomson J	8		8
Thomson R	28	1	29
Whitelaw	7	1	8
Whitney	4		4
Wilson	32	3	35

Goalscorers

PLAYER	LEAGUE	CUP COMPETITION S CUP	TOTAL
McGrory	28		28
Napier	21	5	26
Thomson A	9	1	10
O'Donnell	9		9
Scarff	6		6
Thomson r	4		4
Solis	3		3
Hughes	3		3
Kavanagh	3		3
McGhee	2		2
McDonall	2		2
Whitney	1		1
Wilson	1		1
Opps' o.gs.	2	1	3

Fact File

John Thomson died in hospital after injuries sustained in the Old Firm game on 5 September 1931. Thirty thousand mourners attended the funeral and men and boys walked from Glasgow to his home town of Fife to pay their respects.

MANAGER: Willie Maley
CAPTAIN: Jimmy McStay
TOP SCORER: Jimmy McGrory
BIGGEST WIN: 7-0 v Cowdenbeath, 26 August 1931, league
HIGHEST ATTENDANCE: 80,000 v Rangers, 5 September 1931, league
MAJOR TRANSFERS IN: Joe Kennaway from New Bedford (USA)

Final Scottish League Div 1 Table

		P	W	D	L	F	A	Pts
1	MOTHERWELL	38	30	6	2	119	31	66
2	RANGERS	38	28	5	5	118	42	61
3	CELTIC	38	20	8	10	94	50	48
4	THIRD LANARK	38	21	4	13	92	81	46
5	ST MIRREN	38	20	4	14	77	56	44
6	PARTICK T	38	19	4	15	58	59	42
7	ABERDEEN	38	16	9	13	57	49	41
8	HEARTS	38	17	5	16	63	61	39
9	KILMARNOCK	38	16	7	15	68	70	39
10	HAMILTON A	38	16	6	16	84	65	38
11	DUNDEE	38	14	10	14	61	72	38
12	COWDENBEATH	38	15	8	15	66	78	38
13	CLYDE	38	13	9	16	58	70	35
14	AIRDRIEONIANS	38	13	6	19	74	81	32
15	MORTON	38	12	7	19	78	87	31
16	QUEEN'S PARK	38	13	5	20	59	79	31
17	AYR U	38	11	7	20	70	90	29
18	FALKIRK	38	11	5	22	70	76	27
19	DUNDEE U	38	6	7	25	40	118	19
20	LEITH ATH.	38	6	4	28	46	137	16

Season 1932-33

Scottish League Divison 1

DATE	OPPONENTS	SCORE	GOALSCORERS	ATTENDANCE
Aug 13	ABERDEEN	W 3-0	McGrory, Cameron, Napier (pen)	-
Aug 16	THIRD LANARK	W 4-2	McGrory 2, Napier, Cameron	-
Aug 20	Hamilton Ac.	D 1-1	McGrory	-
Aug 24	PARTICK THISTLE	L 1-2	Napier	-
Aug 27	MORTON	W 7-1	Napier 3, McGrory 2, Thomson R, Thomson A	-
Aug 30	AYR UNITED	W 4-1	Napier 2 (1 pen), McGillivray, McGrory	-
Sep 3	Falkirk	D 1-1	McGillivray	-
Sep 10	RANGERS	D 1-1	McGrory	-
Sep 14	East Stirling	W 3-1	Napier 3 (1 pen)	-
Sep 17	Queen's Park	L 1-4	O'Donnell	-
Sep 24	KILMARNOCK	D 0-0		-
Oct 1	Hearts	D 1-1	Napier	-
Oct 8	ST JOHNSTONE	W 5-0	O'Donnell H 2, O'Donnell F, Napier 2 (1 pen)	-
Oct 15	Clyde	W 2-0	Geatons, O'Donnell F	-
Oct 22	MOTHERWELL	W 4-1	Crom 2, Thomson A, Smith	-
Oct 29	St Mirren	L 1-3	Napier (pen)	-
Nov 5	Partick Thistle	L 0-3		30,000
Nov 12	EAST STIRLING	W 3-0	Thomson A 3	-
Nov 19	COWDENBEATH	W 3-0	Napier 2, McGrory	-
Nov 26	Third. Lanark	W 4-0	Napier 2, McGrory 2	-
Dec 3	Airdrie	W 3-0	Thomson R 2, Napier (pen)	-
Dec 10	DUNDEE	W 3-2	McGrory, Geatons, o.g.	-
Dec 17	Ayr United	W 1-0	McGrory	-
Dec 24	Aberdeen	L 0-1		-
Dec 26	QUEEN'S PARK	W 2-0	O'Donnell F, O'Donnell H	-
Dec 31	HAMILTON AC.	L 0-3		-
Jan 2	Rangers	D 0-0		42,000
Jan 7	Morton	W 1-0	McGrory	-
Jan 14	FALKIRK	L 0-1		-
Jan 28	Kilmarnock	D 2-2	O'Donnell H, McGonagle (pen)	-
Feb 11	HEARTS	W 3-2	McGrory 2, Thomson R	-
Feb 25	St Johnstone	L 0-1		-
Mar 11	Motherwell	L 2-4	O'Donnell F, McGrory	-
Mar 25	Cowdenbeath	W 5-1	McGrory 3, Thomson R 2	-
Apr 3	ST MIRREN	D 0-0		-
Apr 10	CLYDE	W 2-1	McGrory 2	-
Apr 18	AIRDRIE	W 2-1	Paterson, Thomson A	-
Apr 22	Dundee	L 0-3		-

Scottish Cup

DATE	OPPONENTS		SCORE	GOALSCORERS	ATTENDANCE
Jan 21	Dunfermline Ath.	(Rd1)	W 7-1	McGrory 3, O'Donnell H 3, Thomson R	8,384
Feb 4	FALKIRK	(Rd2)	W 2-0	McGrory 2	26,744
Feb 18	PARTICK THISTLE	(Rd3)	W 2-1	McGrory, Thomson R	55,595
Mar 4	Albion Rovers	(Rd4)	D 1-1	Napier	14,000
Mar 8	ALBION ROVERS	(R)	W 3-1	Napier 2 (1 pen), Thomson A	23,810
Mar 18	Hearts	(SF)	D 0-0		87,000
Mar 22	Hearts	(R)	W 2-1	McGrory, Thomson A	63,756
Apr 15	Motherwell	(F)	W 1-0	McGrory	102,339

League & Cup Appearances

PLAYER	LEAGUE	CUP COMPETITION S CUP	TOTAL
Cameron	4		4
Connor	1		1
Cook	23		23
Crum	3		3
Geatons	34	4	38
Hogg	19	8	27
Hughes	6	4	10
Kennaway	28	5	33
McDonald	6		6
McGillivray	4		4
McGonagle	31	8	39
McGrory	25	8	33
McStay	34	8	42
Morrison	3		3
Napier	35	8	43
O'Donnell F	13		13
O'Donnell H	27	8	35
Paterson	2		2
Smith	9		9
Thomson A	36	8	44
Thomson R	29	8	37
Wallace	10	3	13
Wilson	36	8	44

Goalscorers

PLAYER	LEAGUE	CUP COMPETITION S CUP	TOTAL
McGrory	22	8	30
Napier	20		20
Thomson A	6	2	8
Thomson R	6	2	8
O'Donnell H	4	3	7
O'Donnel F	5		5
Cameron	2		2
McGillivray	2		2
Geatons	2		2
Crum	2		2
McGonagle	1		1
Paterson	1		1
Smith	1		1
Opps' o.gs.	1		1

Fact File

On 19 September 1932 Bertie Thomson asked for a transfer and refused to train. He was suspended (but not forgiven) for two months.

MANAGER: Willie Maley

CAPTAIN: Jimmy McStay

TOP SCORER: Jimmy McGrory

BIGGEST WIN: 7-1 v Morton, 27 August 1932, league; 7-1 v Dunfermline, 21 January 1933, Scottish Cup

HIGHEST ATTENDANCE: 102,339 v Motherwell, 15 April 1933, Scottish Cup

MAJOR TRANSFERS OUT: Paddy Connolly to Hibernian, Willie Cook to Everton

Final Scottish League Div 1 Table

		P	W	D	L	F	A	Pts
1	RANGERS	38	26	10	2	113	43	62
2	MOTHERWELL	38	27	5	6	114	53	59
3	HEARTS	38	21	8	9	84	51	50
4	CELTIC	38	20	8	10	75	44	48
5	ST JOHNSTONE	38	17	10	11	70	55	44
6	ABERDEEN	38	18	6	14	85	58	42
7	ST MIRREN	38	18	6	14	73	60	42
8	HAMILTON A	38	18	6	14	90	78	42
9	QUEEN'S PARK	38	17	7	14	78	79	41
10	PARTICK T	38	17	6	15	75	55	40
11	FALKIRK	38	15	6	17	70	70	36
12	CLYDE	38	15	5	18	69	75	35
13	THIRD LANARK	38	14	7	17	70	80	35
14	KILMARNOCK	38	13	9	16	72	86	35
15	DUNDEE	38	12	9	17	60	77	33
16	AYR U	38	13	4	21	62	95	30
17	COWDENBEATH	38	10	5	23	65	111	25
18	AIRDRIEONIANS	38	10	3	25	55	102	23
19	MORTON	38	6	9	23	49	97	21
20	EAST STIRLINGSHIRE	38	7	3	28	55	115	17

Season 1933-34

Scottish League Divison 1

DATE	OPPONENTS	SCORE	GOALSCORERS	ATTENDANCE
Aug 12	Queen of the South	L 2-3	McGrory, McGonagle (pen)	10,948
Aug 19	FALKIRK	D 2-2	McGrory, McGonagle (pen)	-
Aug 23	Partick Thistle	W 3-0	McGrory, Crum, O'Donnell F	25,000
Aug 26	Kilmarnock	L 3-4	McGonagle, Connor, Crum	-
Sep 2	HEARTS	D 0-0		
Sep 9	Rangers	D 2-2	McGrory 2	49,000
Sep 19	COWDENBEATH	W 7-0	McGrory 3, Napier 3 (2 pens), O'Donnell H	-
Sep 23	St Johnstone	D 1-1	Buchan	-
Sep 30	QUEEN'S PARK	W 3-1	O'Donnell H, McStay, Thomson A	-
Oct 7	Aberdeen	L 0-3		18,000
Oct 21	Motherwell	D 1-1	Crum	18,000
Oct 28	HIBERNIAN	W 2-1	Crum 2	-
Nov 4	PARTICK THISTLE	W 2-0	McGrory, O'Donnell F	-
Nov 11	Cowdenbeath	W 1-0	O'Donnell F	-
Nov 18	Ayr United	L 1-3	O'Donnell F	11,000
Nov 25	THIRD LANARK	W 3-1	O'Donnell F 2 (1 pen), McGrory	-
Dec 2	AIRDRIE	W 4-2	Thomson A, Crum, McGrory, Hughes	-
Dec 9	Dundee	L 2-3	O'Donnell F, Crum	-
Dec 23	QUEEN OF THE SOUTH	L 0-1		-
Dec 25	Queen's Park	W 3-2	O'Donnell F, Napier, McGrory	-
Dec 30	Falkirk	L 0-2		-
Jan 1	RANGERS	D 2-2	McGrory, McGonagle	45,000
Jan 6	KILMARNOCK	W 4-1	McGrory 2, McDonald, Napier	-
Jan 13	Hearts	L 1-2	McGonagle (pen)	-
Jan 27	ST JOHNSTONE	D 0-0		-
Feb 24	ABERDEEN	D 2-2	Crum, Dunn	-
Mar 10	MOTHERWELL	W 3-0	O'Donnell H 2, O'Donnell F	-
Mar 17	Hibernian	W 2-1	McGrory, O'Donnell H	-
Mar 24	AYR UNITED	L 0-3		-
Mar 31	Third Lanark	D 1-1	McGrory	-
Apr 2	CLYDE	W 2-1	O'Donnell F 2 (1 pen)	-
Apr 7	Airdrie	W 4-2	Murphy 2, O'Donnell F 2 (1 pen)	-
Apr 11	ST MIRREN	W 3-0	O'Donnell F 3	-
Apr 14	Hamilton Ac.	D 1-1	O'Donnell F (pen)	-
Apr 18	Clyde	D 1-1	O'Donnell F	-
Apr 21	DUNDEE	W 3-2	Divers 2, O'Donnell F	-
Apr 23	HAMILTON AC.	W 5-1	O'Donnell F 2, Crum 2, Divers	-
Apr 28	St Mirren	W 2-1	O'Donnell F, Geatons	-

Scottish Cup

DATE	OPPONENTS	SCORE	GOALSCORERS	ATTENDANCE
Jan 20	Dalbeattie Star	(Rd1) W 6-0	Crum 4, O'Donnell F 2	2,376
Feb 3	Ayr United	(Rd2) W 3-2	McGonagle (pen), O'Donnell F, O'Donnell H	25,261
Feb 17	FALKIRK	(Rd3) W 3-1	O'Donnell F 2, McGrory	43,000
Mar 3	St Mirren	(Rd4) L 0-2		33,434

League & Cup Appearances

PLAYER	LEAGUE	CUP COMPETITION S CUP	TOTAL
Bucan	6	1	7
Connor	3		3
Crum	30	3	33
Dawson	4	2	6
Divers	8		8
Dunn	6		6
Geatons	14	2	16
Hogg	38	4	42
Hughes	35	3	38
Kennaway	33	4	37
McDonald	14	1	15
McGonagle	35	4	39
McGrory	26	3	29
McStay	33	4	37
Morrison	4		4
Murphy	2		2
Napier	15	2	17
O'Donnell F	33	4	37
O'Donnell H	20	3	23
Smith	4		4
Thomson A	23	4	27
Thomson R	2		2
Wallace	5		5
Wilson	25	1	26

Goalscorers

PLAYER	LEAGUE	CUP COMPETITION S CUP	TOTAL
O'Donnell F	22	5	27
McGrory	17	1	18
Crum	10	4	14
McGonagle	5	1	6
O'Donnell H	5	1	6
Napier	5		5
Divers	3		3
Murphy	2		2
Thomson A	2		2
Buchan	1		1
Connor	1		1
Dunn	1		1
Geatons	1		1
Hughes	1		1
McDonald	1		1
McStay	1		1

Fact File

John Thomson's replacement Joe Kennaway represented Canada, USA and Scotland at international level.

MANAGER: Willie Maley
CAPTAIN: Jimmy McStay
TOP SCORER: Frank O'Donnell
BIGGEST WIN: 7-0 v Cowdenbeath, 19 September 1933, league
HIGHEST ATTENDANCE: 49,000 v Rangers, 9 September 1933, league
MAJOR TRANSFERS OUT: Bertie Thomson to Blackpool

Final Scottish League Div 1 Table

		P	W	D	L	F	A	Pts
1	RANGERS	38	30	6	2	118	41	66
2	MOTHERWELL	38	29	4	5	97	45	62
3	CELTIC	38	18	11	9	78	53	47
4	Q OF S	38	21	3	14	75	78	45
5	ABERDEEN	38	18	8	12	90	57	44
6	HEARTS	38	17	10	11	86	59	44
7	KILMARNOCK	38	17	9	12	73	64	43
8	AYR U	38	16	10	12	87	92	42
9	ST JOHNSTONE	38	17	6	15	74	53	40
10	FALKIRK	38	16	6	16	73	68	38
11	HAMILTON A	38	15	8	15	65	79	38
12	DUNDEE	38	15	6	17	68	64	36
13	PARTICK T	38	14	5	19	73	78	33
14	CLYDE	38	10	11	17	56	70	31
15	QUEEN'S PARK	38	13	5	20	65	85	31
16	HIBERNIAN	38	12	3	23	51	69	27
17	ST MIRREN	38	9	9	20	46	75	27
18	AIRDRIEONIANS	38	10	6	22	59	103	26
19	THIRD LANARK	38	8	9	21	62	103	25
20	COWDENBEATH	38	5	5	28	58	118	15

Season 1934-35

Scottish League Divison 1

DATE	OPPONENTS	SCORE	GOALSCORERS	ATTENDANCE
Aug 11	KILMARNOCK	W 4-1	McGrory 2, McInally, O'Donnell H	16,000
Aug 18	Hearts	D 0-0		-
Aug 22	MOTHERWELL	L 0-1		15,000
Aug 25	ST JOHNSTONE	D 0-0		-
Sep 1	Queen's Park	L 0-1		-
Sep 8	RANGERS	D 1-1	Hughes	36,000
Sep 11	HIBERNIAN	W 4-0	McGrory, Morrison (pen), Delaney, McDonald	-
Sep 15	Hamilton Ac.	L 2-4	McGrory, Delaney	15,000
Sep 22	ABERDEEN	W 4-1	O'Donnell F 2, Murphy, McInally	-
Sep 29	Albion Rovers	L 1-2	Murphy	-
Oct 1	Dundee	D 0-0		18,000
Oct 6	QUEEN OF THE SOUTH	L 1-2	Delaney	-
Oct 13	Clyde	W 3-0	McGrory, Delaney, Buchan	25,000
Oct 20	Partick Thistle	W 3-1	O'Donnell F 2, O'Donnell	-
Oct 27	DUNFERMLINE ATH.	W 3-0	O'Donnell F 2, Buchan	-
Nov 3	AYR UNITED	W 7-0	O'Donnell F 2, Delaney 2, O'Donnell H, Buchan, Paterson (pen)	-
Nov 10	Falkirk	W 2-1	O'Donnell F, Napier	-
Nov 17	Airdrie	W 2-0	O'Donnell F, Paterson (pen)	-
Nov 24	DUNDEE	W 4-0	Buchan 4	13,000
Dec 1	St Mirren	W 4-2	Paterson 2 (2 pens), Buchan, O'Donnell F	12,000
Dec 8	MOTHERWELL	W 3-2	O'Donnell H 2, McGrory	32,000
Dec 15	Hibernian	L 2-3	O'Donnell F, McGrory	-
Dec 22	Kilmarnock	W 3-2	Paterson (pen), Napier, O'Donnell F	-
Dec 25	QUEEN'S PARK	W 4-1	Delaney 2, Crum, McGrory	-
Dec 29	HEARTS	W 4-2	McGrory 3, Crum	-
Jan 1	Rangers	L 1-2	Paterson (pen)	83,000
Jan 5	St Johnstone	W 1-0	McGrory	-
Jan 12	HAMILTON AC.	W 3-1	Delaney 2, McGrory	25,000
Jan 19	Aberdeen	L 0-2	-	-
Feb 2	ALBION ROVERS	W 5-1	Delaney 3, Dunn, O'Donnell H	-
Feb 16	Queen of the South	W 4-3	McGrory, O'Donnell F, Paterson (pen), Buchan	-
Feb 23	PARTICK THISTLE	W 3-1	McGrory, O'Donnell H, Buchan	-
Mar 2	CLYDE	L 0-2		-
Mar 16	Dunfermline Ath.	W 3-1	McGrory, O'Donnell H, Buchan	-
Mar 23	Ayr United	L 0-1		-
Apr 13	AIRDRIE	W 2-0	Buchan, O'Donnell H	-
Apr 17	FALKIRK	W 7-3	McGrory 2, Delaney 2, Buchan, O'Donnell F, O'Donnell H	-
Apr 27	ST MIRREN	W 2-1	O'Donnell H, McInally	-

Scottish Cup

DATE	OPPONENTS		SCORE	GOALSCORERS	ATTENDANCE
Jan 26	MONTROSE	(Rd1)	W 4-1	O'Donnell F 2, Paterson (pen), Buchan	15,000
Feb 9	PARTICK THISTLE	(Rd2)	D 1-1	O'Donnell H	54,180
Feb 13	Partick Thistle	(R)	W 3-1	O'Donnell H 2, McGrory	39,644
Mar 9	Aberdeen	(Rd3)	L 1-3	McGrory	40,105

League & Cup Appearances

PLAYER	LEAGUE	CUP COMPETITION S CUP	TOTAL
Buchan	28	4	32
Crum	10	2	12
Dawson	8	1	9
Delaney	30	3	33
Dunn	3		3
Fagan	1		1
Geatons	31	3	34
Hogg	36	4	40
Hughes	10		10
Kennaway	38	4	42
McDonald	30	4	34
McGonagle	31	3	34
McGrory	27	4	31
McInally	7		7
Morrison	13		13
Murphy	6		6
Napier	27	2	29
O'Donnell F	23	1	24
O'Donnell H	28	4	32
Paterson	31	4	35

Goalscorers

PLAYER	LEAGUE	CUP COMPETITION S CUP	TOTAL
McGrory	18	2	20
O'Donnell F	15	2	17
Delaney	15		15
Buchan	13	1	14
O'Donnell H	11	3	14
Paterson	7	1	8
McInally	3		3
Crum	2		2
Murphy	2		2
Napier	2		2
Dunn	1		1
Hughes	1		1
Morrison	1		1
McDonald	1		1

Fact File

Celtic great Jimmy McMenemy took over as coach on 15 October 1934. Celtic won their first nine games under his direction.

MANAGER: Willie Maley

CAPTAIN: Peter McGonagle

TOP SCORER: Jimmy McGrory

BIGGEST WIN: 7-0 v Ayr, 3 November 1934, league

HIGHEST ATTENDANCE: 83,000 v Rangers, 1 January 1935, league

MAJOR TRANSFERS OUT: Alec Thomson to Dunfermline, Peter Wilson to Hibernian

Final Scottish League Div 1 Table

		P	W	D	L	F	A	Pts
1	RANGERS	38	25	5	8	96	46	55
2	CELTIC	38	24	4	10	92	45	52
3	HEARTS	38	20	10	8	87	51	50
4	HAMILTON A	38	19	10	9	87	67	48
5	ST JOHNSTONE	38	18	10	10	66	46	46
6	ABERDEEN	38	17	10	11	68	54	44
7	MOTHERWELL	38	15	10	13	83	64	40
8	DUNDEE	38	16	8	14	63	63	40
9	KILMARNOCK	38	16	6	16	76	68	38
10	CLYDE	38	14	10	14	71	69	38
11	HIBERNIAN	38	14	8	16	59	70	36
12	QUEEN'S PARK	38	13	10	15	61	80	36
13	PARTICK T	38	15	5	18	61	68	35
14	AIRDRIEONIANS	38	13	7	18	64	72	33
15	DUNFERMLINE ATH	38	13	5	20	56	96	31
16	ALBION R	38	10	9	19	62	77	29
17	Q OF S	38	11	7	20	52	72	29
18	AYR U	38	12	5	21	61	112	29
19	ST MIRREN	38	11	5	22	49	70	27
20	FALKIRK	38	9	6	23	58	82	24

Season 1935-36

Scottish League Divison 1

DATE	OPPONENTS	SCORE	GOALSCORERS	ATTENDANCE
Aug 10	Aberdeen	L 1-3	McGrory	25,000
Aug 17	HAMILTON AC.	W 1-0	McGrory	-
Aug 24	St Johnstone	W 3-2	McGrory 2, Delaney	-
Aug 28	THIRD LANARK	W 6-0	McGrory 3, Buchan 2, Crum	-
Aug 31	QUEEN'S PARK	W 3-0	Delaney 2, McGrory	-
Sep 7	Queen of the South	W 3-1	Geatons, Delaney, McGrory	12,000
Sep 14	ALBION ROVERS	W 4-0	McGrory 3, Delaney	-
Sep 16	DUNFERMLINE ATH.	W 5-3	McGrory 3, Buchan, Delaney	-
Sep 21	Rangers	W 2-1	Murphy, Crum	72,000
Sep 28	HEARTS	W 2-1	Delaney, Crum	-
Oct 5	Kilmarnock	D 1-1	McInally	-
Oct 19	AIRDRIE	W 4-0	McGrory 2, Buchan, Delaney	-
Oct 26	Motherwell	W 2-1	Murphy, McGrory	16,000
Nov 2	DUNDEE	W 4-2	Delaney 2, McGrory, Crum	-
Nov 9	Hibernian	W 5-0	McGrory 2, Buchan, Murphy, Delaney	20,000
Nov 16	ARBROATH	W 5-0	McGrory 2, Delaney, Lyon (pen), Murphy	-
Nov 23	Ayr United	W 2-0	McGrory, Delaney	-
Nov 30	PARTICK THISTLE	D 1-1	Murphy	-
Dec 7	Third Lanark	W 3-1	Murphy, McGrory, o.g.	-
Dec 14	Dunfermline Ath.	L 0-1		-
Dec 21	ABERDEEN	W 5-3	McGrory 3, Buchan, Murphy	40,000
Dec 28	HAMILTON AC.	W 2-0	Buchan, Hughes	-
Jan 1	RANGERS	L 3-4	McGrory 2, Delaney	65,000
Jan 4	ST JOHNSTONE	W 2-0	Murphy, Lyon (pen)	-
Jan 11	QUEEN OF THE SOUTH	W 5-0	McGrory 3, Crum, Murphy	-
Jan 18	Albion Rovers	W 3-0	Fagan, McGrory, Murphy	12,000
Feb 1	Hearts	L 0-1		30,000
Feb 15	KILMARNOCK	W 4-0	Lyon, Buchan, Delaney, McGrory	-
Feb 22	Queen's Park	W 3-2	McGrory 2, Murphy	-
Feb 29	Clyde	W 4-0	Crum, Buchan, McGrory, Hughes	-
Mar 7	Airdrie	W 3-2	McGrory 2, Crum	-
Mar 14	MOTHERWELL	W 5-0	McGrory 3, Delaney, Buchan	-
Mar 21	Dundee	W 2-0	Delaney, McGrory	-
Mar 28	HIBERNIAN	W 4-1	Lyon (pen), Crum, Murphy, McGrory	-
Apr 11	Arbroath	W 2-0	Delaney, McGrory	-
Apr 13	CLYDE	W 2-1	Delaney, McGrory	-
Apr 18	AYR UNITED	W 6-0	McGrory 3, Murphy, Lyon, Buchan	-
Apr 25	Partick Thistle	W 3-1	Fagan 2, Lyon (pen)	-

Scottish Cup

Feb 8	ST JOHNSTONE	(Rd1) L 1-2	Buchan	26,647

League & Cup Appearances

PLAYER	LEAGUE	CUP COMPETITION S CUP	TOTAL
Buchan	38	1	39
Crum	38	1	39
Delaney	30	1	31
Divers	2		2
Fagan	5		5
Fitzsimons	2		2
Foley	5		5
Geatons	34	1	35
Hogg	38	1	39
Hughes	4		4
Kennaway	33	1	34
Lyon	38	1	39
McDonald	10		10
McGonagle	14		14
McGrory	32	1	33
McInally	1		1
Millar	1		1
Mills	1		1
Morrison	27	1	28
Murphy	29	1	30
Paterson	36	1	37

Goalscorers

PLAYER	LEAGUE	CUP COMPETITION S CUP	TOTAL
McGrory	50		50
Delaney	19		19
Murphy	13		13
Buchan	11	1	12
Crum	8		8
Lyon	6		6
Fagan	3		3
Hughes	2		2
Geatons	1		1
McInally	1		1
Opps' o.gs.	1		1

Fact File

On 19 October 1935 Jimmy McGrory overtook Steve Bloomer's world record of 352 first-class goals.

MANAGER: Willie Maley

CAPTAIN: Willie Lyon

TOP SCORER: Jimmy McGrory

BIGGEST WIN: 6-0 v Third Lanark, 28 August 1935, league; 6-0 v Ayr United, 18 April 1936, league

HIGHEST ATTENDANCE: 72,000 v Rangers, 21 September 1935, league

MAJOR TRANSFERS IN: Willie Lyons from Queen's Park

MAJOR TRANSFERS OUT: Charlie Napier to Derby, Frank O'Donnell to Preston, Hugh O'Donnell to Preston

Final Scottish League Div 1 Table

		P	W	D	L	F	A	Pts
1	CELTIC	38	32	2	4	115	33	66
2	RANGERS	38	27	7	4	110	43	61
3	ABERDEEN	38	26	9	3	96	50	61
4	MOTHERWELL	38	18	12	8	77	58	48
5	HEARTS	38	20	7	11	88	55	47
6	HAMILTON A	38	15	7	16	77	74	37
7	ST JOHNSTONE	38	15	7	16	70	81	37
8	KILMARNOCK	38	14	7	17	69	64	35
9	THIRD LANARK	38	15	5	18	63	65	35
10	PARTICK T	38	12	10	16	64	72	34
11	ARBROATH	38	11	11	16	46	69	33
12	DUNDEE	38	11	10	17	67	80	32
13	QUEEN'S PARK	38	11	10	17	58	75	32
14	DUNFERMLINE ATH	38	12	8	18	67	92	32
15	Q OF S	38	11	9	18	54	72	31
16	ALBION R	38	13	4	21	69	92	30
17	HIBERNIAN	38	11	7	20	56	82	29
18	CLYDE	38	10	8	20	63	84	28
19	AIRDRIEONIANS	38	9	9	20	68	91	27
20	AYR U	38	11	3	24	53	98	25

Season 1936-37

Scottish League Divison 1

DATE	OPPONENTS	SCORE	GOALSCORERS	ATTENDANCE
Aug 8	ST JOHNSTONE	W 3-2	Murphy 2, Buchan	-
Aug 15	Clyde	D 1-1	Fagan	22,000
Aug 19	St Johnstone	L 1-2	Buchan	19,000
Aug 22	QUEEN OF THE SOUTH	W 5-0	Fagan 2, Crum, Delaney, Buchan	
Aug 29	Albion Rovers	W 3-1	Fagan, Crum, Paterson (pen)	-
Sep 5	KILMARNOCK	L 2-4	Fagan 2	
Sep 9	CLYDE	W 3-1	Buchan, Delaney, Paterson (pen)	-
Sep 12	Hamilton Ac.	W 2-1	Crum 2	-
Sep 19	RANGERS	D 1-1	Delaney	60,000
Sep 26	Hearts	W 1-0	Delaney	36,000
Oct 3	ABERDEEN	W 3-2	Delaney 2, Buchan	-
Oct 10	Queen's Park	W 2-0	McGrory, Delaney	-
Oct 17	Dundee	D 0-0		-
Oct 24	HIBERNIAN	W 5-1	Crum 2, Buchan, Delaney, Paterson (pen)	-
Oct 31	Arbroath	W 3-2	McGrory, Buchan, Delaney	8,000
Nov 7	ST MIRREN	W 3-0	Buchan 2, Murphy	5,000
Nov 14	Partick Thistle	D 1-1	Murphy	-
Nov 21	THIRD LANARK	W 6-3	McGrory 3, Crum, Lyon, Buchan	-
Nov 28	DUNFERMLINE ATH.	W 3-1	McGrory 2, Murphy	7,000
Dec 5	Falkirk	W 3-0	McGrory, McInally, Carruth	-
Dec 12	MOTHERWELL	W 3-2	Delaney 2, Crum	-
Dec 19	Queen of the South	L 0-1		-
Dec 26	ALBION ROVERS	W 4-0	Delaney 2, Murphy, McGrory	-
Jan 1	Rangers	L 0-1		95,000
Jan 2	QUEEN'S PARK	W 4-0	McGrory 3 (pen), o.g.	-
Jan 9	Kilmarnock	D 3-3	Carruth 2, o.g.	-
Jan 16	HAMILTON AC.	D 3-3	McDonald, Carruth, Delaney	-
Jan 23	Aberdeen	L 0-1		-
Feb 6	HEARTS	W 3-2	McGrory 2, Buchan	35,000
Feb 20	DUNDEE	L 1-2	McGrory	-
Mar 6	Hibernian	D 2-2	Crum, McGrory	-
Mar 20	St Mirren	W 2-1	McGrory, Murphy	-
Mar 27	PARTICK THISTLE	D 1-1	Divers	-
Mar 29	FALKIRK	W 1-0	Geatons (pen)	-
Apr 6	Third Lanark	L 2-4	Buchan 2	-
Apr 10	Dunfermline Ath.	W 4-3	Crum 2, Divers, Dawson	-
Apr 16	ARBROATH	W 5-1	Dawson 2, Carruth 2, Divers	-
Apr 30	Motherwell	L 0-8		-

Scottish Cup

Jan 30	Stenhousemuir	(Rd1) D 1-1	McGrory	5,000
Feb 3	STENHOUSEMUIR	(R) W 2-0	McGrory 2	8,000
Feb 13	Albion Rovers	(Rd2) W 5-2	McGrory 2, Buchan 2, Delaney	19,000
Feb 27	East Fife	(Rd3) W 3-0	McGrory	12,069
Mar 17	MOTHERWELL	(Rd4) D 4-4	Crum 2, Lyon (pen), Buchan	36,150
Mar 24	Motherwell	(R) W 2-1	McGrory, Buchan	35,023
Apr 3	Clyde	(SF) W 2-0	McGrory, o.g.	76,000
Apr 24	Aberdeen	(F) W 2-1	Crum, Buchan	146,433

League & Cup Appearances

PLAYER	LEAGUE	CUP COMPETITION S CUP	TOTAL
Boyle	9		9
Buchan	32	8	40
Carruth	7	1	8
Crum	37	8	45
Dawson	5		5
Delaney	32	7	39
Divers	5		5
Doyle	3		3
Duffy	1		1
Fagan	6		6
Fitzsimons	2		2
Foley	1		1
Geatons	36	8	44
Hogg	35	8	43
Hughes	1		1
Kennaway	34	8	42
Lyon	35	8	43
McDonald	12		12
McGrory	25	8	33
McInally	1		1
Millar	3		3
Morrison	30	8	38
Murphy	30	8	38
Paterson	36	8	44

Goalscorers

LEAGUE PLAYER	PLAYER	CUP COMPETITION S CUP	TOTAL
McGrory	18	8	26
Buchan	13	5	18
Delaney	14	1	15
Crum	11	3	14
Carruth	6		6
Fagan	6		6
Murphy	6		6
Dawson	3		3
Divers	3		3
Paterson	3		3
Lyon	1	1	2
Geatons	1		1
McInally	1		1
McDonald	1		1
Opps' o.gs.	2	1	3

Fact File

Celtic's 0-8 defeat at Motherwell on 30 April 1937 is their heaviest defeat in any competition.

MANAGER: Willie Maley

CAPTAIN: Willie Lyon

TOP SCORER: Jimmy McGrory

BIGGEST WIN: 5-0 v Queen of the South, 22 August 1936, league

HIGHEST ATTENDANCE: 146,433 v Aberdeen, 24 April 1937, league

MAJOR TRANSFERS OUT: Willie Fagan to Preston

Final Scottish League Div 1 Table

		P	W	D	L	F	A	PTS
1	RANGERS	38	26	9	3	88	32	61
2	ABERDEEN	38	23	8	7	89	44	54
3	CELTIC	38	22	8	8	89	58	52
4	MOTHERWELL	38	22	7	9	96	54	51
5	HEARTS	38	24	3	11	99	60	51
6	THIRD LANARK	38	20	6	12	79	61	46
7	FALKIRK	38	19	6	13	98	66	44
8	HAMILTON A	38	18	5	15	91	96	41
9	DUNDEE	38	12	15	11	58	69	39
10	CLYDE	38	16	6	16	59	70	38
11	KILMARNOCK	38	14	9	15	60	70	37
12	ST JOHNSTONE	38	14	8	16	74	68	36
13	PARTICK T	38	11	12	15	73	68	34
14	ARBROATH	38	13	5	20	57	84	31
15	QUEEN'S PARK	38	9	12	17	51	77	30
16	ST MIRREN	38	11	7	20	68	81	29
17	HIBERNIAN	38	6	13	19	54	83	25
18	Q OF S	38	8	8	22	49	95	24
19	DUNFERMLINE ATH	38	5	11	22	65	98	21
20	ALBION R	38	5	6	27	53	116	16

Season 1937-38

Scottish League Divison 1

DATE	OPPONENTS	SCORE	GOALSCORERS	ATTENDANCE
Aug 14	Queen of the South	D 2-2	McGrory, Buchan	14,000
Aug 18	Hamilton Ac.	W 2-1	McGrory, Murphy	12,000
Aug 21	MORTON	W 4-0	Buchan 2, Crum 2	-
Aug 25	QUEEN OF THE SOUTH	D 2-2	Buchan 2 (1 pen)	19,000
Aug 28	Kilmarnock	L 1-2	Buchan	-
Sep 4	HAMILTON AC.	W 4-2	Carruth 3, Buchan (pen)	-
Sep 11	Rangers	L 1-3	Murphy	-
Sep 15	Morton	W 3-2	Buchan 2, Murphy	-
Sep 18	HEARTS	W 2-1	Crum, Delaney	-
Sep 25	Aberdeen	D 1-1	McGrory	30,000
Oct 2	CLYDE	W 3-1	Buchan, Crum, McGrory	-
Oct 9	Arbroath	L 0-2		-
Oct 16	QUEEN'S PARK	W 4-3	McGrory, McDonald, Crum, o.g.	-
Oct 23	ST JOHNSTONE	W 6-0	Carruth 3, Murphy, Buchan, Crum	-
Nov 6	PARTICK THISTLE	W 6-0	Crum 2, Carruth 2, Buchan, Geatons	-
Nov 13	Third Lanark	D 1-1	Buchan (pen)	30,000
Nov 20	Ayr United	D 1-1	Carruth	11,000
Nov 27	FALKIRK	W 2-0	Delaney, Carruth	-
Dec 4	Motherwell	W 2-1	Murphy, Carruth	-
Dec 18	Hibernian	W 3-0	McDonald, Divers, Carruth	20,000
Dec 25	KILMARNOCK	W 8-0	Crum 2, Divers 2, Murphy 2, Delaney, McDonald	-
Jan 1	RANGERS	W 3-0	Divers 2, McDonald (pen)	82,500
Jan 3	Queen's Park	W 3-0	Murphy, Divers, Crum	-
Jan 8	Hearts	W 4-2	Crum 2, Divers 2	43,128
Jan 15	ABERDEEN	W 5-2	Crum 2, McDonald 2, Carruth	-
Jan 29	Clyde	W 6-1	Divers 2, Crum, Murphy, McDonald, Lynch	15,000
Feb 5	ARBROATH	W 4-0	Crum 3, Divers	7,500
Feb 19	St Johnstone	W 2-1	Divers 2	-
Feb 26	ST MIRREN	W 5-1	McDonald 3 (1 pen), Crum, Divers	-
Mar 12	Partick Thistle	W 6-1	Delaney 2, Crum, Murphy, Divers, Geatons	-
Mar 19	THIRD LANARK	D 1-1	Crum	-
Mar 26	AYR UNITED	D 1-1	McDonald	-
Apr 2	Falkirk	L 0-3		-
Apr 9	MOTHERWELL	W 4-1	Carruth 2, McDonald (pen), Divers	-
Apr 16	Dundee	W 3-2	Divers 2, Carruth	-
Apr 18	DUNDEE	W 3-0	Lyon 2 (2 pens), Divers	-
Apr 23	St Mirren	W 3-1	Crum 2, Delaney	-
Apr 30	HIBERNIAN	W 3-0	Divers, Lyon (pen), Delaney	-

Scottish Cup

Jan 22	Third Lanark	(Rd1)	W 2-1	Crum 2	32,877
Feb 12	NITHSDALE WAND	(Rd2)	W 5-0	Murphy 3, Carruth 2	6,000
Mar 5	KILMARNOCK	(Rd3)	L 1-2	McDonald	39,389

League & Cup Appearances

PLAYER	LEAGUE	CUP COMPETITION S CUP	TOTAL
Boyle	1		1
Buchan	16		16
Carruth	19	2	21
Crum	38	2	40
Davitt	1		1
Delaney	26	1	27
Divers	20	3	23
Doyle	2		2
Duffy	1		1
Fitzsimons	1		1
Geatons	22	1	23
Hogg	38	3	41
Kennaway	36	3	39
Lynch	14	3	17
Lyon	36	3	39
McDonald	27	3	30
McGrory	10		10
Millar	5		5
Morrison	31	3	34
Murphy	37	3	40
Paterson	37	3	40

Goalscorers

PLAYER	LEAGUE	CUP COMPETITION S CUP	TOTAL
Crum	24	2	25
Divers	20		20
Carruth	16	2	18
Buchan	13		13
McDonald	12	1	13
Murphy	10	3	13
Delaney	7		7
McGrory	5		5
Lyon	3		3
Geatons	2		2
Lynch	1		1

Fact File

Celtic celebrated their Golden Jubilee season by winning their 19th league title and the Empire Exhibition trophy.

MANAGER: Willie Maley

CAPTAIN: Willie Lyon

TOP SCORER: John Crum

BIGGEST WIN: 8-0 v Kilmarnock, 25 December 1937, league

HIGHEST ATTENDANCE: 43,877 v Third Lanark, 22 January 1938, Scottish Cup

MAJOR TRANSFERS OUT: Willie Buchan to Blackpool

Final Scottish League Div 1 Table

		P	W	D	L	F	A	Pts
1	CELTIC	38	27	7	4	114	42	61
2	HEARTS	38	26	6	6	90	50	58
3	RANGERS	38	18	13	7	75	49	49
4	FALKIRK	38	19	9	10	82	52	47
5	MOTHERWELL	38	17	10	11	78	69	44
6	ABERDEEN	38	15	9	14	74	59	39
7	PARTICK T	38	15	9	14	68	70	39
8	ST JOHNSTONE	38	16	7	15	78	81	39
9	THIRD LANARK	38	11	13	14	68	73	35
10	HIBERNIAN	38	11	13	14	57	65	35
11	ARBROATH	38	11	13	14	58	79	35
12	QUEEN'S PARK	38	11	12	15	59	74	34
13	HAMILTON A	38	13	7	18	81	76	33
14	ST MIRREN	38	14	5	19	58	66	33
15	CLYDE	38	10	13	15	68	78	33
16	Q OF S	38	11	11	16	58	71	33
17	AYR U	38	9	15	14	66	85	33
18	KILMARNOCK	38	12	9	17	65	91	33
19	DUNDEE	38	13	6	19	70	74	32
20	MORTON	38	6	3	29	64	127	15

Season 1938-39

Scottish League Divison 1

DATE	OPPONENTS	SCORE	GOALSCORERS	ATTENDANCE
Aug 13	KILMARNOCK	W 9-1	Delaney 2, Divers 2, Lyon (pen), Murphy, Geatons, McDonald, Grum (pen)	-
Aug 20	Hamilton Ac.	W 1-0	Delaney	-
Aug 24	Kilmarnock	D 0-0		-
Aug 27	ABERDEEN	L 1-2	Delaney	-
Sep 3	Hearts	W 5-1	McDonald 2, Crum, Divers, Murphy	45,000
Sep 10	RANGERS	W 6-2	McDonald 3, Lyon 2 (1 pen), Delaney	74,500
Sep 14	HAMILTON AC.	L 1-2	Delaney	-
Sep 17	Clyde	W 4-1	McDonald, Crum, Divers, Lynch	30,000
Sep 24	RAITH ROVERS	W 6-1	Crum 3, McDonald 2, Murphy	-
Oct 1	Albion Rovers	W 8-1	Crum 5, Delaney 2, Geatons	-
Oct 12	QUEEN OF THE SOUTH	W 5-1	Divers 2, Delaney 2, Lyon (pen)	12,000
Oct 22	Partick Thistle	D 0-0		-
Oct 29	THIRD LANARK	W 6-1	McDonald 2, Crum, Birrell, Divers, o.g.	-
Nov 5	AYR UNITED	D 3-3	Murphy, Delaney, McDonald	-
Nov 12	Falkirk	D 1-1	o.g.	-
Nov 19	MOTHERWELL	L 1-3	Delaney	-
Nov 26	Arbroath	W 2-0	Geatons, Crum	-
Dec 3	HIBERNIAN	W 5-4	Watter 2, Murphy 2, Delaney	-
Dec 10	St Johnstone	D 1-1	Murphy	-
Dec 17	ST MIRREN	W 3-2	Divers 2, Murphy (pen)	-
Dec 24	Aberdeen	L 1-3	Delaney	-
Dec 31	HEARTS	D 2-2	Watters 2	-
Jan 2	Rangers	L 1-2	Carruth	118,730
Jan 3	QUEEN'S PARK	L 0-1		-
Jan 7	Raith Rovers	L 0-4		-
Jan 25	ALBION ROVERS	W 4-1	Divers 4	-
Jan 28	Queen of the South	D 1-1	Divers	-
Feb 11	CLYDE	W 3-1	Birrell, McDonald, Anderson	-
Feb 25	PARTICK THISTLE	W 3-1	Carruth 3	-
Mar 8	Third Lanark	W 2-0	Carruth, Lyon	-
Mar 11	Ayr United	W 4-1	Delaney, Murphy, Divers, Carruth	-
Mar 18	FALKIRK	L 1-2	Murphy	-
Apr 1	ARBROATH	W 2-0	Divers, McDonald	-
Apr 5	Motherwell	W 3-2	Murphy 2, Anderson	-
Apr 8	Hibernian	L 0-1		-
Apr 10	Queen's Park	W 2-1	Anderson, o.g.	-
Apr 22	ST JOHNSTONE	D 1-1	Crum	-
Apr 29	St Mirren	L 1-2	Divers	-

Scottish Cup

Jan 21	Burntisland	(Rd1) W 8-3	Crum 3, McDonald 2, Delaney, Murphy (pen), Watters	1,427
Feb 4	Montrose	(Rd2) W 7-1	Crum 3, Divers 2, Delaney, McDonald	6,389
Feb 18	Hearts	(R3) D 2-2	Delaney, McDonald	49,572
Feb 22	HEARTS	(R) W 2-1	Divers 2	80,840
Mar 4	Motherwell	(Rd4) L 1-3	Delaney	31,000

League & Cup Appearances

PLAYER	LEAGUE	CUP COMPETITION S CUP	TOTAL
Anderson	11		11
Birrell	6		6
Carruth	13		13
Crum	29	5	34
Delaney	25	5	30
Divers	35	4	39
Doherty	2		2
Duffy	2		2
Geatons	30	1	31
Hogg	38	5	43
Kennaway	36	5	41
Lynch	16	5	21
Lyon	33	5	38
McDonald	30	5	35
Millar	1		1
Morrison	34	5	39
Murphy	35	5	40
O'Neill	4		4
Paterson	29	4	33
Watters	9	1	10

Goalscorers

PLAYER	LEAGUE	CUP COMPETITION S CUP	TOTAL
Divers	17	4	21
Crum	14	6	20
McDonald	15	4	19
Delaney	14	4	18
Murphy	12	1	13
Carruth	6		6
Lyon	5		5
Watters	4	1	5
Geatons	3		3
Anderson	3		3
Birrell	2		2
Lynch	1		1
Opps' o.gs.	3		3

Final Scottish League Div 1 Table

		P	W	D	L	F	A	Pts
1	RANGERS	38	25	9	4	112	55	59
2	CELTIC	38	20	8	10	99	53	48
3	ABERDEEN	38	20	6	12	91	61	46
4	HEARTS	38	20	5	13	98	70	45
5	FALKIRK	38	19	7	12	73	63	45
6	Q OF S	38	17	9	12	69	64	43
7	HAMILTON A	38	18	5	15	67	71	41
8	ST JOHNSTONE	38	17	6	15	85	82	40
9	CLYDE	38	17	5	16	78	70	39
10	KILMARNOCK	38	15	9	14	73	86	39
11	PARTICK T	38	17	4	17	74	87	38
12	MOTHERWELL	38	16	5	17	82	86	37
13	HIBERNIAN	38	14	7	17	68	69	35
14	AYR U	38	13	9	16	76	83	35
15	THIRD LANARK	38	12	8	18	80	96	32
16	ALBION R	38	12	6	20	65	90	30
17	ARBROATH	38	11	8	19	54	75	30
18	ST MIRREN	38	11	7	20	57	80	29
19	QUEEN'S PARK	38	11	5	22	57	83	27
20	RAITH R	38	10	2	26	65	99	22

Fact File

On 17 September 1938 in the match against Clyde John Morrison became the first Division 1 player to be sent off in Scotland.

MANAGER: Willie Maley

CAPTAIN: Willie Lyon

TOP SCORER: John Divers

BIGGEST WIN: 9-1 v Kilmarnock, 13 August 1938, league

HIGHEST ATTENDANCE: 118,730 v Rangers, 2 January 1939, league

Season 1939-1940

Scottish League Division A

DATE	OPPONENTS	SCORE	GOALSCORERS	ATTENDANCE
Aug 12	Aberdeen	L 1-3	Crum	-
Aug 19	HEARTS	W 2-0	Divers, Lyon	-
Aug 23	ABERDEEN	L 1-3	Murphy	-
Aug 26	Cowdenbeath	W 2-1	Crum, Lynch	-
Sep 2	CLYDE	W 1-0	Divers	-

The Scottish League and Cup were suspended for the duration of the Second World War – regional leagues were in operation until the end of 1946-47.

League Appearances

PLAYER	LEAGUE	TOTAL
Anderson	2	2
Crum	5	5
Divers	5	5
Geatons	5	5
Hogg	5	5
Kelly J	1	1
Kelly JC	1	1
Kennaway	5	5
Lynch	4	4
Lyon	4	4
McDonald	4	4
Morrison	4	4
Murphy	5	5
O'Neill	1	1
Paterson	4	4

Goalscorers

PLAYER	LEAGUE	TOTAL
Crum	2	2
Divers	2	2
Lynch	1	1
Lyon	1	1
Murphy	1	1

Fact File

The war-truncated season was notable only for the appearance of two players called John Kelly in the Celtic line-up.

MANAGER: Willie Maley
CAPTAIN: Willie Lyon

Final Scottish League Div A Table

		P	W	D	L	F	A	Pts
1	RANGERS	5	4	1	0	14	3	9
2	FALKIRK	5	4	0	1	20	10	8
3	HEARTS	5	2	2	1	14	9	6
4	ABERDEEN	5	3	0	2	9	9	6
5	PARTICK T	5	2	2	1	7	7	6
6	CELTIC	5	3	0	2	7	8	6
7	ALBION R	5	2	1	2	12	7	5
8	MOTHERWELL	5	2	1	2	14	12	5
9	THIRD LANARK	5	2	1	2	9	8	5
10	KILMARNOCK	5	2	1	2	10	9	5
11	Q OF S	5	2	1	2	10	9	5
12	ST MIRREN	5	1	3	1	8	8	5
13	HAMILTON A	5	2	1	2	7	11	5
14	ARBROATH	5	2	0	3	9	9	4
15	ST JOHNSTONE	5	2	0	3	7	8	4
16	HIBERNIAN	5	2	0	3	11	13	4
17	ALLOA ATH	5	2	0	3	8	13	4
18	AYR U	5	2	0	3	10	17	4
19	CLYDE	5	1	0	4	10	14	2
20	COWDENBEATH	5	1	0	4	6	18	2

Season 1946-47

Scottish League Division A

DATE	OPPONENTS	SCORE	GOALSCORERS	ATTENDANCE
Aug 10	MORTON	L 1-2	Rae	33,000
Aug 14	Clyde	D 2-2	Cantwell 2	15,000
Aug 17	Aberdeen	L 2-6	Kiernan 2	35,000
Aug 21	HEARTS	L 2-3	Bogan, Evans	30,000
Aug 28	Hamilton Ac.	D 2-2	Cantwell, Kiernan (pen)	-
Aug 31	St Mirren	W 1-0	Cantwell	12,000
Sep 4	THIRD LANARK	L 1-4	Cantwell	20,000
Sep 7	RANGERS	L 2-3	Kiernan, Bogan	28,000
Sep 14	Queen of the South	L 1-3	Kiernan	15,000
Nov 2	Falkirk	W 4-1	Rae, McAloon, Evans, Kiernan	15,000
Nov 9	HIBERNIAN	W 4-1	McAloon 2, Evans, Kiernan	45,000
Nov 16	Partick Thistle	L 1-4	McAloon	40,000
Nov 23	Motherwell	W 2-1	McAloon, Rae	15,000
Nov 30	KILMARNOCK	W 4-2	Kiernan 2 (1 pen), Rae, McAloon	15,000
Dec 7	Morton	L 1-2	Jordan	-
Dec 14	CLYDE	D 3-3	Airlie 2, o.g.	18,000
Dec 21	Hearts	L 1-2	Airlie	20,000
Dec 25	QUEEN'S PARK	W 1-0	Rae	-
Dec 28	HAMILTON AC.	W 2-1	McAloon 2	15,000
Jan 1	Rangers	D 1-1	Hazlett	75,000
Jan 2	ABERDEEN	L 1-5	Hazlett	-
Jan 4	QUEEN OF THE SOUTH	W 2-0	McAloon, Rae (pen)	10,000
Jan 11	Queen's Park	W 3-1	Rae 2, McAloon	12,000
Jan 18	Third Lanark	D 0-0		30,000
Feb 22	ST MIRREN	W 2-1	Kiernan, Hazlett	10,000
Mar 22	PARTICK THISTLE	W 2-0	Evans, o.g.	15,000
Mar 29	Kilmarnock	W 2-1	Kiernan, McAloon	12,000
Apr 12	Hibernian	L 0-2		25,000
Apr 26	FALKIRK	D 0-0		12,000
May 3	MOTHERWELL	W 3-2	Sirrel, McAloon, Rae (pen)	7,000

Scottish Cup

Jan 25	Dundee	(Rd1) L 1-2	McAloon	36,000

Scottish League Cup

Sep 21	Hibernian	L 2-4	Bogan, Gallagher	20,000
Sep 28	THIRD LANARK	D 0-0		15,000
Oct 5	Hamilton Ac.	D 2-2	Kiernan 2	18,000
Oct 12	HIBERNIAN	D 1-1	McAloon	40,000
Oct 19	Third Lanark	W 3-2	Kiernan 2 (1 pen), Bogan	35,000
Sep 26	HAMILTON AC.	W 3-1	Kiernan 2, Rae	15,000

Celtic failed to qualify for quarter-finals.

League & Cup Appearances

PLAYER	LEAGUE	CUP COMPETITIONS		TOTAL
		S CUP	SL CUP	
Airlie	6			3
Baillie	1			1
Bogan	10		6	16
Cannon	3			3
Cantwell	8		1	9
Corbert	19	1	1	21
Docherty	3	1		4
Evans	21	1		22
Gallagher	14		1	15
Hazlett	18		2	20
Hogg	26	1	6	33
Jordan	3			3
Kiernan	22	1	6	29
Lamb	1			1
Lynch	14	1	6	21
McAloon	19	1	4	24
McAuley	10		5	15
McDonald	9		3	12
McMillan	12		5	17
McPhail	3			3
Mallan	14	1		15
Miller	29	1	5	35
Milne	29	1	4	34
O'Sullivan	4			4
Paton			4	4
Quinn F	5			5
Quinn R	2			2
Rae	15	1	5	21
Shields	3			3
Sirrel	6		1	7
Ugolini	1		1	2

Goalscorers

PLAYER	LEAGUE	CUP COMPETITIONS		TOTAL
		S CUP	SL CUP	
Kiernan	11		6	17
McAloon	12	1	1	14
Rae	9		1	11
Cantwell	5			5
Evans	4			4
Airlie	3			3
Bogan	2		2	3
Hazlett	3			3
Gallagher			1	1
Jordan	1			1
Sirrel	1			1
Opps' o.gs.	2			2

Fact File

Appalling weather conditions meant Celtic were only able to play one match between 25 January and 15 March 1947.

MANAGER: Jimmy McGrory

CAPTAIN: Bobby Hogg

TOP SCORER: Tommy Kiernan

BIGGEST WIN: 4-1 v Falkirk, 2 November 1946, league; 4-1 v Hibernian, 9 November 1946, league

HIGHEST ATTENDANCE: 75,000 v Rangers, 1 January 1947, league

MAJOR TRANSFERS IN: Gerry McAloon from Brentford

Final Scottish League Div A Table

		P	W	D	L	F	A	PTS
1	RANGERS	30	21	4	5	76	26	46
2	HIBERNIAN	30	19	6	5	69	33	44
3	ABERDEEN	30	16	7	7	58	41	39
4	HEARTS	30	16	6	8	52	43	38
5	PARTICK T	30	16	3	11	74	59	35
6	MORTON	30	12	10	8	58	45	34
7	CELTIC	30	13	6	11	53	55	32
8	MOTHERWELL	30	12	5	13	58	54	29
9	THIRD LANARK	30	11	6	13	56	64	28
10	CLYDE	30	9	9	12	55	65	27
11	FALKIRK	30	8	10	12	62	61	26
12	Q OF S	30	9	8	13	44	69	26
13	QUEEN'S PARK	30	8	6	16	47	60	22
14	ST MIRREN	30	9	4	17	47	65	22
15	KILMARNOCK	30	6	9	15	44	66	21
16	HAMILTON A	30	2	7	21	38	85	11

Season 1947-48

Scottish League Division A

DATE	OPPONENTS	SCORE	GOALSCORERS	ATTENDANCE
Aug 13	Airdrie	L 2-3	McAuley, Kiernan (pen)	20,000
Aug 27	QUEEN'S PARK	W 4-0	Paton, Rae, McPhail, Evans	15,000
Sep 20	Rangers	L 0-2		50,000
Sep 27	MOTHERWELL	L 0-1		25,000
Oct 4	Aberdeen	L 0-2		25,000
Oct 11	MORTON	W 3-2	Bogan, Paton, McLaughlan	14,000
Oct 18	Clyde	L 0-2		20,000
Oct 25	QUEEN OF THE SOUTH	W 4-3	Paton 2, Sirrel, McDonald	12,000
Nov 8	FALKIRK	L 0-3		14,000
Nov 15	Partick Thistle	W 5-3	McDonald 2, Corbett (pen), Bogan, Walsh	32,000
Nov 22	St Mirren	W 2-1	McAuley, Walsh	20,000
Dec 6	DUNDEE	D 1-1	McDonald	20,000
Dec 13	Hibernian	D 1-1	Paton	38,000
Dec 20	AIRDRIE	D 0-0		12,000
Dec 25	HEARTS	W 4-2	McDonald 2, Bogan, Walsh	-
Dec 27	Queen's Park	L 2-3	Paton, McDonald	18,000
Jan 2	RANGERS	L 0-4		60,000
Jan 3	Hearts	L 0-1		40,000
Jan 10	ABERDEEN	W 1-0	Corbett	25,000
Jan 17	Morton	L 0-4		12,000
Jan 24	PARTICK THISTLE	L 1-2	McPhail	15,000
Jan 31	CLYDE	D 0-0		15,000
Feb 14	Queen of the South	L 0-2		13,500
Feb 28	Falkirk	W 1-0	Corbett (pen)	20,000
Mar 13	ST MIRREN	D 0-0		18,000
Mar 20	Motherwell	W 3-0	McPhail 2, Weir	20,000
Mar 29	Third Lanark	L 1-5	Evans	25,000
Apr 3	HIBERNIAN	L 2-4	Lavery, Evans	30,000
Apr 10	THIRD LANARK	L 1-3	Bogan	10,000
Apr 17	Dundee	W 3-2	Weir 3	31,000

Scottish Cup

Feb 7	COWDENBEATH	(Rd2) W 3-0	McPhail 2, Gallagher	19,331
Feb 21	MOTHERWELL	(Rd3) W 1-0	Paton	55,231
Mar 6	MONTROSE	(QF) W 4-0	McPhail 2, Weir, Paton	39,077
Mar 27	Morton	(SF) L 0-1		80,000

Scottish League Cup

Aug 9	Rangers	L 0-2		75,000
Aug 16	DUNDEE	D 1-1	Paton	25,000
Aug 23	THIRD LANARK	W 3-1	Gallacher 2, Quinn R	25,000
Sep 1	RANGERS	W 2-0	Gallacher, Paton	60,000
Sep 6	Dundee	L 1-4	Bogan	35,000
Sep 13	Third Lanark	L 2-3	Gallacher, o.g.	25,000

Celtic failed to qualify for quarter-finals.

League & Cup Appearances

PLAYER	LEAGUE	CUP COMPETITIONS		TOTAL
		S CUP	SL CUP	
Baillie	5			5
Boden	2		2	4
Bogan	23	4	3	30
Corbett	29	4	6	39
Evans	27	3	5	35
Ferguson	5			5
Fraser	1			1
Gallacher	3		4	7
Gallagher	11	3		14
Gormely	1			1
Hazlett	3			3
Hogg	5		4	9
Kapler	7		1	8
Kiernan	1		2	3
Lavery	2			2
McAloon	1		1	2
McAuley	27	4	6	37
McDonald P			2	2
McDonald T	13	1		14
McLaughlin	2			2
McMillan	4	2		6
McPhail	25	4	6	35
Mallan	24	4	4	32
Miller	27	4	6	37
Milne	23	4	1	28
Mitchell	1			1
Paton	28	4	5	37
Quinn F			1	1
Quinn R	4		3	7
Rae	4		1	5
Sirrel	4		3	7
Ugolini	3			3
Walsh	10			10
Weir	5	3		8

Goalscorers

PLAYER	LEAGUE	CUP COMPETITIONS		TOTAL
		S CUP	SL CUP	
Paton	6	2	2	10
McPhail	4	4		8
McDonald T	7			7
Bogan	4		1	5
Weir	4	1		5
Gallacher			4	4
Gallagher	1			1
Corbett	3			3
Evans	3			3
Walsh	3			3
McAuley	2			2
Kiernan	1			1
Lavery	1			1
McLaughlin	1			1
Quinn R			1	1
Rae	1			1
Sirrel	1			1
Opps' o.gs.			1	1

Fact File

On 6 September 1947 Celtic were forced to field three different players in goal against Dundee. Miller, injured after 11 minutes, was replaced by right back Hogg who was replaced by centre forward Rae.

MANAGER: Jimmy McGrory

CAPTAIN: John McPhail

TOP SCORER: Johnny Paton

BIGGEST WIN: 4-0 v Queen's Park, 27 August 1947, league; 4-0 v Montrose, 6 March 1948, Scottish Cup

HIGHEST ATTENDANCE: 80,000 v Morton, 27 March 1948, Scottish Cup

MAJOR TRANSFERS IN: Leslie Johnston from Clyde, Jock Weir from Blackburn

MAJOR TRANSFERS OUT: Seton Airlie to FC Cannes, Tommy Kiernan to Stoke City

Final Scottish League Div A Table

		P	W	D	L	F	A	PTS
1	HIBERNIAN	30	22	4	4	86	27	48
2	RANGERS	30	21	4	5	64	28	46
3	PARTICK T	30	16	4	10	61	42	36
4	DUNDEE	30	15	3	12	67	51	33
5	ST MIRREN	30	13	5	12	54	58	31
6	CLYDE	30	12	7	11	52	57	31
7	FALKIRK	30	10	10	10	55	48	30
8	MOTHERWELL	30	13	3	14	45	47	29
9	HEARTS	30	10	8	12	37	42	28
10	ABERDEEN	30	10	7	13	45	45	27
11	THIRD LANARK	30	10	6	14	56	73	26
12	CELTIC	30	10	5	15	41	56	25
13	Q OF S	30	10	5	15	49	74	25
14	MORTON	30	9	6	15	47	43	24
15	AIRDRIEONIANS	30	7	7	16	40	78	21
16	QUEEN'S PARK	30	9	2	19	45	75	20

Season 1948-49

Scottish League Division A

DATE	OPPONENTS	SCORE	GOALSCORERS	ATTENDANCE
Aug 14	MORTON	D 0-0		55,070
Aug 18	Aberdeen	L 0-1		35,000
Aug 21	RANGERS	L 0-1		50,000
Aug 28	Hearts	W 2-1	McPhail 2 (1 pen)	40,000
Sep 1	QUEEN OF THE SOUTH	D 2-2	Gallacher 2	40,000
Sep 4	Albion Rovers	D 3-3	Weir 2, Tully	25,000
Oct 23	DUNDEE	L 0-1		25,000
Oct 30	Hibernian	W 2-1	Johnston 2	32,000
Nov 6	Clyde	W 4-0	Gallacher J 2, Paton 2	30,000
Nov 13	EAST FIFE	L 0-1		45,000
Nov 20	Third Lanark	L 2-3	Paton, Gallacher	20,000
Nov 27	FALKIRK	D 4-4	Gallagher 3, Weir	50,000
Dec 4	Partick Thistle	W 2-1	Gallacher, Johnston	33,000
Dec 11	St Mirren	D 1-1	Tully	34,000
Dec 18	MOTHERWELL	W 3-2	Johnston, McAuley (pen), Paton	45,000
Dec 25	ABERDEEN	W 3-0	McPhail, Paton, Johnston	35,000
Jan 1	Rangers	L 0-4		85,000
Jan 3	HEARTS	W 2-0	Tully, Gallacher	50,000
Jan 8	Morton	D 0-0		15,000
Jan 15	ALBION ROVERS	W 3-0	Docherty T, Gallacher, Weir	15,000
Jan 29	Queen of the South	L 0-1		16,500
Feb 12	HIBERNIAN	L 1-2	McPhail (pen)	40,000
Feb 26	East Fife	L 2-3	Johnston, Docherty T	18,360
Mar 12	Falkirk	D 2-2	Docherty T	16,000
Mar 19	PARTICK THISTLE	W 3-0	Weir 2, Gallacher	25,000
Mar 26	ST MIRREN	W 2-1	Weir, o.g.	28,000
Apr 2	Motherwell	W 1-0	Gallacher	20,000
Apr 11	Dundee	L 2-3	Johnston, Gallacher	29,000
Apr 16	THIRD LANARK	L 1-2	Tully	30,000
Apr 18	CLYDE	W 2-1	Weir, Johnston	25,000

Scottish Cup

Jan 22	Dundee United	(Rd1) L 3-4	Gallacher 2, Tully	25,000

Scottish League Cup

Sep 11	HIBERNIAN	W 1-0	Weir	55,000
Sep 18	Clyde	W 2-0	Gallacher, Gallagher	26,000
Sep 25	RANGERS	W 3-1	Gallacher, Gallagher, Weir	65,000
Oct 2	Hibernian	L 2-4	Gallacher 2	53,000
Oct 9	CLYDE	L 3-6	Gallacher 2, Paton	30,000
Oct 16	Rangers	L 1-2	McPhail	105,000

Celtic failed to qualify for quarter-finals.

League & Cup Appearances

PLAYER	LEAGUE	CUP COMPETITIONS		TOTAL
		S CUP	SL CUP	
Baillie	7			7
Boden	27	1	5	33
Bogan	1			1
Bonnar	9			9
Docherty J	1			1
Docherty T	9			9
Evans	24	1	6	31
Gallacher	19	1	6	26
Gallagher	3	1	5	9
Johnston	23	1		24
Lavery	2			2
McAuley	24	1	6	31
McGrory			1	1
McGuire	10			10
McMillan	2			2
McPhail	18	1	1	20
Mallan	21	1	6	28
Miller	21	1	6	28
Milne	24		6	30
Paton	24	1	6	31
Sirrel	3		1	4
Tully	30	1	5	36
Weir D	1			1
Weir J	27	1	6	34

Goalscorers

PLAYER	LEAGUE	CUP COMPETITIONS		TOTAL
		S CUP	SL CUP	
Gallacher	11	2	6	22
Weir	8		2	10
Johnston	8			8
Paton	5		1	6
McPhail	4		1	5
Tully	4	1		5
Docherty T	3			3
Gallagher	3		2	2
McAuley	1			1
Opps' o.gs.	1			1

Fact File

Celtic did not score their first goal until 297 minutes into the season – after a penalty against Hearts.

MANAGER: Jimmy McGrory

CAPTAIN: John McPhail

TOP SCORER: Jackie Gallacher

BIGGEST WIN: 4-0 v Clyde, 6 November 1948, league

HIGHEST ATTENDANCE: 105,000 v Rangers, 16 October 1947, Scottish League Cup

MAJOR TRANSFERS IN: Charlie Tully from Belfast Celtic

MAJOR TRANSFERS OUT: Tommy Bogan to Preston, Willie Corbett to Preston, Gerry McAloon to Belfast Celtic

Final Scottish League Div A Table

		P	W	D	L	F	A	PTS
1	RANGERS	30	20	6	4	63	32	46
2	DUNDEE	30	20	5	5	71	48	45
3	HIBERNIAN	30	17	5	8	75	52	39
4	EAST FIFE	30	16	3	11	64	46	35
5	FALKIRK	30	12	8	10	70	54	32
6	CELTIC	30	12	7	11	48	40	31
7	THIRD LANARK	30	13	5	12	56	52	31
8	HEARTS	30	12	6	12	64	54	30
9	ST MIRREN	30	13	4	13	51	47	30
10	Q OF S	30	11	8	11	47	53	30
11	PARTICK T	30	9	9	12	50	63	27
12	MOTHERWELL	30	10	5	15	44	49	25
13	ABERDEEN	30	7	11	12	39	48	25
14	CLYDE	30	9	6	15	50	67	24
15	MORTON	30	7	8	15	39	51	22
16	ALBION R	30	3	2	25	30	105	8

Season 1949-50

Scottish League Division A

DATE	OPPONENTS	SCORE	GOALSCORERS	ATTENDANCE
Sep 10	Queen of the South	W 2-0	Taylor, Haughney	20,250
Sep 17	HEARTS	W 3-2	Haughney, Taylor, Collins	30,000
Sep 24	Rangers	L 0-4		64,000
Oct 1	RAITH ROVERS	D 2-2	Taylor, Haughney	30,000
Oct 8	Motherwell	W 2-1	Collins, McPhail	30,000
Oct 15	ABERDEEN	W 4-2	McPhail 2, Collins, Haughney	25,000
Oct 22	Dundee	L 0-3		35,000
Oct 29	HIBERNIAN	D 2-2	McPhail, Evans	45,000
Nov 5	CLYDE	W 4-1	Rennet 3, Haughney	35,000
Nov 12	Stirling Albion	L 1-2	McPhail	25,000
Nov 19	THIRD LANARK	W 2-1	McPhail, Haughney	18,000
Nov 26	Falkirk	D 1-1	Haughney	20,000
Dec 3	PARTICK THISTLE	W 1-0	Rennet	25,000
Dec 10	St Mirren	D 0-0		30,000
Dec 17	East Fife	L 1-5	Gallacher	14,000
Dec 24	QUEEN OF THE SOUTH	W 3-0	Haughney 2, Collins	14,000
Dec 31	Hearts	L 2-4	Collins 2	45,000
Jan 2	RANGERS	D 1-1	Weir	65,000
Jan 3	Raith Rovers	D 1-1	Haughney	20,000
Jan 7	MOTHERWELL	W 3-1	Taylor, McAuley, o.g.	40,000
Jan 14	Aberdeen	L 0-4		25,000
Jan 21	DUNDEE	W 2-0	Tully, Evans	25,000
Feb 4	Hibernian	L 1-4	Collins (pen)	41,000
Feb 18	STIRLING ALBION	W 2-1	Weir 2	20,000
Mar 4	FALKIRK	W 4-3	McPhail 3 (1 pen), Weir	16,000
Mar 11	Third Lanark	L 0-1		20,000
Mar 18	St Mirren	W 1-0	Haughney	20,000
Mar 25	EAST FIFE	W 4-1	McPhail 4 (1 pen)	25,000
Apr 10	Partick Thistle	L 0-1		34,000
Apr 15	Clyde	D 2-2	Fernie, Tully	25,000

Scottish Cup

Jan 28	Brechin City	(Rd1) W 3-0	Weir 2, McPhail	6,000
Feb 15	Third Lanark	(Rd2) D 1-1	Weir	35,000
Feb 20	THIRD LANARK	(R) W 4-1	McPhail 3, Tully	33,000
Feb 25	ABERDEEN	(QF) L 0-1		65,112

Scottish League Cup

Aug 13	RANGERS	W 3-2	McPhail 2 (1 pen), Haughney	70,000
Aug 17	Aberdeen	W 5-4	Haughney 3, Collins, McPhail	40,000
Aug 20	St Mirren	L 0-1		47,500
Aug 27	Rangers	L 0-2		95,000
Aug 31	ABERDEEN	L 1-3	Haughney	15,000
Sep 3	ST MIRREN	W 4-1	Haughney, Tully, McAuley, McPhail	20,000

Celtic failed to qualify for quarter-finals.

League & Cup Appearances

PLAYER	LEAGUE	CUP COMPETITIONS		TOTAL
		S CUP	SL CUP	
Baillie	23	4	6	33
Boden	27	4	5	36
Bonnar	13	4		17
Cairney	1			1
Collins	26	4	6	36
Docherty	1			1
Evans	27	4	6	37
Fallon	1			1
Fernie	4			4
Gallacher	1			1
Haughney	23	1	6	30
Johnston	1		4	5
McAuley	17	4	5	26
McGrory	25	4	1	30
McGuire	4	4		8
McPhail	22	4	6	32
Mallan	9		2	11
Miller	17		6	23
Milne	16		1	17
Peacock	4		1	5
Rennett	14	1		15
Taylor	14	2	1	17
Toner	2			2
Tully	25	4	5	34
Weir	13	4		17

Goalscorers

PLAYER	LEAGUE	CUP COMPETITIONS		TOTAL
		S CUP	SL CUP	
McPhail	13	4	4	21
Haughney	11		6	17
Collins	7		1	8
Weir	4	3		7
Rennett	4			4
Taylor	4			4
Tully	2	1	1	4
Evans	2			2
McAuley	1		1	2
Fernie	1			1
Gallacher	1			1
Opps' o.gs.	1			1

Fact File

In the game against Hibernian on 4 February 1950 five penalties were taken. Bobby Collins had to retake his *after* scoring.

MANAGER: Jimmy McGrory

CAPTAIN: John McPhail

TOP SCORER: John McPhail

BIGGEST WIN: 4-1 v Clyde, 5 November 1949, league; 4-1 v East Fife, 25 March 1950, league; 4-1 v Third Lanark, 20 February 1950, Scottish Cup; 4-1 v St Mirren, 3 September 1949, Scottish League Cup

HIGHEST ATTENDANCE: 95,000 v Rangers, 27 August 1949, Scottish League Cup

MAJOR TRANSFERS IN: Bertie Peacock from Glentoran

MAJOR TRANSFERS OUT: Johnny Paton to Brentford

Final Scottish League Div A Table

		P	W	D	L	F	A	PTS
1	RANGERS	30	22	6	2	58	26	50
2	HIBERNIAN	30	22	5	3	86	34	49
3	HEARTS	30	20	3	7	86	40	43
4	EAST FIFE	30	15	7	8	58	43	37
5	CELTIC	30	14	7	9	51	50	35
6	DUNDEE	30	12	7	11	49	46	31
7	PARTICK T	30	13	3	14	55	45	29
8	ABERDEEN	30	11	4	15	48	56	26
9	RAITH R	30	9	8	13	45	54	26
10	MOTHERWELL	30	10	5	15	53	58	25
11	ST MIRREN	30	8	9	13	42	49	25
12	THIRD LANARK	30	11	3	16	44	62	25
13	CLYDE	30	10	4	16	56	73	24
14	FALKIRK	30	7	10	13	48	72	24
15	Q OF S	30	5	6	19	31	63	16
16	STIRLING A	30	6	3	21	38	77	15

Season 1950-51

Scottish League Division A

DATE	OPPONENTS	SCORE	GOALSCORERS	ATTENDANCE
Sep 9	MORTON	L 3-4	McPhail 3 (2 pen)	50,000
Sep 23	RANGERS	W 3-2	Weir D, McPhail (pen), Peacock	53,789
Sep 30	Raith Rovers	W 2-1	Weir J, Peacock	13,500
Oct 7	RAITH ROVERS	L 2-3	Peacock 2	20,000
Oct 14	Aberdeen	L 1-2	McPhail	30,000
Oct 21	DUNDEE	D 0-0		30,000
Oct 28	Morton	W 2-0	Collins, McPhail	20,000
Nov 5	Clyde	W 3-1	Weir J, McPhail, Collins	30,000
Nov 11	FALKIRK	W 3-0	McPhail, Collins (pen) Peacock	11,000
Nov 18	Airdrie	W 4-2	Collins 2 (1 pen), McPhail Tully	20,000
Nov 25	THIRD LANARK	D 1-1	McPhail	15,000
Dec 2	Partick Thistle	W 1-0	Weir J	38,000
Dec 9	St Mirren	D 0-0		30,000
Dec 16	EAST FIFE	W 6-2	McPhail 3, Collins 3	18,000
Dec 30	HEARTS	D 2-2	McAlinden 2	40,000
Jan 1	Rangers	L 0-1		55,000
Jan 6	Motherwell	L 1-2	Weir J	25,500
Jan 13	ABERDEEN	L 3-4	Tully 2, Collins (pen)	60,000
Jan 20	Dundee	L 1-3	o.g.	29,000
Feb 3	HIBERNIAN	L 0-1		60,000
Feb 17	Falkirk	W 2-0	Haughney, Collins	12,000
Mar 3	Third Lanark	L 0-2		35,000
Mar 17	ST MIRREN	W 2-1	Collins (pen), Weir J	30,000
Mar 24	East Fife	L 0-3		12,000
Apr 7	Hearts	D 1-1	Collins	18,000
Apr 11	AIRDRIE	L 0-1		-
Apr 16	PARTICK THISTLE	L 0-3		-
Apr 25	MOTHERWELL	W 3-1	Collins (2 pen), Weir J	-
Apr 28	CLYDE	W 1-0	Collins	24,000
Apr 30	Hibernian	L 1-3	Weir J	22,000

Scottish Cup

Jan 27	East Fife	(Rd1) D 2-2	Weir J, Collins	14,000
Jan 31	EAST FIFE	(R) W 4-2	McPhail 2, Peacock, Collins	36,000
Feb 10	DUNS	(Rd2) W 4-0	Weir J 2, Peacock, Weir D	22,907
Feb 24	Hearts	(Rd3) W 2-1	Weir J, McPhail	47,000
Mar 10	ABERDEEN	(Rd4) W 3-0	McPhail 2, Tully	75,000
Mar 31	Raith Rovers	(SF) W 3-2	Weir J, McPhail, Tully	84,237
Apr 21	Motherwell	(F) W 1-0	McPhail	131,943

Scottish League Cup

Aug 12	EAST FIFE	W 2-0	Peacock, McPhail	60,000
Aug 16	Third Lanark	W 2-1	Collins, Fernie	40,000
Aug 19	RAITH ROVERS	W 2-1	McPhail 2	35,000
Aug 26	East Fife	D 1-1	McPhail	15,000
Aug 30	THIRD LANARK	W 3-1	McPhail (2 pen), Collins	30,000
Sep 2	Raith Rovers	D 2-2	Collins, Peacock	16,000
Sep 16	MOTHERWELL	(QF/FL) L 1-4	McPhail	50,000
Sep 30	Motherwell	(QF/SL) W 1-0	McPhail	29,000

League & Cup Appearances

PLAYER	LEAGUE	CUP COMPETITIONS		TOTAL
		S CUP	SL CUP	
Baillie	28	7	8	43
Boden	10	5	1	16
Bonnar	19	1	8	28
Collins	27	7	8	42
Evans	28	7	8	43
Fallon	27	7	1	35
Fernie	7		7	14
Haughney	6	1	7	14
Hunter	11	6		17
McAlindon	5			5
McDowall	1			1
McGrory	3	2	7	12
McPhail	17	5	8	30
Mallan	19		1	20
Millsopp	6	1		7
Milne	16		8	24
Peacock	30	7	8	45
Rollo	14	7		21
Tully	27	6	7	40
Walsh	1			1
Weir D	4	1		5
Weir J	24	7	1	32

Goalscorers

PLAYER	LEAGUE	CUP COMPETITIONS		TOTAL
		S CUP	SL CUP	
McPhail	13	7	8	28
Collins	15	2	3	20
Weir J	7	5		12
Peacock	5	2	2	9
Tully	3	2		5
McAlindon	2			2
Weir D	1	1		2
Fernie	1		1	1
Haughney	1			1
Opps' o.gs.	1			1

Fact File

Bobby Collins, a cobbler by trade, devised a boot strap to protect Alec Boden's injured foot.

MANAGER: Jimmy McGrory

CAPTAIN: John McPhail

TOP SCORER: John McPhail

BIGGEST WIN: 6-2 v East Fife, 16 December 1950, league

HIGHEST ATTENDANCE: 131,943 v Motherwell, 21 April 1951, Scottish Cup

MAJOR TRANSFERS OUT: Willie Miller to Clyde, Pat McAuley to Luton

Final Scottish League Div A Table

		P	W	D	L	F	A	Pts
1	HIBERNIAN	30	22	4	4	78	26	48
2	RANGERS	30	17	4	9	64	37	38
3	DUNDEE	30	15	8	7	47	30	38
4	HEARTS	30	16	5	9	72	45	37
5	ABERDEEN	30	15	5	10	61	50	35
6	PARTICK T	30	13	7	10	57	48	33
7	CELTIC	30	12	5	13	48	46	29
8	RAITH R	30	13	2	15	52	52	28
9	MOTHERWELL	30	11	6	13	58	65	28
10	EAST FIFE	30	10	8	12	48	66	28
11	ST MIRREN	30	9	7	14	35	51	25
12	MORTON	30	10	4	16	47	59	24
13	THIRD LANARK	30	11	2	17	40	51	24
14	AIRDRIEONIANS	30	10	4	16	52	67	24
15	CLYDE	30	8	7	15	37	57	23
16	FALKIRK	30	7	4	19	35	81	18

Season 1951-52

Scottish League Division A

DATE	OPPONENTS	SCORE	GOALSCORERS	ATTENDANCE
Sep 8	Motherwell	D 2-2	Peacock, Tully	28,000
Sep 22	Rangers	D 1-1	Collins	86,000
Sep 29	HEARTS	L 1-3	Peacock	50,000
Oct 10	Morton	W 1-0	Millsopp	-
Oct 20	Dundee	L 1-2	o.g.	32,000
Oct 27	HIBERNIAN	D 1-1	McPhail	40,000
Nov 3	THIRD LANARK	D 2-2	Walsh, o.g.	-
Nov 10	Stirling Albion	L 1-2	McAlindon	-
Nov 17	AIRDRIE	W 3-1	Walsh, Peacock, McPhail	20,000
Nov 24	Queen of the South	L 0-4		14,500
Dec 1	PARTICK THISTLE	W 2-1	Collins, Walsh	30,000
Dec 8	ST MIRREN	W 2-1	Lafferty 2	20,000
Dec 15	East Fife	L 1-3	Walsh	15,000
Dec 22	MOTHERWELL	D 2-2	Lafferty, Peacock	28,000
Dec 29	Aberdeen	W 4-3	Collins 2 (1 pen), Walsh, o.g.	25,000
Jan 1	RANGERS	L 1-4	Tully	45,000
Jan 2	Hearts	L 1-2	Collins	-
Jan 12	Raith Rovers	L 0-1		16,000
Jan 19	DUNDEE	D 1-1	Walsh	35,000
Feb 2	Hibernian	L 1-3	Walsh	40,000
Feb 16	STIRLING ALBION	W 3-1	Collins 2 (1 pen), McPhail	20,000
Feb 23	RAITH ROVERS	L 0-1		20,000
Feb 27	Airdrie	L 1-2	Collins	-
Mar 1	QUEEN OF THE SOUTH	W 6-1	Weir J 2, McPhail, Collins, Tully, Peacock	-
Mar 5	MORTON	D 2-2	McPhail, Peacock	12,000
Mar 8	Partick Thistle	W 4-2	McPhail 2, Millsopp, Collins	30,000
Mar 15	St Mirren	L 1-3	McPhail	37,000
Mar 22	EAST FIFE	W 2-1	Tully, McPhail	30,000
Mar 29	ABERDEEN	W 2-0	Weir J, McPhail	18,000
Apr 12	Third Lanark	D 3-3	Collins 2 (1 pen), McPhail	35,000

Scottish Cup

DATE	OPPONENTS		SCORE	GOALSCORERS	ATTENDANCE
Jan 30	THIRD LANARK	(Rd1)	D 0-0		24,000
Feb 4	Third Lanark	(R)	L 1-2	Rollo	27,344

Scottish League Cup

DATE	OPPONENTS		SCORE	GOALSCORERS	ATTENDANCE
Aug 11	THIRD LANARK		D 1-1	Fallon	45,000
Aug 15	Airdrie		D 1-1	Peacock	-
Aug 18	MORTON		W 2-0	Evans, Heron	40,000
Aug 25	Third Lanark		W 1-0	Walsh	35,000
Aug 29	AIRDRIE		W 2-0	Walsh, Heron	25,000
Sep 1	Morton		L 0-2		
Sep 15	FORFAR ATHLETIC	(QF/FL)	W 4-1	Peacock, Collins, Baillie, Walsh	28,000
Sep 19	Forfar Athletic	(QF/SL)	D 1-1	Peacock	6,900
Oct 13	Rangers	(SF)	L 0-3		83,235

League & Cup Appearances

PLAYER	LEAGUE	CUP COMPETITIONS		TOTAL
		S CUP	SL CUP	
Baillie	30	2	9	41
Bell	13			13
Boden	12		1	13
Bonnar	16	2	7	25
Collins	30	2	8	40
Devanney	1		2	3
Evans	25	2	9	36
Fallon	30	2	9	41
Fernie	6			6
Haughney	1		2	3
Heron	1		4	5
Jack	3			3
Lafferty	6			6
McAlindon	4			4
McPhail	21	2	3	26
Mallan	3		8	11
Millsopp	12		1	13
Morrison	1			1
Peacock	25	2	9	36
Rollo	17	2	9	28
Stein	17	2		19
Tully	23	2	9	34
Walsh	21	2	8	31
Weir D	1			1
Weir J	11		1	12

Goalscorers

PLAYER	LEAGUE	CUP COMPETITIONS		TOTAL
		S CUP	SL CUP	
Collins	12		1	13
McPhail	11			11
Walsh	7		3	10
Peacock	6		3	9
Tully	4			4
Lafferty	3			3
Weir J	3			3
Heron			2	2
Millsopp	2			2
Baillie			1	1
Evans			1	1
Fallon			1	1
McAlindon	1			1
Rollo		1		1
Opps' o.gs.	3			3

Fact File

When goalkeeper Andy Bell turned up for his debut on 20 October 1951 he only knew two of the Celtic team. He was introduced to the others on the bus to Dundee.

MANAGER: Jimmy McGrory
CAPTAIN: John McPhail
TOP SCORER: Bobby Collins
BIGGEST WIN: 6-1 v Queen of the South, 1 March 1952, league
HIGHEST ATTENDANCE: 83,235 v Rangers, 13 October 1951, Scottish League Cup
MAJOR TRANSFERS IN: Jock Stein from Llanelly

Final Scottish League Div A Table

		P	W	D	L	F	A	Pts
1	HIBERNIAN	30	20	5	5	92	36	45
2	RANGERS	30	16	9	5	61	31	41
3	EAST FIFE	30	17	3	10	71	49	37
4	HEARTS	30	14	7	9	69	53	35
5	RAITH R	30	14	5	11	43	42	33
6	PARTICK T	30	12	7	11	48	51	31
7	MOTHERWELL	30	12	7	11	51	57	31
8	DUNDEE	30	11	6	13	53	52	28
9	CELTIC	30	10	8	12	52	55	28
10	Q OF S	30	10	8	12	50	60	28
11	ABERDEEN	30	10	7	13	65	58	27
12	THIRD LANARK	30	9	8	13	51	62	26
13	AIRDRIEONIANS	30	11	4	15	54	69	26
14	ST MIRREN	30	10	5	15	43	58	25
15	MORTON	30	9	6	15	49	56	24
16	STIRLING A	30	5	5	20	36	99	15

Season 1952-53

Scottish League Division A

DATE	OPPONENTS	SCORE	GOALSCORERS	ATTENDANCE
Sep 6	FALKIRK	W 5-3	McPhail 3, Fernie, Tully	20,000
Sep 13	Raith Rovers	D 1-1	Tully	10,000
Sep 20	RANGERS	W 2-1	Walsh, Rollo	48,000
Sep 27	Aberdeen	D 2-2	Peacock, Fallon	27,000
Oct 4	MOTHERWELL	W 3-0	Peacock, Fallon, Walsh (pen)	30,000
Oct 11	Clyde	W 2-1	Peacock 2	31,000
Oct 18	QUEEN OF THE SOUTH	D 1-1	Peacock	25,000
Oct 25	Hearts	L 0-1		40,000
Nov 1	St Mirren	W 2-1	Fernie, Duncan	36,000
Nov 8	THIRD LANARK	W 5-4	Peacock, Lafferty, Walsh Tully, o.g.	30,000
Nov 15	Partick Thistle	L 0-3		38,500
Nov 22	Airdrie	D 0-0		18,000
Dec 6	Hibernian	D 1-1	McIlroy	32,000
Dec 13	DUNDEE	W 5-0	Fernie 3, Tully, McIlroy	25,000
Dec 20	Falkirk	W 3-2	Collins, McIlroy, Peacock	14,000
Dec 27	RAITH ROVERS	L 0-1		25,000
Jan 1	Rangers	L 0-1		73,000
Jan 10	Motherwell	L 2-4	Fernie, Peacock	20,600
Jan 17	CLYDE	L 2-4	McGrory, Tully	30,000
Jan 31	Queen of the South	L 1-2	Tully	-
Feb 14	HEARTS	D 1-1	McPhail (pen)	30,000
Feb 28	Third Lanark	W 3-1	McGrory 2, Walsh	30,000
Mar 7	PARTICK THISTLE	W 3-1	Walsh 2, Tully	35,000
Mar 18	AIRDRIE	L 0-1		-
Mar 21	East Fife	L 1-4	o.g.	13,000
Mar 28	HIBERNIAN	L 1-3	Collins (pen)	-
Apr 4	Dundee	L 0-4		28,000
Apr 11	ST MIRREN	W 3-2	Fernie, Fallon, Collins	10,000
Apr 14	ABERDEEN	L 1-3	McPhail	10,000
Apr 18	EAST FIFE	D 1-1	Walsh	20,000

Scottish Cup

Jan 24	Eyemouth Utd	(Rd1) W 4-0	McGrory 4		4,131
Feb 7	Stirling Albion	(Rd2) D 1-1	McGrory		24,763
Feb 11	STIRLING ALBION	(R) W 3-0	McGrory 2, Peacock		24,500
Feb 21	Falkirk	(Rd3) W 3-2	Tully, Fernie, McGrory		23,100
Mar 14	Rangers	(QF) L 0-2			95,000

Scottish League Cup

Aug 9	St Mirren	W 1-0	McDonald	25,000
Aug 13	PARTICK THISTLE	L 2-5	Tully, McDonald	40,000
Aug 16	HIBERNIAN	W 1-0	McPhail	49,000
Aug 23	ST MIRREN	W 3-1	McPhail, Peacock, Fernie	25,000
Aug 27	Partick Thistle	W 1-0	McPhail, Peacock, Fernie	25,000
Aug 30	Hibernian	L 0-3		51,000

Celtic failed to qualify for quarter-finals.

League & Cup Appearances

PLAYER	LEAGUE	CUP COMPETITIONS		TOTAL
		S CUP	SL CUP	
Baillie	12		6	18
Boden	15	2	6	23
Bonnar	13	4	6	23
Collins	14	5		19
Conroy	1			1
Duffy	2			2
Duncan	2			2
Evans	30	5	6	41
Fallon	20	1	6	27
Fernie	24	5	4	33
Haughney	13	2	1	16
Hepburn	6			6
Hunter	17	1		18
Jack	4	2		6
Lafferty	1			1
McDonald			2	2
McGrory	10	5		15
McIlroy	8			8
McPhail	15	4	4	23
Mallan	1			1
Meechan	19	4	1	24
Millsopp	1		3	4
Peacock	22	2	5	29
Rollo	5	1		6
Stein	28	5	5	38
Tully	25	5	6	36
Walsh	22	2	2	26
Weir			2	2
Whyte			1	1

Goalscorers

PLAYER	LEAGUE	CUP COMPETITIONS		TOTAL
		S CUP	SL CUP	
McGrory	3	8		11
Peacock	8	1	2	11
Fernie	7	1	1	9
Tully	7	1	1	9
McPhail	5		2	7
Walsh	7			7
Collins	3			3
Fallon	3			3
McIlroy	3			3
McDonald			2	2
Duncan	1			1
Lafferty	1			1
Rollo	1			1
Opps' o.gs.	2			2

Fact File

On 21 February 1953 Charlie Tully scored direct from a corner in the match against Falkirk. Ordered to re-take it, he scored again.

MANAGER: Jimmy McGrory

CAPTAIN: Jock Stein

TOP SCORERS: John McGrory and Bertie Peacock

BIGGEST WIN: 5-0 v Dundee, 13 December 1952, league

HIGHEST ATTENDANCE: 95,000 v Rangers, 14 March 1953, Scottish Cup

MAJOR TRANSFERS IN: Neil Mochan from Middlesbrough

MAJOR TRANSFERS OUT: Jock Weir to Falkirk, John McAlindon to Worcester City

Final Scottish League Div A Table

		P	W	D	L	F	A	Pts
1	RANGERS	30	18	7	5	80	39	43
2	HIBERNIAN	30	19	5	6	93	51	43
3	EAST FIFE	30	16	7	7	72	48	39
4	HEARTS	30	12	6	12	59	50	30
5	CLYDE	30	13	4	13	78	78	30
6	ST MIRREN	30	11	8	11	52	58	30
7	DUNDEE	30	9	11	10	44	37	29
8	CELTIC	30	11	7	12	51	54	29
9	PARTICK T	30	10	9	11	55	63	29
10	Q OF S	30	10	8	12	43	61	28
11	ABERDEEN	30	11	5	14	64	68	27
12	RAITH R	30	9	8	13	47	53	26
13	FALKIRK	30	11	4	15	53	63	26
14	AIRDRIEONIANS	30	10	6	14	53	75	26
15	MOTHERWELL	30	10	5	15	57	80	25
16	THIRD LANARK	30	8	4	18	52	75	20

Season 1953-54

Scottish League Division A

DATE	OPPONENTS	SCORE	GOALSCORERS	ATTENDANCE
Sep 5	Hamilton Ac.	L 0-2		20,000
Sep 12	CLYDE	W 1-0	Collins	23,000
Sep 19	Rangers	D 1-1	Duncan	59,000
Sep 26	ABERDEEN	W 3-0	Collins 3 (3 pens)	26,000
Oct 10	RAITH ROVERS	W 3-0	Fernie 2, Collins	20,000
Oct 17	Queen of the South	L 1-2	Collins	16,000
Oct 24	HEARTS	W 2-0	McPhail, Walsh	30,000
Oct 31	Dundee	D 1-1	McPhail	27,000
Nov 7	HIBERNIAN	D 2-2	Collins, Stein	40,000
Nov 14	East Fife	L 1-4	Fernie	15,000
Nov 21	AIRDRIE	W 4-1	Mochan 3, McPhail	20,000
Nov 28	PARTICK THISTLE	W 2-1	Fernie 2	27,000
Dec 5	Stirling Albion	L 1-2	Peacock	18,000
Dec 12	ST MIRREN	W 4-0	Walsh 2, Mochan, Hemple	25,000
Dec 26	Clyde	W 7-1	Mochan 2, Higgins 2, Collins 2, Hemple	21,500
Jan 1	RANGERS	W 1-0	Mochan	-
Jan 2	Aberdeen	L 0-2		30,000
Jan 9	FALKIRK	W 1-0	Higgins	28,000
Jan 16	Raith Rovers	L 0-2		13,000
Jan 23	QUEEN OF THE SOUTH	W 3-1	Mochan 2, McPhail	28,000
Feb 6	Hearts	L 2-3	Haughney (2 pens)	47,519
Feb 20	DUNDEE	W 5-1	Mochan 2, Walsh, Fernie Higgins	32,000
Mar 6	EAST FIFE	W 4-1	Higgins 2, Fernie, Walsh	25,000
Mar 17	Airdrie	W 6-0	Mochan 3, Fallon, Higgins Fernie	13,000
Mar 20	Partick Thistle	W 3-1	Fallon 2, Fernie	30,000
Mar 29	STIRLING ALBION	W 4-0	Mochan 2, Fallon, Fernie	-
Apr 7	St Mirren	W 3-1	Tully, Collins, Haughney (pen)	18,000
Apr 14	Falkirk	W 3-0	Mochan 2, Fallon	22,000
Apr 17	Hibernian	W 3-0	Mochan 2, Higgins	45,000
Apr 26	HAMILTON AC.	W 1-0	Haughney	20,000

Scottish Cup

Feb 17	Falkirk	(Rd2) W 2-1	Fernie, Higgins	22,000
Feb 27	Stirling Albion	(Rd3) W 4-3	Mochan 2, Haughney (pen), Higgins	25,750
Mar 13	Hamilton Ac.	(QF) W 2-1	Haughney (pen), Fernie	22,000
Mar 27	Motherwell	(SF) D 2-2	Mochan, Fallon	100,000
Apr 5	Motherwell	(R) W 3-1	Fernie, Mochan, o.g.	92,662
Apr 24	Aberdeen	(F) W 2-1	Fallon, o.g.	129,926

Scottish League Cup

Aug 8	ABERDEEN	L 0-1		55,000
Aug 12	East Fife	D 1-1	Peacock	16,000
Aug 15	Airdrie	L 1-2	Walsh (pen)	22,000
Aug 22	Aberdeen	L 2-5	Walsh, Mochan	30,000
Aug 26	EAST FIFE	L 0-1		-
Aug 29	AIRDRIE	W 2-0	Walsh, McPhail	18,000

Celtic failed to qualify for quarter-finals.

League & Cup Appearances

PLAYER	LEAGUE	CUP COMPETITIONS		TOTAL
		S CUP	SL CUP	
Baillie	1		1	2
Bell	6	3		9
Boden	2			2
Bonnar	20	3	5	28
Collins	25		4	29
Duncan	6	1		7
Evans	29	6	6	41
Fallon	12	3		15
Fernie	26	6	5	37
Haughney	28	6	6	40
Hemple	4			4
Higgins	14	6		20
Hunter	4		1	5
McIlroy	3		1	4
McMillan			2	2
McPhail	15		6	21
Meechan	24	6	2	32
Mochan	22	6	5	33
Peacock	30	6	6	42
Rollo	1		4	5
Ryan	1			1
Stein	27	6	5	38
Tully	11			11
Walsh	19	3	5	27
Whyte			1	1

Goalscorers

PLAYER	LEAGUE	CUP COMPETITIONS		TOTAL
		S CUP	SL CUP	
Mocahn	20	4	1	25
Fernie	10	3		13
Collins	10			10
Higgins	8	2		10
Walsh	5		3	8
Fallon	5	2		7
Haughney	4	2		6
McPhail	4		1	5
Hemple	2			2
Peacock	1		1	2
Duncan	1			1
Stein	1			1
Tully	1			1
Opps' o.gs.		2		2

MANAGER: Jimmy McGrory
CAPTAIN: Jock Stein
TOP SCORER: Neil Mochan
BIGGEST WIN: 7-1 v Clyde, 26 December 1953, league
HIGHEST ATTENDANCE: 129,926 v Aberdeen, 24 April 1954, Scottish Cup

Final Scottish League Div A Table

		P	W	D	L	F	A	PTS
1	CELTIC	30	20	3	7	72	29	43
2	HEARTS	30	16	6	8	70	45	38
3	PARTICK T	30	17	1	12	76	54	35
4	RANGERS	30	13	8	9	56	35	34
5	HIBERNIAN	30	15	4	11	72	51	34
6	EAST FIFE	30	13	8	9	55	45	34
7	DUNDEE	30	14	6	10	46	47	34
8	CLYDE	30	15	4	11	64	67	34
9	ABERDEEN	30	15	3	12	66	51	33
10	Q OF S	30	14	4	12	72	58	32
11	ST MIRREN	30	12	4	14	44	54	28
12	RAITH R	30	10	6	14	56	60	26
13	FALKIRK	30	9	7	14	47	61	25
14	STIRLING A	30	10	4	16	39	62	24
15	AIRDRIEONIANS	30	5	5	20	41	92	15
16	HAMILTON A	30	4	3	23	29	94	11

Season 1954-55

Scottish League Division A

DATE	OPPONENTS	SCORE	GOALSCORERS	ATTENDANCE
Sep 11	Clyde	D 2-2	Fernie, Walsh	30,000
Sep 18	RANGERS	W 2-0	Walsh, Higgins	45,000
Sep 25	Raith Rovers	W 3-1	Haughney (2 pens), Mochan	18,000
Oct 2	KILMARNOCK	W 6-3	Higgins 2, Fernie 2, Walsh, Mochan	30,000
Oct 9	Aberdeen	W 2-0	Mochan, Haughney (pen)	38,000
Oct 16	QUEEN OF THE SOUTH	D 1-1	Higgins	23,000
Oct 30	FALKIRK	W 3-1	Walsh, Higgins, Haughney (pen)	30,000
Nov 6	St Mirren	D 1-1	Walsh	35,000
Nov 13	STIRLING ALBION	W 7-0	Walsh 3, Higgins 2, Fernie, Tully	15,000
Nov 20	Partick Thistle	L 2-4	Walsh, Collins	33,000
Nov 27	Motherwell	D 2-2	Higgins, Walsh	20,000
Dec 4	EAST FIFE	D 2-2	Walsh, Mochan	23,500
Dec 11	Hibernian	W 5-0	Walsh 2, Fernie 2, Higgins	33,000
Dec 18	DUNDEE	W 4-1	Haughney (pen), Fernie, Rowan, o.g.	14,000
Dec 25	Clyde	D 2-2	Boden, Collins	32,000
Jan 1	Rangers	L 1-4	Fernie	65,000
Jan 3	RAITH ROVERS	W 4-1	Evans, Collins, Walsh, Tully	-
Jan 8	Kilmarnock	W 2-1	Tully, o.g.	24,518
Jan 22	Queen of the South	W 2-0	Fernie 2	12,500
Jan 29	HEARTS	W 2-0	Walsh 2	49,300
Feb 12	Falkirk	D 1-1	Fernie	20,223
Feb 26	ST MIRREN	W 5-2	Walsh, Fernie, Collins, Smith, Haughney (pen)	36,000
Mar 9	Stirling Albion	W 3-2	Haughney (pen), Boden, Stein	6,000
Mar 12	PARTICK THISTLE	D 0-0		38,000
Mar 19	Motherwell	W 1-0	Mochan	35,000
Mar 30	East Fife	W 4-3	Walsh 2, Mochan 2	-
Apr 2	HIBERNIAN	L 1-2	Tully	31,000
Apr 9	Dundee	W 1-0	Reid	23,000
Apr 16	ABERDEEN	W 2-1	McPhail 2	40,000
Apr 30	Hearts	W 3-0	Mochan 2, Collins	18,000

Scottish Cup

Feb 5	Alloa Athletic	(Rd2)	W 4-2	Walsh 2, Haughney (pen), Peacock	15,000
Feb 19	Kilmarnock	(Rd3)	D 1-1	Smith	30,000
Feb 23	KILMARNOCK	(R)	W 1-0	Walsh	40,000
Mar 5	HAMILTON AC.	(QF)	W 2-1	Fernie, Collins	49,000
Mar 26	Airdrie	(SF)	D 2-2	Fernie, Walsh	80,040
Apr 4	Airdrie	(R)	W 2-0	McPhail 2	71,000
Apr 23	Clyde	(F)	D 1-1	Walsh	106,234
Apr 27	Clyde	(R)	L 0-1		68,831

Scottish League Cup

Aug 14	FALKIRK	W 3-0	Fallon 2, Higgins	46,000
Aug 18	Dundee	L 1-3	Mochan	28,000
Aug 21	HEARTS	L 1-2	Higgins	55,000
Aug 28	Falkirk	D 2-2	Fernie, Haughney (pen)	15,000
Sep 1	DUNDEE	L 0-1		30,000
Sep 4	Hearts	L 2-3	Tully, Collins	32,000

Celtic failed to qualify for quarter-finals.

League & Cup Appearances

PLAYER	LEAGUE	CUP COMPETITIONS		TOTAL
		S CUP	SL CUP	
Baillie			1	1
Bell	7			7
Boden	9			9
Bonnar	22	8	6	36
Collins	20	7	2	29
Conroy	2			2
Duncan			1	1
Evans	30	8	6	44
Fallon	20	5	6	31
Fernie	23	8	5	36
Haughney	30	8	6	44
Higgins	14		4	18
Jack			1	1
McMahon	1			1
McPhail	4	3		7
Meechan	18	8	4	30
Mochan	17	2	5	24
Peacock	29	8	6	43
Reid	3			3
Rowan	1			1
Smith	3			3
Stein	28	8	6	42
Tully	21	5	6	32
Walsh	28	7	1	36

Goalscorers

PLAYER	LEAGUE	CUP COMPETITIONS		TOTAL
		S CUP	SL CUP	
Walsh	19	5		24
Fernie	12	2	1	15
Higgins	9		2	11
Mochan	9		1	10
Haughney	7	1	1	9
Collins	5	1	1	7
Tully	4		1	5
McPhail	2	2		4
Boden	2			2
Fallon			2	2
Smith	1	1		2
Evans	1			1
Peacock		1		1
Reid	1			1
Rowan	1			1
Stein	1			1
Opps' o.gs.	2			2

Fact File

On 25 September 1954, Neil Mochan scored Celtic's 4,000th league goal, in the league match against Raith Rovers.

MANAGER: Jimmy McGrory

CAPTAIN: Jock Stein

TOP SCORER: Jimmy Walsh

BIGGEST WIN: 7-0 v Stirling Albion, 13 November 1954, league

HIGHEST ATTENDANCE: 106,234 v Clyde, 23 April 1955, Scottish Cup

MAJOR TRANSFERS OUT: Joe Baillie to Wolverhampton

Final Scottish League Div A Table

		P	W	D	L	F	A	Pts
1	ABERDEEN	30	24	1	5	73	26	49
2	CELTIC	30	19	8	3	76	37	46
3	RANGERS	30	19	3	8	67	33	41
4	HEARTS	30	16	7	7	74	45	39
5	HIBERNIAN	30	15	4	11	64	54	34
6	ST MIRREN	30	12	8	10	55	54	32
7	CLYDE	30	11	9	10	59	50	31
8	DUNDEE	30	13	4	13	48	48	30
9	PARTICK T	30	11	7	12	49	61	29
10	KILMARNOCK	30	10	6	14	46	58	26
11	EAST FIFE	30	9	6	15	51	62	24
12	FALKIRK	30	8	8	14	42	54	24
13	Q OF S	30	9	6	15	38	56	24
14	RAITH R	30	10	3	17	49	57	23
15	MOTHERWELL	30	9	4	17	42	62	22
16	STIRLING A	30	2	2	26	29	105	6

Season 1955-56

Scottish League Division A

DATE	OPPONENTS	SCORE	GOALSCORERS	ATTENDANCE
Sep 10	Falkirk	L 1-3	Mochan	10,000
Sep 17	STIRLING ALBION	W 3-0	Tully 2, McPhail	14,000
Sep 24	Rangers	D 0-0		47,000
Oct 1	RAITH ROVERS	W 2-0	McVittie, Sharkey	15,000
Oct 8	Hearts	L 1-2	Fernie	30,000
Oct 15	MOTHERWELL	D 2-2	Fernie, McVittie	22,000
Oct 22	Clyde	W 3-1	Higgins, Fernie (pen), McPhail	25,000
Oct 29	DUNFERMLINE ATHLETIC	W 4-2	Walsh 3, Tully	28,000
Nov 5	EAST FIFE	D 0-0		27,000
Nov 12	Dundee	W 2-1	Mochan 2	24,000
Nov 19	ST MIRREN	W 3-0	Fernie, Sharkey, Mochan	29,000
Nov 26	Airdrie	W 2-1	Sharkey, o.g.	17,500
Dec 3	Stirling Albion	W 3-0	Mochan, Fernie, Walsh	11,000
Dec 10	KILMARNOCK	L 0-2		15,000
Dec 17	PARTICK THISTLE	W 5-1	Mochan 3, Sharkey, Haughney (pen)	20,500
Dec 24	Hibernian	W 3-2	Mochan 2, Sharkey	29,000
Dec 31	Queen of the South	W 3-1	Mochan, Sharkey, Collins	12,500
Jan 2	RANGERS	L 0-1		47,000
Jan 7	Aberdeen	L 0-1		36,000
Jan 21	Raith Rovers	D 1-1	Sharkey	16,000
Jan 28	HEARTS	D 1-1	Walsh	40,000
Feb 11	Motherwell	D 2-2	Tully, Smith	19,000
Feb 25	CLYDE	W 4-1	Haughney (pen), Mochan, Collins, Walsh	30,000
Mar 7	Dunfermline Athletic	D 1-1	Collins	10,000
Mar 10	East Fife	L 0-3		11,000
Mar 17	DUNDEE	W 1-0	Collins	24,000
Mar 28	St Mirren	W 2-0	Peacock, Mochan	10,000
Mar 31	AIRDRIE	W 3-1	Mochan 2, McAlindon	20,000
Apr 10	ABERDEEN	D 1-1	McAlindon	14,000
Apr 13	Kilmarnock	D 0-0		-
Apr 23	Partick Thistle	L 0-2		-
Apr 25	HIBERNIAN	L 0-3		9,500
Apr 28	QUEEN OF THE SOUTH	L 1-3	Walsh	9,000
Apr 30	FALKIRK	W 1-0	Fernie	4,000

Scottish Cup

Feb 4	Morton	(Rd2) W 2-0	Tully, Collins	17,000
Feb 18	Ayr United	(Rd3) W 3-0	Collins 2, Mochan	24,000
Mar 3	AIRDRIE	(QF) W 2-1	Collins, Tully	59,000
Mar 24	Clyde	(SF) W 2-1	Sharkey, Haughney (pen)	65,200
Apr 21	Hearts	(F) L 1-3	Haughney	132,842

Scottish League Cup

Aug 13	QUEEN OF THE SOUTH	W 4-2	Mochan, Walsh, Collins, Fernie	40,000
Aug 17	Queen of the South	W 2-0	Walsh, o.g.	12,000
Aug 20	FALKIRK	W 5-1	Collins 2, Tully, Mochan, Fernie	40,000
Aug 27	Rangers	W 4-1	Smith 2, McPhail, Mochan	75,000
Aug 31	RANGERS	L 0-4		61,000
Sep 3	Falkirk	D 1-1	Mochan	17,000

Celtic failed to qualify for quarter-finals.

League & Cup Appearances

PLAYER	LEAGUE	CUP COMPETITIONS		TOTAL
		S CUP	SL CUP	
Beattie	31	5	1	37
Boden	17	4		21
Bonnar	3		5	8
Collins	26	4	6	36
Conroy	1		1	2
Craig	1	1		1
Docherty	1		1	2
Evans	31	5	6	42
Fallon	20	3	5	28
Fernie	32	5	5	42
Goldie	10	1		11
Haughney	24	5	6	35
Higgins	7			7
Jack	4			4
Kennedy	1			1
McAlindon	4	1	1	6
McPhail	2		3	5
McVittie	4		1	5
Meechan	6	1	1	8
Mochan	31	4	6	41
Peacock	33	5	5	43
Reid	1			1
Rowan	1			1
Sharkey	19	2		21
Smith	13	2	3	18
Stein	6		4	10
Tully	17	5	3	25
Walsh	16	2	3	21
Whyte	7			7

Goalscorers

PLAYER	LEAGUE	CUP COMPETITIONS		TOTAL
		S CUP	SL CUP	
Mochan	15	1	4	20
Collins	4	4	3	11
Walsh	7		2	9
Fernie	6		2	8
Sharkey	7	1		8
Tully	4	2	1	7
Haughney	2	2		4
McPhail	2		1	3
Smith	1		2	3
McAlindon	2			2
McVittie	2			2
Higgins	1			1
Peacock	1			1
Opps' o.gs.	1		1	2

Fact File

At the end of the season Celtic released John McPhail after 15 years' service and signed his brother Billy from Clyde.

MANAGER: Jimmy McGrory

CAPTAIN: Bobby Evans

TOP SCORER: Neil Mochan

BIGGEST WIN: 5-1 v Partick Thistle, 17 December 1955, league; 5-1 v Falkirk, 20 August 1955, Scottish League Cup

HIGHEST ATTENDANCE: 132,842 v Hearts, 21 April 1956, Scottish Cup

MAJOR TRANSFERS IN: Billy McPhail from Clyde

Final Scottish League Div A Table

		P	W	D	L	F	A	Pts
1	RANGERS	34	22	8	4	85	27	52
2	ABERDEEN	34	18	10	6	87	50	46
3	HEARTS	34	19	7	8	99	47	45
4	HIBERNIAN	34	19	7	8	86	50	45
5	CELTIC	34	16	9	9	55	39	41
6	Q OF S	34	16	5	13	69	73	37
7	AIRDRIEONIANS	34	14	8	12	85	96	36
8	KILMARNOCK	34	12	10	12	52	45	34
9	PARTICK T	34	13	7	14	62	60	33
10	MOTHERWELL	34	11	11	12	53	59	33
11	RAITH R	34	12	9	13	58	75	33
12	EAST FIFE	34	13	5	16	61	69	31
13	DUNDEE	34	12	6	16	56	65	30
14	FALKIRK	34	11	6	17	58	75	28
15	ST MIRREN	34	10	7	17	57	70	27
16	DUNFERMLINE ATH	34	10	6	18	42	82	26
17	CLYDE	34	8	6	20	50	74	22
18	STIRLING A	34	4	5	25	23	82	13

Season 1956-57

Scottish League Division 1

DATE	OPPONENTS	SCORE	GOALSCORERS	ATTENDANCE
Sep 8	QUEEN'S PARK	W 2-0	Mochan, Collins	28,000
Sep 22	RANGERS	L 0-2		53,000
Sep 29	Motherwell	L 0-1		18,000
Oct 13	Falkirk	W 1-0	Collins	20,000
Oct 20	RAITH ROVERS	D 1-1	McPhail	16,000
Nov 3	Dundee	L 1-2	Mochan	22,000
Nov 10	EAST FIFE	W 4-0	Mochan, Haughney, Ryan, Higgins	17,000
Nov 17	Ayr United	W 3-1	McPhail, Tully, Haughney	17,000
Nov 24	PARTICK THISTLE	D 1-1	Mochan	20,000
Dec 1	HEARTS	D 1-1	McPhail	32,000
Dec 8	St Mirren	W 2-0	Mochan, Higgins	21,500
Dec 15	DUNFERMLINE ATHLETIC	W 3-1	Higgins, Mochan, Fernie	11,000
Dec 22	Airdrie	W 7-3	Higgins 4, Fernie, Ryan, Mochan	16,000
Dec 29	Hibernian	D 3-3	Ryan, Smith, Mochan	31,000
Jan 1	Rangers	L 0-2		60,000
Jan 2	KILMARNOCK	D 1-1	Mochan-	
Jan 5	Queen's Park	L 0-2		21,174
Jan 12	MOTHERWELL	W 2-1	Haughney, Sharkey	32,000
Jan 19	Queen of the South	L 3-4	Higgins, Mochan, o.g.	11,000
Jan 26	FALKIRK	W 4-0	Mochan, McPhail, Higgins, o.g.	18,000
Feb 9	Raith Rovers	L 1-3	Fernie	20,000
Feb 23	ABERDEEN	W 2-1	McPhail, Mochan	12,000
Mar 6	DUNDEE	D 1-1	Haughney	7,000
Mar 9	East Fife	L 0-2		9,000
Mar 17	AYR UNITED	W 4-0	Byrne 2, Haughney, Collins	10,000
Mar 30	Hearts	L 1-3	Collins	25,000
Apr 10	Partick Thistle	L 1-3	Byrne	18,000
Apr 13	Dunfermline Athletic	W 1-0	McAlindon	12,000
Apr 17	ST MIRREN	L 2-3	Haughney, Fernie	-
Apr 20	AIRDRIE	W 3-0	Haughney, McAlindon, Collins	6,000
Apr 22	Aberdeen	W 1-0	Higgins	15,000
Apr 26	Kilmarnock	D 0-0		-
Apr 27	HIBERNIAN	W 2-1	Fernie, Haughney	12,000
Apr 29	QUEEN OF THE SOUTH	D 0-0		3,000

Scottish Cup

Feb 2	Forres Mechanics	(Rd2) W 5-0	McPhail 3, Higgins, Mochan	7,000
Feb 16	RANGERS	(Rd3) D 4-4	McPhail, Higgins, Collins, Fernie	50,000
Feb 20	Rangers	(R) W 2-0	Higgins, Mochan	88,000
Mar 2	ST MIRREN	(QF) W 2-1	Peacock, Higgins	49,000
Mar 23	Kilmarnock	(SF) D 1-1	Higgins	109,145
Mar 27	Kilmarnock	(F) L 1-3	Collins	76,963

Scottish League Cup

Aug 11	Aberdeen	W 2-1	Fernie, Higgins	35,000
Aug 15	RANGERS	W 2-1	Collins, Tully	45,000
Aug 18	EAST FIFE	W 2-1	Fernie, McPhail	28,000
Aug 25	ABERDEEN	W 3-2	Collins, Tully, Fernie	36,000
Aug 29	Rangers	D 0-0		84,000
Sep 1	East Fife	W 1-0	McPhail	16,535
Sep 12	DUNFERMLINE ATHLETIC	(QF/FL) W 6-0	Mochan 2, McPhail 2, Collins, o.g.	23,000
Sep 15	Dunfermline Athletic	(QF/SL) L 0-3		16,000
Oct 6	Clyde	(SF) W 2-0	McPhail 2	36,697
Oct 27	Partick Thistle	(F) D 0-0		58,794
Oct 31	Partick Thistle	(R) W 3-0	McPhail 2, Collins	31,156

League & Cup Appearances

PLAYER	LEAGUE	CUP COMPETITIONS		TOTAL
		S CUP	SL CUP	
Beattie	29	6	11	46
Bonnar	4			4
Byrne	5	2		7
Collins	20	6	11	37
Craig	2			2
Evans	31	6	11	48
Fallon	22	6	10	38
Fernie	32	6	11	49
Goldie	1			1
Haughney	34	6	11	51
Higgins	19	6	3	28
Jack	33	6	11	50
Kennedy	4		1	5
McAlindon	3			3
McCreadie	1			1
McPhail	13	4	10	27
Meechan	8			8
Mochan	31	6	6	43
Peacock	31	6	11	48
Ryan	15			15
Sharkey	3			3
Smith	10		4	14
Tully	21		8	29
Walsh	2		2	4

Goalscorers

PLAYER	LEAGUE	CUP COMPETITIONS		TOTAL
		S CUP	SL CUP	
McPhail	5	4	8	17
Higgins	10	5	1	16
Mochan	12	2	2	16
Collins	5	2	4	11
Fernie	5	1	3	9
Haughney	8			8
Byrne	3			3
Ryan	3			3
Tully	1		2	3
McAlindon	2			2
Peacock		1		1
Sharkey	1			1
Smith	1			1
Opps' o.gs.	2		1	3

Fact File

Celtic won their first Scottish League Cup in October 1956, but were not presented with their medals until 10 January 1957.

Final Scottish League Div 1 Table

		P	W	D	L	F	A	Pts
1	RANGERS	34	26	3	5	96	48	55
2	HEARTS	34	24	5	5	81	48	53
3	KILMARNOCK	34	16	10	8	57	39	42
4	RAITH R	34	16	7	11	84	58	39
5	CELTIC	34	15	8	11	58	43	38
6	ABERDEEN	34	18	2	14	79	59	38
7	MOTHERWELL	34	16	5	13	72	66	37
8	PARTICK T	34	13	8	13	53	51	34
9	HIBERNIAN	34	12	9	13	69	56	33
10	DUNDEE	34	13	6	15	55	61	32
11	AIRDRIEONIANS	34	13	4	17	77	89	30
12	ST MIRREN	34	12	6	16	58	72	30
13	QUEEN'S PARK	34	11	7	16	55	59	29
14	FALKIRK	34	10	8	16	51	70	28
15	EAST FIFE	34	10	6	18	59	82	26
16	Q OF S	34	10	5	19	54	96	25
17	DUNFERMLINE ATH	34	9	6	19	54	74	24
18	AYR U	34	7	5	22	48	89	19

MANAGER: Jimmy McGrory

CAPTAIN: Bobby Evans

TOP SCORER: Billy McPhail

BIGGEST WIN: 6-0 v Dunfermline Athletic, 12 September 1956, Scottish League Cup

HIGHEST ATTENDANCE: 109,145 v Kilmarnock, 23 March 1957, Scottish Cup

MAJOR TRANSFERS IN: Sammy Wilson from Falkirk

MAJOR TRANSFERS OUT: Jimmy Walsh to Leicester

Season 1957-58

Scottish League Division 1

DATE	OPPONENTS	SCORE	GOALSCORERS	ATTENDANCE
Sep 7	Falkirk	W 1-0	Fernie	14,000
Sep 21	Rangers	W 3-2	Collins, McPhail, Wilson	60,000
Oct 12	RAITH ROVERS	D 1-1	Mochan	20,000
Oct 26	Third Lanark	W 2-0	Collins 2	24,000
Nov 2	KILMARNOCK	W 4-0	Mochan 2, Wilson, McPhail	35,000
Nov 9	East Fife	W 3-0	McPhail 2, Mochan	9,000
Nov 16	ST MIRREN	D 2-2	Divers, Wilson	30,000
Nov 23	Hibernian	W 1-0	Wilson	40,000
Nov 30	Airdrie	W 5-2	Collins 2, Wilson 2, Peacock	22,000
Dec 7	DUNDEE	D 0-0		20,000
Dec 14	Clyde	W 6-3	McPhail 2, Smith 2, Wilson, o.g.	26,500
Dec 21	PARTICK THISTLE	L 2-3	Mochan 2	18,000
Dec 25	QUEEN OF THE SOUTH	L 1-2	Conway	15,000
Dec 28	HEARTS	L 0-2		43,000
Jan 1	RANGERS	L 0-1		50,000
Jan 2	Queen's Park	W 3-0	Wilson 2, McVittie	10,000
Jan 4	FALKIRK	D 2-2	Byrne, Colrain	18,000
Jan 11	Motherwell	W 3-1	Mochan, Collins, o.g.	16,000
Jan 18	ABERDEEN	D 1-1	Collins	20,000
Jan 25	Raith Rovers	W 2-1	Collins, Bryne	10,000
Feb 22	Kilmarnock	D 1-1	Wilson	21,000
Mar 5	EAST FIFE	W 4-0	Byrne 3, Collins	4,000
Mar 8	St Mirren	D 1-1	Collins	12,000
Mar 14	Hearts	L 3-5	Byrne, Collins, Smith	30,000
Mar 19	HIBERNIAN	W 4-0	Wilson 3, McPhail	-
Mar 22	AIRDRIE	W 4-2	Collins 3, Byrne	15,000
Mar 29	Dundee	L 3-5	Collins, McVittie, Wilson	5,000
Apr 5	Aberdeen	W 1-0	Byrne	12,000
Apr 7	QUEEN'S PARK	W 5-1	Wilson 2, McVitie, Byrne, Smith	4,000
Apr 9	CLYDE	W 6-2	Collins 2, Fernie, McVittie, Wilson, McPhail	-
Apr 12	Partick Thistle	W 1-0	Collins	26,000
Apr 16	Queen of the South	L 3-4	Wilson 2, McPhail	7,000
Apr 21	MOTHERWELL	D 2-2	Wilson 2	-
Apr 30	THIRD LANARK	W 4-1	Wilson 2, Peacock, Collins	-

Scottish Cup

Feb 1	Airdrie	(Rd1) W 4-3	Byrne 2, Collins, Fernie	26,000
Feb 15	STIRLING ALBION	(Rd2) W 7-2	Smith 2, Wilson 2, Byrne 2, Mochan	30,200
Mar 1	CLYDE	(Rd3) L 0-2		-

Scottish League Cup

Aug 10	AIRDRIE	W 3-2	McPhail, Mochan, Peacock	38,000
Aug 14	East Fife	W 4-1	McPhail 3, Collins	-
Aug 17	Hibernian	L 1-3	Collins	35,000
Aug 24	Airdrie	W 2-1	Smith, Fernie	16,000
Aug 28	EAST FIFE	W 6-1	McPhail 2, Wilson 2, Auld, Collins	18,000
Aug 31	HIBERNIAN	W 2-0	Wilson, McPhail	50,000
Sep 11	THIRD LANARK	(QF/FL) W 6-1	McPhail 2, Collins 2, Wilson, Auld	20,000
Sep 14	Third Lanark	(QF/SL) W 3-0	Collins, McPhail, Wilson	20,000
Sep 28	Clyde	(SF) W 4-2	Wilson, McPhail, Collins, Fernie	42,000
Oct 19	Rangers	(F) W 7-1	McPhail 3, Mochan 2, Wilson, Fernie	82,293

Fact File

The 7-1 defeat of Rangers in the Scottish League Cup on 19 October is the highest ever score in a major UK final.

MANAGER: Jimmy McGrory

CAPTAIN: Bertie Peacock

TOP SCORER: Sammy Wilson

BIGGEST WIN: 7-1 v Rangers, 19 October 1957, Scottish League Cup

HIGHEST ATTENDANCE: 82,293 v Rangers, 19 October 1957, Scottish League Cup

League & Cup Appearances

PLAYER	LEAGUE	CUP COMPETITIONS		TOTAL
		S CUP	SL CUP	
Auld	2		6	8
Beattie	33	3	10	46
Byrne	13	3		16
Collins	30	3	10	43
Colrain	4			4
Conroy	3			3
Conway	3			3
Divers	1			1
Donnelly	19	3	7	29
Evans	33	3	10	46
Fallon	26	3	10	39
Fernie	27	3	9	39
Goldie	2			2
Haffey	1			1
Jack	2			2
Jackson	1			1
Kennedy	4			4
McPhail	20		10	30
McVittie	11			11
Meechan	9		3	12
Mochan	26	3	4	33
Peacock	31	3	10	44
Ryan	6			6
Sharkey	1		2	3
Smith	23	3	3	29
Tully	10		9	19
Wilson	33	3	7	43

Goalscorers

PLAYER	LEAGUE	CUP COMPETITIONS		TOTAL
		S CUP	SL CUP	
Wilson	23	2	7	32
Collins	19	1	7	27
McPhail	9		14	23
Byrne	9	4		13
Mochan	7	1	3	11
Smith	4	2	1	7
Fernie	2	1	3	6
McVittie	4			4
Peacock	2		1	3
Auld			2	2
Colrain	1			1
Conway	1			1
Divers	1			1
Opps' o.gs.	2			2

Final Scottish League Div 1 Table

		P	W	D	L	F	A	Pts
1	HEARTS	34	29	4	1	132	29	62
2	RANGERS	34	22	5	7	89	49	49
3	CELTIC	34	19	8	7	84	47	46
4	CLYDE	34	18	6	10	84	61	42
5	KILMARNOCK	34	14	9	11	60	55	37
6	PARTICK T	34	17	3	14	69	71	37
7	RAITH R	34	14	7	13	66	56	35
8	MOTHERWELL	34	12	8	14	68	67	32
9	HIBERNIAN	34	13	5	16	59	60	31
10	FALKIRK	34	11	9	14	64	82	31
11	DUNDEE	34	13	5	16	49	65	31
12	ABERDEEN	34	14	2	18	68	76	30
13	ST MIRREN	34	11	8	15	59	66	30
14	THIRD LANARK	34	13	4	17	69	88	30
15	Q OF S	34	12	5	17	61	72	29
16	AIRDRIEONIANS	34	13	2	19	71	92	28
17	EAST FIFE	34	10	3	21	45	88	23
18	QUEEN'S PARK	34	4	1	29	41	114	9

Season 1958-59

Scottish League Division 1

DATE	OPPONENTS	SCORE	GOALSCORERS	ATTENDANCE
Aug 20	Clyde	L 1-2	Auld	-
Sep 6	RANGERS	D 2-2	Collins, Smith	50,000
Sep 13	Kilmarnock	W 4-1	Colrain 2, Smith, Auld	20,000
Sep 20	RAITH ROVERS	W 3-2	Fernie 2, Smith	30,000
Sep 27	Aberdeen	L 1-3	Peacock	20,000
Oct 4	QUEEN OF THE SOUTH	W 3-1	Divers, Conway, Auld	20,000
Oct 11	FALKIRK	L 3-4	Divers 2, Fernie	23,000
Oct 18	Airdrie	W 4-1	Fernie, Byrne, Smith, Divers	16,000
Oct 25	THIRD LANARK	W 3-1	Wilson, Mochan, Auld	20,000
Nov 1	Dundee	D 1-1	Higgins	22,500
Nov 8	Dunfermline Athletic	L 0-1		16,500
Nov 15	ST MIRREN	D 3-3	Auld 2, o.g.	17,000
Nov 22	Partick Thistle	L 0-2		24,794
Nov 29	Hibernian	L 2-3	Colrain, Higgins	22,000
Dec 13	STIRLING ALBION	W 7-3	Colrain 3, Divers 2, Jackson, McVittie	13,000
Dec 20	Hearts	D 1-1	Higgins	25,000
Dec 27	CLYDE	W 3-1	Colrain 2, McVittie	20,000
Jan 1	Rangers	L 1-2	Peacock	55,000
Jan 2	MOTHERWELL	D 3-3	Divers 2, Colrain	36,000
Jan 21	KILMARNOCK	W 2-0	Peacock, o.g.	9,000
Jan 24	Queen of the South	D 2-2	Auld, Colrain	7,500
Feb 7	Falkirk	L 2-3	Colrain, Divers	11,500
Feb 21	Third Lanark	D 1-1	McVittie	18,000
Mar 4	DUNDEE	D 1-1	Mochan	9,000
Mar 7	DUNFERMLINE ATHLETIC	W 3-1	Jackson 2, Mochan	14,000
Mar 10	AIRDRIE	L 1-2	Colrain	4,000
Mar 18	St Mirren	L 0-1		-
Mar 21	PARTICK THISTLE	W 2-0	Slater, Colrain	15,000
Mar 25	ABERDEEN	W 4-0	Lochhead, Mochan, Colrain, McVittie	6,000
Mar 28	HIBERNIAN	W 3-0	Wilson 2, Lochhead	18,000
Apr 6	Raith Rovers	L 1-3	Mochan	8,000
Apr 8	Motherwell	L 0-2		-
Apr 11	Stirling Albion	W 1-0	McVittie	7,500
Apr 18	HEARTS	W 2-1	Auld, Smith	19,500

Scottish Cup

Jan 31	ALBION ROVERS	(Rd1) W 4-0	Wilson 2, Jackson, o.g.	27,000
Feb 18	CLYDE	(Rd2) D 1-1	McVittie	32,000
Feb 23	Clyde	(R) W 4-3	Wilson 2, McVittie, Peacock	26,087
Feb 28	RANGERS	(Rd3) W 2-1	Divers, McVittie	42,500
Mar 16	Stirling Albion	(QF) W 3-1	Divers, Wilson, Lochhead	28,000
Apr 4	St Mirren	(SF) L 0-4		73,885

Scottish League Cup

Aug 9	Clyde	W 4-1	Tully, Collins, Wilson, Auld	26,500
Aug 13	AIRDRIE	D 3-3	Auld, Conway, Collins	-
Aug 16	ST MIRREN	W 3-0	Collins, Conway, Tully	-
Aug 23	CLYDE	W 2-0	Wilson, Auld	39,000
Aug 27	Airdrie	W 2-1	Peacock, Conway	15,000
Aug 30	St Mirren	L 3-6	Collins 2, Auld	20,000
Sep 10	COWDENBEATH	(QF/FL) W 2-0	Collins, Auld	-
Sep 17	Cowdenbeath	(QF/SL) W 8-1	Wilson 4, Colrain 2, Auld, o.g.	10,000
Oct 1	Partick Thistle	(SF) L 1-2	Conway	45,000

League & Cup Appearances

PLAYER	LEAGUE	CUP COMPETITIONS		TOTAL
		S CUP	SL CUP	
Auld	27	2	9	38
Beattie	20		6	26
Byrne	5			5
Chalmers	1			1
Collins	2		7	9
Colrain	25	3	1	29
Conway	9	1	7	17
Crerand	4			4
Divers	20	4	1	25
Donnelly	4		1	5
Evans	20	6	3	29
Fernie	12		9	21
Haffey	14	6	3	23
Higgins	10			10
Jack	1			1
Jackson	17	4	1	22
Kennedy	1		1	2
Kurila	1			1
Lochhead	7	4		11
MacKay	30	6	8	44
McNeill	17		6	23
McVittie	17	5		22
Mochan	33	6	8	47
Paton	1			1
Peacock	27	6	9	42
Slater	4			4
Smith	27	6	3	36
Tully	5	1	9	15
Wilson	14	5	7	26

Goalscorers

PLAYER	LEAGUE	CUP COMPETITIONS		TOTAL
		S CUP	SL CUP	
Colrain	14		2	16
Auld	8		6	14
Wilson	3	5	6	14
Divers	9	2		11
McVittie	5	3		8
Collins	1		6	7
Conway	1		4	5
Mochan	5			5
Peacock	3	1	1	5
Smith	5			5
Fernie	4			4
Jackson	3	1		4
Higgins	3			3
Lochhead	2	1		3
Tully			2	2
Byrne	1			1
Slater	1			1
Opps' o.gs.	2	1	1	4

Fact File

As Celtic scored seven against Stirling Albion at Celtic Park on 13 December, the reserves scored nine against their reserves at Annfield.

MANAGER: Jimmy McGrory

CAPTAIN: Bertie Peacock

TOP SCORER: John Colrain

BIGGEST WIN: 8-1 v Cowdenbeath, 17 September 1958, Scottish League Cup

HIGHEST ATTENDANCE: 73,885 v St Mirren, 4 April 1959, Scottish Cup

MAJOR TRANSFERS OUT: Bobby Collins to Everton, Willie Fernie to Middlesbrough

Final Scottish League Div 1 Table

		P	W	D	L	F	A	PTS
1	RANGERS	34	21	8	5	92	51	50
2	HEARTS	34	21	6	7	92	51	48
3	MOTHERWELL	34	18	8	8	83	50	44
4	DUNDEE	34	16	9	9	61	51	41
5	AIRDRIEONIANS	34	15	7	12	64	62	37
6	CELTIC	34	14	8	12	70	53	36
7	ST MIRREN	34	14	7	13	71	74	35
8	KILMARNOCK	34	13	8	13	58	51	34
9	PARTICK T	34	14	6	14	59	66	34
10	HIBERNIAN	34	13	6	15	68	70	32
11	THIRD LANARK	34	11	10	13	74	83	32
12	STIRLING A	34	11	8	15	54	64	30
13	ABERDEEN	34	12	5	17	63	66	29
14	RAITH R	34	10	9	15	60	70	29
15	CLYDE	34	12	4	18	62	66	28
16	DUNFERMLINE ATH	34	10	8	16	68	87	28
17	FALKIRK	34	10	7	17	58	79	27
18	Q OF S	34	6	6	22	38	101	18

Season 1959-60

Scottish League Division 1

DATE	OPPONENTS	SCORE	GOALSCORERS	ATTENDANCE
Aug 19	KILMARNOCK	W 2-0	Conway, Divers	-
Sep 5	Rangers	L 1-3	Jackson	65,000
Sep 12	HEARTS	L 3-4	Auld, Divers, Conway	40,000
Sep 19	Raith Rovers	W 3-0	Chalmers 2, Jackson	13,000
Sep 26	CLYDE	D 1-1	Mackle	27,000
Oct 3	Arbroath	W 5-0	Chalmers 2, Jackson 2, Conway	9,000
Oct 10	ABERDEEN	D 1-1	Conway	25,000
Oct 17	Third Lanark	L 2-4	Divers, Jackson	22,000
Oct 24	MOTHERWELL	W 5-1	Divers 2, Jackson, Auld, Colrain	25,000
Oct 31	Hibernian	D 3-3	Peacock, Jackson, Colrain	28,000
Nov 7	AYR UNITED	L 2-3	Auld, Divers	23,000
Nov 14	DUNFERMLINE ATHLETIC	W 4-2	Divers 3, Jckson	16,000
Nov 21	Stirling Albion	D 2-2	Colrain, o.g.	18,000
Nov 28	Partick Thistle	L 1-3	Divers	30,000
Dec 5	DUNDEE	L 2-3	Chalmers, Mochan	10,000
Dec 12	AIRDRIE	D 0-0		13,000
Dec 19	St Mirren	W 3-0	O'Hara, Colrain, Mochan	19,000
Dec 26	Kilmarnock	L 1-2	Mochan	15,000
Jan 1	RANGERS	L 0-1		50,000
Jan 2	Hearts	L 1-3	Peacock	28,000
Jan 9	RAITH ROVERS	W 1-0	Mochan	15,000
Jan 16	Clyde	D 3-3	Byrne 2, Mochan	25,000
Jan 23	ARBROATH	W 4-0	Divers 2, Byrne, Carroll	16,000
Feb 6	Aberdeen	L 2-3	Mochan 2	14,000
Mar 7	HIBERNIAN	W 1-0	Conway	19,000
Mar 16	Ayr United	D 1-1	Crerand	-
Mar 19	Dunfermline Athletic	L 2-3	Conway, Byrne	10,000
Mar 21	Motherwell	W 2-1	Mochan 2	-
Mar 26	STIRLING ALBION	D 1-1	Mochan	12,000
Mar 28	THIRD LANARK	W 4-0	Chalmers 2, Colrain, Mochan	8,000
Apr 12	PARTICK THISTLE	L 2-4	Chalmers 2	5,000
Apr 16	Dundee	L 0-2		15,000
Apr 18	Airdrie	W 5-2	Chalmers 3, Mochan, o.g.	4,000
Apr 30	ST MIRREN	D 3-3	Chalmers 2, Mochan	10,000

Scottish Cup

Feb 13	St Mirren	(Rd2) D 1-1	Byrne	37,000
Feb 24	ST MIRREN	(R) D 4-4	Mochan 2, Divers 2	28,000
Feb 29	ST MIRREN	(2R) W 5-2	Mochan 5	51,000
Mar 5	Elgin City	(Rd3) W 2-1	Divers, Smith	12,000
Mar 12	PARTICK THISTLE	(QF) W 2-0	Smith, Colrain	41,000
Apr 2	Rangers	(SF) D 1-1	Chalmers	79,786
Apr 6	Rangers	(R) L 1-4	Mochan	70,977

Scottish League Cup

Aug 8	Raith Rovers	L 1-2	Mackle	17,000
Aug 12	PARTICK THISTLE	L 1-2	Mochan	25,000
Aug 15	Airdrie	L 2-4	Carroll, o.g.	15,000
Aug 22	RAITH ROVERS	W 1-0	o.g.	24,000
Aug 26	Partick Thistle	W 2-0	Jackson 2	20,000
Aug 29	AIRDRIE	D 2-2	Divers, Auld	24,500

Celtic failed to qualify for quarter-finals.

League & Cup Appearances

PLAYER	LEAGUE	CUP COMPETITIONS		TOTAL
		S CUP	SL CUP	
Auld	20	1	3	24
Byrne	14	5	3	22
Carroll	10		2	12
Chalmers	17	2		19
Clark	2			2
Colrain	17	7	3	27
Conway	12		2	14
Crerand	8			8
Curran	3			3
Divers	23	7	3	33
Donnelly	5			5
Evans	30	7	6	43
Fallon	14			14
Gallagher	4		1	5
Haffey	20	7	6	33
Jackson	13	1	2	16
Kennedy	20	7	3	30
Kurila	1			1
Lochhead	1		1	2
MacKay	29	7	6	42
Mackle	3		2	5
McNeill	19	7	6	39
O'Hara	6		2	8
Peacock	33	7	4	44
Slater	1			1
Smith	21	5	3	29

Goalscorers

PLAYER	LEAGUE	CUP COMPETITIONS		TOTAL
		S CUP	SL CUP	
Mochan	13	8	1	22
Divers	12	3	1	16
Chalmers	14	1		15
Jackson	8		2	10
Colrain	5	1		6
Conway	6			6
Byrne	4	1		5
Auld	3			4
Carroll	1		1	2
Mackle	1		1	2
Peacock	2			2
Smith		2		2
Crerand	1			1
O'Hara	1			1
Opps' o.gs.	2		2	4

Fact File

45,000 turned up on 12 October 1959 to see the first ever floodlit game at Celtic Park. Celtic lost 0-2 to Wolverhampton Wanderers in a friendly played to celebrate the occasion.

MANAGER: Jimmy McGrory

CAPTAIN: Bertie Peacock

TOP SCORER: Neil Mochan

BIGGEST WIN: 5-0 v Arbroath, 3 October 1959, league

HIGHEST ATTENDANCE: 79,786 v Rangers, 2 April 1960, Scottish Cup

MAJOR TRANSFERS IN: Johnny Kelly from Crewe

MAJOR TRANSFERS OUT: Dick Beattie to Portsmouth, Matt McVittie to St Johnstone, Bobby Evans to Chelsea, Eric Smith to Leeds

Final Scottish League Div 1 Table

		P	W	D	L	F	A	Pts
1	HEARTS	34	23	8	3	102	51	54
2	KILMARNOCK	34	24	2	8	67	45	50
3	RANGERS	34	17	8	9	72	38	42
4	DUNDEE	34	16	10	8	70	49	42
5	MOTHERWELL	34	16	8	10	71	61	40
6	CLYDE	34	15	9	10	77	69	39
7	HIBERNIAN	34	14	7	13	106	85	35
8	AYR U	34	14	6	14	65	73	34
9	CELTIC	34	12	9	13	73	59	33
10	PARTICK T	34	14	4	16	54	78	32
11	RAITH R	34	14	3	17	64	62	31
12	THIRD LANARK	34	13	4	17	75	83	30
13	DUNFERMLINE ATH	34	10	9	15	72	80	29
14	ST MIRREN	34	11	6	17	78	86	28
15	ABERDEEN	34	11	6	17	54	72	28
16	AIRDRIEONIANS	34	11	6	17	56	80	28
17	STIRLING A	34	7	8	19	55	72	22
18	ARBROATH	34	4	7	23	38	106	15

Season 1960-61

Scottish League Division 1

DATE	OPPONENTS	SCORE	GOALSCORERS	ATTENDANCE
Aug 24	Kilmarnock	D 2-2	Carroll, Mochan	20,000
Sep 10	RANGERS	L 1-5	Chalmers	40,000
Sep 17	Third Lanark	L 0-2		15,000
Sep 24	ABERDEEN	D 0-0		19,000
Oct 1	Airdrie	L 0-2		12,000
Oct 8	ST MIRREN	W 4-2	Auld 2, Divers, Chalmers	32,000
Oct 15	Hibernian	W 6-0	Carroll 2, Chalmers 2, Fernie, Auld	28,000
Oct 22	Clyde	W 3-0	Auld, Carroll, Peacock	23,500
Oct 29	AYR UNITED	W 2-0	Carroll, Divers	16,000
Nov 5	Raith Rovers	D 2-2	Fernie, Chalmers	10,000
Nov 12	PARTICK THISTLE	L 0-1		23,000
Nov 19	Dunfermline Athletic	D 2-2	Carroll, Chalmers	11,000
Nov 26	St Johnstone	L 1-2	Chalmers	15,000
Dec 10	DUNDEE UNITED	D 1-1	Hughes	15,000
Dec 17	Hearts	L 1-2	Crerand	24,000
Dec 24	MOTHERWELL	W 1-0	Divers	20,500
Dec 26	DUNDEE	W 2-1	Conway, Byrne	11,000
Dec 31	KILMARNOCK	W 3-2	Chalmers 2, Gallagher	30,000
Jan 2	Rangers	L 1-2	Divers	79,000
Jan 7	THIRD LANARK	L 2-3	Divers, Chalmers	22,000
Jan 14	Aberdeen	W 3-1	Gallagher, Chalmers, Divers	22,000
Jan 21	AIRDRIE	W 4-0	Chalmers 2, Divers, Crerand	21,000
Feb 4	St Mirren	L 1-2	Peacock	27,000
Feb 18	HIBERNIAN	W 2-0	Chalmers 2	33,000
Feb 27	CLYDE	W 6-1	Hughes 2, Byrne, Peacock, Gallagher, Chalmers	-
Mar 4	Ayr United	W 3-1	McNeill, Peacock, Fernie	15,500
Mar 18	Partick Thistle	W 2-1	Byrne, Chalmers	27,000
Mar 20	RAITH ROVERs	D 1-1	Chalmers	-
Mar 25	DUNFERMLINE ATHLETIC	W 2-1	Fernie, Byrne	20,000
Apr 5	ST JOHNSTONE	D 1-1	Fernie	8,000
Apr 8	Dundee	W 1-0	Chalmers	17,500
Apr 10	Dundee United	D 1-1	Hughes	15,000
Apr 29	Motherwell	D 2-2	Chalmers, Fernie	14,000
May 2	HEARTS	L 1-3	Divers	7,000

Scottish Cup

Jan 28	Falkirk	(Rd1)	W 3-1	Peacock 2, o.g.	20,000
Feb 11	MONTROSE	(Rd2)	W 6-0	Hughes 2, Chalmers 2, Byrne, o.g.	26,000
Feb 25	Raith Rovers	(Rd3)	W 4-1	Chalmers, Fernie, Hughes, o.g.	19,359
Mar 11	HIBERNIAN	(QF)	D 1-1	Chalmers	56,000
Mar 15	Hibernian	(R)	W 1-0	Clark	39,243
Apr 1	Airdrie	(SF)	W 4-0	Hughes 2, Chalmers, Fernie	72,612
Apr 22	Dunfermline Athletic	(F)	D 0-0		113,328
Apr 26	Dunfermline Athletic	(R)	L 0-2		87,866

Scottish League Cup

Aug 13	THIRD LANARK	W 2-0	Hughes, Mochan	25,000
Aug 17	Partick Thistle	D 1-1	Carroll	20,000
Aug 20	Rangers	W 3-2	Carroll, Divers, Hughes	60,000
Aug 27	Third Lanark	W 3-1	Hughes 2, Divers	31,000
Aug 31	PARTICK THISTLE	L 1-2	Hughes	26,000
Sep 3	RANGERS	L 1-2	Chalmers	

Celtic failed to qualify for quarter-finals.

League & Cup Appearances

PLAYER	LEAGUE	CUP COMPETITIONS		TOTAL
		S CUP	SL CUP	
Auld	15	1		16
Byrne	16	7		23
Carroll	17		5	22
Chalmers	32	7	6	45
Clark	10	4		14
Conway	7		1	8
Crerand	31	8	6	45
Curran	1			1
Divers	23	2	6	31
Donnelly	1			1
Fallon	4		3	7
Fernie	22	7		29
Gallagher	15	8		23
Goldie	1			1
Haffey	29	8	3	40
Hughes	19	8	6	33
Jackson	1			1
Kelly	3			3
Kennedy	32	7	6	45
Kurila	3		2	5
MacKay	32	8	6	46
McNamee	1			1
McNeill	31	8	4	43
Mochan	2		6	8
O'Neill	2	1		3
Peacock	24	4	6	34

Goalscorers

PLAYER	LEAGUE	CUP COMPETITIONS		TOTAL
		S CUP	SL CUP	
Chalmers	20	5	1	26
Hughes	4	5	5	14
Divers	8		2	10
Carroll	6		2	8
Fernie	6	2		8
Peacock	4	2		6
Byrne	4	1		5
Auld	4			4
Gallagher	3			3
Crerand	2			2
Clark		1		1
Conway	1			1
McNeill	1			1
Mochan	1		1	1
Opps' o.gs.		3		3

Fact File

Willie O'Neill made his Celtic debut in the Scottish Cup final.

MANAGER: Jimmy McGrory

CAPTAIN: Bertie Peacock

TOP SCORER: Steve Chalmers

BIGGEST WIN: 6-0 v Hibernian, 15 October 1960, league; 6-0 v Montrose, 11 February 1961, Scottish Cup

HIGHEST ATTENDANCE: 113,328 v Dunfermline, 22 April 1961, Scottish Cup

MAJOR TRANSFERS IN: Willie Fernie from Middlesbrough

MAJOR TRANSFERS OUT: Neil Mochan to Dundee United, John Colrain to Clyde, Jim Conway to Norwich, Bertie Auld to Birmingham

Final Scottish League Div 1 Table

		P	W	D	L	F	A	Pts
1	RANGERS	34	23	5	6	88	46	51
2	KILMARNOCK	34	21	8	5	77	45	50
3	THIRD LANARK	34	20	2	12	100	80	42
4	CELTIC	34	15	9	10	64	46	39
5	MOTHERWELL	34	15	8	11	70	57	38
6	ABERDEEN	34	14	8	12	72	72	36
7	HEARTS	34	13	8	13	51	53	34
8	HIBERNIAN	34	15	4	15	66	69	34
9	DUNDEE U	34	13	7	14	60	58	33
10	DUNDEE	34	13	6	15	61	53	32
11	PARTICK T	34	13	6	15	59	69	32
12	DUNFERMLINE ATH	34	12	7	15	65	81	31
13	AIRDRIEONIANS	34	10	10	14	61	71	30
14	ST MIRREN	34	11	7	16	53	58	29
15	ST JOHNSTONE	34	10	9	15	47	63	29
16	RAITH R	34	10	7	17	46	67	27
17	CLYDE	34	6	11	17	55	77	23
18	AYR U	34	5	12	17	51	81	22

Season 1961-62

Scottish League Division 1

DATE	OPPONENTS	SCORE	GOALSCORERS	ATTENDANCE
Aug 23	Kilmarnock	L 2-3	Divers, Chalmers	20,000
Sep 9	THIRD LANARK	W 1-0	Divers	29,000
Sep 16	Rangers	D 2-2	Divers, Fernie	70,000
Sep 23	DUNDEE UNITED	W 3-1	Hughes, Chalmers, Jackson	24,000
Sep 30	Falkirk	L 1-3	Hughes	13,000
Oct 14	STIRLING ALBION	W 5-0	Hughes 3, Carroll, Divers	22,000
Oct 18	St Johnstone	W 3-0	Divers, Jackson, Carroll	7,000
Oct 21	Hearts	L 1-2	Hughes	22,000
Oct 28	DUNFERMLINE ATHLETIC	W 2-1	Carroll 2	26,000
Nov 4	Dundee	L 1-2	Carroll	24,500
Nov 15	ST MIRREN	W 7-1	Chalmers 2, Carroll 2, Jackson 2, Hughes	22,000
Nov 18	AIRDRIE	W 3-0	Jackson 2, Hughes	26,000
Nov 25	Aberdeen	D 0-0		15,000
Dec 2	PARTICK THISTLE	W 5-1	Chalmers 2, Hughes, Jackson, Divers	20,000
Dec 16	HIBERNIAN	W 4-3	Divers 3, Hughes	28,000
Dec 23	Raith Rovers	W 4-0	Divers 2, Chalmers, Carroll	14,000
Jan 6	KILMARNOCK	D 2-2	Carroll, Chalmers	35,000
Jan 10	Third Lanark	D 1-1	Hughes	-
Jan 13	Dundee United	W 5-4	Jackson 2, Hughes 2, Crerand	20,000
Jan 20	FALKIRK	W 3-0	Divers, Jackson, Crerand	27,000
Jan 22	MOTHERWELL	D 1-1	Jackson	23,000
Feb 3	ST JOHNSTONE	W 3-1	Divers 2, Hughes	19,000
Feb 10	Stirling Albion	L 0-1		11,000
Feb 21	HEARTS	D 2-2	Divers, Hughes	23,000
Feb 24	Dunfermline Athletic	W 3-0	Hughes 2, Divers	15,000
Mar 3	DUNDEE	W 2-1	Brogan, McNeill	39,000
Mar 17	Airdrie	L 0-1		24,000
Mar 24	ABERDEEN	W 2-0	Brogan 2	21,000
Mar 26	St Mirren	W 5-0	Divers 2, Chalmers 2, Carroll	-
Apr 4	Partick Thistle	W 2-1	Brogan, Hughes	7,200
Apr 7	Hibernian	D 1-1	Divers	50,000
Apr 9	RANGERS	D 1-1	Hughes	50,000
Apr 21	RAITH ROVERS	L 0-1		11,000
Apr 23	Motherwell	W 4-0	Carroll 2, Chalmers, o.g.	-

Scottish Cup

Dec 13	COWDENBEATH	(Rd1) W 5-1	Chalmers 2, Jackson, Hughes, Divers	19,000
Jan 27	Morton	(Rd2) W 3-1	Carroll, Divers, Jackson	21,000
Feb 17	Hearts	(Rd3) W 4-3	Divers 2, Chalmers, Crerand	35,045
Mar 10	THIRD LANARK	(QF) D 4-4	Chalmers 2, Brogan, Hughes	42,500
Mar 14	Third Lanark	(R) W 4-0	Hughes 2, Chalmers, Byrne	51,518
Mar 31	St Mirren	(SF) L 1-3	Byrne	56,000

Scottish League Cup

Aug 12	Partick Thistle	W 3-2	Jackson 2, Hughes	33,549
Aug 16	ST JOHNSTONE	L 0-1		23,000
Aug 19	Hibernian	D 2-2	Hughes, Chalmers	28,000
Aug 26	PARTICK THISTLE	W 3-2	Hughes 2, Carroll	27,000
Aug 30	St Johnstone	L 0-2		-
Sep 2	HIBERNIAN	W 2-1	Divers 2	31,000

Celtic failed to qualify for quarter-finals.

Fact File

Due to injuries, goalkeeper Frank Connor was re-signed after being released. He was subsequently released again.

MANAGER: Jimmy McGrory
CAPTAIN: Duncan MacKay
TOP SCORER: John Hughes
BIGGEST WIN: 7-1 v St Mirren, 15 November 1961, league
HIGHEST ATTENDANCE: 70,000 v Rangers, 16 September 1961, league
MAJORS TRANSFERS OUT: Willie Fernie to St Mirren

League & Cup Appearances

PLAYER	LEAGUE	CUP COMPETITIONS		TOTAL
		S CUP	SL CUP	
Brogan	10	3		13
Byrne	8	2		10
Carroll	28	4	5	37
Chalmers	31	6	6	43
Clark	12	3	5	20
Connor	2		6	8
Crerand	31	6	1	38
Divers	34	6	6	46
Donnelly	3		1	4
Fernie	3		4	7
Gallagher	1			1
Haffey	32	6		38
Hughes	31	6	6	43
Jackson	24	3	5	32
Kennedy	32	6	6	44
Kurila			2	2
Lennox	1			1
MacKay	32	6	5	43
McNamee	5			5
McNeill	29	6	6	41
Price	23	3	2	28

Goalscorers

PLAYER	LEAGUE	CUP COMPETITIONS		TOTAL
		S CUP	SL CUP	
Hughes	18	4	4	26
Divers	19	4	2	25
Chalmers	12	6	1	19
Jckson	11	2	2	15
Carroll	12	1	1	14
Brogan	4	1		5
Crerand	2	1		3
Byrne		2		2
Fernie	1			1
McNeill	1			1
Opps' o.gs.	1			1

Final Scottish League Div 1 Table

		P	W	D	L	F	A	PTS
1	DUNDEE	34	25	4	5	80	46	54
2	RANGERS	34	22	7	5	84	31	51
3	CELTIC	34	19	8	7	81	37	46
4	DUNFERMLINE ATH	34	19	5	10	77	46	43
5	KILMARNOCK	34	16	10	8	74	58	42
6	HEARTS	34	16	6	12	54	49	38
7	PARTICK T	34	16	3	15	60	55	35
8	HIBERNIAN	34	14	5	15	58	72	33
9	MOTHERWELL	34	13	6	15	65	62	32
10	DUNDEE U	34	13	6	15	70	71	32
11	THIRD LANARK	34	13	5	16	59	60	31
12	ABERDEEN	34	10	9	15	60	73	29
13	RAITH R	34	10	7	17	51	73	27
14	FALKIRK	34	11	4	19	45	68	26
15	AIRDRIEONIANS	34	9	7	18	57	78	25
16	ST MIRREN	34	10	5	19	52	80	25
17	ST JOHNSTONE	34	9	7	18	35	61	25
18	STIRLING A	34	6	6	22	34	76	18

Season 1962-63

Scottish League Division 1

DATE	OPPONENTS	SCORE	GOALSCORERS	ATTENDANCE
Aug 22	Falkirk	W 3-1	Jackson, Byrne, Hughes	5,000
Sep 8	RANGERS	L 0-1		72,000
Sep 15	Clyde	W 3-1	Divers 2, Chalmers	23,000
Sep 22	ABERDEEN	L 1-2	Hughes	29,000
Sep 29	Raith Rovers	W 2-0	Murdoch, McNeill	9,000
Oct 6	KILMARNOCK	D 1-1	Carroll	36,000
Oct 13	Motherwell	W 2-0	Gallagher, Carroll	18,000
Oct 20	DUNDEE UNITED	W 1-0	Chalmers	21,000
Oct 27	Airdrie	W 6-1	Divers 2, Craig 2, Chalmers, Gallagher	16,000
Nov 3	St Mirren	W 7-0	Chalmers 3, Divers, MacKay, Price, Gallagher	25,000
Nov 10	QUEEN OF THE SOUTH	L 0-1		29,000
Nov 17	Dundee	D 0-0		14,000
Nov 24	PARTICK THISTLE	L 0-2		40,000
Dec 1	Hibernian	D 1-1	Murdoch	20,000
Dec 8	HEARTS	D 2-2	Hughes, Price	30,000
Dec 15	Third Lanark	L 0-2		15,000
Dec 26	DUNFERMLINE ATHLETIC	W 2-1	Hughes, o.g.	-
Dec 29	FALKIRK	W 2-1	Hughes 2	18,000
Jan 1	Rangers	L 0-4		55,000
Jan 5	Aberdeen	W 5-1	Hughes 3, Craig 2	16,000
Mar 2	AIRDRIE	W 3-1	Divers 2, o.g.	23,000
Mar 9	ST MIRREN	D 1-1	Murdoch	25,000
Mar 16	Queen of the South	W 5-2	Craig 3, Brogan, McNamee	8,000
Mar 19	RAITH ROVERS	W 4-1	Brogan 2, McNamee, Chalmers	8,000
Mar 23	DUNDEE	W 4-1	Hughes, Brogan, Craig, o.g.	42,000
Mar 27	Kilmarnock	L 0-6		-
Apr 2	Partick Thistle	W 5-1	Craig 2, Murdoch, MacKay, Divers	-
Apr 6	HIBERNIAN	W 2-0	Price, MacKay	14,000
Apr 20	THIRD LANARK	W 2-1	Craig 2	14,000
Apr 27	Dunfermline Athletic	D 1-1	Divers	12,000
Apr 29	Hearts	L 3-4	Chalmers, Divers, Johnstone	-
May 6	CLYDE	W 2-0	MacKay, Hughes	-
May 11	Dundee United	L 0-3		12,000
May 13	MOTHERWELL	W 6-0	Chalmers 3, Craig, Divers, o.g.	-

Scottish Cup

Jan 28	Falkirk	(Rd1) W 2-0	Hughes, Gallagher	13,500
Mar 6	HEARTS	(Rd2) W 3-1	Murdoch, McNamee, Hughes	38,000
Mar 13	GALA FAIRYDEAN	(Rd3) W 6-0	Murdoch 3, Hughes 2, Divers	-
Mar 30	St Mirren	(QF) W 1-0	Brogan	34,988
Apr 13	Raith Rovers	(SF) W 5-2	MacKay 2, Divers, Chalmers, Brogan	35,681
May 4	Rangers	(F) D 1-1	Murdoch	129,527
May 15	Rangers	(R) L 0-3		120,263

Scottish League Cup

Aug 11	HEARTS	W 3-1	Murdoch, Gallagher, Hughes	41,000
Aug 15	Dundee	L 0-1		-
Aug 18	DUNDEE UNITED	W 4-0	Hughes 2, Crerand, Gallagher	35,000
Aug 25	Hearts	L 2-3	Murdoch, Hughes	33,000
Aug 29	DUNDEE	W 3-0	Hughes 2, Gallagher	28,000
Sep 1	Dundee United	D 0-0		-

Celtic failed to qualify for quarter-finals.

Inter-Cities Fairs Cup

Sep 26	Valencia	(Rd1/FL) L 2-4	Carroll, o.g.	40,000
Oct 24	VALENCIA	(Rd1/SL) D 2-2	Crerand, o.g.	45,000

MANAGER: Jimmy McGrory

CAPTAIN: Duncan MacKay

TOP SCORER: John Hughes

BIGGEST WIN: 7-0 v St Mirren, 3 November 1962, league

HIGHEST ATTENDANCE: 129,527 v Rangers, 4 May 1963, Scottish Cup

MAJOR TRANSFERS IN: Bobby Craig from Blackburn, Paddy Turner from Morton

MAJOR TRANSFERS OUT: Bobby Carroll to St Mirren, Pat Crerand to Manchester United, Mike Jackson to St Johnstone

League & Cup Appearances

PLAYER	LEAGUE	CUP COMPETITIONS			TOTAL
		S CUP	SL CUP	ICFC	
Brogan	18	5			23
Byrne	9		6	2	17
Carroll	6			1	7
Chalmers	27	4	1	2	34
Clark	2			1	3
Craig	17	3		1	21
Crerand	17		6	2	25
Cushley	2				2
Divers	27	7		1	35
Fallon				1	1
Gallagher	17	3	6	2	27
Gemmell	2	1			3
Haffey	33	7	6	1	47
Hughes	16	6	6		28
Jackson	2			1	3
Jeffrey	4				4
Johnstone	4	1			5
Kennedy	25	5	6	1	37
Lennox	4		5		9
McCarron	1				1
MacKay	29	6	6	2	43
McNamee	19	7		1	27
McNeill	28	7	6	1	42
Madden	1				1
Murdoch	19	6	6		31
O'Neill	13	1		2	16
Price	27	7	6		40
Young	5	1			6

Goalscorers

PLAYER	LEAGUE	CUP COMPETITIONS			TOTAL
		S CUP	SL CUP	ICFC	
Hughes	11	4	6		21
Craig	13				13
Divers	11	2			13
Chalmers	11	1			12
Murdoch	4	5	2		11
Gallagher	3	1	3		7
Brogan	4	2			6
MacKay	4	2			6
Carroll	2			1	3
McNamee	2	1			3
Price	3				3
Crerand			1	1	2
Byrne	1				1
Jackson	1				1
Johnstone	1				1
McNeill	1				1
Opps' o.gs.	4			2	6

Fact File

Celtic made their first appearance in European competition.

Final Scottish League Div 1 Table

		P	W	D	L	F	A	Pts
1	RANGERS	34	25	7	2	94	28	57
2	KILMARNOCK	34	20	8	6	92	40	48
3	PARTICK T	34	20	6	8	66	44	46
4	CELTIC	34	19	6	9	76	44	44
5	HEARTS	34	17	9	8	85	59	43
6	ABERDEEN	34	17	7	10	70	47	41
7	DUNDEE U	34	15	11	8	67	52	41
8	DUNFERMLINE ATH	34	13	8	13	50	47	34
9	DUNDEE	34	12	9	13	60	49	33
10	MOTHERWELL	34	10	11	13	60	63	31
11	AIRDRIEONIANS	34	14	2	18	52	76	30
12	ST MIRREN	34	10	8	16	52	72	28
13	FALKIRK	34	12	3	19	54	69	27
14	THIRD LANARK	34	9	8	17	56	68	26
15	Q OF S	34	10	6	18	36	75	26
16	HIBERNIAN	34	8	9	17	47	67	25
17	CLYDE	34	9	5	20	49	83	23
18	RAITH R	34	2	5	27	35	118	9

Season 1963-64

Scottish League Division 1

DATE	OPPONENTS	SCORE	GOALSCORERS	ATTENDANCE
Aug 21	QUEEN OF THE SOUTH	W 4-0	Chalmers 2, Turner, Jeffrey	-
Sep 7	Rangers	L 1-2	Chalmers	55,000
Sep 14	THIRD LANARK	D 4-4	Divers, Lennox, Turner, Brogan F	19,000 19,000
Sep 21	Falkirk	L 0-1		11,000
Sep 28	St Mirren	L 1-2	Chalmers	16,000
Oct 5	DUNFERMLINE ATHLETIC	D 2-2	Murdoch, Brogan F	17,000
Oct 12	ABERDEEN	W 3-0	Chalmers 2, MacKay	15,000
Oct 19	Dundee United	W 3-1	Hughes, Murdoch, o.g.	16,000
Oct 26	AIRDRIE	W 9-0	Hughes 3, Divers 3, Gallagher, Murdoch, Chalmers	13,000
Nov 2	East Stirling	W 5-1	Chalmers 3, Divers, Hughes	7,000
Nov 9	PARTICK THISTLE	W 5-3	Chalmers 3, Johnstone, Hughes	28,000
Nov 16	Hibernian	D 1-1	Murdoch	25,000
Nov 23	KILMARNOCK	W 5-0	Hughes 3, Divers, Johnstone	28,000
Nov 30	Dundee	D 1-1	Murdoch	25,000
Dec 7	ST JOHNSTONE	W 3-1	Murdoch 3	24,000
Dec 14	Hearts	D 1-1	Divers	23,000
Dec 21	MOTHERWELL	W 2-1	Divers, Clark	25,000
Dec 28	Queen of the South	W 2-0	Johnstone, Chalmers	7,000
Jan 1	RANGERS	L 0-1		65,000
Jan 2	Third Lanark	D 1-1	Divers	-
Jan 4	FALKIRK	W 7-0	Chalmers 3, Divers 2, Johnstone, Hughes	16,000
Jan 18	ST MIRREN	W 3-0	Chalmers, Johnstone, Divers	20,000
Feb 1	Dunfermline Athletic	L 0-1		16,000
Feb 8	Aberdeen	W 3-0	Brogan F, Divers, o.g.	18,000
Feb 19	DUNDEE UNITED	W 1-0	Chalmers	10,000
Feb 22	Airdrie	W 2-0	Brogan F 2	8,000
Feb 29	EAST STIRLING	W 5-2	Chalmers 3, Murdoch 2	15,000
Mar 1	Partick Thistle	D 2-2	Divers, Murdoch	-
Mar 14	HIBERNIAN	W 5-0	Murdoch 2, Chalmers 2, Divers	11,000
Mar 21	Kilmarnock	L 0-4		12,000
Mar 28	Motherwell	W 4-0	Chalmers 2, Murdoch, Johnstone	8,000
Apr 1	DUNDEE	W 2-1	Gallagher, Chalmers	-
Apr 4	St Johnstone	D 1-1	Murdoch	9,500
Apr 18	HEARTS	D 1-1	Chalmers	20,000

Scottish Cup

DATE	OPPONENTS	SCORE	GOALSCORERS	ATTENDANCE
Jan 11	EYEMOUTH	(Rd1) W 3-0	Chalmers 2, Gallagher	17,000
Jan 25	Morton	(Rd2) W 3-1	Hughes, Gallagher, Johnstone	21,000
Feb 15	AIRDRIE	(Rd3) W 4-1	Chalmers, Murdoch, Johnstone, Hughes	32,000
Mar 7	Rangers	(QF) L 0-2		84,724

Scottish League Cup

DATE	OPPONENTS	SCORE	GOALSCORERS	ATTENDANCE
Aug 10	RANGERS	L 0-3		60,000
Aug 14	Kilmarnock	D 0-0		23,000
Aug 17	QUEEN OF THE SOUTH	D 1-1	Brogan F	18,000
Aug 24	Rangers	L 0-3		65,000
Aug 28	KILMARNOCK	W 2-0	Divers, Gallagher	12,000
Aug 31	Queen of the South	W 3-2	Chalmers 2, Gallagher	6,500

Celtic failed to qualify for quarter-finals.

European Cup-Winners' Cup

DATE	OPPONENTS	SCORE	GOALSCORERS	ATTENDANCE
Sep 17	Basle	(Rd1/FL) W 5-1	Hughes 3, Divers, Lennox	15,000
Oct 10	BASLE	(Rd1/SL) W 5-0	Divers 2, Johnstone, Murdoch, Chalmers	8,000
Dec 4	DINAMO ZAGREB	(Rd2/FL) W 3-0	Chalmers 2, Hughes	42,000
Dec 11	Dinamo Zagreb	(Rd2/SL) L 1-2	Murdoch	10,000
Feb 16	SLOVAN BRATISLAVA	(QF/FL) W 1-0	Murdoch	53,000
Mar 4	Slovan Bratislava	(QF/SL) W 1-0	Hughes	30,000
Apr 15	MTK BUDAPEST	(SF/FL) W 3-0	Chalmers 2, Johnstone	51,000
Apr 29	MTK Budapest	(SF/SL) L 0-4		10,000

MANAGER: Jimmy McGrory

CAPTAIN: Billy McNeill

TOP SCORER: Steve Chalmers

BIGGEST WIN: 9-0 v Airdrie, 26 October 1963, league

HIGHEST ATTENDANCE: 84,724 v Rangers, 7 March 1964, Scottish Cup

MAJOR TRANSFERS OUT: Bobby Craig to St Johnstone, John McNamee to Hibernian, Frank Brogan to Ipswich, Paddy Turner to Glentoran

---

League & Cup Appearances

PLAYER	LEAGUE	CUP COMPETITIONS			TOTAL
		S CUP	SL CUP	ECWC	
Brogan F	9	1	1	1	12
Brogan J	3				3
Chalmers	34	4	6	8	52
Clark	26	3	5	7	41
Cushley	5				5
Divers	29	2	3	6	40
Fallon	34	4		6	34
Gallagher	10	3	3	2	18
Gemmell	31	4	6	8	49
Haffey	10		6	2	18
Henderson	2				2
Hughes	23	4	3	8	38
Jeffrey	1		3		4
Johnstone	25	4	2	7	38
Kennedy	29	4		7	40
Lennox	6			1	7
MacKay	9		6	2	17
McNamee	2		2	1	5
McNeill	28	4	6	8	46
Murdoch	26	2	3	7	38
O'Neill	5				5
Price	1		5		6
Turner	7	1	6		14
Young	29	4		7	40

Goalscorers

PLAYER	LEAGUE	CUP COMPETITIONS			TOTAL
		S CUP	SL CUP	ECWC	
Chalmers	28	2	3	5	38
Divers	15	1		3	19
Murdoch	15		1	3	19
Hughes	10		2	5	17
Johnstone	6		2	2	10
Brogan F	5	1			6
Gallagher	2	2	2		6
Lennox	1			1	2
Turner	2				2
Clark	1				1
Jeffrey	1				1
MacKay	1				1
Opps' o.gs.	2				2

Fact File

Goalkeeper Frank Haffey missed a penalty in Celtic's 9-0 defeat of Airdrie in October 1963.

Final Scottish League Div 1 Table

		P	W	D	L	F	A	Pts
1	RANGERS	34	25	5	4	85	31	55
2	KILMARNOCK	34	22	5	7	77	40	49
3	CELTIC	34	19	9	6	89	34	47
4	HEARTS	34	19	9	6	74	40	47
5	DUNFERMLINE ATH	34	18	9	7	64	33	45
6	DUNDEE	34	20	5	9	94	50	45
7	PARTICK T	34	15	5	14	55	54	35
8	DUNDEE U	34	13	8	13	65	49	34
9	ABERDEEN	34	12	8	14	53	53	32
10	HIBERNIAN	34	12	6	16	59	66	30
11	MOTHERWELL	34	9	11	14	51	62	29
12	ST MIRREN	34	12	5	17	44	74	29
13	ST JOHNSTONE	34	11	6	17	54	70	28
14	FALKIRK	34	11	6	17	54	84	28
15	AIRDRIEONIANS	34	11	4	19	52	97	26
16	THIRD LANARK	34	9	7	18	47	74	25
17	Q OF S	34	5	6	23	40	92	16
18	EAST STIRLINGSHIRE	34	5	2	27	37	91	12

Season 1964-65

Scottish League Division 1

DATE	OPPONENTS	SCORE	GOALSCORERS	ATTENDANCE
Aug 19	Motherwell	W 3-1	Murdoch, Chalmers, Lennox	13,000
Sep 5	RANGERS	W 3-1	Chalmers 2, Hughes	58,000
Sep 12	Clyde	D 1-1	Chalmers	22,000
Sep 19	DUNDEE UNITED	D 1-1	Chalmers	26,500
Sep 26	Hearts	L 2-4	Murdoch, Lennox	22,000
Oct 10	Aberdeen	W 3-1	Hughes, Murdoch, Chalmers	12,000
Oct 12	MORTON	W 1-0	Divers	35,000
Oct 17	ST MIRREN	W 4-1	Divers 2, Hughes, Murdoch	23,000
Oct 28	Kilmarnock	L 2-5	Gemmell, Gallagher	16,000
Oct 31	AIRDRIE	W 2-1	Chalmers 2	12,000
Nov 7	St Johnstone	L 0-3		11,000
Nov 14	DUNDEE	L 0-2		14,500
Nov 21	FALKIRK	W 3-0	Hughes 2, Maxwell	16,000
Nov 28	Third Lanark	W 3-0	Murdoch, Hughes, o.g.	11,000
Dec 12	Partick Thistle	W 4-2	Hughes 2, Gallagher, Maxwell	
Dec 19	DUNFERMLINE ATHLETIC	L 1-2	Gallagher	15,000
Dec 26	MOTHERWELL	W 2-0	Hughes 2	9,500
Jan 1	Rangers	L 0-1		64,400
Jan 2	CLYDE	D 1-1	Hughes	13,500
Jan 9	Dundee United	L 1-3	Hughes	18,000
Jan 16	HEARTS	L 1-2	Gemmell	21,000
Jan 23	Morton	D 3-3	Lennox, Hughes, Gemmell	17,000
Jan 30	ABERDEEN	W 8-0	Hughes 5, Auld, Murdoch, Lennox	14,000
Feb 13	St Mirren	W 5-1	Chalmers, Lennox, Brogan J, Hughes, Murdoch	12,000
Feb 27	KILMARNOCK	W 2-0	Chalmers, Hughes	23,000
Mar 10	Airdrie	W 6-0	Auld 5, Hughes	18,000
Mar 13	ST JOHNSTONE	L 0-1		-
Mar 20	Dundee	D 3-3	Lennox 2, Johnstone	18,000
Mar 22	HIBERNIAN	L 2-4	Lennox 2	19,000
Apr 3	THIRD LANARK	W 1-0	o.g.	12,000
Apr 7	Hibernian	W 4-0	Auld 2, Chalmers, Murdoch	16,500
Apr 14	Falkirk	L 2-6	Auld 2	
Apr 17	PARTICK THISTLE	L 1-2	Chalmers	11,500
Apr 28	Dunfermline Athletic	L 1-5	Hughes	10,000

Scottish Cup

Feb 6	St Mirren	(Rd1)	W 3-0	Lennox 2, Chalmers	28,300
Feb 20	Queen's Park	(Rd2)	W 1-0	Lennox	27,343
Mar 6	KILMARNOCK	(QF)	W 3-2	Lennox, Auld, Hughes	47,000
Mar 27	Motherwell	(SF)	D 2-2	Lennox, Auld	52,000
Mar 31	Motherwell	(R)	W 3-0	Chalmers, Hughes, Lennox	58,959
Apr 24	Dunfermline Athletic	(F)	W 3-2	Auld 2, McNeill	108,800

Scottish League Cup

Aug 8	PARTICK THISTLE		D 0-0		29,000
Aug 12	Hearts		W 3-0	Murdoch 2, Chalmers	20,000
Aug 15	KILMARNOCK		W 4-1	Gallagher 2, Chalmers, Johnstone	23,000
Aug 22	Partick Thistle		W 5-1	Chalmers 3, Gallagher, Johnstone	28,000
Aug 26	HEARTS		W 6-1	Murdoch 3, Gallagher 2, Kennedy	28,000
Aug 29	Kilmarnock		L 0-2		18,000
Sep 9	East Fife	(QF/FL)	L 0-2		-
Sep 16	EAST FIFE	(QF/SL)	W 6-0	Chalmers 5, Kennedy	32,000
Sep 29	Morton	(SF)	W 2-0	Lennox, Gallagher	60,000
Oct 24	Rangers	(F)	L 1-2	Johnstone	91,423

Inter-Cities Fairs Cup

Sep 23	LEIXOES	(Rd1/FL)	D 1-1	Murdoch	
Oct 7	LEIXSOES	(Rd1/SL)	W 3-0	Chalmers 2, Murdoch	33,000
Nov 18	Barcelona	(Rd2/FL)	L 1-3	Hughes	25,000
Dec 2	BARCELONA	(Rd2/SL)	D 0-0		43,000

MANAGER: Jimmy McGrory; Jock Stein (from March 1965)

CAPTAIN: Billy McNeill

TOP SCORER: Steve Chalmers

BIGGEST WIN: 8-0 v Aberdeen, 30 January 1965, league

HIGHEST ATTENDANCE: 108,800 v Dunfermline Athletic, 24 April 1965, Scottish Cup

MAJOR TRANSFERS IN: Hugh Maxwell from Falkirk, Ronnie Simpson from Hibernian, Bertie Auld from Birmingham, Joe McBride from Motherwell

MAJOR TRANSFERS OUT: Frank Haffey to Swindon, Duncan MacKay to Third Lanark, Hugh Maxwell to St Johnstone

League & Cup Appearances

PLAYER	LEAGUE	CUP COMPETITIONS			TOTAL
		S CUP	SL CUP	ICFC	
Auld	12	6			18
Brogan	13	3	3		19
Chalmers	23	5	10	4	42
Clark	27	6	9	3	45
Curley	1				1
Cushley	10		4	3	17
Divers	10		2		12
Fallon	26	6	10	2	44
Gallagher	16	3	9	3	31
Gemmell	30	6	10	4	50
Haverty	1				1
Hughes	29	6	4	2	41
Johnstone	24	1	10	4	39
Kennedy	22		8	3	33
Lennox	22	6	6	3	37
MacKay	1				1
McNeill	22	6	6	2	36
Maxwell	8				8
Murdoch	32	6	9	4	51
O'Neill	4			1	5
Simpson	8			2	10
Young	33	6	10	4	53

Goalscorers

PLAYER	LEAGUE	CUP COMPETITIONS			TOTAL
		S CUP	SL CUP	ICFC	
Chalmers	12	2	10	2	26
Hughes	22	2		1	25
Lennox	9	6	1		16
Murdoch	8		5	2	15
Auld	10	4			14
Gallagher	3		6		9
Johnstone	1		3		4
Divers	3				3
Gemmell	3				3
Kennedy			2		2
Maxwell	2				2
Brogan	1				1
McNeill		1			1
Opps' o.gs.	2				2

Fact File

Celtic's 18th Scottish Cup victory came 11 years to the day since their 17th triumph.

Final Scottish League Div 1 Table

		P	W	D	L	F	A	Pts
1	KILMARNOCK	34	22	6	6	62	33	50
2	HEARTS	34	22	6	6	90	49	50
3	DUNFERMLINE ATH	34	22	5	7	83	36	49
4	HIBERNIAN	34	21	4	9	75	47	46
5	RANGERS	34	18	8	8	78	35	44
6	DUNDEE	34	15	10	9	86	63	40
7	CLYDE	34	17	6	11	64	58	40
8	CELTIC	34	16	5	13	76	57	37
9	DUNDEE U	34	15	6	13	59	51	36
10	MORTON	34	13	7	14	54	54	33
11	PARTICK T	34	11	10	13	57	58	32
12	ABERDEEN	34	12	8	14	59	75	32
13	ST JOHNSTONE	34	9	11	14	57	62	29
14	MOTHERWELL	34	10	8	16	45	54	28
15	ST MIRREN	34	9	6	19	38	70	24
16	FALKIRK	34	7	7	20	43	85	21
17	AIRDRIEONIANS	34	5	4	25	48	110	14
18	THIRD LANARK	34	3	1	30	22	99	7

Season 1965-66

Scottish League Division 1

DATE	OPPONENTS	SCORE	GOALSCORERS	ATTENDANCE
Aug 25	Dundee United	W 4-0	Divers, McBride, Young, Gemmell	18,000
Sep 11	CLYDE	W 2-1	Young, Gemmell	26,500
Sep 18	Rangers	L 1-2	Hughes	76,000
Sep 25	ABERDEEN	W 7-1	Lennox 2, Johnstone 2, Hughes, Auld, McBride	20,000
Oct 9	HEARTS	W 5-2	McBride 2, Lennox 2, Gallagher	30,000
Oct 16	Falkirk	W 4-3	Lennox 2, Murdoch, Johnstone	16,000
Oct 27	Dundee	W 2-1	McBride, Lennox	17,000
Oct 30	STIRLING ALBION	W 6-1	Hughes 3, McBride 2, Murdoch	17,000
Nov 6	PARTICK THISTLE	D 1-1	McBride	26,000
Nov 13	St Johnstone	W 4-1	Hughes 2, McBride, Johnstone	11,700
Nov 20	HAMILTON AC.	W 5-0	Auld, Johnstone, Gemmell, Murdoch, McBride	12,000
Nov 27	KILMARNOCK	W 2-1	Hughes, McBride	24,000
Dec 11	HIBERNIAN	W 2-0	Hughes, McBride	23,000
Dec 18	Dunfermline Athletic	W 2-0	Chalmers 2	15,000
Dec 25	MORTON	W 8-1	McBride 3, Chalmers 2, Hughes 2, Murdoch	21,000
Jan 1	Clyde	W 3-1	McBride 2, Lennox	-
Jan 3	RANGERS	W 5-1	Chalmers 3, Gallagher, Murdoch	65,000
Jan 8	DUNDEE UNITED	W 1-0	Gallagher	36,000
Jan 15	Aberdeen	L 1-3	McBride	20,000
Jan 22	MOTHERWELL	W 1-0	McBride	27,000
Jan 29	Hearts	L 2-3	Hughes, McBride	28,000
Feb 12	FALKIRK	W 6-0	McBride 3, Auld 2, Hughes	19,500
Feb 26	Stirling Albion	L 0-1		17,000
Feb 28	DUNDEE	W 5-0	McBride 3, Chalmers, Gemmell	23,000
Mar 12	ST JOHNSTONE	W 3-2	Chalmers 2, McBride	26,000
Mar 19	Hamilton Ac.	W 7-1	Johnstone 2, McBride 2, Chalmers, Lennox, Auld	17,000
Mar 21	Partick Thistle	D 2-2	Lennox, Auld	26,000
Mar 29	Kilmarnock	W 2-0	Lennox 2	25,000
Apr 5	St Mirren	W 3-0	McBride 2, Chalmers	10,000
Apr 9	ST MIRREN	W 5-0	Auld 2, Chalmers 2, Gallagher	25,000
Apr 16	Hibernian	D 0-0		24,000
Apr 30	Morton	W 2-0	Johnstone, Lennox	18,000
May 4	DUNFERMLINE ATHLETIC	W 2-1	Lennox, Johnstone	30,000
May 7	Motherwell	W 1-0	Lennox	20,000

Scottish Cup

Feb 5	STRANRAER	(Rd1) W 4-0	Gallagher, Murdoch, McBride, Lennox	15,500
Feb 23	Dundee	(Rd2) W 2-0	McBride, Chalmers	22,000
Mar 5	Hearts	(QF) D 3-3	Auld, McBride, Chalmers	45,965
Mar 9	Hearts	(R) W 3-1	Johnstone, Murdoch, Chalmers	72,000
Mar 26	Dunfermline Athletic	(SF) W 2-0	Auld, Chalmers	53,900
Apr 23	Rangers	(F) D 0-0		126,599
Apr 27	Rangers	(R) L 0-1		96,862

Scottish League Cup

Aug 14	Dundee United	L 1-2	Auld	25,000
Aug 18	MOTHERWELL	W 1-0	Divers	32,000
Aug 21	DUNDEE	L 0-2		34,000
Aug 28	DUNDEE UNITED	W 3-0	Young, Chalmers, McBride	36,000
Sep 1	Motherwell	W 3-2	Lennox 2, Hughes	22,000
Sep 4	Dundee	W 3-1	Divers, Hughes, McBride	27,000
Sep 15	Raith Rovers	(QF/FL) W 8-1	McBride 3, Hughes 3, Lennox, Johnstone	15,000
Sep 22	RAITH ROVERS	(QF/SL) W 4-0	Auld 2, Murdoch, Chalmers	9,000
Oct 4	Hibernian	(SF) D 2-2	McBride, Lennox	50,000
Oct 18	Hibernian	(R) W 4-0	McBride, Hughes, Lennox, Murdoch	51,423
Oct 23	Rangers	(F) W 2-1	Hughes 2	107,600

European Cup-Winners' Cup

Sep 29	Go Ahead Deventer	(Rd1/FL) W 6-0	Lennox 3, Johnstone 2, Hughes	25,000
Oct 7	GO AHEAD DEVENTER	(Rd1/SL) W 1-0	McBride	20,000
Nov 3	AGF Aarhus	(Rd2/FL) W 1-0	McBride	11,500
Nov 17	AGF AARHUS	(Rd2/SL) W 2-0	McNeill, Johnstone	27,000
Jan 12	DINAMO KIEV	(QF/FL) W 3-0	Murdoch 2, Gemmell	64,000
Jan 26	Dinamo Kiev	(QF/SL) D 1-1	Gemmell	45,000
Apr 14	LIVERPOOL	(SF/FL) W 1-0	Lennox	80,000
Apr 19	Liverpool	(SF/SL) L 0-2		54,000

League & Cup Appearances

PLAYER	LEAGUE	CUP COMPETITIONS			TOTAL
		S CUP	SL CUP	ECWC	
Auld	17	4	4	2	27
Brogan	2				2
Cattanach	1				1
Chalmers	22	6	6	6	40
Clark	34	7	11	8	60
Craig	15	4		4	23
Cushley	12	1	1	2	16
Divers	3		5		8
Fallon	4		7		11
Gallagher	19	3	6	4	32
Gemmell	34	7	11	8	60
hughes	23	6	8	7	44
Johnstone	32	7	8	7	54
Kennedy			1		1
Lennox	24	2	11	6	43
McBride	30	7	7	7	51
McNeill	25	7	10	7	49
Murdoch	31	7	11	8	57
Simpson	30	7	3	8	48
Young	16	2	11	4	33

Goalscorers

PLAYER	LEAGUE	CUP COMPETITIONS			TOTAL
		S CUP	SL CUP	ECWC	
McBride	31	3	7	2	43
Lennox	15	1	5	4	25
Hughes	13		8	1	22
Chalmers	14	4	2		20
Johnstone	9	1	1	3	14
Auld	8	2	3		13
Murdoch	5	2	2	2	11
Gemmell	4			2	6
Gallagher	4	1			5
Divers	1		2		3
Young	2		1		3
McNeill				1	1

Fact File

Irish airline, Aer Lingus, presented the club with a mascot — an Irish wolfhound pup.

MANAGER: Jock Stein
CAPTAIN: Billy McNeill
TOP SCORER: Joe McBride
BIGGEST WIN: 8-1 v Morton, 25 December 1965 league; 8-1 v Raith Rovers, 15 September 1965, Scottish League Cup
HIGHEST ATTENDANCE: 126,599 v Rangers, 23 April 1966, Scottish Cup

Final Scottish League Div 1 Table

		P	W	D	L	F	A	Pts
1	Celtic	34	27	3	4	106	30	57
2	Rangers	34	25	5	4	91	29	55
3	Kilmarnock	34	20	5	9	73	46	45
4	Dunfermline Ath	34	19	6	9	94	55	44
5	Dundee U	34	19	5	10	79	51	43
6	Hibernian	34	16	6	12	81	55	38
7	Hearts	34	13	12	9	56	48	38
8	Aberdeen	34	15	6	13	61	54	36
9	Dundee	34	14	6	14	61	61	34
10	Falkirk	34	15	1	18	48	72	31
11	Clyde	34	13	4	17	62	64	30
12	Partick T	34	10	10	14	55	64	30
13	Motherwell	34	12	4	18	52	69	28
14	St Johnstone	34	9	8	17	58	81	26
15	Stirling A	34	9	8	17	40	68	26
16	St Mirren	34	9	4	21	44	82	22
17	Morton	34	8	5	21	42	84	21
18	Hamilton A	34	3	2	29	27	117	8

The Essential History of Celtic

Season 1966-67

Scottish League Division 1

DATE	OPPONENTS	SCORE	GOALSCORERS	ATTENDANCE
Sep 10	Clyde	W 3-0	Chalmers, McBride, Hughes	16,500
Sep 17	RANGERS	W 2-0	Auld, Murdoch	65,000
Sep 24	Dundee	W 2-1	Lennox, Chalmers	28,500
Oct 1	ST JOHNSTONE	W 6-1	Johnstone 2, Lennox 2, McBride 2	24,000
Oct 8	Hibernian	W 5-3	McBride 4, Chalmers	43,256
Oct 15	AIRDRIE	W 3-0	Lennox 2, McBride	41,000
Oct 24	AYR UNITED	W 5-1	Johnstone 2, Lennox, Hughes, Gemmell	21,000
Nov 2	STIRLING ALBION	W 7-3	McBride 3, Chalmers 2, Johnstone, Auld	21,000
Nov 5	ST MIRREN	D 1-1	Gemmell	24,000
Nov 12	Falkirk	W 3-0	McBride 2, Auld	12,000
Nov 19	Dunfermline Athletic	W 5-4	McBride 2, Murdoch, Johnstone, Auld	22,000
Nov 26	HEARTS	W 3-0	McBride 2, o.g.	40,000
Dec 3	Kilmarnock	D 0-0		27,000
Dec 10	MOTHERWELL	W 4-2	Chalmers 3, Murdoch	40,000
Dec 17	PARTICK THISTLE	W 6-2	Wallace 2, Chalmers 2, Murdoch, McBride	25,000
Dec 24	Aberdeen	D 1-1	Lennox	31,000
Dec 31	Dundee United	L 2-3	Lennox, Wallace	25,000
Jan 7	DUNDEE	W 5-1	Wallace 2, Johnstone, Gallagher, o.g.	37,000
Jan 11	CLYDE	W 5-1	Chalmers 2, Gallagher, Gemmell, Lennox	38,000
Jan 14	St Johnstone	W 4-0	Johnstone 2, Chalmers, Lennox	19,000
Jan 21	HIBERNIAN	W 2-0	Wallace, Chalmers	41,000
Feb 4	Airdrie	W 3-0	Johnstone, Chalmers, Auld	23,000
Feb 11	Ayr United	W 5-0	Chalmers 3, Johnstone, Hughes	19,000
Feb 25	Stirling Albion	D 1-1	Hughes	16,000
Mar 4	St Mirren	W 5-0	Wallace 2, Lennox, Hughes, Gemmell	18,000
Mar 18	DUNFERMLINE ATHLETIC	W 3-2	Chalmers, Gemmell, Wallace	41,000
Mar 20	FALKIRK	W 5-0	Chalmers 2, Auld, Hughes, Gemmell	25,000
Mar 25	Hearts	W 3-0	Auld, Wallace, Gemmell	-
Mar 27	Partick Thistle	W 4-1	Chalmers 2, Lennox, Wallace	30,000
Apr 8	Motherwell	W 2-0	Wallace, Gemmell	21,000
Apr 19	ABERDEEN	D 0-0		33,000
May 3	DUNDEE UNITED	L 2-3	Gemmell, Wallace	44,000
May 6	Rangers	D 2-2	Johnstone 2	78,000
May 15	KILMARNOCK	W 2-0	Lennox, Wallace	21,000

Scottish Cup

Jan 28	ARBROATH	(Rd1)	W 4-0	Murdoch, Gemmell, Chalmers, Auld	31,000
Feb 18	ELGIN CITY	(Rd2)	W 7-0	Lennox 3, Wallace 2, Chalmers, Hughes	34,000
Mar 11	QUEEN'S PARK	(QF)	W 5-3	Gemmell, Chalmers, Wallace, Murdoch, Lennox	34,000
Apr 1	Clyde	(SF)	D 0-0		56,704
Apr 5	Clyde	(R)	W 2-0	Lennox, Auld	55,138
Apr 29	Aberdeen	(F)	W 2-0	Wallace 2	126,102

Scottish League Cup

Aug 13	Hearts	W 2-0	McBride 2	25,000
Aug 17	CLYDE	W 6-0	McBride 3, Lennox 2, Chalmers	30,000
Aug 20	ST MIRREN	W 8-2	McBride 4, Lennox 2, Auld	31,500
Aug 27	HEARTS	W 3-0	McBride 2, Chalmers	46,000
Aug 31	Clyde	W 3-1	McBride 2, Gemmell	18,000
Sep 3	St Mirren	W 1-0	Murdoch	20,000
Sep 14	DUNFERMLINE ATHLETIC	(QF/FL) W 6-3	Auld 2, McNeill, Hughes, McBride, Johnstone	36,000
Sep 21	Dunfermline Athletic	(QF/SL) W 3-1	Chalmers 2, McNeill	20,000
Oct 17	Airdrie	(SF) W 2-0	Murdoch, McBride	36,930
Oct 29	Rangers	(F) W 1-0	Lennox	94,532

European Cup

Sep 28	FC ZURICH	(Rd1/FL) W 2-0	Gemmell, McBride	50,000
Oct 5	FC Zurich	(Rd1/SL) W 3-0	Gemmell 2, Chalmers	23,000
Nov 30	Nantes	(Rd2/FL) W 3-1	McBride, Lennox, Chalmers	25,000
Dec 7	NANTES	(Rd2/SL) W 3-1	Johnstone, Chalmers, Lennox	41,000
Mar 1	Vojvodina	(QF/FL) L 0-1		30,000
Mar 8	VOJVODINA	(QF/SL) W 2-0	Chalmers, McNeill	75,000
Apr 12	DUKLA PRAGUE	(SF/FL) W 3-1	Wallace 2, Johnstone	75,000
Apr 25	Dukla Prague	(SF/SL) D 0-0		22,000
May 25	Internazionale	(F) W 2-1	Gemmell, Chalmers	55,000

League & Cup Appearances

PLAYER	LEAGUE	CUP COMPETITIONS			TOTAL
		S CUP	SL CUP	E CUP	
Auld	27	5	9	8	49
Brogan	0 (1)				0 (1)
Cattanach		2			2
Chalmers	28 (1)	6	9 (1)	9	53 (2)
Clark	34	6	10	9	59
Craig	17	4	1	5	27
Cushley	1				1
Fallon	1				1
Gallagher	11	3	1	2	17
Gemmell	34	6	10	9	59
Hughes	19	3 (1)	4	5	31 (1)
Johnstone	25	5	10	9	49
Lennox	26 (1)	5	7	7	45 (1)
McBride	14		10	2	26
McNeill	33	6	10	9	58
Murdoch	31	4	10	9	54
O'Neill	18		9 (1)	4	31 (1)
Simpson	33	6	10	9	58
Wallace	21	5 (1)		3	29 (1)

Goalscorers

PLAYER	LEAGUE	CUP COMPETITIONS			TOTAL
		S CUP	SL CUP	E CUP	
Chalmers	23	3	5	5	36
McBride	18		15	2	35
Lennox	13	5	5	2	25
Wallace	14	5		2	21
Gemmell	9	2	1	4	16
Johnstone	13		1	2	16
Auld	7	2	3		12
Hughes	6	1	1		8
Murdoch	4	2	2		8
McNeill			2	1	3
Gallagher	2				2
Opps' o.gs.	2				2

Fact File

Celtic won all five competitions they entered. In addition to those on this page they won the Glasgow Cup.

MANAGER: Jock Stein
CAPTAIN: Billy McNeill
TOP SCORER: Steve Chalmers
BIGGEST WIN: 7-0 v Elgin City, 18 February 1967, Scottish Cup
HIGHEST ATTENDANCE: 126,102 v Aberdeen, 29 April 1967, Scottish Cup
MAJOR TRANSFERS IN: Willie Wallace from Hearts

Final Scottish League Div 1 Table

		P	W	D	L	F	A	Pts
1	CELTIC	34	26	6	2	111	33	58
2	RANGERS	34	24	7	3	92	31	55
3	CLYDE	34	20	6	8	64	48	46
4	ABERDEEN	34	17	8	9	72	38	42
5	HIBERNIAN	34	19	4	11	72	49	42
6	DUNDEE	34	16	9	9	74	51	41
7	KILMARNOCK	34	16	8	10	59	46	40
8	DUNFERMLINE ATH	34	14	10	10	72	52	38
9	DUNDEE U	34	14	9	11	68	62	37
10	MOTHERWELL	34	10	11	13	59	60	31
11	HEARTS	34	11	8	15	39	48	30
12	PARTICK T	34	9	12	13	49	68	30
13	AIRDRIEONIANS	34	11	6	17	41	53	28
14	FALKIRK	34	11	4	19	33	70	26
15	ST JOHNSTONE	34	10	5	19	53	73	25
16	STIRLING A	34	5	9	20	31	85	19
17	ST MIRREN	34	4	7	23	25	81	15
18	AYR U	34	1	7	26	20	86	9

Season 1967-68

Scottish League Division 1

DATE	OPPONENTS	SCORE	GOALSCORERS	ATTENDANCE
Sep 9	CLYDE	W 3-0	McMahon, Lennox, Auld	37,000
Sep 16	Rangers	L 0-1		90,000
Sep 23	ST JOHNSTONE	D 1-1	Murdoch	31,000
Sep 30	Stirling Albion	W 4-0	Auld 2, Wallace, Lennox	16,000
Oct 7	HIBERNIAN	W 4-0	Murdoch 2, Johnstone, Wallace	40,000
Oct 14	Partick Thistle	W 5-1	Lennox 4, McNeill	30,000
Oct 24	MOTHERWELL	W 4-2	Wallace, McNeill, Lennox, Chalmers	23,000
Nov 11	Airdrie	W 2-0	Brogan, Murdoch	18,000
Nov 15	KILMARNOCK	W 3-0	Auld, Hughes, Chalmers	30,000
Nov 18	FALKIRK	W 3-0	Chalmers 2, Hughes	35,000
Nov 25	Raith Rovers	W 2-0	Gemmell, Wallace	18,000
Dec 2	DUNDEE UNITED	D 1-1	Murdoch	37,000
Dec 9	HEARTS	W 3-1	Chalmers, Lennox, o.g.	35,000
Dec 16	Dundee	W 5-4	Wallace 2, McNeill, Lennox, Johnstone	16,000
Dec 23	Morton	W 4-0	McBride 3, Hughes	18,000
Dec 30	DUNFERMLINE ATHLETIC	W 3-2	Chalmers 2, McNeill	36,000
Jan 1	Clyde	W 3-2	Chalmers 2, McBride	15,000
Jan 2	RANGERS	D 2-2	Auld, Murdoch	75,000
Jan 20	Hibernian	W 2-0	Lennox, o.g.	38,077
Feb 3	PARTICK THISTLE	W 4-1	Lennox 2, Gemmell, o.g.	27,000
Feb 10	Motherwell	W 1-0	Hughes	20,000
Feb 14	STIRLING ALBION	W 2-0	Gemmell, Wallace	17,000
Mar 2	Kilmarnock	W 6-0	Lennox 4, Wallace, Quinn	14,000
Mar 6	ABERDEEN	W 4-1	Lennox 3, McNeill	28,000
Mar 13	AIRDRIE	W 4-0	Wallace 3, Lennox	17,000
Mar 16	Falkirk	W 3-0	Gemmell, Wallace, Lennox	-
Mar 23	RAITH ROVERS	W 5-0	Wallace 3, Hughes, Lennox	22,500
Mar 25	St Johnstone	W 6-1	Lennox 4, Johnstone, Wallace	12,000
Mar 30	Dundee United	W 5-0	Lennox 2, Johnstone, Wallace, Cattanach	20,000
Apr 6	Hearts	W 2-0	Johnstone, Lennox	27,000
Apr 10	Aberdeen	W 1-0	Lennox	25,000
Apr 13	DUNDEE	W 5-2	Hughes 2, Lennox 2, o.g.	41,500
Apr 20	MORTON	W 2-1	Wallace, Lennox	51,000
Apr 30	Dunfermline Athletic	W 2-1	Lennox 2	30,000

Scottish Cup

Jan 27	DUNFERMLINE ATHLETIC	(Rd1) L 0-2		47,000

Scottish League Cup

Aug 12	DUNDEE UNITED	W 1-0	Johnstone	54,000
Aug 16	Rangers	D 1-1	Gemmell	94,168
Aug 19	ABERDEEN	W 3-1	Gemmell, Lennox, Auld	50,000
Aug 26	Dundee United	W 1-0	Lennox	30,000
Aug 30	RANGERS	W 3-1	Wallace, Murdoch, Lennox	75,000
Sep 2	Aberdeen	W 5-1	Gemmell, McMahon, Johnstone, Auld, Craig	23,000
Sep 13	AYR UNITED	(QF/FL) W 6-2	Lennox 2, Johnstone 2, Murdoch, McMahon	26,000
Sep 27	Ayr United	(QF/SL) W 2-0	Brogan, Wallace	-
Oct 11	Morton	(SF) W 7-1	Hughes 2, Wallace, Craig 2, Johnstone, Lennox	45,662
Oct 28	Dundee	(F) W 5-2	Chalmers 2, Hughes, Lennox, Wallace	66,600

European Cup

Sep 20	DINAMO KIEV	(Rd1/FL) L 1-2	Lennox	54,000
Oct 4	Dinamo Kiev	(Rd1/SL) D 1-1	Lennox	85,000

World Club Championship

Oct 18	RACING CLUB	(FL) W 1-0	McNeill	90,000
Nov 1	Racing Club	(SL) L 1-2	Gemmell	120,000
Nov 5	Racing Club	(Play-off) L 0-1		75,000

MANAGER: Jock Stein

CAPTAIN: Billy McNeill

TOP SCORER: Bobby Lennox

BIGGEST WIN: 7-1 v Morton, 11 October 1967, Scottish League Cup

HIGHEST ATTENDANCE: 120,000 v Racing Club, 1 November 1967, World Club Championship

---

League & Cup Appearances

PLAYER	LEAGUE	CUP COMPETITIONS				TOTAL
		S CUP	SL CUP	E CUP	WCC	
Auld	19 (1)	1	8 (1)	2	2	32 (2)
Brogan	18 (1)	1	1			20 (1)
Cattanach	4 (2)	1	1 (1)			7 (3)
Chalmers	13 (3)	0 (1)	5	1	1	20 (4)
Clark	18		9	2	3	32
Connelly	0 (1)					0 (1)
Craig	22		8	2	3	35
Fallon	1		1		2	4
Gallagher	13		2			15
Gemmell	34	1	9	2	3	49
Hay	0 (1)					0 (1)
Hughes	31 (1)	1	4	1	2	39 (1)
Johnstone	29	1	8	2	3	43
Lennox	28		9	2	3	42
Macari	0 (1)		0 (1)			0 (1)
McBride	4 (3)	1	1			6 (3)
McMahon	2		2			4
McNeill	34	1	10	2	3	50
Murdoch	34	1	9	2	3	49
O'Neill	6 (1)		3 (1)		1	10 (2)
Quinn	0 (2)					0 (2)
Shevlane	2		1			3
Simpson	33	1	9	2	1	46
Wallace	29 (1)	1	10	2	3	45 (1)

Goalscorers

PLAYER	LEAGUE	CUP COMPETITIONS				TOTAL
		S CUP	SL CUP	E CUP	WCC	
Lennox	32		7	2		41
Wallace	21		4			25
Chalmers	9		2			11
Hughes	7		3			10
Johnstone	5		5			10
Gemmell	4		3		1	8
Murdoch	6		2			8
Auld	5		2			7
McNeill	5				1	6
McBride	4					4
Craig			3			3
McMahon	1		2			3
Brogan	1		1			2
Cattanach	1					1
Quinn	1					1
Opps' o.gs.	4					4

Fact File

Celtic set a club record by scoring over 100 goals for the third successive season.

Final Scottish League Div 1 Table

		P	W	D	L	F	A	Pts
1	CELTIC	34	30	3	1	106	24	63
2	RANGERS	34	28	5	1	93	34	61
3	HIBERNIAN	34	20	5	9	67	49	45
4	DUNFERMLINE ATH	34	17	5	12	64	41	39
5	ABERDEEN	34	16	5	13	63	48	37
6	MORTON	34	15	6	13	57	53	36
7	KILMARNOCK	34	13	8	13	59	57	34
8	CLYDE	34	15	4	15	55	55	34
9	DUNDEE	34	13	7	14	62	59	33
10	PARTICK T	34	12	7	15	51	67	31
11	DUNDEE U	34	10	11	13	53	72	31
12	HEARTS	34	13	4	17	56	61	30
13	AIRDRIEONIANS	34	10	9	15	45	58	29
14	ST JOHNSTONE	34	10	7	17	43	52	27
15	FALKIRK	34	7	12	15	36	50	26
16	RAITH R	34	9	7	18	58	86	25
17	MOTHERWELL	34	6	7	21	40	66	19
18	STIRLING A	34	4	4	26	29	105	12

Season 1968-69

Scottish League Division 1

DATE	OPPONENTS	SCORE	GOALSCORERS	ATTENDANCE
Sep 7	Clyde	W 3-0	Brogan, Lennox, Gemmell	26,000
Sep 14	RANGERS	L 2-4	Wallace 2	75,000
Sep 21	Dunfermline Athletic	D 1-1	Johnstone	25,000
Sep 28	ABERDEEN	W 2-1	Connelly, Lennox	37,000
Oct 5	DUNDEE UNITED	W 2-0	Murdoch, Gemmell	46,000
Oct 12	Hearts	W 1-0	Chalmers	34,000
Oct 19	ST JOHNSTONE	W 2-1	Lennox, McNeill	37,000
Oct 26	Morton	D 1-1	McBride	23,000
Nov 2	DUNDEE	W 3-1	Chalmers 2, Johnstone	37,000
Nov 9	Arbroath	W 5-0	Chalmers 3, McNeill, Wallace	-
Nov 16	RAITH ROVERS	W 2-0	Murdoch 2	31,000
Nov 23	Partick Thistle	W 4-0	Hughes 2, Callaghan, Lennox	29,300
Nov 30	Hibernian	W 5-2	Hughes 2, Gemmell, McNeill, Lennox	34,988
Dec 7	ST MIRREN	W 5-0	Chalmers 2, Johnstone, Hughes, Gemmell	47,000
Dec 14	Falkirk	D 0-0		17,000
Dec 21	KILMARNOCK	D 1-1	Chalmers	40,000
Dec 28	Airdrie	D 0-0		22,000
Jan 1	CLYDE	W 5-0	Callaghan 2, Gemmell, Wallace, Lennox	31,000
Jan 2	Rangers	L 0-1		85,000
Jan 4	DUNFERMLINE ATHLETIC	W 3-1	Wallace 2, Lennox	43,500
Jan 11	Aberdeen	W 3-1	Hughes, Wallace, o.g.	31,000
Jan 18	Dundee United	W 3-1	Lennox, Hughes, McMahon	23,000
Feb 1	HEARTS	W 5-0	Lennox, Wallace, Murdoch, Johnstone, Brogan	37,000
Mar 5	ARBROATH	W 7-1	Wallace 3, Chalmers 2, Johnstone, Hughes	20.000
Mar 8	Raith Roves	W 3-1	Wallace 2, Auld	16,000
Mar 15	PARTICK THISTLE	W 1-0	Hughes	29,000
Mar 24	HIBERNIAN	D 1-1	Wallace	30,000
Mar 29	St Mirren	W 3-0	Craig, Hughes, Hood	24,000
Apr 1	St Johnstone	W 3-2	Wallace, Gemmell, Hood	13,000
Apr 9	FALKIRK	W 5-2	Wallace 2, Lennox 2, Hood	24,000
Apr 19	AIRDRIE	D 2-2	Gemmell, Lennox	34,000
Apr 1	Kilmarnock	D 2-2	Gemmell, o.g.	18,000
Apr 28	MORTON	L 2-4	Wallace, Hood	31,000
Apr 30	Dundee	W 2-1	Macari, Hood	-

Scottish Cup

Jan 25	Partick Thistle	(Rd1) D 3-3	Hughes, Wallace, Murdoch	35,867
Jan 29	PARTICK THISTLE	(R) W 8-1	Callaghan 2, McNeill, Johnstone, Wallace 2, Lennox, Hughes	48,000
Feb 12	Clyde	(Rd2) D 0-0		25,000
Feb 24	CLYDE	(R) W 3-0	Chalmers, Hughes, Murdoch	38,000
Mar 1	ST JOHNSTONE	(QF) W 3-2	Hughes, Lennox, Chalmers	39,000
Mar 22	Morton	(SF) W 4-1	Wallace, McNeill, Chalmers, Johnstone	48,349
Apr 26	Rangers	(F) W 4-0	McNeill, Lennox, Connelly, Chalmers	132,870

Scottish League Cup

Aug 10	Rangers	W 2-0	Wallace 2	80,000
Aug 14	MORTON	W 4-1	Wallace, Hughes, Murdoch, Gemmell	41,000
Aug 17	PARTICK THISTLE	W 4-0	Wallace 4	46,000
Aug 24	RANGERS	W 1-0	Wallace	75,000
Aug 28	Morton	W 3-0	Wallace, Lennox, Hughes	25,000
Aug 31	Partick Thistle	W 6-1	Lennox 5, o.g.	25,000
Sep 11	HAMILTON AC.	(QF/FL) W10-0	Chalmers 5, Lennox 5	26,000
Sep 25	Hamilton Ac.	(QF/SL) W 4-2	McBride 2, McMahon, Clark	4,000
Oct 9	Clyde	(SF) W 1-0	Connelly	34,676
Apr 5	Hibernian	(F) W 6-2	Lennox 3, Wallace, Auld, Craig	74,000

European Cup

Sep 18	St Etienne	(Rd1/FL) L 0-2		34,000
Oct 2	ST ETIENNE	(Rd1/SL) W 4-0	Gemmell, Craig, Chalmers, McBride	75,000
Nov 13	RED STAR BELGRADE	(Rd2/FL) W 5-1	Johnstone 2, Murdoch,	67,000
Nov 27	Red Star Belgrade	(Rd2/SL) D 1-1	Wallace	40,000
Feb 19	AC Milan	(QF/FL) D 0-0		72,402
Mar 12	AC MILAN	(QF/SL) L 0-1		75,000

MANAGER: Jock Stein **CAPTAIN:** Billy McNeill
TOP SCORER: Willie Wallace

League & Cup Appearances

PLAYER	LEAGUE	CUP COMPETITIONS			TOTAL
		S CUP	SL CUP	E CUP	
Auld	9 (4)	2 (1)	1 (1)	0 (2)	12 (8)
Brogan	30	5	9	6	50
Callaghan	12 (3)	3 (2)			15 (5)
Cattanach	1				1
Chalmers	17 (4)	5 (1)	3	4	29 (5)
Clark	9 (1)	1 (1)	2 (2)	4	16 (4)
Connelly	6 (1)	1	7 (1)	2	16 (2)
Craig	32	6	5	6	49
Dalglish			0 (1)		0 (1)
Fallon	22	4	3	4	33
Gallagher	1				1
Gemmell	31	7	8	5	51
Gorman			1		1
Hay	1	1	1		2
Hood	7				7
Hughes	27	5	8	6	46
Johnstone	30 (1)	6	7 (1)	5	48 (2)
Lennox	27 (1)	6	9	4	46 (1)
Macari	1		2 (1)		3 (1)
McBride	4		3		7
McMahon	0 (1)		1		1 (1)
McNeill	34	7	9	6	56
Murdoch	30	7	8	5	50
O'Neill	4	1	6	1	12
Quinn			1		1
Simpson	12	3	6	2	23
Wallace	29 (2)	7	8	5 (1)	49 (3)
Wraith			1		1

Goalscorers

PLAYER	LEAGUE	CUP COMPETITIONS			TOTAL
		S CUP	SL CUP	E CUP	
Wallace	18	4	10	2	34
Lennox	12	3	14	1	30
Chalmers	11	4	5	1	21
Hughes	10	4	2		16
Gemmell	8		1	1	10
Johnstone	5	2		2	9
Murdoch	4	2	1	1	8
McNeill	3	3			6
Callaghan	3	2			5
Hood	5				5
McBride	1		2	1	4
Connelly	1	1	1		3
Craig	1		1	1	3
Auld	1		1		2
Brogan	2				2
McMahon	1		1		2
Clark			1		1
Macari	1				1
Opps' o.gs.	2		1		3

Fact File

The 10-0 victory over Hamilton on 11 September 1968 was Celtic's biggest win for 73 years.

Final Scottish League Div 1 Table

		P	W	D	L	F	A	Pts
1	CELTIC	34	23	8	3	89	32	54
2	RANGERS	34	21	7	6	81	32	49
3	DUNFERMLINE ATH	34	19	7	8	63	45	45
4	KILMARNOCK	34	15	14	5	50	32	44
5	DUNDEE U	34	17	9	8	61	49	43
6	ST JOHNSTONE	34	16	5	13	66	59	37
7	AIRDRIEONIANS	34	13	11	10	46	44	37
8	HEARTS	34	14	8	12	52	54	36
9	DUNDEE	34	10	12	12	47	48	32
10	MORTON	34	12	8	14	58	68	32
11	ST MIRREN	34	11	10	13	40	54	32
12	HIBERNIAN	34	12	7	15	60	59	31
13	CLYDE	34	9	13	12	35	50	31
14	PARTICK T	34	9	10	15	39	53	28
15	ABERDEEN	34	9	8	17	50	59	26
16	RAITH R	34	8	5	21	45	67	21
17	FALKIRK	34	5	8	21	33	69	18
18	ARBROATH	34	5	6	23	41	82	16

Season 1969-70

Scottish League Division 1

DATE	OPPONENTS	SCORE	GOALSCORERS	ATTENDANCE
Aug 30	ST JOHNSTONE	D 2-2	Chalmers, Hood	60,000
Sep 3	Kilmarnock	W 4-2	Wallace 2, Lennox 2	25,000
Sep 6	Dunfermline Athletic	L 1-2	Gemmell	25,000
Sep 13	HIBERNIAN	L 1-2	Johnstone	45,000
Sep 20	Rangers	W 1-0	Hood	75,000
Sep 27	Clyde	W 2-1	Lennox 2	35,000
Oct 4	RAITH ROVERS	W 7-1	Johnstone 2, Lennox 2, Wallace, Callaghan, Hughes	32,000
Oct 11	Airdrie	W 2-0	Chalmers, Wallace	20,000
Oct 29	Aberdeen	W 3-2	Murdoch, Johnstone, Brogan	25,000
Nov 1	Ayr United	W 4-2	Johnstone 2, Murdoch 2	20,000
Nov 8	HEARTS	L 0-2		35,000
Nov 15	Motherwell	W 2-1	Hood, Hughes	23,000
Nov 29	Morton	W 3-0	Macari, Hood, Wallace	22,000
Dec 1	ST MIRREN	W 2-0	Macari 2	23,000
Dec 7	DUNDEE	W 1-0	Gemmell	31,000
Dec 14	St Johnstone	W 4-1	Wallace 2, Gemmell, Hood	15,500
Dec 17	DUNDEE UNITED	W 7-2	Wallace 2, Auld, Hood, Gemmell, Hughes, Murdoch	26,000
Dec 20	KILMARNOCK	W 3-1	Hughes 2, Gemmell	35,000
Dec 27	PARTICK THISTLE	W 8-1	Hughes 3, Wallace 2, Auld, McNeill, o.g.	30,000
Jan 1	Clyde	W 2-0	Hughes, Macari	26,000
Jan 3	RANGERS	D 0-0		72,000
Jan 17	Hibernian	W 2-1	McNeill, Hughes	40,839
Jan 31	DUNFERMLINE ATHLETIC	W 3-1	Wallace, Macari, Lennox	36,000
Feb 16	Partick Thistle	W 5-1	Gemmell 2, Hood, Johnstone, Macari	20,000
Feb 25	Raith Rovers	W 2-0	McNeill, Gemmell	11,000
Feb 28	AIRDRIE	W 4-1	Johnstone 2, Lennox, Wallace	31,000
Mar 7	Dundee United	W 2-0	McNeill 2	20,500
Mar 10	MORTON	W 4-0	Auld, Macari, Lennox, o.g.	21,000
Mar 21	AYR UNITED	W 3-0	Wallace 2, Lennox	27,000
Mar 25	ABERDEEN	L 1-2	Gemmell	33,000
Mar 28	Hearts	D 0-0		26,000
Apr 4	MOTHERWELL	W 6-1	Lennox 3, Wallace, Johnstone, Murdoch	30,000
Apr 6	Dundee	W 2-1	Auld, Lennox	13,000
Apr 18	St Mirren	W 3-2	Hood, Davidson, Callaghan	25,000

Scottish Cup

Jan 24	DUNFERMLINE ATHLETIC	(Rd1) W 2-1	Hughes, Hood	50,000
Feb 7	DUNDEE UNITED	(Rd2) W 4-0	Hughes 2, Macari, Wallace	45,000
Feb 21	RANGERS	(QF) W 3-1	Lennox, Hay, Johnstone	75,000
Mar 14	Dundee	(SF) W 2-1	Macari, Lennox	64,546
Apr 11	Aberdeen	(F) L 1-3	Lennox	108,434

Scottish League Cup

Aug 9	AIRDRIE	W 6-1	Hughes 2, Connelly, Wallace, Hood, Gemmell	40,000
Aug 13	Rangers	L 1-2	Hood	71,645
Aug 16	RAITH ROVERS	W 5-0	Wallace 2, Hood, McNeill, Hughes	37,000
Aug 20	RANGERS	W 1-0	Gemmell	70,000
Aug 23	Airdrie	W 3-0	Wallace, Lennox, McNeill	21,000
Aug 27	Raith Rovers	W 5-2	Chalmers 2, Hood, 2, Brogan	17,000
Sep 10	Aberdeen	(QF/FL) D 0-0		32,000
Sep 24	ABERDEEN	(QF/SL) W 2-1	Lennox, Wallce	47,000
Oct 8	Ayr United	(SF) D 3-3	Hughes, Gemmell, Auld	33,110
Oct 13	Ayr United	(R) W 2-1	Hood, Chalmers	47,831
Oct 25	St Johnstone	(F) W 1-0	Auld	73,067

European Cup

Sep 17	Basle	(Rd1/FL) D 0-0		38,000
Oct 1	BASLE	(Rd1/SL) W 2-0	Hood, Gemmell	52,000
Nov 12	BENFICA	(Rd2/FL) W 3-0	Gemmell, Wallace, Hood	80,000
Nov 26	Benfica	(Rd2/SL) L 0-3*		37,000
Mar 4	FIORENTINA	(QF/FL) W 3-0	Auld, Wallace, o.g.	80,000
Mar 18	Fiorentina	(QF/SL) L 0-1		50,000
Apr 1	Leeds United	(SF/FL) W 1-0	Connelly	45,505
Apr 15	LEEDS UNITED	(SF/SL) W 2-1	Hughes, Murdoch	136,505
May 6	Feyenoord	(F) L 1-2	Gemmell	53,187

*Celtic won on toss of a coin.

MANAGER: Jock Stein **CAPTAIN:** Billy McNeill

TOP SCORER: Willie Wallace

BIGGEST WIN: 8-1 v Partick Thistle, 27 December 1969, league

HIGHEST ATTENDANCE: 136,505 v Leeds, 15 April 1970, European Cup

MAJOR TRANSFERS IN: Evan Williams from Wolverhampton

League & Cup Appearances

PLAYER	LEAGUE	CUP COMPETITIONS			TOTAL
		S CUP	SL CUP	E CUP	
Auld	15 (3)	1 (1)	2 (3)	7	25 (7)
Brogan	27 (1)	5	5 (2)	7	44 (3)
Callaghan	12 (2)	1	4	2 (1)	19 (3)
Cattanach	0 (1)				0 (1)
Chalmers	5		5 (1)	2	12 (1)
Clark	9		9	3	21
Connelly	7	1	4	3 (2)	15 (2)
Craig	19 (4)	1 (2)	6	2	28 (6)
Dalglish	2		2		4
Davidson	1				1
Fallon	16		10	4	30
Gemmell	29	5	10	9	53
Hay	26 (1)	5	6	7	44 (1)
Hood	25 (2)	2 (1)	11	2 (3)	40 (6)
Hughes	20 (1)	4	8	6	38 (1)
Johnstone	27	4	4 (2)	9	44 (2)
Lennox	19 (1)	4	8	7	38 (1)
Macari	12 (3)	2			14 (3)
McNeill	31	5	11	9	56
Murdoch	24 (2)	5	6	7	42 (2)
Quinn	1				1
Simpson	2		1		3
Wallace	29 (1)	5	9 (1)	8	51 (2)
Williams	16	5		5	26

Goalscorers

PLAYER	LEAGUE	CUP COMPETITIONS			TOTAL
		S CUP	SL CUP	E CUP	
Wallace	16	1	5	2	24
Lennox	14	3	2		19
Hughes	10	3	4	1	18
Hood	8	1	6	2	17
Gemmell	9		3	3	15
Johnstone	10	1			11
Macari	7	2			9
Auld	4		2	1	7
McNeill	5		2		7
Murdoch	5			1	6
Chalmers	2		3		5
Brogan	1		1		2
Callaghan	2				2
Connelly			1	1	2
Davidson	1				1
Hay		1			1
Opps' o.gs.	2			1	3

Fact File

By overcoming Fiorentina, Celtic became the first British side to beat an Italian side over two legs in the European Cup.

Final Scottish League Div 1 Table

		P	W	D	L	F	A	Pts
1	CELTIC	34	27	3	4	96	33	57
2	RANGERS	34	19	7	8	67	40	45
3	HIBERNIAN	34	19	6	9	65	40	44
4	HEARTS	34	13	12	9	50	36	38
5	DUNDEE U	34	16	6	12	62	64	38
6	DUNDEE	34	15	6	13	49	44	36
7	KILMARNOCK	34	13	10	11	62	57	36
8	ABERDEEN	34	14	7	13	55	45	35
9	MORTON	34	13	9	12	52	52	35
10	DUNFERMLINE ATH	34	15	5	14	45	45	35
11	MOTHERWELL	34	11	10	13	49	51	32
12	AIRDRIEONIANS	34	12	8	14	59	64	32
13	ST JOHNSTONE	34	11	9	14	50	62	31
14	AYR U	34	12	6	16	37	52	30
15	ST MIRREN	34	8	9	17	39	54	25
16	CLYDE	34	9	7	18	34	56	25
17	RAITH R	34	5	11	18	32	67	21
18	PARTICK T	34	5	7	22	41	82	17

Season 1970-71

Scottish League Division 1

DATE	OPPONENTS	SCORE	GOALSCORERS	ATTENDANCE
Aug 29	MORTON	W 2-0	Lennox 2	35,000
Sep 5	Clyde	W 5-0	Macari 2, Hay, Davison, o.g.	20,000
Sep 12	RANGERS	W 2-0	Murdoch, Hughes	73,000
Sep 19	Hibernian	L 0-2		36,000
Sep 26	DUNDEE	W 3-0	Johnstone 2, Macari	28,000
Oct 3	Dunfermline Athletic	W 2-0	Wallace, Macari	15,000
Oct 10	ST JOHNSTONE	W 1-0	Wallace	37,000
Oct 17	Airdrie	W 3-1	Hood 2, Lennox	20,000
Oct 28	HEARTS	W 3-2	Wallace 2, Hood	18,000
Oct 31	Motherwell	W 5-0	Hood 3, Johnstone, Connelly	15,000
Nov 7	COWDENBEATH	W 3-0	Connelly 2, Wallace	21,000
Nov 14	KILMARNOCK	W 3-0	Murdoch, Johnstone, Wallace	27,000
Nov 21	Falkirk	D 0-0		20,000
Nov 28	ST MIRREN	W 3-0	Davidson 2, Gemmell	25,000
Dec 5	Dundee United	W 2-1	Davidson, o.g.	20,000
Dec 12	ABERDEEN	L 0-1		63,000
Dec 19	Ayr United	W 2-1	Hood, Hughes	15,000
Dec 26	Morton	W 3-0	Chalmers, Wallace, Lennox	18,000
Jan 2	Rangers	D 1-1	Johnstone	80,000
Jan 9	HIBERNIAN	W 2-1	Hood, Callaghan	28,000
Jan 16	Dundee	W 8-1	Johnstone 2, Wallace 2, Hood 2, Callaghan, o.g.	20,000
Jan 22	DUNFERMLINE ATHLETIC	W 1-0	Wallace	25,000
Feb 6	St Johnstone	L 2-3	Wallace, Hood	17,000
Feb 20	AIRDRIE	W 4-1	Wallace 2, Hood, Macari	27,000
Feb 27	Hearts	D 1-1	Hood	25,000
Mar 13	Cowdenbeath	W 5-1	Hood 2, McNeill, Hughes, Lennox	10,000
Mar 20	Kilmarnock	W 4-1	Hood 2, Davidson, Hughes	16,000
Mar 27	FALKIRK	W 4-0	Hood 2, Wallace, Hughes	22,000
Apr 10	DUNDEE UNITED	D 1-1	Wallace	30,000
Apr 12	MOTHERWELL	W 3-0	Johnstone, Wallace, Hood	23,000
Apr 17	Aberdeen	D 1-1	Hood	35,000
Apr 27	St Mirren	D 2-2	Lennox, Hood	20,000
Apr 29	AYR UNITED	W 2-0	Lennox, Wallace	25,000
May 1	CLYDE	W 6-1	Lennox 3, Wallace 2, Chalmers	35,000

Scottish Cup

Jan 23	QUEEN OF THE SOUTH	(Rd3) W 5-1	Hood 2, McNeill, Wallace, Callaghan	25,000
Feb 13	DUNFERMLINE ATHLETIC	(Rd4) D 1-1	Wallace	37,000
Feb 17	Dunfermline Athletic	(R) W 1-0	Hood	22,000
Mar 6	RAITH ROVERS	(QF) W 7-1	Lennox 3, Gemmell, Callaghan, Wallace, Davidson	32,000
Apr 3	Airdrie	(SF) D 3-3	Hood 2, Johnstone	39,000
Apr 7	Airdrie	(R) W 2-0	Johnstone, Hood	47,000
May 8	Rangers	(F) D 1-1	Lennox	120,000
May 12	Rangers	(R) W 2-1	Macari, Hood	103,000

Scottish League Cup

Aug 8	Hearts	W 2-1	Johnstone, Hughes	32,000
Aug 12	CLYDE	W 5-3	Lennox 3, Johnstone 2	25,000
Aug 15	DUNDEE UNITED	D 2-2	Callaghan, Lennox	39,000
Aug 19	Clyde	W 2-0	Gemmell 2	24,000
Aug 22	HEARTS	W 4-2	Hughes 2, Connelly, Macari	40,000
Aug 26	Dundee United	D 2-2	Hay, Macari	15,000
Sep 9	Dundee	(QF/FL) D 2-2	Johnstone 2	22,000
Sep 23	DUNDEE	(QF/SL) W 5-1	Macari 2, Hood, Hughes, Wilson	41,000
Oct 7	Dumbarton	(SF) D 0-0		25,000
Oct 12	Dumbarton	(R) W 4-3	Lennox 2, Wallace, Macari	32,000
Oct 24	Rangers	(F) L 0-1		106,000

European Cup

Sep 16	KPV KOKKOLA	(Rd1/FL) W 9-0	Hood 3, Wilson 2, McNeill Hughes, Davidson, Johnstone	41,000
Sep 30	KPV Kokkola	(Rd1/SL) W 5-0	Wallace 2, Davidson, Callaghan, Lennox	5,000
Oct 21	Waterford	(Rd2/FL) W 7-0	Wallace 3, Macari 2, Murdoch 2	48,000
Nov 4	WATERFORD	(Rd2/SL) W 3-2	Johnstone 2, Hughes	18,000
Mar 10	Ajax	(QF/FL) L 0-3		65,000
Mar 24	AJAX	(QF/SL) W 1-0	Johnstone	83,000

MANAGER: Jock Stein   **CAPTAIN:** Billy McNeill
TOP SCORER: Harry Hood

League & Cup Appearances

PLAYER	LEAGUE	CUP COMPETITIONS			TOTAL
		S CUP	SL CUP	E CUP	
Auld	4 (1)	3		1 (8)	1 (9)
Brogan	26	7 (1)	8	4 (1)	45 (2)
Callaghan	19	8	3	3	33
Cattanach	4			1	5
Chalmers	3			1 (1)	4 (1)
Clark	1				1
Connelly	22 (2)	4 (1)	11	5	42 (3)
Craig	22	3	5	4	34
Dalglish	1 (2)	1			2 (2)
Davidson	6 (1)	2		1 (3)	9 (4)
Fallon	3		2	1	6
Gemmell	19	6	6	3	34
Hay	27 (1)	8	11	5	51 (1)
Hood	27 (3)	8	10	3 (1)	48 (4)
Hughes	14	1	7	3	25
Johnstone	30	8	9	4	51
Lennox	22 (2)	4 (2)	7 (1)	5 (1)	38 (6)
Macari	8 (3)	1	5 (3)	1	15 (6)
McGrain	7		4 (1)	1 (1)	12 (2)
McNeill	31	8	10	5	54
Murdoch	21 (2)	1	8	4	34 (2)
Quinn	0 (2)	2		1	3 (2)
Wallace	25 (1)	7 (1)	3 (3)	5	40 (5)
Williams	31	8	9	5	53
Wilson	1		1 (1)	0 (1)	2 (2)

Goalscorers

PLAYER	LEAGUE	CUP COMPETITIONS			TOTAL
		S CUP	SL CUP	E CUP	
Hood	22	7	1	3	33
Wallace	19	3	1	5	28
Lennox	10	4	6	1	21
Johnstone	8	2	5	4	19
Macari	5	1	5	2	13
Hughes	5		4	2	11
Davidson	5	1		2	8
Callaghan	2		1	1	6
Connelly	3		1		4
Gemmell	1	1	2		4
Murdoch	2			2	4
McNeill	1	1		1	3
Wilson	1		1		3
Chalmers	2				2
Hay	1		1		2
Opps' o.gs.	3				3

Fact File

Jim Craig scored his second own goal in successive Scottish Cup matches against Rangers.

Final Scottish League Div 1 Table

		P	W	D	L	F	A	PTS
1	CELTIC	34	25	6	3	89	23	56
2	ABERDEEN	34	24	6	4	68	18	54
3	ST JOHNSTONE	34	19	6	9	59	44	44
4	RANGERS	34	16	9	9	58	34	41
5	DUNDEE	34	14	10	10	53	45	38
6	DUNDEE U	34	14	8	12	53	54	36
7	FALKIRK	34	13	9	12	46	53	35
8	MORTON	34	13	8	13	44	44	34
9	MOTHERWELL	34	13	8	13	43	47	34
10	AIRDRIEONIANS	34	13	8	13	60	65	34
11	HEARTS	34	13	7	14	41	40	33
12	HIBERNIAN	34	10	10	14	47	53	30
13	KILMARNOCK	34	10	8	16	43	67	28
14	AYR U	34	9	8	17	37	54	26
15	CLYDE	34	8	10	16	33	59	26
16	DUNFERMLINE ATH	34	6	11	17	44	56	23
17	ST MIRREN	34	7	9	18	38	56	23
18	COWDENBEATH	34	7	3	24	33	77	17

Season 1971-72

Scottish League Division 1

DATE	OPPONENTS	SCORE	GOALSCORERS	ATTENDANCE
Sep 4	CLYDE	W 9-1	Lennox 3, Macari 2, Murdoch, McNeill, Dalglish, Callaghan	30,000
Sep 11	Rangers	W 3-2	Johnstone, Dalglish, Macari	69,000
Sep 18	MORTON	W 3-1	Hood, Lennox, o.g.	35,000
Sep 25	Airdrie	W 5-0	Macari 3, Lennox, Dalglish	20,000
Oct 2	ST JOHNSTONE	L 0-1		40,000
Oct 9	Hibernian	W 1-0	Macari	40,000
Oct 16	DUNDEE	W 3-1	Dalglish 3	32,000
Oct 27	Dunfermline Athletic	W 2-1	McNeill, Lennox	18,000
Oct 30	Ayr United	W 1-0	Dalglish	16,000
Nov 6	ABERDEEN	D 1-1	Hood	64,000
Nov 13	Dundee United	W 5-1	Hood 2, Dalglish, Macari, Lennox	18,000
Nov 20	FALKIRK	W 2-0	Dalglish, McNeill	25,000
Nov 27	Partick Thistle	W 5-1	Johnstone, Dalglish, Deans, Hood, o.g.	33,000
Dec 4	KILMARNOCK	W 5-1	Dalglish 2, Johnstone 2, Deans	28,000
Dec 11	EAST FIFE	W 2-1	Deans 2	23,000
Dec 18	Motherwell	W 5-1	Dalglish 2, Johnstone, Lennox, Deans	18,000
Dec 25	HEARTS	W 3-2	Johnstone, Deans, Hood	34,000
Jan 1	Clyde	W 7-0	Deans 2, Hood 2, Dalglish, Davidson, o.g.	15,000
Jan 3	RANGERS	W 2-1	Johnstone, Brogan	66,000
Jan 8	Morton	D 1-1	Hood	18,000
Jan 15	AIRDRIE	W 2-0	Dalglish, Lennox	27,000
Jan 22	St Johnstone	W 3-0	Deans 2, Dalglish	14,000
Jan 29	HIBERNIAN	W 2-1	Deans, Hood	38,000
Feb 19	DUNFERMLINE ATHLETIC	W 1-0	Macari	26,000
Mar 4	AYR UNITED	W 2-0	Deans 2	23,000
Mar 11	Aberdeen	D 1-1	Lennox	32,000
Mar 25	Falkirk	W 1-0	Davidson	15,000
Apr 1	PARTICK THISTLE	W 3-1	Davidson 2, Johnstone	29,000
Apr 8	Kilmarnock	W 3-1	Davidson, Deans, Wilson	13,000
Apr 15	East Fife	W 3-0	Deans 2, Hood	12,000
Apr 22	MOTHERWELL	W 5-2	Murdoch 2, Deans 2, Lennox	20,000
Apr 25	DUNDEE UNITED	W 3-0	Johnstone, Deans, Lennox	13,000
Apr 29	Hearts	L 1-4	Murdoch	10,000
May 1	Dundee	D 1-1	Macari	12,000

Scottish Cup

Feb 5	ALBION ROVERS	(Rd1) W 5-0	Callaghan 2, Murdoch, Macari, Deans	20,000
Feb 26	DUNDEE	(Rd2) W 4-0	Lennox 2, Dalglish, Deans	47,000
Mar 18	HEARTS	(QF) D 1-1	Deans	47,000
Mar 27	Hearts	(R) W 1-0	Macari	40,000
Apr 12	Kilmarnock	(SF) W 3-1	Deans 2, Macari	48,000
May 6	Hibernian	(F) W 6-1	Deans 3, Macari 2, McNeill	106,000

Scottish League Cup

Aug 14	Rangers†	W 2-0	Johnstone, Dalglish	72,000
Aug 18	Morton	W 1-0	Lennox	20,000
Aug 21	Ayr United	W 3-0	Hay, Dalglish, Hughes	20,000
Aug 25	MORTON	L 0-1		27,000
Aug 28	Rangers	W 3-0	Lennox, Dalglish, Callaghan	74,000
Aug 30	AYR UNITED	W 4-1	Hay, Lennox, Dalglish, Macari	16,000
Sep 8	Clydebank	(QF/FL) W 5-0	Macari 2, Hood, Wallace, Callaghan	10,000
Sep 22	CLYDEBANK	(QF/SL) W 6-2	Hoods 3, Macari 2, o.g.	16,000
Oct 6	St Mirren	(SF) W 3-0	Hay, Lennox, Hood	29,000
Oct 23	Partick Thistle	(F) L 1-4	Dalglish	62,000

†Played at Ibrox.

European Cup

Sep 15	B1903 Copenhagen	(Rd1/FL) L 1-2	Macari	6,000
Sep 29	B1903 COPENHAGEN	(Rd1/SL) W 3-0	Wallace 2, Callaghan	53,000
Oct 20	SLIEMA WANDERERS	(Rd2/FL) W 5-0	Hood 2, Gemmell, Brogan, Macari	29,000
Nov 3	Sliema Wanderers	(Rd2/SL) W 2-1	Lennox, Hood	17,000
Mar 8	Ujpest Dozsa	(QF/FL) W 2-1	Macari, o.g.	30,000
Mar 22	UJPEST DOZSA	(QF/SL) D 1-1	Macari	75,000
Apr 5	Inter Milan	(SF/FL) D 0-0		80,000
Apr 19	INTER MILAN	(SF/SL) D 0-0*		75,000

*Lost 4-5 on penalties.

MANAGER: Jock Stein   **CAPTAIN:** Billy McNeill

League & Cup Appearances

PLAYER	LEAGUE	CUP COMPETITIONS			TOTAL
		S CUP	SL CUP	E CUP	
Brogan	20 (1)	4	4	5	33 (1)
Callaghan	28 (2)	6	10	6	50 (2)
Connaghan	14				14
Connelly	32	5	10	8	55
Craig	16	3	4 (1)	5	28 (1)
Dalglish	31	4	7 (1)	7	49 (1)
Davidson	5			1 (1)	6 (1)
Deans	21	5		0 (1)	26 (1)
Gemmell	3		4	3	10
Hancock				0 (1)	0 (1)
Hay	28	4	10	4	46
Hood	24	3	4 (2)	4	35 (2)
Hughes	0 (1)		4 (1)	0 (1)	4 (3)
Johnstone	23	2	8	5 (1)	38 (1)
Lennox	24 (2)	4	9	7 (1)	44 (3)
Macari	19 (1)	5	6	8	38 (1)
McCluskey	2 (2)	1 (1)		1 (1)	4 (4)
McGrain	2 (1)	1	4	2	9 (1)
McLaughlin			1		1
McNeill	34	6	8	7	55
Marshall			1		1
Murdoch	15	6	6	6	33
Quinn	9	0 (1)			9 (1)
Wallace	2 (2)		1 (1)	1 (1)	4 (4)
Williams	20	6	10	7	43
Wilson	2 (2)	1			3 (2)

Goalscorers

PLAYER	LEAGUE	CUP COMPETITIONS			TOTAL
		S CUP	SL CUP	E CUP	
Deans	19	8			27
Macari	10	5	5	4	24
Dalglish	17	1	5		23
Hood	11		5	3	19
Lennox	12	2	4	1	19
Johnstone	9		1		10
Callaghan	1	2	2	1	6
Davidson	5				5
Murdoch	4	1			5
McNeill	3	1			4
Hay			3		3
Wallace			1	2	3
Brogan	1			1	2
Gemmell			1		1
Hughes			1		1
Wilson	1				1
Opps' o.gs.	3		1	1	5

MAJOR TRANSFERS IN: John 'Dixie' Deans from Motherwell

MAJOR TRANSFERS OUT: Steve Chalmers to Morton, John Hughes and Willie Wallace to Crystal Palace, Tommy Gemmell to Nottingham Forest

Final Scottish League Div 1 Table

		P	W	D	L	F	A	Pts
1	CELTIC	34	28	4	2	96	28	60
2	ABERDEEN	34	21	8	5	80	26	50
3	RANGERS	34	21	2	11	71	38	44
4	HIBERNIAN	34	19	6	9	62	34	44
5	DUNDEE	34	14	13	7	59	38	41
6	HEARTS	34	13	13	8	53	49	39
7	PARTICK T	34	12	10	12	53	54	34
8	ST JOHNSTONE	34	12	8	14	52	58	32
9	DUNDEE U	34	12	7	15	55	70	31
10	MOTHERWELL	34	11	7	16	49	69	29
11	KILMARNOCK	34	11	6	17	49	64	28
12	AYR U	34	9	10	15	40	58	28
13	MORTON	34	10	7	17	46	52	27
14	FALKIRK	34	10	7	17	44	60	27
15	AIRDRIEONIANS	34	7	12	15	44	76	26
16	EAST FIFE	34	5	15	14	34	61	25
17	CLYDE	34	7	10	17	33	66	24
18	DUNFERMLINE ATH	34	7	9	18	31	50	23

Season 1972-73

Scottish League Division 1

DATE	OPPONENTS	SCORE	GOALSCORERS	ATTENDANCE
Sep 2	KILMARNOCK*	W 6-2	Hood 3, Deans 2, Murdoch	11,000
Sep 9	Morton	W 2-0	Murdoch 2	15,000
Sep 16	RANGERS*	W 3-1	Johnstone, Dalglish, Macari	50,000
Sep 23	Dundee	L 0-2		18,000
Sep 30	AYR UNITED	W 1-0	Deans	25,000
Oct 7	AIRDRIE	D 1-1	Lennox	22,000
Oct 14	Partick Thistle	W 4-0	Hay, Dalglish, Deans, Lennox	26,000
Oct 21	EAST FIFE	W 3-0	Macari, Deans, Hood	20,000
Oct 28	Aberdeen	W 3-2	Dalglish, Macari, Deans	36,000
Nov 4	DUNDEE UNITED	W 3-1	Johnstone, Dalglish, Macari	32,000
Nov 11	Motherwell	W 5-0	Dalglish 2, Hood 2, o.g.	11,000
Nov 18	HEARTS	W 4-2	Johnstone, Deans, Dalglish, Hood	28,000
Nov 25	Falkirk	W 3-2	Dalglish 2, Deans	15,000
Dec 2	Dumbarton	W 6-1	McCluskey 3, Hood, Johnstone, o.g.	15,000
Dec 16	Arbroath	W 2-1	Hood 2	5,000
Dec 23	HIBERNIAN	D 1-1	Dalglish	45,000
Jan 6	Rangers	L 1-2	Deans	67,000
Jan 13	DUNDEE	W 2-1	Johnstone, Dalglish	27,000
Jan 20	Ayr United	W 3-1	Dalglish 2, Deans	12,000
Jan 27	Airdrie	L 1-2	Deans	15,000
Feb 7	Kilmarnock	W 4-0	Dalglish 2, Johnstone, Callaghan	12,000
Feb 10	PARTICK THISTLE	D 1-1	Murdoch	32,000
Feb 17	East Fife	D 2-2	Deans 2	11,000
Feb 28	ST JOHNSTONE	W 4-0	Lennox 2, Dalglish, Hay	19,000
Mar 3	ABERDEEN	W 2-0	Dalglish, Lennox	38,000
Mar 6	MORTON	W 1-0	Wilson	23,000
Mar 10	Dundee United	D 2-2	Lennox 2	18,000
Mar 24	Hearts	W 2-0	Deans, Lennox	22,000
Mar 31	FALKIRK	W 4-0	Lennox 2, Hood, Deans	19,000
Apr 3	MOTHERWELL	W 2-0	Dalglish, Deans	22,000
Apr 14	St Johnstone	W 3-1	Dalglish 2, Johnstone	14,000
Apr 18	DUMBARTON	W 5-0	Deans 3, Dalglish, Callaghan	27,000
Apr 21	ARBROATH	W 4-0	Hood, Deans, Dalglish, Hay	28,000
Apr 28	Hibernian	W 3-0	Deans 2, Dalglish	45,000

Scottish Cup

Feb 3	EAST FIFE	(Rd3) W 4-1	Deans 2, Dalglish 2	25,000
Feb 24	Motherwell	(Rd4) W 4-0	Deans 2, Dalglish, Lennox	24,000
Mar 17	ABERDEEN	(QF) D 0-0		40,000
Mar 21	Aberdeen	(R) W 1-0	McNeill	33,000
Apr 7	Dundee	(SF) D 0-0		53,000
Apr 11	Dundee	(R) W 3-0	Johnstone 2, Dalglish	47,000
May 5	Rangers	(F) L 2-3	Connelly, Dalglish	122,000

Scottish League Cup

Aug 12	Stirling Albion	W 3-0	Macari 2, Dalglish	17,000
Aug 16	EAST FIFE	D 1-1	Dalglish	5,000
Aug 19	Arbroath	W 5-0	Dalglish 2, Deans 2, Murdoch	8,000
Aug 23	East Fife	W 3-2	Dalglish 2, Lennox	8,000
Aug 26	STIRLING ALBION	W 3-0	Murdoch, Deans, Dalglish	17,000
Aug 28	ARBROATH*	D 3-3	Dalglish, Hood, o.g.	5,000
Sep 20	Stranraer	(Rd2/FL) W 2-1	Davidson, Lennox	5,000
Oct 4	STRANRAER	(Rd2/SL) W 5-2	Lennox 2, Murdoch, Davidson, Deans	9,000
Oct 11	Dundee	(QF/FL) L 0-1		22,000
Nov 1	DUNDEE	(QF/SL) W 3-2	Macari 2, Lennox	39,000
Nov 20	Dundee	(QF Play-off) W 4-1	Deans 2, Dalglish, Hood	36,000
Nov 27	Aberdeen	(SF) W 3-2	Johnstone, Hood, Callaghan	39,000
Dec 9	Hibernian	(F) L 1-2	Dalglish	71,000

European Cup

Sep 13	ROSENBORG*	(Rd1/FL) W 2-1	Deans, Macari	18,000
Sep 27	Rosenborg	(Rd1/SL) W 3-1	Hood, Dalglish, Macari	25,000
Oct 25	UJPEST DOZSA	(Rd2/FL) W 2-1	Dalglish 2	55,000
Nov 8	Ujpest Dozsa	(Rd2/SL) L 0-3		30,000

*Played at Hampden Park due to re-building work at Celtic Park.

Fact File

Kenny Dalglish became the first player to score in all six Scottish League Cup sectional games.

League & Cup Appearances

PLAYER	LEAGUE	CUP COMPETITIONS			TOTAL
		S CUP	SL CUP	E CUP	
Brogan	20	5	5	1	31
Callaghn	27	4	9 (1)	4	44 (1)
Connaghan	4		7		11
Connelly	32	7	12	4	55
Dalglish	32	6	11	4	53
Davidson	1 (1)	0 (1)	3 (1)		4 (3)
Deans	30 (1)	7	10	2 (1)	49 (2)
Hay	21	6	8	2	37
Hood	22 (7)	1 (3)	8 (1)	3 (1)	34 (12)
Hunter	15	7			22
Johnstone	21 (1)	6 (1)	7	3	37 (2)
Lennox	15 (8)	5 (1)	7	1 (2)	28 (11)
Lynch	0 (1)				0 (1)
Macari	10 (1)		6	3	19 (1)
McCluskey	14 (2)		6 (2)	2 (1)	22 (5)
McGrain	30	7	10	4	51
McLaughlin	0 (2)		2 (2)		2 (4)
McNeill	30	7	10	4	51
Murdoch	24	7	7	2	40
Quinn	9 (1)	2	7		18 (1)
Williams	15		6	4	25
Wilson	2 (2)		2 (1)	1	5 (3)

Goalscorers

PLAYER	LEAGUE	CUP COMPETITIONS			TOTAL
		S CUP	SL CUP	E CUP	
Dalglish	23	5	10	3	41
Deans	22	4	6	1	33
Hood	12		3	1	16
Lennox	10	1	5		16
Johntone	7	2	1		10
Macari	4		4	2	10
Murdoch	4		3		7
Callaghan	2		1		3
Hay	3				3
McCluskey	3				3
Davidson			2		2
Connelly	1				1
McNeill		1			1
Wilson	1				1
Opps' o.gs.	2		1		3

MANAGER: Jock Stein

CAPTAIN: Billy McNeill

TOP SCORER: Kenny Dalglish

BIGGEST WIN: 6-1 v Dumbarton, 2 December 1972, league

HIGHEST ATTENDANCE: 122,000 v Rangers, 5 May 1973, Scottish Cup

MAJOR TRANSFERS IN: Alistair Hunter from Kilmarnock, Steve Murray from Aberdeen

MAJOR TRANSFERS OUT: Jim Craig to Sheffield Wednesday, Lou Macari to Manchester United

Final Scottish League Div 1 Table

		P	W	D	L	F	A	PTS
1	CELTIC	34	26	5	3	93	28	57
2	RANGERS	34	26	4	4	74	30	56
3	HIBERNIAN	34	19	7	8	74	33	45
4	ABERDEEN	34	16	11	7	61	34	43
5	DUNDEE	34	17	9	8	68	43	43
6	AYR U	34	16	8	10	50	51	40
7	DUNDEE U	34	17	5	12	56	51	39
8	MOTHERWELL	34	11	9	14	38	48	31
9	EAST FIFE	34	11	8	15	46	54	30
10	HEARTS	34	12	6	16	39	50	30
11	ST JOHNSTONE	34	10	9	15	52	67	29
12	MORTON	34	10	8	16	47	53	28
13	PARTICK T	34	10	8	16	40	53	28
14	FALKIRK	34	7	12	15	38	56	26
15	ARBROATH	34	9	8	17	39	63	26
16	DUMBARTON	34	6	11	17	43	72	23
17	KILMARNOCK	34	7	8	19	40	71	22
18	AIRDRIEONIANS	34	4	8	22	34	75	16

Season 1973-74

Scottish League Division 1

DATE	OPPONENTS	SCORE	GOALSCORERS	ATTENDANCE
Sep 1	Dunfermline Athletic	W 3-2	Hood, Wilson, o.g.	15,000
Sep 8	CLYDE	W 5-0	Lennox 3, McGrain, Dalglish	27,000
Sep 15	Rangers	W 1-0	Johnstone	67,000
Sep 29	St Johnstone	L 1-2	Deans	12,000
Oct 6	MOTHERWELL	W 2-0	Deans, Wilson	32,000
Oct 13	Dundee	W 1-0	Callaghan	17,000
Oct 20	HIBERNIAN	D 1-1	McCluskey	34,000
Oct 27	Hearts	W 3-1	Dalglish 2, Connelly	33,000
Nov 3	EAST FIFE	W 4-2	Deans 2, Hood, Dalglish	23,000
Nov 10	Ayr United	W 1-0	Dalglish	15,000
Nov 17	PARTICK THISTLE	W 7-0	Deans 6, Lennox	22,000
Nov 24	Dumbarton	W 2-0	Lennox, Dalglish	9,000
Dec 1	Arbroath	W 2-1	Wilson, Dalglish	5,000
Dec 8	DUNDEE UNITED	D 3-3	Hood, Callaghan, Dalglish	19,000
Dec 22	FALKIRK	W 6-0	Deans 4, Dalglish, Lennox	11,000
Dec 29	DUNFERMLINE ATHLETIC	W 6-0	Hood 2, Deans 2, Dalglish 2	21,000
Jan 1	Clyde	W 2-0	Dalgish, Lennox	12,000
Jan 5	RANGERS	W 1-0	Lennox	55,000
Jan 19	ST JOHNSTONE	W 3-0	Murray, Lennox, o.g.	19,000
Feb 2	Motherwell	L 2-3	Murray, Lennox	16,000
Feb 10	DUNDEE	L 1-2	Hay	40,000
Feb 23	Hibernian	W 4-2	Deans 2, Dalglish, Wilson	48,000
Mar 2	HEARTS	W 1-0	Deans	32,000
Mar 16	AYR UNITED	W 4-0	Johnstone 2, Deans 2	26,000
Mar 23	Partick Thistle	L 0-2		20,000
Mar 30	DUMBARTON	D 3-3	Deans, Wilson, Dalglish	19,000
Apr 6	ARBROATH	W 1-0	Dalglish	18,000
Apr 13	Dundee United	W 2-0	Murray, Hay	15,000
Apr 17	East Fife	W 6-1	Hood 2, Dalglish 2, Deans, Lennox	8,000
Apr 20	ABERDEEN	W 2-0	Deans, Lennox	31,000
Apr 27	Falkirk	D 1-1	Dalglish	16,000
Apr 29	Aberdeen	D 0-0		15,000
Apr 30	MORTON	D 1-1	McLaughlin	9,000
May 6	Morton	D 0-0		6,000

Scottish Cup

Jan 27	CLYDEBANK	(Rd3) W 6-1	Deans 3, Lennox 2, Davidson	28,000
Feb 17	STIRLING ALBION	(Rd4) W 6-1	Hood 2, Murray 2, Dalglish, Wilson	23,000
Mar 10	MOTHERWELL	(QF) D 2-2	Hood 2	46,000
Mar 13	Motherwell	(R) W 1-0	Deans	28,000
Apr 3	Dundee	(SF) W 1-0	Johnstone	58,000
May 4	Dundee United	(F) W 3-0	Murray, Hood, Deans	76,000

Scottish League Cup

Aug 11	ARBROATH	W 2-1	Lennox, Lynch	18,000
Aug 15	Falkirk	W 2-0	Hay, Lennox	18,000
Aug 18	Rangers	W 2-1	Lennox, Hood	63,000
Aug 22	FALKIRK	W 2-1	Lennox, o.g.	17,000
Aug 25	RANGERS	L 1-3	Lennox	57,000
Aug 29	Arbroath	W 3-1	Dalglish, Callaghan, Wilson	5,000
Sep 12	Motherwell	(Rd2/FL) W 2-1	Murray, Hood	21,000
Oct 10	MOTHERWELL	(Rd2/SL) L 0-1		25,000
Oct 29	MOTHERWELL	(R) W 3-2	Johnstone, Murray, Deans	26,000
Oct 31	ABERDEEN	(QF/FL) W 3-2	Dalglish 2, McCluskey	28,000
Nov 21	Aberdeen	(QF/SL) D 0-0		16,000
Dec 5	Rangers	(SF) W 3-1	Hood 3	54,000
Dec 15	Dundee	(F) L 0-1		30,000

European Cup

Sep 19	TPS Turku	(Rd1/FL) W 6-1	Callaghan 2, Connelly, Johnstone, Hood, Deans	5,000
Oct 3	TPS TURKU	(Rd1/SL) W 3-0	Johnstone 2, Deans	18,000
Oct 24	VEJLE	(Rd2/FL) D 0-0		30,000
Nov 6	Vejle	(Rd2/SL) W 1-0	Lennox	20,000
Feb 27	Basle	(QF/FL) L 2-3	Dalglish, Wilson	25,000
Mar 20	BASLE	(QF/SL) W 4-2	Murray, Deans, Callaghan, Dalglish	71,000
Apr 10	ATLETICO MADRID	(SF/FL) D 0-0		73,000
Apr 24	Atletico Madrid	(SF/SL) L 0-2		70,000

MANAGER: Jock Stein **CAPTAIN:** Billy McNeill

TOP SCORER: 'Dixie' Deans

BIGGEST WIN: 7-0 v Partick Thistle, 17 November 1973, league

HIGHEST ATTENDANCE: 76,000 v Dundee United, 4 May 1974, Scottish Cup

MAJOR TRANSFERS IN: Jimmy Bone from Sheffield United

League & Cup Appearances

PLAYER	LEAGUE	S CUP	SL CUP	E CUP	TOTAL
Bone	3 (1)	1			4 (1)
Brogan	30	6	13	7	56
Callaghan	16 (6)	2 (2)	6 (4)	4 (1)	28 (13)
Connaghan	8	4		3	15
Connelly	14 (1)	3	10 (1)	6	33 (2)
Dalglish	31 (2)	6	10	7	54 (2)
Davidson	3			1 (1)	4 (3)
Deans	24 (2)	6	5 (1)	5 (1)	40 (4)
Hay	25	6	9	7	47
Hood	28 (3)	6	8 (4)	6	48 (7)
Hunter	26	2	13	4	45
Johnstone	13 (2)	2	7 (2)	6	28 (4)
Lennox	17 (2)	1	8	3	29 (2)
Lynch	1 (2)		1 (1)		2 (3)
McCluskey	23 (2)	5 (1)	5 (1)	5 (1)	38 (5)
MacDonald	2	1	2		5
McGrain	29 (1)	3	13	5	50 (1)
McLaughlin	2 (1)		6		8 (1)
McNamara	1 (1)			1	2 (1)
McNeill	30	5	11	7	53
Murdoch			1		1
Murray	32	5	12	8	57
Quinn	3				3
Ritchie	0 (1)				0 (1)
Welsh	3				3
Williams				1	1
Wilson	10 (10)	2 (1)	3 (3)	3 (2)	18 (16)

Goalscorers

PLAYER	LEAGUE	S CUP	SL CUP	E CUP	TOTAL
Deans	24	5	1	3	33
Dalglish	18	1	3	2	24
Lennox	12	2	5	1	20
Hood	7	5	5	1	18
Murray	3	3	2	1	9
Johnstone	3	1		3	8
Wilson	5	1	1	1	8
Callaghan	2		1	3	6
Hay	2		1		3
Connelly	1			1	2
McCluskey	1		1		2
Davidson		1			1
Lynch			1		1
McGrain	1				1
McLaughlin	1				1
Opps' o.gs.	2		1		3

Fact File

On 27 January 1974 Celtic played their first-ever Sunday match – a Scottish Cup tie against Clydebank.

Final Scottish League Div 1 Table

		P	W	D	L	F	A	Pts
1	CELTIC	34	23	7	4	82	27	53
2	HIBERNIAN	34	20	9	5	75	42	49
3	RANGERS	34	21	6	7	67	34	48
4	ABERDEEN	34	13	16	5	46	26	42
5	DUNDEE	34	16	7	11	67	48	39
6	HEARTS	34	14	10	10	54	43	38
7	AYR U	34	15	8	11	44	40	38
8	DUNDEE U	34	15	7	12	55	51	37
9	MOTHERWELL	34	14	7	13	45	40	35
10	DUMBARTON	34	11	7	16	43	58	29
11	PARTICK T	34	9	10	15	33	46	28
12	ST JOHNSTONE	34	9	10	15	41	60	28
13	ARBROATH	34	10	7	17	52	69	27
14	MORTON	34	8	10	16	37	49	26
15	CLYDE	34	8	9	17	29	65	25
16	DUNFERMLINE ATH	34	8	8	18	43	65	24
17	EAST FIFE	34	9	6	19	26	51	24
18	FALKIRK	34	4	14	16	33	58	22

Season 1974-75

Scottish League Division 1

DATE	OPPONENTS	SCORE	GOALSCORERS	ATTENDANCE
Aug 3	KILMARNOCK	W 5-0	Johnstone, Wilson, Murray, Davidson, Dalglish	27,000
Sep 7	Clyde	W 4-2	Davidson, McCluskey, Dalglish, Lennox	15,000
Sep 14	RANGERS	L 1-2	Dalglish	60,000
Sep 21	Motherwell	W 2-1	Lennox 2	13,000
Sep 28	AYR UNITED	W 5-3	Wilson 2, Deans, Dalglish, Hood	20,000
Oct 5	Dumbarton	W 3-1	Johnstone, Deans, Dalglish	13,000
Oct 12	ARBROATH	W 1-0	Murray	16,000
Oct 19	HIBERNIAN	W 5-0	Deans 3, Johnstone, Murray	39,000
Nov 2	ABERDEEN	W 1-0	Wilson	29,000
Nov 6	Partick Thistle	W 2-1	Deans, Dalglish	15,000
Nov 9	Dundee United	D 0-0		15,000
Nov 16	AIRDRIE	W 6-0	Murray 2, McNeill, Glavin, Wilson, Lennox	26,000
Nov 23	Hearts	D 1-1	Wilson	23,000
Nov 30	Morton	W 1-0	Murray	17,000
Dec 7	DUNFERMLINE ATHLETIC	W 2-1	Bone, Hood	20,000
Dec 14	Dundee	W 6-0	Dalglish 3, Johnstone 2, Wilson	15,000
Dec 21	ST JOHNSTONE	W 3-1	Dalglish, Murray, McCluskey	20,000
Dec 28	Kilmarnock	W 1-0	Dalglish	17,000
Jan 1	CLYDE	W 5-1	Callaghan 2, Deans, Dalglish, Glavin	20,000
Jan 4	Rangers	L 0-3		70,000
Jan 11	MOTHERWELL	L 2-3	Hood 2	26,000
Jan 18	Ayr United	W 5-1	Deans 2, Murray, Hood, o.g.	15,000
Feb 8	Arbroath	D 2-2	Hood, Dalglish	7,000
Feb 11	DUMBARTON	D 2-2	Hood, Wilson	15,000
Feb 22	Hibernian	L 1-2	Wilson	29,000
Mar 1	PARTICK THISTLE	W 3-2	Hood, Dalglish, McCluskey	21,000
Mar 12	Aberdeen	L 2-3	Lynch 2	16,000
Mar 15	DUNDEE UNITEd	L 0-1		20,000
Mar 22	Airdrie	L 0-1		14,000
Mar 29	HEARTS	W 4-1	Dalglish 2, Wilson, Glavin	21,000
Apr 5	MORTON	D 1-1	Wilson	13,000
Apr 12	Dunfermline Athletic	W 3-1	Wilson 2, Lennox	105,000
Apr 19	DUNDEE	L 1-2	Glavin	13,000
Apr 26	St Johnstone	L 1-2	Glavin	11,000

Scottish Cup

DATE	OPPONENTS		SCORE	GOALSCORERS	ATTENDANCE
Jan 25	Hibernian	(Rd3)	W 2-0	Deans, Murray	36,000
Feb 15	CLYDEBANK	(Rd4)	W 4-1	Dalglish 2, McNamara, MacDonald	21,000
Mar 8	Dumbarton	(QF)	W 2-1	Glavin, Wilson	16,000
Apr 2	Dundee	(SF)	W 1-0	Glavin	40,000
May 3	Airdrie	(F)	W 3-1	Wilson 2, McCluskey	75,000

Scottish League Cup

DATE	OPPONENTS		SCORE	GOALSCORERS	ATTENDANCE
Aug 10	MOTHERWELL		W 2-1	Dalglish, Wilson	27,000
Aug 14	Ayr United		L 2-3	Murray, Connelly	6,000
Aug 17	DUNDEE UNITED		W 1-0	McNamara	26,000
Aug 21	AYR UNITED		W 5-2	Johnstone 2, Wilson 2, Lennox	16,000
Aug 24	Dundee United		W 1-0	Wilson	15,000
Aug 28	Motherwell		D 2-2	Dalglish 2	8,000
Sep 11	HAMILTON AC.	(QF/FL)	W 2-0	Hood 2	12,000
Sep 25	Hamilton Ac.	(QF/SL)	W 4-2	Deans, Callaghan, McNamara, Lennox	8,000
Oct 9	Airdrie	(SF)	W 1-0	Murray	19,000
Oct 26	Hibernian	(F)	W 6-3	Deans 3, Wilson, Murray, Johnstone	53,000

European Cup

DATE	OPPONENTS		SCORE	GOALSCORERS	ATTENDANCE
Sep 18	OLYMPIAKOS	(Rd1/FL)	D 1-1	Wilson	40,000
Oct 2	Olympiakos	(Rd1/SL)	L 0-2		42,000

MANAGER: Jock Stein

CAPTAIN: Billy McNeill

TOP SCORER: Paul Wilson

BIGGEST WIN: 6-0 v Airdrie, 16 November 1974, league; 6-0 v Dundee, 14 December 1974, league

HIGHEST ATTENDANCE: 75,000 v Airdrie, 3 May 1975, Scottish Cup

MAJOR TRANSFES IN: Ronnie Glavin from Partick Thistle, Peter Latchford from West Bromwich Albion

League & Cup Appearances

PLAYER	LEAGUE	CUP COMPETITIONS			TOTAL
		S CUP	SL CUP	E CUP	
Barclay		1			1
Bone	2 (1)		2 (1)		4 (2)
Brogan	19 (1)	1	7	2	29 (1)
Burns	0 (1)				0 (1)
Callaghan	19 (3)	3	7	2	31 (3)
Connaghan	6		6	2	14
Connelly	15	3	5		23
Dalglish	33	5	7 (1)	2	47 (1)
Davidson	4		2		6
Deans	18 (1)	2	4	1	25 (1)
Glavin	19 (1)	3 (1)			22 (2)
Hood	21 (6)	5	6 (2)	1 (1)	33 (9)
Hunter	18	1	4		23
Johnstone	15 (6)		7	2	24 (6)
Latchford	10	3			13
Lennox	9 (5)	2	4 (3)	0 (2)	15 (10)
Lynch	5 (2)	2			7 (2)
McCluskey	28 (1)	4	10	2	44 (1)
MacDonald	12 (3)	2	1		15 (3)
McGrain	30	5	7	2	44
McLaughlin	0 (1)				0 (1)
McNamara	1	1	4 (2)		6 (2)
McNeill	30	4	9	2	45
Murray	28	3	8	2	41
Welsh	1 (1)				1 (1)
Wilson	31 (2)	5	10	2	48 (2)

Goalscorers

PLAYER	LEAGUE	CUP COMPETITIONS			TOTAL
		S CUP	SL CUP	E CUP	
Wilson	13	3	5	1	22
Dalglish	16	2	3		21
Deans	9	1	4		14
Murray	8	1	3		12
Hood	8		2		10
Johnstone	5		3		8
Glavin	5	2			7
Lennox	5		2		7
McCluskey	3	1			4
Callaghan	2		1		3
McNamara	1		2		3
Davidson	2				2
Lynch	2				2
Bone	1				1
Connelly			1		1
MacDonald		1			1
McNeill	1				1
Opps' o.gs.	1				1

Fact File

The Scottish Cup final was Billy McNeill's 832nd and final appearance.

Final Scottish League Div 1 Table

		P	W	D	L	F	A	Pts
1	RANGERS	34	25	6	3	86	33	56
2	HIBERNIAN	34	20	9	5	69	37	49
3	CELTIC	34	20	5	9	81	41	45
4	DUNDEE U	34	19	7	8	72	43	45
5	ABERDEEN	34	16	9	9	66	43	41
6	DUNDEE	34	16	6	12	48	42	38
7	AYR U	34	14	8	12	50	61	36
8	HEARTS	34	11	13	10	47	52	35
9	ST JOHNSTONE	34	11	12	11	41	44	34
10	MOTHERWELL	34	14	5	15	52	57	33
11	AIRDRIEONIANS	34	11	9	14	43	55	31
12	KILMARNOCK	34	8	15	11	52	68	31
13	PARTICK T	34	10	10	14	48	62	30
14	DUMBARTON	34	7	10	17	44	55	24
15	DUNFERMLINE ATH	34	7	9	18	46	66	23
16	CLYDE	34	6	10	18	40	63	22
17	MORTON	34	6	10	18	31	62	22
18	ARBROATH	34	5	7	22	34	66	17

FIRST TEN CLUBS FORMED A NEW PREMIER DIVISION; REMAINING EIGHT PLUS TOP SIX FROM DIV 2 FORMED NEW DIV 1.

Season 1975-76

Scottish League Premier Division

DATE	OPPONENTS	SCORE	GOALSCORERS	ATTENDANCE
Aug 30	Rangers	L 1-2	Dalglish	69,000
Sep 6	DUNDEE	W 4-0	Lennox 3, McNamara	25,000
Sep 13	Motherwell	D 1-1	Dalglish	18,000
Sep 20	St Johnstone	W 2-1	McCluskey 2	12,000
Sep 27	DUNDEE UNITED	W 2-1	Dalglish, Macdonald	21,000
Oct 4	HEARTS	W 3-1	Deans, Hood, Wilson	20,000
Oct 11	Aberdeen	W 2-1	Dalglish, Deans	18,000
Nov 1	RANGERS	D 1-1	Wilson	55,000
Nov 8	Dundee	L 0-1		16,000
Nov 12	Ayr United	W 7-2	Edvaldsson 3, Deans 2, Dalglish, Macdonald	15,000
Nov 15	MOTHERWELL	L 0-2		33,000
Nov 22	ST JOHNSTONE	W 3-2	Lennox 2, Dalglish	20,000
Nov 29	Dundee United	W 3-1	Deans, Lennox, Lynch	11,000
Dec 6	Hearts	W 1-0	Deans	21,000
Dec 10	HIBERDIAN	D 1-1	Deans	21,000
Dec 13	ABERDEEN	L 0-2		24,000
Dec 20	Hibernian	W 3-1	Edvaldsson, Deans, McNamara	21,000
Dec 27	AYR UNITED	W 3-1	Edvaldsson 2, Dalglish	22,000
Jan 1	Rangers	L 0-1		57,000
Jan 3	DUNDEE	D 3-3	Dalglish 2, Deans	21,000
Jan 10	Motherwell	W 3-1	Deans 2, Dalglish	15,000
Jan 17	St Johnstone	W 4-3	Dalglish, Deans, Macdonald, Edvaldsson	9,000
Jan 31	DUNDEE UNITED	W 2-1	Dalglish, Wilson	18,000
Feb 7	HEARTS	W 2-0	Dalglish 2	22,000
Feb 21	Aberdeen	W 1-0	Lennox	18,000
Feb 28	HIBERNIAN	W 4-0	Dalglish, Lennox, Wilson, Deans	33,000
Mar 20	Dundee	W 1-0	Dalglish	14,000
Mar 27	MOTHERWELL	W 4-1	Dalglish 2, Lennox, Deans	29,000
Apr 3	ST JOHNSTONE	W 1-0	Dalglish	16,000
Apr 10	Dundee United	L 2-3	Dalglish 2	12,000
Apr 17	ABERDEEN	D 1-1	Dalglish	29,000
Apr 21	Hibernian	L 0-2		17,000
Apr 24	AYR UNITED	L 1-2	Deans	16,000
Apr 26	RANGERS	D 0-0		51,000
May 1	Ayr United	W 5-3	Dalglish 2, Ritchie, Lennox, McCluskey	6,800
May 3	Hearts	L 0-1		9,000

Scottish Cup

Jan 24	Motherwell	(Rd3) L 2-3	Dalglish, Lynch	25,000

Scottish League Cup

Aug 9	ABERDEEN	W 1-0	Dalglish	32,000
Aug 13	Hearts	L 0-2		19,000
Aug 16	DUMBARTON	W 3-1	Wilson, Lennox, Edvaldsson	23,000
Aug 20	HEARTS	W 3-1	Glavin, Lynch, Edvaldsson	28,000
Aug 23	Dumbarton	W 8-0	Hood 2, Wilson 2, Dalglish 2, Callaghan, McGrain	12,000
Aug 27	Aberdeen	W 2-0	Lennox, Ritchie	13,000
Sep 10	Stenhousemuir	(QF/FL) W 2-0	Lennox, Dalglish	4,000
Sep 24	STENHOUSEMUIR	(QF/SL) W 1-0	Lynch	6,000
Oct 6	Partick Thistle	(SF) W 1-0	Edvaldsson	31,000
Oct 25	Rangers	(F) L 0-1		58,000

European Cup-Winners' Cup

Sep 16	Valur	(Rd1/FL) W 2-0	Wilson, Macdonald	8,000
Oct 1	VALUR	(Rd1/SL) W 7-0	Hood 2, Edvaldsson, Dalglish, McCluskey P, Deans, Callaghan	16,000
Oct 22	Boavista	(Rd2/FL) D 0-0		37,000
Nov 5	BOAVISTA	(Rd2/SL) W 3-1	Dalglish, Edvaldsson, Deans	37,000
Mar 3	SACHSENRING ZWICKAU	(QF/FL) D 1-1	Dalglish	46,000
Mar 17	Sachsenring Zwickau	(QF/SL) L 0-1		40,000

CARETAKER/MANAGER: Sean Fallon (Jock Stein injured after car crash)

CAPTAIN: Kenny Dalglish

TOP SCORER: Kenny Dalglish

BIGGEST WIN: 8-0 v Dumbarton, 23 August 1975, Scottish League Cup

HIGHEST ATTENDANCE: 69,000 v Rangers, 30 August 1975, league

MAJOR TRANSFERS IN: Johannes Edvaldsson from Holbeck, John Doyle from Ayr United

MAJOR TRANSFERS OUT: 'Dixie' Deans to Luton

League & Cup Appearances

PLAYER	LEAGUE	CUP COMPETITIONS			TOTAL
		S CUP	SL CUP	ECWC	
Aitken	12		1 (1)	2	15 (1)
Burns	5				5
Callaghan	22		4 (1)	5	31 (1)
Casey	1		0 (1)	0 (2)	1 (3)
Connelly	1 (2)		1 (1)		2 (3)
Dalglish	35	1	10	5	51
Deans	29	1	2	3	35
Doyle	5				5
Edvaldsson	35	1	10	6	52
Glavin	10	1	7 (1)	1 (1)	19 (2)
Hannah	0 (2)				0 (2)
Hood	7 (7)		6	5	18 (7)
Hunter	1				1
Latchford	35	1	10	6	52
Lennox	25 (5)	1	7 (2)	2 (1)	35 (8)
Lynch	34	1	10	5	50
McCluskey G	2 (2)*			1 (1)	3 (3)
McCluskey P	34	1	9	6	50
Macdonald	27	1	9	5	42
McGrain	35	1	9	6	51
McNamara	16 (2)	1	6 (2)	3 (1)	26 (5)
Murray	2 (1)				2 (1)
Ritchie	5 (3)		0 (1)		5 (4)
Wilson	18 (8)		9	5	32 (8)

Goalscorers

PLAYER	LEAGUE	CUP COMPETITIONS			TOTAL
		S CUP	SL CUP	ECWC	
Dalglish	24	1	4	3	32
Deans	15			2	17
Lennox	10		3		13
Edvaldsson	7		3	2	12
Wilson	4		3	1	8
Hood	1		2	2	5
Lynch	1	1	2		4
McCluskey P	3			1	4
Macdonald	3			1	4
Callaghan			1	1	2
McNamara	2				2
Ritchie	1		1		2
Glavin			1		1
McGrain			1		1

Fact File

In September Celtic missed four penalties in four games.

Final Scottish Premier Division Table

		P	W	D	L	F	A	Pts
1	RANGERS	36	23	8	5	60	24	54
2	CELTIC	36	21	6	9	71	42	48
3	HIBERNIAN	36	18	7	11	55	43	43
4	MOTHERWELL	36	16	8	12	57	49	40
5	HEARTS	36	13	9	14	39	45	35
6	AYR U	36	14	5	17	46	59	33
7	ABERDEEN	36	11	10	15	49	50	32
8	DUNDEE U	36	12	8	16	46	48	32
9	DUNDEE	36	11	10	15	49	62	32
10	ST JOHNSTONE	36	3	5	28	29	79	11

Season 1976-77

Scottish League Premier Division

DATE	OPPONENTS		SCORE	GOALSCORERS	ATTENDANCE
Sep 4	RANGERS		D 2-2	Wilson 2	57,000
Sep 11	Dundee United		L 0-1		15,000
Sep 18	HEARTS		D 2-2	Glavin, G McCluskey	27,000
Sep 25	Kilmarnock		W 4-0	Glavin, Craig, Doyle, Macdonald	14,000
Oct 2	HIBERNIAN		D 1-1	Dalglish	29,000
Oct 16	Ayr United		W 2-0	Glavin, Craig	12,000
Oct 20	DUNDEE UNITED		W 5-1	Glavin 3, Craig, Lennox	23,000
Oct 23	Aberdeen		L 1-2	Dalglish	19,000
Oct 30	MOTHERWELL		W 2-0	Dalglish 2	31,000
Nov 20	Hearts		W 4-3	Dalglish, Macdonald, Lennox, Glavin	20,000
Nov 24	Rangers		W 1-0	Craig	43,000
Nov 27	KILMARNOCK		W 2-1	Craig, Wilson	22,000
Dec 18	AYR UNITED		W 3-0	Doyle, Wilson, Dalglish	18,000
Dec 26	ABERDEEN		D 2-2	Craig 2	47,000
Jan 8	Dundee United		W 2-1	Dalglish, Doyle	16,000
Jan 11	RANGERS		W 1-0	o.g.	52,000
Jan 22	Kilmarnock		W 3-1	Glavin 2, Wilson	14,000
Feb 5	HIBERNIAN		W 4-2	Glavin 2, Edvaldsson, Craig	28,000
Feb 7	HEARTS		W 5-1	Glavin, Edvaldsson, Craig, Dalglish, Lynch	21,000
Feb 12	PARTICK THISTLE		W 2-0	Glavin, Dalglish	26,000
Feb 19	Ayr United		W 4-2	Dalglish 2, Craig, Lynch	13,000
Feb 22	Partick Thistle		W 4-2	Edvaldsson, Glavin, Craig, Aitken	13,000
Mar 5	Aberdeen		L 0-2		21,000
Mar 9	PARTICK THISTLE		W 2-1	Conn, Doyle	22,000
Mar 16	MOTHERWELL		D 2-2	Glavin, Edvaldsson	23,000
Mar 19	Rangers		D 2-2	Aitlen 2	51,000
Mar 26	DUNDEE UNITED		W 2-0	Glavin, Craig	37,000
Mar 30	Hibernian		D 1-1	Glavin	11,000
Apr 2	Hearts		W 3-0	Glavin, Craig, Aitken	17,000
Apr 9	KILMARNOCK		W 1-0	Craig	20,000
Apr 13	Motherwell		L 0-3		13,000
Apr 16	Hibernian		W 1-0	Craig	22,000
Apr 20	ABERDEEN		W 4-1	Glavin, Conn, Craig, Dalglish	27,000
Apr 23	Partick Thistle		D 1-1	Aitken	18,000
Apr 30	AYR UNITED		W 2-0	Dalglish, Edvaldsson	17,000
May 10	Motherwell		D 2-2	Dalglish, Burns	12,000

Scottish Cup

Jan 29	Airdrie	(Rd3) D 1-1	Doyle	18,000
Feb 2	AIRDRIE	(R) W 5-0	Craig 4, Glavin	20,000
Feb 27	AYR UNITED	(Rd4) D 1-1	Glavin	38,000
Mar 2	Ayr United	(R) W 3-1	Glavin, Doyle, Aitken	13,000
Mar 13	QUEEN OF THE SOUTH	(QF) W 5-1	Glavin 3, Craig, Dalglish	27,000
Apr 6	Dundee	(SF) W 2-0	Craig 2	29,000
May 7	Rangers	(F) W 1-0	Lynch	54,000

Scottish League Cup

Aug 14	Dundee United	W 1-0	Dalglish	13,000
Aug 18	DUMBARTON	W 3-0	Dalglish 2, Doyle	15,000
Aug 21	Arbroath	W 5-0	Dalglish, Wilson, McGrain, Glavin, Edvaldsson	6,000
Aug 25	Dumbarton	D 3-3	Wilson, Macdonald, Doyle	12,000
Aug 28	ARBROATH	W 2-1	Wilson, Doyle	17,000
Sep 1	DUNDEE UNITED	D 1-1	Macdonald	15,000
Sep 22	Albion Rovers	(QF/FL) W 1-0	Callaghan	8,000
Oct 6	Albion Rovers	(QF/SL) W 5-0	Dalglish 3, Doyle 2	7,000
Oct 26	Hearts	(SF) W 2-1	Dalglish 2	21,000
Nov 6	Aberdeen	(F) L 1-2	Dalglish	69,000

UEFA Cup

Sep 15	WISLA KRAKOW	(Rd1/FL) D 2-2	Macdonald, Dalglish	30,000
Sep 29	Wisla Krakow	(Rd1/SL) L 0-2		45,000

League & Cup Appearances

PLAYER	LEAGUE	CUP COMPETITIONS			TOTAL
		S CUP	SL CUP	UEFA	
Aitken	33	7	5 (1)	1	46 (1)
Baines	5	1			6
Burns	13 (9)	1 (2)	6	1	21 (11)
Callaghan	0 (1)		4		4 (1)
Casey		0 (1)			0 (1)
Conn	13 (1)	2			15 (1)
Connaghan			2		2
Craig	34	7			41
Dalglish	35	7	9	2	53
Doyle	33 (1)	6	9	2	50 (1)
Edvaldsson	13 (4)	3 (1)	8 (1)	2	26 (6)
Gibson	1 (2)	0 (1)			1 (3)
Glavin	34	6	10	2	52
Henderson			1 (1)		1 (1)
Latchford	31	6	8	2	47
Lennox	2 (3)		3 (3)	1 (1)	6 (7)
Lynch	30	6	9	2	47
McCluskey G	0 (1)		3 (1)		3 (2)
McCluskey P	4 (4)	1	5 (3)	1	11 (7)
Macdonald	24	5	10	2	41
McGrain	36	7	10	2	55
Stanton	36	7			43
Wilson	19 (5)	5	8 (1)	2	34 (6)

Goalscorers

PLAYER	LEAGUE	CUP COMPETITIONS			TOTAL
		S CUP	SL CUP	UEFA	
Dalglish	14	1	10	1	26
Glavin	19	6	1		26
Craig	16	7			23
Doyle	4	2	5		11
Wilson	5		3		8
Aitken	5	1			6
Edvaldsson	5		1		6
Macdonald	2		2	1	5
Lynch	2	1			3
Conn	2				2
Lennox	2				2
Burns	1				1
Callaghan			1		1
McCluskey G	1				1
McGrain			1		1
Opps' o.gs.	1				1

MANAGER: Jock Stein

CAPTAIN: Kenny Dalglish

TOP SCORERS: Kenny Dalglish and Ronnie Glavin

BIGGEST WIN: 5-0 v Airdrie, 2 February 1977, Scottish Cup; 5-0 v Arbroath, 21 August 1976, Scottish League Cup

HIGHEST ATTENDANCE: 69,000 v Aberdeen, 6 November 1976, Scottish League Cup

MAJOR TRANSFERS IN: Pat Stanton from Hibernian, Joe Craig from Partick Thistle, Roy Baines from Morton, Alfie Conn from Tottenham

MAJOR TRANSFERS OUT: Tom Callaghan to Clydebank, Denis Connaghan to Clydebank

Final Scottish Premier Division Table

		P	W	D	L	F	A	Pts
1	CELTIC	36	23	9	4	79	39	55
2	RANGERS	36	18	10	8	62	37	46
3	ABERDEEN	36	16	11	9	56	42	43
4	DUNDEE U	36	16	9	11	54	45	41
5	PARTICK T	36	11	13	12	40	44	35
6	HIBERNIAN	36	8	18	10	34	35	34
7	MOTHERWELL	36	10	12	14	57	60	32
8	AYR U	36	11	8	17	44	68	30
9	HEARTS	36	7	13	16	49	66	27
10	KILMARNOCK	36	4	9	23	32	71	17

Fact File

Atholl Henderson made his debut on 1 September in the match against Dundee United, after John Doyle injured himself in the pre-match warm-up.

Season 1977-78

Scottish League Premier Division

DATE	OPPONENTS	SCORE	GOALSCORERS	ATTENDANCE
Aug 13	DUNDEE UNITED	D 0-0		34,000
Aug 20	Ayr United	L 1-2	Craig	14,000
Aug 27	MOTHERWELL	L 0-1		29,000
Sep 10	Rangers	L 2-3	Edvaldsson 2	48,000
Sep 17	Aberdeen	L 1-2	o.g.	25,000
Sep 24	CLYDEBANK	W 1-0	McAdam	20,000
Oct 1	HIBERNIAN	W 3-1	Edvaldsson, Glavin, Craig	26,000
Oct 8	Partick Thistle	L 0-1		19,000
Oct 15	ST MIRREN	L 1-2	McAdam	29,000
Oct 22	Dundee United	W 2-1	Glavin, Wilson	17,000
Oct 29	AYR UNITED	W 3-2	McAdam, Glavin, Macdonald	20,000
Nov 5	Motherwell	W 3-2	Craig 2, Macdonald	16,000
Nov 12	RANGERS	D 1-1	McAdam	56,000
Nov 19	ABERDEEN	W 3-2	Aitken, Edvaldsson, Lynch	27,000
Dec 10	PARTICK THISTLE	W 3-0	McAdam, Macdonald, Lynch	27,000
Dec 17	St Mirren	D 3-3	McAdam, Craig, Lynch	17,000
Dec 24	DUNDEE UNITED	W 1-0	Edvaldsson	21,000
Dec 31	Ayr United	L 1-2	Edvaldsson	14,000
Jan 2	MOTHERWELL	L 0-1		23,000
Jan 7	Rangers	L 1-3	Edvaldsson	51,000
Jan 14	Aberdeen	L 1-2	Macdonald	24,000
Feb 25	ST MIRREN	L 1-2	McCluskey	22,000
Mar 4	Dundee United	W 1-0	o.g.	12,000
Mar 11	AYR UNITED	W 3-0	Edvaldsson, Glavin, McCluskey	15,000
Mar 22	Motherwell	L 1-2	Craig	9,000
Mar 25	RANGERS	W 2-0	Glavin, Macdonald	50,000
Mar 29	Partick Thistle	W 4-0	Burns 2, Macdonald, McAdam	12,000
Apr 1	ABERDEEN	D 2-2	Glavin, Edvaldsson	24,000
Apr 5	HIBERNIAN	W 2-1	McCluskey 2	20,000
Apr 8	Clydebank	L 2-3	McCluskey, Burns	8,000
Apr 12	Hibernian	D 1-1	McCluskey	10,000
Apr 15	Hibernian	L 1-4	Conroy	16,000
Apr 17	CLYDEBANK	W 5-2	Edvaldsson, Aitken, McAdam, Glavin, Macdonald	7,000
Apr 22	PARTICK THISTLE	W 5-2	Doyle 2, Craig 2, Glavin	16,000
Apr 26	Clydebank	D 1-1	Conroy	4,000
Apr 29	St Mirren	L 1-3	Glavin	13,000

Scottish Cup

Feb 6	DUNDEE	(Rd3) W 7-1	McCluskey 3, McAdam 2, Burns, Macdonald	22,000
Feb 27	KILMARNOCK	(Rd4) D 1-1	Macdonald	25,000
Mar 6	Kilmarnock	(R) L 0-1		14,000

Scottish League Cup

Aug 31	MOTHERWELL	(Rd2) D 0-0		23,000
Sep 3	Motherwell	(R) W 4-2	Wilson, Burns, Gray, o.g.	20,000
Oct 5	Stirling Albion	(Rd3) W 2-1	Doyle, Aitken	8,000
Oct 26	STIRLING ALBION	(R) D 1-1	o.g.	12,000
Nov 9	St Mirren	(QF/FL) W 3-1	Craig 2, Edvaldsson	18,000
Nov 16	ST MIRREN	(QF/SL) W 2-0	Wilson, Doyle	17,000
Mar 1	Hearts	(SF) W 2-0	Craig, McCluskey	18,000
Mar 18	Rangers	(F) L 1-2	Edvaldsson	60,000

European Cup

Sep 14	JEUNESSE ESCH	(Rd1/FL) W 5-0	Craig 2, Macdonald, Wilson, McLaughlin	22,000
Sep 28	Jeunesse Esch	(Rd1/SL) W 6-1	Glavin 2, Edvaldsson 2, Lennox, Craig	3,000
Oct 19	SW INNSBRUCK	(Rd2/FL) W 2-1	Craig, Burns	30,000
Nov 2	Sw Innsbruck	(Rd2/SL) L 0-3		22,000

League & Cup Appearances

PLAYER	LEAGUE	CUP COMPETITIONS			TOTAL
		S CUP	SL CUP	E CUP	
Aitken	33	3	6	4	46
Burns	22 (2)	3	6	3	34 (2)
Casey	2 (2)	1	3	3	9 (2)
Conn	9 (1)	2	3 (1)	0 (1)	14 (3)
Conroy	5				5
Coyne	0 (1)				0 (1)
Craig	19 (1)	0 (1)	5 (2)	4	28 (4)
Dowie	12 (2)	1	2 (1)		15 (3)
Doyle	20 (6)		6 (2)	3	29 (8)
Edvaldsson	33 (3)	3	6 (1)	3	45 (1)
Filippi	11 (1)	1 (1)			12 (2)
Glavin	28	1	5 (1)	4	3
Kay	5		4	1	10
Latchford	5	3	4	4	51
Lennox	1 (2)		3 (1)	1 (2)	5 (5)
Lynch	26 (1)		4	3	33 (1)
McAdam	32 (1)	3			35 (1)
McCluskey G	12 (3)	3	2 (1)		17 (4)
McCluskey J			0 (1)		0 (1)
Macdonald	36	3	8	4	51
McGrain	7		2	2	11
Mackie	1 (1)		1 (1)		2 (2)
McLaughlin	1			0 (2)	1 (2)
McWilliams	1		1 (1)	1	3 (1)
Munro	14 (1)	2	5		21 (1)
Sneddon	15	3	2		20
Stanton	1				1
Wilson	14 (6)	1	6 (1)	4	25 (7)

Goalscorers

PLAYER	LEAGUE	CUP COMPETITIONS			TOTAL
		S CUP	SL CUP	E CUP	
Craig	8		4	4	16
Edvaldsson	10		2	2	14
Glavin	9			2	11
McAdam	8	2			10
McCluskey G	6	3	1		10
Macdonald	7	2		1	10
Burns	3	1	1	1	6
Doyle	2		2		4
Wilson	1		2	1	4
Aitken	2		1		3
Lynch	3				3
Conroy	2				2
Lennox	1			1	1
McLaughlin	1			1	1
Opps' o.gs.	1		2		3

Fact File

On 29 March 1978, Roddie Macdonald scored Celtic's 6000th league goal in the match against Partick Thistle.

MANAGER: Jock Stein

CAPTAIN: Danny McGrain

TOP SCORER: Joe Craig

BIGGEST WIN: 7-1 v Dundee, 6 February 1978, Scottish Cup

HIGHEST ATTENDANCE: 60,000 v Rangers, 18 March 1978, Scottish League Cup

MAJOR TRANSFERS IN: John Dowie from Fulham, Tom McAdam from Dundee United

MAJOR TRANSFERS OUT: Kenny Dalglish to Liverpool

Final Scottish Premier Division Table

		P	W	D	L	F	A	Pts
1	RANGERS	36	24	7	5	76	39	55
2	ABERDEEN	36	22	9	5	68	29	53
3	DUNDEE U	36	16	8	12	42	32	40
4	HIBERNIAN	36	15	7	14	51	43	37
5	CELTIC	36	15	6	15	63	54	36
6	MOTHERWELL	36	13	7	16	45	52	33
7	PARTICK T	36	14	5	17	52	64	33
8	ST MIRREN	36	11	8	17	52	63	30
9	AYR U	36	9	6	21	36	68	24
10	CLYDEBANK	36	6	7	23	23	64	19

Season 1978-79

Scottish League Premier Division

DATE	OPPONENTS	SCORE	GOALSCORERS	ATTENDANCE
Aug 12	Morton	W 2-1	Glavin, Macdonald	16,000
Aug 19	HEARTS	W 4-0	Conn 2, Burns, McAdam	24,000
Aug 26	Motherwell	W 5-1	Conn 2, Aitken 2, McAdam	19,000
Sep 9	RANGERS	W 3-1	McAdam 2, McCluskey	60,000
Sep 16	HIBERNIAN	L 0-1		27,000
Sep 23	Partick Thistle	W 3-2	Lynch, Aitken, Macdonald	23,000
Sep 30	ST MIRREN	W 2-1	Lynch, Conn	26,000
Oct 7	Aberdeen	L 1-4	McAdam	25,000
Oct 14	Dundee United	L 0-1		17,000
Oct 21	MORTON	D 0-0		24,000
Oct 28	Hearts	L 0-2		18,000
Nov 4	MOTHERWELL	L 1-2	McAdam	21,000
Nov 11	Rangers*	D 1-1	Lynch	52,000
Nov 18	Hibernian	D 2-2	Provan, MacLeod	22,000
Nov 25	PARTICK THISTLE	W 1-0	McAdam	26,000
Dec 9	ABERDEEN	D 0-0		24,000
Dec 16	DUNDEE UNITED	D 1-1	Lynch	21,000
Dec 23	Morton	L 0-1		13,000
Mar 3	ABERDEEN	W 1-0	Conn	26,000
Mar 17	MOTHERWELL	W 2-1	Lennox 2	16,000
Mar 28	MORTON	W 3-0	Provan, Burns, Glavin	16,000
Mar 31	Hibernian	L 1-2	Glavin	18,000
Apr 4	Motherwell	W 4-3	Doyle, Lennox, McGrain, Davidson	8,000
Apr 7	PARTICK THISTLE	W 2-0	Conroy, Lynch	19,000
Apr 11	Dundee United	L 1-2	Davidson	14,000
Apr 14	St Mirren	W 1-0	McCluskey	19,000
Apr 18	Hearts	W 3-0	MacLeod, Conroy, Burns	21,000
Apr 21	ABERDEEN	D 1-1	Lynch	19,000
Apr 25	ST MIRREN	W 2-1	Edvaldsson, Aitken	18,000
Apr 28	DUNDEE UNITED	W 2-1	Doyle, Lynch	37,000
May 2	HIBERNIAN	W 3-1	Conroy, Provan, McGrain	23,000
May 5	Rangers*	L 0-1		52,000
May 7	Partick Thistle	W 2-1	Provan, McCluskey	18,000
May 11	St Mirren†	W 2-0	Lennox, McCluskey	22,000
May 14	HEARTS	W 1-0	Conroy	18,000
May 21	RANGERS	W 4-2	Aitken, McCluskey, MacLeod, o.g.	52,000

*Played at Hampden Park (Ibrox unavailable). †Played at Ibrox (Love St. unavailable).

Scottish Cup

Jan 31	Montrose	(Rd3) W 4-2	McCluskey 3, Lynch	3,000
Feb 26	BERWICK RANGERS	(Rd4) W 3-0	Lynch, Burns, o.g.	13,000
Mar 10	Aberdeen	(QF) D 1-1	Doyle	24,000
Mar 14	ABERDEEN	(R) L 1-2	Lennox	37,000

Scottish League Cup

Aug 16	DUNDEE	(Rd1/FL) W 3-1	McAdam 2, Glavin	12,000
Aug 23	Dundee	(Rd1/SL) W 3-0	Doyle 2, Conn	12,000
Aug 30	Dundee United	(Rd2/FL) W 3-2	Lynch, Macdonald, Conroy	12,000
Sep 2	DUNDEE UNITED	(Rd2/SL) W 1-0	Glavin	30,000
Oct 4	MOTHERWELL	(Rd3/FL) L 0-1		19,000
Oct 11	Motherwell	(Rd3/SL) W 4-1	McAdam 2, Lennox, Aitken	17,000
Nov 8	Montrose	(QF/FL) D 1-1	Lynch	3,000
Nov 15	MONTROSE	(QF/SL) W 3-1	Lynch, McAdam, Edvaldsson	10,000
Dec 13	Rangers	(SF) L 2-3	Doyle, McAdam	49,000

League & Cup Appearances

PLAYER	LEAGUE	CUP COMPETITIONS		TOTAL
		S CUP	SL CUP	
Aitken	36	3	9	52
Baines	7		3	10
Bonner	2			2
Burns	28 (1)	3	8	43 (1)
Casey	1 (4)		1 (3)	2 (7)
Conn	12 (1)	2	5	22 (1)
Conroy	20 (1)		5	27 (1)
Davidson	12			12
Doyle	23 (2)	4	6 (1)	34 (3)
Edvaldsson	34	4	9	51
Filippi	19 (1)	1	8	29 (1)
Glavin	9 (1)		4 (2)	16 (3)
Latchford	27	4	6	41
Lennox	6 (8)	1	1 (1)	9 (10)
Lynch	27 (1)	4	7	41 (1)
McAdam	24 (4)	0 (1)	9	37 (5)
McCluskey	16 (5)	2	1 (1)	22 (8)
Macdonald	18	4	9	23
McGrain	18	4	1	24
Mackie	0 (2)			0 (2)
MacLeod	23	4		27
Provan	30	4	5	40
Sneddon	4		1	7
Wilson	0 (1)		1 (1)	1 (3)

Goalscorers

PLAYER	LEAGUE	CUP COMPETITIONS		TOTAL
		S CUP	SL CUP	
McAdam	7		6	13
Lynch	7	2	3	12
McCluskey	5	3		8
Conn	6		1	7
Aitken	5		1	6
Doyle	2	1	3	6
Lennox	4	1	1	6
Conroy	4		1	5
Glavin	3		2	5
Burns	3	1		4
Provan	4			4
Macdonald	2		1	3
MacLeod	3			3
Davidson	2			2
Edvaldsson	1		1	2
McGrain	2			2
Opps' o.gs.	1	1		2

Fact File

Celtic won the league in the last game of the season playing with 10 men for 35 minutes and trailing Rangers 0-1.

MANAGER: Billy McNeill

CAPTAIN: Danny McGrain

TOP SCORER: Tom McAdam

BIGGEST WIN: 5-1 v Motherwell, 26 August 1978, league

HIGHEST ATTENDANCE: 60,000 v Rangers, 9 September 1978, league

MAJOR TRANSFERS IN: Davie Provan from Kilmarnock, Murdo MacLeod from Dumbarton

MAJOR TRANSFERS OUT: Joe Craig to Blackburn, Paul Wilson to Motherwell, Ronnie Glavin to Barnsley, Roy Baines to Morton

Final Scottish Premier Division Table

		P	W	D	L	F	A	Pts
1	CELTIC	36	21	6	9	61	37	48
2	RANGERS	36	18	9	9	52	35	45
3	DUNDEE U	36	18	8	10	56	37	44
4	ABERDEEN	36	13	14	9	59	36	40
5	HIBERNIAN	36	12	13	11	44	48	37
6	ST MIRREN	36	15	6	15	45	41	36
7	MORTON	36	12	12	12	52	53	36
8	PARTICK T	36	13	8	15	42	39	34
9	HEARTS	36	8	7	21	39	71	23
10	MOTHERWELL	36	5	7	24	33	86	17

Scottish League Premier Division

DATE	OPPONENTS	SCORE	GOALSCORERS	ATTENDANCE
Aug 11	MORTON	W 3-2	McCluskey, Provan, MacLeod	26,000
Aug 18	Rangers	D 2-2	Sneddon, McAdam	36,000
Aug 25	KILMARNOCK	W 5-0	McCluskey 3, Davidson 2	26,000
Sep 8	DUNDEE UNITED	D 2-2	McCluskey 2	27,000
Sep 15	Hibernian	W 3-1	Lennox, Conroy, MacLeod	18,000
Sep 22	Aberdeen	W 2-1	Aitken, Doyle	23,000
Sep 29	ST MIRREN	W 3-1	MacLeod, Macdonald, McAdam	29,000
Oct 6	Partick Thistle	D 0-0		21,000
Oct 13	DUNDEE	W 3-0	McAdam 2, MacLeod	25,000
Oct 20	Morton	L 0-1		18,000
Oct 27	RANGERS	W 1-0	Macdonald	56,000
Nov 3	Kilmarnock	L 0-2		18,000
Nov 10	Dundee United	W 1-0	Edvaldsson	18,000
Nov 17	HIBERNIAN	W 3-0	Edvaldsson 2, Lennox	25,000
Dec 1	St Mirren	L 1-2	Macdonald	20,000
Dec 15	PARTICK THISTLE	W 5-1	McAdam 2, Macdonald, Lennox, Sullivan	19,000
Dec 22	MORTON	W 3-0	McAdam, Sullivan, Doyle	27,000
Dec 29	Rangers	D 1-1	Lennox	34,000
Jan 5	DUNDEE UNITED	W 1-0	MacLeod	25,000
Jan 12	Hibernian	D 1-1	Aitken	21,000
Jan 19	Aberdeen	D 0-0		24,000
Feb 9	Partick Thistle	D 1-1	MacLeod	17,000
Feb 23	DUNDEE	D 2-2	MacLeod, McCluskey	23,000
Mar 1	Morton	W 1-0	Doyle	20,000
Mar 12	ST MIRREN	D 2-2	Doyle, McCluskey	30,000
Mar 15	Kilmarnock	D 1-1	Lennox	15,000
Mar 29	HIBERNIAN	W 4-0	Lennox, Doyle, McGarvey, Macdonald	22,000
Apr 2	RANGERS	W 1-0	McGarvey	52,000
Apr 5	ABERDEEN	L 1-2	Doyle	40,000
Apr 8	Dundee United	L 0-3		14,000
Apr 16	KILMARNOCK	W 2-0	Macdonald, Doyle	18,000
Apr 19	Dundee	L 1-5	Aitken	14,000
Apr 23	ABERDEEN	L 1-3	McCluskey	48,000
Apr 26	PARTICK THISTLE	W 2-1	McCluskey, McAdam	20,000
Apr 30	Dundee	W 2-0	Conroy, Sullivan	10,000
May 3	St Mirren	D 0-0		20,000

Scottish Cup

Jan 26	RAITH ROVERS	(Rd3) W 2-1	Lennox, Doyle	18,000
Feb 16	ST MIRREN	(Rd4) D 1-1	MacLeod	32,000
Feb 20	St Mirren	(R) W 3-2	Doyle 2, Lennox	27,000
Mar 8	MORTON	(QF) W 2-0	Casey, McCluskey	35,000
Apr 12	Hibernian	(SF) W 5-0	Lennox, Provan, Doyle, McAdam, MacLeod	32,000
May 10	Rangers	(F) W 1-0	McCluskey	70,000

Scottish League Cup

Aug 20	Falkirk	(Rd2/FL) W 2-1	McCluskey, Provan	9,000
Sep 1	FALKIRK	(Rd2/SL) W 4-1	Conroy 2, Lennox, Doyle	17,000
Sep 26	Stirling Albion	(Rd3/FL) W 2-1	McAdam, Doyle	8,000
Oct 10	STIRLING ALBION	(Rd3/SL) W 2-0	MacLeod, Doyle	11,000
Oct 31	Aberdeen	(QF/FL) L 2-3	Edvaldsson, Provan	24,000
Nov 24	ABERDEEN	(QF/SL) L 0-1		39,000

European Cup

Sep 10	Partizan Tirana	(Rd1/FL) L 0-1		25,000
Oct 3	PARTIZAN TIRANA	(Rd1/SL) W 4-1	Aitken 2, Macdonald, Davidson	51,000
Oct 24	DUNDALK	(Rd2/FL) W 3-2	Macdonald, McCluskey, Burns	33,000
Nov 7	Dundalk	(Rd2/SL) D 0-0		16,000
Mar 5	REAL MADRID	(QF/FL) W 2-0	McCluskey, Doyle	67,000
Mar 19	Real Madrid	(QF/SL) L 0-3		110,000

League & Cup Appearances

PLAYER	LEAGUE	CUP COMPETITIONS			TOTAL
		S CUP	SL CUP	E CUP	
Aitken	35	5	6	6	52
Burns	12 (3)	1 (1)		2 (1)	15 (5)
Casey	2 (1)	1			3 (1)
Conroy	13 (5)	1 (1)	3 (1)	2	19 (7)
Davidson	5		4	3 (1)	12 (1)
Doyle	22 (2)	6	4 (1)	3 (1)	35 (4)
Edvaldsson	5 (4)	1	2	1	9 (4)
Latchford	36	6	6	6	54
Lennox	19 (10)	5 (1)	3 (3)	4 (2)	31 (16)
Lynch	1		1		2
McAdam	34	5	6	6	51
McCluskey	22 (1)	3 (2)	5	5	34 (3)
Macdonald	27 (2)	5	4 (1)	5	41 (3)
McGarvey	11 (1)	2			13 (1)
McGrain	34	6	6	6	52
MacLeod	36	6	6	6	54
Provan	35	6	5	6	52
Sneddon	32	6	6	4	48
Sullivan	15	1			16

Goalscorers

PLAYER	LEAGUE	CUP COMPETITIONS			TOTAL
		S CUP	SL CUP	E CUP	
Doyle	7	4	3	1	15
McCluskey	10	2	1	2	15
Lennox	6	3	1		10
McAdam	8	1	1		10
MacLeod	7	2	1		10
Macdonald	6			2	8
Aitken	3			2	5
Conroy	2		2		4
Edvaldsson	3		1		4
Provan	1	1	2		4
Davidson	2			1	2
Sullivan	3				3
McGarvey	2				2
Burns	1			1	1
Casey		1			1
Sneddon	1				1

MANAGER: Billy McNeill

CAPTAIN: Danny McGrain

TOP SCORERS: George McCluskey and John Doyle

BIGGEST WIN: 5-0 v Kilmarnock, 25 August 1979, league;

5-0 v Hibernian, 12 April 1980, Scottish Cup

HIGHEST ATTENDANCE: 110,000 v Real Madrid, 19 March 1980, European Cup

MAJOR TRANSFERS IN: Frank McGarvey from Liverpool, Dominic Sullivan from Aberdeen

MAJOR TRANSFERS OUT: Johannes Edvardsson to Tulsa, Andy Lynch to Philadelphia

Final Scottish Premier Division Table

		P	W	D	L	F	A	Pts
1	ABERDEEN	36	19	10	7	68	36	48
2	CELTIC	36	18	11	7	61	38	47
3	ST MIRREN	36	15	12	9	56	49	42
4	DUNDEE U	36	12	13	11	43	30	37
5	RANGERS	36	15	7	14	50	46	37
6	MORTON	36	14	8	14	51	46	36
7	PARTICK T	36	11	14	11	43	47	36
8	KILMARNOCK	36	11	11	14	36	52	33
9	DUNDEE	36	10	6	20	47	73	26
10	HIBERNIAN	36	6	6	24	29	67	18

Fact File

In the European Cup tie in Tirana, Celtic handed over a pennant to Partizan and, in return, received a book on Albanian architecture.

Season 1980-81

Scottish League Premier Division

DATE	OPPONENTS		SCORE	GOALSCORERS	ATTENDANCE
Aug 9	MORTON		W 2-1	McCluskey, MacLeod	20,000
Aug 16	Kilmarnock		W 3-0	McGarvey 2, Sullivan	13,000
Aug 23	RANGERS		L 1-2	Burns	58,000
Sep 6	PARTICK THISTLE		W 4-1	Nicholas 2, McGarvey, MacLeod	20,000
Sep 13	Hearts		W 2-0	Nicholas, Provan	17,000
Sep 20	AIRDRIE		D 1-1	Nicholas	18,000
Sep 27	Aberdeen		D 2-2	Nicholas, Burns	23,000
Oct 4	DUNDEE UNITED		W 2-0	Nicholas, McGarvey	21,000
Oct 11	St Mirren		W 2-0	o.g. 2	18,000
Oct 18	Morton		W 3-2	Nicholas, Provan, Aitken	16,000
Oct 25	KILMARNOCK		W 4-1	Nicholas 2, McGarvey 2	18,000
Nov 1	Rangers		L 0-3		33,000
Nov 8	ABERDEEN		L 0-2		29,000
Nov 15	Airdrie		W 4-1	Nicholas, Aitken, McGarvey, McAdam	15,000
Nov 22	ST MIRREN		L 1-2	McCluskey	16,000
Nov 29	Dundee United		W 3-0	McAdam, Weir, o.g.	15,000
Dec 6	Partick Thistle		W 1-0	McCluskey	12,000
Dec 13	HEARTS		W 3-2	McCluskey, Macdonald, McGarvey	13,000
Dec 20	AIRDRIE		W 2-1	McCluskey, McAdam	11,000
Dec 27	Aberdeen		L 1-4	Nicholas	23,000
Jan 1	Kilmarnock		W 2-1	McGarvey 2	8,000
Jan 3	MORTON		W 3-0	McGarvey 2, Provan	14,000
Jan 10	DUNDEE UNITED		W 2-1	McGarvey, Nicholas	22,000
Jan 31	Hearts		W 3-0	McGarvey, Burns, Sullivan	14,000
Feb 21	RANGERS		W 3-1	Nicholas 2, Aitken	52,000
Feb 28	Morton		W 3-0	McGvvey 2, Provan	14,000
Mar 14	ST MIRREN		W 7-0	McGarvey 3, McCluskey 2, Aitken, Nicholas	18,000
Mar 18	PARTICK THISTLE		W 4-1	MacLeod 2, McGarvey, Sullivan	15,000
Mar 21	Airdrie		W 2-1	McGarvey, MacLeod	13,000
Mar 28	ABERDEEN		D 1-1	McCluskey	35,000
Apr 1	HEARTS		W 6-0	McCluskey 2, MacLeod 2, McGarvey, Provan	13,000
Apr 5	Partick Thistle		W 1-0	McAdam	17,000
Apr 18	Rangers		W 1-0	Nicholas	34,000
Apr 22	Dundee United		W 3-2	McGarvey, MacLeod, Burns	15,000
Apr 25	KILMARNOCK		D 1-1	Provan	22,000
May 2	St Mirren		L 1-3	Provan	14,000

Scottish Cup

Jan 24	Berwick Rangers	(Rd3) W 2-0	Nicholas, Burns	9,000
Feb 14	STIRLING ALBION	(Rd4) W 3-0	McGarvey, McCluskey, Burns	14,000
Mar 8	EAST STIRLING	(QF) W 2-0	Conroy, MacLeod	18,000
Apr 11	Dundee United	(SF) D 0-0		40,000
Apr 15	Dundee United	(SF) L 2-3	Nicholas 2	32,000

Scottish League Cup

Aug 27	Stirling Albion	(Rd2/FL) L 0-1		5,000
Aug 30	STIRLING ALBION	(Rd2/SL) W 6-1	Burns 2, Nicholas 2, Provan, Sullivan	16,000
Sep 22	Hamilton Ac.	(Rd3/FL) W 3-1	Burns, Nicholas, Doyle	9,000
Sep 24	HAMILTON AC.	(Rd3/SL) W 4-1	McGarvey 2, Burns, Nicholas	10,000
Oct 8	Partick Thistle	(QF/FL) W 1-0	Nicholas	15,000
Oct 20	PARTICK THISTLE	(QF/SL) W 2-1	Burns, Macdonald	12,000
Nov 12	Dundee United	(SF/FL) D 1-1	Nicholas	14,000
Nov 19	DUNDEE UNITED	(SF/SL) L 0-3		21,000

European Cup-Winners' Cup

Aug 20	DIOSGYORI MISKOLC	(PR/FL) W 6-0	McGarvey 3, McCluskey 2, Sullivan	28,000
Sep 3	Diosgyori Miskolc	(PR/SL) L 1-2	Nicholas	8,000
Sep 17	POLITEHNICA TIMISOARA	(Rd1/FL) W 2-1	Nicholas 2	32,000
Oct 1	Politehnica Timisoara	(Rd1/SL) L 0-1		50,000

MANAGER: Billy McNeill

CAPTAIN: Danny McGrain

TOP SCORER: Frank McGarvey

BIGGEST WIN: 7-0 v St Mirren, 14 March 1981, league

HIGHEST ATTENDANCE: 58,000 v Rangers, 23 August 1980, league

MAJOR TRANSFERS OUT: Roddie Macdonald to Hearts, Alan Sneddon to Hibernian

League & Cup Appearances

PLAYER	LEAGUE	CUP COMPETITIONS			TOTAL
		S CUP	SL CUP	ECWC	
Aitken	33	5	8	4	50
Bonner	36	5	8	3	52
Burns	32 (1)	5	7	3	47 (1)
Conroy	14 (1)	4	0 (3)	0 (1)	18 (5)
Doyle	1 (4)	0 (2)	4 (1)	0 (1)	5 (8)
Latchford				1	1
McAdam	35	5	8	4	52
McCluskey	16 (7)	1 (1)	5	2	24 (8)
Macdonald	14		5 (1)	1	20 (1)
McGarvey	33	4	4 (3)	3	44 (3)
McGrain	33	3	8	4	48
MacLeod	14 (4)	2 (2)	3	4	23 (6)
Nicholas	26 (3)	5	5 (2)	3 (1)	39 (6)
Provan	31 (2)	5	7	4	47 (2)
Reid	22	5	2		29
Sneddon	15		6	4	25
Sullivan	30	5	6	4	45
Weir	11	1	2		14

Goalscorers

PLAYER	LEAGUE	CUP COMPETITIONS			TOTAL
		S CUP	SL CUP	ECWC	
McGarvey	23	1	2	3	29
Nicholas	16	3	6	3	28
McCluskey	10	1		2	13
Burns	4	2	5		11
MacLeod	8	1			9
Provan	7		1		8
Sullivan	3		1	1	5
Aitken	4				4
McAdam	4				4
Macdonald	1		1		2
Conroy		1			1
Doyle			1		1
Weir	1				1
Opps' o.gs.	3				3

Fact File

The match on 8 November against Aberdeen was Celtic's first sponsored game – courtesy of Morris Furnishing.

Final Scottish Premier Division Table

		P	W	D	L	F	A	Pts
1	CELTIC	36	26	4	6	84	37	56
2	ABERDEEN	36	19	11	6	61	26	49
3	RANGERS	36	16	12	8	60	32	44
4	ST MIRREN	36	18	8	10	56	47	44
5	DUNDEE U	36	17	9	10	66	42	43
6	PARTICK T	36	10	10	16	32	48	30
7	AIRDRIEONIANS	36	10	9	17	36	55	29
8	MORTON	36	10	8	18	36	58	28
9	KILMARNOCK	36	5	9	22	23	65	19
10	HEARTS	36	6	6	24	27	71	18

Season 1981-82

Scottish League Premier Division

DATE	OPPONENTS	SCORE	GOALSCORERS	ATTENDANCE
Aug 29	AIRDRIE	W 5-2	McCluskey 2, Burns, McGarvey, Nicholas	21,000
Sep 5	Aberdeen	W 3-1	McGarvey 2, Burns	18,000
Sep 12	MORTON	W 2-1	MacLeod, McAdam	19,000
Sep 19	Rangers	W 2-0	McAdam, MacLeod	40,000
Sep 26	PARTICK THISTLE	W 2-0	Nicholas, Burns	15,000
Oct 3	Dundee	W 3-1	McCluskey 2, McGarvey	13,000
Oct 10	St Mirren	W 2-1	McCluskey, Nicholas	16,000
Oct 17	DUNDEE UNITED	D 1-1	McCluskey	23,000
Oct 24	Hibernian	L 0-1		18,000
Oct 31	Airdrie	W 3-1	McCluskey, Sullivan, Burns	13,000
Nov 7	ABERDEEN	W 2-1	McCluskey, McGarvey	29,000
Nov 14	Morton	D 1-1	McCluskey	12,000
Nov 21	RANGERS	D 3-3	McAdam, McGarvey, MacLeod	48,000
Nov 28	Partick Thistle	W 2-0	McCluskey, Provan	13,000
Dec 5	DUNDEE	W 3-1	McGarvey 2, Conroy	14,000
Jan 9	Rangers	L 0-1		42,000
Jan 30	Aberdeen	W 3-1	McCluskey, MacLeod, McStay	20,000
Feb 2	HIBERNIAN	D 0-0		16,000
Feb 6	Dundee	W 3-1	MacLeod 2, McGarvey	11,000
Feb 20	PARTICK THISTLE	D 2-2	McCluskey, Aitken	14,000
Feb 27	Hibernian	L 0-1		15,000
Mar 3	MORTON	W 1-0	McGarvey	9,000
Mar 13	St Mirren	W 5-2	MacLeod 2, Burns, Sullivan, McCluskey	17,000
Mar 20	AIRDRIE	W 2-0	Sullivan, Burns	12,000
Mar 27	ABERDEEN	L 0-1		30,000
Mar 31	Dundee United	W 2-0	Burns 2	15,000
Apr 3	Morton	D 1-1	Crainie	10,000
Apr 10	RANGERS	W 2-1	Crainie, McAdam	49,000
Apr 14	Airdrie	W 5-1	Crainie, Aitken, McCluskey, Reid, Provan	12,000
Apr 17	DUNDEE	W 4-2	McCluskey 2, Provan, Reid	14,000
Apr 21	DUNDEE UNITED	W 3-1	McCluskey 2, Provan	14,000
Apr 24	Partick Thistle	W 3-0	Crainie 3	14,000
May 1	HIBERNIAN	W 6-0	MacLeod 2, Crainie, McCluskey, Aitken, Burns	16,000
May 3	ST MIRREN	D 0-0		27,000
May 8	Dundee United	L 0-3		16,000
May 15	ST MIRREN	W 3-0	McCluskey 2, McAdam	39,000

Scottish Cup

Jan 23	QUEEN OF THE SOUTH	(Rd3) W 4-0	McGarvey, McGrain, McCluskey, Halpin	11,000
Feb 13	Aberdeen	(Rd4) L 0-1		24,000

Scottish League Cup

Aug 8	ST MIRREN	L 1-3	McGarvey	26,000
Aug 12	St Johnstone	L 0-2		10,000
Aug 15	HIBERNIAN	W 4-1	MacLeod 2, Nicholas 2	19,000
Aug 19	ST JOHNSTONE	W 4-1	Provan 2, McGarvey, Nicholas	14,000
Aug 22	St Mirren	W 5-1	McCluskey 3, MacLeod 2	18,000
Aug 26	Hibernian	W 4-1	McGarvey 2, Sullivan, MacLeod	13,000

Celtic did not quality for the quarter-finals.

European Cup

Sep 16	JUVENTUS	(Rd1/FL) W 1-0	MacLeod	60,000
Sep 30	Juventus	(Rd1/SL) L 0-2		69,000

MANAGER: Billy McNeill

CAPTAIN: Danny McGrain

TOP SCORER: George McCluskey

BIGGEST WIN: 6-0 v Hibernian, 1 May 1982, league

HIGHEST ATTENDANCE: 69,000 v Juventus, 30 September 1981, European Cup

League & Cup Appearances

PLAYER	LEAGUE	CUP COMPETITIONS			TOTAL
		S CUP	SL CUP	E CUP	
Aitken	33	2	6	2	43
Bonner	36	2	6	2	46
Burns	33	2	6	2	43
Conroy	6 (2)		0 (1)		6 (3)
Crainie	14 (2)				14 (2)
Garner	1		2		3
Halpin	2 (1)	1 (1)			3 (2)
McAdam	33 (1)	2	3	2	40 (1)
McCluskey	35	2	3 (1)	2	42 (1)
McGarvey	25 (1)	2	6	1	34 (1)
McGrain	27	2	5	1	35
MacLeod	36	2	6	2	46
McStay	7 (3)	2			9 (3)
Moyes	15 (4)		3 (1)	1	19 (5)
Nicholas	7 (3)		3	1	11 (3)
Provan	19 (1)		6	2	27 (1)
Reid	36	2	5	2	45
Sullivan	31	1	6	2	40

Goalscorers

PLAYER	LEAGUE	CUP COMPETITIONS			TOTAL
		S CUP	SL CUP	E CUP	
McCluskey	21	1	3		25
MacLeod	10		5	1	16
McGarvey	10	1	4		15
Burns	9				9
Crainie	7				7
Nicholas	3		3		6
Provan	4		2		6
McAdam	5				5
Sullivan	3		1		4
Aitken	3				3
Reid	2				2
Conroy	1				1
Halpin		1			1
McGrain		1			1
McStay	1				1

Fact File

For the first time in 18 years, Celtic failed to qualify for the Scottish League Cup quarter-finals.

Final Scottish Premier Division Table

		P	W	D	L	F	A	Pts
1	CELTIC	36	24	7	5	79	33	55
2	ABERDEEN	36	23	7	6	71	29	53
3	RANGERS	36	16	11	9	57	45	43
4	DUNDEE U	36	15	10	11	61	38	40
5	ST MIRREN	36	14	9	13	49	52	37
6	HIBERNIAN	36	11	14	11	38	40	36
7	MORTON	36	9	12	15	31	54	30
8	DUNDEE	36	11	4	21	46	72	26
9	PARTICK T	36	6	10	20	35	59	22
10	AIRDRIEONIANS	36	5	8	23	31	76	18

Season 1982-83

Scottish League Premier Division

DATE	OPPONENTS		SCORE	GOALSCORERS	ATTENDANCE
Sep 4	DUNDEE		W 2-0	Provan, Aitken	19,000
Sep 11	St Mirren		W 2-1	Nicholas 2	15,000
Sep 18	Motherwell		W 7-0	Nicholas 3, Aitken 2, McGarvey, MacLeod	17,000
Sep 25	HIBERNIAN		W 2-0	McStay P, MacLeod	16,000
Oct 2	Dundee United		D 2-2	McStay P, Aitken	20,000
Oct 9	ABERDEEN		L 1-3	Nicholas	29,000
Oct 16	KILMARNOCK		W 2-1	Nicholas 2	11,000
Oct 23	Morton		W 2-1	Nicholas, McGarvey	12,000
Oct 30	RANGERS		W 3-2	McStay P, McGarvey, MacLeod	60,000
Nov 6	Dundee		W 3-2	Nicholas, McGarvey, Burns	11,000
Nov 13	ST MIRREN		W 5-0	Nicholas 3, Aitken, Burns	15,000
Nov 20	MOTHERWELL		W 3-1	Nicholas, McStay P, Burns	14,000
Nov 27	Hibernian		W 3-2	McGarvey 2, McStay P	17,000
Dec 11	Aberdeen		W 2-1	MacLeod, Provan	25,000
Dec 18	Kilmarnock		W 4-0	Provan, McAdam, McGarvey, Burns	9,000
Dec 27	MORTON		W 5-1	McGarvey 2, Nicholas, MacLeod, Reid	19,000
Jan 1	Rangers		W 2-1	McStay P, Nicholas	44,000
Jan 3	DUNDEE		D 2-2	Burns, Nicholas	16,000
Jan 8	St Mirren		W 1-0	MacLeod	14,000
Jan 15	Motherwell		L 1-2	MacLeod	15,000
Jan 22	HIBERNIAN		W 4-1	McGarvey 2, Nicholas, McCluskey	17,000
Feb 5	Dundee United		D 1-1	Nicholas	17,000
Feb 12	ABERDEEN		L 1-3	Nicholas	42,000
Feb 26	KILMARNOCK		W 4-0	McGarvey 2, Nicholas, MacLeod	10,000
Mar 5	Morton		W 3-0	Sullivan, MacLeod, McCluskey	8,000
Mar 19	Dundee		L 1-2	McGarvey	11,000
Mar 23	RANGERS		D 0-0		51,000
Mar 26	ST MIRREN		D 1-1	Provan	15,000
Apr 2	MOTHERWELL		W 3-0	McGarvey, McAdam, o.g.	15,000
Apr 6	DUNDEE UNITED		W 2-0	McGarvey, Nicholas	34,000
Apr 9	Hibernian		W 3-0	Nicholas 2, Provan	15,000
Apr 20	DUNDEE UNITED		L 2-3	Nicholas, Burns	23,000
Apr 23	Aberdeen		L 0-1		24,000
Apr 30	Kilmarnock		W 5-0	MacLeod 2, McGrain, Nicholas, Burns	7,000
May 7	MORTON		W 2-0	Nicholas, Aitken	12,000
May 14	Rangers		W 4-2	Nicholas 2, McAdam, McGarvey	39,000

Scottish Cup

Jan 28	Clydebank	(Rd3)	W 3-0	Nicholas 2, McCluskey	9,000
Feb 19	DUNFERMLINE ATHLETIC	(Rd4)	W 3-0	McGarvey 2, McCluskey	12,000
Mar 12	HEARTS	(QF)	W 4-1	Nicholas 2, MacLeod, McGarvey	25,000
Apr 16	Aberdeen	(SF)	L 0-1		51,000

Scottish League Cup

Aug 14	DUNFERMLINE ATHLETIC		W 6-0	McCluskey 2, Provan 2, McGarvey, Reid	14,000
Aug 18	Alloa Athletic		W 5-0	McCluskey, McStay P, Burns, McGrain, Reid	4,000
Aug 21	Arbroath		W 3-0	McCluskey, Nicholas, Crainie	5,000
Aug 25	ALLOA ATHLETIC		W 4-1	Nicholas, MacLeod, Aitken, Burns	6,000
Aug 28	Dunfermline Athletic		W 7-1	Nicholas 4, Burns, McCluskey, o.g.	8,000
Sep 1	ARBROATH		W 4-1	Nicholas, McCluskey, Dobbin, MacLeod	5,000
Sep 8	PARTICK THISTLE	(QF/FL)	W 4-0	Provan, Nicholas, MacLeod, McGarvey	9,000
Sep 22	Partick Thistle	(QF/SL)	W 3-0	Nicholas 2, MacLeod	8,000
Oct 27	DUNDEE UNITED	(SF/FL)	W 2-0	Nicholas, McGarvey	19,000
Nov 10	Dundee United	(SF/SL)	L 1-2	Nicholas	15,000
Dec 4	Rangers	(F)	W 2-1	Nicholas, MacLeod	55,000

European Cup

Sep 15	AJAX	(Rd1/FL)	D 2-2	Nicholas, McGarvey	56,000
Sep 29	Ajax	(Rd1/SL)	W 2-1	Nicholas, McCluskey	65,000
Oct 20	Real Sociedad	(Rd2/FL)	L 0-2		31,000
Nov 3	REAL SOCIEDAD	(Rd2/SL)	W 2-1	MacLeod 2	54,000

League & Cup Appearances

PLAYER	LEAGUE	CUP COMPETITIONS			TOTAL
		S CUP	SL CUP	E CUP	
Aitken	33	4	11	3	51
Bonner	36	4	10	4	54
Buckley			1		1
Burns	17	1	8	1 (1)	27 (1)
Conroy	1				1
Crainie	3 (4)	0 (1)	1 (3)		4 (8)
Dobbin			1		1
Halpin			0 (1)		0 (1)
McAdam	35	4	7	4	50
McCluskey	7 (13)	2 (1)	6 (1)	0 (2)	15 (17)
McGarvey	32 (2)	4	8 (2)	4	48 (4)
McGrain	34	3	10	4	51
McInally	0 (1)		1		2 (1)
MacLeod	35	4	11	4	54
McStay P	36	4	9	4	53
McStay W	0 (1)				0 (1)
Moyes	4 (1)		5	1 (1)	10 (2)
Nicholas	35	4	8 (2)	4	50 (2)
Provan	33	4	10	4	51
Reid	24 (2)	2	8 (1)	4	38 (3)
Sinclair	25	3	4 (1)	3	35 (1)
Sullivan	7 (1)	1 (1)	0 (1)	0 (1)	8 (4)

Goalscorers

PLAYER	LEAGUE	CUP COMPETITIONS			TOTAL
		S CUP	SL CUP	E CUP	
Nicholas	29	4	13	2	48
McGarvey	17	3	3	1	24
MacLeod	11	1	5	2	19
McCluskey	2	2	6	1	11
Burns	7		3		10
Provan	5		3		8
Aitken	6		1		7
McStay P	6		1		7
McAdam	3				3
Reid	1		2		3
McGrain	1		1		2
Dobbin			1		1
Crainie			1		1
Sullivan	1				1
Opps' o.gs.	1		1		2

Fact File

Davie Provan's reward for being Man of the Match in the Scottish League Cup final against Rangers was a holiday for two in the USA.

MANAGER: Billy McNeill

CAPTAIN: Danny McGrain

TOP SCORER: Charlie Nicholas

BIGGEST WIN: 7-0 v Motherwell, 18 September 1982, league

HIGHEST ATTENDANCE: 65,000 v Ajax, 29 September 1982, European Cup

MAJOR TRANSFERS IN: Graeme Sinclair from Dumbarton

Final Scottish Premier Division Table

		P	W	D	L	F	A	Pts
1	DUNDEE U	36	24	8	4	90	35	56
2	CELTIC	36	25	5	6	90	36	55
3	ABERDEEN	36	25	5	6	76	24	55
4	RANGERS	36	13	12	11	52	41	38
5	ST MIRREN	36	11	12	13	47	51	34
6	DUNDEE	36	9	11	16	42	53	29
7	HIBERNIAN	36	7	15	14	35	51	29
8	MOTHERWELL	36	11	5	20	39	73	27
9	MORTON	36	6	8	22	30	74	20
10	KILMARNOCK	36	3	11	22	28	91	17

Scottish League Premier Division

DATE	OPPONENTS	SCORE	GOALSCORERS	ATTENDANCE
Aug 20	Hibernian	W 2-0	MacLeod, Melrose	14,000
Sep 3	RANGERS	W 2-1	Aitken, McGarvey	50,000
Sep 10	ST JOHNSTONE	W 5-2	Burns 2, McGarvey, Melrose, o.g.	11,000
Sep 17	Motherwell	W 3-0	Burns, McGarvey, McStay P	14,000
Sep 24	Dundee	W 6-2	McClair 4, Burns, Melrose	11,000
Oct 1	ST MIRREN	D 1-1	Whittaker	15,000
Oct 8	Dundee United	L 1-2	Melrose	20,000
Oct 15	HEARTS	D 1-1	McGarvey	20,000
Oct 22	Aberdeen	L 1-3	Aitken	23,000
Oct 20	HIBERNIAN	W 5-1	McClair 2, Provan, Whittaker, MacLeod	13,000
Nov 5	Rangers	W 2-1	McGarvey, Burns	40,000
Nov 12	MOTHERWELL	W 4-0	McClair 2, MacLeod, McGarvey	13,000
Nov 19	St Mirren	L 2-4	Burns, Aitken	13,000
Nov 26	DUNDEE	W 1-0	Reid	14,000
Dec 3	St Johnstone	W 3-0	Dobbin, Melrose, Aitken	8,000
Dec 10	ABERDEEN	D 0-0		25,000
Dec 17	Hearts	W 3-1	McClair 2, Dobbin	15,000
Dec 27	DUNDEE UNITED	D 1-1	McClair	25,000
Dec 31	Hibernian	W 1-0	o.g	11,000
Jan 7	Motherwell	D 2-2	McGarvey, McStay P	11,000
Feb 4	Aberdeen	L 0-1		22,000
Feb 11	ST JOHNSTONE	W 5-2	McClair 2, MacLeod 2, McGarvey	9,000
Feb 14	ST MIRREN	W 2-0	McGarvey 2	9,000
Feb 25	HEARTS	W 4-1	McClair 3, Colquhoun	17,000
Mar 3	Dundee United	L 1-3	Aitken	15,000
Mar 20	Dundee	L 2-3	Burns, Reid	7,000
Mar 31	ABERDEEN	W 1-0		19,000
Apr 2	RANGERS	W 3-0	McStay P, McStay W, Provan	53,000
Apr 7	St Johnstone	D 0-0		6,000
Apr 10	MOTHERWELL	W 4-2	McClair 2, MacLeod, Archdeacon	5,000
Apr 18	St Mirren	W 4-2	McClair 2, Burns, Sinclair	6,000
Apr 21	Rangers	L 0-1		40,000
Apr 24	DUNDEE	W 3-0	McClair, Melrose, McAdam	4,000
Apr 28	HIBERNIAN	W 3-2	McClair 2, Colquhoun	9,000
May 5	Hearts	D 1-1	Burns	12,000
May 12	DUNDEE UNITED	D 1-1	MacLeod	10,000

Scottish Cup

Jan 28	Berwick Rangers	(Rd3) W 4-0	McClair 2, McGarvey, Melrose	5,000
Feb 18	East Fife	(Rd4) W 6-0	Burns 2, McGarvey, Colquhoun, McClair, MacLeod	10,000
Mar 17	Motherwell	(QF) W 6-0	McClair 2, Reid, Burns, McGarvey, MacLeod	14,000
Apr 14	St Mirren	(SF) W 2-1	McClair, McStay P	24,000
May 19	Aberdeen	(F) L 1-2	McStay P	58,000

Scottish League Cup

Aug 2	Brechin City	W 1-0	Melrose	3,000
Aug 7	BRECHIN CITY	D 0-0		8,000
Aug 31	Airdrie	W 6-1	MacLeod, Provan, McStay P, McGarvey, Whittaker, o.g.	11,000
Sep 7	HIBERNIAN	W 5-1	Reid 2, Melrose, McStay P, McGarvey	5,000
Oct 5	KILMARNOCK	D 1-1	MacLeod	9,000
Oct 16	Hibernian	D 0-0		5,000
Nov 9	AIRDRIE	D 0-0		9,000
Nov 30	Kilmarnock	W 1-0	Melrose	23,000
Feb 22	Aberdeen	(SF/FL) D 0-0		41,000
Mar 10	ABERDEEN	(SF/SL) W 1-0	Reid	66,000
Mar 25	Rangers	(F) L 2-3	McClair, Reid	66,369

UEFA Cup

Sep 14	AARHUS GF	(Rd1/FL) W 1-0	Aitken	23,000
Sep 28	Aarhus GF	(Rd1/SL) W 4-1	MacLeod, McGarvey, Aitken, Provan	15,000
Oct 19	Sporting Lisbon	(Rd2/FL) L 0-2		57,000
Nov 2	SPORTING LISBON	(Rd2/SL) W 5-0	Burns, McAdam, McClair, MacLeod, McGarvey	39,000
Nov 23	Nottingham Forest	(Rd3/FL) D 0-0		32,000
Dec 7	NOTTINGHAM FOREST	(Rd3/SL) L 1-2	MacLeod	66,000

Fact File

On 17 September against Motherwell, Jim Melrose came on as a substitute and was booked immediately because he came on without permission.

League & Cup Appearances

PLAYER	LEAGUE	CUP COMPETITIONS			TOTAL
		S CUP	SL CUP	UEFA	
Aitken	31	4	16	6	51
Archdeacon	0 (1)				0 (1)
Bonner	33	5	11	6	55
Burns	31 (1)	5	11	6	53 (1)
Colquhoun	11 (1)	1			12 (1)
Crainie	0 (2)		1 (1)		1 (3)
Dobbin	1 (1)		3		4 (2)
Grant	2 (1)				2 (1)
Halpin	1 (3)		1 (3)	0 (1)	2 (7)
Latchford	3				3
McAdam	28	4	7	5	44
McClair	28 (7)	5	8 (1)	3 (3)	44 (11)
McGarvey	28 (2)	4 (1)	10	6	48 (3)
McGrain	33	5	10	6	54
McGugan	1				1
MacLeod	34	5	10	6	55
McStay P	34	5	8	6	53
McStay W	15 (3)	2	5	1	23 (3)
Melrose	20 (9)	2 (2)	6 (1)	3 (3)	31 (15)
Provan	14 (4)	3	5 (1)	4	26 (5)
Reid	23 (1)	5	5 (1)	4 (1)	37 (3)
Sinclair	15 (5)	0 (2)	4 (1)	4	23 (8)
Whittaker	10		6		16

Goalscorers

PLAYER	LEAGUE	CUP COMPETITIONS			TOTAL
		S CUP	SL CUP	UEFA	
McClair	23	6	1	1	31
McGarvey	10	3	2	2	17
MacLeod	7	2	2	3	14
Burns	9	3		1	13
Melrose	6	1	3		10
Aitken	5			2	7
McStay P	3	2	2		7
Reid	2	1	4		7
Provan	2		1	1	4
Colquhoun	2	1			3
Whittaker	2		1		3
Dobbin	2				2
McAdam	1			1	2
Archdeacon	1				1
McStay W	1				1
Sinclair	1				1
Opps' o.gs.	2		1		3

MANAGER: Davie Hay

CAPTAIN: Danny McGrain

TOP SCORER: Brian McClair

BIGGEST WIN: 6-1 v Airdrie, 31 August 1983, Scottish League Cup

HIGHEST ATTENDANCE: 66,639 v Rangers, 25 May 1984, Scottish League Cup

MAJOR TRANSFERS IN: Brian McClair from Motherwell, John Colquhoun from Stirling Albion

MAJOR TRANSFERS OUT: Charlie Nicholas to Arsenal, George McCluskey to Leeds

Final Scottish Premier Division Table

		P	W	D	L	F	A	Pts
1	ABERDEEN	36	25	7	4	78	21	57
2	CELTIC	36	21	8	7	80	41	50
3	DUNDEE U	36	18	11	7	67	39	47
4	RANGERS	36	15	12	9	53	41	42
5	HEARTS	36	10	16	10	38	47	36
6	ST MIRREN	36	9	14	13	55	59	32
7	HIBERNIAN	36	12	7	17	45	55	31
8	DUNDEE	36	11	5	20	50	74	27
9	ST JOHNSTONE	36	10	3	23	36	81	23
10	MOTHERWELL	36	4	7	25	31	75	15

Season 1984-85

Scottish League Premier Division

DATE	OPPONENTS	SCORE	GOALSCORERS	ATTENDANCE
Aug 11	Hibernian	D 0-0		15,000
Aug 18	DUNDEE UNITED	D 1-1	McClair	19,000
Aug 25	Rangers	D 0-0		44,000
Sep 1	MORTON	W 5-0	McClair 2, McGarvey 2, Grant	12,000
Sep 8	Dumbarton	D 1-1	McGarvey	8,000
Sep 15	HEARTS	W 1-0	McGarvey	18,000
Sep 22	St Mirren	W 2-1	McClair, Colquhoun	12,000
Sep 27	Dundee	W 3-2	Burns, Colquhoun, Grant (pen)	13,000
Oct 6	ABERDEEN	W 2-1	McGarvey, Provan	31,420
Oct 13	HIBERNIAN	W 3-0	Burns, McClair, Grant (pen)	27,863
Oct 20	Dundee United	W 3-1	Johnston, MacLeod, Grant	16,729
Nov 3	Morton	L 1-2	Johnston	8,503
Nov 10	DUMBARTON	W 2-0	Johnston, McGarvey	13,792
Nov 17	Hearts	W 5-1	McClair 3, Johnston, Burns	20,117
Nov 24	ST MIRREN	W 7-1	McGarvey 3, McStay P, Burns, Provan, McClair	16,418
Dec 1	DUNDEE	W 5-1	Johnston 3, McGarvey, Burns	15,889
Dec 8	Aberdeen	L 2-4	Johnston (pen), McGarvey	23,000
Dec 15	Hibernian	W 1-0	Johnston	10,000
Dec 22	RANGERS	D 1-1	McClair	43,748
Dec 29	DUNDEE UNITED	L 1-2	Burns	22,894
Jan 1	Rangers	W 2-1	Johnston, McClair	45,000
Feb 2	St Mirren	W 2-0	Johnston, Burns	14,026
Feb 9	Dundee	L 0-2		12,087
Feb 19	MORTON	W 4-0	McGarvey, McStay P, Provan, Chalmers	10,197
Feb 23	ABERDEEN	W 2-0	Johnston, McStay P (pen)	48,824
Mar 2	Dundee United	D 0-0		16,493
Mar 16	HIBERNIAN	L 0-1		15,820
Mar 20	HEARTS	W 3-2	Johnston, MacLeod, McClair	11,522
Mar 23	Morton	W 7-2	McClair 4, McGarvey 2, Archdeacon	8,000
Apr 3	Dumbarton	W 2-0	McClair, Johnston	7,000
Apr 6	Hearts	W 2-0	McClair, McStay P	14,883
Apr 20	ST MIRREN	W 3-0	Aitken 2 (pen), McGarvey	11,746
Apr 27	Aberdeen	D 1-1	Aitken (pen)	23,000
May 1	RANGERS	D 1-1	McInally	40,079
May 4	DUNDEE	L 0-1		8,815
May 11	DUMBARTON	W 2-0	McClair, McStay W	6,514

Scottish Cup

Jan 30	Hamilton Ac.	(Rd3)	W 2-1	McGarvey 2	10,000
Feb 16	INVERNESS THISTLE	(Rd4)	W 6-0	McStay P 3, Johnston, McGarvey, MacLeod	14,927
Mar 9	Dundee	(QF)	D 1-1	Johnston	21,301
Mar 13	DUNDEE	(R)	W 2-1	McGarvey, Johnston	37,930
Apr 13	Motherwell	(SF)	D 1-1	Burns	30,536
Apr 17	Motherwell	(R)	W 3-0	Johnston 2, Aitken	25,677
May 18	Dundee United	(F)	W 2-1	Provan, McGarvey	60,346

Scottish League Cup

Aug 22	Dunfermline Athletic	(Rd2)	W 3-2	McClair 2, McInally	7,230
Aug 29	Airdrie	(Rd3)	W 4-0	Burns, McInally, Grant, McClair	11,411
Sep 4	Dundee United	(QF)	L 1-2	McInally	21,182

European Cup-Winners' Cup

Sep 19	KAA Gent	(Rd1/FL)	L 0-1		22,500
Oct 3	KAA GENT	(Rd1/SL)	W 3-0	McGarvey 2, McStay P	32,749
Oct 24	Rapid Vienna	(Rd2/FL)	L 1-3	McClair	16,000
Dec 12	Rapid Vienna*	(Rd2/P-o)	L 0-1		51,500

*2nd leg Play-off, played at Old Trafford. Celtic won the original 2nd leg 3-0, but because of crowd trouble the game was expunged from records by UEFA and replayed at a neutral venue.

MANAGER: Davie Hay

CAPTAIN: Danny McGrain

TOP SCORER: Brian McClair

BIGGEST WIN: 7-1 v St Mirren, 24 November 1984, league

HIGHEST ATTENDANCE: 60,346 v Dundee United, 18 May 1985, Scottish Cup

MAJOR TRANSFERS IN: Maurice Johnston from Watford, Pierce O'Leary from Vancouver

MAJOR TRANSFERS OUT: Mark Reid to Charlton

League & Cup Appearances

PLAYER	LEAGUE	CUP COMPETITIONS			TOTAL
		S CUP	SL CUP	ECWC	
Aitken	33	5	3	4	45
Archdeacon	1 (2)	0 (1)			1 (3)
Bonner	34	6	3	4	47
Burns	25 (2)	4 (2)	3 (1)	3	35 (5)
Chalmers	0 (1)				0 (1)
Colquhoun	14 (5)			1 (1)	18 (6)
Coyle	0 (1)				0 (1)
Grant	19 (1)	2 (1)	3	4	26 (2)
Johnston	27	7			34
Latchford	2	1			3
McAdam	25 (1)	6 (1)	3	3	37 (2)
McClair	25 (7)	3 (3)	3	4	35 (10)
McGarvey	30 (3)	4 (3)	1 (1)	4	39 (7)
McGrain	30	7	3	4	44
McGugan	3				3
McInally	4 (8)	1 (1)	2 (1)	0 (1)	6 (11)
McKechnie	1 (1)				1 (1)
MacLeod	30 (1)	7		4	41 (1)
McStay P	32 (2)	7		4	45 (2)
McStay W	11 (3)	4	1 (1)	1	17 (4)
Melrose			0 (1)		0 (1)
O'Leary	11	4 (1)			15 (1)
Provan	19 (6)	7		2 (1)	28 (7)
Reid	15 (1)	3	1	2	21 (1)
Sinclair	5 (1)		2		7 (1)

Goalscorers

PLAYER	LEAGUE	CUP COMPETITIONS			TOTAL
		S CUP	SL CUP	ECWC	
McClair	19		3	1	23
McGarvey	15	5		2	22
Johnston	14	5			19
Burns	7	1	1		9
McStay P	4	3		1	8
Grant	4		1		5
Aitken	3	1			4
McInally	1		3		4
Provan	3	1			4
MacLeod	2	1			3
Colquhoun	2				2
Archdeacon	1				1
Chalmers	1				1
McStay W	1				1

Fact File

Celtic jerseys were adorned with an advertising slogan for the first time this season.

Final Scottish Premier Division Table

		P	W	D	L	F	A	Pts
1	ABERDEEN	36	27	5	4	89	26	59
2	CELTIC	36	22	8	6	77	30	52
3	DUNDEE U	36	20	7	9	67	33	47
4	RANGERS	36	13	12	11	47	38	38
5	ST MIRREN	36	17	4	15	51	56	38
6	DUNDEE	36	15	7	14	48	50	37
7	HEARTS	36	13	5	18	47	64	31
8	HIBERNIAN	36	10	7	19	38	61	27
9	DUMBARTON	36	6	7	23	29	64	19
10	MORTON	36	5	2	29	29	100	12

Season 1985-86

Scottish League Premier Division

DATE	OPPONENTS	SCORE	GOALSCORERS	ATTENDANCE
Aug 10	Hearts	D 1-1	McStay P	21,780
Aug 17	MOTHERWELL	W 2-1	McClair, Provan	20,198
Aug 24	Clydebank	W 2-0	Johnston 2	9,100
Aug 31	RANGERS	D 1-1	McStay P	58,365
Sep 7	Hibernian	W 5-0	McClair 2, Johnston, Archdeacon, o.g.	13,150
Sep 14	ABERDEEN	W 2-1	McClair 2	39,540
Sep 28	Dundee	W 2-0	McClair, Johnston	15,378
Oct 5	ST MIRREN	W 2-0	McClair, McGugan	25,651
Oct 12	HEARTS	L 0-1		26,638
Oct 19	Motherwell	W 2-1	McStay P 2 (1 pen)	13,902
Oct 26	DUNDEE UNITED	L 0-3		25,967
Nov 2	Aberdeen	L 1-4	Provan	23,000
Nov 9	Rangers	L 0-3		42,054
Nov 16	CLYDEBANK	W 2-0	McGhee 2	14,418
Nov 23	HIBERNIAN	D 1-1	Johnston	21,000
Dec 14	Hearts	D 1-1	McGhee	22,361
Dec 23	Dundee United	L 0-1		15,074
Dec 28	CLYDEBANK	W 2-0	Johnston, McStay P (pen)	13,822
Jan 1	RANGERS	W 2-0	McGugan, McClair	49,000
Jan 4	Dundee United	L 2-4	McClair 2	16,113
Jan 11	ABERDEEN	D 1-1	Grant	31,317
Jan 15	MOTHERWELL	W 3-2	McGhee, Johnston, McClair	12,000
Jan 18	Hibernian	D 2-2	Archdeacon, Burns	13,500
Feb 1	Dundee	W 3-1	Johnston, McStay P, McClair	12,295
Feb 8	ST MIRREN	D 1-1	Burns	18,103
Feb 22	HEARTS	D 1-1	Johnston	45,366
Mar 15	DUNDEE UNITED	D 1-1	MacLeod	22,956
Mar 22	Rangers	D 4-4	Johnston, McClair, Burns, MacLeod	41,006
Mar 29	Clydebank	W 5-0	McClair 3 (2 pen), Burns, McInally	7,969
Apr 2	DUNDEE	W 2-1	Johnston, Burns	12,506
Apr 5	St Mirren	W 2-1	MacLeod, McStay P	11,286
Apr 12	Aberdeen	W 1-0	Johnston	22,000
Apr 19	HIBERNIAN	W 2-0	Archdeacon, McClair	15,966
Apr 26	DUNDEE	W 2-0	McClair, Johnston	14,511
Apr 30	Motherwell	W 2-0	McClair 2 (1 pen)	10,545
May 3	St Mirren	W 5-0	McClair 2, Johnston 2, McStay P	17,577

Scottish Cup

Jan 25	ST JOHNSTONE	(Rd3) W 2-0	Grant, Johnston	15,008
Feb 15	QUEEN'S PARK	(Rd4) W 2-1	McClair, Aitken	11,656
Mar 8	Hibernian	(QF) L 3-4	McClair 2 (1 pen), McGhee	20,000

Scottish League Cup

Aug 21	Queen of the South	(Rd2) W 4-1	Johnston 2, McClair, McInally	6,404
Aug 28	BRECHIN CITY	(Rd3) W 7-0	Johnston 2, Aitken (pen), McInally, Burns, McStay P, Provan	9,292
Sep 4	Hibernian	(QF) D 4-4*	Johnston 2, Provan, Aitken	15,500
			*Lost on penalties.	

European Cup-Winners' Cup

Sep 18	Atletico Madrid	(Rd1/FL) D 1-1	Johnston	55,000
Oct 2	ATLETICO MADRID	(Rd1/SL) L 1-2	Aitken	(Behind closed doors)

League & Cup Appearances

PLAYER	LEAGUE	CUP COMPETITIONS			TOTAL
		S CUP	SL CUP	ECWC	
Aitken	36	3	3	2	43
Archdeacon	19 (4)	3			22 (4)
Bonner	30		3	2	35
Burns	34	3	3	2	42
Chalmers	0 (3)				0 (3)
Coyle	1				1
Grant	26 (4)	2	3	2	33 (4)
Johnston	31 (1)	3	3	2	39 (1)
Latchford	6	3			9
McAdam	5	1	2 (1)	0 (1)	8 (2)
McClair	33 (1)	2 (1)	3	2	40 (2)
McGhee	13 (5)	3 (1)			16 (6)
McGrain	27 (1)	2	2	2	33 (1)
McGugan	19 (2)	1		2	22 (2)
McInally	5 (1)	1 (2)	1	1 (1)	7 (14)
MacLeod	29 (1)	2	3	2	36 (1)
McStay P	34	2	2	2	40
McStay W	14 (4)	1	1		16 (4)
O'Leary	12 (1)	1	1 (2)		14 (3)
Provan	11 (1)		3	2	16 (1)
Shepherd	0 (1)	1			1 (1)
Whyte	11				11

Goalscorers

PLAYER	LEAGUE	CUP COMPETITIONS			TOTAL
		S CUP	SL CUP	ECWC	
McClair	22	3	1		26
Johnston	15	1	6	1	23
McStay P	8		1		9
Burns	5		1		6
McGhee	4	1			5
Provan	2		2		4
Archdeacon	3				3
MacLeod	3				3
McInally	1		2		3
Aitken			2		2
Grant	1	1			2
McGugan	2				2
Opps' o.gs.	1				1

Fact File

The European Cup-Winners' Cup home match against Atletico Madrid was ordered to be played behind closed doors.

MANAGER: Davie Hay

CAPTAIN: Danny McGrain

TOP SCORER: Brian McClair

BIGGEST WIN: 7-0 v Brechin City, 28 August 1985, Scottish League Cup

HIGHEST ATTENDANCE: 58,365 v Rangers, 31 August 1985, league

MAJOR TRANSFERS IN: Mark McGhee from Hamburg

Final Scottish Premier Division Table

		P	W	D	L	F	A	PTS
1	CELTIC	36	20	10	6	67	38	50
2	HEARTS	36	20	10	6	59	33	50
3	DUNDEE U	36	18	11	7	59	31	47
4	ABERDEEN	36	16	12	8	62	31	44
5	RANGERS	36	13	9	14	53	45	35
6	DUNDEE	36	14	7	15	45	51	35
7	ST MIRREN	36	13	5	18	42	63	31
8	HIBERNIAN	36	11	6	19	49	63	28
9	MOTHERWELL	36	7	6	23	33	66	20
10	CLYDEBANK	36	6	8	22	29	77	20

Season 1986-87

Scottish League Premier Division

DATE	OPPONENTS	SCORE	GOALSCORERS	ATTENDANCE
Aug 9	DUNDEE	W 1-0	Johnston	35,433
Aug 13	Motherwell	W 4-0	McClair 2 (1 pen), Johnston 2	13,325
Aug 11	Clydebank	W 1-0	Johnston	9,850
Aug 23	ABERDEEN	D 1-1	MacLeod	46,073
Aug 31	Rangers	L 0-1		43,502
Sep 6	HAMILTON AC.	W 4-1	McInally 3, Johnston	17,036
Sep 13	Dundee United	D 2-2	McClair, McStay P	19,972
Sep 20	HIBERNIAN	W 5-1	McClair 2, McStay P, Johnston, McInally	22,140
Sep 27	Falkirk	W 1-0	Johnston	16,400
Oct 4	ST MIRREN	W 2-0	Johnston, McClair	20,526
Oct 8	HEARTS	W 2-0	Johnston, McClair (pen)	34,382
Oct 11	Dundee	W 3-0	Johnston 2, McClair	13,351
Oct 18	MOTHERWELL	W 3-1	McInally 2, Shepherd	19,935
Oct 29	CLYDEBANK	W 6-0	McInally 2, McClair 2, McGhee, MacLeod	10,161
Nov 1	RANGERS	D 1-1	McClair	60,000
Nov 8	Hamilton Ac.	W 2-1	Johnston, McClair (pen)	10,000
Nov 15	DUNDEE UNITED	W 1-0	Johnston	34,930
Nov 19	Hibernian	W 1-0	McClair	17,800
Nov 22	FALKIRK	W 4-0	Johnston 2, McInally, Grant	16,545
Nov 26	Aberdeen	D 1-1	McClair (pen)	22,040
Nov 29	St Mirren	W 1-0	O'Leary	16,233
Dec 3	Hearts	L 0-1		25,686
Dec 6	DUNDEE	W 2-0	Johnston 2	19,300
Dec 13	Motherwell	D 1-1	McClair	11,760
Dec 20	ABERDEEN	D 1-1	McInally	35,624
Dec 27	Clydebank	D 1-1	McClair	8,367
Jan 1	Rangers	L 0-2		43,206
Jan 3	HAMILTON AC.	W 8-3	McClair 4, McInally 2, MacLeod 2	16,380
Jan 10	Dundee United	L 2-3	McClair 2	18,576
Jan 21	HIBERNIAN	W 1-0	Rogan	21,583
Jan 24	Falkirk	W 2-1	Johnston 2	15,500
Feb 7	ST MIRREN	W 3-0	Johnston 2, McClair	20,143
Feb 14	HEARTS	D 1-1	McClair	38,198
Feb 28	Dundee	L 1-4	McClair	12,545
Mar 7	MOTHERWELL	W 3-1	Shepherd, Aitken, o.g.	14,840
Mar 14	Aberdeen	L 0-1		20,000
Mar 21	CLYDEBANK	W 3-0	McClair 2 (1 pen), McInally	13,029
Mar 28	Hamilton Ac.	W 3-2	McClair, McInally, Archdeacon	8,505
Apr 4	RANGERS	W 3-1	McClair (2 pen), Archdeacon	60,800
Apr 11	Hibernian	W 4-1	McClair, Johnston, McInally, McStay P	14,000
Apr 18	DUNDEE UNITED	D 1-1	McClair	30,798
Apr 25	St Mirren	W 3-1	McClair 2, Johnston	11,868
May 2	FALKIRK	L 1-2	McClair (pen)	14,238
May 9	Hearts	L 0-1		12,596

Scottish Cup

Feb 1	Aberdeen	(Rd3) D 2-2	McClair, McInally	23,000
Feb 4	ABERDEEN	(R) D 0-0		55,405
Feb 9	Aberdeen	(2R) W 1-0	McClair	21,255
Feb 21	Hearts	(Rd4) L 0-1		28,891

Scottish League Cup

Aug 20	AIRDRIE	(Rd2) W 2-0	McClair 2	15,000
Aug 28	DUMBARTON	(Rd3) W 3-0	Johnston 2, McStay P	11,300
Sep 3	Aberdeen	(QF) D 1-1*	Johnston	23,500
Sep 23	Motherwell	(SF) D 2-2*	McClair, Aitken	26,541
Oct 26	Rangers	(F) L 1-2	McClair	74,216

*Won on penalties.

European Cup

Sep 17	Shamrock Rovers	(Rd1/FL) W 1-0	MacLeod	18,000
Oct 1	SHAMROCK ROVERS	(Rd1/SL) W 2-0	Johnston 2	27,670
Oct 22	DINAMO KIEV	(Rd2/FL) D 1-1	Johnston	48,000
Nov 5	Dinamo Kiev	(Rd2/SL) L 1-3	McGhee	107,000

MANAGER: Davie Hay

CAPTAIN: Danny McGrain

TOP SCORER: Brian McClair

BIGGEST WIN: 6-0 v Clydebank, 29 October 1986, league

HIGHEST ATTENDANCE: 107,000 v Dinamo Kiev, 5 November 1986, European Cup

League & Cup Appearances

PLAYER	LEAGUE	CUP COMPETITIONS			TOTAL
		S CUP	SL CUP	E CUP	
Aitken	42	4	5	4	55
Archdeacon	12 (17)		1 (2)	0 (1)	13 (20)
Bonner	43	4	5	4	56
Burns	14 (3)		3	2	19 (3)
Grant	32 (5)	4	2 (1)	3	41 (6)
Johnston	39 (1)	4	5	4	52 (1)
Latchford	1				1
McClair	43 (1)	4	5	4	56 (1)
McGhee	6 (11)	0 (3)	1	1 (1)	8 (15)
McGrain	21 (5)	4	1	3	29 (5)
McGugan	21 (1)	0 (1)	3	1	25 (2)
McGuire	0 (1)				0 (1)
McInally	29 (9)	4	2 (3)	2	37 (12)
MacLeod	37 (1)	4	5	4	50 (1)
McStay P	43	4	5	4	56
McStay W	15 (1)		4	2	21 (1)
O'Leary	15 (1)			0 (2)	15 (3)
Rogan	10				10
Shepherd	16 (5)	0 (1)	1 (2)	3	20 (8)
Smith	3 (3)		2		5 (3)
Whyte	42	4	5	3	54

Goalscorers

PLAYER	LEAGUE	CUP COMPETITIONS			TOTAL
		S CUP	SL CUP	E CUP	
McClair	35	2	4		41
Johnston	23		3	3	29
McInally	15	1			16
MacLeod	4			1	5
McStay P	3		1		4
Aitken	1		1		2
Archdeacon	2				2
McGhee	1			1	2
Shepherd	2				2
Grant	1				1
O'Leary	1				1
Rogan	1				1
Opps' o.gs.	1				1

Fact File

On 25 April in the match against St Mirren, McClair's first goal gave him a club post-war record of 33.

Final Scottish Premier Division Table

		P	W	D	L	F	A	Pts
1	RANGERS	44	31	7	6	85	23	69
2	CELTIC	44	27	9	8	90	41	63
3	DUNDEE U	44	24	12	8	66	36	60
4	ABERDEEN	44	21	16	7	63	29	58
5	HEARTS	44	21	14	9	64	43	56
6	DUNDEE	44	18	12	14	74	57	48
7	ST MIRREN	44	12	12	20	36	51	36
8	MOTHERWELL	44	11	12	21	43	64	34
9	HIBERNIAN	44	10	13	21	44	70	33
10	FALKIRK	44	8	10	26	31	70	26
11	CLYDEBANK	44	6	12	26	35	93	24
12	HAMILTON A	44	6	9	29	39	93	21

Season 1987-88

Scottish League Premier Division

DATE	OPPONENTS	SCORE	GOALSCORERS	ATTENDANCE
Aug 8	Morton	W 4-0	Walker 2, McGhee, Stark	15,500
Aug 12	HEARTS	W 1-0	McGhee	29,945
Aug 15	MOTHERWELL	W 4-0	Walker 2, McGhee, Stark	24,486
Aug 22	Dunfermline Athletic	L 1-2	Walker (pen)	18,070
Aug 29	RANGERS	W 1-0	Stark	60,800
Sep 5	Dundee United	D 0-0		16,182
Sep 12	Falkirk	W 1-0	Burns	17,500
Sep 19	ABERDEEN	D 2-2	Burns, Stark	38,944
Sep 22	St Mirren	W 1-0	Whyte	18,011
Oct 3	HIBERNIAN	D 1-1	Walker	31,805
Oct 7	Dundee	D 1-1	Walker (pen)	13,382
Oct 10	MORTON	W 3-1	Walker, Whyte, McAvennie	22,788
Oct 17	Rangers	D 2-2	Walker, o.g.	44,000
Oct 24	DUNDEE UNITED	L 1-2	Shepherd	31,032
Oct 28	FALKIRK	W 3-2	Stark 2, Archdeacon	11,381
Oct 31	Aberdeen	W 1-0	McAvennie	21,000
Nov 7	Hearts	D 1-1	McGhee	29,000
Nov 14	DUNDEE	W 5-0	Walker 2, McAvennie 2, Miller	31,446
Nov 17	Motherwell	W 2-0	Walker, Whyte	17,261
Nov 21	DUNFERMLINE ATHLETIC	W 4-0	Walker (2 pen), McAvennie, Stark	28,534
Nov 25	ST MIRREN	W 1-0	Grant	26,713
Nov 28	Hibernian	W 1-0	McAvennie	23,500
Dec 5	Morton	W 4-0	McAvennie 4	15,500
Dec 12	HEARTS	D 2-2	Walker (pen), McStay	43,968
Dec 19	ABERDEEN	D 0-0		37,721
Dec 22	Falkirk	W 2-0	Walker, McStay	12,000
Dec 26	Dundee United	W 2-1	Walker (pen), Miller	18,485
Jan 2	RANGERS	W 2-0	McAvennie 2	60,800
Jan 9	St Mirren	D 1-1	o.g.	19,300
Jan 16	HIBERNIAN	W 2-0	McStay, Miller	34,986
Feb 6	MOTHERWELL	W 1-0	Walker	25,035
Feb 13	Dundee	W 2-1	McAvennie, Morris	17,106
Feb 27	MORTON	W 1-0	Aitken (pen)	23,210
Mar 2	Dunfermline Athletic	W 4-0	McAvennie 2, Walker, Stark	17,446
Mar 5	FALKIRK	W 2-0	McGhee, Walker	23,174
Mar 20	Rangers	W 2-1	McStay, Walker	43,650
Mar 26	DUNDEE UNITED	D 0-0		34,933
Mar 30	Aberdeen	W 1-0	Walker	22,700
Apr 2	Hibernian	W 2-0	Walker, Grant	19,500
Apr 5	ST MIRREN	W 2-0	Walker, McStay	45,465
Apr 16	Hearts	L 1-2	McGhee	26,200
Apr 23	DUNDEE	W 3-0	Walker 2, Morris	72,000
Apr 30	Motherwell	W 1-0	Rogan	13,874
May 7	DUNFERMLINE ATHLETIC	W 1-0	Morris	44,482

Scottish Cup

Jan 30	STRANRAER	(Rd3) W 1-0	McAvennie	21,625
Feb 21	HIBERNIAN	(Rd4) D 0-0		30,755
Feb 24	Hibernian	(R) W 1-0	Stark	24,000
Mar 12	Partick Thistle	(QF) W 3-0	Walker, Burns, Stark	16,800
Apr 9	Hearts	(SF) W 2-1	McGhee, Walker	65,886
May 14	Dundee United	(F) W 2-1	McAvennie 2	74,000

Scottish League Cup

Aug 19	FORAR ATHLETIC	(Rd2) W 3-1	Walker 2, Stark	15,000
Aug 26	Dumbarton	(Rd3) W 5-1	Stark 2, Burns, Walker, McGhee	10,000
Sep 1	Aberdeen	(QF) L 0-1		24,000

UEFA Cup

Sep 15	BORUSSIA DORTMUND	(Rd1/FL) W 2-1	Walker, Whyte	16,800
Sep 29	Borussia Dortmund	(Rd1/SL) L 0-2		54,000

MANAGER: Billy McNeill

CAPTAIN: Roy Aitken

TOP SCORER: Andy Walker

BIGGEST WIN: 5-0 v Dundee, 14 November 1987, league

HIGHEST ATTENDANCE: 74,000 v Dundee United, 14 May 1988, Scottish Cup

MAJOR TRANSFERS IN: Joe Miller from Aberdeen, Frank McAvennie from West Ham, Mick McCarthy from Manchester City, Chris Morris from Sheffield Wednesday, Billy Stark from Aberdeen, Andy Walker from Motherwell

---

League & Cup Appearances

PLAYER	LEAGUE	CUP COMPETITIONS			TOTAL
		S CUP	SL CUP	UEFA	
Aitken	43	6	3	2	54
Archdeacon	4 (6)		0 (1)		4 (7)
Baillie	11 (2)	2			13 (2)
Bonner	32	5	1		38
Burns	21 (6)	5	3	2	31 (6)
Grant	36 (1)	2	3	2	43 (1)
McAvennie	32	6			38
McCarrison	1				1
McCarthy	22	3		1	26
McGhee	15 (9)	2 (2)	3	1	21 (11)
McGugan	1 (1)		2		3 (1)
McGuire	0 (1)		0 (1)	0 (1)	0 (3)
McKnight	12	1	2	2	17
McStay P	44	6	2	2	54
Miller	24 (3)	5 (1)			29 (4)
Morris	44	6	3	2	55
Rogan	25 (8)	4	3	2	34 (8)
Shepherd	0 (6)		1 (1)		1 (7)
Stark	34 (3)	3 (2)	3	2	42 (5)
Walker	42	4	3	2	51
Whyte	41	5	2	2	50

Goalscorers

PLAYER	LEAGUE	CUP COMPETITIONS			TOTAL
		S CUP	SL CUP	UEFA	
Walker	26	2	3	1	32
McAvennie	15	3			18
Stark	8	2	3		13
McGhee	6	1	1		8
McStay	5				5
Burns	2	1	1		4
Whyte	3			1	4
Miller	3				3
Morris	3				3
Grant	2				2
Aitken	1				1
Archdeacon	1				1
Rogan	1				1
Shepherd	1				1
Opps' o.gs.	2				2

Fact File

Celtic did the League and Cup double in their centenary season.

MAJOR TRANSFERS OUT: Maurice Johnston to Nantes, Brian McClair to Manchester United, Alan McInally to Aston Villa, Murdo MacLeod to Borussia Dortmund

---

Final Scottish Premier Division Table

		P	W	D	L	F	A	PTS
1	CELTIC	44	31	10	3	79	23	72
2	HEARTS	44	23	16	5	74	32	62
3	RANGERS	44	26	8	10	85	34	60
4	ABERDEEN	44	21	17	6	56	25	59
5	DUNDEE U	44	16	15	13	54	47	47
6	HIBERNIAN	44	12	19	13	41	42	43
7	DUNDEE	44	17	7	20	70	64	41
8	MOTHERWELL	44	13	10	21	37	56	36
9	ST MIRREN	44	10	15	19	41	64	35
10	FALKIRK	44	10	11	23	41	75	31
11	DUNFERMLINE ATH	44	8	10	26	41	84	26
12	MORTON	44	3	10	31	27	100	16

Season 1988-89

Scottish League Premier Division

DATE	OPPONENTS	SCORE		GOALSCORERS	ATTENDANCE
Aug 13	HEARTS	W	1-0	McAvennie	46,846
Aug 20	Dundee United	L	0-1		18,769
Aug 27	Rangers	L	1-5	McAvennie	42,867
Sep 3	HAMILTON AC.	W	2-1	McAvennie, Miller	24,084
Sep 17	ABERDEEN	L	1-3	Miller (pen)	37,769
Sep 24	Dundee	L	0-1		15,515
Sep 28	MOTHERWELL	W	3-1	McAvennie 2, Walker	20,137
Oct 1	Hibernian	L	1-3	Walker	24,000
Oct 8	ST MIRREN	W	7-1	McGhee 3, Stark 2, McStay, Miller	26,091
Oct 12	DUNDEE UNITED	W	1-0	Miller	36,750
Oct 22	Hearts	W	2-0	McGhee, McAvennie	24,013
Oct 29	DUNDEE	L	2-3	Stark, Morris	23,843
Nov 2	Aberdeen	D	2-2	Stark 2	22,000
Nov 5	Hamilton Ac.	W	8-0	McGhee 3, McAvennie 3 (1 pen), Miller, Stark	10,500
Nov 12	RANGERS	W	3-1	McGhee, Stark, o.g.	60,113
Nov 19	HIBERNIAN	W	1-0	McAvennie	35,251
Nov 26	St Mirren	W	3-2	Burns 2, McAvennie	21,266
Dec 3	Motherwell	W	3-1	McGhee, McInally, McStay	16,392
Dec 10	ABERDEEN	D	0-0		42,347
Dec 17	Dundee United	L	0-1		18,745
Dec 31	HEARTS	W	4-2	McGhee 2, Stark 2	44,636
Jan 3	Rangers	L	1-4	Morris	42,515
Jan 7	HAMILTON AC.	W	2-0	Walker, Miller	18,679
Jan 14	ST MIRREN	W	2-1	Walker (pen), Morris	26,956
Jan 21	Hibernian	W	3-1	Walker, McGhee, McStay	23,500
Feb 11	MOTHERWELL	L	1-2	Walker	21,445
Feb 25	Dundee	W	3-0	Walker, McStay, McCarrison	14,559
Mar 11	Hearts	W	1-0	McGhee	23,087
Mar 25	DUNDEE UNITED	W	1-0	McGhee	32,589
Apr 1	RANGERS	L	1-2	Walker	60,800
Apr 8	Hamilton Ac.	L	0-2		9,301
Apr 12	Motherwell	D	2-2	McGhee, McStay	10,507
Apr 22	DUNDEE	W	2-1	McGhee, Rogan	16,000
Apr 29	Aberdeen	D	0-0		21,500
May 6	HIBERNIAN	W	1-0	Miller	18,316
May 13	St Mirren	W	1-0	Miller	13,057

Scottish Cup

					GOALSCORERS	ATTENDANCE
Jan 28	DUMBARTON	(Rd3)	W	2-0	Walker, Burns	24,844
Feb 18	CLYDEBANK	(Rd4)	W	4-1	Burns 2, McAvennie, Stark	23,120
Mar 18	HEARTS	(QF)	W	2-1	McGhee, Aitken (pen)	46,348
Apr 16	Hibernian	(SF)	W	3-1	McCarthy, McGhee, Walker	42,160
May 20	Rangers	(F)	W	1-0	Miller	72,069

Scottish League Cup

Aug 17	AYR UNITED	(Rd2)	W	4-1	Walker 2, McAvennie, Burns	25,044
Aug 24	HAMILTON AC.	(Rd3)	W	7-2	Walker 2, McAvennie 2, Stark, Burns, Archdeacon	23,109
Aug 31	Dundee United	(QF)	L	0-2		21,350

European Cup

Sep 7	Honved	(Rd1/FL)	L	0-1		10,000
Oct 5	HONVED	(Rd1/SL)	W	4-0	Stark, Walker, McAvennie, McGhee	42,673
Oct 26	WERDER BREMEN	(Rd2/FL)	L	0-1		50,624
Nov 8	Werder Bremen	(Rd2/SL)	D	0-0		40,000

League & Cup Appearances

PLAYER	LEAGUE	CUP COMPETITIONS			TOTAL
		S CUP	SL CUP	E CUP	
Aitken	32	4	2	4	42
Andrews	5			1	6
Archdeacon	2 (8)		0 (1)	0 (1)	2 (10)
Baillie	8 (1)	0 (1)			8 (2)
Bonner	26	5		2	33
Burns	30 (2)	5	3	2 (1)	40 (3)
Coyne	4 (3)				4 (3)
Elliot	2 (2)				2 (2)
Fulton	1 (2)	1			2 (2)
Grant	20 (1)	5	2	1	29 (1)
McAvennie	23	2	3	4	32
McCahill	4 (1)				4 (1)
McCarrison	0 (1)				0 (1)
McCarthy	26	5	3	4	38
McGhee	28 (1)	5	0 (1)	2 (1)	35 (3)
McStay	33	5	3	4	45
Mathie	0 (1)				0 (1)
Miller	16 (6)	3	3	2 (1)	24 (7)
Morris	33	4	3	4	44
Rogan	34	4	3	4	45
Rough	5		1	1	7
Stark	22 (3)	3 (1)	0 (1)	3	28 (5)
Traynor	3 (1)				3 (1)
Walker	19 (3)	2	3	2 (1)	26 (4)
Whyte	20 (2)	2	1	4	27 (2)

Goalscorers

PLAYER	LEAGUE	CUP COMPETITIONS			TOTAL
		S CUP	SL CUP	E CUP	
McGhee	16	2		1	19
McAvennie	12	1	3	1	17
Walker	8	2	4	1	15
Stark	9	1	1	1	12
Miller	8	1			9
Burns	2	3	2		7
McStay	5				5
Morris	3				3
Aitken		1			1
Archdeacon			1		1
McCarrison	1				1
McCarthy		1			1
Rogan	1				1
Opps' o.gs.	1				1

Fact File

David Syme, the referee for the game against Hearts on 18 March 1989, tore his calf muscle and had to retire. His grandfather, David, played in goal for Celtic in 1918.

MANAGER: Billy McNeill

CAPTAIN: Roy Aitken

TOP SCORER: Mark McGhee

BIGGEST WIN: 8-0 v Hamilton Ac., 5 November 1988, league

HIGHEST ATTENDANCE: 72,069 v Rangers, 20 May 1989, Scottish Cup

MAJOR TRANSFERS IN: Ian Andrews from Leicester City, Tommy Coyne from Dundee, Alan Rough from Orlando Lions

Final Scottish Premier Division Table

		P	W	D	L	F	A	PTS
1	RANGERS	36	26	4	6	62	26	56
2	ABERDEEN	36	18	14	4	51	25	50
3	CELTIC	36	21	4	11	66	44	46
4	DUNDEE U	36	16	12	8	44	26	44
5	HIBERNIAN	36	13	9	14	37	36	35
6	HEARTS	36	9	13	14	35	42	31
7	ST MIRREN	36	11	7	18	39	55	29
8	DUNDEE	36	9	10	17	34	48	28
9	MOTHERWELL	36	7	13	16	35	44	27
10	HAMILTON A	36	6	2	28	19	76	14

Season 1989-90

Scottish League Premier Division

DATE	OPPONENTS	SCORE	GOALSCORERS	ATTENDANCE
Aug 12	Hearts	W 3-1	Coyne 3 (pen)	25,932
Aug 19	DUNFERMLINE ATHLETIC	W 1-0	Galloway	34,000
Aug 26	RANGERS	D 1-1	Dziekanowski	54,000
Sep 9	St Mirren	L 0-1		19,673
Sep 16	Dundee United	D 2-2	Morris, Coyne	16,428
Sep 23	MOTHERWELL	D 1-1	McStay	29,000
Sep 30	Aberdeen	D 1-1	Miller	21,374
Oct 4	HIBERNIAN	W 3-1	Walker 2, Dziekanowski	36,000
Oct 14	Dundee	W 3-1	Aitken, Coyne, Dziekanowski	16,215
Oct 21	HEARTS	W 2-1	Aitken, Coyne	38,106
Oct 28	Dunfermline Athletic	L 0-2		19,588
Nov 4	Rangers	L 0-1		41,598
Nov 18	DUNDEE UNITED	L 0-1		32,350
Nov 22	ST MIRREN	D 1-1	Miller	23,100
Nov 25	Motherwell	D 0-0		16,039
Dec 2	ABERDEEN	W 1-0	Walker (pen)	38,300
Dec 9	Hibernian	W 3-0	Dziekanowski, Walker, Wdowczyk	18,000
Dec 16	DUNDEE	W 4-1	Dziekanowski, Walker, Miller, McStay	17,860
Dec 26	Hearts	D 0-0		23,259
Dec 30	DUNFERMLINE ATHLETIC	L 0-2		30,548
Jan 2	RANGERS	L 0-1		54,000
Jan 6	St Mirren	W 2-0	Dziekanowski, Miller	14,813
Jan 13	Dundee United	L 0-2		16,438
Jan 27	MOTHERWELL	L 0-1		23,000
Feb 3	Dundee	D 0-0		14,100
Feb 10	HIBERNIAN	D 1-1	Dziekanowski	25,000
Feb 17	Aberdeen	D 1-1	McStay	22,100
Mar 3	DUNDEE UNITED	W 3-0	Galloway, Whyte, Miller	23,541
Mar 10	HEARTS	D 1-1	Coyne	34,792
Mar 24	Dunfermline Athletic	D 0-0		14,044
Apr 1	Rangers	L 0-3		41,926
Apr 7	ST MIRREN	L 0-3		18,481
Apr 17	Hibernian	L 0-1		11,000
Apr 21	DUNDEE	D 1-1	Creaney	15,115
Apr 28	Motherwell	D 1-1	Dziekanowski	10,322
May 2	ABERDEEN	L 1-3	Walker	20,154

Scottish Cup

Jan 20	Forfar Athletic	(Rd3)	W 2-1	Morris (pen), Dziekanowski	8,388
Feb 24	RANGERS	(Rd4)	W 1-0	Coyne	52,565
Mar 17	Dunfermline Athletic	(QF)	D 0-0		19,542
Mar 24	DUNFERMLINE ATHLETIC	(R)	W 3-0	McStay, Coyne, Miller	40,798
Apr 14	Clydebank	(SF)	W 2-0	Walker 2	34,768
May 12	Aberdeen	(F)	D 0-0*		60,493

*Lost on penalties.

Scottish League Cup

Aug 15	Dumbarton	(Rd2)	W 3-0	McStay, Dziekanowski, Burns	8,500
Aug 22	QUEEN OF THE SOUTH	(Rd3)	W 2-0	Grant, Dziekanowski	20,074
Aug 30	Hearts	(QF)	D 2-2*	Dziekanowski, Walker	25,218
Sep 20	Aberdeen	(SF)	L 0-1		45,367

*Won on penalties.

European Cup-Winners' Cup

Sep 12	Partizan Belgrade	(Rd1/FL)	L 1-2	Galloway	15,000
Sep 27	PARTIZAN BELGRADE	(Rd1/SL)	W 5-4	Dziekanowski 4, Walker	49,500

League & Cup Appearances

PLAYER	LEAGUE	CUP COMPETITIONS			TOTAL
		S CUP	SL CUP	ECWC	
Aitken	18		4	2	24
Bonner	36	6	4	2	48
Burns	8 (1)		3	1	12 (1)
Coyne	17 (6)	3	3	1	24 (6)
Creaney	2 (4)				2 (4)
Dziekanowski	31 (2)	6	4	2	43 (2)
Elliot	0 (2)				0 (2)
Elliott	25	4		1	30
Fulton	13 (3)	2	1 (1)		16 (4)
Galloway	29 (4)	3	4	2	38 (4)
Grant	24 (2)	5	3	2	34 (2)
Hewitt	8 (4)		3		11 (4)
McCahill	2	1	1		4
McStay P	35	6	4	2	47
Mathie	5 (1)	1			6 (1)
Miller	16	6	0 (1)	1	23 (1)
Morris	32	5	4	1	42
Rogan	16 (2)	3	2 (1)	2	23 (3)
Stark	2	1			3
Walker	19 (13)	2	1 (3)	1 (1)	23 (17)
Wdowczyk	23	6			29
Whyte	35	6	3	2	46

Goalscorers

PLAYER	LEAGUE	CUP COMPETITIONS			TOTAL
		S CUP	SL CUP	ECWC	
Dziekanowski	8	1	3	4	16
Walker	6	2	1	1	10
Coyne	7	2			9
Miller	5	1			6
McStay P	3	1	1		5
Galloway	2			1	3
Aitken	2				2
Morris	1	1			2
Burns			1		1
Creaney	1				1
Grant			1		1
Whyte	1				1
Wdowczyk	1				1

MANAGER: Billy McNeill

CAPTAIN: Roy Aitken

TOP SCORER: Dariusz Dziekanowski

BIGGEST WIN: 4-1 v Dundee, 16 December 1989, league

HIGHEST ATTENDANCE: 60,493 v Aberdeen, 12 May 1990, Scottish Cup

MAJOR TRANSFERS IN: Dariusz Dziekanowski from Legia Warsaw, Paul Elliott from Pisa, Mike Galloway from Hearts, Dariusz Wdowczyk from Gwardia Warsaw

MAJOR TRANSFERS OUT: Frank McAvennie to West Ham United, Mark McGhee to Newcastle, Mick McCarthy to Lyon, Roy Aitken to Newcastle, Tommy Burns to Kilmarnock

Fact File

Chris Morris scored Celtic's 1000th Premier League goal in the match against Dunfermline Athletic on 28 October.

Final Scottish Premier Division Table

		P	W	D	L	F	A	Pts
1	RANGERS	36	20	11	5	48	19	51
2	ABERDEEN	36	17	10	9	56	33	44
3	HEARTS	36	16	12	8	54	35	44
4	DUNDEE U	36	11	13	12	36	39	35
5	CELTIC	36	10	14	12	37	37	34
6	MOTHERWELL	36	11	12	13	43	47	34
7	HIBERNIAN	36	12	10	14	34	41	34
8	DUNFERMLINE ATH	36	11	8	17	37	50	30
9	ST MIRREN	36	10	10	16	28	48	30
10	DUNDEE	36	5	14	17	41	65	24

Season 1990-91

Scottish League Premier Division

DATE	OPPONENTS	SCORE	GOALSCORERS	ATTENDANCE
Aug 25	Motherwell	L 0-1		17,437
Sep 1	ABERDEEN	L 0-3		45,223
Sep 8	HIBERNIAN	W 2-0	Miller, Dziekanowski	28,068
Sep 15	Rangers	D 1-1	Whyte	38,445
Sep 22	HEARTS	W 3-0	Miller 2, Creaney	38,409
Sep 29	St Mirren	W 3-2	Creaney 2, McStay	20,097
Oct 6	ST JOHNSTONE	D 0-0		27,014
Oct 13	Dunfermline Athletic	D 1-1	McStay	16,068
Oct 20	DUNDEE UNITED	D 0-0		34,363
Nov 3	Aberdeen	L 0-3		21,500
Nov 6	MOTHERWELL	W 2-1	Coyne 2	20,317
Nov 10	Hearts	L 0-1		19,189
Nov 17	ST MIRREN	W 4-1	Billie, Miller, Creaney, Coyne	25,665
Nov 25	RANGERS	L 1-2	Elliott	52,265
Dec 1	Hibernian	W 3-0	Coyne 2, Nicholas	16,219
Dec 8	Dundee United	L 1-3	Coyne	16,748
Dec 15	DUNFERMLINE ATHLETIC	L 1-2	Nicholas	18,870
Dec 22	St Johnstone	L 2-3	Coyne, Collins	10,260
Dec 29	HEARTS	D 1-1	Coyne	28,106
Jan 2	Rangers	L 0-2		38,389
Jan 5	HIBERNIAN	D 1-1	Coyne	20,521
Jan 19	ABERDEEN	W 1-0	Coyne	28,187
Jan 30	Motherwell	D 1-1	Dziekanowski	13,452
Feb 2	DUNDEE UNITED	W 1-0	Coyne	26,127
Mar 2	ST JOHNSTONE	W 3-0	Coyne, Elliott, Miller	24,560
Mar 6	Dunfermline Athletic	W 1-0	Creaney	12,468
Mar 9	Hibernian	W 2-0	Miller 2	11,500
Mar 12	St Mirren	W 2-0	Creaney 2	11,268
Mar 24	RANGERS	W 3-0	Rogan, Miller, Coyne	52,000
Mar 30	MOTHERWELL	L 1-2	Coyne	21,252
Apr 6	Aberdeen	L 0-1		22,500
Apr 13	Dundee United	L 1-2	o.g.	12,603
Apr 20	DUNFERMLINE ATHLETIC	W 5-1	Coyne 2, Nicholas 2, Whyte	14,268
Apr 27	Hearts	W 1-0	Nicholas	17,085
May 5	ST MIRREN	W 1-0	Coyne	17,200
May 11	St Johnstone	W 3-2	Nicholas, Galloway, Coyne (pen)	9,484

Scottish Cup

Jan 26	Forfar Athletic	(Rd3) W 2-0	Wdowczyk, Coyne	8,000
Feb 26	ST MIRREN	(Rd4) W 3-0	Miller, Creaney, o.g.	27,199
Mar 17	RANGERS	(QF) W 2-0	Creaney, Wdowczyk	52,286
Apr 3	Motherwell	(SF) D 0-0		41,756
Apr 9	Motherwell	(R) L 2-4	Rogan, o.g.	31,342

Scottish League Cup

Aug 22	AYR UNITED	(Rd2) W 4-0	Elliott 2, Dziekanowski 2	21,462
Aug 29	Hamilton Ac.	(Rd3) W 1-0	Dziekanowski	9,168
Sep 5	QUEEN OF THE SOUTH	(QF) W 2-1	Dziekanowski, Miller	18,669
Sep 25	Dundee United	(SF) W 2-0	Creaney, McStay	49,956
Oct 28	Rangers	(F) L 1-2	Elliott	62,281

League & Cup Appearances

PLAYER	LEAGUE	CUP COMPETITIONS		TOTAL
		S CUP	SL CUP	
Baillie	8 (1)	1		9 (1)
Bonner	36	5	5	46
Britton	0 (2)	0 (2)		0 (4)
Collins	35	5	5	45
Coyne	24 (2)	5		29 (2)
Creaney	22 (9)	4	2	28 (9)
Dziekanowski	11 (3)	1	5	17 (3)
Elliott	27	4	5	36
Fulton	19 (2)	0 (1)	2	21 (3)
Galloway	3 (4)		0 (1)	3 (5)
Grant	27 (1)	1	5	33 (1)
Hayes	3 (4)		3	6 (4)
Hewitt	1 (3)		0 (2)	1 (5)
McCarrison	0 (1)			0 (1)
McLaughlin	2 (1)		2	4 (1)
McNally	17 (2)	3		20 (2)
McStay	30	5	5	40
Mathie	2 (2)			2 (2)
Miller	24 (6)	5	2 (2)	31 (8)
Morris	15 (3)	3	3 (1)	21 (4)
Nicholas	12 (2)		1	13 (2)
Rogan	25 (2)	4	2	31 (2)
Walker	6 (5)		2 (2)	8 (7)
Wdowczyk	23 (1)	4	2	29 (1)
Whyte	24	5	4	33

Goalscorers

PLAYER	LEAGUE	CUP COMPETITIONS		TOTAL
		S CUP	SL CUP	
Coyne	18	1		19
Creaney	7	2	1	10
Miller	8	1	1	10
Dziekanowski	2		4	6
Nicholas	6			6
Elliott	2		3	5
McStay	2		1	3
Rogan	1	1		2
Wdowczyk		2		2
Whyte	2			2
Baillie	1			1
Collins	1			1
Galloway	1			1
Opps' o.gs.	1	2		3

Fact File

Celtic beat Rangers in successive weeks as a total of 5 players were sent off. Peter Grant was the only Celt to get his marching orders.

MANAGER: Billy McNeill

CAPTAIN: Paul McStay

TOP SCORER: Tommy Coyne

BIGGEST WIN: 5-1 v Dunfermline, 20 April 1990, league

HIGHEST ATTENDANCE: 62,281 v Rangers, 28 October 1990, Scottish League Cup

MAJOR TRANSFERS IN: John Collins from Hibernian, Martin Hayes from Arsenal, Charlie Nicholas from Aberdeen

Final Scottish Premier Division Table

		P	W	D	L	F	A	Pts
1	RANGERS	36	24	7	5	62	23	55
2	ABERDEEN	36	22	9	5	62	27	53
3	CELTIC	36	17	7	12	52	38	41
4	DUNDEE U	36	17	7	12	41	29	41
5	HEARTS	36	14	7	15	48	55	35
6	MOTHERWELL	36	12	9	15	51	50	33
7	ST JOHNSTONE	36	11	9	16	41	54	31
8	DUNFERMLINE ATH	36	8	11	17	38	61	27
9	HIBERNIAN	36	6	13	17	24	51	25
10	ST MIRREN	36	5	9	22	28	59	19

Season 1991-92

Scottish League Premier Division

DATE	OPPONENTS	SCORE	GOALSCORERS	ATTENDANCE
Aug 10	Dundee United	W 4-3	Collins 2, Nicholas, Coyne	16,531
Aug 13	Dunfermline Athletic	W 3-1	Nicholas 2, Coyne	13,264
Aug 17	FALKIRK	W 4-1	Coyne 2, Gillespie, Collins	32,548
Aug 24	Aberdeen	L 0-1		21,800
Aug 31	RANGERS	L 0-2		51,382
Sep 7	ST MIRREN	D 0-0		21,233
Sep 14	St Johnstone	L 0-1		9,986
Sep 21	AIRDRIE	W 3-1	Miller, Galloway, Nicholas (pen)	17,552
Sep 28	Hibernian	D 1-1	Nicholas	19,000
Oct 5	HEARTS	W 3-1	McNally, Nicholas (pen), Cascarino	33,106
Oct 8	Motherwell	W 2-0	Coyne, Nicholas	13,238
Oct 12	DUNDEE UNITED	W 4-1	Nicholas 2, Coyne, Galloway	27,845
Oct 19	Falkirk	L 3-4	McStay 2, Collins	11,600
Oct 26	St Mirren	W 5-0	Coyne 2, McStay, Creaney, O'Neil	10,442
Oct 30	ST JOHNSTONE	W 4-0	Nicholas 2 (1 pen), Collins, Coyne	18,240
Nov 2	Rangers	D 1-1	Cascarino	37,378
Nov 9	ABERDEEN	W 2-1	Nicholas, Creaney	36,387
Nov 16	Hearts	L 1-3	Coyne	22,646
Nov 20	MOTHERWELL	D 2-2	Nicholas 2	16,215
Nov 23	Airdrie	W 3-0	Cascarino, Coyne, Creaney	10,102
Nov 30	DUNFERMLINE ATHLETIC	W 1-0	Coyne	20,452
Dec 4	HIBERNIAN	D 0-0		22,067
Dec 7	Dundee United	D 1-1	Morris	11,145
Dec 14	ST MIRREN	W 4-0	Creaney 2, Collins, o.g.	16,813
Dec 28	Aberdeen	D 2-2	Mowbray, Cascarino	20,422
Jan 1	RANGERS	L 1-3	Mowbray	51,833
Jan 4	HEARTS	L 1-2	Collins	30,154
Jan 8	St Johnstone	W 4-2	McStay, Gillespie, Coyne, Collins	9,283
Jan 11	Motherwell	D 0-0		12,115
Jan 18	Dunfermline Athletic	W 1-0	Coyne	9,863
Feb 1	FALKIRK	W 2-0	Coyne, McStay	16,929
Feb 8	AIRDRIE	W 2-0	Creaney 2	18,854
Feb 22	Hibernian	W 2-0	Creaney, Nicholas	16,317
Feb 29	Hearts	W 2-1	Creaney 2	20,863
Mar 14	ABERDEEN	W 1-0	Collins	29,202
Mar 17	MOTHERWELL	W 4-1	Nicholas, McStay, Creaney, Miller	15,521
Mar 21	Rangers	W 2-0	Nicholas, Creaney	42,160
Mar 28	DUNDEE UNITED	W 3-1	Creaney, Nicholas, Whyte	22,513
Apr 4	Falkirk	W 3-0	Creaney, Nicholas, Collins	8,842
Apr 8	St Mirren	D 1-1	Boyd	7,316
Apr 11	ST JOHNSTONE	W 3-2	Nicholas 2, Fulton	13,326
Apr 18	Airdrie	D 0-0		9,000
Apr 25	DUNFERMLINE ATHLETIC	W 2-0	McStay, Collins	12,649
May 2	HIBERNIAN	L 1-2	Fulton	25,527

Scottish Cup

Jan 22	MONTROSE	(Rd3)	W 6-0	Creaney 3, Coyne 3	18,578
Feb 11	DUNDEE UNITED	(Rd4)	W 2-1	Creaney, Coyne	26,225
Mar 3	MORTON	(QF)	W 3-0	Creaney 2, Collins	28,016
Mar 31	Rangers	(SF)	L 0-1		45,196

Scottish League Cup

Aug 21	Morton	(Rd2)	W 4-2	Nicholas 2, Creaney 2	9,518
Aug 27	RAITH ROVERS	(Rd3)	W 3-1	Miller, Creaney, Fulton	21,083
Sep 3	Airdrie	(QF)	D 0-0*		10,200

*Lost on penalties.

UEFA Cup

Sep 18	GERMINAL EKEREN	(Rd1/FL)	W 2-0	Nicholas 2 (1 pen)	27,410
Oct 1	Germinal Ekeren	(Rd1/SL)	D 1-1	Galloway	7,000
Oct 22	Neuchatel Xamax	(Rd2/FL)	L 1-5	O'Neil	11,300
Nov 6	NEUCHATEL XAMAX	(Rd2/SL)	W 1-0	Miller	25,446

MANAGER: Liam Brady

CAPTAIN: Paul McStay

TOP SCORER: Charlie Nicholas

BIGGEST WIN: 6-0 v Montrose, 22 January 1992, Scottish Cup

HIGHEST ATTENDANCE: 51,833 v Rangers, 1 January 1992, league

MAJOR TRANSFERS IN: Tom Boyd from Chelsea, Tony Cascarino from Aston Villa, Gordon Marshall from Falkirk, Gary Gillespie from Liverpool

---

League & Cup Appearances

PLAYER	LEAGUE	CUP COMPETITIONS			TOTAL
		S CUP	SL CUP	UEFA	
Bonner	19		3	4	26
Boyd	12 (1)	2			14 (1)
Cascarino	13 (11)	0 (1)	1	2 (1)	16 (13)
Collins	36 (2)	4	2	3	45 (2)
Coyne	32 (7)	3 (1)	2	3 (1)	40 (9)
Creaney	21 (11)	4	2 (1)	0 (2)	27 (14)
Dziekanowski	0 (1)				0 (1)
Fulton	18 (12)	1 (1)	3	2 (1)	24 (14)
Galloway	26 (8)	1 (3)	2 (1)	2	31 (12)
Gillespie	24	2	2	2	30
Grant	20 (2)		2	3	23 (2)
McNally	21 (3)		0 (1)	2 (1)	23 (5)
McStay	32		4	2	38
Marshall	25		4		29
Miller	23 (3)	4	2 (1)	2 (1)	31 (5)
Morris	29 (3)	4	3	2	38 (3)
Mowbray	14 (1)	2			16 (1)
Nicholas	32 (5)	1 (2)	2	4	39 (7)
O'Neil	25 (3)	3	0 (1)	3	31 (4)
Rogan	5		2		7
Smith	1 (2)				1 (2)
Walker	0 (1)		0 (1)		0 (2)
Wdowczyk	18 (1)	1	2	4	25 (1)
Whyte	38 (2)	4	3	4	49 (2)

Goalscorers

PLAYER	LEAGUE	CUP COMPETITIONS			TOTAL
		S CUP	SL CUP	UEFA	
Nicholas	21		2	2	25
Creaney	14	6	3		23
Coyne	15	4			19
Collins	11	1			12
McStay	7				7
Cascarino	4				4
Miller	2		1	1	4
Fulton	2		1		3
Galloway	2			1	3
Gillespie	2				2
Mowbray	2				2
O'Neil	1			1	2
Boyd	1				1
Morris	1				1
McNally	1				1
Whyte	1				1
Opps' o.gs.	1				1

Fact File

Celtic suffer their biggest defeat in Europe, losing 1-5 to Neuchatel on 22 October in the UEFA Cup.

MAJOR TRANSFERS OUT: Tony Cascarino to Chelsea, Anton Rogan to Sunderland, Andy Walker to Bolton, Paul Elliott to Chelsea

---

Final Scottish Premier Division Table

		P	W	D	L	F	A	Pts
1	RANGERS	44	33	6	5	101	31	72
2	HEARTS	44	27	9	8	60	37	63
3	CELTIC	44	26	10	8	88	42	62
4	DUNDEE U	44	19	13	12	66	50	51
5	HIBERNIAN	44	16	17	11	53	45	49
6	ABERDEEN	44	17	14	13	55	42	48
7	AIRDRIEONIANS	44	13	10	21	50	70	36
8	ST JOHNSTONE	44	13	10	21	52	73	36
9	FALKIRK	44	12	11	21	54	73	35
10	MOTHERWELL	44	10	14	20	43	61	34
11	ST MIRREN	44	6	12	26	33	73	24
12	DUNFERMLINE ATH	44	4	10	30	22	80	18

Season 1992-93

Scottish League Premier Division

DATE	OPPONENTS	SCORE	GOALSCORERS	ATTENDANCE
Aug 1	Hearts	W 1-0	o.g.	18,510
Aug 5	Aberdeen	D 1-1	Creaney	15,200
Aug 8	MOTHERWELL	D 1-1	Mowbray	24,935
Aug 15	DUNDEE UNITED	W 2-0	Creaney 2	30,250
Aug 22	Rangers	D 1-1	Creaney	43,239
Aug 29	Airdrie	D 1-1	Payton	10,500
Sep 2	ST JOHNSTONE	W 3-1	Collins 2, Creaney	21,823
Sep 12	HIBERNIAN	L 2-3	Wdowczyk, McStay	28,149
Sep 19	Falkirk	W 5-4	Creaney 2, Wdowczyk (pen), Payton, Collins	9,756
Sep 26	PARTICK THISTLE	L 1-2	Payton	21,468
Oct 3	Dundee	W 1-0	Payton	12,866
Oct 7	HEARTS	D 1-1	Miller	26,059
Oct 17	Motherwell	W 3-1	Galloway (pen), Grant, o.g.	10,016
Oct 24	AIRDRIE	W 2-0	Collins, McStay	19,568
Oct 31	St Johnstone	D 0-0		9,783
Nov 7	RANGERS	L 0-1		51,952
Nov 11	Dundee United	D 1-1	Nicholas	11,096
Nov 21	FALKIRK	W 3-2	Gillespie, Creaney, O'Neil	15,979
Nov 28	Hibernian	W 2-1	O'Neil 2	13,008
Dec 2	ABERDEEN	D 2-2	Slater, Vata	21,193
Dec 5	Partick Thistle	W 3-2	Payton, Grant, Creaney	13,128
Dec 12	DUNDEE	W 1-0	Payton	16,717
Dec 19	Hearts	L 0-1		13,554
Dec 26	DUNDEE UNITED	L 0-1		22,852
Jan 2	Rangers	L 0-1		46,059
Jan 23	Airdrie	W 1-0	Coyne	7,200
Jan 30	MOTHERWELL	D 1-1	McStay	18,513
Feb 3	ST JOHNSTONE	W 5-1	Coyne (2 pens), McAvennie, Wdowczyk, Collins	12,931
Feb 13	Aberdeen	D 1-1	Payton	15,600
Feb 20	PARTICK THISTLE	D 0-0		15,561
Feb 23	Dundee	W 1-0	Payton	7,370
Feb 27	Falkirk	W 3-0	Payton 2, McAvennie	8,500
Mar 10	HEARTS	W 1-0	Payton	16,984
Mar 16	HIBERNIAN	W 2-1	Payton 2	12,178
Mar 20	RANGERS	W 2-1	Collins, Payton	53,137
Mar 27	Dundee United	W 3-2	McAvennie, Galloway, Collins	11,353
Apr 3	Motherwell	L 0-2		10,102
Apr 6	AIRDRIE	W 4-0	Slater, Collins, McAvennie, Vata	12,183
Apr 10	St Johnstone	D 1-1	McAvennie	8,608
Apr 17	Hibernian	L 1-3	Nicholas	11,183
Apr 20	FALKIRK	W 1-0	McAvennie	12,201
May 1	ABERDEEN	W 1-0	McAvennie	20,642
May 8	Partick Thistle	W 1-0	McAvennie (pen)	10,424
May 15	DUNDEE	W 2-0	McStay, McAvennie	19,436

Scottish Cup

Jan 9	Clyde	(Rd3) D 0-0		7,000
Jan 20	CLYDE	(R) W 1-0	Coyne	16,559
Feb 6	Falkirk	(Rd4) L 0-2		13,012

Scottish League Cup

Aug 12	Stirling Albion	(Rd2) W 3-0	Creaney 2, Coyne	2,630
Aug 19	DUNDEE	(Rd3) W 1-0	Payton	30,849
Aug 26	Hearts	(QF) W 2-1	Payton, Creaney	21,502
Sep 23	Aberdeen	(SF) L 0-1		40,618

UEFA Cup

Sep 15	Cologne	(Rd1/FL) L 0-2		26,000
Sep 30	COLOGNE	(Rd1/SL) W 3-0	McStay, Creaney, Collins	30,747
Oct 20	Borussia Dortmund	(Rd2/FL) L 0-1		35,800
Nov 3	BORUSSIA DORTMUND	(Rd2/SL) L 1-2	Creaney	31,578

MANAGER: Liam Brady

CAPTAIN: Paul McStay

TOP SCORER: Andy Payton

BIGGEST WIN: 5-1 v St Johnstone, 3 February 1993, league

HIGHEST ATTENDANCE: 53,137 v Rangers, 20 March 1993, league

MAJOR TRANSFERS IN: Andy Payton from Middlesbrough, Rudi Vata from Dinamo Tirana, Stuart Slater from West Ham

MAJOR TRANSFERS OUT: Derek Whyte to Middlesbrough, Chris Morris to Middlesbrough, Martin Hayes to Swansea, Tommy Coyne to Tranmere, Steve Fulton to Bolton, Joe Miller to Aberdeen

League & Cup Appearances

PLAYER	LEAGUE	CUP COMPETITIONS			TOTAL
		S CUP	SL CUP	UEFA	
Bonner	33	3	1	2	39
Boyd	42	3	4	4	53
Collins	43	3	4	4	54
Coyne	5 (5)	2 (1)	0 (1)		7 (7)
Creaney	23 (3)	1 (1)	4	3 (1)	31 (5)
Fulton	3 (3)		1 (1)	0 (1)	4 (5)
Galloway	29 (1)	3	3	3	28 (1)
Gillespie	18	1	1	3	23
Grant	27 (4)	1 (2)	3 (1)	3 (1)	34 (8)
Gray	1				1
McAvennie	19	1			20
McCarrison	0 (1)				0 (1)
McNally	25 (2)	3	2 (1)	2	32 (3)
McQuilken	1				1
McStay	43	3	3	4	53
Marshall	11		3	2	16
Miller	10 (13)	1 (1)	1 (1)	0 (2)	12 (17)
Morris	3				3
Mowbray	26	4	3	4	37
Nicholas	12 (4)		1	2 (1)	15 (5)
O'Neil	11 (6)	1	3	2	17 (6)
Payton	19 (10)	1 (1)	3	1	2 (11)
Slater	37 (2)	3	1 (2)	4	45 (4)
Smith	4 (2)				4 (2)
Vata	15 (7)	1			16 (7)
Wdowczyk	24 (1)	2	3	1	30 (1)
Whyte	0 (1)				0 (1)

Goalscorers

PLAYER	LEAGUE	CUP COMPETITIONS			TOTAL
		S CUP	SL CUP	UEFA	
Payton	13		2		15
Creaney	9		3	2	14
Collins	8			1	9
McAvennie	9				9
McStay	4			1	5
Coyne	3	1	1		5
Galloway	3				3
O'Neil	3				3
Wdowczyk	3				3
Grant	2				2
Nicholas	2				2
Slater	2				2
Vata	2				2
Gillespie	1				1
Miller	1				1
Mowbray	1				1
Opps' o.gs.	2				2

Fact File

On 28 November 1992, Brian O'Neil's second goal against Hibernian was Celtic's 7000th in league football.

Final Scottish Premier Division Table

		P	W	D	L	F	A	Pts
1	RANGERS	44	33	7	4	97	35	73
2	ABERDEEN	44	27	10	7	87	36	64
3	CELTIC	44	24	12	8	68	41	60
4	DUNDEE U	44	19	9	16	56	49	47
5	HEARTS	44	15	14	15	46	51	44
6	ST JOHNSTONE	44	10	20	14	52	66	40
7	HIBERNIAN	44	12	13	19	54	64	37
8	PARTICK T	44	12	12	20	50	71	36
9	MOTHERWELL	44	11	13	20	46	62	35
10	DUNDEE	44	11	12	21	48	68	34
11	FALKIRK	44	11	7	26	60	86	29
12	AIRDRIEONIANS	44	6	17	21	35	70	29

Season 1993-94

Scottish League Premier Division

DATE	OPPONENTS	SCORE	GOALSCORERS	ATTENDANCE
Aug 7	Motherwell	D 2-2	Slater, McAvennie	14,596
Aug 14	HIBERNIAN	D 1-1	Nicholas	27,690
Aug 21	RANGERS	D 0-0		47,942
Aug 28	Partick Thistle	W 1-0	McNally	14,733
Sep 4	ABERDEEN	L 0-1		34,311
Sep 11	Raith Rovers	W 4-1	Nicholas 2, Payton 2	8,200
Sep 18	DUNDEE UNITED	D 1-1	Creaney	26,377
Sep 25	Hearts	L 0-1		14,761
Oct 2	KILMARNOCK	D 0-0		23,395
Oct 6	St Johnstone	L 1-2	Creaney	7,386
Oct 9	DUNDEE	W 2-1	Creaney, McGinlay	15,994
Oct 16	Hibernian	D 1-1	Creaney	14,588
Oct 30	Rangers	W 2-1	Collins, O'Neil	47,522
Nov 6	PARTICK THISTLE	W 3-1	McGinlay 2, Nicholas	21,629
Nov 9	Aberdeen	D 1-1	O'Neil	21,000
Nov 13	Kilmarnock	D 2-2	McGinlay, Nicholas	16,649
Nov 20	HEARTS	D 0-0		25,981
Nov 24	MOTHERWELL	W 2-0	McGinlay 2	16,654
Nov 27	RAITH ROVERS	W 2-0	Collins 2	17,453
Nov 30	DUNDEE UNITED	L 0-1		10,108
Dec 4	ST JOHNSTONE	W 1-0	McGinlay	16,751
Dec 11	Dundee	D 1-1	Creaney	8,250
Dec 18	HIBERNIAN	W 1-0	McStay	16,793
Jan 1	RANGERS	L 2-4	Collins, Nicholas	48,506
Jan 8	Partick Thistle	L 0-1		13,092
Jan 12	Motherwell	L 1-2	McNally	13,159
Jan 19	ABERDEEN	D 2-2	Byrne, McStay	19,083
Jan 22	DUNDEE UNITED	D 0-0		17,235
Feb 5	Raith Rovers	D 0-0		7,678
Feb 12	Hearts	W 2-0	Nicholas 2	14,049
Mar 1	KILMARNOCK	W 1-0	Collins	10,882
Mar 5	St Johnstone	W 1-0	Byrne	8,622
Mar 19	Hibernian	D 0-0		14,704
Mar 26	MOTHERWELL	L 0-1		36,199
Mar 30	RAITH ROVERS	W 2-1	Donnelly 2	14,140
Apr 2	Dundee United	W 3-1	Collins, Falconer, Mowbray	9,713
Apr 6	DUNDEE	D 1-1	Donnelly	16,585
Apr 9	HEARTS	D 2-2	Collins, Vata	18,761
Apr 16	Kilmarnock	L 0-2		11,576
Apr 23	Dundee	W 2-0	McGinlay 2	5,982
Apr 27	ST JOHNSTONE	D 1-1	Donnelly	10,602
Apr 30	Rangers	D 1-1	Collins	45,853
May 7	PARTICK THISTLE	D 1-1	McGinlay	16,827
May 14	Aberdeen	D 1-1	Donnelly	16,500

Scottish Cup

Jan 29	Motherwell	(Rd3) L 0-1		14,061

Scottish League Cup

Aug 10	Stirling Albion	(Rd2) W 2-0	McAvennie, McGinlay	8,611
Aug 25	Arbroath	(Rd3) W 9-1	McAvennie 3, Payton 3,	5,364
			McNally, McGinlay, Nicholas	
Aug 31	AIRDRIE	(QF) W 1-0	McAvennie	25,738
Sep 22	Rangers	(SF) L 0-1		47,420

UEFA Cup

Sep 14	Young Boys (Berne)	(Rd1/FL) D 0-0		7,300
Sep 29	YOUNG BOYS (BERNE)	(Rd1/SL) W 1-0	o.g.	21,500
Oct 20	SPORTING LISBON	(Rd2/FL) W 1-0	Creaney	31,321
Nov 3	Sporting Lisbon	(Rd2/SL) L 0-2		65,000

League & Cup Appearances

PLAYER	LEAGUE	CUP COMPETITIONS			TOTAL
		S CUP	SL CUP	UEFA	
Biggins	4 (5)	0 (1)			4 (6)
Bonner	31		4	4	39
Boyd	38	1	4	4	47
Byrne	18 (4)	1		2	21 (4)
Collins	38	1	3	3	45
Creaney	17 (1)		1	3	21 (1)
Donnelly	10 (2)				10 (2)
Falconer	14				14
Galloway	15 (6)		4	2	21 (6)
Gillespie	25 (2)	1		3	29 (2)
Grant	27 (1)		4	4	35 (1)
Hay	2				2
McAvennie	8 (3)	1	4		13 (3)
McGinlay	37 (2)	1	3 (1)	4	45 (3)
McLaughlin	0 (8)				0 (8)
McNally	30 (2)	1	4	2	37 (2)
McStay P	35	1	4	4	44
Marshall	1				1
Martin	15				15
Mowbray	23 (2)	1		2	26 (2)
Muggleton	12	1			13
Nicholas	30 (5)		3	3 (1)	36 (6)
O'Neil	14 (13)	1	0 (2)	1 (3)	16 (18)
Payton	1 (6)		0 (2)	2	3 (8)
Slater	3 (2)		2		5 (2)
Smith	6 (1)				6 (1)
Vata	6 (4)				6 (4)
Wdowczyk	24 (1)		4	1 (1)	29 (2)

Goalscorers

PLAYER	LEAGUE	CUP COMPETITIONS			TOTAL
		S CUP	SL CUP	UEFA	
McGinlay	10		2		12
Nicholas	8		1		9
Collins	8				8
Creaney	5			1	6
McAvennie	1		5		6
Donnelly	5				5
Payton	2		3		5
McNally	2		1		3
Byrne	2				2
McStay	2				2
O'Neil	2				2
Falconer	1				1
Mowbray	1				1
Slater	1				1
Vata	1				1
Opps' o.gs.			1		1

Fact File

Frank Connor took charge for 3 games prior to the arrival of Lou Macari on the 30 October.

MANAGER: Liam Brady (until Oct 1993), Lou Macari

CAPTAIN: Paul McStay

TOP SCORER: Pat McGinlay

BIGGEST WIN: 9-1 v Arbroath, 25 August 1993, Scottish League Cup

HIGHEST ATTENDANCE: 65,000 v Sporting Lisbon, 3 November 1993, UEFA Cup

MAJOR TRANSFERS IN: Pat McGinlay from Hibernian, Wayne Biggins from Barnsley, Carl Muggleton from Leicester, Lee Martin from Manchester United, Willie Falconer from Sheffield United

MAJOR TRANSFERS OUT: Stuart Slater to Ipswich, Andy Payton to Barnsley, Gerry Creaney to Portsmouth, Wayne Biggins to Stoke City

Final Scottish Premier Division Table

		P	W	D	L	F	A	Pts
1	RANGERS	44	22	14	8	74	41	58
2	ABERDEEN	44	17	21	6	58	36	55
3	MOTHERWELL	44	20	14	10	58	43	54
4	CELTIC	44	15	20	9	51	38	50
5	HIBERNIAN	44	16	15	13	53	48	47
6	DUNDEE U	44	11	20	13	47	48	42
7	HEARTS	44	11	20	13	37	43	42
8	KILMARNOCK	44	12	16	16	36	45	40
9	PARTICK T	44	12	16	16	46	57	40
10	ST JOHNSTONE	44	10	20	14	35	47	40
11	RAITH R	44	6	19	19	46	80	31
12	DUNDEE	44	8	13	23	42	57	29

Season 1994-95

Scottish League Premier Division

(Due to ground improvements at Celtic Park, all home games played at Hampden Park).

DATE	OPPONENTS	SCORE	GOALSCORERS	ATTENDANCE
Aug 13	Falkirk	D 1-1	Walker	12,200
Aug 20	DUNDEE UNITED	W 2-1	Walker, Mowbray	25,817
Aug 27	Rangers	W 2-0	Collins, McStay	45,466
Sep 10	Partick Thistle	W 2-1	O'Donnell 2	14,883
Sep 17	KILMARNOCK	D 1-1	McGinlay	28,457
Sep 24	HIBERNIAN	W 2-0	Collins, O'Donnell	28,170
Oct 1	Motherwell	D 1-1	Walker	10,869
Oct 8	ABERDEEN	D 0-0		29,024
Oct 15	Hearts	L 0-1		12,086
Oct 22	FALKIRK	L 0-2		23,719
Oct 30	RANGERS	L 1-3	Byrne	32,171
Nov 5	Dundee United	D 2-2	Collins 2	11,000
Nov 9	PARTICK THISTLE	D 0-0		21,462
Nov 19	Kilmarnock	D 0-0		12,602
Nov 30	Hibernian	D 1-1	Collins	12,200
Dec 3	MOTHERWELL	D 2-2	Falconer, o.g.	21,465
Dec 26	Aberdeen	D 0-0		21,000
Dec 31	FALKIRK	W 2-0	Grant, Walker	21,152
Jan 4	Rangers	D 1-1	Byrne	45,794
Jan 7	DUNDEE UNITED	D 1-1	Collins	21,429
Jan 11	HEARTS	D 1-1	van Hooijdonk	26,491
Jan 14	KILMARNOCK	W 2-1	Collins, Falconer	25,342
Jan 21	Partick Thistle	D 0-0		12,760
Feb 4	Motherwell	L 0-1		10,771
Feb 11	HIBERNIAN	D 2-2	Collins, Falconer	24,284
Feb 25	Hearts	D 1-1	O'Donell	11,195
Mar 5	ABERDEEN	W 2-0	van Hooijdonk 2	25,863
Mar 21	Kilmarnock	W 1-0	Walker	10,112
Apr 1	MOTHERWELL	D 1-1	Walker	24,047
Apr 15	Aberdeen	L 0-2		14,500
Apr 19	HEARTS	L 0-1		18,638
Apr 29	Falkirk	W 2-1	Boyd, O'Donnell	9,000
May 2	PARTICK THISTLE	L 1-3	Grant	18,900
May 7	RANGERS	W 3-0	van Hooijdonk, Vata, o.g.	31,025
May 10	Hibernian	W 1-0	Falconer	6,101
May 13	Dundee United	W 1-0	O'Donnell	10,420

Scottish Cup

Jan 28	ST MIRREN	(Rd3) W 2-0	Falconer, van Hooijdonk	28,449
Feb 18	MEADOWBANK THISTLE	(Rd4) W 3-0	van Hooijdonk 2, Falconer	23,710
Mar 10	KILMARNOCK	(QF) W 1-0	Collins (pen)	30,873
Apr 7	Hibernian	(SF) D 0-0		40,950
Apr 11	Hibernian	(R) W 3-0	Collins, Falconer, O'Donnell	32,000
May 27	Airdrie	(F) W 1-0	van Hooijdonk	36,915

Scottish League Cup

Aug 16	Ayr United	(Rd2) W 1-0	Grant	8,182
Aug 31	Dundee	(Rd3) W 2-1	Collins, Walker	25,817
Sep 2	DUNDEE UNITED	(QF) W 1-0	Collins	28,859
Oct 26	Aberdeen	(SF) W 1-0	O'Neil	44,000
Nov 27	Raith Rovers	(F) D 2-2*	Walker, Nicholas	45,384

*Lost on penalties.

League & Cup Appearances

PLAYER	LEAGUE	CUP COMPETITIONS		TOTAL
		S CUP	SL CUP	
Bonner	20	5		25
Boyd	35	5	5	45
Byrne	6		1 (1)	7 (1)
Collins	33 (1)	6	5	44 (1)
Craig		0 (1)		0 (1)
Donnelly	7 (10)	1 (1)	4 (1)	12 (12)
Falconer	19 (6)	4 (2)	1 (1)	24 (9)
Galloway	11		4	15
Grant	27 (1)	5 (1)	4	36 (2)
Gray	8 (3)	1		9 (3)
Hay	2 (3)			2 (3)
McGinlay	7 (1)		2 (1)	9 (2)
Mackay	1			1
McKinlay	17	5		22
McLaughlin	19 (2)	6		25 (2)
McNally	19 (1)	3	5	27 (1)
McStay	28 (1)	4	5	37 (1)
Marshall	16	1	5	22
Martin	4		1	5
Mowbray	15	2	4	21
Nicholas	5 (6)		1 (3)	6 (9)
O'Donnell	25 (2)	3 (2)		28 (4)
O'Neil	24 (2)	5	2 (1)	31 (3)
O'Neill	0 (1)			0 (1)
Slavin	3			3
Smith	3		1	4
van Hooijdonk	13	5		18
Vata	7	3		10
Walker	22 (4)	2 (2)	5	29 (6)

Goalscorers

PLAYER	LEAGUE	CUP COMPETITIONS		TOTAL
		S CUP	SL CUP	
Collins	8	2	2	12
van Hooijdonk	4	4		8
Walker	6		2	8
Falconer	4	3		7
O'Donnell	6	1		7
Grant	2		1	3
Byrne	2			2
Boyd	1			1
McGinlay	1			1
McStay	1			1
Mowbray	1			1
Nicholas			1	1
O'Neil			1	1
Vata	1			1
Opps' o.gs.	2			2

MANAGER: Tommy Burns

CAPTAIN: Paul McStay

TOP SCORER: John Collins

BIGGEST WIN: 3-0 v Rangers, 7 May 1995, league; 3-0 v Meadowbank, 18 February 1995, Scottish Cup; 3-0 v Hibernian, 11 April 1995, Scottish Cup

HIGHEST ATTENDANCE: 45,794 v Rangers, 4 January 1995, league

MAJOR TRANSFERS IN: Phil O'Donnell from Motherwell, Tosh McKinlay from Hearts, Pierre van Hooijdonk from Breda

MAJOR TRANSFERS OUT: Carl Muggleton to Stoke, Pat McGinlay to Hibernian

Final Scottish Premier Division Table

		P	W	D	L	F	A	Pts
1	RANGERS	36	20	9	7	60	35	69
2	MOTHERWELL	36	14	12	10	50	50	54
3	HIBERNIAN	36	12	17	7	49	37	53
4	CELTIC	36	11	18	7	39	33	51
5	FALKIRK	36	12	12	12	48	47	48
6	HEARTS	36	12	7	17	44	51	43
7	KILMARNOCK	36	11	10	15	40	48	43
8	PARTICK T	36	10	13	13	40	50	43
9	ABERDEEN	36	10	11	15	43	46	41
10	DUNDEE U	36	9	9	18	40	56	36

Season 1995-96

Scottish League Premier Division

DATE	OPPONENTS	SCORE	GOALSCORERS	ATTENDANCE
Aug 26	Raith Rovers	W 1-0	van Hooijdonk	9,300
Sep 10	Aberdeen	W 3-2	Collins 2, Thom	20,000
Sep 16	MOTHERWELL	D 1-1	O'Donnell	33,377
Sep 23	Hearts	W 4-0	McLaughlin 2, Walker 2	13,696
Sep 30	RANGERS	L 0-2		34,250
Oct 4	Falkirk	W 1-0	Hughes	9,096
Oct 7	PARTICK THISTLE	W 2-1	van Hooijdonk, Collins	33,585
Oct 14	HIBERNIAN	D 2-2	van Hooijdonk, Collins	34,123
Oct 21	Kilmarnock	D 0-0		14,011
Oct 28	ABERDEEN	W 2-0	McLaughlin, van Hooijdonk (pen)	34,010
Nov 4	Motherwell	W 2-0	Collins, Donnelly	12,077
Nov 8	RAITH ROVERS	D 0-0		31,119
Nov 11	Partick Thistle	W 2-1	van Hooijdonk 2	12,059
Nov 19	Rangers	D 3-3	Thom, Collins (pen), van Hooijdonk	46,460
Nov 25	HEARTS	W 3-1	Collins 3 (1 pen)	33,936
Dec 2	KILMARNOCK	W 4-2	van Hooijdonk 2, Grant, Thom	33,812
Dec 9	Hibernian	W 4-0	Donnelly, McNamara, O'Donnell, van Hooijdonk	14,117
Dec 16	FALKIRK	W 1-0	van Hooijdonk	35,012
Jan 3	RANGERS	D 0-0		36,944
Jan 6	MOTHERWELL	W 1-0	van Hooijdonk	35,370
Jan 9	Raith Rovers	W 3-1	Collins, O'Donnell, van Hooijdonk	9,300
Jan 14	Aberdeen	W 2-1	Collins, van Hooijdonk	17,100
Jan 17	Hearts	W 2-1	van Hooijdonk, Walker	15,871
Jan 20	Kilmarnock	D 0-0		15,716
Feb 2	HIBERNIAN	W 2-1	McStay, van Hooijdonk	37,142
Feb 10	Falkirk	D 0-0		10,400
Feb 24	PARTICK THISTLE	W 4-0	van Hooijdonk 2 (1 pen), Grant, Wieghorst	36,430
Mar 2	HEARTS	W 4-0	Donnelly, McLaughlin, McStay, van Hooijdonk	37,193
Mar 17	Rangers	D 1-1	Hughes	47,312
Mar 23	Motherwell	D 0-0		12,394
Apr 1	ABERDEEN	W 5-0	Donnelly 2, van Hooijdonk 2, Cadete	35,994
Apr 10	KILMARNOCK	D 1-1	van Hooijdonk	36,372
Apr 14	Hibernian	W 2-1	van Hooijdonk 2	10,472
Apr 20	FALKIRK	W 4-0	Thom 2, Cadete, Donnelly	35,895
Apr 27	Partick Thistle	W 4-2	van Hooijdonk 2 (1 pen), Cadete, Mackay	13,940
May 4	RAITH ROVERS	W 4-1	Cadete 2, Grant, Gray	37,423

Scottish Cup

Jan 28	Whitehill Welfare	(Rd3) W 3-0	van Hooijdonk 2, Donnelly	13,100
Feb 17	RAITH ROVERS	(Rd4) W 2-0	Donnelly, Thom	31,870
Mar 10	DUNDEE UNITED	(QF) W 2-1	Thom, van Hooijdonk	32,750
Apr 7	Rangers	(SF) L 1-2	van Hooijdonk	36,333

Scottish League Cup

Aug 19	Ayr United	(Rd2) W 3-0	Collins, Thom, van Hooijdonk	9,128
Aug 31	RAITH ROVERS	(Rd3) W 2-1	Donnelly, van Hooijdonk	27,546
Sep 9	RANGERS	(QF) L 0-1		32,399

European Cup-Winners' Cup

Sep 14	Dinamo Batumi	(Rd1/FL) W 3-2	Thom 2, Donnelly	18,000
Sep 28	DINAMO BATUMI	(Rd1/SL) W 4-0	Thom 2, Donnelly, Walker	34,033
Oct 19	Paris St-Germain	(Rd2/FL) L 0-1		30,000
Nov 2	PARIS ST-GERMAIN	(Rd2/SL) L 0-3		34,573

Fact File

John Hughes became the third player of that name to play for Celtic – they were all unrelated.

MANAGER: Tommy Burns
CAPTAIN: Paul McStay
TOP SCORER: Pierre van Hooijdonk
BIGGEST WIN: 5-0 v Aberdeen, 1 April 1996, league
HIGHEST ATTENDANCE: 47,312 v Rangers, 17 March 1996, league

League & Cup Appearances

PLAYER	LEAGUE	CUP COMPETITIONS			TOTAL
		S CUP	SL CUP	ECWC	
Boyd	34	3	3	4	44
Cadete	2 (4)				2 (4)
Collins	26 (3)	2	3	3	34 (3)
Donnelly	35	3 (1)	2 (1)	2 (2)	42 (4)
Falconer	0 (2)				0 (2)
Grant	30	4	3	4	41
Gray	3 (2)			0 (1)	3 (3)
Hay	1 (3)	0 (1)		0 (1)	1 (5)
Hughes	26	3	3	4	36
Mackay	9 (2)		0 (1)		9 (3)
McKinlay	33	4	3	4	44
McLaughlin	11 (15)	2 (1)	1 (2)	1 (2)	15 (21)
McNamara	26	4			30
McQuilken	3 (1)				3 (1)
McStay	29 (1)	4	1	3	37 (1)
Marshall	36	4	3	4	47
O'Donnell	13 (1)	0 (1)	2	2	17 (2)
O'Neil	3 (3)	2 (1)			5 (4)
Thom	31 (1)	3	3	4	41 (1)
van Hooijdonk	34	4	2 (1)	3	43 (1)
Vata	5 (1)		3	4	12 (1)
Walker	4 (12)	1	1 (1)	2 (1)	8 (14)
Wieghorst	2 (7)	1 (1)			3 (8)

Goalscorers

PLAYER	LEAGUE	CUP COMPETITIONS			TOTAL
		S CUP	SL CUP	UEFA	
van Hooijdonk	26	4	2		32
Collins	11		1		12
Thom	5	2	1	4	12
Donnelly	6	2	1	2	11
Cadete	5				5
McLaughlin	4				4
Walker	3		1		4
Grant	3				3
O'Donnell	3				3
Hughes	2				2
McStay	2				2
Gray	1				1
Mackay	1				1
McNamara	1				1
Wieghorst	1				1

MAJOR TRANSFERS IN: Andreas Thom from Bayer Leverkusen, John Hughes from Falkirk, Morten Wieghorst from Dundee, Jackie McNamara from Dunfermline, Jorge Cadete from Sporting Lisbon

MAJOR TRANSFERS OUT: Charlie Nicholas to Clyde, Paul Byrne to Southend, Tony Mowbray to Ipswich, Jamie McQuilken to Dundee United, Barry Smith to Dundee, Mark McNally to Southend, Willie Falconer to Motherwell, Andy Walker to Sheffield United, Rudi Vata to Apollon Limassol, John Collins to Monaco

Final Scottish Premier Division Table

		P	W	D	L	F	A	Pts
1	RANGERS	36	27	6	3	85	25	87
2	CELTIC	36	24	11	1	74	25	83
3	ABERDEEN	36	16	7	13	52	45	55
4	HEARTS	36	16	7	13	55	53	55
5	HIBERNIAN	36	11	10	15	43	57	43
6	RAITH R	36	12	7	17	41	57	43
7	KILMARNOCK	36	11	8	17	39	54	41
8	MOTHERWELL	36	9	12	15	28	39	39
9	PARTICK T	36	8	6	22	29	62	30
10	FALKIRK	36	6	6	24	31	60	24

Season 1996-97

Scottish League Premier Division

DATE	OPPONENTS	SCORE	GOALSCORERS	ATTENDANCE
Aug 10	Aberdeen	D 2-2	van Hooijdonk, Thom	18,500
Aug 15	RAITH ROVERS	W 4-1	Thom 2, van Hooijdonk, Donnelly	47,200
Aug 24	Kilmarnock	W 3-1	Thom, Cadete, Di Canio	15,900
Sep 7	HIBERNIAN	W 5-0	Cadete 2, O'Neil, van Hooijdonk, o.g.	47,002
Sep 14	Dundee United	W 2-1	van Hooijdonk, Mackay	12,152
Sep 21	DUNFERMLINE ATHLETIC	W 5-1	van Hooijdonk 2, Di Canio 2, Cadete	50,032
Sep 28	Rangers	L 0-2		50,210
Oct 10	MOTHERWELL	W 1-0	van Hooijdonk	49,422
Oct 20	Hearts	D 2-2	van Hooijdonk 2	13,352
Oct 26	Hibernian	W 4-0	Thom 2, van Hooijdonk, Donnelly	14,135
Nov 2	ABERDEEN	W 1-0	Di Canio	50,136
Nov 14	RANGERS	L 0-1		50,041
Nov 30	HEARTS	D 2-2	Di Canio (pen), O'Neil	50,034
Dec 7	Motherwell	L 1-2	Hay	11,589
Dec 21	DUNDEE UNITED	W 1-0	O'Donnell	46,590
Dec 26	Aberdeen	W 2-1	Di Canio, Cadete	19,000
Dec 28	DUNFERMLINE ATHLETIC	W 4-2	Di Canio 2, van Hooijdonk, Cadete	45,818
Jan 2	Rangers	L 1-3	Di Canio	52,019
Jan 4	MOTHERWELL	W 5-0	Cadete 2, van Hooijdonk, Di Canio (pen), Wieghorst	45,374
Jan 8	KILMARNOCK	W 6-0	Cadete 3, Hay, McNamara, Wieghorst	45,724
Jan 11	Hearts	W 2-1	Cadete 2	15,424
Jan 14	Raith Rovers	W 2-1	Cadete, Hay	8,544
Jan 18	HIBERNIAN	W 4-1	van Hooijdonk 2, Cadete, McLaughlin	49,092
Jan 29	Dunfermline Athletic	D 2-2	McStay, Cadete	18,000
Feb 1	Dundee United	L 0-1		12,600
Feb 6	RAITH ROVERS	W 2-0	Di Canio, Cadete	45,233
Feb 22	Motherwell	W 1-0	Cadete	12,131
Mar 1	HEARTS	W 2-0	Di Canio, Cadete	49,729
Mar 11	Kilmarnock	L 0-2		15,087
Mar 16	RANGERS	L 0-1		49,929
Mar 22	Dunfermline Athletic	D 2-2	O'Donnell, Donnelly	12,447
Apr 5	Raith Rovers	D 1-1	Di Canio	7,912
Apr 20	ABERDEEN	W 3-0	Cadete 2, Donnelly	47,293
May 4	Hibernian	W 3-1	Cadete 2, Di Canio	10,603
May 7	KILMARNOCK	D 0-0		42,994
May 10	DUNDEE UNITED	W 3-0	Johnson, Hay, Cadete	47,765

Scottish Cup

Jan 26	Clydebank	(Rd3)	W 5-0	Cadete 2, van Hooijdonk, Mackay, Di Canio (pen)	16,102
Feb 17	Hibernian	(Rd4)	D 1-1	O'Donnell	16,000
Feb 26	HIBERNIAN	(R)	W 2-0	O'Donnell, Di Canio	46,424
Mar 3	RANGERS	(QF)	W 2-0	Mackay, Di Canio (pen)	49,591
Apr 12	Falkirk	(SF)	D 1-1	Johnson	45,261
Apr 23	Falkirk	(R)	L 0-1		35,879

Scottish League Cup

Aug 8	Clyde	(Rd2)	W 3-1	Cadete 2, Thom	8,300
Sep 4	Alloa Athletic	(Rd3)	W 5-1	Cadete 3, Thom, van Hooijdonk	12,582
Sep 17	Hearts	(QF)	L 0-1		14,422

UEFA Cup

Aug 8	Kosice	(QR/FL)	D 0-0		16,000
Aug 20	KOSICE	(QR/SL)	W 1-0	Cadete	46,752
Sep 10	HAMBURG	Rd1(FL)	L 0-2		45,412
Sep 24	Hamburg	(Rd1/SL)	L 0-2		35,000

MANAGER: Tommy Burns (until 2 May), Billy Stark

CAPTAIN: Paul McStay

TOP SCORER: Jorge Cadete

BIGGEST WIN: 6-0 v Kilmarnock 8 January 1997, league

HIGHEST ATTENDANCE: 50,210 v Rangers, 28 September 1996, league

MAJOR TRANSFERS IN: Paolo Di Canio from AC Milan, Alan Stubbs from Bolton, David Hannah from Dundee United, Enrico Annoni from Roma, Tommy Johnson from Aston Villa

MAJOR TRANSFERS OUT: John Hughes to Hibernian, Pierre van Hooijdonk to Nottingham Forest, Brian O'Neil to Aberdeen

League & Cup Appearances

PLAYER	LEAGUE	CUP COMPETITIONS			TOTAL
		S CUP	SL CUP	UEFA	
Annoni	3	2			5
Anthony	0 (2)		0 (1)		0 (3)
Boyd	31	5	3	4	43
Cadete	30 (1)	5	3	4	42 (1)
Di Canio	25 (1)	6	2	2 (1)	35 (2)
Donnelly	20 (9)	2	1 (2)	1 (1)	24 (12)
Elliot	0 (1)				0 (1)
Grant	21 (2)	2	3	4	30 (2)
Gray	7 (4)		1		8 (4)
Hannah	14 (4)	3 (2)			17 (6)
Hay	4 (10)	0 (2)			4 (12)
Hughes	5 (1)		2	3	10 (1)
Johnson	3 (1)	1 (1)			4 (2)
Kelly	1				1
Kerr	25 (1)	6			31 (1)
McBride	0 (2)				0 (2)
Mackay	18 (2)	4	1	1 (1)	24 (3)
McKinlay	24 (3)	6	1	3	34 (3)
McLaughlin	8 (12)	1 (2)	0 (2)	1 (1)	10 (17)
McNamara	30	4 (1)	3	3 (1)	40 (2)
McStay	14 (1)	4	1	1	20 (1)
Marshall	11		3	4	18
O'Donnell	19	6		1	26
O'Neil	15 (1)		1	3	19 (1)
Stubbs	20	4	1	1	26
Thom	18 (5)	3 (2)	3	4	28 (7)
van Hooijdonk	19 (2)	2	3	2 (2)	26 (4)
Wieghorst	11 (6)		1 (2)	2 (2)	14 (10)

Goalscorers

PLAYER	LEAGUE	CUP COMPETITIONS			TOTAL
		S CUP	SL CUP	UEFA	
Cadete	25	2	5	1	33
van Hooijdonk	14	1	1		16
Di Canio	12	3			15
Thom	6		2		8
Donnelly	5				5
O'Donnell	2	2			4
Hay	4				4
Mackay	1	2			3
Johnson	1	1			2
O'Neil	2				2
Wieghorst	2				2
McNamara	1				1
McStay	1				1
McLaughlin	1				1
Opps' o.gs.	1				1

Fact File

Billy Stark took charge of Celtic as caretaker manager for their last three league games.

Final Scottish Premier Division Table

		P	W	D	L	F	A	Pts
1	RANGERS	36	25	5	6	85	33	80
2	CELTIC	36	23	6	7	78	32	75
3	DUNDEE U	36	17	9	10	46	33	60
4	HEARTS	36	14	10	12	46	43	52
5	DUNFERMLINE ATH	36	12	9	15	52	65	45
6	ABERDEEN	36	10	14	12	45	54	44
7	KILMARNOCK	36	11	6	19	41	61	39
8	MOTHERWELL	36	9	11	16	44	55	38
9	HIBERNIAN	36	9	11	16	38	55	38
10	RAITH R	36	6	7	23	29	73	25

Season 1997-98

Scottish League Premier Division

DATE	OPPONENTS	SCORE	GOALSCORERS	ATTENDANCE
Aug 3	Hibernian	L 1-2	MacKay	13,051
Aug 16	DUNFERMLINE ATHLETIC	L 1-2	Thom (pen)	46,206
Aug 23	St Johnstone	W 2-0	Larsson, Jackson	10,265
Sep 13	Motherwell	W 3-2	Burley 2, Donnelly	11,550
Sep 20	ABERDEEN	W 2-0	Larsson 2	49,017
Sep 27	Dundee United	W 2-1	Donnelly, O'Donnell	11367
Oct 4	KILMARNOCK	W 4-0	Larsson 2, Donnelly, Wieghorst	48,165
Oct 18	Hearts	W 2-1	Rieper, Larsson	16,977
Oct 25	ST JOHNSTONE	W 2-0	Larsson, Donnelly	48,545
Nov 1	Dunfermline Athletic	W 2-0	Larsson, Blinker	12,627
Nov 8	Rangers	L 0-1		50,082
Nov 15	MOTHERWELL	L 0-2		48,010
Nov 19	RANGERS	D 1-1	Stubbs	49,509
Nov 22	DUNDEE UNITED	W 4-0	Larsson 2, Thom 2 (1 pen)	48,581
Dec 6	Kilmarnock	D 0-0		15,632
Dec 9	Aberdeen	W 2-0	Larsson, Johnson	16,981
Dec 13	HEARTS	W 1-0	Burley	50,035
Dec 20	HIBERNIAN	W 5-0	Burley 2, McNamara, Larsson, Wieghorst	49,094
Dec 27	St Johnstone	L 0-1		10,455
Jan 2	RANGERS	W 2-0	Burley, Lambert	49,350
Jan 10	Motherwell	D 1-1	Lambert	12,350
Jan 27	Dundee United	W 2-1	Burley, Donnelly	14,004
Feb 2	ABERDEEN	W 3-1	Larsson, Wieghorst, Jackson	46,606
Feb 8	Hearts	D 1-1	McNamara	17,653
Feb 21	KILMARNOCK	W 4-0	Brattbakk 4	49,231
Feb 25	DUNFERMLINE ATHLETIC	W 5-1	Brattbakk 2, Larsson, Wieghorst, O'Donnell	48,502
Feb 28	Hibernian	W 1-0	Rieper	17,137
Mar 15	DUNDEE UNITED	D 1-1	Donnelly	48,656
Mar 21	Aberdeen	W 1-0	Burley (pen)	18,009
Mar 28	HEARTS	D 0-0		50,038
Apr 8	Kilmarnock	W 2-1	Donnelly, Larsson	18,076
Apr 12	Rangers	L 0-2		50,042
Apr 18	MOTHERWELL	W 4-1	Donnelly 2, Burley 2	49,541
Apr 25	HIBERNIAN	D 0-0		50,034
May 3	Dunfermline Athletic	D 1-1	Donnelly	12,866
May 9	ST JOHNSTONE	W 2-0	Larsson, Brattbakk	50,032

Scottish Cup

Jan 24	MORTON	(Rd3) W 2-0	Brattbakk, Jackson	40,014
Feb 16	Dunfermline Athletic	(Rd4) W 2-1	Mahe, Brattbakk	12,000
Mar 8	Dundee United	(QF) W 3-2	Brattbakk, Wieghorst, o.g.	14,000
Apr 5	Rangers	(SF) L 1-2	Burley	48,993

Scottish League Cup

Aug 9	Berwick Rangers	(Rd2) W 7-0	Donnelly 2, Wieghorst, Larsson, Jackson, Thom, Blinker	6,267
Aug 19	St Johnstone	(Rd3) W 1-0	Donnelly (pen)	7,488
Sep 10	MOTHERWELL	(QF) W 1-0	Larsson	37,006
Oct 14	Dunfermline Athletic	(SF) W 1-0	Burley	27,796
Nov 30	Dundee United	(F) W 3-0	Rieper, Larsson, Burley	49,305

UEFA Cup

Jul 23	Inter CableTel	(1QR/FL) W 3-0	Thom (pen), Johnson, Wieghorst	4,980
Jul 29	INTER CABLETEL	(1QR/SL) W 5-0	Jackson, Thom (pen), Johnson, Hannah, Hay	41,537
Aug 12	Tirol Innsbruck	(2QR/FL) L 1-2	Stubbs	6,200
Aug 26	TIROL INNSBRUCK	(2QR/SL) W 6-3	Donnelly 2, Burley 2, Wieghorst, Thom	47,017
Sep 16	LIVERPOOL	(Rd1/FL) D 2-2	McNamara, Donnelly	48,625
Sep 30	Liverpool	(Rd1/SL) D 0-0		38,205

MANAGER: Wim Jansen   **CAPTAIN:** Tom Boyd

TOP SCORER: Henrik Larsson

BIGGEST WIN: 7-0 v Berwick Rangers, 9 August 1997, Scottish League Cup

HIGHEST ATTENDANCE: 50,082 v Rangers, 8 November 1997, league

MAJOR TRANSFERS IN: Regi Blinker from Sheffield Wednesday, Harald Brattbakk from Rosenborg, Craig Burley from Chelsea, Jonathan Gould from Bradford City, Darren Jackson from Hibernian, Paul Lambert from Borussia Dortmund, Henrik Larsson from Feyenoord, Stephane Mahe from Rennes, Marc Rieper from West Ham

League & Cup Appearances

PLAYER	LEAGUE	CUP COMPETITIONS			TOTAL
		S CUP	SL CUP	UEFA	
Annoni	14 (6)	1 (1)	0 (1)	1 (1)	16 (9)
Blinker	13 (2)	1 (1)	4	1	19 (3)
Boyd	33	4	5	5	47
Brattbakk	11 (6)	4			15 (6)
Burley	35	4	5	4	48
Donnelly	21 (9)	2 (1)	3 (2)	5 (1)	31 (13)
Gould	35	4	5	4	48
Grant			0 (1)		0 (1)
Gray				2	2
Hannah	9 (6)	0 (1)	2 (1)	5 (1)	16 (9)
Hay				0 (1)	0 (1)
Jackson	9 (14)	0 (3)	2	2 (1)	13 (18)
Johnson	1 (1)			2	3 (1)
Lambert	25 (1)	4	0 (1)		29 (2)
Larsson	34 (1)	4	5	4	47 (1)
McBride			0 (1)		0 (1)
Mackay	3 (1)		3	2	8 (1)
McKinlay	2 (3)		0 (1)	4	6 (4)
McNamara	28 (3)	2	2 (2)	4 (2)	36 (7)
Mahe	23	3	5	4	35
Marshall	1			2	3
O'Donnell	6 (9)	1	3 (1)	1 (1)	11 (11)
Rieper	30	4	2		36
Stubbs	29	4	3	5 (1)	41 (1)
Thom	8 (7)		3 (2)	4	15 (9)
Wieghorst	26 (5)	2 (1)	3	5	36 (6)

Goalscorers

PLAYER	LEAGUE	CUP COMPETITIONS			TOTAL
		S CUP	SL CUP	UEFA	
Larsson	16		3		19
Donnelly	10		3	3	16
Burley	10	1	2	2	15
Brattbakk	7	3			10
Wieghorst	4	1	1	2	8
Thom	3		1	3	7
Jackson	3	1	1	1	6
McNamara	2			1	6
Rieper	2		1		3
Blinker	1		1		2
Johnson				2	2
Lambert	2				2
O'Donnell	2				2
Stubbs	1			1	2
Hannah				1	1
Hay				1	1
Mackay	1				1
Mahe		1			1
Opps' o.gs.		1			1

MAJOR TRANSFERS OUT: Paolo Di Canio to Sheffield Wednesday, Peter Grant to Norwich, Jorge Cadete to Celta Vigo, Andreas Thom to Hertha Berlin, Gordon Marshall to Kilmarnock

Final Scottish Premier Division Table

		P	W	D	L	F	A	PTS
1	CELTIC	36	22	8	6	64	24	74
2	RANGERS	36	21	9	6	76	38	72
3	HEARTS	36	19	10	7	70	46	67
4	KILMARNOCK	36	13	11	12	40	52	50
5	ST JOHNSTONE	36	13	9	14	38	42	48
6	ABERDEEN	36	9	12	15	39	53	39
7	DUNDEE U	36	8	13	15	43	51	37
8	DUNFERMLINE ATH	36	8	13	15	43	68	37
9	MOTHERWELL	36	9	7	20	46	64	38
10	HIBERNIAN	36	6	12	18	38	59	30

Season 1998-99

Scottish League Premier Division

DATE	OPPONENTS	SCORE	GOALSCORERS	ATTENDANCE
Aug 1	DUNFERMLINE ATHLETIC	W 5-0	Burley 3, Donnelly, Mackay	59,220
Aug 16	Aberdeen	L 2-3	Larsson 2 (1 pen)	16,640
Aug 22	DUNDEE UNITED	W 2-1	Burley, Burchill	59,738
Aug 29	Dundee	D 1-1	Burley	9,853
Sep 12	KILMARNOCK	D 1-1	Blinker	58,361
Sep 20	Rangers	D 0-0		50,026
Sep 23	ST JOHNSTONE	L 0-1		55,889
Sep 26	HEARTS	D 1-1	Donnelly	60,077
Oct 3	Motherwell	W 2-1	Brattbakk, Lambert	12,103
Oct 17	Dunfermline Athletic	D 2-2	Stubbs, Brattbakk	10,968
Oct 24	ABERDEEN	W 2-0	Donnelly 2	60,081
Oct 31	Kilmarnock	L 0-2		16,695
Nov 7	DUNDEE	W 6-1	Larsson 3 (2 pens), Burchill 2, Donnelly	58,093
Nov 14	St Johnstone	L 1-2	Larsson	9,762
Nov 21	RANGERS	W 5-1	Larsson 2, Moravcik 2, Burchill	59,783
Nov 28	MOTHERWELL	W 2-0	Larsson, O'Donnell	59,227
Dec 6	Hearts	L 1-2	O'Donnell	17,334
Dec 12	Dundee United	D 1-1	Larsson	11,612
Dec 19	DUNFERMLINE ATHLETIC	W 5-0	Larsson 2, Moravcik 2, Mjallby	59,024
Dec 27	Dundee	W 3-0	Larsson, O'Donnell, Riseth	10,043
Jan 3	Rangers	D 2-2	Stubbs, Larsson	50,059
Jan 31	ST JOHNSTONE	W 5-0	Brattbakk 3, Moravcik, Larsson	60,092
Feb 6	HEARTS	W 3-0	Larsson 3 (1 pen)	59,815
Feb 17	KILMARNOCK	W 1-0	Riseth	59,126
Feb 21	Motherwell	W 7-1	Larsson 4 (1 pen), Moravcik, Burley, Burchill	11,963
Feb 27	DUNDEE UNITD	W 2-1	Larsson, Burley	59,902
Mar 14	Aberdeen	W 5-1	Larsson 2, Viduka 2, Burley	16,825
Mar 21	Kilmarnock	D 0-0		14,722
Apr 3	DUNDEE	W 5-0	Larsson 2, Burley, Blinker, Viduka	59,269
Apr 14	Hearts	W 4-2	Viduka 2, Blinker, Riseth	16,388
Apr 17	MOTHERWELL	W 1-0	Larsson (pen)	59,588
Apr 24	St Johnstone	L 0-1		10,379
May 2	RANGERS	L 0-3		59,918
May 8	Dunfermline Athletic	W 2-1	Johnson 2	8,809
May 15	ABERDEEN	W 3-2	Johnson, Blinker, Burchill	59,138
May 23	Dundee United	W 2-1	Burchill 2	-

Scottish Cup

Jan 23	AIRDRIE	(Rd3) W 3-1	Larsson, O'Donnell, o.g.	43,642
Feb 13	DUNFERMLINE ATHLETIC	(Rd4) W 4-0	Larsson 3, Brattbakk	47,194
Mar 8	Morton	(QF) W 3-0	Viduka 2, Larsson	14,000
Apr 10	Dundee United	(SF) W 2-0	Blinker, Viduka	43,491
May 29	Rangers	(F) L 0-1		51,746

Scottish League Cup

Aug 19	Airdrie	(Rd2) L 0-1		9,500

Champions League

Jul 22	ST PATRICK'S ATHLETIC	(1QR/FL) D 0-0		56,864
Jul 29	St Patrick's Athletic	(1QR/SL) W 2-0	Larsson, Brattbakk	9,700
Aug 12	CROATIA ZAGREB	(2QR/FL) W 1-0	Jackson	51,782
Aug 26	Croatia Zagreb	(2QR/SL) L 0-3		27,000

UEFA Cup

Sep 15	Vitoria Guimaraes	(Rd1/FL) W 2-1	Larsson, Donnelly	9,000
Sep 29	VITORIA GUIMARAES	(Rd1/SL) W 2-1	Stubbs, Larsson	38,076
Oct 24	FC ZURICH	(Rd2/FL) D 1-1	Brattbakk	44,121
Nov 3	FC Zurich	(Rd2/SL) L 2-4	Larsson, O'Donnell	19,000

League & Cup Appearances

PLAYER	LEAGUE	CUP COMPETITIONS			TOTAL
		S CUP	SL CUP	CL/UEFA	
Annoni	9 (5)	2	0 (1)	0 (2)	11 (8)
Blinker	13 (2)	3 (2)	1	4	21 (4)
Boyd	31	4	1	6	42
Brattbakk	16 (9)	1 (1)		6 (1)	23 (11)
Burchill	5 (16)	0 (2)	0 (1)		5 (19)
Burley	20 (1)	2	1	7	30 (1)
Corr	0 (1)				0 (1)
Donnelly	20 (3)	1 (1)	1	5 (3)	27 (7)
Gould	28	5	1	8	42
Hannah	5 (4)	0 (1)		2 (1)	7 (6)
Healy	2 (1)				2 (1)
Jackson	4 (2)	1		4 (4)	9 (6)
Johnson	3	0 (1)			3 (1)
Kerr	4			0 (1)	4 (1)
Lambert	33	5	1	8	47
Larsson	35	5		8	48
McBride	1				1
McCondichie	1				1
Mackay	1		1	1	3
McKinlay	11 (7)	2 (1)	0 (1)	3 (1)	16 (10)
McNamara	15 (1)	2	1	6	24 (1)
Mahe	24	5	1	6	36
Marshall	1 (1)				1 (1)
Mjallby	17	4			21
Moravcik	14	3			17
O'Donnell	13 (2)	2 (1)	1	3	19 (3)
Rieper	7			5	12
Riseth	26 (1)	3			29 (1)
Stubbs	22 (1)	3		6	31 (1)
Viduka	8 (1)	2			10 (1)
Warner	3				3
Wieghorst	5 (2)	1 (1)			6 (3)

Goalscorers

PLAYER	LEAGUE	CUP COMPETITIONS			TOTAL
		S CUP	SL CUP	CL/UEFA	
Larsson	28	5		4	37
Burley	9				9
Brattbakk	5	1		2	8
Burchill	8				8
Viduka	5	3			8
Donnelly	5			1	6
Moravcik	6				6
Blinker	4	1			5
O'Donnell	3	1		1	5
Johnson	3				3
Riseth	3				3
Stubbs	2		1		3
Jackson			1		1
Lambert	1				1
Mackay	1				1
Mjallby	1				1
Opps' o.gs.		1			1

MAJOR TRANSFERS OUT: Simon Donnelly to Sheffield Wednesday, Phil O'Donnell to Sheffield Wednesday, David Hannah to Dundee United, Malky Mackay to Norwich, Darren Jackson to Hearts, Brian McLaughlin to Dundee United

MANAGER: Doctor Jozef Venglos

CAPTAIN: Tom Boyd

TOP SCORER: Henrik Larsson

BIGGEST WIN: 7-1 v Motherwell, 21 February 1999, league

HIGHEST ATTENDANCE: 60,092 v St Johnstone, 31 January 1998, league

MAJOR TRANSFERS IN: Johan Mjallby from AIK Solna, Lubomir Moravcik from MSV Durisburg, Vidar Riseth from Lask Linz, Mark Viduka from Croatia Zagreb

Final Scottish Premier Division Table

		P	W	D	L	F	A	Pts
1	RANGERS	36	23	8	5	76	31	77
2	CELTIC	36	21	8	7	84	35	71
3	ST JOHNSTONE	36	15	12	9	39	38	57
4	KILMARNOCK	36	14	14	8	47	29	56
5	DUNDEE	36	13	7	16	36	56	46
6	HEARTS	36	11	9	16	44	50	42
7	MOTHERWELL	36	10	11	15	35	54	41
8	ABERDEEN	36	10	7	19	43	71	37
9	DUNDEE UTD	36	8	10	18	37	48	34
10	DUNFERMLINE	36	4	16	16	28	59	28

Season 1999-2000

Scottish League Premier Division

DATE	OPPONENTS	SCORE	GOALSCORERS	ATTENDANCE
Aug 1	Aberdeen	W 5-0	Larsson 2, Viduka 2, Burchill	16,080
Aug 7	ST JOHNSTONE	W 3-0	Viduka, Wieghorst, Mjallby	60,253
Aug 15	Dundee United	L 1-2	Berkovic	12,375
Aug 21	Dundee	W 2-1	Larsson, Mahe	10,531
Aug 29	HEARTS	W 4-0	Berkovic 2, Larsson, Viduka	59,837
Sep 12	Kilmarnock	W 1-0	Burchill	14,328
Sep 25	Hibernian	W 2-0	Viduka 2	14,743
Oct 16	ABERDEEN	W 7-0	Larsson 3, Viduka 3, Berkovic	60,033
Oct 24	St Johnstone	W 2-1	Burchill, Wieghorst	-
Oct 27	MOTHERWELL	L 0-1		58,731
Oct 30	KILMARNOCK	W 5-1	Viduka 3, Burley, Wright	59,720
Nov 7	Rangers	L 2-4	Berkovic 2	50,026
Nov 20	Hearts	W 2-1	Moravcik, Wright	17,184
Nov 27	Motherwell	L 2-3	Berkovic, Viduka (pen)	12,775
Dec 4	HIBERNIAN	W 4-0	Moravcik 2, Viduka (pen), Weighorst	60,092
Dec 11	Aberdeen	W 6-0	Viduka, Moravcik, Mahe, Lambert, Blinker, Wright	16,532
Dec 18	DUNDEE UNITED	W 4-1	Viduka, Moravcik, Burchill, Blinker	59,120
Dec 27	RANGERS	D 1-1	Viduka	59,772
Jan 22	Kilmarnock	D 1-1	Viduka	14,126
Feb 5	HEARTS	L 2-3	Viduka, Moravcik	59,896
Feb 12	Dundee	W 3-0	Viduka, Mjallby, Healy	10,044
Mar 1	DUNDEE	W 6-2	Johnson 3, Viduka 2 (1 pen), Petrov	56,228
Mar 5	Hibernian	L 1-2	Viduka	12,236
Mar 8	RANGERS	L 0-1		59,800
Mar 11	ST JOHNSTONE	W 4-1	Viduka 2, Burchill 2	59,530
Mar 26	Rangers	L 0-4		5,039
Apr 2	KILMARNOCK	W 4-2	Johnson, Berkovic, Blinker, Burchill	40,569
Apr 5	MOTHERWELL	W 4-0	Johnson 2, Blinker, Berkovic	46,862
Apr 8	Hearts	L 0-1		16,046
Apr 15	DUNDEE	D 2-2	Mahe, Burchill	47,163
Apr 22	HIBERNIAN	D 1-1	Mahe	43,229
Apr 29	Motherwell	D 1-1	Burchill	8,115
May 2	Dundee United	W 1-0	Burchill	7,449
May 6	ABERDEEN	W 5-1	Johnson 3, Moravcik 2	41,786
May 13	St Johnstone	D 0-0		6,729
May 21	DUNDEE UNITED	W 2-0	Lynch, Burchill	47,586

Scottish Cup

Feb 8	INVERNESS CALEDONIAN THISTLE	(Rd3) L 1-3	Burchill	34,389

Scottish League Cup

Oct 13	Ayr United	(Rd 3) W 4-0	Viduka, Mjallby, Blinker, Petta	8,421
Dec 1	DUNDEE	(QF) W 1-0	Wieghorst	40,260
Feb 16	Kilmarnock	(SF) W 1-0	Moravcik	22,926
Mar 19	Aberdeen	(F) W 2-0	Riseth, Johnson	50,073

UEFA Cup

Aug 12	Cwmbran Town	(Rd1/SL) W 6-0	Larsson 2, Berkovic, Tebily, Viduka, Brattbakk	8,920
Aug 26	CWMBRAN TOWN	(Rd1/SL) W 4-0	Brattbakk, Mjallby, Johnson, Smith	46,757
Sep 16	HAPOEL TEL AVIV	(Rd2/SL) W 2-0	Larsson 2 (1 pen)	45,171
Sep 30	Hapoel Tel Aviv	(Rd2/SL) W 1-0	Larsson	7,000
Oct 21	Olympique Lyonnais	(Rd3/SL) L 0-1		35,000
Nov 4	OLYMPIQUE LYONNAIS	(Rd3/SL) L 0-1		54,291

League & Cup Appearances

PLAYER	LEAGUE	CUP COMPETITIONS			TOTAL
		S CUP	SL CUP	UEFA	
Berkovic	27 (1)	1	0 (1)	2 (1)	30 (3)
Blinker	11 (7)	1	1	1 (4)	14 (11)
Boyd	10	1	2		13
Brattbakk	0 (2)	0 (1)		1 (1)	1 (4)
Burchill	10 (16)	1	2 (1)	3 (1)	16 (18)
Burley	6 (2)		1	5	12 (2)
Convery	0 (1)				0 (1)
Crainey	5 (4)				5 (4)
De Ornelas	0 (2)				0 (2)
Fotheringham	1 (1)				1 (1)
Goodwin	1				1
Gould	28 (1)	1	3	5	37 (1)
Healy	8 (2)	1	0 (1)	1	10 (3)
Johnson	7 (3)		1	0 (2)	8 (5)
Kennedy	1 (4)				1 (4)
Kerr	4				4
Kharine	4		1	1	6
Lambert	26			5	31
Larsson	8 (1)			4	12 (1)
Lynch	1 (1)				1 (1)
McCann	1				1
McColligan	1				1
McKinlay		0 (1)		1	1 (1)
McNamara	23		4	4	31
Mahe	20	1	3	2	26
Miller	0 (1)				0 (1)
Mjallby	26 (4)		4	2	32 (4)
Moravcik	29 (1)	1	4	4	38 (1)
Petrov	20 (6)		1 (1)	1	22 (7)
Petta	2 (10)		0 (1)	3 (1)	5 (12)
Riseth	28	1	4	5	38
Scheidt	1 (2)				1 (2)
Shields	0 (1)				0 (1)
Smith	0 (1)			0 (1)	0 (2)
Stubbs	23		3 (1)	6	32 (1)
Tebily	19 (4)	1	3	5	28 (4)
Viduka	28	1	4	4	37
Wieghorst	13 (3)	0 (1)	2 (1)	1 (1)	16 (6)
Wright	4 (4)		1		5 (4)

Goalscorers

PLAYER	LEAGUE	CUP COMPETITIONS			TOTAL
		S CUP	SL CUP	UEFA	
Viduka	25		1	1	27
Burchill	11	1			12
Larsson	7			5	12
Johnson	9		1	1	11
Berkovic	9			1	10
Moravcik	8		1		9
Blinker	4		1		5
Mahe	4				4
Mjallby	2		1	1	4
Wieghorst	3		1		4
Wright	3				3
Brattbakk				2	2
Burley	1				1
Healy	1				1
Lambert	1				1
Lynch	1				1
Petrov	1				1
Petta			1		1
Riseth			1		1
Smith				1	1
Tebily				1	1

MANAGER: John Barnes (until Feb 2000), Kenny Dalglish took over for the rest of the season

CAPTAIN: Tom Boyd   **TOP SCORER:** Mark Viduka

BIGGEST WIN: 7-0 v Aberdeen, 16 October 1999, league

HIGHEST ATTENDANCE: 60,253 v St Johnstone, 7 August 1999, league

MAJOR TRANSFERS IN: Eyal Berkovic from West Ham, Dmitri Kharine from Chelsea, Stilian Petrov from CSKA Sofia, Bobby Petta from Ipswich, Rafael Scheidt from Gremio, Brazil, Olivier Tebily from Sheffield United, Ian Wright from West Ham

MAJOR TRANSFERS OUT: Tosh McKinlay to Grasshoppers, Zurich, Craig Burley to Derby, Harald Brattbakk to FC Copenhagen, Ian Wright to Burnley

Final Scottish Premier Division Table

		P	W	D	L	F	A	Pts
1	RANGERS	36	28	6	2	96	26	90
2	CELTIC	36	21	6	9	90	38	69
3	HEARTS	36	15	9	12	47	40	54
4	MOTHERWELL	36	14	10	12	49	63	52
5	ST JOHNSTONE	36	10	12	14	36	44	42
6	HIBERNIAN	36	10	11	15	49	61	41
7	DUNDEE	36	12	5	19	45	64	41
8	DUNDEE UTD	36	11	6	19	34	57	39
9	KILMARNOCK	36	8	13	15	38	52	37
10	ABERDEEN	36	9	6	21	44	83	33

Season 2000-01

Scottish League Premier Division

DATE	OPPONENTS	SCORE	GOALSCORERS	ATTENDANCE
July 30	Dundee United	W 2-1	Larsson, Sutton	11,761
Aug 5	MOTHERWELL	W 1-0	Petrov	59,057
Aug 13	KILMARNOCK	W 2-1	Larsson, Johnson	58,054
Aug 19	Hearts	W 4-2	Sutton 2, Larsson, Moravcik	16,744
Aug 27	RANGERS	W 6-2	Sutton 2, Larsson 2, Petrov, Lambert	59,476
Sep 9	HIBERNIAN	W 3-0	Larsson 2 (1 pen), Burchill	60,091
Sep 18	Dunfermline Athletic	W 2-1	Larsson 2 (1 pen)	9,452
Sep 23	DUNDEE	W 1-0	Petrov	59,634
Oct 1	Aberdeen	D 1-1	Larsson	18,239
Oct 14	ST MIRREN	W 2-0	Sutton, Larsson	60,002
Oct 17	St Johnstone	W 2-0	Valgaeren, Larsson (pen)	8,946
Oct 21	DUDEE UNITED	W 2-1	Larsson, Thompson	59,427
Oct 29	Motherwell	D 3-3	Mjallby, Valgaeren, McNamara	10,820
Nov 5	Kilmarnock	W 1-0	Thompson	13,413
Nov 12	ST JOHNSTONE	W 4-1	Larsson 2, Sutton, Moravcik	57,137
Nov 18	HEARTS	W 6-1	Larsson 2, Valgaeren, Moravcik, Mjallby, Petrov	59,813
Nov 26	Rangers	L 1-5	Larsson	50,083
Nov 29	Hibernian	D 0-0		14,939
Dec 2	DUNFERMLINE ATHLETIC	W 3-1	Moravcik, Larsson, Johnson	59,244
Dec 10	Dundee	W 2-1	Petrov, Agathe	10,736
Dec 16	ABERDEEN	W 6-0	Larsson 3, Vega 2, Smith	60,013
Dec 23	St Mirren	W 2-0	Agathe, Larsson	9,487
Dec 26	Dundee United	W 4-0	Sutton 2, Larsson (pen), Petrov	10,200
Jan 2	KILMARNOCK	W 6-0	Larsson 4, Sutton 2	59,380
Feb 4	Hearts	W 3-0	Larsson 3	13,077
Feb 11	RANGERS	W 1-0	Thompson	59,486
Feb 21	MOTHERWELL	W 1-0	Moravcik	58,880
Feb 25	HIBERNIAN	D 1-1	Mjallby	60,063
Mar 4	Dunfermline Athletic	W 3-0	Petrov, Larsson, Lennon	9,096
Mar 14	St Johnstone	W 2-1	Johnson, Larsson	8,991
Apr 1	Aberdeen	W 1-0	Agathe	16,067
Apr 4	DUNDEE	W 2-1	Johnson, Mjallby	59,562
Apr 7	ST MIRREN	W 1-0	Johnson	60,440
Apr 22	HEARTS	W 1-0	Moravcik	59,298
Apr 29	Rangers	W 3-0	Moravcik 2, Larsson	50,057
May 6	Hibernian	W 5-2	McNamara 2, Larsson, Stubbs, Moravcik	8,728
May 13	DUNDEE	L 0-2		59,435
May 20	Kilmarnock	L 0-1		12,675

Scottish Cup

Jan 28	Stranraer	(Rd3) W 4-1	Valgaeren, McNamara, Moravcik, o.g.	5,600
Feb 17	Dunfermline Athletic	(Rd4) D 2-2	Larsson 2	11,222
Mar 7	DUNFERMLINE ATHLETIC	(R) W 4-1	Larsson (2 pen) Vega 2	31,940
Mar 11	HEARTS	(QF) W 1-0	Larsson	34,672
Apr 15	Dundee United	(SF) W 3-1	Larsson 2 (1 pen), McNamara	38,699
May 26	Hibernian	(F) W 3-0	Larsson 2 (1 pen), McNamara	51,824

Scottish League Cup

Sep 5	RAITH ROVERS	(Rd2) W 4-0	Johnson 2, Thompson (pen), Sutton	30,753
Nov 1	Hearts	(QF) W 5-2	McNamara, Healy, Crainey, Smith, Moravcik	13,076
Feb 7	Rangers	(SF) W 3-1	Larsson 2, Sutton	50,000
Mar 18	Kilmarnock	(F) W 3-0	Larsson 3	48,830

UEFA Cup

Aug 10	Jeunesse Esch	(Rd1/FL) W 4-0	Moravcik 2, Larsson, Petta	4,004
Aug 24	JEUNESSE ESCH	(Rd1/SL) W 7-0	Burchill 3, Berkovic 2, Riseth, Petrov	40,282
Sep 14	HJK HELSINKI	(Rd2/FL) W 2-0	Larsson 2	40,454
Sep 28	HJK Helsinki	(Rd2/SL) L 1-2	Sutton	6,530
Oct 26	Bordeaux	(Rd3/FL) D 1-1	Larsson (pen)	21,318
Nov 9	BORDEAUX	(Rd3/SL) L 1-2	Moravcik	51,242

MANAGER: Martin O'Neill

CAPTAIN: Tom Boyd

TOP SCORER: Henrik Larsson

MAJOR TRANSFERS IN: Didier Agathe from Hibernian, Robert Douglas from Dundee, Neil Lennon from Leicester, Chris Sutton from Chelsea, Alan Thompson from Aston Villa, Ramon Vega from Tottenham Hotspur

MAJOR TRANSFERS OUT: Vidar Riseth to 1860 Munich, Mark Viduka to Leeds, Alan Stubbs to Everton, Ramon Vega to Watford

League & Cup Appearances

PLAYER	LEAGUE	CUP COMPETITIONS			TOTAL
		S CUP	SL CUP	UEFA	
Agathe	26 (1)	6		2	34 (1)
Berkovic	2 (2)		0 (1)	2 (2)	4 (5)
Boyd	21 (9)	2 (3)	2 (2)	4 (1)	29 (15)
Burchill	0 (2)		1	1	2 (2)
Crainey	0 (2)	0 (1)	1 (1)		1 (4)
Douglas	22	6			28
Fotheringham	1				1
Gould	15		3	6	24
Healy	4 (8)		3	1 (5)	8 (13)
Johnson	9 (7)	1 (3)	2 (1)	0 (2)	12 (11)
Kerr			1		1
Kharine	1				1
Lambert	27	4 (2)	2	5	38 (2)
Larsson	37	6	2	5	50
Lennon	17	6	2		25
Lynch				1	1
McNamara	18 (12)	2 (2)	3	5	28 (14)
Mahe	7 (3)		1	2	10 (3)
Maloney	1 (3)				1 (3)
Miller				0 (1)	0 (1)
Mjallby	30 (5)	4 (1)	2	6	42 (6)
Moravcik	16 (11)	4 (1)	2 (1)	4 (1)	26 (14)
Petrov	27 (1)	1 (2)	1 (1)	4 (1)	33 (5)
Petta	20	2	2 (2)	5	29 (2)
Riseth	0 (1)		1	2 (1)	3 (2)
Scheidt			0 (1)	1 (1)	1 (2)
Smith	2 (5)		1 (1)		3 (6)
Stubbs	7 (3)		1		8 (3)
Sutton	24	4	3	4	35
Tebily	2 (2)	0 (1)	0 (1)	1	3 (4)
Thompson	29 (1)	6	3		38 (1)
Valgaeren	35	6	3	5	49
Vega	18	6	2		26

Goalscorers

PLAYER	LEAGUE	CUP COMPETITIONS			TOTAL
		S CUP	SL CUP	UEFA	
Larsson	35	9	5	4	53
Moravcik	9	1	1	3	14
Sutton	11		2	1	14
Petrov	7			1	8
Johnson	5		2		7
McNamara	3	3	1		7
Burchill	1			3	4
Mjallby	4				4
Thompson	3		1		4
Valgaeren	3	1			4
Vega	2	2			4
Agathe	3				3
Berkovic				2	2
Smith	1		1		2
Crainey			1		1
Healy			1		1
Lambert	1				1
Lennon	1				1
Petta				1	1
Riseth				1	1
Stubbs	1				1
Opps' o.gs.		1			1

Final Scottish Premier Division Table

		P	W	D	L	F	A	Pts
1	CELTIC	38	31	4	3	90	9	97
2	RANGERS	38	26	4	8	76	36	82
3	HIBERNIAN	38	18	12	8	57	35	66
4	KILMARNOCK	38	15	9	14	44	53	54
5	HEARTS	38	14	10	14	56	50	52
6	DUNDEE	38	13	8	17	51	49	47
7	ABERDEEN	38	11	12	15	45	52	45
8	MOTHERWELL	38	12	7	19	42	56	43
9	DUNFERMLINE	38	11	9	18	34	54	42
10	ST JOHNSTONE	38	9	13	16	40	56	40
11	DUNDEE UTD	38	9	8	21	38	63	35
12	ST MIRREN	38	8	6	24	32	72	30

Season 2001-02

Scottish League Premier Division

DATE	OPPONENTS	SCORE	GOALSCORERS	ATTENDANCE
July 28	ST JOHNSTONE	W 3-0	Lambert 2, Mjallby	58,005
Aug 4	Kilmarnock	W 1-0	Larsson	13,201
Aug 11	HEARTS	W 2-0	Larsson 2	58,243
Aug 18	Livingston	D 0-0		10,024
Aug 25	Hibernian	W 4-1	Sutton 2, Moravcik, Larsson	14,701
Sep 8	DUNFERMLINE ATHLETIC	W 3-1	Moravcik 2, Sutton	57,936
Sep 15	Dundee	W 4-0	Larsson 2, Petrov, Maloney	9,842
Sep 22	ABERDEEN	W 2-0	Larsson, Petrov	59,197
Sep 30	Rangers	W 2-0	Petrov, Thompson	50,097
Oct 13	Motherwell	W 2-1	Moravcik, Larsson (pen)	9,922
Oct 20	DUNDEE UNITED	W 5-1	Hartson 3, Balde, Maloney	59,900
Oct 27	KILMARNOCK	W 1-0	Valgaeren	58,897
Nov 3	St Johnstone	W 2-1	Larsson, o.g.	9,031
Nov 17	Hearts	W 1-0	Larsson (pen)	15,570
Nov 25	RANGERS	W 2-1	Valgaeren, Larsson (pen)	59,609
Dec 1	HIBERNIAN	W 3-0	Hartson 2, Lennon	59,415
Dec 9	Dunfermline Athletic	W 4-0	Hartson 2, Balde, Thompson	8,207
Dec 15	DUNDEE	W 3-1	Sutton, Larsson, Hartson	57,198
Dec 22	Aberdeen	L 0-2		18,610
Dec 26	LIVINGSTON	W 3-2	Larsson 2, Moravcik	59,000
Dec 29	Dundee United	W 4-0	Hartson, Petrov, Thompson, Larsson	12,165
Jan 2	MOTHERWELL	W 2-0	Larsson, Hartson	57,695
Jan 11	Kilmarnock	W 2-0	Hartson (pen), Lambert	11,689
Jan 19	ST JOHNSTONE	W 2-1	Larsson, Thompson	58,547
Jan 23	HEARTS	W 2-0	Larsson 2	57,203
Jan 30	Livingston	W 3-1	Moravcik, Larsson, Hartson	10,000
Feb 2	Hibernian	D 1-1	Hartson	12,313
Feb 9	DUNFERMLINE ATHLETIC	W 5-0	Larsson 3, Hartson, Agathe	58,590
Feb 17	Dundee	W 3-0	Larsson, Mjallby, Hartson	10,642
Mar 2	ABERDEEN	W 1-0	Thompson (pen)	59,564
Mar 10	Rangers	D 1-1	Petrov	49,765
Mar 16	DUNDEE UNITED	W 1-0	Petrov	58,392
Mar 19	Motherwell	W 4-0	Larsson 2 (1 pen), Lambert, Mjallby	10,134
Apr 6	LIVINGSTON	W 5-1	Larsson 3, Hartson 2	59,752
Apr 13	DUNFERMLINE ATHLETIC	W 3-0	Hartson 2, Lambert, Smith, Sylla	57,016
Apr 21	RANGERS	D 1-1	Thompson	59,384
Apr 28	Hearts	W 4-1	Lynch 2, Maloney 2	12,391
May 12	Aberdeen	W 1-0	Maloney	15,332

Scottish Cup

Jan 8	Alloa Athletic	(Rd3) W 5-0	Balde, Wieghorst, Maloney, Petta, Sylla	5,498
Jan 26	Kilmarnock	(Rd4) W 2-0	Larsson, o.g.	11,269
Feb 25	Aberdeen	(QF) W 2-0	Hartson, Petrov	18.000
Mar 23	Ayr United	(SF) W 3-0	Thompson 2, Larsson	26,774
May 4	Rangers	(F) L 2-3	Hartson, Balde	

Scottish League Cup

Nov 6	STIRLING ALBION	(Rd2) W 8-0	Maloney 4, Hartson 2, Tebily, Healy	29,933
Dec 19	Livingston	(QF) W 2-0	Balde, Hartson	8,146
Feb 5	Rangers	(SF) L 1-2	Balde	43,457

Champions League

Aug 8	Ajax	(3QR/FL) W 3-1	Petta, Agathe, Sutton	51,324
Aug 22	AJAX	(3QR/SL)) L 0-1		59,000
Sep 18	Juventus	(Gp E) L 2-3	Petrov, Larsson (pen)	39,945
Sep 25	PORTO	(Gp E) W 1-0	Larsson	58,500
Oct 10	ROSENBORG	(Gp E) W 1-0	Thompson	57,233
Oct 17	Porto	(Gp E) L 0-3		30,303
Oct 23	Rosenborg	(Gp E) L 0-2		21,540
Oct 31	JUVENTUS	(Gp E) W 4-3	Sutton 2, Valgaeren, Larsson (pen)	57,717

Celtic failed to qualify from Group E.

UEFA Cup

Nov 22	Valencia	(Rd3/FL) L 0-1		39,000
Dec 6	VALENCIA	(Rd3/SL) W 1-0*	Larsson	57,299

*Celtic lost on penalties.

Fact File

Celtic became the first team ever to amass 103 league points.

MANAGER: Martin O'Neill   **CAPTAIN:** Paul Lambert

League & Cup Appearances

PLAYER	LEAGUE	CUP COMPETITIONS			TOTAL
		S CUP	SL CUP	CL/UEFA	
Agathe	20	3	1	8	32
Balde	22	5	3	8	38
Boyd	9	1		2	12
Crainey	10 (4)	1 (1)	1	1	13 (5)
Douglas	35	4	2	10	51
Gould	1	1	0 (1)		2 (1)
Guppy	10 (6)	2	2	1 (2)	15 (8)
Hartson	26 (5)	4	3	2 (3)	35 (8)
Healy	2 (1)	0 (1)	1		3 (2)
Kennedy	1				1
Kharine	2 (1)		1		3 (1)
Lambert	33 (1)	4	1	10	48 (1)
Larsson	33	3	1	10	47
Lennon	32 (1)	4	1 (1)	10	47 (2)
Lynch	1				1
McNamara	9 (12)	2 (2)	2	3 (1)	16 (15)
Maloney	3 (13)	1 (1)	1	0 (1)	5 (15)
Mjallby	35	4	2	10	51
Moravcik	16 (7)	1	2 (1)	3 (3)	22 (11)
Petrov	26 (2)	5	2 (1)	7 (1)	40 (4)
Petta	12 (6)	1 (1)	0 (1)	4 (2)	17 (10)
Smith	3 (8)	0 (1)			3 (9)
Sutton	18	2	1 (1)	8	29 (1)
Sylla	7 (2)	1 (1)	1	0 (1)	9 (4)
Tebily	8 (3)	1	1		10 (3)
Thompson	22 (3)	3 (1)	1	4 (2)	30 (6)
Valgaeren	20	1	2	9	32
Wieghorst	2 (1)	1	1		4 (1)

Goalscorers

PLAYER	LEAGUE	CUP COMPETITIONS			TOTAL
		S CUP	SL CUP	CL/UEFA	
Larsson	29	2		4	35
Hartson	19	2	3		24
Maloney	5	1	4		10
Thompson	6	2		1	9
Petrov	6	1		1	8
Sutton	4			3	7
Balde	2	2	2		6
Moravcik	6				6
Lambert	5				5
Mjallby	3				3
Valgaeren	2		1		3
Agathe	1			1	2
Petta		1		1	2
Sylla	1	1			2
Lynch	2				2
Healy			1		1
Lennon	1				1
Smith	1				1
Tebily			1		1
Wieghorst		1			1
Opps' o.gs.	1	1			2

TOP SCORER: Henrik Larsson

MAJOR TRANSFERS IN: John Hartson from Coventry, Mohammed Sylla from St Johnstone, Steve Guppy from Leicester

MAJOR TRANSFERS OUT: Eyal Berkovic to Manchester City, Mark Burchill to Portsmouth

Final Scottish Premier Division Table

		P	W	D	L	F	A	PTS
1	CELTIC	38	33	4	1	94	18	103
2	RANGERS	38	25	10	3	82	27	85
3	LIVINGSTON	38	16	10	12	50	47	58
4	ABERDEEN	38	16	7	15	51	49	55
5	KILMARNOCK	38	13	10	15	44	54	49
6	HEARTS	38	14	6	18	52	57	48
7	DUNDEE UTD	38	12	10	16	38	59	46
8	DUNFERMLINE	38	12	9	17	41	44	45
9	DUNDEE	38	12	8	18	41	55	44
10	HIBERNIAN	38	10	11	17	51	56	41
11	MOTHERWELL	38	11	7	20	49	69	40
12	ST JOHNSTONE	38	5	6	27	24	62	21

Complete Players' Career Records

These records cover all players who have played a senior competitive match for Celtic since they first entered the Scottish Cup in 1888 until summer 2002. 'Period' covers the seasons in which a competitive appearance was made, thus 1922-29 covers seasons 1922-23 to 1928-29 inclusive. 'League' covers all major League competitions – Scottish League Division

Player		Birthplace	From	Year Joined	Year Left	To	League Apps	Sub	Goals
Adams	Davie	Oathlaw	Dunipace Juniors	1902	1912	retired	248		0
Agathe	Didier	Réunion Island	Hibernian	2000		Still at club	46	1	4
Airlie	Seton	Carmyle	Greyfrairs	1939	1947	FC Cannes	6		3
Aitken	Roy	Irvine	Celtic Boys Club	1972	1990	Newcastle United	483		40
Allan	George	Linlithgow Bridge	Liverpool	1897	1898	Liverpool	17		15
Allan	Thomas	Carlute	Carlute Milton Rovers	1910	1913		2		0
Anderson	Oliver	Glasgow	Arthurlie	1937	1946	Alloa Athletic	13		3
Andrews	Ian	Nottingham	Leicester City	1988	1990	Southampton	5		0
Annoni	Enrico	Guissano, Italy	AS Roma	1997	1999	Serie C	26		11
Anthony	Marc	Edinburgh	Celtic Boys Club	1995	1999	Berwick Rangers	0	2	0
Archdeacon	Owen	Greeenock	Gourock United	1982	1989	Barnsley	38	38	7
Arnott	Walter	Glasgow	St. Bernard's	1895	1895	Notts County	1		0
Atkinson	John	Cambuslang	Hamilton Acad	1909	1910	Hamilton Acad	1		0
Auld*	Bertie	Glasgow	Maryhill Harp	1955	1971	Hibernian	167	9	50
Baillie	Joe	Dumfries	St. Roch's Juniors	1945	1954	Wolverhampton W	107		0
Baillie	Lex	Hamilton	Burnbank Boys Club	1982	1991	St Mirren	27	4	1
Baines	Roy	Derby	Morton	1976	1979	Morton	12		0
Balde	Dianbobo	Marseille	Toulouse	2001		Still at club	22		0
Barber	Tom	Derby	Aston Villa	1918	1919	Partick Thistle	5		0
Barclay	Graham	Bothwell	Blantyre Victoria	1973	1977	released	0		0
Barrie	Jim	Old Kilpatrick	Fall River (USA)	1930	1930	released	1		0
Battles*	Barney	Glasgow	Hearts	1895	1897	Dundee	110		6
Bauchop	James	Sauchie	Alloa Athletic	1906	1918	Bradford City	14		5
Beattie	Dick	Glasgow	Duntocher Hibs	1954	1959	Portsmouth	114		0
Bell	Andrew		Arthurlie Juniors	1951	1955	released	25		0
Bell	James	Mauchline	Dumbarton	1890	1891	Hurlford	15		0
Bell	John	Dumbarton	Everton	1898	1900	New Brighton	35		16
Bennett	Alec	Rutherglen	Glencairn	1903	1908	Rangers	126		44
Berkovic	Eyal	Haifa, Israel	West Ham United	1999	2000	Manchester City	29	3	9
Biggins	Wayne	Sheffield	Barnsley	1993	1994	Stoke City	4	5	0
Birrell	Jimmy	Dunfermline	Blairhall Colliery	1938	1940	registration cancelled	6		2
Black	John	Glasgow	Benburb	1912	1914	Clyde	4		1
Black	Willie	Flemington	Queen's Park	1904	1905	Everton	10		0
Blackwood	John	Maine, USA	Petershill	1899	1900	Arsenal	1		0
Blair	Dan	Glasgow	St. Anthony's	1924	1927	released	3		0
Blair	John		Belfast Celtic	1910	1911	Motherwell	1		0
Blessington	Jimmy	Linlithgow	Hibernian	1892	1898	Preston North End	82		31
Blinker	Regi	Surinam	Sheffield Wed	1997	2000	Rosendaal	37	11	9
Boden	Alec	Hardgate	Duntocher St. Mary	1943	1956	Ayr United	122		2
Bogan	Tommy	Glasgow	Hibernian	1946	1948	Preston North End	34		5
Bone	Jimmy	Bridge of Allan	Sheffield United	1974	1975	Arbroath	5	2	1
Bonnar	John	Edinburgh	Arbroath	1946	1958	Dumbarton	120		0
Bonner	Pat	Clochglas, Co Donegal	Keadue Rovers	1978	1994	retired	483		0
Boyd	Tom	Glasgow	Chelsea	1991		Still at club	296	10	2
Boyle	James	Glasgow	Towerhill	1890	1893	Clyde	9		0
Boyle	John	Bathgate	1933	1938	released	10		0
Boyle	Robert	Cowie	Cowie Wanderers	1912	1913	Alloa	10		0
Brady	Alec	Cathcart	Everton	1891	1892	Sheffield Wed	19		4
Brattbakk	Harald	Trondheim	Rosenborg	1997	2000	FC Copenhagen	27	17	12
Breslin	Pat	Maryhill	Johnstone	1899	1899		1		0
Britton	Gerry	Glasgow	Celtic Boys Club	1987	1992	Partick Thistle	0	2	0
Brodie	John	Dumbarton	Dumbarton Harp	1916	1919	Chelsea	2		1
Brogan	Frank	Stepps	St. Roch's	1960	1964	Ipswich Town	37		0
Brogan	Jim	Glasgow	St. Roch's	1962	1975	Coventry City	208	5	6
Brown	Hugh	Glasgow	St. Anthony's	1916	1921	Dunfermline Ath	98		2
Brown	John	Dysart	Falkirk	1911	1913	Chelsea	40		7
Brown	Willie	Glasgow	Parkhead Juniors	1916	1919	Dundee	2		2
Browning	John	Dumbarton	Vale of Leven	1911	1919	Chelsea	210		64
Buchan	Willie	Grangemouth	Grange Rovers	1933	1937	Blackpool	120		38
Buckley	John	East Kilbride	Queen's Park	1978	1983	Partick Thistle	0		0

One, 'A' or the Premier League. 'League Cup' includes all names by which the competition has been known. 'Europe' covers the European Cup, Champions League, European Cup-Winners' Cup and UEFA Cup and also includes the 1967 World Club Championship matches.

Scottish League Cup			Scottish Cup			European			Totals		
Apps	Sub	Goals	Apps	Sub	Goals	Apps	Sub	Goals	Apps	Sub	Goals
0		0	43		0	0		0	291		0
1		0	9		0	10		1	66	1	5
0		0	0		0	0		0	6		3
82	2	6	55	2		50		0	670	2	53
0		0	2	1	0	0			19		16
0		0	0		0	0		0	2		0
0		0	0		0	0		0	13		3
2		0	0		0	1		0	8		0
0		2	5	1	1			3	32		17
0	1	0	0		0	0		0	0	3	0
1	4	1	3	1	0	0	2	0	42	45	8
0		0	0		0	0		0	1		0
0		0	0		0	0		0	1		2
42	5	20	26	2	8	22	2	0	257	18	79
31		1	13		0	0		0	151		1
0		0	3	1	0	0			30	5	1
3		0	1		0	0		0	16		0
3		2	5		2	8		0	38	6	0
0		0	0		0	0		0	5		0
0		0	1		0	0		0	1		0
0		0	0		0	0		0	1		0
0		0	26		0	0		0	136		6
0		0	0		0	0		0	14		5
28		0	14		0	0		0	156		0
0		0	3		0	0		0	28		0
0		0	7		0	0		0	22		0
0		0	11		7	0		0	46		23
0		0	26		6	0		0	152		50
0	2	0	1		0	4	3	3	34	8	12
0		0	0	1	0	0		0	4	6	0
0		0	0		0	0		0	6		2
0		0	0		0	0		0	4		1
0		0	1		0	0		0	11		0
0		0	0		0	0		0	1		0
0		0	0		0	0		0	3		0
0		0	0		0	0		0	1		0
0		0	17		8	0		0	99		39
6	2		6	1	1	8		0	57	16	12
20		0	16		0	0		0	158		2
9	3	4	0		0	0			47		8
2	1	0	1		0	0		0	8	3	1
38		0	22		0	0		0	180		0
64		0	55		0	39		0	641		0
29	2	0	31	3	0	33	1	0	389	16	2
0		0	0		0	0		0	9		0
0		0	0		0	0		0	10		0
0		0	0		0	0		0	10		0
0		0	5		6	0		0	24		10
0		0	5	2	4	7	2	4	39	21	20
0		0	0		0	0		0	0		0
0		0	0	2	0	0		0	0	4	0
0		0	0		0	0		0	2		1
1		0	9		0	1		0	48		0
55	2	2	37	1	0	32	1	1	332	9	9
0		0	0		0	0		0	98		2
0		0	7		3	0		0	47		10
0		0	0		0	0		0	2		2
0		0	7		2	0		0	217		66
0		0	14		7	0		0	134		45
1		0	0		0	0		0	1		0

Player		Birthplace	From	Year Joined	Year Left	To	League Apps	Sub	Goals
Burchill	Mark	Broxburn	Celtic Boys Club	1997	2001	Portsmouth	15	34	20
Burley	Craig	Ayr	Chelsea	1997	1999	Derby Dounty	61	3	20
Burns	John		St. Anthony's	1918	1920	Queen of the South	13		3
Burns	Tommy	Glasgow	Maryhill Juniors	1973	1989	Kilmarnock	325	32	52
Byrne	Alec	Greenock	Gourock Juniors	1954	1963	Morton	70		22
Byrne	Paul	Dublin	Bangor, NI	1993	1995	Southend	24	4	4
Cadete	Jorge	Mozambique	Sporting Lisbon	1995	1997	Celta Vigo	32	5	30
Cairney	Charles	Blantyre	Cambuslang Rangers	1949	1950	Leyton Orient	1		0
Cairney	James	Glasgow	St. Anthony's	1922	1923	Arthurlie	3		0
Callachan	Harry	Madras	Parthead Juniors	1925	1927	Leicester City	11		0
Callaghan	Tommy	Cowdenbeath	Dunfermline Ath	1968	1976	Clydebank	143	14	14
Cameron	James	Lochee	Shelbourne	1932	1933	Arbroath	4		2
Campbell	John		Benburb	1890	1903	Third Lanark	169		88
Campbell	Robert	Ellon	Queen's Park	1905	1906	Rangers	11		0
Cannon	Bernard	Buncrana	Blantyre Celtic	1947	1948	Derry City	3		0
Cantwell	Jack		Glenboig St. Joseph's	1946	1947	Dumbarton	8		5
Carlin	James	Glasgow	Paisley Celtic	1896	1897	Victoria United	1		0
Carroll	Bobby	Glasgow	Irvine Meadow	1957	1963	St Mirren	61		21
Carruth	Joe	Glasgow	Petershill	1936	1945	Stirling Albion	39		27
Cascarino	Tony	St Paul's, Cray	Aston Villa	1990	1992	Chelsea	13	11	4
Casey	Jim	Glasgow	Maryhill Juniors	1974	1980	Phoenix Inferno	6	7	0
Cassidy	Jimmy	Dalry	Bolton Wanderers	1892	1898	retired	1		0
Cassidy	Joe	Dalziel	Newton Heath	1893	1895	Newton Heath	28		13
Cassidy	Joe	Cadder	Vale of Clyde	1912	1924	Bolton Wanderers	189		90
Cattanach	Dave	Falkirk	Stirling Albion	1963	1972	Falkirk	10	3	1
Chalmers	Paul	Glasgow	'S'-form	1979	1986	St Mirren	0	4	1
Chalmers	Steve	Glasgow	Ashfield Juniors	1959	1971	Morton	253	8	147
Clark	Joe	Glasgow	St. Anthony's	1912	1913	Abercorn	2		0
Clark	John	Edinburgh	Clyde	1903	1903	Clyde	2		0
Clark	John	Bellshill	Larkhall Thistle	1958	1971	Morton	162	1	1
Clifford	Hugh	Carfin	Stoke	1892	1893	Stoke	5		0
Coen	Joseph	Glasgow	Clydebank	1931	1932	Guildford City	3		0
Coleman	James		Dumbarton Ath	1888	1888	Dumbarton Ath	1		0
Coleman	Johnny	Cardross	Hibernian	1888	1895	retired	7		2
Collins	Alec	Port Glasgow		1888			0		0
Collins	Bobby	Glasgow	Pollok Juniors	1949	1958	Everton	220		81
Collins	Frank	Dublin	Jacob's, Dublin	1921	1922	Jacob's, Dublin	2		0
Collins	John	Galashiels	Hibernian	1990	1996	Monaco	211	6	47
Colquhoun	John	Stirling	Stirling Albion	1983	1985	Hearts	25	6	4
Colrain	John	Glasgow	Duntocher Hibs	1957	1960	Clyde	44		21
Conn	Alfie	Edinburgh	Tottenham Hotspur	1977	1979	Derby County	34	3	10
Connachan	James	Glasgow	Duntocher Hibs	1897	1898	Airdrie	1		0
Connaghan	Denis	Glasgow	St Mirren	1971	1977	Clydebank	32		0
Connelly	George	High Valleyfield	Tulliallan Thistle	1965	1978	Released	129	7	5
Connolly	Barney	Glasgow	Vale of Clyde	1913	1919	Cambuslang Rangers	13		4
Connolly	Paddy	Hamilton	Kirkintillock Rob Roy	1921	1933	Hibernian	259		40
Connor	Frank	Blantyre	Blantyre Celtic	1960	1962	Portadown	2		0
Connor	John		St. Roch's Juniors	1932	1936	Plymouth Argyle	4		1
Conroy	Mike (1)	Port Glasgow	St. Anthony's	1953	1960	retired	7		0
Conroy	Mike (2)	Johnstone	Port Glasgow Juniors	1978	1982	Hibernian	59	9	7
Convery	John	Newtonards	Glenavon	1997	2002	released	0	1	0
Conway	Jim	Motherwell	Coltness United	1957	1961	Norwich City	32		9
Cook	Willie	Coleraine	Port Glasgow Juniors	1930	1932	Everton	100		0
Corbett	Willie	Falkirk	Maryhill Juniors	1940	1948	Preston North End	48		0
Corcoran	Patrick	Glasgow	Clyde	1918	1919	Hamilton Acad	3		0
Corr	Barry J.	Glasgow	Celtic Boys Club	1997	1997	released	0	1	0
Corrigan	Edwards	New Monkland	Petershill Juniors	1924	1926	Dundee	4		0
Cowan	Joseph	Prestonpans	Wellesley Juniors	1929	1931	Raith Rovers	1		1
Coyle	Ronnie	Glasgow	Celtic Boys Club	1979	1987	Middlesbrough	1	1	0
Coyne	Brian	Glasgow	St. Roch's Juniors	1977	1979	Shrewsbury Town	0	1	0
Coyne	Tommy	Glasgow	Dundee	1989	1993	Tranmere Rovers	82	23	43
Craig	Billy		St. Anthony's	1953	1957	Third Lanark	8		0
Craig	Bobby	Airdrie	Blackburn Rovers	1962	1963	St. Johnstone	17		0
Craig	Jim	Glasgow	Glasgow University	1963	1972	Hellenic	143	4	1
Craig	Joe	Bridge of Allan	Partick Thistle	1972	1978	Blackburn Rovers	53	1	24
Craig	Michael	Glasgow	Deeside Boys Club	1993	1995	Aberdeen	0		0
Craig	Robert	Beith	Vale of Garnock	1906	1909	Brighton & Hove Alb	13		0
Craig	Tully	Falkirk	Grange Rovers	1919	1922	Alloa Athletic	9		3
Crainey	Stephen	Glasgow	Celtic Boys Club				15	10	0

Scottish League Cup			Scottish Cup			European			Totals		
Apps	Sub	Goals	Apps	Sub	Goals	Apps	Sub	Goals	Apps	Sub	Goals
3	2	0	1	2	1	4	1	3	23	39	24
7		2	6		1	16		2	90	3	25
0		0	0		0	0		0	13		3
70	1	15	38	5	12	34	3	3	467	41	82
9		0	19		8	2		0	100		30
1	1	0	1		0	2		0	28	4	4
3		5	5		2	4		1	44	5	38
0	0	0	0		0	0		0	1		0
0		0	1		0	0		0	4		0
0		0	0		0	0		0	11		0
47	6	8	24	2	6	26	2	6	240	24	34
0	0	0	0		0	0		0	4		2
0		0	46		25	0		0	215		113
0	0	0	0		0	0		0	11		0
0		0	0		0	0		0	3		0
1		0	0		0	0		0	9		5
0		0	0		0	0		0	1		0
12		4	4		1	1		1	78		27
0		0	3		2	0		0	42		29
1		0	0	1	0	2	1	0	16	13	4
4	4	0	2	1	1	3	2	0	15	14	1
0		0	0		0	0		0	1		0
0		0	8		4	0		0	36		17
0		0	15		13	0		0	204		103
1	1	0	3		0	1		0	15	4	1
0		0	0		0	0		0	0	4	1
57	2	31	45	2	28	38	1	13	393	13	219
0		0	0		0	0		0	2		1
0		0	0		0	0		0	2		0
55	2	1	23	1	1	40		0	280	4	3
0		0	0		0	0		0	5		0
0		0	0		0	0		0	3		0
0		0	0		0	0		0	1		0
0		0	11		0	0		0	18		2
0		0	2		0	0		0	2		0
62		26	38		10	0		0	320		117
0		0	0		0	0		0	2		0
22		3	21		3	13		1	267	6	54
3		0	1		1	1	1	0	30	6	5
4		2	10		0	0		0	58		23
8	1	3	6		0	3	1	0	51	5	13
0		0	0		0	0		0	1		0
15		0	4		0	5		0	56		0
60	3	4	24	1	2	28	2	2	241	13	13
0		0	0		0	0		0	13		4
0		0	37		7	0		0	296		47
6		0	0		0	0		0	8		0
0		0	0		0	0		0	4		1
1		0	0		0	0		0	8		0
8	5	1	5	1	1	4	1	0	76	16	9
0		0	0		0	0		0	0	1	0
10		4	1		0	0		0	43		13
0		0	10		0	0		0	110		0
7		0	5		0	0		0	60		0
0		0	0		0	0		0	3		0
0		0	0		0	0		0	0	1	0
0		0	0		0	0		0	4		0
0		0	0		0	0		0	1		1
0		0	0		0	0		0	1	1	0
0		0	0		0	0		0	0	1	0
5	1	1	13	2	8	4	1	0	104	27	52
0		0	1		0	0		0	9		0
0		0	3		0	1		0	21		0
29	1	4	21	2	0	31		0	224	7	6
5	2	4	7	1	7	4		0	69	4	39
0		0	0	1	0	0		0	0	1	0
0		0	0		0	0		0	13		0
0		0	0		0	0		0	9		3
2	1	0	1	2	0	1		0	19	13	0

Player		Birthplace	From	Year Joined	Year Left	To	League Apps	Sub	Goals
Crainie	Danny	Kilsyth	Celtic Boys Club	1979	1983	Wolverhampton	17	8	7
Crawford	Alec		Clyde	1901	1902	Partick Thistle	10		3
Creaney	Gerry	Coatbridge	Celtic Boys Club	1987	1994	Portsmouth	85	28	36
Crerand	Pat	Glasgow	Duntocher Hibs	1957	1963	Manchester United	91		5
Crilly	Willie	Glasgow	Alloa Athletic	1922	1922	Alloa Athletic	3		0
Cringan	Willie	Ponfeigh	Sunderland	1917	1923	Third Lanark	202		9
Crone	Willie	Dublin	Belfast Celtic	1913	1916	Distillery	17		9
Crossan*	Barney		Benburb	1890	1891	Preston North End	8		3
Crozier	James	Glasgow	Hull City	1928	1929	Derry City	2		0
Crum	John	Glasgow	Ashfield Juniors	1932	1942	Morton	190		73
Cullen	Joe		Benburb	1892	1897	Tottenham Hotspur	58		0
Cunningham	Johnny	Glasgow	Glasgow Hibernian	1890	1892	Partick Thistle	7		0
Curley	Tom	Glasgow	Portsmouth	1961	1965	Brentford	1		0
Curran	John	Bellshill	Benburb	1892	1894	Liverpool	21		0
Curran	John	Glasgow	Duntocher Hibs	1958	1962	Derry City	4		0
Cushley	John	Hamilton	Blantyre Celtic	1960	1967	West Ham United	30		0
Dalglish	Kenny	Glasgow	Cumbernauld United	1968	1977	Liverpool	200	4	112
Davidson	Andrew		Rutherglen Glencairn	1913	1914	St Mirren	5		0
Davidson	James	Edinburgh	Leith Athletic	1892	1895	Burnley	21		10
Davidson	Robert	West Calder	Dykehead	1898	1902	Manchester City	43		0
Davidson	Vic	Glasgow	Ashfield	1968	1981	Phoenix Inferno	37	2	17
Davitt	Michael		St. Francis Juniors	1935	1941	Renfrew Juniors	1		0
Dawson	Daniel	Larkhall	Larkhall Thistle	193	1938	Queen of the South	17	3	0
De Ornales	Fernando	Caracas, Venezuela	Zaragoza	2000	2000	Hong Kong	0	2	0
Deans	John	Linwood	Motherwell	1971	1976	Luton Town	122	5	89
Delaney	Jimmy	Cleland	Stoneyburn Juniors	1933	1946	Manchester United	143		69
Devanny	Alex	Glasgow	Glasgow Perthshires	1949	1952	Berwick Rangers	1		0
Devlin*	James		Blackstoun Rangers	1890	1895	Royal Albert	2		0
Devlin	John		Mossend Celtic	1895	1895	Airdrie	2		1
Di Canio	Paolo	Rome	AC Milan	1996	1997	Sheffield Wed	25	1	12
Divers	Johnny		Hibernian	1893	1901	Hibernian	64		37
Divers	John	Clydebank	Renfrew Juniors	1932	1945	Morton	75		44
Divers	John	Clydebank	Renfrew Juniors	1956	1966	Partick Thistle	171		78
Dobbin	Jim	Dunfermline	'S'-form	1980	1984	Doncaster Rovers	1	2	0
Docherty	James		Duntocher Hibs	1954	1954	Alloa Athletic	1		0
Docherty	Jim	Clydebank	Renfrew Juniors	1947	1950	Northampton Town	2		0
Docherty	John		Dumbarton	1898	1900	Vale of Leven	11		0
Docherty	Tommy	Glasgow	Shettleston Juniors	1948	1949	Preston North End	9		3
Dodds*	Joe	Carlute	Carlute Milton Rovers	1908	1923	Queen of the South	351		28
Doherty	Hugh	Buncrana	Dundalk	1946	1947	Blackpool	3		0
Doherty	John	Derry	Derry City	1937	1939	Coleraine	2		0
Dolan	Frank	Old Monkland		1890	1894	Coatdyke Gaelic	2		0
Dolan	Michael	Uddingston	Drumpellier	1888	1888	Uddingston	3		0
Donaldson	Andy	Airdrie	Airdrie	1911	1912	Airdrie	17		6
Donlevey	Pat		Glasgow Perthshire	1898	1898	Airdrie	1		0
Donnelly	John	W. Lothian	Armadale Thistle	1956	1962	Preston North End	31		0
Donnelly	Simon	Glasgow	Queen's Park	1993	1999	Sheffield Wed	113	33	31
Donnelly	Willie	Magherafelt	Clyde	1900	1901	Belfast Celtic	3		0
Donoghue*	John	New York	Shawfield Juniors	1926	1933	Roubaix	42		1
Douglas	Robert	Lanark	Dundee	2001		Still at club	57		0
Dowds	Peter		Broxburn Shamrock	1889	1894	retired	36		16
Dowie	John	Hamilton	Fulham	1977	1979	Doncaster Rovers	12	2	0
Doyle	Dan	Paisley	Everton	1891	1899	retired	112		3
Doyle	Frank	Glasgow	Fulham	1926	1933	retired	17		2
Doyle	Johnny	Caldercruix	Ayr United	1976	1981	deceased	82	13	15
Doyle	Tom	Uddingston	Blantyre Celtic	1935	1938	Rochdale	5		0
Drummond	James	Bellshill	Bellshill Athletic	1901	1902	Manchester City	4		1
Duff	Tom	Ayr	Cowlairs	1891	1892	Cowlairs	8		0
Duffy	John	Dundee	Dunkeld Amat	1948	1954	Southend United	2		0
Duffy	Robert	Dundee	Lochee Harp	1935	1947	released	4		0
Dunbar	Michael	Cathcart	Hibernian	1888	1893	retired	15		4
Dunbar*	Tom	Busby	Busby Cartvale	1890	1898	Busby Cartvale	51		3
Duncan	James	Glasgow	Baillieston Juniors	1951	1955	St Mirren	8		2
Duncan	Scott	Dumbarton	Rangers	1919	1919	Dumbarton	2		0
Duncan	Willie	Kilsyth	Airdrie	1910	1915	Bethlehem Steel (USA)	9		0
Dunn	Willie	Glasgow	Ashfield Juniors	1933	1935	Brentford	9		2
Dunning	Willie	Arthurlie	Johnstone Juniors	1888	1889	Glasgow Hibernian	0		0
Dziekanowski	Dariusz	Poland	Legia Warsaw	1989	1992	Bristol City	42	6	10
Edvaldsson	Johannes	Reykjavik	Holbek, Denmark	1975	1980	Tulsa Roughnecks	120	9	26

Complete Players' Career Records: Crainie – Edvaldsson

Scottish League Cup			Scottish Cup			European			Totals		
Apps	Sub	Goals	Apps	Sub	Goals	Apps	Sub	Goals	Apps	Sub	Goals
2	4	1	0	1	0	0		0	19	13	8
0		0	0		0	0		0	10		3
9	1	7	9	1	8	6	3	2	109	33	53
13		1	14	1	2	2		1	120		8
0		0	0		0	0		0	3		0
0		0	12		0	0		0	214		10
0		0	0		0	0		0	17		9
0		0	7		4	0		0	15		7
0		0	0		0	0		0	2		0
0		0	21		14	0		0	211		87
0		0	15		0	0		0	73		0
0		0	1		0	0		0	8		1
0		0	0		0	0		0	1		0
0		0	5		0	0		0	26		0
0		0	0		0	0		0	4		0
5		0	1		0	5		0	41		0
56	3	35	30	11	0	27	9	0	313	7	167
0		0	1		0	0		0	6		0
0		0	0		0	0		0	21		10
0		0	13		0	0		0	56		0
9	1	2	2	3	2	6	6	3	54	12	24
0		0	0		0	0		0	1		0
0		0	3		0	0		0	20		3
0		0	0		0	0		0	0	2	0
21	1	11	21		18	11	3	6	175	9	124
0		0	17		5	0		0	160		74
2		0	0		0	0		0	3		0
0		0	0		0	0		0	2		0
0		0	0		0	0		0	2		1
2		0	6	3	3	2	1	0	35	2	15
0		0	23		8	0		0	87		45
0		0	7		4	0		0	82		48
26		8	28		11	7		3	232		100
4	1	0	0		0	0		0	5	2	1
1		0	0		0	0		0	2		0
0		0	0		0	0		0	2		0
0		0	0		0	0		0	11		0
0		0	0		0	0		0	9		3
0		0	27		2	0		0	378		30
0		0	1		0	0		0	4		0
0		0	0		0	0		0	2		0
0		0	0		0	0		0	2		0
0		0	1		0	0		0	4		0
0		0	0		0	0		0	17		6
0		0	0		0	0		0	1		0
9		0	3		0	0		0	43		0
11	6	4	9	4	2	13	7	6	146	50	43
0		0	2		0	0		0	5		0
0		0	8		0	0		0	50		1
2		0	10		0	10		0	79		0
0		0	13		3	0		0	49		19
2	1	0	1		0	0		0	15	3	0
0		0	21		2	0		0	123		5
0		0	4		1	0		0	21		3
25	4	14	10	2	7	6	1	1	123	20	37
0		0	0		0	0		0	5		0
0		0	0		0	0		0	4		1
0		0	1		0	0		0	9		0
0		0	0		0	0		0	2		0
0		0	0		0	0		0	4		0
0		0	17		6	0		0	32		10
0		0	9		1	0		0	60		4
1		0	0		0	0		0	9		2
0		0	0		0	0		0	2		0
0		0	0		0	0		0	9		0
0		0	0		0	0		0	9		2
0		0	6		0	0		0	6		0
9		7	7	1		2		4	60	6	22
35	2	8	12	1	0	16		4	183	12	38

Player		Birthplace	From	Year Joined	Year Left	To	League Apps	Sub	Goals
Elliot	Barry	Carlisle	Celtic Boys Club	1995	2000	Dundee	0	1	0
Elliot	David	Glasgow	Celtic Boys Club	1987	1990	Partick Thistle	2	4	0
Elliott	George	Sunderland	Middlesbrough	1918	1925	retired	1		0
Elliott	Paul	Lewisham	Pisa	1989	1991	Chelsea	52		2
Evans	Bobby	Glasgow	St. Anthony's Juniors	1944	1960	Chelsea	384		10
Fagan	Willie	Musselburgh	Wellesley Juniors	1934	1936	Preston North End	12		9
Falconer	John	Govan	Cowdenbeath	1931	1934	Creetown	7		0
Falconer	Willie	Aberdeen	Sheffield United	1994	1996	Motherwell	33	8	5
Fallon	John	Blantyre	Fauldhouse United	1958	1972	Motherwell	125		0
Fallon	Sean	Sligo	Glenavon	1950	1958	retired	177		8
Farrell	Paddy		Distillery	1896	1897	Arsenal	1		0
Ferguson	George		St. Anthony's	1945	1948	Dumbarton	5		0
Ferguson	John		Jordanhill Juniors	1895	1895	Blackburn Rovers	1		1
Ferguson	Willie	Glasgow	Maryhill Juniors	1895	1897	Burnley	25		11
Fernie*	Willie	Kinglassie	Kinglassie Colliery	1948	1961	St Mirren	219		54
Fillipi	Joe	Ayrshire	Ayr United	1977	1979	Clyde	30	2	0
Findlay	Robert	Galston	Kilmarnock	1900	1901	Kilmarnock	14		6
Fisher*	James	Denny	Aston Villa	1898	1900	Newton Heath	10		3
Fitzsimmons	Tom	Annbank	Annbank	1892	1892	Newton Heath	1		0
Fitzsimmons	John	Glasgow	St. Roch's	1934	1938	Alloa Athletic	5		0
Flannaghan	M		Benburb	1892			4		1
Fleming	William	Alexandria	Vale of Leven	1924	1925	Ayr United	19		10
Foley	James	Cork	Cork FC	1934	1936	Plymouth Argyle	6		0
Foran	Joseph	Paisley	Greenlaw Strollers	1890	1894	Johnstone FC	2		1
Fotheringham	Mark	Dundee	Celtic Boys Club	1999		Still at club	2	1	0
Fraser	Bet	Dundee	Lochee Harp	1948	1949	Hearts	1		0
Fullarton	Alex	Stevenston	Saltcoats Victoria	1916	1917	Clydebank	1		0
Fulton	Steve	Greenock	Celtic Boys Club	1987	1993	Bolton Wanderers	54	22	2
Gallacher	Jackie		Armadale Thistle	1943	1951	Kettering Town	22		15
Gallacher	Patsy	Ramelton, Co. Donegal	Clydebank Juniors	1911	1926	Falkirk	432		186
Gallagher	Antony		Johnstone FC	1893			2		1
Gallagher	Charlie	Glasgow	Yoker Athletic	1958	1970	Dumbarton	107		17
Gallagher	Hugh	Girvan	Maybole	1889	1890	Preston North End	1		1
Gallagher	Jimmy	Coatbridge	Shettleston Celtic	1929	1932	Nithsdale Wand	2		0
Gallagher	Paddy	Johnstone	Hibernian	1888	1893	retired	30		0
Gallagher	Pat	Johnstone	Johnstone FC	1892	1893	Johnstone FC	2		0
Gallagher	Willie	Renfrew	St. Anthony's	1937	1949	Falkirk	29		0
Galloway	Mike	Oswestry	Hearts	1989	1996	retired	113	23	8
Garden	William	Kilsyth	Kilsyth Rangers	1925	1926	Kilsyth Rangers	1		0
Garner	Willie	Denny	Aberdeen	1981	1982	Alloa Athletic	1		0
Garry	Edward	Renton	Galston	1905	1907	Derby County	6		1
Geatons	Charlie	Lochgelly	Lochgelly Celtic	1927	1941	retired	286		11
Geddes	John	Lochgelly	Lochgelly Celtic	1927	1929	Gillingham	2		0
Geehrin	Pat	Musselburgh	Bonnyrigg Thistle	1910	1911	Bristol City	1		0
Gemmell	Tommy	Craigneuk	Coltness United	1961	1971	Nottingham Forest	247		38
Gibson	Andrew	Glasgow	Southampton	1912	1912	Leeds City	2		1
Gibson	Johnny	Hull	St Mirren	1976	1978	East Fife	1	2	0
Gilchrist	John	Glasgow	St. Anthony's	1919	1923	Preston North End	127		7
Gilfeather	Eddie	Auchterderan	Cowdenbeath	1922	1926	Hibernian	2		0
Gilgun	Paddy	West Shotts	Law Scotia	1924	1925	Brighton & Hove Alb	3		1
Gilhooly	Pat	Draffan	Cambuslan Hibs	1896	1900	Sheffield United	46		17
Gillespie	Gary	Bonnybridge	Liverpool	1991	1994	Coventry City	67	2	3
Gilligan	Sam	Dundee	Dundee	1903	1904	Bristol City	13		13
Glancey	Lawrence	Cowdenbeath	Hearts o' Beath	1921	1923	Bo'ness	1		0
Glasgow	Sam	Leadhills	Nithsdale Wanderers	1920	1922	St. Johnstone	2		0
Glavin	Ronnie	Glasgow	Partick Thistle	1974	1979	Barnsley	100	2	36
Goldie	Hugh	Dalry	Everton	1897	1899	Dundee	25		0
Goldie	Peter	Dumbarton	Duntocher Hibs	1952	1958	Aldershot	13		0
Goldie	Willie	Newmains	Airdrie	1960	1961	Albion Rovers	1		0
Goodwin	Jim	Waterford	Tramore	1997	2002	Stockport County	1		0
Gorman	John	Winchburgh	Uphall Saints	1967	1970	Carlisle United	0		0
Gormley	Phil	Greenock	Kirkintillock Rob Roy	1948	1950	Aldershot	1		0
Gould	Jonathon	London	Bradford City	1997		Still at club	107	1	0
Graham	John	Dalry	Bristol Rovers	1903	1904	Millwall	4		0
Granger	John	Dumbarton	Vale of Leven	1922	1925	Vale of Leven	13		0
Grant	Peter	Bellshill	Celtic Boys Club	1982	1997	Norwich City	338	26	15
Grassam	Willie	Larbert	West Ham United	1903	1903	Manchester United	2		0
Gray*	Alec	Bainsford	Stenhousemuir	1912	1918	Kilmarnock	13		5
Gray	John	Stenhousemuir	Elder Park	1900	1902	Cape Caledonians	2	1	0

Scottish League Cup			Scottish Cup			European			Totals		
Apps	Sub	Goals	Apps	Sub	Goals	Apps	Sub	Goals	Apps	Sub	Goals
0		0	0		0	0		0	0	1	0
0		0	0		0	0		0	2	4	0
0		0	0		0	0		0	1		0
5		3	8		1	0		0	66		5
87		0	64		0	0		0	535		10
0		0	0		0	0		0	12		9
0		0	1		0	0		0	8		0
1	1	0	4	2	3	0		0	38	11	8
36		0	14		0	20		0	195		0
46		3	31		2	0		0	254		13
0		0	0		0	0		0	1		0
0		0	0		0	0		0	5		0
0		0	0		0	0		0	1		1
0		0	2	1	0	0		0	27		12
59		11	39		10	0		0	317		75
8		0	2	1	0	1		0	41	3	0
0		0	3	2	0	0		0	17		8
0		0	0		0	0		0	10		3
0		0	0		0	0		0	1		0
0		0	0		0	0		0	5		0
0		0	0		0	0		0	4		1
0		0	0		0	0		0	19		10
0		0	0		0	0		0	6		0
0		0	0		0	0		0	2		1
0		0	0		0	0		0	2	1	0
0		0	0		0	0		0	1		0
0		0	0		0	0		0	1		0
7	2	1	4	2	0	2	2	0	67	28	3
10		10	1		2	0		0	33		27
0		0	32		6	0		0	464		192
0		0	0		0	0		0	2		1
28		11	23		4	13		0	171		32
0		0	0		0	0		0	1		1
0		0	0		0	0		0	2		0
0		0	15		1	0		0	45		1
0		0	0		0	0		0	2		0
6		3	4		0	0		0	39		3
17	2	0	7	3	0	9	2	0	146	28	10
0		0	0		0	0		0	1		0
2		0	0		0	0		0	3		0
0		0	0		0	0		0	6		1
0		0	33		0	0		0	319		11
0		0	0		0	0		0	2		0
0		0	0		0	0		0	1		0
74		10	43		3	54		12	418		63
0		0	0		0	0		0	2		1
0		0	0	1	0	0		0	1	3	0
0		0	7		0	0		0	134		7
0		0	0		0	0		0	2		0
0		0	0		0	0		0	3		1
0		0	4		3	0		0	50		20
3		0	4		0	8		0	82	2	3
0		0	1		0	0		0	14		0
0		0	0		0	0		0	1		0
0		0	0		0	0		0	2		0
26	4	4	11	1	8	10	1	2	147	8	50
0		0	2		1	0		0	27		1
0		0	1		0	0		0	14		0
0		0	0		0	0		0	1		0
0		0	0		0	0		0	1		0
1		0	0		0	0		0	1		0
0		0	0		0	0		0	1		0
12	1	0	11		0	23		0	153	2	0
0		0	0		0	0		0	4		0
0		0	0		0	0		0	13		0
40	3	3	34	4	1	32	1	0	444	34	19
0		0	0		0	0		0	2		0
0		0	1		0	0		0	14		5
0		0	0		0	0		0	2		1

Player		Birthplace	From	Year Joined	Year Left	To	League Apps	Sub	Goals
Gray	Stuart	Harrogate	'S'-form	1992	1994	Reading	19	9	1
Gray	William	Glasgow	Maryhill Hibs	1927	1929	Hamilton Acad	26		12
Groves*	Willie	Leith	Hibernian	1888	1898	Rushden	4		3
Guppy	Steve	Winchester	Leicester City	2001		Still at Club	10	6	0
Haffey	Frank	Glasgow	Campsie Black Watch	1958	1964	Swindon Town	140		0
Halpin	John	Broxburn	Armadale Thistle	1978	1984	Carlisle United	3	4	0
Hamill*	Micky	Belfast	Manchester United	1918	1920	Manchester City	7		0
Hamilton	Davie	Glasgow	Cambuslang Hibs	1902	1912	Dundee	221		53
Hancock	Steve	Sheffield	Newtongrange Star	1970	1974	Sheffield Wed	0		0
Hannah	David	Coatbridge	Dundee United	1996	1999	Dundee United	28	14	0
Hannah	Robert		Celtic Boys Club	1974	1977	Ayr United	0	2	0
Hartson	John	Swansea	Coventry City	2001		Still at club	26	5	19
Hastie	John		Glenbuck Cherrypickers	1910	1912	Nithsdale Wanderers	16		3
Haughney	Mike	Paisley	Newtongrange Star	1949	1957	retired	159		32
Haverty	Joe	Dublin	Millwall	1964	1964	Bristol Rovers	1		0
Hay	Chris	Glasgow	Giffnock North	1993	1997	Swindon Town	9	16	4
Hay	David	Paisley	St Mirren's BG	1966	1974	Chelsea	106	3	6
Hay	James	Beith	Glossop	1903	1918	Newcastle United	214		14
Hayes	Martin	Walthamstow	Arsenal	1990	1993	Swansea City	3	4	0
Hazlett	George	Glasgow	Glasgow Perthshire	1946	1948	Belfast Celtic	21		0
Healy	James	Craigneuk	Sheildmuir Celtic	1924	1925	Plymouth Argyle	2		0
Healy	Colin	Cork	Wilton United	1998		Still at club	16	12	1
Hemple	Sam	Glasgow	Rutherglen Glencairn	1952	1954	Albion Rovers	4		2
Henderson	Adam	Darlington	Preston North End	1897	1898	Bristol St. George's	9		4
Henderson	Athol	Perth	St. Johnstone	1976	1977	Dunfermline Ath	0		0
Henderson	John	Dumfries	Dumfries FC	1895	1897	Victoria United	3		0
Henderson	Sam	Glasgow	Ashfield	1962	1968	Stirling Albion	2		0
Hepburn	Anthony	Glasgow	Clydebank Juniors	1952	1954	Ayr United	6		0
Heron	Gil	Kingston, Jamaica	Detroit Corinthians	1951	1952	Third Lanark	1		0
Hewitt	John	Aberdeen	Aberdeen	1989	1992	St Mirren	9	7	0
Higgins	John	Uddingston	St. John's BG	1950	1959	Queen of the South	65		31
Hill	John	Dumbarton	Dumbarton Harp	1913	1913	Vale of Leven	2		0
Hilley	Hugh	Glasgow	St. Anthony's	1921	1930	retired	171		0
Hodge	John	Greenock	Port Glasgow Ath	1899	1902	Portsmouth	34		19
Hogg	Bobby	Larkhall	Royal Albert	1931	1948	Alloa Athletic	278		0
Hood	Harry	Glasgow	Clyde	1969	1976	San Antonio	161	28	74
Hughes	John	Barrhead	Parkhead Juniors	1922	1925	Alloa Athletic	5		0
Hughes	John	Coatbridge	Shotts Bon Accord	1959	1971	Crystal Palace	233	3	115
Hughes	John	Edinburgh	Falkirk	1995	1996	Hibernian	31	1	2
Hughes	Willie	Winchburgh	Bathgate	1929	1936	Clyde	94		11
Hunter	Alistair	Glasgow	Kilmarnock	1973	1976	Motherwell	60		0
Hunter	George	Troon	Neilston Juniors	1949	1954	Derby County	31		0
Hutchison	Tom	Glasgow	West Bromwich Albion	1896	1896	Abercorn	2		0
Hynds*	Tom	Hurlford	Hurlford Thistle	1898	1902	Manchester City	28		2
Jack	Peter		Newtown Thistle	1895	1895	Vale of Clyde	1		0
Jack	John	Bellshill	Stonehouse Violet	1950	1959	Morton	48		0
Jackson	Darren	Edinburgh	Hibernian	1997	1999	Hearts	13	16	3
Jackson	John	Dalry	Clyde	1908	1919	Motherwell	27		4
Jackson	Mike	Glasgow	Benburb	1957	1963	St. Johnstone	57		23
Jarvis	George	Glasgow	Cambuslang Rangers	1912	1919	Stoke	7		0
Jeffrey	Bobby	Ayr	Coltness United	1961	1963	Airdrie	5		0
Johnson	Tommy	Newcastle	Aston Villa	1997	2001	Sheffield Wed	23	12	18
Johnston	Leslie	Glasgow	Clyde	1948	1949	Stoke City	24		8
Johnston	Maurice	Glasgow	Watford	1984	1987	Nantes	97	2	52
Johnstone	Jimmy	Viewpark	Blantyre Celtic	1961	1975	San José (USA)	298	10	82
Johnstone	Peter	Collessie	Glencraig Celtic	1908	1917	killed in action	211		23
Jordan	Jackie	Glasgow	Queen's Park	1946	1947	Edinburgh City	3		1
Kapler	Konrad	Poland	Forres Mechanics	1947	1949	Rochdale	7		0
Kavanagh	Peter	Dublin	Bohemians	1929	1932	Northampton Town	32		5
Kay	Roy	Edinburgh	Hearts	1977	1978	York City	5		0
Kelly	Charlie	Airdrie	Hibernian	1891	1893	Busby Cartvale	2		0
Kelly	Frank	Glasgow	Motherwell	1918		deceased	2		0
Kelly	James	Renton	Renton	1888	1897	retired	104		3
Kelly	John	Mearns	Busby Cartvale	1888			0		0
Kelly	John	Wishaw	Nithsdale Wand.	1929	1930	Carlisle United	9		0
Kelly	John C.	Paisley	Arthurlie	1938	1941	Morton	1		0
Kelly	John		Shawfield Juniors	1939	1940	Shawfield Juniors	1		0
Kelly	Johnny	Glasgow	Crewe Alexandra	1960	1962	Morton	3		0
Kelly	Paddy	Kirkcaldy	Celtic Boys Club	1995	1997	Newcastle United	1		0

| Scottish League Cup | | | Scottish Cup | | | European | | | Totals | | |
Apps	Sub	Goals	Apps	Sub	Goals	Apps	Sub	Goals	Apps	Sub	Goals
1		0	1		0	2	1	0	23	2	1
0		0	5		0	0		0	31		12
0		0	14		13	0		0	18		16
2		0	2		0	1	2	0	15	8	0
24		0	34		0	3		0	201		0
1	4	0	1	1	1	0	1	0	5	10	1
0		0	0		0	0		0	7		0
0		0	39		7	0		0	260		60
0		0	0		0	0	1	0	0	1	0
2	1	0	3	4	0	7	2	1	40	21	1
0		0	0		0	0		0	0	2	0
3		3	4		2	2	3	0	35	8	24
0		0	3		1	0		0	19		4
45		7	29		5	0		0	233		44
0		0	0		0	0		0	1		0
0		0	0	3	0	0	2	1	9	21	5
37		5	24		1	23		0	190	3	12
0		0	41		5	0		0	255		19
3		0	0		0	0		0	6	4	0
2		0	0		0	0		0	23		0
0		0	0		0	0		0	2		0
4	1	2	1	1	0	2	5	0	23	19	3
0		0	0		0	0		0	4		2
0		0	1		2	0		0	10		6
1	1	0	0		0	0		0	1	1	0.
0		0	1		0	0		0	4		0
0		0	0		0	0		0	2		0
0		0	0		0	0		0	6		0
4		2	0		0	0		0	5		2
3	2	0	0		0	0		0	12	9	0
7		3	12		7	0		0	84		41
0		0	0		0	0		0	2		0
0		0	24		0	0		0	195		0
0		0	8		5	0		0	42		24
10		0	34		0	0		0	322		0
53	9	22	25	4	13	24	6	12	263	47	121
0		0	0		0	0		0	5		0
62	1	38	42	1	25	40	1	10	377	6	188
5		0	3		0	7		0	46	1	2
0		0	10		1	0		0	104		12
17		0	10		0	4		0	91		0
0		0	7		0	0		0	38		0
0		0	0		0	0		0	2		0
0		0	3		0	0		0	31		2
0		0	0		0	0		0	1		0
12		0	8		0	0		0	68		0
3		1	0	3	1	6	5	2	22	24	7
0		0	0		0	0		0	27		4
8		4	8		3	1		0	74		30
0		0	0		0	0		0	7		0
3		0	0		0	0		0	8		0
3	1	3	2	5	1	2	4	3	30	22	25
4		0	1		0	0		0	29		8
8		9	14		6	6		4	125	2	71
87	5	21	47	1	11	66	1	16	498	17	130
0		0	22		2	0		0	233		25
0		0	0		0	0		0	3		1
1		0	0		0	0		0	8		0
0		0	3		0	0		0	35		5
4		0	0		0	1		0	10		0
0		0	0		0	0		0	2		0
0		0	0		0	0		0	2		0
0		0	35		1	0		0	139		4
0		0	2		0	0		0	2		0
0		0	1		0	0		0	10		0
0		0	0		0	0		0	1		0
0		0	0		0	0		0	1		0
0		0	0		0	0		0	3		0
0		0	0		0	0		0	1		0

Player		Birthplace	From	Year Joined	Year Left	To	League Apps	Sub	Goals
Kennaway	Joe	Montreal	New Bedford, US	1931	1940	SA Healey FC (USA)	263		0
Kennedy	Jim	Johnstone	Duntocher Hibs	1955	1965	Morton	170		0
Kennedy	John	Newtonards	Distillery	1965	1967	Lincoln City	0		0
Kennedy	John	Bellshill	Celtic Boys Club	1999		Still at club	2	4	0
Kerr	Stuart	Bellshill	Celtic Boys Club	1994	2001	Wigan Athletic	34	1	0
Kharine	Dmitri	Moscow	Chelsea	1999		Still at club	7	1	0
Kiernan	Tommy	Coatbridge	Albion Rovers	1945	1947	Stoke City	23		12
King	Alex	Dykehead	Hearts	1896	1900	Dykehead	56		11
King	John	Shotts	Dykehead	1895	1897	East Stirling	9		0
Kivlichan	Willie	Galashields	Rangers	1907	1911	Bradford PA	76		20
Kurila	John	Glasgow	St. Francis BG	1958	1962	Northampton Town	5		0
Kyle	James	Glasgow	Benburb	1890			2		0
Lafferty	James	Barrhead	Arthurlie	1951	1953	Lincoln City	7		4
Lamb	Peter	New Monkland	St. Anthony's	1945	1947	Alloa Athletic	1		0
Lambert	Paul	Glasgow	Borussia Dortmund	1997		Still at club	144	1	10
Larsson	Henrik	Helsingborgs, Swe	Feyenoord	1997		Still at club	147	2	116
Latchford	Peter	Birmingham	West Bromwich Albion	1975	1987	Clyde	186		0
Lavery	Dan	Sydney, Aus	Antrim GAA	1948	1949	Ballymena United	4		1
Lawrie*	Willie	Dumfries	Clydebank Juniors	1919	1921	Aberdeen	3		0
Lees*	Walter		Cronberry Eglinton	1892	1894	Lincoln City	4		3
Leitch	William	Saltcoats	Saltcoats Victoria	1923	1926	Kilmarnock	5		1
Lennon	Neil	Lurgan	Leicester City	2000		Still at club	49	1	2
Lennox*	Bobby	Saltcoats	Ardeer Recreation	1961	1980	retired	297	50	167
Livingstone	Dugald	Alexandria	Ashfield	1916	1921	Everton	44		0
Livingstone	George	Dumbarton	Sunderland	1901	1902	Liverpool	17		4
Lochhead	Ian	Glasgow	Drumchapel Am	1958	1961	Dumbarton	7		2
Loney	Willie	Denny	Denny Athletic	1900	1913	Motherwell	254		28
Longmuir	Archie	Ardrossan	Ardrossan Winton Rov	1920	1921	Blackburn Rovers	10		6
Lynch	Allan	Portobello	Scottish Rifles	1897	1899	Clyde	2		0
Lynch	Andy	Glasgow	Hearts	1973	1980	Philadelphia Fury	124	7	15
Lynch	Matt		St. Anthony's	1934	1948	Dumbarton	48		3
Lynch	Simon	Montreal	Celtic Boys Club	1999		Still at club	2	1	3
Lyon	Willie	Birkenhead	Queen's Park	1935	1944	retired	146		16
McAdam	Tom	Glasgow	Dundee United	1977	1986	Motherwell	251	7	36
McAldindon	John	Carlisle	Penrith Amateurs	1948	1957	Shrewbury Town	16		7
McAloon	Gerry	Glasgow	Brentford	1946	1948	Belfast Celtic	20		12
McArdle	John	Glasgow	St. Anthony's	1926	1927	St. Roch's	1		0
McArthur	Dan	Old Monkland	Parkhead Juniors	1892	1903	Clyde	104		0
McAtee	Andy	Cumbernauld	Mossend Hibs	1910	1925	New Bedford (USA)	407		65
McAteer	Tom	Glasgow	Clyde	1910	1912	Wishaw Thistle	24		4
McAulay	Willie	Glasgow	Cambusland Hibs	1898	1898	Sheffield Wed	1		1
McAulay	Pat	New Stevenston	Arthurlie	1942	1950	Luton Town	78		4
McAvennie*	Frank	Glasgow	West Ham United	1987	1993	released	82	3	37
McBride	Joe	Glasgow	Motherwell	1965	1968	Hibernian	52	3	54
McBride	John Paul	Hamilton	Celtic Boys Club	1995		St. Johnstone	1	2	0
McCabe	Pat		East Stirling	1915	1916	East Stirling	2		0
McCafferty	Willie	Rutherglen	Rutherglen Glencairn	1902	1903	Stenhousemuir	1		0
McCahill	Steve	Greenock	Dumbarton	1989	1992	Morton	6	1	0
McCallum	Denis	Alexandria	Dumbarton	1926	1932	Glentoran	39		3
McCallum*	Neil	Bonhill	Renton	1888	1892	Nottingham Forest	20		12
McCallum	Willie	Kilbirnie	Hibernian	1890	1911	West Bromwich Albion	1		0
McCann	Dan	Hurlford	Dundee	1910	1911	Dundee Hibs	7		1
McCann	Eddie		Broxburn Shamrock	1893	1893	Broxburn Shamrock	1		0
McCann	John	Uphall	Broxburn Shamrock	1893	1893	Hibernian	3		0
McCann	Ryan	Bellshill	Celtic Boys Club	1998		Still at club	1		0
McCann	William		Strathclyde	1894	1895	Clydebank	3		0
McCarrison	Dugald	Lanark	Celtic Boys Club	1987	1993	Kilmarnock	1	3	1
McCarron	Frank	Glasgow	school	1962	1967	Carlisle United	0		0
McCarthy	Mick	Barnsley	Manchester City	1987	1989	Olympique Lyonnais	48		0
McClair	Brian	Airdrie	Motherwell	1983	1987	Manchester United	86	15	99
McCluskey	George	Hamilton	Celtic Boys Club	1973	1983	Leeds United	110	32	55
McCluskey	John	Hamilton	Celtic Boys Club	1976	1979	retired	0		0
McCluskey	Pat	Kilsyth	Maryhill Juniors	1969	1977	Dumbarton	105	11	10
McColgan	Dan	Baillieston	Baillieston Juniors	1925	1928	Third Lanark	2		0
McColl	Jimmy	Glasgow	St. Anthony's	1913	1920	Stoke City	165		117
McColligan	Brian	Glasgow	Celtic Boys Club	1997	2001	Clydebank	1		0
McCondichie	Andy	Glasgow	Celtic Boys Club	1995	1999	Albion Rovers	1		0
McCormack	Arthur	Perth	St. Johnstone	1911	1912	Merthyr Town	1		0
McCormack	Harry		Denny Hibs	1917	1919	Albion Rovers	2		1

Scottish League Cup			Scottish Cup			European			Totals		
Apps	Sub	Goals	Apps	Sub	Goals	Apps	Sub	Goals	Apps	Sub	Goals
0		0	32		0	0		0	295		0
31		2	29		0	11		0	241		2
1		0	0		0	0		0	1		0
0		0	0		0	0		0	2	4	0
0		0	6		0	0	1	0	40	2	0
2		0	0		0	1		0	10	1	0
8		5	1		0	0		0	32		17
0		0	6		2	0		0	62		13
0		0	1		0	0		0	10		0
0		0	16		7	0		0	92		27
4		0	0		0	0		0	9		0
0		0	0		0	0		0	2		0
0		0	0		0	0		0	7		4
0		0	0		0	0		0	1		0
4	1	0	17	2	0	28		0	193	4	10
8		8	18		16	31		17	204	2	157
39		0	27		0	23		0	275		0
0		0	0		0	0		0	4		1
0		0	0		0	0		0	3		0
0		0	0		0	0		0	4		3
0		0	1		0	0		0	6		1
3	1	0	10		0	10		0	72	1	2
107	14	61	46	4	31	58	13	14	508	81	273
0		0	3		0	0		0	47		0
0		0	6		3	0		0	23		7
1		0	4		1	0		0	12		3
0		0	41		2	0		0	305		30
0		0	0		0	0		0	10		6
0		0	0		0	0		0	2		0
31	1	6	13		4	16		0	184	8	25
6		0	9		0	0		0	63		3
0		0	0		0	0		0	3	1	3
0		0	17		1	0		0	163		17
45	1	7	30	2	3	28	1	0	354	11	46
1		0	1		0	0		0	18		7
5		1	1		1	0		0	26		14
0		0	0		0	0		0	1		0
0		0	16		0	0		0	120		0
0		0	32		2	0		0	439		67
0		0	4		1	0		0	28		5
0		0	0		0	0		0	1		1
22		0	9		0	0		0	109		4
7		8	10		4	4		1	103	3	50
21		24	8		3	9		5	90	3	86
0		0	0		0	0	1	0	1	3	0
0		0	0		0	0		0	2		0
0		0	0		0	0		0	1		0
1		0	1		0	0		0	8	1	0
0		0	1		0	0		0	40		3
0		0	13		7	0		0	33		19
0		0	2		0	0		0	3		0
0		0	0		0	0		0	7		1
0		0	0		0	0		0	1		0
0		0	0		0	0		0	3		0
0		0	0		0	0		0	1		0
0		0	0		0	0		0	3		0
0		0	0		0	0		0	1	3	1
0		0	0		0	0		0	0		0
3		0	8		1	5		0	64		1
14	1	9	10	4	11	9	3	2	119	23	121
25	7	11	13	4	12	13	3	5	161	46	83
0		0	0		0	0	1	0	0	1	0
35	6	1	12	2	1	17	3	1	169	22	13
0		0	0		0	0		0	2		0
0		0	4		6	0		0	169		123
0		0	0		0	0		0	1		0
0		0	0		0	0		0	1		0
0		0	0		0	0		0	1		0
0		0	0		0	0		0	2		1

Player		Birthplace	From	Year Joined	Year Left	To	League Apps	Sub	Goals
McCreadie	Bernard	Dumbarton	Renfrew Juniors	1955	1957	Rochdale	1		0
McDermott	Thomas	Glasgow	Dundee	1901	1903	Everton	12		2
MacDonald	Malcolm	Glasgow	St. Anthony's	1932	1945	Kilmarnock	134		31
MacDonald	Roddy	Alness	Brora Rangers	1972	1981	Hearts	160	5	21
McDonald	John	Glasgow	Petershill	1951	1953	St Mirren	0		0
McDonald	Pat	Cambuslang	Airdrie	1942	1947	Dunfermline Ath	9		0
McDonald	Tommy		Third Lanark	1947	1948	Alloa Athletic	13		7
McDonald	Willie		Dumbarton Fern	1893	1895	Eveton	3		0
McDowall	Daniel	Kirkintilloch	Kilmarnock	1950	1951	Workington Town	1		0
McEleny*	Charlie	Glasgow	Abercorn	1893	1897	New Brighton	30		1
McElhaney	Ralph		Third Lanark	1895	1895	Clyde	2		0
McEvoy	Pat	Glasgow	St. Anthony's	1917	1921		10		0
McFarlane	John	Bathgate	Wellesley Juniors	1919	1929	Middlesbrough	268		12
McFarlane	Robert	Greenock	Grimsby Town	1901	1902	Middlesbrough	17	0	0
McGarvey	Frank	Glasgow	Liverpool	1980	1985	St Mirren	159	9	77
McGee	Robert	Mearns	E. Kilbride Thistle	1923	1924	released	1		0
McGhee	James	Lurgar	Hibernian	1890	1908	Hearts (manager)	10		4
McGhee	Joe	Galston	Hurlford Juveniles	1929	1932	Sheffield Wed	5		2
McGhee	Mark	Glasgow	Hamburg	1985	1989	Newcastle United	62	26	27
McGillivray	Charlie	E. Whitburn	Ayr United	1932	1933	Manchester United	4		2
McGinlay	Pat	Glasgow	Hibernian	1993	1994	Hibernian	44	3	11
McGinn	James		Mossend Celtic	1893	1894	Airdrie	2		0
McGinnigle	Willie	Paisley	Hibernian	1918	1919	Hibernian	1		0
McGonagle	Peter	Hamilton	Duntocher Hibs	1926	1936	Hamilton Acad	286		8
McGonagle	Tommy	Glasgow	Maryhill Hibs	1931	1932	Glentoran	1		0
McGrain	Danny	Glasgow	Maryhill Juniors	1967	1987	released	433	8	4
McGregor	Alec	Renfrew	Clydebank Juniors	1914	1916	Clydebank	1		0
McGregor	Tom	Lauvieston	Kilsyth Emmet	1910	1919	Motherwell	77		0
McGrogan*	Vincent	Paisley	Lrgs Thistle	1925	1925	retired	5		0
McGrory*	Jimmy	Glasgow	St. Roch's Juniors	1921	1937	retired	378		395
McGrory	John	Linwood	Maryhill Harp	1946	9153	Albion Rovers	38		3
McGugan	Paul	Glasgow	Eastercraigs Am	1980	1987	Barnsley	45	4	2
McGuire	Dougie	Bathgate	Celtic Boys Club	1984	1988	Coventry City	0	2	0
McGuire	Jimmy	Plains	Aberdeen	948	1950	Shamrock Rovers	14		0
McIlroy	James	Glasgow	Duntocher Hibs	1950	1956	Third Lanark	11		3
McIlvenny*	Harry		Parkhead Juniors	1895	1905	Hamilton Acad	9		1
McInally	Alan	Ayr	Ayr United	1984	1987	Aston Villa	38	28	17
McInally	Arthur	Barrhead	Croy Celtic	1917	1918	St Mirren	1		0
McInally	Jim	Glasgow	Celtic Boys Club	1980	1984	Nottingham Forest	0	1	0
McInally	John	Blantyre	Wishaw Juniors	1934	1937	Arbroath	9		5
McInally*	Tommy	Glasgow	St. Anthony's	1919	1925	Sunderland	188		110
McIntosh	James	Glasgow	Aberdeen	1909	1910	Hull City	8		0
MacKay	Duncan	Glasgow	Maryhill Harp	1955	1964	Third Lanark	162		0
McKay	Johnnie	Glasgow	St. Anthony's	1919	1921	Blackburn Rovers	10		6
MacKay	Malcolm	Glasgow	Queen's Park	1993		Norwich City	32	5	4
McKechnie	Jim	Glasgow	Nottingham Forest	1984	1986	Derry City	1	1	0
McKeown	Mick	Dalmellington	Hibernian	1888	1891	Blackburn Rovers	14		0
McKinlay	Tom	Glasgow	Hearts	1994	1999	Grasshoppers (Switz)	87	13	0
McKnight	Allen	Co. Antrim	Distillery	1986	1988	West Ham United	12		0
McLaren*	James	Lugar	Hibernian	1888	1896	retired	3		0
McLaughlan			Benburb	1892	1893	Albion Rovers	1		0
McLaughlin	Brian	Falkirk	Linlithgow Rose	1971	1977	Ayr United	3	4	1
McLaughlin	Brian	Bellshill	Celtic Boys Club	1992	1999	Wigan Ath	38	37	5
McLaughlin	George	Glasgow	Greenhead Thistle	1923	1924	Clydebank	1		0
McLaughlin*	James		Hibernian	1888	1890	Battlefield	0		0
McLaughlin	Jim	Paisley	Renfrew Juniors	1947	1948	Walsall	2		0
McLaughlin	Paul	Johnstone	Queen's Park	1989	1991	Partick Thistle	2	1	0
McLean	Adam	Greenock	Anderston Thornbank	1917	1928	Sunderland	367		128
McLean	Davie	Forfar	Forfar Athletic	1907	1909	Preston North End	28		13
McLean	Finlay		Hamilton Acad	1904	1905	Hamilton Acad	15		4
McLean	Lachlan		Clachnacuddin	1909	1910	Preston North End	3		0
Macleod	Murdo	Glasgow	Dumbarton	1978	1987	Borussia Dortmund	274	7	55
McLeod	Donald	Laurieston	Stenhousemuir	1902	1908	Middlesbrough	131		0
McMahon	Eamon	Lurgan	Clann nan Gael	1953	1955	Glentoran	1		0
McMahon	Pat	Kilsyth	Kilsythe Rangers	1967	1969	Aston Villa	2	1	2
McMahon	Sandy	Selkirk	Hibernian	1890	1903	Partick Thistle	174		130
McManus	Peter	Winchburgh	St. Bernard's	1895	1895	St. Bernard's	1		0
McMaster	John	Port Glasgow	Clydebank Juniors	1913	1923	Queen of the South	204		6
McMenemy	Jimmy	Rutherglen	Rutherglen Glencairn	1902	1920	Partick Thistle	456		144

Scottish League Cup			Scottish Cup			European			Totals		
Apps	Sub	Goals	Apps	Sub	Goals	Apps	Sub	Goals	Apps	Sub	Goals
0		0	0		0	0		0	0		0
0		0	9		3	0		0	21		5
0		0	13		5	0		0	147	36	0
48	2	4	21		3	19		5	248	7	33
2		2	0		0	0		0	2		2
5		0	0		0	0		0	14		0
0		0	1		0	0		0	14		7
0		0	0		0	0		0	3		0
0		0	0		0	0		0	1		0
0		0	4		0	0		0	34		1
0		0	0		0	0		0	2		0
0		0	0		0	0		0	10		0
0		0	36		2	0		0	304		14
0		6	0		0	0		0	23		0
29	6	11	20	4	13	18		8	226	19	109
0		0	0		0	0		0	1		0
0		0	0		0	0		0	10		4
0		0	1		0	0		0	6		2
4	1	1	10	6	4	4	2	2	80	35	34
0		0	0		0	0		0	4		2
5	2	2	1		0	4		0	54	5	13
0		0	0		0	0		0	2		0
0		0	0		0	0		0	1		0
0		0	39		1	0		0	325		9
0		0	0		0	0		0	1		0
105	1	3	60		0	55	1	0	653	10	7
0		0	0		0	0		0	1		0
0		0	3		0	0		0	80		0
0		0	1		0	0		0	6		0
0		0	67		73	0		0	445		468
9		0	11		8	0		0	58		11
5		0	1	1	0	3		0	54	4	2
0	1	0	0		0	0	1	0	0	4	0
4		0	0		0	0		0	18		0
1		0	0		0	0		0	12		3
0		0	2		1	0		0	11		2
6	6	5	4	1	1	3	2	0	51	37	23
0		0	0		0	0		0	1		0
1		0	1		0	0		0	2	1	0
0		0	0		0	0		0	9		5
0		0	25		16	0		0	213		126
0		0	3		0	0		0	11		0
37		0	33		0	4		0	236		0
0		0	0		0	0		0	10		6
5	1	0	4		2	4	1	0	45	7	6
0		0	0		0	0		0	1	1	0
0		0	16		0	0		0	30		0
4	2	0	17	2	0	15	1	0	123	18	0
2		0	1		0	2		0	17		0
0		0	13		2	0		0	16		2
0		0	0		0	0		0	1		0
9	2	0	0		0	0	2	1	12	8	2
1	4	0	9	4	0	2	3	0	50	48	5
0		0	0		0	0		0	1		0
0		0	3		0	0		0	3		0
0		0	0		0	0		0	2		1
2		0	0		0	0		0	4	1	0
0		0	41		20	0		0	408		148
0		0	0		0	0		0	28		13
0		0	0		0	0		0	15		4
0		0	0		0	0		0	3		0
44	13		36	2	7	32		7	386	9	82
0		0	24		0	0		0	155		0
0		0	0		0	0		0	1		0
3	3	0	0		0	0		0	5	1	5
0		0	43		47	0		0	217		177
0		0	0		0	0		0	1		0
0		0	14		0	0		0	218		6
0		0	59		24	0		0	515		168

Player		Birthplace	From	Year Joined	Year Left	To	League Apps	Sub	Goals
McMenemy	John	Glasgow	St. Roch's	1925	1928	Motherwell	15		2
McMillan	Duncan	Glasgow	Maryhill Harp	1945	1949	Grimsby Town	18		0
McMillan	Thomas	Glasgow	Bailleston Juniors	1952	1954	Norwich City	0		0
McNair	Alec	Bo'ness	Stenhousemuir	1904	1925	retired	548		9
McNair	Willie	Renfrew	Forth Rangers	1905	1906	East Stirling	1		0
McNally	Mark	Motherwell	Celtic Boys Club	1987	1995	Southend United	112	10	3
McNally*	Owen	Denny	Denny Hibs	1927	1930	Bray Unknowns	11		4
McNamara	Jackie	Glasgow	Cumbernauld Juniors	1972	1976	Hibernian	19	3	2
McNamara	Jackie	Glasgow	Dunfermline Ath	1995		Still at club	149	8	7
McNamee	John	Coatbridge	Bellshill Ath	1959	1964	Hibernian	27		0
McNeill	Billy	Bellshill	Blantyre Victoria	1957	1975	retired	486		21
McNeil	Hugh		Motherwell	1900	1901	Hamilton Acad	2		0
McOustra	Willie		Ashfield	1899	1902	Manchester City	23		8
McPhail	Billy	Glasgow	Clyde	1956	1958	retired	33		14
McPhail	John	Glasgow	Strathclyde Juniors	1941	1956	retired	142		58
McPherson	Andrew	Greenock	Morton	1902	1904	Hibernian	27		0
McPherson	James	Kilmarnock	Cowlairs	1890	1894	Kilmarnock	0		0
McQuilken	Jamie	Glasgow	Celtic Boys Club	1991	1995	Dundee United	4	1	0
McStay	Jimmy	Netherburn	Larkhall Thistle	1920	1934	Hamilton Acad	409		6
McStay	Paul	Hamilton	Celtic Boys Club	1981	1997	retired	509	6	57
McStay*	Willie	Netherburn	Larkhall Thistle	1912	1929	Hearts	399		37
McStay	Willie	Hamilton	Celtic Boys Club	1979	1987	Huddersfield	55	12	2
McVittie	Matt	Calderbank	Wishaw Juniors	1953	1959	St. Johnstone	33		11
McWilliams*	Bobby	Camelon	Denny Hibs	1928	1932	Yeovil United	7		0
McWilliams	Ian	Malta	Queen's Park	1977	1978	Seiko (Hong Kong)	1		0
Macari	Lou	Edinburgh	Kilwinning Am	1966	1973	Manchester United	50	8	27
Mackie	Peter	Glasgow	Cumbernauld United	1976	1979	Dundee	1	3	0
Mackle	Tommy		Johnstone Burgh	1959	1961	Dundee	3		1
Madden	Johnny	Dumbarton	Dumbarton	1889	1897	Dundee	92		33
Madden	Richad	Blantyre	Blantyre Celtic	1962	1964	Albion Rovers	1		0
Mahe	Stephane	Puteaux, France	Rennes	1997	2001	Hearts	74	3	4
Mair	Matt	Dunlop	Newmilns	1901	1902	Kilmarnock	1		0
Maley	Tom	Portsmouth	Clydesdale Harriers	1888	1891	retired	2		0
Maley	Willie	Newry	Third Lanark	1888	1897	retired	75		0
Mallan	Jimmy	Glasgow	Pollok Juniors	1942	1953	St Mirren	90		0
Malloy	Willie	Gateshead	Dumbarton Harp	1925	1928	Dumbarton	7		1
Maloney	Shaun	Malaysia	Celtic Boys Club	1999		Still at club	4	16	5
Marshall	Gordon	Farnham	Hibernian	1971	1972	Aberdeen	0		0
Marshall	Gordon	Edinburgh	Falkirk	1992	1998	Kilmarnock	101		0
Marshall*	Harry	Portobello	Hearts	1899	1903	Clyde	29		40
Marshall	Scott	Edinburgh	Southampton	1999	1999	Southampton	1	1	0
Martin	Allan		Hibernian	1895	1896	Hibernian	17		18
Martin	Lee	Hyde	Manchester United	1994	1996	Bristol Rovers	19		0
Mathie	Alex	Bathgate	Celtic Boys Club	1987	1991	Morton	7	4	0
Maxwell	Hugh	Rigghead	Falkirk	1964	1965	St. Johnstone	8		0
Meechan	Frank	Condorrat	Petershill	1952	1959	released	86		0
Merhan	Peter	Broxburn	Sunderland	1895	1897	Everton	25		1
Melrose	Jim	Glasgow	Coventry City	1983	1984	Manchester City	20	9	7
Millar	Alex	Mossend	Shawfield Juniors	1935	1938	Preston North End	9		0
Miller	Andrew	Bo'ness	Croy Celtic	1920	1924	Nottingham Forest	5		1
Miller	Joe	Glasgow	Aberdeen	1987	1993	Aberdeen	113	31	27
Miller	Liam								
Miller	Willie	Glasgow	Maryhill Harp	1942	1950	Clyde	94		0
Mills	Hugh	Bonhill	West Ham United	1935	1936	Luton Town	1		0
Millsopp	John		Blantyre Celtic	1948	1952	deceased	19		2
Milne	Roy	Camelon	Polkemmet Juniors	1940	1952	New York Americans	108		0
Mitchell	John		Baillieston Thistle	1906	1913	Cowdenbeath	89		0
Mitchell	Ronald	Renfrew	Renfrew Waverley	1946	1949	Exeter City	1		0
Mitchell	William		St. Anthony's	1918	1919	Partick Thistle	5		0
Mjallby	Johan	Stockholm	AIK Solna	1998		Still at club	108	9	10
Mochan	Neil	Larbert	Middlesbrough	1953	1960	Dundee United	191		81
Moir*	James	Bonhill	Vale of Leven	1898	1903	Blackburn Rovers	34		0
Moran*	Martin	Bannockburn	Benburb	1898	1909	Hamilton Acad	3		0
Moravcik	Lubomir	Nitra, Slovakia	Duisburg	1998	2002	JEF United (Japan)	75	19	29
Morris	Chris	Newquay	Sheffield Wed	1987	1992	Middlesbrough	156	6	8
Morrison	Alex	Campsie	Ayr FC	1907	1907	Clyde	1		0
Morrison	John	Kilsyth	Croy Celtic	1929	1941	released	161		1
Morrison	Tommy	Belfast	Burnley	1895	1897	Burnley	15		1
Morrison	William		Loanhead Mayflower	1951	1953	Loanhead Mayflower	1		0

Complete Players' Career Records: McMenemy, John – Morrison, William

Scottish League Cup			Scottish Cup			European			Totals		
Apps	Sub	Goals	Apps	Sub	Goals	Apps	Sub	Goals	Apps	Sub	Goals
0		0	1		0	0		0	16		2
5		0	2		0	0		0	25		0
2		0	0		0	0		0	2		0
0		0	56		0	0		0	604		9
0		0	0		0	0		0	1		0
11	2	1	10		0	6	1		129	13	4
0		0	0		0	0		0	11		4
16	4	2	2		1	3	1	0	40	8	5
15	2	1	16	5	3	25	4	1	205	29	12
2		0	7		0	2			38		0
138		4	94		7	72		3	790		35
0		0	0		0	0		0	2		0
0		0	7		3	0		0	30		11
20		22	4		4	0		0	57		40
38		21	24		13	0		0	204		92
0		0	5		0	0		0	32		0
0		0	1		0	0		0	1		0
0		0	0		0	0		0	4	1	0
0		0	63		2	0		0	472		8
54		7	66		6	42		2	671	6	72
0		0	47		2	0		0	446		39
11	1	0	7		0	4		0	77	13	1
6		0	5		3	0		0	44		14
0		0	0		0	0		0	7		0
1	1	0	0		0	1		0	3	1	0
19	5	14	8		8	12		8	89	13	57
1	1	0	0		0	0		0	2	4	0
2		1	0		0	0		0	5		2
0		0	26		16	0		0	118		49
0		0	0		0	0		0	1		0
10	0	9	1		14	0		0	107	3	5
0		0	0		0	0		0	1		0
0		0	7		6	0		0	9		6
0		0	21		1	0		0	96		1
21		0	6		0	0		0	117		0
0		0	1		0	0		0	8		1
1		4	1	1	1	0	1	0	6	18	10
0		0	0		0	1		0	1		0
14		0	9		0	12		0	136		0
0		0	17		0	0		0	46		4
0		0	0		0	0		0	1	1	0
0		0	1		0	0		0	18		18
1		0	0		0	0		0	20		0
0		0	1		0	0		0	8	4	0
0		0	0		0	0		0	8		0
11		0	19		0	0		0	116		0
0		0	0		0	0		0	25		1
6	2	3	2	2	1	3	3	0	31	16	11
0		0	0		0	0		0	9		0
0		0	0		0	0		0	5		1
8	5	2	24	2	3	5	4	1	150	42	33
23		0	6		0	0		0	123		0
0		0	0		0	0		0	1		0
4		0	3		0	0		0	26		2
20		0	5		0	0		0	133		0
0		0	6		0	0		0	95		0
0		0	0		0	0		0	1		0
0		0	0		0	0		0	5		0
8		1	12	1	0	18		1	146	10	12
43		12	34		16	0		0	268		109
0		0	4		0	0		0	38		0
0		0	0		0	0		0	3		0
8	2	2	9	1	1	11	4	3	103	26	35
16	1	0	22		1	9		0	203	7	9
0		0	0		0	0		0	1		0
0		0	17		0	0		0	178		1
0		0	1		0	0		0	16		1
0		0	0		0	0		0	1		0

Player		Birthplace	From	Year Joined	Year Left	To	League Apps	Sub	Goals
Mowbray	Tony	Saltburn	Middlesbrough	1991	1995	Ipswich Town	78	3	5
Moyes	Davie	Glasgow	Drumchapel Am	1978	1983	Cambridge United	19	5	0
Muggleton	Carl	Leicester	Leicester City	1994	1994	Stoke City	12		0
Muir	Bob	Kilmarnock	Bristol Rovers	1903	1904	Notts County	20		4
Mulrooney	John	Hamilton	Earnock Rovers	1911	1914	deceased	42		0
Mulvey	Mick	Glasgow	Carfin Shamrock	1892	1893	Dundee Harp	4		4
Munro	Dan	Peterhead	Forres Mechanics	1905	1910	Bradford City	30		6
Munro	Frank	Broughty Ferry	Wolverhampton W	1977	1978	released	14	1	0
Murdoch	Bobby	Bothwell	Cambuslang Rangers	1959	1973	Middlesbrough	287	4	61
Murphy	Frank	Gartcosh	St. Roch's	1933	1946	Limerick	144		46
Murphy	James B	Glasgow	Parkhead Juniors	1920	1923	Clydebank	35		0
Murphy	James F	Hamilton	E. Kilbride Thistle	1921	1924	Ayr United	6		2
Murray	Michael	Stirling	Glasgow Hibs	1892	1893	Abercorn	2		0
Murray	Patrick	Currie	Nottingham Forest	1902	1903	Portsmouth	11		2
Murray	Steve	Dumbarton	Aberdeen	1973	1976	retired	62	1	11
Napier	Charlie	Bainsford	Maryhill Hibs	1928	1935	Derby County	176		82
Neison	John	Renfrew	Abercorn	1897	1897	Abercorn	1		0
Nichol	Willie	Easington	Aberdeen	1911	1912	Bristol City	16		8
Nicholas*	Charlie	Glasgow	Celtic Boys Club	1979	1996	Clyde	159	28	85
Nicol	Davie		Maryhill Hibs	1927	1929	Hamilton Acad	1		0
O'Brien	John		Mossend Juniors	1895	1895	Benburb	1		0
O'Byrne	Fergus	West Calder	Broxburn Shamrock	1893	1894	Broxburn Shamrock	7		0
O'Connor*	John	Greenock	Vale of Leven Hibs	1888	1892	Nottingham Forest	1		0
O'Donnell	Frank	Buckhaven	Wellesley Juniors	1930	1935	Preston North End	78		51
O'Donnell	Hugh		Wellesley Juniors	1932	1935	Preston North End	75		20
O'Donnell	Phil	Bellshill	Motherwell	1994	1999	Sheffield Wed	76	14	16
O'Hara	Don	Airdrie	Fauldhouse Juniors	1959	1962	Albion Rovers	7		1
O'Kane*	Joe	Glasgow	Maryhill Juniors	1914	1926	Helensburgh	20		13
O'Leary	Pierce	Dublin	Vancouver Whitecaps	1984	1988	retired	38	2	1
O'Neil	Brian	Paisley	Celtic Boys Club	1989	1997	Aberdeen	92	28	8
O'Neill*	Felix	Motherwell	Shotts United	1910	1912	Bathgate	1		0
O'Neill	Hugh	Motherwell	St. Andrews	1937	1940	Arthurlie	5		0
O'Neill	John	Glasgow	Queen's Park	1993	1995	Bournemouth	0	1	0
O'Neill	Willie	Glasgow	St. Anthony's	1959	1969	Carlisle United	49	1	0
O'Rourke	Peter	Newmilus	Mossend Celtic	1895	1897	Burnley	9		0
O'Sullivan	Pat		Airdrie	1945	1947	Alloa Athletic	4		0
Oliver	Jim	Dumfries	Creetown Volunteers	1909	1909	Greetown Volunteers	2		0
Orr	Jim	Dalry	Darwen	1895	1898	Kilmarnock Ath	7		0
Orr	Willie	Shotts	Preston North End	1897	1908	retired	165		17
Owers	Ebenezer	West Ham	Clyde	1913	1914	Clyde	13		8
Paterson	George	Denny	Dunipace Thistle Juv	1932	1946	Brentford	175		9
Paton*	Johnny	Glasgow	Dennistoun Waverley	1942	1952	Watford	52		11
Paton	Roy	Glasgow	Maryhill Harp	1957	1961	Derry City	0		0
Payton	Andy	Burnley	Middlesbrough	1992	1993	Barnsley	20	16	15
Peacock	Bertie	Coleraine	Glentoran	1949	1961	Coleraine	318		32
Petrov	Stilian	Montana, Bulgaria	CSKA Sofia	1999		Still at club	73	9	14
Petta	Bobby	Rotterdam	Ipswich	1999		Still at club	34	16	0
Power	Pat	Glasgow	Blantyre Victoria	1894	1895	Airdrie	1		0
Pratt	David	Lochore	Hearts O'Beath	1919	1921	Bradford City	22		0
Prentice	David	Alloa	Alva Albion Rangers	1928	1930	Plymouth Argyle	6		1
Price	Billy	Tarbolton	Falkirk	1961	1964	Berwick Rangers	51		0
Price	James	Annbank	Cumnock Juniors	1918	1921	Airdrie	6		0
Provan	Davie	Gourock	Kilmarnock	1978	1987	retired	192	14	28
Quinn	Frank	Saltcoats	Saltcoats Victoria	1946	1948	Dundee United	6		0
Quinn	Jimmy	Croy	Smithston Albion	1901	1915	retired	273		187
Quinn	Jimmy	Kilsyth	Groy BG	1964	1975	Sheffield Wed	23	5	1
Quinn	Robert	Earnock	Blantyre Celtic	1943	1947	Arbroath	6		0
Rae	Joe	Glasgow	Arthurlie	1942	1948	Torquay United	19		11
Reid	Ian	Edinburgh	Armadale Thistle	1953	1957	Airdrie	4		1
Reid	Mark	Kilwinning	Celtic Boys Club	1977	1985	Charlton Ath	120	4	5
Rennet	Willie	Perth	Perth Celtic	1949	1951	Arbroath	14		4
Reynolds	Jack	Blackburn	Aston Villa	1897	1898	So'ton St. Mary's	4	1	0
Reynolds	Jerry	Maryhill	Carfin Shamrock	1889	1895	Burnley	74		0
Ribchester*	Willie	Glasgow	Parkhead Juniors	1916	1919	Albion Rovers	2		0
Rieper	Marc	Copenhagen	West Ham United	1997	1998	retired	37		2
Riley	Joseph J.		Maryhill Hibs	1928	1930	St Mirren	10		2
Riseth	Vidar	Levanger, Norway	Linz	1998	2001	1860 Munich	54	2	3
Ritchie	Andy	Bellshill		1973	1976	Morton	5	4	1
Robertson	David	Kirkcaldy	Rosslyn Juniors	1930	1931	Cowdenbeath	2		0

Complete Players' Career Records: Mowbray – Robertson, David

Scottish League Cup			Scottish Cup			European			Totals		
Apps	Sub	Goals	Apps	Sub	Goals	Apps	Sub	Goals	Apps	Sub	Goals
7		0	9		0	6		0	100	3	5
8	1	0	0		0	2	1	0	29	7	0
0		0	1		0	0		0	13		0
0		0	5		3	0		0	25		7
0		0	9		0	0		0	51		0
0		0	0		0	0		0	4		4
0		0	6		0	0		0	36		6
5		0	2		0	0		0	21	1	0
84		17	52		13	57		11	480	4	102
0		0	17		4	0		0	161		50
0		0	3		0	0		0	38		0
0		0	1		0	0		0	7		2
0		0	0		0	0		0	2		0
0		0	5		1	0		0	16		3
20		5	8		4	10		1	100	1	21
0		0	24		10	0		0	200		92
0		0	0		0	0		0	1		0
0		0	0		0	0		0	16		8
24	7	26	9	2	7	17	3	7	209	40	125
0		0	0		0	0		0	1		0
0		0	0		0	0		0	1		0
0		0	0		0	0		0	7		0
0		0	1		0	0		0	2		0
0		0	5		7	0		0	83		58
0		0	15		7	0		0	90		27
6	1	0	12	4	4	7	1	1	101	20	21
0		0	2		0	0		0	9		1
0		0	0		0	0		0	20		13
1	2	0	5	1	0	0	2	0	44	7	1
6	4	1	12	1	0	9	3	1	119	36	10
0		0	0		0	0		0	1		0
0		0	0		0	0		0	5		0
0		0	0		0	0		0	0	1	0
18	2	0	3		0	9		0	79	3	0
0		0	0		0	0		0	9		0
0		0	0		0	0		0	4		0
0		0	0		0	0		0	2		0
0		0	0		0	0		0	7		0
0		0	47		6	0		0	212		23
0		0	3		1	0		0	16		9
0		0	20		1	0		0	195		10
15		3	5		2	0		0	72		16
0		0	1		0	0		0	1		0
3	2	5	1	1	0	3		0	27	19	20
79		10	56		8	0		0	453		50
4	3	0	6	2	1	12	2	1	95	16	16
2	4	1	3	1	1	12	3	1	51	24	3
0		0	0		0	0		0	1		0
0		0	0		0	0		0	22		0
0		0	0		0	0		0	6		1
13		0	10		0	0		0	74		0
0		0	0		0	0		0	6		0
41	1	10	29		1	25	1	2	287	16	41
1		0	0		0	0		0	7		0
0		0	58		30	0		0	331		217
9		0	2	1	0	1		0	35	6	1
3		0	0		0	0		0	9		0
6	1		1		0	0		0	25		12
0		0	0		0	0		0	4		1
21	2	6	17		1	12	1	0	170	7	12
0		0	1		0	0		0	15		4
0		0	0		0	0		0	4	1	0
0		0	25		0	0		0	99		0
0		0	0		0	0		0	2		0
2	1		4		0	5		0	48		3
0		0	0		0	0		0	10		2
5	1		4		0	7	1	1	70	3	5
0	1	1	0		0	0		0	5	5	2
0		0	0		0	0		0	2		0

Player		Birthplace	From	Year Joined	Year Left	To	League Apps	Sub	Goals
Robertson	Graham	Buckhaven	Wellesley Juniors	1929	1931	Cowdenbeath	34		1
Robertson	William	Stirling	Denny Hibs	1909	1910	Preston North End	3		0
Rogan	Anton	Belfast	Distillery	1986	1991	Sunderland	115	12	4
Rollo	Alec	Dumbarton	Ashfield	1948	1954	Kilmarnock	37		1
Roose	Leigh R.	Holt, Wales	Sunderland	1910	1911	Huddersfield Town	0		0
Ross	Andrew	Hurlford	Hurlford Thistle	1898	1900	Galston	1		0
Rough	Alan	Glasgow	Orlando Lions	1988	1988	Hamilton Acad	5		0
Rowan	Jim	Glasgow	Shettleston Juniors	1952	1956	Clyde	2		1
Russell*	Davie	Airdrie	Hearts	1896	1899	Broxburn	71		12
Ryan	Vincent	Dublin	Home Farm, Dublin	1953	1958	St Mirren	22		3
Sanderson	Robert	Peebles	Peebles Rovers	1908	1909	Spennymoor United	2		0
Scarff	Peter	Linwood	Maryhill Hibs	1928	1933	deceased	97		51
Scheidt	Rafael	Brazil	Gremio (Brazil)	1999	2000	Corinthians (Brazil)	1	3	0
Scott	Robert		Airdrie	1893	1899	retired	1		0
Semple	Willie	West Maryston	Baillieston Thistle	1907	1909	Millwall	8		2
Sharkey	Jim	Glasgow	Rutherglen Glencairn	1954	1957	Airdrie	23		8
Shaw	Charlie	Twechar	Queens Park Rangers	1913	1925	New Bedford (USA)	420		0
Shaw	Hugh	Uddingston	Rangers	1906	1906	Kilmarnock	1		0
Shea	Danny	Wapping	Blackburn Rovers	1919	1920	West Ham United	1		0
Shepherd	Tony		Celtic Boys Club	1983	1989	Carlisle United	16	12	3
Shevlane	Chris	Edinburgh	Hearts	1967	1968	Hibernian	2		0
Shevlin	Peter	Wishaw	St. Roch's	1924	1927	South Shields	86		0
Shields	Jimmy		Arthurlie	1939	1947	Dumbarton	3		0
Shields	Paul	Dunfermline	Raith Rovers	2000		Still at club	0	1	0
Simpson	Ronnie	Glasgow	Hibernian	1964	1970	retired	118		0
Sinclair	Graeme	Paisley	Dumbarton	1982	1985	St Mirren	45	6	1
Sinclair	Tom	Glasgow	Rangers	1906	1907	Newcastle United	6		0
Sinclair	Tommy	Alva	Alva Albion Rangers	1927	1928	South Shields	2		0
Sirrel	Jimmy	Glasgow	Renfrew Juniors	1945	1949	Bradford PA	13		2
Slater	Malcolm	Buckie	Buckie Thistle	1958	1960	Buckie Thistle	5		1
Slater	Stuart	Sudbury	West Ham United	1992	1993	Ipswich Town	40	4	3
Slaven	Pat	Rutherglen	Fauldhouse Hibs	1897	1897	Motherwell	1		0
Slavin	Jim	Lanark	Celtic Boys Club	1992	1996	Partick Thistle	3		0
Smith	Barry	Paisley	Giffnock North	1991	1995	Dundee	14	5	0
Smith	Eric	Glasgow	Benburb	1953	1960	Leeds United	95		13
Smith	Hugh	Port Glasgow	Port Glasgow Juniors	1930	1934	Ayr United	25		1
Smith	Jamie	Alexandria	Celtic Boys Club	1997		Still at club	5	14	2
Smith	Mark	Bellshill	Queen's Park	1986	1987	Dunfermline Ath	3	3	0
Sneddon	Alan	Billieston	Larkhall Thistle	1997	1981	Hibernian	66		1
Solis	Jerome	Glasgow	Maryhill Hibs	1931	1932	Coleraine	9		3
Somers*	Peter	Avondale	Hamilton Acad	1897	1910	Hamilton Acad	186		52
Stanton	Pat	Edinburgh	Hibernian	1976	1978	retired	37		0
Stark	Billy	Glasgow	Aberdeen	1987	1990	Kilmarnock	58	6	17
Stein	Jock	Earnock	Llanelly	1951	1957	retired	106		2
Stewart	Tom	Renfrew	Dumbarton Harp	1918	1918	Dumbarton Harp	1		0
Storrier	Dave	Arbroath	Eveton	1898	1901	Dundee	34		0
Strang	William	Dunfermline	Dunfermline Ath	1903	1905	Calgary Caledonians	2		0
Stubbs	Alan	Kirkby	Bolton Wanderers	1996	2001	Everton	101	4	0
Sullivan	Dominic	Glasgow	Aberdeen	1979	1983	Morton	83	7	10
Sutton	Chris	Nottingham	Chelsea	2000		Still at club	42		15
Sylla	Moha'med	Bouakake, Ivory Coast	St. Johnstone	2001		Still at club	7	2	1
Syme	David	Glasgow	St. Anthony's	1918	1919	Irvine Meadow	2		0
Taylor	David	Glasgow	Burnley	1918	1920	Burnley	5		0
Taylor	William		Glencairn Juv	1948	1951	Alloa Athletic	14		4
Tebily	Olivier	Abidjan, Ivory Coast	Sheffield United	1999	2002	Birmingham City	29	9	0
Templeton	Bobby	Coylton	Arsenal	1906	1907	Kilmrnock	29		5
Thom	Andreas	Rudersdorf, Germany	Bayer Leverkusen	1995	1998	Hertha Berlin	57	13	14
Thom	James		Parkhead Juniors	1895	1895	Parkhead Juniors	1		0
Thomas	Danny	Glasgow	Mossend Celtic	1895	1895	Hibernian	1		0
Thompson	Alan	Newcastle	Aston Villa	2000		Still at club	51	4	9
Thomson	Alec	Buckhaven	Wellesley Juniors	1922	1934	Dunfermline Ath	392		87
Thomson	Bertie	Johnstone	Glasgow Perthshire	1929	1933	Blackpool	113		22
Thomson	John	Buckhaven	Wellesley Juniors	1926	1931	deceased	163		0
Thomson	William		Wilshaw Hibs	1895	1895	Wilshaw Hibs	1		0
Tierney	Con	Kilbirnie	Bo'ness	1930	1932	Guildford City	7		0
Toner	Willie	Glasgow	Queen's Park	1948	1951	Sheffield United	2		0
Towie*	Tom		Renton	1892	1893	Derby County	0		0
Travers	Paddy	Beith	Aberdeen	1911	1912	Aberdeen	18		5
Traynor	John	Glasgow	Celtic Boys Club	1983		Clydebank	3	1	0

Complete Players' Career Records: Robertson, Graham – Traynor

Scottish League Cup			Scottish Cup			European			Totals		
Apps	Sub	Goals	Apps	Sub	Goals	Apps	Sub	Goals	Apps	Sub	Goals
0		0	3	0	0	0		0	37		1
0		0	1	0	0	0		0	4		0
12	1	0	15	0	0	6	1	0	148	13	5
13		0	9	1	0	0		0	59		2
0		0	1	0	0	0		0	1		0
0		0	0	0	0	0		0	1		0
1		0	0	0	0	1		0	7		0
0		0	0	0	0	0		0	2		1
0		0	13	0	0	0		0	84		12
0		0	0	0	0	0		0	22		3
0		0	0	0	0	0		0	2		0
0		0	15	4	0	0		0	112		55
0		0	0	0	0	1	1	0	2	4	0
0		0	0	0	0	0		0	1		0
0		0	0	0	0	0		0	8		2
2		0	2	1	0	0		0	27		9
0		0	16	0	0	0		0	436		0
0		0	0	0	0	0		0	1		0
0		0	0	0	0	0		0	1		0
2	3	0	1	1	0	3		0	22	16	3
1		0	0	0	0	0		0	3		0
0		0	17	0	0	0		0	103		0
0		0	0	0	0	0		0	3		0
0		0	0	0	0	0		0	0	1	0
29		0	17	0	0	24		0	188		0
10	2	0	3	2	0	7		0	65	10	1
0		0	0	0	0	0		0	6		0
0		0	0	0	0	0		0	2		0
0		0	5	0	0	0		0	18		2
0		0	0	0	0	0		0	5		1
3	2	0	3	0	0	4		0	50	6	3
0		0	0	0	0	0		0	1		0
0		0	0	0	0	0		0	3		0
1		0	0	0	0	0		0	15	5	0
16	3		9	4	0	0		0	130		20
0		0	2	0	0	0		0	27		1
1	1	1	0	1	0	0	1	0	6	17	3
2		0	0	0	0	0		0	5	3	0
15		0	9	0	0	10		0	100		1
0		0	0	0	0	0		0	9		3
0		0	33	10	0	0		0	219		62
0		0	7	0	0	0		0	44		0
3	1	4	7	3	3	5		1	74	10	25
21		0	21	0	0	0		0	148		2
0		0	0	0	0	0		0	1		0
0		0	6	0	0	0		0	40		0
0		0	0	0	0	0		0	2		0
8	1	0	11		0	18	1	0	138	6	0
12	1	1	8	1	0	6	1	1	109	10	12
4	1	2	6		0	12		4	64	1	21
1		0	1	1	1	0	1	0	9	4	2
0		0	0	0	0	0		0	2		0
0		0	0	0	0	0		0	5		0
1		0	2		0	0		0	17		4
4	1	1	2	1	0	6		1	41	11	2
0	7		0	0	0	0		0	36		5
9	2	4	6	2	2	12		7	84	17	27
0		0	0	0	0	0		0	1		0
0		0	0	0	0	0		0	1		0
4		1	9	1	2	4	2	1	68	7	13
0		0	59	13	0	0		0	451		100
0		0	18	8	0	0		0	131		30
0		0	25	0	0	0		0	188		0
0		0	0	0	0	0		0	1		0
0		0	0	0	0	0		0	7		0
0		0	0	0	0	0		0	2		0
0		0	5	2	0	0		0	5		2
0		0	4	3	0	0		0	22		8
0		0	0	0	0	0		0	3	1	0

Player		Birthplace	From	Year Joined	Year Left	To	League Apps	Sub	Goals
Trodden	Paddy		Kilsyth Hibs	1895	1895	Kilmarnock Ath	1		0
Tully	Charlie	Belfast	Belfast Celtic	1948	1959	Cork Hibs	216		30
Turnbull	David	Hurlford	Kilbirnie Ladeside	1927	1928	Ayr United	2		0
Turnbull	Tom		East Stirling	1899	1900	Sheffield United	11		0
Turner	Paddy	Dublin	Morton	1963	1964	Glentoran	7		0
Ugolini	Rolando	Lucca, Italy	Armadale Thistle	1944	1948	Middlesbrough	4		0
Valgaeren	Joos	Louvain, Belgium	Roda JC	2000		Still at club	55		5
Van Hooijdonk	Pierre	Steenbergen, Neth	NAC Breda	1995	1997	Nottingham Forest	66	2	44
Vata	Rudi	Shkodai, Albania	Dinamo Tirana	1992	1996	Apollon Limassol	33	12	4
Vega	Ramon	Zurich	Tottenham Hotspur	2000	2001	Watford	18		2
Viduka	Mark	Footscray, Australia	Croatia Zagreb	1998	2000	Leeds United	36	1	30
Walker*	Andy	Glasgow	Motherwell	1987	1996	Sheffield United	112	38	49
Wallace	John	Falkirk	Stonehouse Violet	1932	1934	Coleraine	15		0
Wallace	Willie	Kirkintilloch	Hearts	1966	1971	Crystal Palace	135	6	88
Walls	James	Beith	Hamilton Acad	1902	1903	Ayr	4		0
Walsh	Frank	Wishaw	Kilmarnock	1947	1949	Southport	10		3
Walsh	Jimmy	Glasgow	Bo'ness United	1949	1956	Leicester City	108		45
Warner	Tony	Liverpool	Liverpool	1998	1999	Millwall	3		0
Watson	Charlie	Coatbridge	Dumbarton Harp	1919	1922	Bathgate	18		4
Watson	Hugh	Maybole	Trabboch Thistle	1901	1905	Kilmarnock	49		0
Watson	Phil	Dykehead	Dykehead	1902	1903	Ayr	3		0
Watters	Jackie	Waterside	St. Roch's	1937	1947	Airdrie	9		4
Wdowczyk	Dariusz	Warsaw	Gwardia Warsaw	1989	1994	Reading	112	4	4
Weir	Donald	Cadder East	Kilwinning Rangers	1948	1952	Portadown	6		1
Weir	James	Muirkirk	Ayr	1907	1910	Middlesbrough	82		1
Weir	Jock	Fauldhouse	Blackburn Rovers	1948	1952	Falkirk	81		26
Weir	John	Coatbridge	Petershill	1978	1982	Airdrie	11		1
Welford	Jim	Barnard Castle	Aston Villa	1897	1900	Distillery	38		0
Welsh	Frank		Shettleston Juniors	1971	1976	Kilmarnock	4	1	0
Whitehead	George	Galashiels	Hearts	1913	1913	Motherwell	7		2
Whitelaw*	Robert		Doncaster Rovers	1930	1934	Cowdenbeath	17		0
Whitney	Tom	at sea	Bridgeton Waveley	1931	1933	Larne	4		1
Whittaker	Brian	Glasgow	Partick Thistle	1983	1984	Hearts	10		2
Whyte	Derek	Glasgow		1985	1992	Middlesbrough	211	5	7
Whyte	Frank	Glasgow	Maryhill Harp	1951	1956	Swindon Town	7		0
Wieghorst	Morten	Glostrup, Denmark	Dundee	1995	2002	Brondby (Denmark)	59	24	10
Williams	Evan	Dumbarton	Wolverhampton W.	1969	1974	Clyde	82		0
Wilson	Alex	Muirkirk	Cambuslang Rangers	1905	1907	Kilmarnock	14		0
Wilson*	James	Glasgow	Cambuslang Rangers	1913	1919	Albion Rovers	47		0
Wilson	Paul	Milngavie	Maryhill Juniors	1967	1978	Motherwell	97	36	30
Wilson	Peter	Beith	Beith Juniors	1923	1934	Hibernian	344		14
Wilson	Sammy	Glasgow	St Mirren	1957	1959	Millwall	48		26
Wraith	Bobby	Largs	Dalry Thistle	1968	1969	Southport	0		0
Wright	Ian	Woolwich	Nottingham Forest	1999	2000	Burnley	4	4	3
Young	Ian	Neilston Juniors		1961	1968	St Mirren	84		2
Young	James		Lochgelly United	1918	1918	Rangers	1		0
Young	Jim	Kilmarnock	Bristol Rovers	1903	1917	retired	392		14
Young	John		Strathclyde Juniors	1908	1911	Dundee Hibs	3		0

*Denotes players who have spent more than one spell at the club.

(Left) Alec McNair, Jimmy McMenemy and Paddy Travers in training, 1913.

(Right) Steve Chalmers climbs to head Celtic's first in a 5-3 win against Dundee in the Scottish League Cup final, 1967.

(Far right) Ronnie Simpson – Celtic's European Cup-winning keeper.

Scottish League Cup			Scottish Cup			European			Totals		
Apps	Sub	Goals	Apps	Sub	Goals	Apps	Sub	Goals	Apps	Sub	Goals
0		0	0		0	0		0	1		0
68		7	35		6	0		0	319		43
0		0	0		0	0		0	2		0
0		0	0		0	0		0	11		0
6		0	1		0	0		0	14		0
1		0	0		0	0		0	5		0
5		0	7		1	14		1	81		7
5	1	3	11		9	5	2	0	87	5	56
3		0	4		0	4		0	44	12	4
2		0	6		2	0		0	26		4
4	1		3		3	4		1	47	1	35
15	7	10	11	2	6	7	3	4	145	50	69
0		0	3		0	0		0	18		0
31	5	21	24	2	12	27	2	13	217	15	134
0		0	1		0	0		0	5		0
0		0	0		0	0		0	10		3
21		8	15		5	0		0	144		58
0		0	0		0	0		0	3		0
0		0	0		0	0		0	18		4
0		0	9		1	0		0	58		1
0		0	0		0	0		0	3		0
0		0	1		1	0		0	10		5
11		0	13		2	6	1	0	142	5	6
0		0	1		1	0		0	7		2
0		0	14		0	0		0	96		1
10		2	15		9	0		0	106		37
2		0	1		0	0		0	14		1
0		0	6		0	0		0	44		0
0		0	0		0	0		0	4	1	0
0		0	0		0	0		0	7		2
0		0	1		0	0		0	18		0
0		0	0		0	0		0	4		1
6		1	0		0	0		0	16		3
18		0	26		0	15		1	270	5	8
2		0	0		0	0		0	9		0
7	3	2	5	4	2	8	3	2	79	34	16
25		0	19		0	22		0	148		0
0		0	0		0	0		0	14		0
0		0	0		0	0		0	47		0
40	8	15	14	1	4	17	4	6	168	49	55
0		0	51		1	0		0	395		15
14		13	8		7	0		0	70		46
1		0	0		0	0		0	1		0
1		0	0		0	0		0	5	4	3
21		1	13		0	15		0	133		3
0		0	0		0	0		0	1		0
0		0	51		0	0		0	443		14
0		0	0		0	0		0	3		0

Appearance Records

Top Ten Appearances (League)

1. A. McNair   548
2. P. McStay   515
3. B. McNeill   486
4. R. Aitken   = 483
5. P. Bonner   = 483
6. J. McMenemy   456
7. D. McGrain   441
8. P. Gallacher   432
9. C. Shaw   420
10. J. McStay   409

Top Ten Penalty Scorers (all Competitions)

1. T. Gemmell   31
2. W. McStay (senior)   28
3. C. Napier   26
4. M. Haughney   24
5. B. Collins   = 22
6. H. Larsson   = 22
7. C. Nicholas   = 22
8. J. Dodds   16
9. G. Paterson   16
10. B. Murdoch   15

Top Ten Goalscorers (League)

1. J. McGrory   395
2. J. Quinn   187
3. P. Gallacher   186
4. B. Lennox   167
5. S. Chalmers   147
6. J. McMenemy   144
7. S. McMahon   130
8. A. McLean   128
9. H. Larsson   116*
10. J. Hughes   115

*As at end of season 2001-02.

Top Ten Goalkeeper's Clean Sheets (League)

1. C. Shaw   227
2. P. Bonner   172
3. D. Adams   100
4. J. Kennaway   75
5. J. Thompson   57
6. R. Simpson   54
7. P. Latchford   52
8. F. Haffey   41
9. J. Bonnar   40
10. J. Gould   = 36
10. E. Williams   = 36

Tommy Gemmell scores one of his 31 goals from the spot, v Falkirk in March 1967.

Top Ten Internationals

1.	P. Bonner	80
2.	P. McStay	76
3.	T. Bond	66
4.	D. McGrain	62
5.	R. Aitken	50
6.	K. Dalglish	47
7.	B. Evans	45
8.	H. Larsson	43
9.	J. Collins	= 32
10.	J. Mjallby	= 32

Top Ten U-21 Caps

1.	R. Aitken	16
2.	M. Burchill	15
3.	G. Creaney	= 11
4.	S. Donnelly	= 11
5.	P. Grant	= 10
6.	S. Kerr	= 10
7.	D. Whyte	9
8.	B. McClair	= 8
9.	B. McLaughlin	= 8
10.	S. Fulton	= 7
10.	B. O'Neill	= 7

Brothers who have Played for Celtic

Brogan	Frank/Jim
Devlin	James/John
Dolan	Frank/Mick
Maley	Tom/Willie
McCluskey	George/John
McPhail	John/Billy
McStay	Willie/Jimmy†
McStay	Paul/Willie
O'Donnell	Frank/Hugh

†Great Uncles of Paul/Willie McStay.

Fathers and Sons who have Played for Celtic

Chalmers	Steve/Paul
Conroy	Mike/Mike
Divers	John/John*
Gallacher	Patsy/Willie*
Kelly	Jimmy/Frank
Lynch	Andy/Simon
Marshall	Gordon/Gordon and Scott
McMenemy	Jimmy/John
McNamara	Jackie/Jackie

*John senior, nephew of Patsy.

Celtic's top league goalscorer of all time, Jimmy McGrory, arrives for work at Celtic Park, 1964.

Flying keeper Frank Haffey kept 41 clean sheets during his time at the club.

OTHER TITLES IN THE SERIES

The Essential History of...

Aston Villa	Adam Ward/Jeremy Griffin	*0 7553 1140 X*
Blackburn Rovers	Mike Jackman	*0 7553 1022 5*
Charlton Athletic	Paul Clayton	*0 7553 1020 9*
England	Andrew Mourant/Jack Rollin	*0 7553 1142 6*
Ipswich Town	Paul Voller/Mel Henderson	*0 7553 1021 7*
Leeds United	Andrew Mourant	*0 7553 1170 1**
Leicester City	Tony Matthews	*0 7553 1023 3*
Manchester City	Ian Penney	*0 7553 1168 X**
Middlesbrough	Richard Jones	*0 7553 1143 4*
Nottingham Forest	Bob Bickerton	*0 7553 1144 2*
Rangers	Stephen Halliday	*0 7553 1145 0*
Tottenham Hotspur	Bob Goodwin	*0 7553 1019 5*
West Bromwich Albion	Gavin McOwan	*0 7553 1146 9*
West Ham United	Kirk Blows/Tony Hogg	*0 7553 1169 8**

* Trade paperback editions

Please contact your local WHSmith store for details about ordering any of these titles